SECOND EDITION

German

A
Structural
Approach

Walter F. W. Lohnes
and F. W. Strothmann

STANFORD UNIVERSITY

German

A Structural Approach

SECOND EDITION

W · W · NORTON & COMPANY · INC · NEW YORK

SECOND EDITION

"Klatsch am Sonntagmorgen" by Horst Bienek, "der tisch ist oval" by Franz Mon, and "Reisen" by Peter Otto Chotjewitz, from *Die Meisengeige,* ed. Günter Bruno Fuchs, Carl Hanser Verlag, Munich.

"Sachliche Romanze," "Die Entwicklung der Menschheit," and "Das Eisenbahngleichnis" by Erich Kästner, from *Dr. Erich Kaestners Lyrische Hausapotheke,* Atrium Verlag, Zurich.

"Wenn die Haifische Menschen wären" and "Freundschaftsdienste," from *Prosa I* by Bertolt Brecht. Copyright 1965 by Stefan S. Brecht. All rights reserved by Suhrkamp Verlag, Frankfurt/Main.

"If Sharks Were People" and "Good Turns," trans. Yvonne Kapp. Reprinted from the copyrighted works of Bertolt Brecht by permission of Pantheon Books, a Division of Random House, Inc., and Methuen & Company, Ltd. Copyright © 1962 by Methuen & Company, Ltd.

"Heimkehr." Reprinted by permission of Schocken Books Inc., from *Beschreibung eines Kampfes* by Franz Kafka. Copyright © 1946 by Schocken Books Inc.

"Das Gleichnis vom verlornen Sohn." Reprinted from *Die Heilige Schrift* by permission of Theologischer Verlag und Buchhandlungen AG, Zurich.

"The Prodigal Son." Reprinted by permission from *The New English Bible.* Copyright © 1961, 1970 by The Delegates of the Oxford University Press and the Syndics of the Cambridge University Press.

"Ein Tisch ist ein Tisch" by Peter Bichsel, from *Kindergeschichten.* Copyright © 1969 by Hermann Luchterhand Verlag, Neuwied and Darmstadt.

Library of Congress Cataloging in Publication Data
Lohnes, Walter F W
    German: a structural approach.
    1. German language—Grammar—1950–
I. Strothmann, Friedrich Wilhelm, 1904– joint author. II. Title.
PF3112.L6 1973   438'.2'421   72–13799
ISBN 0–393–09345–X

1 2 3 4 5 6 7 8 9 0

Contents

Unit 1 The Present Tense—**sein** and **haben**—Gender—Plural of Nouns—Basic Sentence Structure—Intonation Patterns—**auch**—**denn.**   **1**

The Infinitive.   Personal Pronouns.   Inflected Verb Forms.   Absence of Progressive and Emphatic Forms in German.   Future Meaning of Present-Tense Forms. Variations in Personal Endings.   **sein** and **haben.**   Gender of Nouns.   Singular and Plural Forms of Nouns.   The Inflected Verb and Its Position.   The Element in Front of the Inflected Verb.   News Value.   Word Stress.   Syntactical Stress. Intonation of Assertions.   The Structure of Questions.   The Intonation of Questions. **auch.**   **denn.**

Unit 2 Nominative and Accusative of Personal Pronouns and of **ein**-Words and **der**-Words—Adverbs and Predicate Adjectives—Verbal Complements—Sentence Structure—**doch.**   **25**

Unit 3   aber, oder, denn, und—Negation by kein and nicht— The Modals—Contrast Intonation—The Imperative.   **49**

Unit 4 The Dative—Prepositions with Dative and Accusative—Word Order in the Inner Field—The Perfect—Time Phrases.   **81**

The Dative Case.   Verbs with Only a Dative Object.   Verbs Governing the Dative and Accusative.   Adjectives Governing the Dative.   Prepositions Governing the Accusative.   Prepositions Governing the Dative.   Word Order within the Inner Field.   The German Perfect Formation of the German Participle.   The Use of **sein** and **haben** as Auxiliaries.   Position of the Participle.   The Use of the German Perfect.   Point-of-Time Phrases.   Scanning the Past: Frequency Phrases.   Stretch-of-Time Phrases.   **für**-Phrases.   Replacement of **er, sie, es** by **der, die, das. es** and **das**, Followed by Plural Verb Forms.

Unit 5 Numbers—The Past—The Pluperfect—Verb-Last Position—Open Conditions—**um . . . zu**—**mit**—Word Formation.   **121**

Cardinal Numbers.   The Past Tense of Weak Verbs.   Regular Deviations in the Past of Weak Verbs.   Past Tense of Strong Verbs.   The Principal Parts of Strong and Irregular Weak Verbs.   The Difference between the Past and the Perfect.   The Use of the Past Tense of **haben, sein,** and the Modals.   The Use of the Past in Dependent Clauses.   The Formation of the Pluperfect.   The Use of the Pluperfect.   Dependent Clauses.   Verb-Last Position.   **wenn** and **wann.**   The Conjunction **ob.**   Dependent Clauses in the Front Field.   Position of the Subject in Dependent Clauses.   Intonation of Dependent Clauses.   Open Conditions.

um . . . zu. **mit** as a Verbal Complement. Word Formation. The Suffixes **-chen** and **-lein.** The Suffix **-er.** Infinitives as Neuter Nouns. Compound Nouns.

Unit 8   Relative Pronouns—**wann, ob, als, wenn**—**gar**—**da**-Compounds— **wo**-Compounds—Prepositional Objects.   **229**

Unit 9   Negation—Present and Past Infinitives—Subjective and Objective Use of Modals—Reflexive Pronouns—Contrary-to-Fact Conditions without **wenn**.   **261**

Unit 10 Adjectives.   **299**

Unit 11 Infinitive Constructions—**hin** and **her**—Comparison of Adjectives—The Rhetorical **nicht**—Numbers.   **339**

Unit 12 Reflexive Verbs—Imperatives.   **389**

Preface

SINCE THE FIRST publication of *German: A Structural Approach,* we have received numerous comments and suggestions on how to improve the usefulness of the book. We ourselves have constantly gone over the text with an eye toward possible modifications. The result of this double scrutiny is the present second edition.

We have not altered our basic approach to contemporary German; we still believe that the interaction of active practice and intellectual comprehension of the language best suits the interests and capabilities of college-age students. We have, however, made some rather significant changes in the text. Most important perhaps is the inclusion of a number of unedited short literary pieces by, for example, Kafka and Brecht. Some reading material of the first edition had to be omitted, to the relief of some users and probably to the disappointment of others. A large number of analysis sections were completely rewritten, and, we think, made clearer, including the presentations of time phrases, the subjunctive, and the reflexive verb. Some material, especially in the second half of the book, has been rearranged for easier classroom sequencing. The vocabulary is now set in double columns, as requested by a number of students, to facilitate memorization, and cross references to the analysis have been provided for most of the exercises.

Both the general format and the size of this edition follow the Shorter Edition of 1969.* Many minor changes were made in the patterns and exercises to bring them up to date and to eliminate references that have become somewhat alien to today's students. The illustrations have been updated as well, with a stronger emphasis on pictures that convey a linguistic message, and there is a new endpaper map of the German-speaking areas of Europe. Place names in the text as well as the new illustrations now refer the student to both Germanies, to Austria, and to Switzerland.

We have also made considerable changes in the materials that accompany the text. A new tape program is available for this edition. The Study Guide has been expanded to include, in addition to laboratory exercises, short programmed exercises to be used for independent study, and further exercises

---

* The Regular Edition of the original text will be kept in print for the benefit of those who want a more detailed introduction to German.

for homework assignments. A revised version of the Teacher's Manual can be obtained upon request to the publishers.

We wish to thank all those teachers and students who have written to us during the past five years, often at great length. Without their help, many of the present changes could not have been made. Obviously, we could not take all suggestions into account; to do so would have been to please some at the expense of displeasing others. But that does not lessen our gratitude for both the substance and the spirit of the assistance that has been rendered us. We are particularly indebted to Udo A. Münnich (Michigan State University), Herbert L. Kaufman (Queens College), and Alvin Hall (University of South Carolina), who critically read the manuscript of the second edition and made numerous valuable suggestions. Jutta E. McCormick again undertook the arduous task of bringing order into the constant flow of manuscript, often rewritten two or three times, and of typing the final version.

Most of the illustrations, particularly those demonstrating linguistic principles, we provided ourselves; for others, we are grateful to the Deutsche Zentrale für Fremdenverkehr, the German Information Center, and the Embassy of Lebanon.

W.F.W.L

F.W.S.

Stanford, California

December 1972

Introduction

THIS SECOND EDITION OF *German: A Structural Approach* has the same aims as its parent volume: developing the skills of listening, speaking, reading, and writing, while at the same time giving the student a clear understanding of the principles underlying his language performance. Our approach thus goes beyond the audio-lingual method without, however, abandoning basic audio-lingual techniques. Our experience has shown that the combination of the "how" and the "why" of language acquisition produces good results. An introductory course that makes the student aware of how language is organized and why speech patterns develop systematically can be far more stimulating than one that attempts to turn the student into an automaton.

In learning our native language, we absorb its syntactical principles without any clear conceptual knowledge of many of these principles, and we certainly do not think of them every time we utter a sentence. Nevertheless, we know when to say *He thinks not* and when to say *He doesn't think.* By a series of "pattern drills" that stretches from birth into adulthood we learn how to use a linguistic code without necessarily having a conceptual knowledge of that code. The learning of a second language resembles this process in some ways, but we can never really repeat our first performance.

It is true that one can drill the structural patterns of German intensively over a long period of time and thus approach active control and native fluency. But since college students are linguistic adults who already speak one language, they should not be exposed to the nonconceptual learning process a German child is exposed to.

In the first place, there is not that much time. In one year of college German, an American student cannot afford to learn the language by trial and error and from context only; he has to resort to grammar if he wants to master German quickly.

Secondly, the linguistic code of English acts as a perpetual source of interference; it prevents the student both from understanding many German sentences he hears and from actively using German sentence patterns correctly. This is to be expected, for once we have absorbed one linguistic code, we cannot learn a totally different code without some contrastive analytical knowledge of that new code.

In the third place, college students have reached an age at which they are both able and eager to grasp the systematic concept behind the individual phenomenon. When they encounter the simple sentence **Ich bleibe heute natürlich zu Hause,** they want to know why it is perfectly acceptable to say **Zu Hause bleibe ich heute natürlich nicht,** but impossible to say **Zu Hause bleibe ich heute natürlich.** A conceptual understanding of German sentence structure is a time-saving short cut, and we see no virtue in postponing the immediate comprehension of German syntax by refusing to tell the student, as he manipulates structural patterns, what the principles underlying these patterns are. We are very much in favor of "keeping grammar out of the classroom"; but since we are also against "teaching grammar behind closed doors," we suggest that structural analysis be handled in a new way.

PATTERN SENTENCES make up the first large part of each unit. Work with these patterns must occupy a great amount of classroom time, for it is here that the student will transform his concept of the language into an instrument of communication. Each pattern group contains a sufficient number of examples to illustrate a grammatical point, and there are cross references in the page margins to relevant discussions in the analysis.

From the very beginning, we aim at the student's ability to acquire not only the German he will see in formal print, but also the German he will hear in informal speech, and we have not shied away from the colloquial German used by educated people in everyday speech. Colloquial as well as literary German is recognized as equally acceptable, and the students are taught that **Wo kommen Sie denn her?** and **Wo willst du denn hin?** are just as correct as **Woher kommen Sie?** and **Wohin willst du?**

We have tried not to write typical classroom German, and we have never yielded to the temptation to produce unidiomatic expressions for the sake of making our patterns fit into a preconceived mold. For instance, the use of the attributive genitive must obviously be illustrated, but this is no excuse for introducing sentences like **Die Farbe meines Kugelschreibers ist blau** as starting points for pattern drills as long as there is available a wealth of idiomatic phrases such as **ein Freund meines Mannes, gegen Ende des Jahres,** and **der Erfolg der neuen Methode.** We have mitigated the rigidity—and perhaps also the boredom—of many pattern drills by insisting that the student create sentences that could occur in actual speech. It serves no purpose to have a substitution drill end with **Sie werden ihre Tränen getrocknet haben.** On the other hand, we do expect the student to be able to handle complex structures such as **Seine Frau soll sehr aufgeregt gewesen sein** or **Ich hätte natürlich auch zu Hause bleiben können,** for such structures do belong to the living language as it is actually spoken and written.

Some pattern sections contain built-in variations or are followed by a separate set of variations. These are designed in such a way that they can be used in class immediately after a group of pattern sentences has been introduced.

ANALYSIS is the intellectual core of each unit. The analysis sections have intentionally been written as detailed and unhurried discussions of grammatical points. Pains have been taken to explain grammar in terms the student will understand. We have avoided short, terse rules that cannot be applied without elaboration in the classroom. The analysis sections should be assigned as outside reading as the new patterns are introduced in class, so that the student, while he works on the patterns, will have the feeling that he knows what he is doing and why he is doing it.

In the analysis, our first and foremost concern is syntax. After an introductory section on the pronunciation of individual sounds, Unit 1 deals with sentence intonation; in the following units, the basic structure of German sentences is developed. A discussion of the two-part predicate, the most characteristic feature of German syntax, is followed by an analysis of word order in the inner field of a sentence. Negation and time phrases are dealt with at length. Modal auxiliaries and the subjunctive—indispensable in "real" German—are introduced very early. A number of sections deal with sentence adverbs like **doch, ja,** or **denn.** Other sections are devoted to principles of word formation.

In order to contrast German structures with corresponding English structures, we have occasionally spent much time analyzing English usage from a German point of view. We want to call attention to those features of English that differ from German, and are therefore the primary cause of error.

The broad coverage of the analysis sections reflects our desire to avoid unidiomatic German. This should not detract from the fact, however, that the major building blocks of German grammar have received the greatest emphasis. Some important grammatical categories, for example the subjective use of modals or the relationship of tenses and time phrases, are not treated in other introductory grammars; some have been considered "too advanced" for the beginner. We firmly believe that these categories must be included in a beginning text, for without them the student cannot acquire a totally satisfactory knowledge of basic German.

EXERCISES are provided in addition to the variations in order to reinforce the student's control of each structural element. Their sequence is the same as that of the patterns and the analysis sections. Unlike the variations, however, the exercises should not be done until the student has thoroughly drilled and studied the corresponding patterns. We have intentionally included more exercises than most teachers will want to use, in order to save the teacher the time-consuming effort of writing practice drills of his own.

A separate set of laboratory exercises appears in the Study Guide. These exercises are keyed to each unit; the student is given full instructions for these exercises, but their texts appear only in the Teacher's Manual. Thus their use is not restricted to the language laboratory; they can also be used for further oral drill in the classroom.

CONVERSATIONS are included in all but the last few units; they are based upon the contents of the unit in which they appear, and demonstrate to the student how the material he has learned can produce lively, colloquial, and idiomatic talk. Most of the conversations are set up in such a way that they can be used for memorization if so desired.

READING, as the book progresses, becomes a major concern. We have used a wide variety of topics in our reading selections, some of which, such as passages from German newspapers, give brief glimpses of the contemporary German scene. To meet a frequently expressed desire, we have included a number of short literary pieces in this edition. For most of these, we have added translations to keep the student from getting discouraged when he faces reading selections he cannot master with ease.

WRITING should be practiced from the very beginning. At first the student should be encouraged simply to copy from the text. Later on, dictations should be given regularly. A number of the lab exercises are dictations as well. From Unit 7 on, we have provided a number of structured compositions, based on the material of the conversations and the reading.

VOCABULARY study is essential to the successful completion of a German course. In the pattern sentences the vocabulary has purposely been restricted so that the student can concentrate on learning the structures introduced; the conversations and reading selections provide most of the new words and phrases. All vocabulary is introduced in the context of whole sentences, and vocabulary should be *practiced* in context only. We do, however, recommend very strongly that the student memorize the "basic vocabulary" at the end of each unit. Less frequently used words and phrases appear under the heading "Additional Vocabulary."

ILLUSTRATIONS for the book have been selected mainly to demonstrate linguistic points. We have favored posters, signs, and other material that show language in action in contrast to typical "tourist" pictures, devoid of any linguistic message.

THE STUDY GUIDE for the second edition contains not only lab exercises, but also a series of programmed exercises which should be used in conjunction with the study of the analysis. Through these exercises, the student can check his own progress as he studies, and he can use them for quick review. All answers to the programmed exercises are contained in the Study Guide. In addition, there are a number of tear-out exercises that can be assigned as homework and handed in, if the instructor so chooses.

A TEACHER'S MANUAL is available which contains a number of detailed suggestions on how to teach individual parts of this book, outlines for typical lesson plans, and the scripts for all those lab exercises that do not appear in the printed text.

The Sounds of German

THROUGHOUT THIS BOOK, major emphasis is placed on the intonation of entire utterances, on the characteristic sound of whole German sentences. The pronunciation of the individual sounds that make up those complete sentences is dealt with only in this section. It is imperative that you practice these sounds, with the help of your teacher, and that you listen to the accompanying tapes until you have mastered the sounds. You should review this section frequently as you work your way through the book. After four weeks or four months you will find that this section on pronunciation may be even more useful to you than at the outset.

We have avoided all technical discussion of the German sounds; instead, we have provided a large number of contrastive drills to show the distinction between two or more different German sounds which, to the ear of an American student, very often sound alike when he first hears them. Many German sounds are sufficiently similar to English sounds so as not to cause the beginner great trouble. Our main concern will be those German sounds which either have no equivalent at all in English or tend to cause an American accent if pronounced like their English spelling equivalents. In many cases, an American accent will not make the German sound unintelligible (though you shouldn't take this as an excuse to retain an American accent); in some cases, however, the wrong pronunciation of certain sounds will produce unintended results. If you mispronounce the **ch**-sound in **Nacht**, as many Americans tend to do, you will not produce the German word for *night*, but the word **nackt**, which means *naked*.

Good pronunciation is essential if you want to speak German correctly and naturally. With patience and lots of practice, you should easily be able to overcome your initial difficulties. Don't worry about making mistakes at the beginning; you'll learn more from them than from not speaking at all.

German Vowels

German has long and short vowels, and diphthongs. The distinction between long and short vowels is very important, but unfortunately it is not always indicated by spelling. As a rule of thumb, however, you can assume that a vowel is short if it is followed by a double consonant (for example, **bitte**) or by two or more consonants (**binde**). German vowels are either quite long or very short.

In the following table, all German vowel sounds appear in words. On the tape, this is Pronunciation Drill 1. All the pronunciation drills in this section appear on tape. You should listen to them repeatedly and review them periodically. It is just as important, however, that you listen carefully to your instructor as he drills these exercises with you in class.

PRONUN-CIATION DRILL 1

	LONG	SHORT	UNSTRESSED ONLY
a	Saat	satt	
e	Beet	Bett	
/ə/*			-be (gebe)
/ʌ/*			-ber (Geber)
i	ihn	in	
o	Ofen	offen	
u	Buhle	Bulle	
ä	bäte		
ö	Höhle	Hölle	
ü	fühle	fülle	

	DIPHTHONGS
au	Baum
ei (ai)	kein (Kain)
eu (äu)	Heu (Häuser)

Note: The two dots over **ä, ö,** and **ü** are called Umlaut. Occasionally, especially in names, these sounds are spelled **ae, oe, ue.**

As the table shows, there are twenty different vowel sounds, of which two occur only in unstressed positions. These two are here represented by the symbols /ə/ and /ʌ/, which are not letters in the German alphabet, but are written as **-e** and **-er.**

All German vowels are "pure"; that is, they are monophthongs and do not have any diphthongal glide at the end as do the English letters *a* and *o*. As you hear the following examples, the difference will become clear.

PRONUN-CIATION DRILL 2

ENGLISH *a*	GERMAN LONG **e**		ENGLISH *o*	GERMAN LONG **o**
gay	geh		moan	Mohn
ray	Reh		tone	Ton
stay	steh		tote	tot
baited	betet		boat	Boot

Long **a** vs. short **a**

Many American students have real difficulty in hearing the difference between these two sounds and consequently have trouble pronouncing them. Yet very often the difference between long **a** and short **a** is the difference between two totally unrelated words, as the following examples show.

* We are using phonemic symbols here; in the alphabet /ə/ is **-e** and /ʌ/ is **-er.**

LONG a	vs.	SHORT a
Saat (planting)		**satt** (satisfied)
rate (guess)		**Ratte** (rat)
Rabe (raven)		**Rappe** (black horse)
Wahn (insanity)		**wann** (when)
fahl (pale)		**Fall** (fall)
kam (came)		**Kamm** (comb)
Maße (measures)		**Masse** (mass)
Bahn (track)		**Bann** (ban)

Now say these words again, but stretch the long a sound. Instead of **Saat,** say **Saaaat,** etc. You cannot do this with the short a: if you stretch the words in the second column, you have to stretch the consonant; for example, **Kamm** will become **Kammmm.**

Long e, long ä, short e and ä, unstressed e /ə/ and er /ʌ/

This group of vowel sounds will need your special attention.

Remember that the long e, like all other vowels, does not end in a glide: **geh,** not *gay.*

Some Germans do not really distinguish long ä from long e, except where there is a difference in meaning, for example, in **Gräte** (fishbone) vs. **Grete** (the girl's name Greta).

Short e and short ä represent the same sound: the e in **Kette** is indistinguishable from the ä in **hätte.**

The unstressed /ə/ occurs most frequently in endings and in prefixes; it is quite similar to the unstressed English *a* in *the sofa.* If /ə/ appears in front of final -n, it often all but disappears; thus **nennen** sounds like **nenn'n** and **kommen** like **komm'n.** These forms are hard to hear and hard to distinguish from forms without the -en ending. Yet very often it is essential to realize the distinction, as in **ihn** vs. **ihn(e)n, den** vs. **den(e)n.**

The unstressed /ʌ/, which is written as **er,** is one of the most difficult sounds for most Americans to produce. At first, you will have difficulty hearing the difference between /ə/ and /ʌ/, but the distinction is there and may be crucial, as in **bitte** (*please*) vs. **bitter** (*bitter*).

The following drills are designed to show you the differences between the various sounds of this group.

LONG e	vs.	SHORT e		LONG e	vs.	SHORT e
Beet		**Bett**		**wen**		**wenn**
Wesen		**wessen**		**den**		**denn**
reden		**retten**		**stehen**		**stellen**

Note again that short **e** and **ä** represent the same sound:

SHORT **e** vs.	SHORT **ä**
Wetter	Blätter
kenne	sänne
hemme	Kämme
Schwemme	Schwämme

LONG **ä** vs.	LONG **e** vs.	SHORT **e** OR **ä**
Gräte	Grete	rette
Ähren	ehren	Herren
bäte	bete	bette
wähne	Vene	Wände

/ə/ vs.	/ʌ/	/ə/ vs.	/ʌ/
bete	Beter	gute	guter
Rede	Reeder	Güte	Güter
nehme	Nehmer	Liebe	Lieber
gebe	Geber	Spitze	Spitzer
Esse	Esser	Pfarre	Pfarrer
Messe	Messer		
Summe	Summer	gehören	(erhören)
Hüte	Hüter	gearbeitet	(erarbeitet)
führe	Führer	gegessen	vergessen
Kutte	Kutter	gestört	zerstört

Long i and ü, short i and ü, long and short u

The two i-sounds are not very difficult to produce. They resemble the English vowel sounds in *bean* and *bin.*

The ü-sound, on the other hand, does not exist in English. To produce it, say i (as in English *key*); then freeze your tongue in that position and round your lips; or, to put it another way, say English *ee* with your lips in the English *oo* position. If you are musical and can get B above C above middle C on a piano, whistle it, and your tongue and lips will be in perfect ü-position. The letter y, which occurs mostly in foreign words, is usually pronounced like ü.

The long u-sound is similar to English *oo* in *noon;* the short u-sound is—to oversimplify matters a bit—just a very short version of the same English *oo*-sound, but again both sounds are much more clearly articulated in German.

LONG i	VS.	SHORT i				PRONUN-CIATION DRILL 8
Miete		Mitte				
biete		Bitte				
riete		ritte				
ihnen		innen				

LONG i	VS.	LONG ü (y)				PRONUN-CIATION DRILL 9
Miete		mühte				
Miete		Mythe				
Kiel		kühl				
schiebe		Schübe				
Stiele		Stühle				

SHORT i	VS.	SHORT ü	SHORT i	VS.	SHORT ü	PRONUN-CIATION DRILL 10
Kissen		küssen	Liste		Lüste	
missen		müssen	Gericht		Gerücht	
sticken		Stücken	springe		Sprünge	
Bitte		Bütte	Kiste		Küste	

LONG ü	VS.	SHORT ü	LONG ü	VS.	SHORT ü	PRONUN-CIATION DRILL 11
Hüte		Hütte	Wüste		wüßte	
rügen		rücken	Düne		dünne	
pflügen		pflücken	Füßen		Füssen	
kühnste		Künste	fühle		Fülle	

LONG u	VS.	SHORT u	LONG u	VS.	SHORT u	PRONUN-CIATION DRILL 12
Mus		muß	schuf		Schuft	
Ruhm		Rum	spuken		spucken	
sucht		Sucht	Buhle		Bulle	
Fuder		Futter	Buße		Busse	

LONG u	VS.	LONG ü	LONG u	VS.	LONG ü	PRONUN-CIATION DRILL 13
Mut		Mythe	Schub		Schübe	
Hut		Hüte	tuten		Tüten	
gut		Güte	Huhn		Hühner	
Schwur		Schwüre	Kuhle		Kühle	

SHORT u	VS.	SHORT ü	SHORT u	VS.	SHORT ü	PRONUN-CIATION DRILL 14
Mutter		Mütter	mußte		müßte	
Kunst		Künste	wußte		wüßte	
durfte		dürfte	Bund		Bünde	
kurze		Kürze	Luft		Lüfte	

Long and short o, long and short ö

Remember that the German o-sound does not end in a glide toward u: **Mohn**, not *moan*. To produce an ö, say a long German **e**, then freeze your tongue and round your lips. Note also the clear distinction between German **a** and German **o**. An American would be likely not to distinguish between **Bann, Bahn,** and **Bonn,** but the three sounds are clearly different.

PRONUN-CIATION DRILL 15

LONG o	vs.	SHORT o
wohne		Wonne
Schote		Schotter
Ton		Tonne
Lote		Lotte

PRONUN-CIATION DRILL 16

SHORT o	vs.	LONG a	vs.	SHORT a
Bonn		Bahn		Bann
komm		kam		Kamm
Sonne		Sahne		Susanne
hoffen		Hafen		haften
Schollen		Schalen		schallen
locken		Laken		Schlacken
ob		gab		ab

PRONUN-CIATION DRILL 17

LONG e	vs.	LONG ö
redlich		rötlich
heben		höben
bete		böte
lege		löge

PRONUN-CIATION DRILL 18

LONG o	vs.	LONG ö
Ton		Töne
Lohn		Löhne
Hof		Höfe
Not		Nöte
Bogen		Bögen

PRONUN-CIATION DRILL 19

SHORT e	vs.	SHORT ö
stecken		Stöcken
Recke		Röcke
westlich		östlich
helle		Hölle

PRONUN-
CIATION
DRILL 20

LONG ö	VS.	SHORT ö
Goethe		Götter
Schöße		schösse
Öfen		öffnen
Höhle		Hölle

PRONUN-
CIATION
DRILL 21

LONG ö	VS.	LONG ü	VS.	LONG i
Söhne		Sühne		Kusine
löge		Lüge		liege
Öl		kühl		Kiel
schöbe		Schübe		schiebe

PRONUN-
CIATION
DRILL 22

SHORT ö	VS.	SHORT ü
Stöcke		Stücke
schösse		Schüsse
Röcken		Rücken
Hölle		Hülle

PRONUN-
CIATION
DRILL 23

SHORT u	VS.	SHORT ü	VS.	SHORT i
mußte		müßte		mißte
Stuck		Stück		Stickstoff
Kummer		Kümmel		Kimme
Kunde		künde		Kinder

Diphthongs

There are three German diphthongs, two of which can be spelled in two different ways: **ei (ai)**, **eu (äu)**, and **au**. They will not present much of a problem. They are similar to *i* in English *light,* *oi* in English *foible,* and *ou* in English *mouse,* but, like all German vowels, they are more precise, more clearly defined, and not as drawn-out as their English counterparts.

PRONUN-
CIATION
DRILL 24

ei (ai)	eu (äu)	au
leiten	läuten	lauten
freien	freuen	Frauen
zeigen	zeugen	saugen
leise	Läuse	Laus
Meise	Mäuse	Maus

You will be bothered by the fact that the combination **ei** represents a diphthong, but the combination **ie** is simply a long **i**. The following drill should help you overcome this difficulty. To keep the two sounds straight, think of the English phrase *The hEIght of my nIEce* or of the German phrase **wEIn und bIEr.**

ei	vs.	**ie**		**ei**	vs.	**ie**
meine		Miene		Zeit		zieht
deine		diene		bereiten		berieten
leider		Lieder		keimen		Kiemen
reimen		Riemen		verzeihen		verziehen

Read the following words, distinguishing carefully between **ei** and **ie**:

Viel, Kleid, sieben, Liebe, Leib, leider, Lieder, Seife, siegen, zeigen, liegen, schieben, scheiden, Tier, einheitlich, einseifen, einfrieren, vierseitig, Bierseidel, Zeitspiegel, Spieglein, Meineid, Kleinigkeit.

German Consonants

In presenting the German vowel system, we have, of necessity, had to use almost all German consonant sounds. As you worked through the preceding section, you doubtless noticed that some German consonants, such as **m** and **n,** differ hardly at all from their English equivalents. Others, such as **z,** have probably surprised you because they are not pronounced the way you expected them to sound. The combination of sounds represented by German **z,** however, does exist in English: if you can say *cats* in English, you should be able to say "Tsoh" in German, even though it is spelled **Zoo.**

There are only two consonant sounds in German which have no equivalent in English; they are both graphically represented by **ch.** The following notes and drills will introduce the German consonants and show you where you will encounter difficulties. We shall start with the two **ch**-sounds.

ch after a, o, u, au

This sound is relatively easy for Americans to produce; it corresponds to the **ch** in the Scottish word *loch.* To produce it, start with the sound **h,** let the air flow freely, and then, without diminishing the air flow, reduce the space between the back of your tongue and the roof of your mouth.

Most Americans tend to substitute a *k* for this **ch**-sound. The following drill will show you the difference. Note that the vowels preceding the **ch** are sometimes long and sometimes short.

LONG VOWEL	SHORT VOWEL	DIPHTHONG
nach	Bach	auch
hoch	noch	Lauch
Buch	Bruch	Bauch

k	vs.	ch		k	vs.	ch
nackt		Nacht		Kokken		kochen
Akt		acht		Pocken		pochen
Laken		lachen		zuckt		Zucht
lockt		locht		pauken		brauchen
dockt		Docht				

ch in combination with other letters; chs

For most Americans, this is the most difficult German consonant to produce. There are several ways of learning how to produce it. Say the English word *you* with an extended *y: y-y-y-you*. This *y* is a voiced sound; if you take the voice out of it, you'll produce something very close to this second **ch**-sound. (You can figure out the difference between a voiced and an unvoiced consonant by comparing the *s*-sounds in English *see* and *zee* (the letter *z*) or *Sioux* and *Zoo*.) Another way of getting at this second German **ch** is by starting with a word like *Hubert* or *huge*. Strongly aspirate the *h* and stretch it out: *h-h-huge;* the result will be quite similar to the **ch**-sound. Try the following combinations:

a human
say Hugh
the hue
see Hubert

Again, you must be careful not to substitute *k* for **ch**:

k	vs.	ch		k	vs.	ch
Bäcker		Becher		siegt		Sicht
Leck		Lech		nickt		nicht
schleckt		schlecht		Brücke		Brüche
häkeln		hecheln				

The following drill contrasts the two **ch**-sounds. The words in the second column are the plurals of the words in the first column.

Dach	Dächer		Buch	Bücher
Bach	Bäche		Bruch	Brüche
Loch	Löcher		Brauch	Bräuche

In the following drill, the **ch**-sound occurs after consonants.

München	solcher
mancher	Milch
welcher	Furcht

Another difficulty arises when the **ch**-sound appears initially, as in the suffix **-chen**. Note that if the preceding consonant is an **s** or **sch**-sound, the **ch** in **-chen** is pronounced almost like an English *y*.

<table>
<tr><td rowspan="3">PRONUN-
CIATION
DRILL 32</td><td>Männchen</td><td>bißchen</td></tr>
<tr><td>Frauchen</td><td>Häuschen</td></tr>
<tr><td>Säckchen</td><td>Tischchen</td></tr>
</table>

Finally, the combination **chs** is pronounced like English *x*.

<table>
<tr><td rowspan="3">PRONUN-
CIATION
DRILL 33</td><td>sechs</td><td>Sachsen</td></tr>
<tr><td>Luchs</td><td>wachsen</td></tr>
<tr><td>Lachs</td><td>Büchse</td></tr>
</table>

b, d, g and p, t, k; pf, ps, ng, kn

You will have no trouble pronouncing these sounds, but there is one area where you must watch out: if **b, d, g** appear at the end of a syllable or in front of **t**, they are pronounced like **p, t, k.** In the following drill, the German words are not translations of the English words.

<table>
<tr><td rowspan="6">PRONUN-
CIATION
DRILL 34</td><td>ENGLISH
b, d, g</td><td>vs.</td><td>GERMAN
b, d, g</td></tr>
<tr><td>glib</td><td></td><td>gib</td></tr>
<tr><td>glide</td><td></td><td>Kleid</td></tr>
<tr><td>lied</td><td></td><td>Leid</td></tr>
<tr><td>lead</td><td></td><td>Lied</td></tr>
<tr><td>bug</td><td></td><td>Bug</td></tr>
</table>

Compare the pronunciation of **b, d, g** in the following two columns:

<table>
<tr><td rowspan="9">PRONUN-
CIATION
DRILL 35</td><td>b, d, g</td><td>vs.</td><td>p, t, k</td><td>b, d, g</td><td>vs.</td><td>p, t, k</td></tr>
<tr><td>lieben</td><td></td><td>lieb, liebt</td><td>kriegen</td><td></td><td>Krieg, kriegt</td></tr>
<tr><td>heben</td><td></td><td>hob, hebt</td><td>fliegen</td><td></td><td>flog, fliegt</td></tr>
<tr><td>sieben</td><td></td><td>Sieb, siebt</td><td>lügen</td><td></td><td>log, lügt</td></tr>
<tr><td>Abend</td><td></td><td>ab</td><td>beobachten</td><td></td><td>Obdach</td></tr>
<tr><td>loben</td><td></td><td>Lob, lobt</td><td>aber</td><td></td><td>abfahren</td></tr>
<tr><td>leiden</td><td></td><td>Leid</td><td>radeln</td><td></td><td>Radfahrer</td></tr>
<tr><td>Lieder</td><td></td><td>Lied</td><td>Tage</td><td></td><td>täglich</td></tr>
<tr><td>baden</td><td></td><td>Bad</td><td>sagen</td><td></td><td>unsagbar</td></tr>
<tr><td>Süden</td><td></td><td>Süd</td><td></td><td></td><td></td></tr>
</table>

Now read the following words:

Bad Soden, Abendland, wegheben, abheben, Aberglaube, Staubwedel, Abwege, Feldweg, Feldwege, Waldwege, Laubwald, Laubwälder.

The **p** in the combinations **pf** and initial **ps** is always pronounced; the latter occurs only in foreign words:

Pfeife	**Psychologie**
Pfarrer	**Psychiater**
hüpfen	**Psalm**
Köpfe	**Pseudonym**
Topf	
Napf	

PRONUN-CIATION DRILL 36

The combination **ng** is pronounced as in English *singer,* not as in *finger.*

Finger	**lange**
Sänger	**England**
Ringe	

PRONUN-CIATION DRILL 37

The **k** in **kn** must be pronounced.

ENGLISH	GERMAN	ENGLISH	GERMAN
knave	**Knabe**	knee	**Knie**
knack	**knacken**	knight	**Knecht**
knead	**kneten**	knob	**Knopf**

PRONUN-CIATION DRILL 38

z

The German letter **z** represents the combination **ts,** which, in English, does not occur at the beginning of words. To learn to produce it in initial position start with the English word *cats;* say it again, but make a break between *ca-* and *-ts.* Then do the same with *Betsy: Be/tsy.* If you only say *tsy,* you almost have the first syllable of the German word **Ziege.**

INITIAL	MEDIAL	FINAL
ziehen	**heizen**	**Kranz**
zog	**duzen**	**Pfalz**
gezogen	**geizig**	**Salz**
zu	**Lanze**	**Kreuz**
Zug	**Kanzel**	**Malz**
Züge	**Kerze**	**Pelz**
Zahn	**Kreuzung**	**stolz**

PRONUN-CIATION DRILL 39

However, if it occurs in the middle or at the end of a word, the **ts**-sound is usually represented by **tz.**

Katze	**Platz**
putzen	**Fritz**
sitzen	

PRONUN-CIATION DRILL 40

s, ß, sp, st, sch

German s does not present much of a problem. It is neither as strongly voiceless as the English s-sound as in *see* nor as strongly voiced as the s-sound as in *zoo*.

PRONUN- CIATION DRILL 41

INITIAL	MEDIAL	FINAL
so	lesen	das
sie	blasen	los
sagen	gewesen	Glas
sicher	Käse	Mus

The s-sound may be represented by the symbol ß (instead of ss). It is called an s-z (ess-zet) and is used:

(a) between two vowels of which the first is long:

PRONUN- CIATION DRILL 42

LONG VOWEL + ß	SHORT VOWEL + ss
Maße	Masse
Buße	Busse
Straße	Rasse
große	Rosse

(b) after a vowel or a diphthong before a consonant (mostly in verbs whose stem ends in -ss):

weißt	paßt
mußt	heißt

(c) in final position:

Fuß	weiß
Roß	daß

Many Germans no longer use the ß symbol, but write ss instead.

The s in German sp and st at the beginning is pronounced like English *sh*.

PRONUN- CIATION DRILL 43

Spaß	Start	Strand
Sport	stehen	Strom
spät	still	streng
Spinne	Stock	streichen
Spule	Stück	streuen

German sch is pronounced like English *sh*.

PRONUN- CIATION DRILL 44

schön
waschen
Busch

sch	vs.	ch
Tisch		dich
mischen		mich
Esche		Echo
Büsche		Bücher

w, v, f

There is no German equivalent of the English *w*-sound as in *water*. German w is pronounced like English *v*.

wann	wie
wer	warum
wo	

PRONUN-CIATION DRILL 45

German v is usually pronounced like English *f*.

Vater	voll
verliebt	von
viel	

In some foreign words, German v corresponds to English *v*.

Vase
Villa

German f always corresponds to English *f,* as does the *ph*-sound in foreign words.

fallen	fünf
Fell	Philosophie
fliegen	Physik

w	vs.	f		w	vs.	f
Wein		fein		Wort		fort
Wand		fand		Wunde		Funde
winden		finden				

l and r

These two consonants are mispronounced by most Americans. Such mispronunciations will not normally lead to a misunderstanding, but they do in large measure contribute to a "typical American accent." Constant practice with these two consonants is therefore essential.

The English *l* is a "dark," back *l,* and the German l is a "clear," front **l.** Listen to the difference:

PRONUN-CIATION DRILL 46	ENGLISH *l* VS.	GERMAN l	ENGLISH *l* VS.	GERMAN l
	feel	viel	hell	hell
	stool	Stuhl	lewd	lud
	mall	Mal	light	Leid
	fall	Fall	long	lang
	toll	toll	bald	bald
	still	still	built	Bild

In some parts of Germany, the **r** is trilled, but the preferred sound is a uvular **r.** To produce it, say **Buchen,** with the **ch**-sound as far back as possible. Then add voice to it and you should be saying **Buren.**

PRONUN-CIATION DRILL 47	ENGLISH *r* VS.	GERMAN r	ENGLISH *r* VS.	GERMAN r
	run	ran	fry	frei
	rudder	Ruder	fresh	frisch
	reef	rief	creek	Krieg
	rest	Rest	warn	warnen
	ray	Reh	start	Start
	row	roh	stork	Storch
	brown	braun	worst	Wurst
	dry	drei		

We introduced the **er**-sound (ʌ) under the vowels. Many Germans use this same sound for **r** before **t.**

<table>
<tr><td>PRONUN-CIATION DRILL 48</td><td>er fährt</td><td>er bohrt</td><td>er knurrt</td></tr>
<tr><td></td><td>er lehrt</td><td>er irrt</td><td></td></tr>
</table>

PRONUN-CIATION DRILL 49	INITIAL r	r AFTER CONSONANT	MEDIAL r	r BEFORE t	FINAL r (ʌ)
	raffen	graben	fahren	fahrt	fahr'
	Rebe	Bregenz	Beeren	fährt	Bär
	riefen	Friesen	vieren	viert	vier
	rot	Thron*	Toren	bohrt	Tor
	Ruhe	Bruder	Uhren	fuhrt	Uhr

PRONUN-CIATION DRILL 50	ch VS.	r	ch VS.	r
	Buchen	Buren	Sucht	surrt
	suchen	Suren	Dach	dar
	fachen	fahren	Loch	Lohr
	Acht	Art	Tuch	Tour
	Docht	dort		

* The combination **th,** which occurs in a few German words, is always pronounced as **t:** English *throne,* German **Thron.**

PRONUN-
CIATION
DRILL 51

l	vs.	r		l	vs.	r
wild		wird		Spalt		spart
Geld		Gert		spülen		spüren
halt		hart		fühlen		führen
hold		Hort		fallen		fahren
bald		Bart		tollen		Toren

h

At the beginning of a word or syllable, h is pronounced as in English *house*. It is never silent as in English *honor*. The symbol h, however, is also used to indicate that the preceding vowel is long.

PRONUN-
CIATION
DRILL 52

sehen	seht	steh'
fehlen	fehlt	geh'
Lehrer	lehrt	Reh

q

As in English, q appears only with a following u, but it is pronounced like English *kv*, not *kw*.

PRONUN-
CIATION
DRILL 53

ENGLISH	GERMAN
quicksilver	Quecksilber
quadrant	Quadrant
Quaker	Quäker
qualify	qualifizieren
quality	Qualität
quarter	Quartier

j

This letter is pronounced like English *y*.

PRONUN-
CIATION
DRILL 54

ENGLISH	GERMAN
yes	ja
year	Jahr
young	jung
youth	Jugend
yacht	Jacht
yoke	Joch

The Glottal Stop

The glottal stop is a phenomenon much more common in German than in English. In certain parts of the eastern United States, the word *bottle* is pronounced *bo-'l* with a very short open *o*, after which the glottis is closed and then suddenly reopened. This sudden release of air occurs in German in front of all initial vowels: **ein alter Affe.** Most Americans tend to run these words together: **[einalteraffe]**; this is another contributory factor in a "typical American accent." If you neglect to use the glottal stop, you may get yourself into embarrassing situations. For instance, if you don't use the stop in front of -'au, you will interpret the name of the village of **Himmelsau** as *Celestial Pig* instead of *Heavenly Meadow.*

PRONUN-CIATION DRILL 55

ein alter Affe	**alle anderen Uhren**
Himmelsau	**es erübrigt sich**
der erste Akt	**es ist aber veraltet**
ein alter Omnibus	**eine alte Eule sitzt unter einer alten Ulme**
er aber aß Austern	

Note the difference in

 vereisen (*to get covered with ice*) and **verreisen** (*to go on a trip*)
 verengen (*to narrow*)   **verrenken** (*to sprain*)

Sentence Intonation

Since sentence intonation is closely connected with syntax, it is dealt with in various units of this book, as new syntactical patterns are introduced. A few prefatory remarks, however, are in order, to explain the symbols used in the intonation graphs.

Like English, German is spoken on three basic levels of pitch; these levels are indicated by three horizontal lines:

Unstressed syllables are indicated by dots (•), stressed syllables by short lines with a stress mark (✓). Thus the English sentence *He lives in Munich* would be diagrammed as follows:

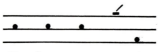

He lives in Munich

If this same sentence is spoken as a question, the last syllable, though un-stressed, shows a rise in pitch. This rise is indicated by the symbol (♪). If the last syllable is stressed, rising pitch is indicated by (⟋) and falling pitch by (⟍).

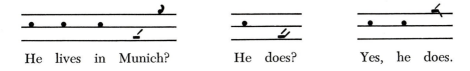

He lives in Munich?   He does?   Yes, he does.

Syllabication

German syllabication is considerably simpler than English syllabication. A few basic rules will suffice to see you through this book.

German words are divided before single consonants and between double consonants.

Va - ter	kom - men
Da - me	reg - nen
Te - le - fon	Mün - chen

The only exception to this rule is **st**, which is never separated.

fe - ster
mei - stens
Fen - ster

Unlike English, German does not consider suffixes independent units; thus it is **Woh - nung**, not **[Wohn - ung]**.

Compound words are divided according to their individual parts.

Brief - trä - ger
Glas - au - ge
Sams - tag

Punctuation

Generally speaking, most German punctuation marks are used as in English. Only the use of the comma is different. The comma may be used to separate main clauses if the second clause contains a new subject, especially in front of coordinating conjunctions. The comma *must* be used to separate dependent clauses from main clauses. Relative clauses are dependent clauses, and German does not distinguish between restrictive and nonrestrictive relative clauses. In contrast to English, the comma is not used in front of **und** in series: **Männer, Frauen und Kinder.**

The first of a pair of quotation marks in German appears below the base line in writing or printing, the second appears at the top: "Be quiet!" „**Sei ruhig!**"

SECOND EDITION

German

A
Structural
Approach

Unit 1
The Present Tense—**sein** and **haben**—
Gender—Plural of Nouns—Basic Sentence Structure—
Intonation Patterns—**auch**—**denn**

Patterns

Practice and read aloud the following sentences until you have
mastered the intonation pattern.

[1] Assertions: Basic Intonation Pattern

Intonation sample:	**Es *reg*net.**

Es *reg*net.	It is *raining*.	
Wir *kom*men.	We are *coming*.	
Er *kommt* schon.	He is *coming* already.	
Er *braucht* es.	He *needs* it.	
Ihr *glaubt* es.	You *believe* it.	
Er *wohnt* hier.	He *lives* here.	

SEE
ANALYSIS
1–15

(pp. 6-16)

[2] Assertions: Enlarged Pattern

Intonation sample:	**Wir brauchen *alle* Geld.**

Sie hat *Hun*ger.	She is *hungry*.
Das ist Frau *Mey*er.	That's Mrs. *Meyer*.
Das ist *Herr* Meyer.	That's *Mr.* Meyer.
Wir brauchen *Re*gen.	We need *rain*.
Wir *ar*beiten heute.	We are *working* today.
Wir bleiben heute zu *Hau*se.	We are staying *home* today.
Wir brauchen *alle* Geld.	We *all* need money.

SEE
ANALYSIS
1–15

(pp. 6-16)

An advertising poster in Vienna. The 2 slimmers: sour milk and yogurt.

1

[3] Assertions: Syntactical Stress on Last Syllable

Intonation sample:  **Er ist in *Köln*.**

SEE
ANALYSIS
1–15

(pp. 6-16)

Sie *kommt*.	She is *coming*.
Er hat *Geld*.	He has *money*.
Sie lernen *Deutsch*.	They are learning *German*.
Er ist in *Köln*.	He is in *Cologne*.
Er wohnt in Ber*lin*.	He is living in *Berlin*.
Das glaube ich *auch*.	I believe that, *too*.
Ich studiere Medi*zin*.	I am studying *medicine*.
Ich bin Stu*dent*.	I am a *student*.

[4] Assertions: Syntactical Stress on First Syllable

Intonation sample: 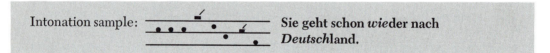 ***Fritz* ist schon hier.**

SEE
ANALYSIS
1–15

(pp. 6-16)

*Va*ter ist hier!	*Father* is here!
Du bist's!	It is *you!*
*Mey*er kommt morgen.	*Meyer* is coming tomorrow.

[5] Syntactical Stress on More than One Syllable

Intonation sample: 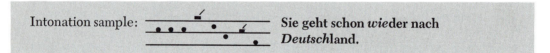 **Sie geht schon *wieder* nach *Deutsch*land.**

SEE
ANALYSIS
1–15

(pp. 6-16)

Sie geht schon *wieder* nach *Deutsch*land.	She is going to *Germany again*.
Übrigens gehen wir *nächs*tes Jahr nach *Deutsch*land.	By the way, we are going to *Germany next* year. (Not *this* year.)
Sonntags gehen wir na*tür*lich in die *Kir*che.	On Sundays we go to *church*, of *course*.

[6] Word Questions

Intonation samples:  **Wann kommt *ihr* denn nach Köln?**

Wo ist Frau *Mann*?

		SEE ANALYSIS 16–17 (pp. 16-18)
Wo *bist* du denn?	Where *are* you?	
Was *hast* du denn?	What do you *have?*	
Wo *wohnt* er denn?	Where does he *live?*	
Wann *kommt* er denn?	When is he *coming?*	
Wo *wohnt* ihr denn?	Where do you *live?*	
Wo *arbeiten* Sie?	Where do you *work?*	
Wann kommst du denn nach *Hause?*	When are you coming *home?*	
Wann kommt *ihr* denn nach Köln?	When are *you* coming to Cologne?	
Wo ist denn die *Zeitung?*	Where is the *newspaper?*	
Wo ist Frau *Mann?*	Where is Mrs. *Mann?*	
Wer ist denn *das?*	Who is *that?*	

[7] Yes-or-No Questions

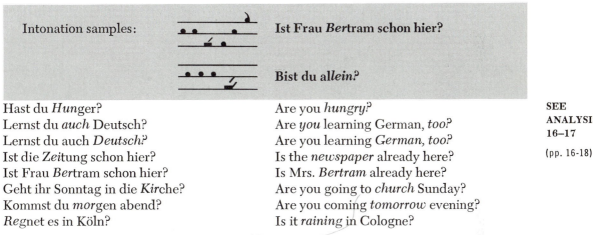

Hast du *Hunger?*	Are you *hungry?*	SEE ANALYSIS 16–17 (pp. 16-18)
Lernst du *auch* Deutsch?	Are *you* learning German, *too?*	
Lernst du auch *Deutsch?*	Are you learning *German, too?*	
Ist die *Zeitung* schon hier?	Is the *newspaper* already here?	
Ist Frau *Bertram* schon hier?	Is Mrs. *Bertram* already here?	
Geht ihr Sonntag in die *Kirche?*	Are you going to *church* Sunday?	
Kommst du *morgen* abend?	Are you coming *tomorrow* evening?	
Regnet es in Köln?	Is it *raining* in Cologne?	

[8] Assertions Intonated as Questions

Du wohnst *auch* in München?	You live in Munich, *too?*	SEE ANALYSIS 16–17 (pp. 16-18)
Er arbeitet jetzt in *München?*	He works in *Munich* now?	
Ihr arbeitet *heute?*	You are working *today?*	
Ihr *arbeitet* heute?	You are *working* today?	
Er braucht *Geld?*	He needs *money?*	
Erika ist hier?	*Erika* is here?	
Erika ist hier in *Köln?*	Erika is here in *Cologne?*	

[9] Front Field Elements

Practice reading these sentences until you can read them rapidly and
with correct intonation.

SEE
ANALYSIS
10–11
(pp. 11-13)

Natürlich	**bleibe**	ich morgen abend zu Hause.
Ich	**bleibe**	morgen abend natürlich zu Hause.
Morgen abend	**bleibe**	ich natürlich zu Hause.

Wir	**gehen**	natürlich Sonntag morgen in die Kirche.
Natürlich	**gehen**	wir Sonntag morgen in die Kirche.
Sonntag morgen	**gehen**	wir natürlich in die Kirche.

Übrigens	**gehen**	wir Sonntag abend ins Kino.
Wir	**gehen**	übrigens Sonntag abend ins Kino.
Sonntag abend	**gehen**	wir übrigens ins Kino.

[10] Numbers; Plural of Nouns

Invent your own variations:

SEE
ANALYSIS
9
(pp. 10-11)

Herr Meyer hat zwei Büros, ein Büro in Köln, und ein Büro in Bonn.

Mr. Meyer has two offices, one office in Cologne and one office in Bonn.

Schmidts haben zwei Kinder. Der Sohn heißt Peter, und die Tochter heißt Sylvia.

The Schmidts have two children. The son's name is Peter, and the daughter's name is Sylvia.

Meyers haben zwei Söhne. Sie heißen Paul und Gerhardt.

The Meyers have two sons. Their names are Paul and Gerhardt.

Müllers haben zwei Töchter.—Wie heißen sie denn?—Sie heißen Andrea und Ingrid.

The Müllers have two daughters.—What are their names?—Their names are Andrea and Ingrid.

Wir bleiben zwei Jahre in Deutschland.

We are staying in Germany for two years.

Wir bleiben zwei Tage in Berlin.

We are staying in Berlin for two days.

Sind Herr Schmidt und Herr Müller schon hier?—Ja, Herr Doktor, die Herren sind schon hier.

Are Mr. Schmidt and Mr. Müller here already?—Yes, Doctor, the gentlemen are already here.

Der Mann arbeitet in München. Die Männer arbeiten alle in München.

The man is working in Munich. The men are all working in Munich.

Frau Meyer und Frau Schmidt sind zu Hause. Die zwei Frauen bleiben heute zu Hause.

Mrs. Meyer and Mrs. Schmidt are at home. The two women are staying at home today.

Conversation

Practice reading these conversations aloud until you have memorized them.

I

SCHMIDT (answering the telephone):
Alfred Schmidt!

Alfred Schmidt.

MEYER: Hier Meyer. Guten Morgen, Herr Schmidt! Also, Sie sind noch in Hamburg! Wie ist denn das Wetter in Hamburg?

Meyer speaking. Good morning, Mr. Schmidt. So, you are still in Hamburg. How is the weather in Hamburg?

SCHMIDT: Hier in Hamburg regnet es, schon seit Sonntag. Und kalt ist es auch.

It's raining here in Hamburg; it has been since Sunday. And it is cold, too.

MEYER: Hier in Köln regnet es auch! Kommen Sie heute zurück?

Here in Cologne it's raining, too. Are you coming back today?

SCHMIDT: Nein, heute noch nicht! Aber morgen! Morgen um elf bin ich im Büro.

No, not today. But tomorrow. I'll be at the office tomorrow at 11.

MEYER: Gut, also dann bis morgen!

O.K., until tomorrow then.

II

KURT: Ja Erika! Was tust *du* denn hier in Köln?

Well, Erika! What are *you* doing here in Cologne?

ERIKA: Was ich hier in Köln tue? Ich studiere* hier Medizin. Hans studiert auch hier in Köln.

What I am doing here in Cologne? I'm going to med school here. Hans is going to school here, too.

KURT: So! Studiert Hans auch Medizin?

Oh! Is Hans studying medicine, too?

ERIKA: Nein, Hans studiert Mathematik!

No, Hans is in math.

KURT: *Wohnt* ihr auch hier in Köln?

Are you *living* here in Cologne too?

ERIKA: Ja, *ich* wohne hier in Köln. Aber Hans wohnt noch in Bonn.

Yes, *I* live here in Cologne. But Hans is still living in Bonn.

* The basic meaning of **studieren** is *to attend a university.*

Analysis

1 The Infinitive

The *infinitive* is that form of the verb which is used as a dictionary entry. Thus the English forms *am, is,* and *was* are found in the dictionary under *be; bought* is found under *buy;* and *does* is found under *do.*

Most German infinitives end in **-en: arbeiten, bleiben, brauchen.** The infinitives **sein, tun,** and certain others to be introduced later end in **-n.** That part of the verb which precedes the infinitive ending **-en** or **-n** is called the *stem.* Thus:

STEM	+	INFINITIVE ENDING	=	INFINITIVE
arbeit-		**-en**		**arbeiten**
bleib-		**-en**		**bleiben**
brauch-		**-en**		**brauchen**
tu-		**-n**		**tun**

2 Personal Pronouns

SINGULAR		PLURAL	
ich	I	**wir**	we
du	you	**ihr**	you
er	he	**sie**	they
sie	she		
es	it	**Sie**	you

English *you:* du, ihr, Sie

Modern English alone among all the Indo-European languages has just one form (*you*) for the second person. English *you* is both singular and plural, formal and informal. In German, there are three mutually exclusive forms:

1. **du** (corresponding to the archaic English *thou*) is the familiar singular. It expresses intimacy and is therefore used in the family, with close friends, and in prayer. It is also used with *all* children up to the age of about fourteen and with animals (pets).

2. **ihr** is the plural of **du.**

3. **Sie,** on the other hand, implies a certain formality and the recognition of social considerations. It is always used with **Herr, Frau, Fräulein,** or other

titles. This polite **Sie,** which is both singular and plural, sounds like the plural **sie** (*they*) and it takes the same verb form. When written, it is always capitalized.

Brauchst du Geld, Maria?	Do you need money, Mary?
Brauchst du Geld, Karl?	Do you need money, Karl?
Braucht ihr Geld, Kinder?	Do you need money, children?
Du bist mein Gott.	Thou art my God. (Ps. 31:14)
Brauchen Sie Geld, Herr Meyer?	Do you need money, Mr. Meyer?
Wohnen Sie in München, Herr Doktor?	Do you live in Munich, Dr. Meyer?

Beware!   **[Brauchst du Geld, Herr Meyer?]**   DO NOT USE!
Americanism!   **[Brauchst du Geld, Frau Meyer?]***

NOTE: Germans love titles. If **Herr Meyer** has earned any kind of doctorate, he is addressed as **Herr Doktor** (no last name), and he is referred to as **Herr Dr. Meyer** or as **Dr. Meyer.**

3 Inflected Verb Forms

The predicate verb of a sentence or a clause is always an *inflected* form—that is, a form modified by a personal ending. (With the exception of *-s,* as in *he lives,* all personal endings have been dropped in English.)

The present tense of regular verbs is formed as follows:

PRONOUN	STEM	+	PERSONAL ENDING	=	INFLECTED FORM	
ich	glaub-		e		ich glaube	I believe
du	glaub-		st		du glaubst	you believe
er					er	he
sie	glaub-		t		sie } glaubt	she } believes
es					es	it
wir	glaub-		en		wir glauben	we believe
ihr	glaub-		t		ihr glaubt	you believe
sie	glaub-		en		sie glauben	they believe
Sie	glaub-		en		Sie glauben	you believe

4 Absence of Progressive and Emphatic Forms in German

A native speaker of English will always differentiate between the *simple present* and the *progressive form.* The simple present usually expresses either a timeless fact:

* Brackets are used in this book to indicate unacceptable forms—either Germanisms in English or Americanisms in German.

Typical street signs: "Straight ahead and right turn only. Begin. No parking from 7 p.m. to 7 a.m. and no stopping from 7 a.m. to 7 p.m."

Water boils at 100° C

or some habitual attitude or activity:

He is usually nasty.
He smokes only cigars.
I just love our new house.

Use of the progressive form, on the other hand, expresses the idea of "being in the middle of" a temporary activity. Thus, it would make no sense to say *I am just loving our new house,* but it is possible to say:

He is being nasty again.
The water is boiling.
This week we are reading Hemingway.
Dad is working in the garden.

Standard German cannot express the difference between *boils* and *is boiling* by verb forms. You should not "translate" *he is having, he is being, he is working* into German. Otherwise you will start by saying **er ist . . .** and end up with an Americanism. **Er arbeitet** means both *he works* and *he is working,* and **es regnet** means both *it rains* and *it is raining.*

German also has no emphatic form. It cannot express the difference between *I go* and *I do go* by different verb forms. Instead, German relies on intonation and on certain particles. The unaccented **ja,** for instance, adds the flavor of *indeed,* implied in *we do go.*

Wir gehen jeden Sonntag in die Kirche.	We go to church *every* Sunday.
Aber Vater, wir gehen ja jeden Sonntag in die Kirche.	But, Father, we *do* go to church every Sunday.

5 Future Meaning of Present-Tense Forms

Just as the progressive form *I am going* has a future meaning in *I am going to Germany next year,* so the present tense of German verbs frequently assumes a future meaning.

Morgen abend gehen wir ins Kino.   We are going to the movies tomorrow night.

6 Variations in Personal Endings

In the case of **er glaubt** or **er kommt**, the ending **-t** is easily pronounced and heard. However, in the case of such verbs as **arbeiten** and of all other verbs whose stems end in **-d** or **-t**, the vowel **-e-** is inserted between the stem and the endings **-st** and **-t** to make these endings clearly audible. For similar reasons (so that the second syllable of all forms of **regnen** starts with an **n-**), it is **es regnet**, not [**es regnt**].

NORMAL VERBS		VERBS WITH STEMS IN -d OR -t	
du	glaubst	du	arbeitest
er		er	
sie	glaubt	sie	arbeitet
es		es	
ihr	glaubt	ihr	arbeitet

Since the infinitive **tun** ends in **-n** and not in **-en**, the **wir**-form and the **sie**-form also end in **-n: wir tun, sie tun.**

7 sein and haben

A few of the most frequently used German verbs are quite irregular. In this unit, we introduce **sein** (*to be*) and **haben** (*to have*). In the present tense, they are inflected as follows:

ich	bin	ich	habe
du	bist	du	hast
er		er	
sie	ist	sie	hat
es		es	
wir	sind	wir	haben
ihr	seid	ihr	habt
sie	sind	sie	haben
Sie	sind	Sie	haben

8 Gender of Nouns

Indo-European, the ancestor of most modern European languages, including English, distinguished between three classes of nouns, which we call masculines, feminines, and neuters. All Indo-European languages, including Old English, inherited this distinction. Modern English is the only Indo-European language which has given up the difference almost completely. All nouns in French and Spanish are either feminine or masculine. German, Russian, and some other languages have kept all three classes alive. Usually, the German nouns themselves can no longer be recognized as masculine, feminine, or neuter just by looking at their dictionary forms: **Winter** (masculine), **Butter** (feminine), and **Wetter** (neuter) all end in **-er.** However, the articles (and also the pronouns and the adjectives) used with nouns still show the old difference:

MASCULINE	*der* **Winter**	(*the* winter)	*der* **Löffel**	(*the* spoon)
FEMININE	*die* **Butter**	(*the* butter)	*die* **Gabel**	(*the* fork)
NEUTER	*das* **Wetter**	(*the* weather)	*das* **Messer**	(*the* knife)

"Gender" is a linguistic, not a biological term. There is obviously nothing "masculine" about a spoon, nothing "feminine" about a fork, and nothing "neuter" about a knife, though the genders of the German nouns are masculine, feminine, and neuter respectively. To be sure, it is **der Mann** (*the man*), **die Frau** (*the woman*), and **das Kind** (*the infant*), and this is the reason why the term "masculine" came to be applied to *all* nouns used with **der,** the term "feminine" to *all* nouns used with **die,** and the term "neuter" to *all* nouns used with **das.** German children are not conscious of gender, and they never hear the term until they go to school. But they always hear their elders and the other children say **der Löffel, die Gabel,** and **das Messer.** They imitate what they hear and thus learn gender without effort. For the English-speaking student there is only one thing to do: learn the article together with the noun.

All German nouns are capitalized; but note that the pronoun **ich** is never capitalized except at the beginning of a sentence.

9 Singular and Plural Forms of Nouns

With a few exceptions, English nouns form the plural by adding *-s* or *-es* to the singular: *house, houses; glass, glasses;* but *foot, feet.*

In German, the plural form of a noun usually does not end in **-s.** It may be the same as the singular form, as in the case of English *sheep,* or it may be different from the singular form, as in the case of English *mouse, mice* or *child, children.*

Since there are no rules by which to tell the plural form of a given singular, there is only one safe way to learn the plural: memorize it together with the singular.

The plural forms are indicated in the vocabulary as follows:

der Vater, ⸚ means that the plural of **der Vater** is **die Väter**

das Kind, –er	**das Kind**	**die Kinder**
der Hund, –e	**der Hund**	**die Hunde**

The articles preceding plural nouns are the same for all three genders; the nominative plural article is **die.**

Nouns of non-German origin may have a plural ending in **-s:**

das Auto, –s   **das Büro, –s**   **das Kino, –s**

10 The Inflected Verb and Its Position

In spite of a few exceptions like *There goes Joe,* it makes sense to state categorically: In English assertions the inflected verb is always preceded by its subject, and the subject may be preceded or followed by some other syntactical unit, usually a time phrase. Thus, the inflected verb may be the second or the third unit of an English assertion.

	She	*lives*	in Munich.
Now	she	*lives*	in Munich.
She	now	*lives*	in Munich.

In German, the inflected verb is always the second syntactical unit. There are no exceptions. This means that one cannot imitate the word order of the last two English sentences above and say:

Beware!	[**Sie jetzt wohnt in München.**]	DO NOT USE!
Americanism!	[**Jetzt sie wohnt in München.**]	

A German verb can be preceded by the subject *or* by a time phrase, but not by the subject *and* a time phrase. This is where the trouble starts, because the one syntactical unit in front of a German verb is very frequently *not* the subject. The sentences

Jetzt wohnt sie in München
Morgen fliegen wir nach München

where the subject *follows* the verb, are just as idiomatic as

Sie wohnt jetzt in München
Wir fliegen morgen nach München

where the subject *precedes* the verb. What is the position of the subject if it does not precede the verb? This question is easily answered: If pronoun subjects like **ich** or **wir** or **sie** do not precede the verb, they immediately follow it. Noun subjects *may* come later. But for the time being, it will be safe to place noun subjects like **Herr Meyer** or **die Zeitung** immediately after the verb.

11 The Element in Front of the Inflected Verb

Are there any syntactical units which cannot precede a German verb? With normal intonation (and that's all we will be using for a while), any syntactical unit which cannot precede an *English* verb cannot precede a *German* verb either. For instance, you cannot, in German or in English, answer the question

Wo arbeitet Herr Meyer heute?   Where is Mr. Meyer working today?

by a statement starting with **in München.** However, you could answer the question *What do the Scotch drink in Munich?* by saying:

In München trinken sie Bier.   In Munich they drink beer.

In other words, if you are tempted to start an English assertion with *next year . . .* , feel free to start the corresponding German assertion with **nächstes Jahr . . . .** Just don't forget that the next unit must be the verb.

Nächstes Jahr fliegen wir nach Deutschland.

You must realize, however, that the English sentence

Next year we are going to fly to Germany

cannot be used to answer a question starting with *when.* This sentence may be used as an unsolicited news item or to answer a question like *Do you have any plans for next year?*, but the question *When are you going to Germany?* can only be answered by *We are going to Germany next year* or—shorter— by *Next year.* Similarly, to answer the German **wann**-question

Wann fliegst du nach München?

you can simply say **Morgen!** But if you answer with a complete sentence you will have to say:

Ich fliege *morgen* nach München.

(The question why **nach München** comes last will be answered later.) The general rule, for both English and German, is: Whenever you want to answer a question by a complete sentence, do *not* start that sentence with the phrase containing the answer.

QUESTION

Wo seid ihr jetzt?   Where are you now?

INTERCHANGEABLE ANSWERS

In Ber*lin!*   In Berlin!
Wir sind in Ber*lin!*   We are in Berlin!
Wir sind jetzt in Ber*lin.*   We are in Berlin now.
Jetzt sind wir in Ber*lin.*   Now we are in Berlin.

There is one exception to the general rule. Questions like

Who is going to come tomorrow?

or

Is anybody going to come tomorrow?

ask for the subject of the verb used. Since the subject always precedes the English verb, the only answer in English is

The *Meyers* are coming tomorrow.

In this case—that is, when the subject contains the news value—you can start the German sentence with the subject, too.

***Meyers* kommen morgen!**

However, the answer

Morgen kommen *Mey*ers!

is just as idiomatic.

12 News Value

Most English and German sentences contain one element of new information that the speaker wants to "put across." This one element is always stressed, because without it there would be no reason to make the statement. This element then contains what we call the news value of the statement.

13 Word Stress

Almost all simple (noncompound) German words stress the first syllable: **A′bend** (*evening*), **ar′beiten** (*to work*), **heu′te** (*today*). Words composed of two nouns stress the first noun much more strongly than the second: **Haus′frau** (*housewife*), **Haus′hund** (*house dog*), **Hun′dehaus** (*doghouse*).

Words of non-German origin frequently do not stress the first syllable: **natür′lich, die Natur′, studie′ren.** The vocabulary will indicate which syllable is stressed in these cases.

14 Syntactical Stress

Word Stress versus Syntactical Stress

If one analyzes the stress situation in a short sentence like

August wohnt in Berlin   Gus lives in Berlin

one can either look at the individual words as words, or one can look at the sentence as a whole.

Looking at the words **Au′gust** and **Berlin′** as words, we find that **Au′gust** is stressed on the first and **Berlin′** on the second syllable. This is a question of word stress. Word stress is fixed, and it is simply a mistake to say **August'** or **Ber'lin.** In fact, **Au'gust** is a personal name and **August'** is the name of a month.

Looking at the sentence as a whole—that is, as one single unit of thought— we find it ambiguous in its written form. The speaker may want to say:

1. *August* **wohnt in Berlin.**   *Gus* lives in Berlin.
2. **August** *wohnt* **in Berlin.**   Gus *lives* in Berlin.
3. **August wohnt in Ber***lin.***   Gus lives in *Berlin.*

The one written sentence turns out to be at least three spoken sentences, which are not interchangeable. Each of them is used in situations where the other two cannot be used.

In all three sentences, **August** is stressed on the first, and **Berlin** on the second syllable. But the stress on **Au'gust** in the first sentence above is so strong that, in comparison, the stress on **Berlin'** becomes insignificant. For in each sentence the speaker singles out at least one word into which he packs the major news value and upon which he therefore places such a strong emphasis that, as far as the sentence as a whole is concerned, all other syllables can be regarded as unstressed. Syntactical stress, by which the speaker distinguishes between important and unimportant words, over-shadows word stress; and whereas word stress is fixed, syntactical stress can shift from one word to another, depending on which word is chosen by the speaker to be the important one in a certain situation. The stressed syllable of this important word is called the *stress point* of a sentence.

15 Intonation of Assertions

The Basic Pattern

As long as only one syllable of an assertion receives syntactical stress, this one syllable (the stress point) is also the syllable with the highest pitch.

Pitch in German (and English) is usually distributed over three levels, symbolized by the three lines below.* An assertion usually starts on level 2, moves up to level 3 for the stress point, and then falls to level 1. By using dots for the syllables without syntactical stress, and a short line with an accent over it for the stress point, the pitch distribution can be diagrammed as follows:

Sie   *wohnt*   **hier**   She   *lives*   here

* For a full explanation of the symbols used in the intonation diagrams, see the intro-ductory section on the sounds of German.

The Enlarged Pattern

Depending on which syllable is selected by the speaker to assume the role
of the stress point, the sentence **Maria wohnt in München** can be pronounced
with the following three intonations:

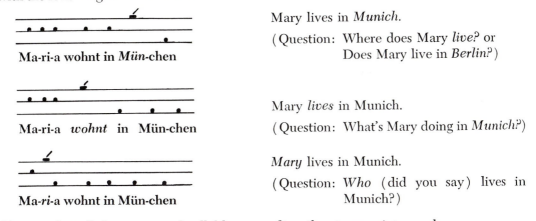

Mary lives in *Munich.*

(Question: Where does Mary *live?* or
                Does Mary live in *Berlin?*)

Mary *lives* in Munich.

(Question: What's Mary doing in *Munich?*)

Mary lives in Munich.

(Question: *Who* (did you say) lives in
                Munich?)

Observe that all the unstressed syllables preceding the stress point may be
spoken with even level-2 pitch, and that all the unstressed syllables following
the stress point show level-1 pitch.

Syntactical Stress on the Last Syllable

The drop from level 3 to level 1 at the end of a sentence functions as a signal
meaning "This is the end of the sentence." This drop must therefore be
maintained, even if the last syllable is the stress point. The last syllable
itself must then show a downward glide.

Er wohnt in Ber-*lin*

Compare the difference between *No!* (↰) as an answer and *No?* (↙)
as a question.

Assertions with More than One Stressed Syllable

Many German sentences contain more than one syllable which carries a
strong syntactical stress. The sentence **Sie arbeiten alle in München,** for
instance, may be pronounced in the following ways:

ONE STRESSED SYLLABLE

They all *work* in Munich.

(Question: What are they all doing in *Munich?*)

Sie *ar*-bei-ten al-le in Mün-chen

They *all* work in Munich.

(Question: How *many* of them work in Munich?)

Sie ar-bei-ten *al*-le in Mün-chen

They all work in *Munich.*

(Question: Where do they all *work?*)

Sie ar-bei-ten al-le in *Mün*-chen

TWO STRESSED SYLLABLES

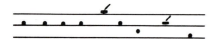

They *all* work in *Munich.*

(Question: What do they do for a *living?*)

Sie ar-bei-ten *al*-le in *Mün*-chen

As the last example shows, if a German sentence contains more than one stressed syllable, the first one has level-3 pitch, and the ones following are lower than the first. The end of the sentence provides the usual signal: the intonation falls to level 1 and thereby indicates the end of the assertion. All stressed syllables express items which have significant news value for the specific situation in which the sentence is spoken.

16 The Structure of Questions

As far as grammatical structure is concerned, German, like English, uses three types of questions.

Yes-or-No Questions

Questions which can be answered by **ja** (*yes*) or **nein** (*no*) may start with an inflected verb in both English and German. However, there is an important difference. The opening verb in English can only be (1) a form of *to be* (*Is Bob in?*), (2) a form of *to have* (*Has he gone?*), (3) a modal (*Can he play?*), or (4) a form of *to do* (*Does he want to play?*). In German, *any* verb can open a yes-or-no question, and the use of **tun** as an auxiliary is impossible. The German questions

Regnet es heute?   **Arbeitet er in Berlin?**   **Brauchst du Geld?**

correspond in English to the unacceptable Germanisms

[Rains it today?]   [Works he in Berlin?]   [Need you money?]

Conversely, the English questions

Does he work?   Do you need money?

correspond in German to the unacceptable Americanisms

Beware!   **[Tut er arbeiten?]**

Americanism!   **[Tust du brauchen Geld?]**   DO NOT USE!

Word Questions

Questions which start with interrogatives (question words) such as **wer** (*who*), **wann** (*when*), **wo** (*where*), or **wie** (*how*) we shall call word questions. In word questions, the inflected verb follows immediately after the interrogative.

Wann kommt ihr?   When are you coming?
Wer ist das?   Who is that?
Wo wohnt sie?   Where does she live?

NOTE: Any German verb can follow the interrogative, and the use of **tun** as an auxiliary is again impossible.

Beware!   **[Wann tust du kommen?]**

Americanism!   **[Wo tut sie wohnen?]**   DO NOT USE!

Questions Structured like Assertions

German assertions, as we pointed out in **10,** are characterized by the fact that the inflected verb is always the second unit in the sentence. Any such assertion can be changed into a yes-or-no question by changing its intonation (see **17**).

17 The Intonation of Questions

Word Questions

Normally, German word questions follow the intonation pattern of assertions.

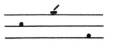

Wo *wohnst* **du?**
Where do you *live?*

Wann kom-men *Sie* **nach Köln?**
When will *you* come to Cologne?

Yes-or-No Questions
──────────

Yes-or-no questions, including assertions changed by intonation into questions, show an upward movement after the last stressed syllable. Although there are several other possibilities, the beginner, after starting as usual on level 2, should place the last stressed syllable on level 1 and then move upward.

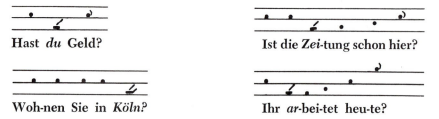

Hast *du* Geld?   Ist die **Zei**-tung schon hier?

Woh-nen Sie in *Köln?*   Ihr *ar*-bei-tet heu-te?

Note that after a stressed syllable on level 1 no other stressed syllables can follow.

18 auch

German **auch,** meaning *also* or *too*, is one of the most frequently used words. The stressed **auch** refers *back* to a preceding unit, regardless of whether that unit is stressed or not. The unstressed **auch** refers *forward* to a *stressed* unit, except in one case: Since the inflected verb is always the second unit in a German sentence, one cannot imitate the English sentence *He also likes money,* or *He also lives in Munich.* Instead, the stressed verb precedes the unstressed **auch.**

    Er *wohnt* auch in München.   He also *lives* in Munich.
                                                                              He *lives* in Munich, too.

Here are some further examples:

    Sie ist *auch* intelligent.   *She, too,* is intelligent.
    Sie ist auch intellig*ent*.   She is also *intelligent.*
    Er hat *auch* ein Büro in Köln.   *He, too,* has an office in Cologne.
    Er hat auch ein Bü*ro* in Köln.   He also has an *office* in Cologne.
    Er hat auch ein Büro in *Köln*.   He also has an office in *Cologne.*

19 denn

Idiomatic German is characterized by the very frequent use of "particles" which, in addition to their definable dictionary meaning, have a psychological meaning sometimes hard to define. English occasionally uses such particles, too. Thus, *there* has a definable dictionary meaning in *She is there.*

However, when a mother runs up to her crying baby, pats it on the back, and says, "There, there!" *there* is no longer the same word as in *She is there.*

The particles used most frequently in German will be introduced one by one; use them as often as possible in spoken German. We shall start with **denn.**

The unstressed German **denn** occurs most frequently in word questions. It expresses either impatience or interest.

IMPATIENCE	A:	**Ist Meyer hier?**	Is Meyer here?
	B:	**Nein, Meyer ist noch nicht hier.**	No, Meyer is not here yet.
	A:	**Wo bleibt er denn?**	Well, where is he? (I have been waiting long enough.)
INTEREST	A:	**Fritz ist hier!**	Fritz is here!
	B:	**Wo ist er denn?**	Where is he? (I am interested in finding out.)

The use of this **denn** is so frequent in spoken German that most word questions contain it. It follows the inflected verb and the personal pronouns, and it may even follow unstressed nouns, but it precedes the first stressed element of importance unless the inflected verb is stressed.

Wann *brauchst* du es denn?
Wo *ist* das Büro denn?
Wo ist denn das Bü*ro?*

In yes-or-no questions, **denn** implies a feeling of surprise or incredulity.

***Arbeitet* ihr denn heute?**	You are *working* today? (I can't believe it.)
Hat er denn *Geld?*	Does he have *money?* (I thought he was on relief.)

Exercises

A. Write out, and say aloud, the following German sentences. Be prepared to go through these sentences in class without your book.

> **Ich studiere, und du studierst *auch*.**
> **Du studierst, und er studiert *auch*.**
> **Er studiert, und wir studieren *auch*.**
> **Wir studieren, und ihr studiert *auch*.**
> **Ihr studiert, und sie studieren *auch*.**

1. Ich arbeite heute, und du _____ heute *auch.*
   Du_____ heute, und er _____ heute *auch.*
   Er _____ heute, und sie (*she*) _____ heute *auch.*
   Sie (*she*) _____ heute, und wir _____ heute *auch.*
   Wir _____ heute, und ihr _____ heute *auch.*
   Ihr _____ heute, und sie (*they*) _____ heute *auch.*

2. Ich bin allein. _____ du *auch* allein, Erika?
   Er _____ allein. _____ Erika *auch* allein?
   Wir _____ allein. _____ ihr *auch* allein?
   Ihr _____ allein. _____ Meyers *auch* allein?
   Wir _____ allein. _____ Sie *auch* allein, Frau Meyer?

3. Ich habe Geld. _____ du *auch* Geld?
   Du _____ Geld. _____ er *auch* Geld?
   Er _____ Geld. _____ sie (*she*) *auch* Geld?
   Wir _____ Geld. _____ ihr *auch* Geld?
   Ihr _____ Geld. _____ sie (*they*) *auch* Geld?
   Frau Fischer _____ Geld. _____ Sie *auch* Geld, Frau Meyer?

4. Ich gehe *heute* ins Kino, und ich _____ auch *morgen* ins Kino.
   Du _____ *heute* ins Kino, und du _____ auch *morgen* ins Kino.
   Er _____ *heute* ins Kino, und er _____ auch *morgen* ins Kino.
   Wir _____ *heute* ins Kino, und wir _____ auch *morgen* ins Kino.
   Ihr _____ *heute* ins Kino, und ihr _____ auch *morgen* ins Kino.
   Sie _____ *heute* ins Kino, und sie _____ auch *morgen* ins Kino.

5. Ich gehe heute ins Kino, und du _____ heute *auch* ins Kino.
   Du _____ heute ins Kino, und er _____ heute *auch* ins Kino.
   Er _____ heute ins Kino, und wir _____ heute *auch* ins Kino.
   Wir _____ heute ins Kino, und ihr _____ heute *auch* ins Kino.
   Ihr _____ heute ins Kino, und sie _____ heute *auch* ins Kino.

6. Ich tue das, und du _____ es *auch.*
   Du _____ das, und er _____ es *auch.*
   Er _____ das, und wir _____ es *auch.*
   Wir _____ das, und ihr _____ es *auch.*
   Ihr _____ das, und sie _____ es *auch.*

B. Write down the answers to the following questions. Be prepared
to answer these questions in class, orally and at normal speed,
without looking at your book or paper.

Wohnen Sie in Berlin?	**Ja, ich wohne in Berlin.**
	Nein, ich wohne in München.
Wo ist Fritz?	**Fritz ist zu Hause.**
	Er ist in Bonn.

1. Ist Fritz zu Hause? Ja, _____. Nein, _____ im Büro.
2. Wer ist das? Das _____.
3. Arbeiten Sie in Köln? Ja, ich _____, Nein, ich _____ in Bonn.
4. Wo arbeiten Sie? Ich _____.
5. Bleibst du heute abend zu Hause? Ja, _____. Nein, ich gehe _____ ins Kino.
6. Studiert sie in Heidelberg? Ja, _____. Nein, _____ in Hamburg.
7. Wann kommt ihr denn? Wir _____.
8. Wohnen Schmidts *auch* in Köln? Ja, _____. Nein, _____ in München.

C. Write down one *yes-or-no* question which could be answered
by the assertions printed. Copy the assertions also. Be prepared
to ask these questions orally in class.

Haben wir (habt ihr, haben Sie) Geld?	Ja, wir haben Geld.

1. _____ Nein, wir wohnen in Berlin.
2. _____ Ja, sie arbeiten heute.
3. _____ Nein, das ist Frau Meyer.
4. _____ Natürlich ist Meyer intelligent.
5. _____ Ja, sie (die Zeitung) ist schon hier.
6. _____ Ja, sie (Erika) wohnt *auch* in München.
7. _____ Nein!
8. _____ Ja!

SEE
ANALYSIS
16

(pp. 16-17)

D. Write down the *word* questions which could be answered by
the statements printed. Be prepared to ask these questions in
class at normal speed when you hear the statement.

Wo arbeitet Herr Meyer?	Er arbeitet in Berlin.

1. Wo _____   Wir wohnen in Berlin.
2. Wo _____   Zu Hause!
3. Wo _____   Ich bin in Köln.
4. Wer _____   Herr Meyer.
5. Wann _____   Ich komme morgen.
6. Was _____   Er studiert Psychologie.
7. Wer _____   Herr Meyer kommt heute.
8. Wer _____   Ich bin Anna Meyer.

SEE
ANALYSIS
16

(pp. 16-17)

E. Repeat each sentence, starting as indicated.

1. Ich bleibe zu Hause. Heute _____.
2. Er bleibt morgen zu Hause. Morgen _____.
3. Es regnet. Hier _____.
4. Im Winter regnet es hier. Hier _____.

SEE
ANALYSIS
10–11

(pp. 11-13)

5. Wir arbeiten. Heute _____.
6. Meyers haben Geld. Übrigens _____.
7. Wir gehen sonntags in die Kirche. Sonntags _____.
8. In Kalifornien regnet es im Winter. Im Winter _____.
9. Nächstes Jahr gehen wir nach Deutschland. Nach Deutschland _____.

F. Supply the correct plural forms.

SEE
ANALYSIS
9
(pp. 10-11)

1. Ich bleibe ein Jahr in Deutschland. Fritz bleibt zwei _____ in Deutschland.
2. Herr Meyer hat ein Büro. Schmidt hat zwei _____.
3. Meyers Sohn heißt Peter. Meyers _____ heißen Peter und Paul.
4. Der Mann arbeitet in München. Die _____ arbeiten alle in München.
5. Frau Meyer und Frau Schmidt sind zu Hause. Die zwei _____ bleiben heute zu Hause.

G. Express in German. Be prepared to give the German equivalents instantly without using book or paper.

1. I am hungry.
2. We need money.
3. Hans will come later.
4. The newspaper is here.
5. Where does Dr. Meyer live?
6. We are studying psychology.
7. Hans is here, too.
8. Tomorrow night we are staying home.
9. She, too, is intelligent.
10. Does Meyer *also* live here?
11. Meyer also *lives* here.
12. We are also going to *Munich*.
13. Is it raining in Hamburg?
14. When are you coming to Munich, Mr. Meyer?

Vocabulary

der Abend, –e	evening	brauchen	to need
abends	evenings	das Büro, –s	office
Guten Abend!	Good evening!	im Büro	in the office
aber	but, however	die Butter	butter
alle	all, all of us	dann	then; in that case
allein	alone	das	that (*demonstrative*)
also	therefore; well; in other words	denn	(*see* 19)
arbeiten	to work	Deutsch	German (language)
auch	also, too	Deutschland	Germany
der August'	(month of) August	der Dok'tor, die Dokto'ren	doctor
im August'	in August	elf	eleven
das Auto, –s	automobile, car	fliegen	to fly
bis	until; up to (a point in place or time)	die Frau, –en	woman, wife
		Frau Meyer	Mrs. Meyer
bis morgen	until tomorrow	das Fräulein	Miss
bleiben	to stay, to remain	Fräulein Meyer	Miss Meyer

die Gabel, –n	fork
gehen	to go, to walk
Wie geht's?	How are things going?
das Geld	money
glauben	to think, to believe
der Gott, ‥er	god
Gott	God
gut	good
haben	to have
das Haus, ‥er	house
Ich gehe nach Hause	I go home
Ich bin zu Hause	I am at home
heißen	to be called
Ich heiße Fritz	My name is Fritz
der Herr, –en	gentleman
Herr Meyer	Mr. Meyer
heute	today
heute abend	this evening
heute morgen	this morning
hier	here
der Hund, –e	dog
der Hunger	hunger
Ich habe Hunger	I am hungry
in	in
intelligent'	intelligent
ja	yes; indeed; well
das Jahr, –e	year
jeden Sonntag	every Sunday
jetzt	now
Kalifor'nien	California
kalt	cold
das Kind, –er	child
das Kino, –s	movie house
Ich gehe ins Kino	I go to the movies
die Kirche, –n	church
Ich gehe in die Kirche	I go to church
kommen	to come
lernen	to learn
der Löffel, –	spoon
der Mann, ‥er	man, husband
die Mathematik'	mathematics
die Medizin'	medicine
Medizin'	(science of) medicine
das Messer, –	knife
der Morgen, –	morning
morgen	tomorrow
Guten Morgen!	Good morning!
morgen abend	tomorrow evening, tomorrow night
nach	to, toward; after
nach elf	after eleven
nächst	next
nächstes Jahr	next year
die Natur'	nature
natür'lich	naturally, of course
nein	no
nicht	not
noch	still
noch nicht	not yet
die Psychologie'	psychology
regnen	to rain
der Regen	rain
Es regnet	It is raining
schon	already; as early as
sein	to be
seit	since
der Sohn, ‥e	son
der Sonntag, –e	Sunday
Sonntag abend	Sunday evening, Sunday night
Sonntag morgen	Sunday morning
sonntags	on Sundays
der Student', –en	university student (male)
die Studen'tin, –nen	university student (female)
studie'ren	to study; to attend a university
die Tochter, ‥	daughter
trinken	to drink
tun	to do
übrigens	by the way, incidentally
um	around; about; at
um elf	at eleven o'clock
und	and
der Vater, ‥	father
Wann?	When? (interrogative)
Was?	What?
Wer?	Who?
das Wetter	weather
Wie?	How?
wieder	again (second or third time); back (to the place of)
der Winter, –	winter
im Winter	in winter
Wo?	Where?
wohnen	to reside, to live
die Zeitung, –en	newspaper
zu	to; at
zu Hause	at home
zurück'	back
zurück'fahren	to go back
wieder zurück'	back again
zwei	two

Unit 2 Nominative and Accusative of Personal Pronouns and of **ein**-Words and **der**-Words—Adverbs and Predicate Adjectives—Verbal Complements— Sentence Structure—**doch**

[1] Accusative of Personal Pronouns

Find out the system by which this exercise is constructed. Then practice the sentences aloud until you can say them rapidly, without having to pause for the correct pronoun.

SEE
ANALYSIS
24–25

(pp. 33-34)

du kennst *mich,* und *ich* kenne *dich*
er kennt *mich,* und *ich* kenne *ihn*
sie kennt *mich,* und *ich* kenne *sie*
ihr kennt *mich,* und *ich* kenne *euch*
sie kennen *mich,* und *ich* kenne *sie*
Sie kennen *mich,* und *ich* kenne *Sie*

ich kenne *dich,* und *du* kennst *mich*
er kennt *dich,* und *du* kennst *ihn*
sie kennt *dich,* und *du* kennst *sie*
wir kennen *dich,* und *du* kennst *uns*
sie kennen *dich,* und *du* kennst *sie*

ich kenne *ihn,* und *er* kennt *mich*
du kennst *ihn,* und *er* kennt *dich*
sie kennt *ihn,* und *er* kennt *sie*
wir kennen *ihn,* und *er* kennt *uns*
ihr kennt *ihn,* und *er* kennt *euch*
sie kennen *ihn,* und *er* kennt *sie*
Sie kennen *ihn,* und *er* kennt *Sie*

ich kenne *sie,* und *sie* kennt *mich*
du kennst *sie,* und *sie* kennt *dich*
er kennt *sie,* und *sie* kennt *ihn*
wir kennen *sie,* und *sie* kennt *uns*
ihr kennt *sie,* und *sie* kennt *euch*

Do your wheels need realigning?

du kennst *uns,* und *wir* kennen *dich*
er kennt *uns,* und *wir* kennen *ihn*
sie kennt *uns,* und *wir* kennen *sie*
ihr kennt *uns,* und *wir* kennen *euch*
sie kennen *uns,* und *wir* kennen *sie*
Sie kennen *uns,* und *wir* kennen *Sie*

ich kenne *euch,* und *ihr* kennt *mich*
er kennt *euch,* und *ihr* kennt *ihn*
sie kennt *euch,* und *ihr* kennt *sie*
wir kennen *euch,* und *ihr* kennt *uns*
sie kennen *euch,* und *ihr* kennt *sie*

ich kenne *sie,* und *sie* kennen *mich*
du kennst *sie,* und *sie* kennen *dich*
er kennt *sie,* und *sie* kennen *ihn*
wir kennen *sie,* und *sie* kennen *uns*
ihr kennt *sie,* und *sie* kennen *euch*

[2] **wissen** and **kennen**

SEE
ANALYSIS
22–23
(p. 32)

Ich *weiß,* er *kennt* mich.
Du *weißt,* er *kennt* dich.
Er *weiß,* ich *kenne* ihn.
Sie *weiß,* er *kennt* sie.
Wir *wissen,* er *kennt* uns.
Ihr *wißt,* sie *kennen* euch.
Sie *wissen,* wir *kennen* sie.
Sie *wissen,* er *kennt* Sie.

[3] Accusative of Personal Pronouns in Context

Practice these short conversations until you are ready to assume the
role of either of the two speakers. After these conversations have
been drilled in class, try to invent some variations of your own.

SEE
ANALYSIS
20–25
(pp. 31-34)

A: Erikas Mann heißt Max.
   Kennst du ihn?

Erika's husband's name is Max.
Do you know him?

B: Nein, ich kenne ihn nicht.

No, I don't know him.

A: Aber ich weiß, er kennt dich.

But I know that he knows you.

B: Nein, er kennt mich nicht.

No, he does not know me.

A: Wagners Frau heißt Irene.
   Kennst du sie?

Wagner's wife's name is Irene.
Do you know her?

B: Nein, ich kenne sie nicht.

No, I don't know her.

A: Aber sie sagt, sie kennt dich.   But she says she knows you.

B: Nein, sie kennt mich nicht.   No, she does not know me.

[4] Nominative and Accusative of Possessive Adjectives

SEE
ANALYSIS
26

(pp. 34-36)

Das ist mein Mann.   Das ist meine Frau.   Das ist mein Haus.
Ist das dein Sohn?   Ist das deine Tochter?   Ist das dein Kind?
Peter ist sein Sohn.   Gabriele ist seine Tochter.   Das ist sein Kind.
Peter ist ihr Sohn.   Gabriele ist ihre Tochter.   Das ist ihr Kind.

Das ist unser Sohn.   Das ist unsere Tochter.   Das ist unser Haus.
Ist das euer Sohn?   Ist das eure Tochter?   Ist das euer Haus?
Ihr Sohn heißt Peter.   Ihre Tochter heißt Gabriele.   Das ist ihr Haus.

Ist das Ihr Sohn, Herr   Ist das Ihre Tochter, Herr   Ist das Ihr Haus, Herr
   Klein?   Klein?   Klein?

Meine Söhne wohnen in Lübeck.
Wo wohnen denn deine Töchter jetzt?
Seine Freundinnen wohnen jetzt alle in Wien.
Ihre Freundinnen wohnen auch alle in Wien.

Unsere Kinder wohnen in Mannheim.
Wo wohnen denn eure Kinder jetzt?
Jetzt wohnen ihre Kinder in Salzburg.
Wo wohnen Ihre Freunde denn jetzt, Herr Lehmann?

Ich brauche *meinen* Wagen, und *ihr* braucht *euren* Wagen.
Du brauchst *deinen* Wagen, und *wir* brauchen *unseren* Wagen.
Er braucht *seinen* Wagen, und *sie* brauchen *ihren* Wagen.

Ich lese *mein* Buch, und *du* liest *dein* Buch.
Du liest *dein* Buch, und *er* liest *sein* Buch.
Er liest *sein* Buch, und *sie* liest *ihr* Buch.
Sie liest *ihr* Buch, und *wir* lesen *unsere* Bücher.
Wir lesen *unsere* Bücher, und *ihr* lest *eure* Bücher.
Ihr lest *eure* Bücher, und *sie* lesen *ihre* Bücher.

[5] ein-Words and Personal Pronouns in Context

Practice these brief conversations with another student.

SEE
ANALYSIS
26

(pp. 34-36)

ERNST: Hast du einen *Freund* hier in Mün-   Do you have a friend here in Munich?
chen?

FRITZ: Natürlich habe ich einen *Freund*   Of course, I have a friend here in Munich,
hier in München, und eine *Freund*in   and I also have a girl.
habe ich *auch*.

Sie lernt jetzt
hoffentlich fahren.

FRAU MEYER:	Frau *Schmidt*, Sie kennen doch Frau *Hoff*mann! Kennen Sie auch ihren *Mann?*	Mrs. Smith, you know Mrs. Hoffman, don't you? Do you also know her husband?
FRAU SCHMIDT:	Ja, ihr Mann arbeitet für *mei*nen Mann.	Yes, her husband works for my husband.
HANS:	Was *liest* du denn da, Erika?	What are you reading there, Erika?
ERIKA:	Ein Buch!	A book!
HANS:	Ist es interes*sant?*	Is it interesting?
ERIKA:	Ja! Ein Stu*dent* liebt eine Stu*dentin.*	Yes, a student loves a coed.
HANS:	Und *sie?* Liebt *sie* ihn *auch?*	And does she love him too?
ERIKA:	Nein, diese Stu*dentin* liebt ihren Pro*fes*sor.	No, this coed loves her professor.
HANS:	Und *er,* der Pro*fes*sor?	And the professor?
ERIKA:	Der Pro*fes*sor ist ein Dummkopf und liebt nur seine *Bü*cher!	The professor is a fool and loves only his books.

[6] The Second Prong of the Predicate—The Front Field

Study these sentences carefully. Practice them until you can develop
all variations without having to look at your book.

SEE
ANALYSIS
29–37

(pp. 37-43)

PREDICATE: *fahren lernen*

Sie	**lernt**	doch jetzt	**fahren.**
Jetzt	**lernt**	sie *doch*	**fahren.**
Wann	**lernt**	sie denn	**fahren?**
Hoffentlich	**lernt**	sie jetzt	**fahren.**
Sie	**lernt**	jetzt hoffentlich	**fahren.**
Jetzt	**lernt**	sie hoffentlich	**fahren.**

PREDICATE: *abfahren*

Der Zug	**fährt**	um 6 Uhr 5 (sechs Uhr fünf)	**ab.**
Um 6 Uhr 5	**fahren**	wir	**ab.**
Wo	**fährt**	denn der Zug nach Köln	**ab?**
Wann	**fährst**	du denn	**ab?**
	Fährt	der Zug jetzt	**ab?**
Meyers	**fahren**	schon um sechs Uhr	**ab.**

PREDICATE: *nach Berlin fahren*

Morgen	**fahre**	ich doch	**nach Berlin.**
Leider	**fahre**	ich morgen *doch*	**nach Berlin.**
Ich	**fahre**	morgen leider	**nach Berlin.**

PREDICATE: *ein Dummkopf sein*

Meyer	**ist**	leider	**ein Dummkopf.**
Leider	**ist**	Meyer	**ein Dummkopf.**

PREDICATE: *intelligent sein*

Seine Frau	**ist**	gottseidank	**intelligent.**
Gottseidank	**ist**	seine Frau	**intelligent.**
Gottseidank	**ist**	seine Frau auch	**intelligent.**
Gottseidank	**ist**	seine Frau *auch*	**intelligent.**

Conversation

Memorize this conversation and be ready to recite it in class.

ER: Weißt du *was*, Inge? Erika ist hier in Frankfurt!

You know what, Inge? Erika is here in Frankfurt!

SIE: Erika? Was tut denn Erika hier in Frankfurt?

Erika? What's Erika doing here in Frankfurt?

ER: Sie sagt, sie braucht einen *Sport*wagen!

She says she needs a sports car!

SIE: Einen *Sport*wagen! *Einen* Wagen *hat* sie schon, und *jetzt* braucht sie einen *Sport*wagen! Ja, ja, *sie* hat *al*les, und *wir* haben *nichts!*

A sports car! She already has *one* car, and now she needs a sports car. I tell you, she has everything, and we have nothing.

ER: Aber *Inge! Wer* hat denn *alles?* Du glaubst, Erika hat *alles.* Aber *ich* weiß, Erika ist *unglück*lich. *Erika* weiß es *auch! Sie* glaubt, sie hat *nichts.*

But Inge! Who does have everything? You think Erika has everything. But I know she is unhappy. Erika knows it too. She thinks she has nothing.

SIE: Aber *Geld* hat sie! Ist *Geld* „*nichts*"?

But she has money! Is money "nothing"?

ER: *Geld* ist *viel.* Aber Geld ist nicht *alles. Wir* sind Stu*den*ten. Stu*den*ten haben doch *nie* Geld! Aber ich bin *glück*lich, und *du* bist hoffentlich *auch* glücklich. Na*tür*lich hat Erika *Geld.* Sie ist doch jetzt Frau *Fischer. Frau Dr. Anton Fischer!* Warum bist *du* übrigens nicht Frau *Fischer?* Du weißt doch, Anton—

Money is a great deal. But money is not everything. We are students. Students, after all, never have any money. But I am happy, and I hope you are happy too. Of course Erika has money. She is now Mrs. Fischer, the wife of Dr. Anton Fischer. By the way, why aren't you Mrs. Fischer? You know, don't you, Anton . . .

SIE: *Ich? Frau Fischer? Antons Frau? Nein! Nie!*

I? Mrs. Fischer? Anton's wife? No! Never!

Reading

Gehen Sie mit ins Kino, Frau Lenz?

Frau Lenz kommt zu Frau Bertram:

FRAU B: Guten Morgen, Frau *Lenz! Gut,* daß Sie *kom*men! Was machen Sie heute *abend?* Ich glaube, *ich* gehe ins *Kino.*

Good morning, Mrs. Lenz. I'm glad you came! What are you doing tonight? I think I'll go to the movies.

FRAU L: Ins *Kino!*

5 To the movies!

FRAU B: *Ja,* ich brauche heute abend nicht zu *ar*beiten, und da bleibe ich natürlich nicht zu *Hause.*

Yes, I don't have to work tonight. And so, of course, I'm not staying home.

FRAU L: *So!* Sie gehen ins *Kino! Ich* gehe *nie* ins Kino.

Well! So you're going to the movies! I 10 never go to the movies.

FRAU B: Warum kommen Sie nicht *mit* ins Kino! Frau *Hoff*mann—*ken*nen Sie Frau *Hoff*mann?—Frau Hoffmann kommt *auch* mit.

Why don't you come along to the movies too! Mrs. Hoffmann—do you know Mrs. Hoffmann?—Mrs. Hoffmann is coming along too.

FRAU L: Ja, Frau *Hoff*mann *ken*ne ich. Aber ins Kino? Ich *weiß* nicht. *Her*mann und *ich,* wir gehen *nie* ins Kino. Er sagt, wir haben kein *Geld.* Aber ich *glau*be, er bleibt lieber zu *Hause* und liest die Zei-tung.

15 Yes, I know Mrs. Hoffmann. But to the movies? I don't know! Hermann and I, we never go to a movie. He says we can't afford it. But I think he'd rather stay home and read the paper.

So! Sie gehen ins Kino!

FRAU B: Wo *ist* er denn heute? Wann kommt er denn heute nach *Hause*?

Where is he today? When is he coming home today?

FRAU L: *Heute* kommt er *spät* nach Hause. Er arbeitet heute in *Bonn*.

Today he is coming home late. He is working in Bonn today.

FRAU B: In *Bonn! Das* ist doch *gut. Wir drei, Sie,* Frau *Hoff*mann und *ich,* gehen ins *Kino;* und *er* arbeitet in *Bonn.*

₅ In Bonn! That's just fine! The three of us, you, Mrs. Hoffmann, and I, will go to the movies; and he is working in Bonn.

FRAU L: *Gut,* Frau Bertram. Wir gehen alle *drei* ins Kino.

Fine! All three of us will go to the ₁₀ movies.

Analysis

20 Verbs with Vowel Change

Certain verbs change the stem vowel in the **du**-form and **er**-form. In these cases, the vocabulary at the end of the unit will show in parentheses the correct **du**- and **er**-form. Example: **fahren (du fährst, er fährt)**; **lesen (du liest, er liest)**. Note that if there is a change of vowel, it occurs both with **du** and with **er**, but nowhere else.

ich	fahre	I	go
du	fährst	you	go
er		he	
sie	fährt	she	goes
es		it	

wir	fahren	we	go
ihr	fahrt	you	go
sie	fahren	they	go
Sie	fahren	you	go

ich	lese	I	read
du	liest	you	read
er		he	
sie	liest	she	reads
es		it	

wir	lesen	we	read
ihr	lest	you	read
sie	lesen	they	read
Sie	lesen	you	read

21 Stems Ending in -s

After a stem which ends in -s, like **lesen**, the **du**-form adds -t, not -st, to the stem. As a result, the **du**-form becomes identical with the **er**-form.

  ich lese
  du liest
  er liest

22 **werden** and **wissen**

Like **sein** and **haben**, **werden** (*to become*) and **wissen** (*to know facts*) are irregular. In the present tense, they are inflected as follows:

ich	werde		ich	weiß
du	wirst		du	weißt
er			er	
sie	wird		sie	weiß
es			es	
wir	werden		wir	wissen
ihr	werdet		ihr	wißt
sie	werden		sie	wissen
Sie	werden		Sie	wissen

23 **wissen** and **kennen**

Both these verbs correspond to English *to know*, but German makes a clear distinction between the two. The use of **wissen** in main clauses is largely restricted to such sentences as

  Das weiß ich.
  Ich weiß es.

Frequently, the object of **wissen** is a short clause with normal word order, such as

  Ich weiß, Meyer wohnt in München.
  Ich weiß, er kommt morgen.

For the time being, do not use **wissen** with a following question word like **wer, wann, wo**; these words introduce dependent clauses to be treated in Unit 5.

The verb **kennen** expresses personal acquaintance with people or objects.

  Kennen Sie Herrn Meyer?
  Kennen Sie Deutschland?
  Kennen Sie das Buch?

24 The Nominative and Accusative Cases

In English we don't talk much about "cases" of nouns and pronouns, because the function of a noun in a sentence is ordinarily determined by its position. For instance, how do we know who bites whom in the sentence *The dog bites the cat?* Position alone indicates that *dog* is the subject and that *cat* is the object. By reversing position, the functions of *cat* and *dog* are *also* reversed.

However, in English sentences such as *I love him* the situation is quite different. Here, function is indicated by position *and* by form. Form alone would be sufficient, and, at least in theory, one could say *Him love I* without being misunderstood.

In German, the term "nominative case," or simply "nominative," is used whenever a noun or pronoun, *by virtue of either its form or its position,* is marked as the subject or as the predicate noun. The term "accusative case," or simply "accusative," is used whenever a word, *by form or position,* is marked as the direct object of a verb or of certain prepositions such as **für.**

Whenever function is not indicated by form, German, like English, relies on position. In

> **Meine Mutter kennt diese Frau**   My mother knows this woman

meine Mutter and **diese Frau** can both be either nominative or accusative as far as form is concerned, but position makes **meine Mutter** the subject. In

> **Diese Frau kennt meine Mutter**   This woman knows my mother

position makes **diese Frau** the subject and **meine Mutter** the object.

On the other hand, the two German sentences

> **Er liebt seinen Sohn**

and

> **Seinen Sohn liebt er**

both mean *He loves his son.* The **er** indicates by its form that it is the subject, and **seinen** indicates by its form that **seinen Sohn** must be the object. In this case, therefore, form alone is sufficient to indicate function.

25 The Nominative and Accusative Forms of Personal Pronouns

NOM.	ich	du	er	sie	es	wir	ihr	sie	Sie
ACC.	mich	dich	ihn	sie	es	uns	euch	sie	Sie

There is no difference in form between the nominative and the accusative of **sie, Sie,** and **es.**

Agreement between Nouns and Pronouns

Since **der Kaffee** is a masculine noun, the thing denoted by **dieser Kaffee** (*this coffee*) is, from a German point of view, a "he" and must be referred to by using the masculine pronouns **er** and **ihn.**

> **Er (dieser Kaffee) ist gut. Wo kaufst du ihn?**

Similarly, **die Zeitung** is a "she" and must be referred to by using the feminine pronoun **sie.**

> **Sie (die Zeitung) ist uninteressant. Ich lese sie nie.**

On the other hand, **das Geld** and **das Kind** are both neuter nouns. If these nouns are replaced by pronouns, you must use **es.**

> **Ich brauche es (das Geld).**
> **Ist es (das Kind) gesund?**

26 The Nominative and Accusative of **der**-Words, **ein**-Words, and Nouns

The Nominative and Accusative of **der**-Words

The term "**der**-words" is used for all words which indicate gender, case, and number in the same way in which the definite article **der,** by changing its form, indicates gender, case, and number. For instance, **dieser** and **jeder** are **der**-words.

	MASC.	FEM.	NEUT.	MASC.	FEM.	NEUT.
NOM. SING.	der	die	das	dieser	diese	dieses
ACC. SING.	den	die	das	diesen	diese	dieses
NOM. PL.		die			diese	
ACC. PL.		die			diese	

EXAMPLES:

> **Der Vater kennt diese Frau.**
> **Diese Frau kennt der Vater.**

Father knows this woman.
(Function indicated by form; **der Vater** can only be nominative.)

NOTE:

1. Only the masculine singular of the **der**-words distinguishes the nominative from the accusative.

2. In the plural, all three genders have the same forms.

The Nominative and Accusative of ein-Words

The term "ein-words" is used for all words which indicate case and number in the same way in which the indefinite article **ein** shows case and number. **Kein** (*no, not a*) and the possessive adjectives are **ein**-words.

The possessive adjectives are:

mein	my	**unser**	our
dein	your	**euer**	your
sein	his	**ihr**	their
ihr	her	**Ihr**	your (polite)
sein	its		

	MASC.	FEM.	NEUT.	MASC.	FEM.	NEUT.
NOM. SING.	ein	eine	ein	kein	keine	kein
ACC. SING.	einen	eine	ein	keinen	keine	kein
NOM. PL.	*(no plural)*			keine		
ACC. PL.				keine		

	MASC.	FEM.	NEUT.	MASC.	FEM.	NEUT.
NOM. SING.	mein	meine	mein	euer	eure	euer
ACC. SING.	meinen	meine	mein	euren	eure	euer
NOM. PL.		meine			eure	
ACC. PL.		meine			eure	

EXAMPLES:

Mein Vater kennt diese Frau.	My father knows this woman.
Diese Frau kennt mein Vater.	(Function indicated by form; **mein Vater** can only be nominative.)

However:

Frau Schmitz, meine Freundin versteht Ihre Tochter.	Mrs. Schmitz, my friend understands your daughter.
	(Function indicated by position.)

NOTE:

1. Only the masculine singular of the **ein**-words distinguishes the nominative from the accusative.

2. Remember: The plural of **ein Kind** is **Kinder.**

3. In the accusative of **unser** and **euer,** the **-e-** before the **-r-** is frequently dropped.

unseren or **unsren**   **unsere** or **unsre**

4. In the plural, all three genders have the same forms.

The Accusative of Nouns

Only very few nouns distinguish between nominative and accusative—for example, **der Mensch** and **der Student**, which add **-en** in all cases but the nominative singular. **Der Herr** adds an **-n** in all singular forms and an **-en** in all plural forms.

NOM. SING.	der Mensch	der Student	der Herr
ACC. SING.	den Menschen	den Studenten	den Herrn
NOM. PL.	die Menschen	die Studenten	die Herren
ACC. PL.	die Menschen	die Studenten	die Herren

27 Cardinal Numbers

The cardinal numbers from 1 to 12 are:

1	eins	4	vier	7	sieben	10	zehn
2	zwei	5	fünf	8	acht	11	elf
3	drei	6	sechs	9	neun	12	zwölf

The numeral **eins** is used only for counting, for telephone numbers, in arithmetic, etc; it is never used together with a following noun. In front of a noun, the numeral looks like the indefinite article **ein** and is declined like **ein**. In the sentence **wir haben eine Tochter, eine** means *one* if it is stressed, and *a* if it is not stressed.

NUMERAL	**Ich glaube, Meyers haben zwei *Söhne*.—Nein, sie haben nur *einen* Sohn.**	I believe the Meyers have two sons.—No, they have only *one* son.
INDEFINITE ARTICLE	**Ich glaube, Meyers haben jetzt auch eine *Tochter*.—Nein, sie haben nur einen Sohn.**	I believe the Meyers now have a *daughter*, too.—No, they have only a *son*.

If the other numbers are followed by a noun, they are not changed.

Wir haben drei Kinder, zwei Autos und einen Hund.

28 Adverbs and Predicate Adjectives

In the English sentences

He lived happily ever after
He was happy as long as he lived

the word *happily* is an adverb and characterizes the verbal act, the mode of living. The word *happy* is a predicate adjective. It characterizes the subject, not the verbal act.

German normally makes no distinction in form between a predicate adjective and an adverb.

PREDICATE ADJECTIVE	**Der Mensch ist gut.**	Man is good.
ADVERB	**Er fährt gut.**	He drives well.

NOTE: For the time being, do not use adjectives attributively—that is, in front of the noun to which they belong.

29 Verbal Complements

When a walkie-talkie operator wants to tell his partner that he is through, he says "Over." This single word is a complete utterance. However, it is not a complete sentence. All complete English and German sentences have a predicate that is expressed, completely or partially, by an inflected verb.

Not many verbs contain, by themselves, enough information for a complete predicate. The question *What happened to Joe?* can be fully answered by *He died!* In this case *died,* an inflected form of *to die,* is the complete predicate. Similarly the observation *It took,* made while looking at a baby's small-pox vaccination, is a complete sentence; and *took* is the complete predicate.

But verbal forms like *died* and *took* are the exception. It simply would not make any sense to answer the question *Where is Joe?* by saying *Joe is!* or *Joe got!* It is of the nature of verbal forms like *is* and *got* that they cannot, by themselves, form a complete and meaningful predicate. I have to say at least something like *Joe is at home* or *Joe got the measles.* In other words, forms like *is* and *got* demand some other element to complete them. We shall call such other elements, which are necessary to complete an otherwise meaningless utterance, *verbal complements.* In our examples

Joe is at home
Joe is sick
Joe got the measles

the words *at home, sick,* and *the measles* are complements of the verbs *to be* and *to get;* and only in combination with such complements can the inflected forms *is* and *got* form a complete predicate.

The same is true in German: The sentence

Fritz wohnt in Zürich   Fritz lives in Zurich

contains an inflected form of **wohnen.** Since **wohnen** means *to live* only in the sense of *to reside* or *to dwell,* **Fritz wohnt** would be an incomplete statement. It would not make any sense in English either to tell somebody, *Fritz is residing.* To form a complete predicate, **wohnen** needs an additional element. The phrase **in Zürich** satisfies that need; and **in Zürich,** therefore, is a verbal complement.

Verbal complements also appear in combination with verbs that can very well form a complete predicate by themselves. Thus

Johanna geht   Joan is leaving

is a complete statement. However, in the sentence

Die Lichter gehen an   The lights go on

the inflected forms **gehen** and *go* do not express the complete predicate. The complete predicates are **gehen an** and *go on*. Verbal complements like **an** and *on* change the meaning of the verbs with which they are combined. The **gehen** of **Die Lichter gehen an** does not have the same meaning as the **geht** in **Johanna geht,** and the statement **Die Lichter gehen** makes no more sense than **Fritz wohnt.** We may thus consider the fixed combination of verb plus complement as an "irreducible verbal pattern," because the removal of the complement would destroy the meaning of the verb.

The term "verbal complement" can only be used if the element completing the predicate follows the inflected form of the verb. The *up* in *He upset me* is not a complement but a prefix, but in *He set me up, up* is a complement. Observe the difference in stress: When a prefix is attached to a verb, the prefix is unstressed and the verb is stressed. If a complement follows the verb, the complement is stressed and the verb is not stressed. Again it is the same in German: The complement following the verb is stressed, and the verb is not stressed. In any German railway station, you can hear the announcement

Der Zug fährt jetzt *ab*

where the inflected form **fährt** has no stress at all. Whenever an assertion contains a complement, the inflected verb is called *the first part of the predicate,* and the complement is called *the second part of the predicate.* These two parts belong together. In German, the feeling for this "togetherness" is so strong that the question

Bist du morgen zu Hause?

(where **zu Hause** is the complement of **bist**) can be answered by **Ja!** or by **Ja, ich bin morgen zu Hause.** But it cannot be answered (as in English *Yes, I am*) by

Beware!
Americanism!   **[Ja, ich bin.]**   DO NOT USE!

In spite of all the similarities in the functions of German and English verbal complements, it is nevertheless an unfortunate fact that, in most cases, there is a wide discrepancy between the word order of a German sentence and its English equivalent. It is therefore necessary to learn the basic structure of German assertions and the position of verbal complements in particular.

Das Bier ist aber gut hier in München.

30 The Overall Structure of German Assertions

The structure of the German TV announcement

Wir schalten jetzt um nach Hamburg
We are now switching over to Hamburg

exemplifies the structure of all German assertions. This unvarying structure can be represented by the following schematic diagram:

FRONT FIELD	INFLECTED VERB	INNER FIELD	VERBAL COMPLEMENT	END FIELD
Wir	schalten	jetzt	um	nach Hamburg.
Das Bier	ist	aber	gut	hier in München.

Not all German assertions use this pattern in its entirety, but *no German assertion will disregard it.* The following patterns are possible:

FRONT FIELD	INFLECTED VERB		
Ich	lese.		I am reading.
Es	regnet.		It is raining.
Sie	kommen.		They are coming.

FRONT FIELD	INFLECTED VERB	INNER FIELD	
Da	kommt	Frau Meyer.	That is Mrs. Meyer.
Das	weiß	ich.	That I know.
			I know that.
Heute	kommt	Fritz.	Fritz is coming today.

NOTE: The last two statements cannot be imitated in English. In English, the subject must precede the verb; in German, it must follow the verb if the front field is occupied by some other syntactical unit.

FRONT FIELD	INFLECTED VERB	INNER FIELD	VERBAL COMPLEMENT
Ich	bleibe	heute	zu Hause.
Wir	fahren	morgen	nach Berlin.
Fritz	ist	heute	krank.
Wir	machen	es jetzt	aus.

All of the last four sentences contain a verbal complement. But in no case does the verbal complement in the corresponding English sentences have the position it has in the German sentences.

I   am staying   home   today.

We   are going   to Berlin   tomorrow.

Fritz   is   sick   today.

We   turn   it   off   now.

31 The Position of Verbal Complements

Up to now, we have said that the inflected verb is the first part of the predicate and that the verbal complement is the second part of the predicate. In German, the two parts of the predicate embrace the inner field like a pair of parentheses, or like the prongs that hold the jewel of a ring in place. And since it is inconvenient to always speak of "the first part of the predicate" and "the second part of the predicate," we shall call them the *first prong* and the *second prong*. Now compare the following German sentence with its English equivalent:

Hier   gehen   im Winter um vier die Lichter   an.

During the winter the lights   go   on   here at four.

The comparison shows: In German sentences which do not use the end field (and most of them don't), the verbal complement is the last element of the sentence.

English sentence structure is different. In most sentences, the verbal complement immediately follows the inflected verb, and it can be separated from the inflected verb by only one element.

Music turns me on.
He turned the music off.

In a German dictionary, most verbs and their complements are listed with the complement preceding the infinitive. Thus the infinitive belonging to the sentence **Ich komme nächstes Jahr wieder** is **wiederkommen,** and the infinitive belonging to **Der Zug fährt jetzt ab** is **abfahren.** Note that the stressed complement **ab** does not become an unstressed prefix. Even when joined to a following infinitive this **ab** can be recognized as a complement by the fact that it is stressed, while the infinitive remains unstressed. Prepositions like **an** or **aus,** and other one-word complements like **ab,** or **wieder,** or even a noun like **Rad** (**radfahren**—*to bicycle*) are always joined to the infinitive. Here are the infinitives of some frequently used compound verbs and a short sentence illustrating each one:

*an*gehen	**Das Licht geht an.**	The light goes on.
*an*machen	**Wir machen jetzt das Licht an.**	We're turning the light on now.
*aus*machen	**Wir machen jetzt das Licht aus.**	We're turning the light off now.
*ab*fahren	**Der Zug fährt jetzt ab.**	The train is leaving now.
*zurück*fahren	**Ich fahre morgen zurück.**	I'll go (drive) back tomorrow.
*wieder*kommen	**Ich komme nächstes Jahr wieder.**	I'll come back next year.
*fah*ren lernen	**Sie lernt jetzt fahren.**	She's learning to drive now.
zu *Hau*se bleiben	**Ich bleibe heute abend zu Hause.**	I'll stay home tonight.
nach *Hau*se gehen	**Wir gehen jetzt nach Hause.**	We're going (We'll go) home now.

32 The Front Field and Its Function

It was pointed out in **10** that the front field can be occupied by only one syntactical unit, usually not by the words which contain the answer to a preceding question. The main function of the front field is to state the "topic" of the sentence, that is, the thing the speaker wants to talk about. Thus, if someone tells you:

    Ich fahre im Dezember nach Kalifornien

you might reply:

    Im Dezember *reg*net **es aber meistens in Kalifornien.**

The reply would mean: "Talking about December, the fact is that it usually rains then in California." If you had replied:

    In Kalifornien *reg*net **es im Dezember meistens**

it would mean: "Talking about California I can tell you it usually rains there in December." And if you had replied:

    Meistens *reg*net **es dann in Kalifornien**   It usually rains then in California

the meaning would be: "Talking in terms of statistics, I can tell you that, usually, it then rains in California."

Do not shift the stress peak of a sentence into the front field. That is legitimate only when the subject in the front field carries the major news value.

    Weißt du was? *Mey*er **kommt morgen.**

33 The End Field

Most German sentences end with the second prong and have therefore no end field. The end field is frequently used for specifications or amplifications, especially if the amplifying element contains a preposition. It may also be used to introduce an afterthought.

Wir	schalten	jetzt		um	nach Hamburg.

Das	Bier	ist wirklich		gut	hier in München.

34 Sentence Intonation: Shifting the Stress Point

In German sentences which do not imply or intentionally express a contrast, the verbal complement carries the main stress—just as in English.

Morgen	fliegen	wir	nach *Mün*chen.

Wir	fliegen	morgen	nach *Mün*chen.

Any other intonation implies a contrast. The sentence

Morgen fliegen *wir* nach München

means "Tomorrow it's *our* turn to fly to Munich." The sentence

Nein, wir fliegen *mor*gen nach München

means "No, not next week! Tomorrow!" Without the preceding **Nein** the sentence could also be the answer to a **wann**-question. Finally

Morgen *flie*gen wir nach München

implies "Usually we take the train."

35 Directives as Verbal Complements

The question **Wohin?** (*Where to?*) is frequently answered by a prepositional phrase.

Wohin fährt er denn?—Er fährt nach Köln.

We shall call such prepositional phrases *directives*. All German directives are verbal complements—that is, they form the second prong, and in German sentences not using the end field, they stand at the very end.

FRONT FIELD	1ST PRONG	INNER FIELD	2ND PRONG
Morgen	fahre	ich leider	nach Berlin.
Ich	fahre	leider morgen	nach Berlin.
Leider	fahre	ich morgen	nach Berlin.

36 Predicate Adjectives and Predicate Nouns as Verbal Complements

German predicate adjectives and predicate nouns are verbal complements; they form a second prong and follow the inner field.

Erika	ist	gottseidank	intelligent.
Gottseidank	ist	Erika	intelligent.

Meyer	ist	leider	ein Dummkopf.
Leider	ist	Meyer	ein Dummkopf.

37 Word Order in German Questions

German questions follow the pattern of word order found in assertions.

In word questions, the front field is *always* occupied by an interrogative, and personal pronoun subjects are always placed at the beginning of the inner field.

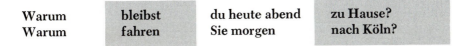

Warum	bleibst	du heute abend	zu Hause?
Warum	fahren	Sie morgen	nach Köln?

Yes-or-no questions have no front field, and again pronoun subjects are placed immediately after the opening verb—that is, at the beginning of the inner field.

	Bleiben	Sie heute abend	zu Hause?
	Fahren	Sie morgen	nach Köln?

38 Sentence Adverbs

In most cases, adverbs modify

a verb:	He lived *happily* ever after.
an adjective:	He is *unusually* intelligent.
another adverb:	It happened *very* suddenly.

However, in order to use German adverbs correctly, it should be noted that certain adverbs, called *sentence adverbs*, express the attitude of the speaker toward the content of the whole sentence.

Thus, *unfortunately, naturally,* and *obviously* are used as sentence adverbs in

Unfortunately he died.
(It is, in my opinion, unfortunate that he died.)

Naturally, he was not at home.
(As I had expected, he was not at home.)

He was obviously not stupid.
(It was clear to all of us that he wasn't stupid.)

Three German sentence adverbs were used in Unit 1: **denn, natürlich,** and **übrigens.** Four more—**doch, gottseidank, hoffentlich,** and **leider**—are introduced in this unit. In both English and German, these sentence adverbs count as *independent syntactical units* as far as word order is concerned.

If a German sentence adverb stands in the front field, nothing else can occupy the front field. The sentence adverbs **doch** and **denn** can appear only in the inner field. If sentence adverbs like **leider, hoffentlich,** and **gottseidank** appear in the end field, they are treated like independent sentences, set off from the main sentence by a comma or period.

Leider wohnt Tante Amalie wieder bei uns.
Tante Amalie wohnt leider wieder bei uns.
Tante Amalie wohnt wieder bei uns. Leider!

Gottseidank fährt Tante Amalie morgen wieder nach Hause.
Tante Amalie fährt gottseidank morgen wieder nach Hause.
Tante Amalie fährt morgen wieder nach Hause, gottseidank!

If a sentence adverb stands in the inner field, it follows unstressed pronouns and, normally, other unstressed elements; it precedes stressed elements, that is, elements with news value, and it precedes the second prong, even if the second prong is unstressed.

Liebt **sie ihn denn?**
Bleibt er denn zu *Hause?*
Bleibt sein Vater denn zu *Hause?*
Bleibt denn sein *Vater* **zu Hause?**

Sie lernt doch *fahren.*
Sie *lernt* **doch fahren.**

39 doch

The word **doch** may be stressed or unstressed. The stressed **doch** stands in front of the second prong (if there is one) or at the end of a sentence (if there is no second prong). It expresses that the fact reported is contrary to expectations. This stressed **doch** is frequently preceded by **also,** which adds the flavor of *so* when used at the beginning of English sentences.

Er kommt *doch!*	He is coming after all! (He said he wouldn't.)
Es regnet also *doch!*	So it's raining after all! (I had hoped it wouldn't.)
Er fährt morgen *doch* **nach München!**	He is going to Munich tomorrow after all! (He first said he wouldn't.)

The unstressed **doch** is a sentence adverb. In assertions it adds the note "Don't you know that . . ." or "Don't forget that . . ." or simply "but."

    Morgen fliegt er doch nach *München!*   But he is flying to *Munich* tomorrow.

When assertions become questions by intonation, the unstressed **doch** expresses the speaker's hope that the opposite is not true.

    Sie *kommen* doch heute abend?   You are *coming* tonight, aren't you?

Do not use the unstressed **doch** in regular questions.

Exercises

A. Complete the following conjugation samples. Be prepared to go through these sentences in class without your book.

1. Ich bin zu Hause. _____ du zu Hause?
   Du _____ zu Hause. _____ er zu Hause?
   Er _____ zu Hause. _____ wir zu Hause?
   Wir _____ zu Hause. _____ ihr zu Hause?
   Ihr _____ zu Hause. _____ sie zu Hause?

2. Ich weiß es. _____ du es *auch?*
   Du _____ es. _____ er es *auch?*
   Wir _____ es. _____ ihr es *auch?*
   Ihr _____ es. _____ sie es *auch?*

3. Ich fahre morgen nach Berlin. _____ du morgen *auch* nach Berlin?
   Du _____ morgen nach Berlin. _____ er morgen *auch* nach Berlin?
   Er _____ morgen nach Berlin. _____ wir morgen *auch* nach Berlin?
   Wir _____ morgen nach Berlin. _____ ihr morgen *auch* nach Berlin?
   Ihr _____ morgen nach Berlin. _____ sie morgen *auch* nach Berlin?

4. Ich lese ein Buch. _____ du *auch* ein Buch?
   Du _____ ein Buch. _____ er *auch* ein Buch?
   Er _____ ein Buch. _____ wir *auch* ein Buch?
   Wir _____ ein Buch. _____ ihr *auch* ein Buch?
   Ihr _____ ein Buch. _____ sie *auch* ein Buch?

B. Express in German.

SEE
ANALYSIS
24–26

(pp. 33-36)

1. We have a dog.
2. Our dog's name is Susi.
3. My father is well again.
4. I need a car.
5. Is that your son, Mrs. Meyer?
6. Is that your daughter, Mrs. Meyer?
7. He loves his son.
8. She loves this student.
9. Does your wife work in Cologne?
10. Do you know my girl friend?
11. Do you know this woman?
12. Do you know this child?
13. That is her father.
14. She loves her father.
15. He loves his daughters.

SEE
ANALYSIS
24–26

(pp. 33-36)

C. In the following sentences, replace the subject by a pronoun.

1. Erika ist jetzt meine Frau.
2. Dieses Buch ist uninteressant.
3. Der Zug fährt nach Frankfurt.
4. Seine Frau hat auch einen Wagen.
5. Herr Meyer ist mein Freund.

SEE
ANALYSIS
24–26

(pp. 33-36)

D. Replace the object by a pronoun.

1. Ich kenne Herrn Lenz nicht.
2. Er liest diese Zeitung nicht.
3. Liebst du Inge?
4. Ich verstehe Hans und Erika gut.
5. Kennen Sie seine Kinder?
6. Ich brauche den Wagen heute abend.

E. Formulate affirmative answers to the following questions, using personal pronouns.

Kennen Sie Frau Bertram?	**Ja, ich kenne sie gut.**

1. Kennen Sie Fritz Bertram?
2. Kennen Sie mich?
3. Kennst du die Frauen da?
4. Hast du das Geld schon?
5. Arbeitet dein Vater in Wien?
6. Verstehst du deine Mutter?
7. Liebst du Sylvia?
8. Brauchst du heute abend den Wagen?
9. Fährt der Zug jetzt ab?
10. Machst du das Licht aus?

SEE
ANALYSIS
39

(pp. 44-45)

F. Insert first a stressed and then an unstressed **doch** into the following sentences. Explain the difference in meaning.

1. Wir fahren nach München.
2. Meyer hat Geld.
3. Herr Lenz wohnt in Köln.
4. Er ist zu Hause.

SEE
ANALYSIS
9

(pp. 10-11)

G. Complete the following sentences with appropriate plural nouns.

1. Erich kauft ein Buch. Fritz kauft zwei _____.
2. Meyers haben zwei _____, Fritz und Karl, und zwei _____, Erika und Sylvia.
3. Sylvia hat einen Freund und zwei _____.
4. Fritz und Erich studieren in Hamburg. Sie sind _____.
5. Erika und Sylvia studieren auch. Sie sind _____.
6. Schmidts haben nur *einen* Wagen. Meyers haben *zwei* _____.

Vocabulary

ab	off
ach!	oh!
ach ja!	oh yes!
alles	everything
an	on; at
angehen	to go on
aus	out
ausgehen	to go out
das Bier	beer
das Buch, ¨er	book
da	there; then, under these circumstances
die Dame, –n	lady, woman
der Dezember	December
im Dezember	in December
dieser, diese, dieses	this
doch	(see 39)
drei	three
der Dummkopf, die Dummköpfe	dumbbell, fool
eins	one (cardinal number)
fahren (du fährst, er fährt)	to drive; to go (by train, boat, plane, car)
abfahren	to depart, to leave
fahren lernen	to learn how to drive
der Film, –e	movie, film
der Freund, –e	friend (male)
die Freundin, –nen	friend (female)
fünf	five
für (with acc.)	for
gesund	well, healthy
glücklich	happy
un'glücklich	unhappy
gottseidank	thank heavens
hoffen	to hope
hoffentlich (sentence adv.)	I hope
interessant'	interesting
un'interessant	uninteresting
jeder, jede, jedes	each, every
der Kaffee	coffee
kaufen	to buy
kein	no (not any)
kennen	to know (to be acquainted with objects or persons)

krank	sick
leider (sentence adv.)	unfortunately
lesen (du liest, er liest)	to read
das Licht, –er	light
lieben	to love
liebhaben	to love (persons only)
lieber	rather
lügen	to tell a lie
machen	to make; to do
anmachen	to turn on
ausmachen	to turn off
der Mensch, –en	man, human being
die Milch	milk
mit	with, along
mitkommen	to come along
die Mutter, ¨	mother
nichts	nothing
nie	never
nur	only
oder	or
der Profes'sor, die Professo'ren	professor
das Rad, ¨er	wheel, bicycle
radfahren	to bicycle
sagen	to say
schalten	to switch
umschalten	to switch over
sechs	six
sofort'	immediately
spät	late
der Sport	sport
die Uhr, –en	clock, watch
um ein Uhr	at one o'clock
um eins	at one o'clock
verstehen	to understand
viel	much
soviel	so much, as much
zuviel	too much
vier	four
der Wagen, –	car, wagon
Warum'?	Why?
werden (du wirst, er wird)	to become
wissen	to know (facts)
Wohin'?	Where? Where to? (asks for a goal, not a location)
der Zug, ¨e	train

Mehr Herz für unsere Kinder

10. September
WELTTAG DES KINDES
1972

Arenbergpark, 3, Dannebergplatz — von 13.00 Uhr bis 17.00 Uhr

DIE KINDERFREUNDE

Unit 3 aber, oder, denn, und—Negation by kein and nicht—The Modals—Contrast Intonation— The Imperative

Patterns

[1] aber, oder, denn, und

Dieses Jahr bleiben wir zu *Hause.*	*This* year we'll stay at *home.*	SEE ANALYSIS 40 (p. 63)

Dieses Jahr bleiben wir zu *Hause.*
Aber *nächstes* Jahr fahren wir nach *Deutsch*land.
*Nächs*tes Jahr fahren wir aber nach *Deutsch*land.
Kommst du *heu*te, oder kommst du *mor*gen?
Alle Menschen sind egoistisch; denn *jeder* Mensch will *glück*lich werden.
Meyers fahren nach *Köln,* und *wir* fahren nach *Mün*chen.

This year we'll stay at *home.*
But *next* year we are going to *Germany.*

Are you coming *today,* or will you come *tomorrow?*
All humans are *egoistic,* for every human being wants to be *happy.*
The Meyers are going to *Cologne,* and *we* are going to *Munich.*

SEE ANALYSIS 40 (p. 63)

[2] nicht, nicht wahr

Wohnen Sie in *Köln?*
Sie wohnen doch in *Köln,* nicht *wahr?*
Sie wohnen doch in *Köln,* *nicht?*

Do you live in *Cologne?*
You live in *Cologne,* don't you?
You live in *Cologne,* don't you?

SEE ANALYSIS 41–42 (p. 63)

[3] nicht ein

Ich kenne hier auch nicht *ei*nen Menschen.
Meyers haben *fünf Töch*ter, aber auch nicht *ei*nen Sohn.

I really don't know a *single* soul here.
The Meyers have *five daughters,* but not *one* son.

SEE ANALYSIS 43 (p. 64)

[4] kein

The following sentences demonstrate the use of **kein.** Study these sentences first; then practice until you can say the sentences with

More heart for our children—World Children's Day 1972.

kein when you hear the sentences without **kein,** and vice versa.

SEE
ANALYSIS
44–45

(pp. 64-65)

Hildegard hat *Geld.*   Hildegard hat *kein* Geld.
Ich trinke *Wein.*   Du trinkst *keinen* Wein.
Sie haben ein *Haus.*   Sie haben *kein* Haus.
Er hat eine *Frau.*   Er hat *keine* Frau.
Sie ist ein *Kind.*   Sie ist *kein* Kind.
Sie haben einen *Sohn,* Frau Meyer?   Nein, wir *ha*ben keinen Sohn. Wir haben
                                                    auch keine *Toch*ter.

Trinken Sie *Bier?*   Nein, ich *trinke* kein Bier.

[5] Negation by **nicht**

Be prepared to produce orally the sentences in one column when you
hear the sentences in the other column.

SEE
ANALYSIS
46–47

(pp. 65-67)

Er *braucht* mich.   Er braucht mich *nicht.*
Hast du mein *Buch?*   Nein, ich *ha*be dein Buch nicht.
*Va*ter ist gottseidank wieder ge*sund.*   *Va*ter ist leider nicht ge*sund.*
Ich *weiß,* Inge ist seine *Toch*ter.   Ich *weiß,* Inge ist *nicht* seine *Toch*ter.
*Sonn*tags gehen wir ins *Ki*no.   *Sonn*tags gehen wir *nicht* ins Kino.
Natürlich bleibe ich heute abend zu *Hause.*   Natürlich bleibe ich heute abend nicht zu
                                                    Hause.

Hoffentlich kommt sie morgen *wie*der.   Hoffentlich kommt sie morgen nicht *wie*der.

[6] schon, noch, immer noch, noch immer, nicht mehr, kein . . . mehr

Be prepared to produce orally the sentences in one column when you
hear the sentences in the other column.

SEE
ANALYSIS
48

(pp. 67-68)

Regnet es *immer* noch?   Nein, es *regnet* nicht mehr.
    Is it *still* raining?   No, it isn't *raining* anymore.

Er ist schon zu *Hause.*   Er ist noch *nicht* zu Hause.
    He is at *home* already.   He is *not* at home yet.

Er ist noch zu *Hause.*   Er ist nicht mehr zu *Hause.*
    He is still at *home.*   He isn't at *home* anymore.

Wir wohnen noch *im*mer in München.   Wir *woh*nen nicht mehr in München.
    We *still* live in Munich.   We don't *live* in Munich anymore.

Ist er *immer* noch krank?   Nein, er ist *nicht* mehr krank.
    Is he *still* sick?   No, he *isn't* sick anymore.

Haben wir noch *Bier?*   Nein, wir *ha*ben kein Bier mehr.
    Do we still have some *beer?*   No, we don't *have* any more beer.

Sie ist noch ein *Kind*.
    She is still a *child*.

Sie ist *im*mer noch ein Kind.
    She is *still* a child.

Sie ist noch *im*mer ein Kind.
    She is *still* a *child*.

Du bist doch noch ein *Kind*, Inge.
    You are still a *child*, Inge.

Ich bin doch kein *Kind* mehr, Mutter.
    But I am not a *child* anymore, mother.

Er ist noch Stu*dent*.
    He is still a *student*.

Er ist schon *Arzt*.
    He is already a *doctor*.

Ich habe noch einen *Bru*der.
    I still have a *brother*.

Ich habe *noch* einen Bruder.
    I have *another* brother.

Sie ist kein *Kind* mehr.
    She is no longer a *child*.

Nein, Mutter, ich bin *kein* Kind mehr.
    No, mother, I'm *not* a child anymore.

Du *bist* noch ein Kind.
    You *are* still a child.

Er ist kein Stu*dent* mehr.
    He is no longer a *student*.

Er ist noch kein *Arzt*.
Er ist noch nicht *Arzt*.
    He is not a *doctor* yet.

Ich *habe* keinen *Bru*der mehr.
    I don't *have* a *brother* anymore.

[7] mehr, mehr als, nicht mehr als

Observe that in the following sentences **mehr** has a quantitative
meaning and not a temporal meaning as in [6] above.

Meine Frau sagt, sie braucht mehr Geld.
Meine Frau braucht mehr Geld als ich.
Frau Meyer braucht viel Geld, aber Herr
    Meyer braucht noch mehr Geld als sie.

My wife says she needs more money.
My wife needs more money than I need.
Mrs. Meyer needs much money, but Mr.
    Meyer needs even more money than she
    does.

Er arbeitet mehr als ich.
Er weiß mehr, als er sagt.
Er hat mehr Geld, als er braucht.
Ich habe nur zehn Mark; ich habe leider
    nicht mehr.
Das kostet nicht mehr als fünf Mark.
Ich habe nicht mehr Geld als du.

He works more than I do.
He knows more than he says.
He has more money than he needs.
I only have ten marks; unfortunately, I don't
    have any more.
That doesn't cost more than five marks.
I don't have more money than you (have).

SEE
ANALYSIS
48
(pp. 67-68)

[8] doch as Answer to a Negative Question

Study these sentences as questions and answers. Be prepared to formulate the answers orally when you hear the questions, and vice versa.

SEE
ANALYSIS
49

(pp. 68-69)

Fahren Sie heute nach *Düsseldorf?*
Fahren Sie *nicht* nach Düsseldorf?

Nein, ich fahre erst *morgen.*
Doch, natürlich fahre ich nach Düsseldorf.

Trinken Sie *Kaff*ee, Frau Schmidt?
Trinken Sie *keinen* Kaffee?

Nein, ich *trinke* keinen Kaffee.
Doch, natürlich trinke ich Kaffee.

Haben Meyers schon *Kinder?*
Haben Meyers noch keine *Kinder?*

Ja, einen *Sohn* und eine *Toch*ter.
Doch, einen *Sohn* und eine *Toch*ter.

Gehst du heute abend ins *Kino?*
Gehst du heute abend *nicht* ins Kino?

Ja, mit Inge.
Doch, aber *nicht* wieder mit *In*ge.

[9] können

Study the following sentences, which contain all the present tense
forms of **können.** Then practice these forms by following the
instruction under "Variations."

SEE
ANALYSIS
51–57

(pp. 69-74)

Ich kann heute *kom*men.
Ich kann heute *nicht* kommen.

I can *come* today.
I *cannot* come today.

Kannst du heute *kom*men?
Kannst du heute nicht *kom*men?

Can you *come* today?
Can't you *come* today?

Kann Herr Bauer heute *ar*beiten?
Nein, er kann heute *nicht* arbeiten.

Will Mr. Bauer be able to *work* today?
No, he will *not* be able to work today.

Wir können das Haus *kau*fen.
Wir können das Haus *nicht* kaufen.

We can *buy* the house.
We *cannot* buy the house.

Ihr könnt das Geld *mor*gen haben.
Ihr könnt das Geld morgen noch *nicht*
  haben.

You can have the money *tomorrow.*
Tomorrow you *can't* have the money yet.

Sie können jetzt das *Licht* ausmachen.
Sie können doch noch nicht das *Licht* ausmachen.

You can switch off the *light* now.
You can't switch off the *light* yet.

VARIATIONS

Ich kann heute kommen.
Er _____ .
Er _____ nicht _____ .
Sie _____ nicht _____ .
_____ Sie _____ ?
Warum _____ du denn _____ nicht _____ ?
Warum _____ ihr denn _____ nicht _____ ?
Wir _____ leider nicht _____ .
Könnt _____ nicht _____ ?

Doch, ich _____.

Nein, wir _____ nicht _____.

Heute _____ ich noch nicht _____.

Form the same variations using (1) **das Haus kaufen,** and (2) **nach München fahren.**

[10] müssen

The following sentences contain all present-tense forms of **müssen.**
Note that **nicht brauchen zu** is used for the negative of **müssen.**

Ich muß *ar*beiten.	I have to *work*.	**SEE ANALYSIS 51–57**
Ich *brau*che nicht zu *ar*beiten.	I don't *have* to work.	(pp. 69-74)

Du mußt *kommen.*
Du *brauchst* nicht zu kommen.

You have to *come.*
You don't *have* to come.

Er muß morgen nach *Wien* fahren.
Er *braucht* morgen nicht nach *Wien* zu fahren.

He has to go to *Vienna* tomorrow.
He does not *have* to go to *Vienna* tomorrow.

Wir müssen morgen leider *ar*beiten.
Wir *brau*chen morgen nicht zu arbeiten.

Unfortunately, we have to *work* tomorrow.
We don't *have* to work tomorrow.

Ihr müßt Tante *Amalie* besuchen.
Ihr *braucht* sie nicht zu be*su*chen.

You have to visit Aunt *Amalie.*
You don't *have* to visit her.

Sie müssen jetzt das *Licht* ausmachen.
Sie brauchen das Licht noch nicht *aus*zumachen.

You have to switch the *light* off now.
You don't have to switch the light *off* yet.

Warum wollen Sie denn bei dem Regen nach *Hamburg* fahren?—Ich *muß!*

Why do you want to drive to *Hamburg* in this rain?—I *have* to!

Sie sagen, Sie arbeiten auch *sonn*tags? Das *brau*chen Sie aber nicht.

You say you work also on *Sundays?* You don't *have* to do that.

Sie *ar*beiten heute? *Müs*sen Sie das?

You are *working* today? Do you *have* to?

VARIATIONS

Mußt du morgen arbeiten?

Nein, morgen _____ ich nicht zu arbeiten.

Ich hoffe, du brauchst morgen nicht zu arbeiten.

Doch, leider _____ ich auch *morgen* arbeiten.

Braucht er denn heute nicht zu arbeiten?

Nein, heute _____.

Müßt ihr heute arbeiten?

Ja, wir _____.

Muß Erika immer noch arbeiten?

Nein, sie _____ nicht mehr _____.

Form the same variations with (1) **nach Berlin fahren,** (2) **zu Hause bleiben,** and (3) **mit Tante Amalie ins Museum gehen.**

[11] wollen

Be prepared to produce orally the negative sentences when you hear
the affirmative sentences and vice versa.

SEE
ANALYSIS
51–57

(pp. 69-74)

Ich will *hei*raten.
   I want to *marry.*

Ich *will* noch nicht heiraten.
   I don't *want* to marry yet.

Willst du jetzt *schla*fen?
   You want to *sleep* now?

Willst du jetzt *nicht* schlafen?
   Don't you want to sleep now?

Sie will *immer Kaf*fee trinken.
   She *always* wants to drink coffee.

Sie *will* keinen Kaffee mehr trinken.
   She doesn't *want* to drink coffee anymore.

Wir wollen heute abend ins *Ki*no gehen.
   We want to go to the *movies* tonight.

Wir wollen heute abend *nicht* ins Kino.
   We *don't* want to go to the movies tonight.

Wann wollt ihr denn *hei*raten?
   When do you intend to get *married?*

Warum *wollt* ihr denn noch nicht heiraten?
   Why don't you *want* to get married yet?

Sie wollen *ar*beiten.
   They want to *work.*

Sie wollen nicht mehr soviel *ar*beiten.
   They no longer want to *work* so much.

VARIATIONS

Hans und Erika wollen heiraten.

Hans _____ ____ heiraten.

Ich _____ noch nicht _____.

Wir _____ erst nächstes Jahr _____.

So, du _____?

Wann _____ ihr denn _____?

[12] sollen

For each sentence, form a parallel example according to the
translation on the right.

SEE
ANALYSIS
51–57

(pp. 69-74)

Ich soll heute abend zu *Hau*se bleiben.
   I am supposed to stay *home* tonight.
   I am supposed to visit Aunt *Amalie* tonight.

_____

Aber *Hans!* Du *sollst* doch keinen Kaffee
   trinken.

But Hans, you're not *supposed* to drink
   coffee.
But Hans, you're not *supposed* to work so
   much.

_____

Sie *soll* sonntags nicht mehr arbeiten.

She's not *supposed* to work on Sundays any-
   more.
She's not *supposed* to go to the movies with
   Hans anymore.

_____

Was sollen wir denn *tun?*

What are we supposed to *do?*
When are we supposed to *visit* them?

Warum sollt ihr ihn denn schon wieder be*such*en?

Why are you supposed to *visit* him again?

Why aren't you supposed to *read* this book?

Herr Meyer, Sie sollen morgen nach Han*nov*er fahren.

Mr. Meyer, you are supposed to go to *Hanover* tomorrow.
Mr. Meyer, you are supposed to stay *here* tomorrow.

---

[13] möchte

After studying these sentences, practice the forms of **möchte** as indicated below.

Ich *möch*te jetzt nichts essen; ich möchte *schlaf*en.—Möchtest du Frau *Mey*er kennenlernen?—Er möchte *Arzt* werden. —Sie möchte nächstes Jahr *hei*raten.— Wir möchten nächstes Jahr *hei*raten.— Wann möchtet ihr denn *hei*raten?—*Alle* Menschen möchten *glück*lich werden.

I don't *want* to eat anything now; I want to *sleep.*—Would you like to meet Mrs. *Meyer?*—He would like to become a *doctor.*—She would like to *marry* next year.—We would like to *marry* next year.—When would you like to get *married?*—All men want to become *happy.*

SEE ANALYSIS 51–57 (pp. 69-74)

Ich möchte eine Tasse *Kaf*fee trinken.— Möchten Sie *auch* eine Tasse Kaffee?

I should like to have (drink) a cup of *coffee.*—Would you *also* like to have a cup of coffee?

Möchtest du heute abend *nicht* ins Kino gehen?—*Nein*, ich möchte *wirk*lich zu *Hause* bleiben.

Would you rather *not* go to the movies tonight?—*No, I really* want to stay at *home.*

Sie *brauchen* das Buch nicht zu *les*en, wenn Sie nicht *wol*len.—Aber ich *möch*te es lesen.

You *need* not *read* the book if you don't *want* to.—But I would *like* to read it.

Er möchte Arzt werden.

VARIATIONS

Ich schlafe.   Ich möchte schlafen.

Ich fahre nächstes Jahr nach Italien.   _____

Morgen gehe ich nicht ins Kino.   _____

Gehst du nach Hause?   _____

Meyer kauft unser Haus.   _____

Wir essen heute abend im Regina.   _____

[14] dürfen

After studying these sentences, go through the variations below.

SEE
ANALYSIS
51–57

(pp. 69-74)

Ich darf ihn nicht besuchen.—Ich darf ihn noch nicht besuchen.—Ich darf ihn nicht mehr besuchen.

I am not permitted to *visit* him.—I am not yet permitted to *visit* him.—I am no longer permitted to *visit* him.

Darfst du *Kaffee* trinken?—Darf er jetzt wieder *Kaffee* trinken?

Can you drink *coffee*?—Can he drink *coffee* again (now)?

Dürfen wir euch morgen besuchen?—Dürft ihr uns besuchen?

May we *visit* you tomorrow?—May you *visit* us?

Sie dürfen ihn nicht besuchen.

They may not *visit* him.

VARIATIONS

Vary each sentence with the new subjects indicated.

Ich darf morgen meinen Mann besuchen.   Du _____

                                           Frau Meyer _____

Wir dürfen keinen Kaffee mehr trinken.   Er _____

                                           Erika _____

Ich darf sonntags nicht ins Kino gehen.   Inge _____

                                           Wir _____

Darf man hier nicht rauchen?

Hier darf man rauchen.

[15] Second Prong

FRONT FIELD	1ST PRONG	INNER FIELD	NICHT	1ST BOX	2ND BOX	
Ich	möchte	das Buch			lesen.	**SEE ANALYSIS 55–56**
Ich	möchte	das Buch	nicht		lesen.	
Ich	darf	Kaffee			trinken.	(pp. 72-74)
Ich	darf	keinen Kaffee			trinken.	
Morgen	kann	sie ihren Mann	noch nicht		besuchen.	
Wir	dürfen	sonntags	nicht mehr		arbeiten.	
Er	scheint	jetzt			zu schlafen.	
Er	scheint	jetzt	nicht		zu schlafen.	
Er	kann		nicht mehr		schlafen.	
Er	scheint		noch nicht		zu schlafen.	
Warum	brauchst	du morgen	nicht		zu arbeiten?	
Seine Frau	scheint	wirklich	nicht	intelligent	zu sein.	
Das	muß			seine Frau	sein.	
Das	kann	doch	nicht	seine Frau	sein.	
Das	scheint			seine Frau	zu sein.	
Das	scheint		nicht	seine Frau	zu sein.	
Erika	möchte	heute abend	nicht	zu Hause	bleiben.	
Ich	möchte	sie		wieder-	sehen.	
Ich	möchte	sie	nicht	wieder-	sehen.	
Ich	möchte	sie wirklich		kennen-	lernen.	
Ich	brauche	sie	nicht	kennen-	zu-lernen.	

[16] Contrast Intonation

Read these sentences aloud until you have thoroughly mastered this
intonation pattern.

Du fährst morgen nach *Ital*ien? *Ich* kann *nicht* nach Italien fahren.

You are going to *Italy* tomorrow? *I cannot* go to Italy.

SEE ANALYSIS 58–59

(pp. 74-76)

Hast *du Geld? Ich* habe *kein* Geld.

Do *you* have *money? I don't* have any money.

Trinken Meyers *Kaf*fee?—*Sie ja*, aber *er nicht*.

Do the Meyers drink *coffee?—She does*, but *he* does *not*.

Ist er intelli*gent* oder interes*sant?*—Intelli*gent ist* er, aber interes*sant* ist er *nicht*.

Is he *intelligent* or *interesting?*—He is *intelligent* all right. But *interesting?* No!

Ich höre, dein Bruder studiert Psycholo*gie*. Was studierst *du?—Ich* studiere Medi*zin*.

I hear your brother is majoring in *psychology*. What are *you* majoring in?—*I am* in *med school*.

Kennen Sie Fritz *Enders*, Frau *Holl*mann?

Do you know Fritz *Enders*, Mrs. *Hollmann?*

—Nein, seine *Mut*ter kenne ich *gut*, aber *ihn* kenne ich *nicht*.

—No, I know his *mother well*, but I do *not* know *him*.

Warum gehst du nie mit *Inge* ins *Kino*? Sie ist doch *so* intelligent.—*Ja*, intelli*gent ist* sie.

Why don't you ever go to the *movies* with *Inge*? She is *so intelligent!*—*Yes*, she is *intelligent* all right.

Warum gehst du so oft mit *Hans* ins Kino? Ist er intelli*gent*?—*Nein*, intelli*gent* ist er *nicht*.

Why do you go to the movies with *Hans* so often? Is he *intelligent*?—*No*, he's not *intelligent*.

[17] Contradiction and Contrast

SEE
ANALYSIS
58–59
(pp. 74-76)

Das ist *Wasser*. Das ist *kein* Wasser. *Wasser* ist das *nicht*.

This is *water*. This is *not* water. This is *no water*.

Wir trinken *Wein*. Wir trinken *keinen* Wein. *Wein* trinken wir *nicht*.

We drink *wine*. We do *not* drink wine. *Wine* we do *not* drink.

Meyers haben einen *Sohn*. Meyers haben *keinen* Sohn. Einen *Sohn* haben Meyers *nicht*.

The Meyers have a *son*. The Meyers do *not* have a son. The Meyers have *no son*.

Wir gehen ins *Kino*. Nein, wir gehen *nicht* ins Kino. Ins *Kino* gehen wir *nicht*.

We're going to the *movies*. No, we're *not* going to the movies. To the *movies* we *won't* go.

Er ist intelli*gent*. Er ist *nicht* intelligent. *Intelligent* ist er *nicht*.

He is *intelligent*. He is *not* intelligent. *Intelligent* he's *not*.

Du fährst morgen nach *München*? Nein, ich fahre morgen *nicht* nach München. Nein, *ich* fahre morgen *nicht* nach München. Nein, nach *München* fahre ich morgen *nicht*.

You are going to *Munich* tomorrow? No, I'm *not* going to Munich tomorrow. No, *I* am *not* going to Munich tomorrow. No, to *Munich* I am *not* going tomorrow.

VARIATIONS

Vary the following sentences in the same manner as above.

Sie haben eine *Toch*ter.
Wir trinken *Bier*.
Ich kenne hier einen *Arzt*.

Wir gehen nach *Hause*.
Er ist zu *Hause*.
Das ist *unser* Hund.

[18] Imperative

SEE
ANALYSIS
60
(pp. 76-77)

Arbeiten Sie nicht soviel!
Bleiben Sie doch hier!
Gehen Sie doch nach Hause!

Don't work so much.
Why don't you stay here?
Why don't you go home?

Kommen Sie doch morgen!	Why don't you come tomorrow?
Lernen Sie Deutsch!	Learn German.
Sagen Sie doch etwas!	Say something.
Seien Sie nicht so egoistisch!	Don't be so selfish.
Tun Sie das doch bitte nicht!	Please don't do that.
Machen Sie bitte das Licht an!	Please turn on the light.
Kaufen Sie doch einen Volkswagen!	Why don't you buy a VW?
Schlafen Sie gut!	Sleep well!
Lassen Sie mich allein!	Leave me alone.

Conversation

I

TANTE AMALIE:	So, Erika, du willst also *hei*raten?	Well, Erika, so you want to get married?
ERIKA:	Ja, Tante Amalie, *Hans* und *ich* wollen *hei*raten.	Yes, Aunt Amalie, Hans and I want to get married.
TANTE AMALIE:	Möchte Hans denn nicht mehr stu*dier*en?	Doesn't Hans want to go to school anymore?
ERIKA:	Na*tür*lich will Hans noch stu*dier*en, und *ich* will *auch* studieren.	Of course, Hans wants to go to school, and so do I.
TANTE AMALIE:	Aber man kann doch nicht heiraten *und* studieren, Erika.	But you can't get married and study, Erika.
ERIKA:	Na*tür*lich kann man das, Tante Amalie.	Of course you can, Aunt Amalie.
TANTE AMALIE:	Dann muß man aber *Geld* haben, Erika, *viel* Geld, und *das habt* ihr nicht.	Then you need money, Erika, lots of money, and that you haven't got.
ERIKA:	Nein, das braucht man *nicht*. Wir können auch *ohne* Geld glücklich sein, Hans und ich. Wir *hei*raten, und wir stu*dier*en, und wir sind *glück*lich.	No, you don't need money. We can be happy without money, too, Hans and I. We'll get married, we'll go to school, and we'll be happy.
TANTE AMALIE:	Ich ver*stehe* dich nicht, Erika. In *mei*ner Jugend . . .	I don't understand you, Erika. In my youth . . .

II

INGE: Du,* Hans, wir haben nicht viel *Zeit*. Sollen wir nicht ein *Ta*xi nehmen?

HANS: Nein, ein Taxi nehmen wir heute *nicht*. Aber wir *fah*ren *doch*. Ich habe einen *Wa*gen!

INGE: Einen *Wa*gen? Du hast einen *Wa*gen? Das ist aber *pri*ma. Ist es *dein* Wagen?

HANS: Nein, nein, es ist nicht *mein* Wagen. Ich habe keinen Wagen. Es ist *Ot*tos Wagen, aber er *braucht* ihn heute nicht. Also brauchen wir heute nicht ins Theater zu *ge*hen, wir können ins Theater *fah*ren.

INGE: Du, das ist *gut*. Jetzt haben wir noch *so* viel Zeit. Es ist ja erst sechs *Uhr*. Jetzt können wir *erst* essen und *dann* ins Theater fahren.

HANS: *Essen will* ich jetzt nichts; ich habe keinen *Hun*ger. Ich möchte jetzt nur eine Tasse *Kaf*fee. Aber *du* sollst natürlich *essen*, wenn du *willst*.

INGE: *Nein*, du mußt *auch* essen. Weißt du, was die Leute *den*ken, wenn *ich* esse und *du* trinkst nur Kaffee? Das ist ein Stu*dent*, denken sie, er hat also kein *Geld* und sagt, er hat keinen *Hun*ger.

HANS: Aber ich habe *wirk*lich keinen Hunger.

INGE: Also gut, dann *esse* ich etwas und *du* trinkst *Kaf*fee, und die *Leu*te sollen *den*ken, was sie *wol*len.

> * German uses the personal pronoun, particularly the familiar **du**, much in the same way as English uses *say* or *you know*.

Reading

Der Mensch, das kann man schon bei Aristoteles lesen, ist ein Tier. Aber dieses Tier, sagt Aristoteles, hat Vernunft.

Man, one can read already in Aristotle, is an animal. But this animal, says Aristotle, has reason.

Und was ist Vernunft? Vernunft ist nicht Intelligenz. Vernunft ist mehr als Intelligenz. ₅

And what is reason? Reason is not intelligence. Reason is more than intelligence.

Wer nur intelligent ist, glaubt: „Alle Menschen sind egoistisch. Ja, sie müssen egoistisch sein. Denn jeder Mensch will glücklich werden. Das heißt aber, der Emil möchte haben, was Fritz hat; und der Fritz ₁₀ möchte sein, was Emil ist. Aber der Emil kann nicht immer alles haben, was er möchte; und Fritz kann nicht sein, was Emil ist. Und darum haßt der Fritz den Emil, und der Emil den Fritz. Darum haßt ein ₁₅ Sohn seinen Vater, und darum haßt Nation A Nation B. Der Krieg zwischen Fritz und Emil, zwischen Sohn und Vater und zwi-

Whoever is merely intelligent believes: "All human beings are egoistic. Indeed, they have to be egoistic. For every human being desires to become happy. But this means: Emil would like to have what Fritz has; and Fritz would like to be what Emil is. But Emil cannot always have what he would like (to have); and Fritz cannot be what Emil is. And for this reason Fritz hates Emil, and Emil hates Fritz. Therefore, a son will hate his father, and Nation A will hate Nation B. War between Fritz and Emil, between father and son, and between Na-schen Nation A und Nation B ist also natürlich. So ist es, und so bleibt es. Leider!"

Aber warum „leider"? Was ist, ist, und es kann nur so sein, wie es ist. Warum also „leider"?

Hier spricht nicht unsere Intelligenz. Hier spricht unsere Vernunft. Unsere Intelligenz sieht nur, was ist. Unsere Vernunft sieht mehr. Sie sieht: Das, was ist, soll und darf nicht sein.

Natürlich will jeder Mensch glücklich werden. Er will es instinktiv. Er muß es wollen. Der Hans will *sein* Glück, und ich will *mein* Glück. Er will also nur, was ich auch will. Ich habe ein Haus und bin glücklich. Hans hat kein Haus und ist unglücklich. Aber, so sagt meine Vernunft, ich kann nicht glücklich sein, wenn Hans unglücklich ist. Denn wenn Hans sagt: „Du hast ein Haus und ich habe kein Haus", dann sagt er auch bald: „Warum sollst du ein Haus haben, und ich habe kein Haus?" Und so beginnen alle Kriege. Aber ich will keinen Krieg; Hans will auch keinen Krieg, er will ein Haus. Ich muß also etwas für ihn tun. Er braucht mich und kann ohne mich nicht glücklich werden; und ich brauche ihn und kann ohne ihn nicht glücklich bleiben. Also muß ich für ihn tun, was ich kann.

Das heißt aber: Ich muß ihn lieben. Denn „lieben" heißt ja „für den Mitmenschen das tun, was gut für ihn ist". Der Krieg, so sagt meine Vernunft, ist nicht natürlich. Natürlich ist nur die Liebe.

Aber leider zwingt mich meine Vernunft nicht. Ich weiß jetzt, was ich soll, aber meine Vernunft läßt mich frei, zu tun oder nicht zu tun, was ich soll. Und das ist unsere Tragik. Wir wollen oft nicht, was wir sollen; und wir können, wenn wir wollen, auch tun, was wir nicht sollen.

Aber wir müssen lernen zu wollen, was wir

tion A and Nation B is therefore natural. That's the way it is, and that's the way it will remain, unfortunately."

But why "unfortunately"? Whatever is, is, and it can only be as it is. Why, therefore, "unfortunately"?

Here (through this "unfortunately") speaks not our intelligence, but our reason. Our intelligence sees only what exists. Our reason sees more. It sees that what is, should not and must not be.

Naturally every human being desires to become happy. He desires it instinctively. He must desire it. Hans wants *his* happiness and I want *my* happiness. Thus he only wants what I want too. I have a house and am happy. Hans does not have a house and is unhappy. But, my reason tells me, I cannot be happy if Hans is unhappy. For if Hans says, "You have a house and I have no house," then he will soon say also, "Why should (shall) you have a house, and I don't have a house?" And thus begin all wars. But I don't want a war; Hans wants no war either, he wants a house. Therefore I have to do something for him. He needs me and cannot become happy without me; and I need him and cannot remain happy without him. Therefore I must do for him what I can.

But this means: I must love him. For "to love" means, after all, "to do that for a fellow man which is good for him." War, says my reason, is not natural. Only love is natural.

But unfortunately my reason does not force me. I now know what I ought to do, but my reason leaves me free to do or not to do what I ought (to do). And that is our tragic fate. We often do not want to do what we ought to do; and we can, if we want to, also do what we ought not to do.

However, we must learn to want to do what

sollen. Ja, der Mensch ist nur dann wirklich frei—frei zu tun, was er will—wenn er will, was er soll.

we ought to do. Indeed, man is only then really free—free to do what he wants to do —when he wants to do what he ought to do.

Zwei Gedichte

The following two poems are from a volume collected and edited by Günter Bruno Fuchs (born 1928 in Berlin) entitled *Die Meisengeige: Zeitgenössische Nonsensverse* (Munich: Carl Hanser Verlag, 1964). In keeping with the subtitle, "Contemporary Nonsense Verses," the title is nonsense: a *Meisengeige*, literally translated, is a "titmouse fiddle."

das Gedicht, –e poem

Horst Bienek (born 1930 in Gleiwitz) and Franz Mon (born 1926 in Frankfurt) are both serious contemporary writers; however, in these two poems they followed G. B. Fuchs's call to play his *Meisengeige* and, obviously, had fun doing it.

HORST BIENEK

Klatsch am Sonntagmorgen

Klatsch gossip

Wer mit wem?
Die mit dem!
Der mit der?
(Ohne Gewähr)
Sie und er?   5
Der und er??
Wer ist wer?

ohne Gewähr without guarantee

Wir mit ihr?
Sie mit dir!
(Am Klavier)   10
Du mit ihm!
Sie mit him!
Ich und du?
Who is who?

am Klavier at the piano

FRANZ MON

der tisch ist oval
das ei ist oval
nicht jeder tisch ist oval
jedes ei ist oval
kaum ein tisch ist oval   5
kaum ein ei ist nicht oval

dieser tisch ist viereckig
dieses ei ist nicht viereckig
viele tische sind viereckig
viele eier sind nicht viereckig   10
die meisten tische sind viereckig
die meisten eier sind nicht viereckig

Analysis

40 aber, oder, denn, und

Aber, oder, denn, and **und** are coordinating conjunctions—that is, conjunctions that connect two clauses of the same type. They precede the front field and are not counted as syntactical units. Of these four conjunctions, only **aber** can also be placed in the inner field. It then follows pronoun subjects and pronoun objects. If **denn** stands in the inner field, it is not the coordinating conjunction **denn** (*for*), but the particle **denn** discussed in **19**.

41 kein, nicht, and nichts

In English, most negative statements contain either *no* or *not*. The most frequently used German words of negation (besides **Nein!**) are **kein** and **nicht**. However, the use of **kein** and **nicht** does not parallel the use of *no* and *not*. You must therefore learn from the very beginning how and when to use **kein,** and how and when to use **nicht**.

German **nichts** means *nothing* or *not anything;* it is the antonym of **etwas,** *something.*

Hast du etwas gegen Erika?	Do you have anything against Erika?
Nein, ich habe nichts gegen Erika.	No, I have nothing against Erika.

42 nicht wahr? and nicht? as Complete Questions

Nicht wahr? (an abbreviation of **ist das nicht wahr?**—*isn't that true?*) corresponds to English *isn't that so?, don't you?, haven't you?, weren't you?,* etc. This **nicht wahr?** is frequently shortened to **nicht?** Since **nicht?** or **nicht wahr?** asks for confirmation, the preceding sentence usually contains **doch** (see **39**).

Sie *kommen* **doch heute abend, nicht wahr?**	You are coming tonight, aren't you?
Sie *kommen* **doch heute abend, *nicht?***	

43 nicht ein

German **nicht ein** does not correspond to English *not a* (see **44**). The **ein** in **nicht ein** is the numeral *one* and is usually stressed. German **nicht ein** therefore means *not one* or *not a single.*

Er hat nicht *ein*en Freund hier.   He doesn't have a *single* friend here.

This **nicht ein** is frequently strengthened by a preceding unstressed **auch,** which may be translated by *even.*

Ich kenne hier auch nicht *ein*en Men-   I don't know even *one* person around here.
schen.

44 Negation by kein

German **kein** is declined like the indefinite article **ein.** For the time being, do not use **kein** without a following noun. When used with a following noun,

$$\text{kein} + \text{noun equals} \begin{cases} no & + \text{noun} \\ not \ any & + \text{noun} \\ not \ a & + \text{noun} \end{cases}$$

Ich habe kein Geld.   I have no money.
                                           I don't have any money.

Ich habe keine Frau.   I have no wife.
                                           I don't have a wife.

Ich habe keinen Wagen.   I have no car.
                                           I don't have a car.

kein after the Inflected Verb

To make a negative statement, **kein** *must* be used in front of a noun object or in front of a predicate noun, *if* in the corresponding affirmative statement the noun would be used *either* with the indefinite article **ein** *or* by itself without any article or possessive adjective.

POSITIVE	NEGATIVE
Das ist Wasser.	Das ist kein Wasser.
Meyers haben einen Sohn.	Meyers haben keinen Sohn.
Meyers haben Geld.	Meyers haben kein Geld.
Meyers haben Kinder.	Meyers haben keine Kinder.

NOTE: The plural of **ein Kind** is **Kinder,** the plural of **kein Kind** is **keine Kinder.** The negation of **zwei Kinder** is **keine zwei Kinder.**

kein in the Front Field

Occasionally, **kein** plus noun is found in the front field: **Kein Mensch weiß, wo Meyer wohnt**—*Nobody knows where Meyer lives.* However, such usage is very restricted. To be safe, *do not use **kein** in the front field.*

45 Intonation of **kein**

The difference in stress distribution between **sie ist** *kein* **Kind** and **sie ist kein** *Kind* parallels the difference between *she is <u>not</u> a child* and *she isn't a <u>child</u>:* **kein** is stressed if it strongly contradicts a preceding affirmative statement; if no strong contradiction is intended or if the noun is mentioned for the first time, the noun itself is stressed.

VATER: **Warum soll Nancy diesen Sommer denn** *nicht* **allein nach Europa fahren?**	FATHER: Why *shouldn't* Nancy go to Europe by herself this summer?
MUTTER: **Sie ist doch noch ein** *Kind.*	MOTHER: She's still a *child.*
VATER: **Nein, sie ist** *kein* **Kind mehr.**	FATHER: No, she *isn't* a child anymore.

46 Negation by **nicht**

To form a negative statement, **nicht** is used whenever **kein** does not have to be used. For instance, the sentences

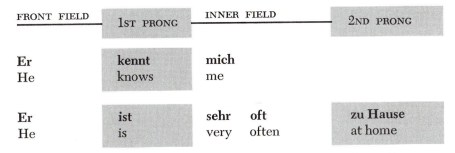

FRONT FIELD	1ST PRONG	INNER FIELD		2ND PRONG
Er He	**kennt** knows	**mich** me		
Er He	**ist** is	**sehr** very	**oft** often	**zu Hause** at home

do not contain a predicate noun like **Wasser** and no noun object like **einen Sohn** (cf. 44). Therefore, they cannot be negated by **kein;** they have to be negated by **nicht.** The problem is where this **nicht** should be placed.

The first sentence does not contain a second prong. In such cases, **nicht** stands at the very end of the sentence.

Er	**kennt**	**mich**	**nicht.**

The second sentence contains the second prong **zu Hause; nicht** always precedes the second prong.

Er	ist	sehr	oft	nicht	zu Hause.
He	is	very	often	not	at home.

Elements preceding **nicht** are not included in the negation. Thus **sehr oft** describes, in a positive way, that the not-being-at-home happens *very often*. On the other hand, all elements following **nicht** are included in the negation. The **zu Hause** constitutes the second prong, and the complete verbal idea in the sentence above is not **sein** but **zu Hause sein.** The position of **nicht** indicates that the complete verbal idea begins with **zu Hause.** Since second prongs are always part of the complete verbal idea, they *always* follow **nicht.**

It is up to the speaker to indicate where the complete verbal idea begins. He may include more than just the second prong. Thus he may say:

Er	ist	nicht	sehr	oft	zu Hause.
He	is	not	very	often	at home.

Now **sehr oft** is included in the negation, and the complete verbal idea is **sehr oft zu Hause sein.** With normal sentence intonation, **nicht** cannot precede pronouns like **mich, dich,** or **uns.** We shall return to this point later.

The following examples show that in most cases **nicht** stands at the end of the inner field and in front of the second prong. For the time being, you can use this statement as a rule of thumb.

Sentences without a Second Prong

Meyer	arbeitet		nicht.
Heute	regnet	es	nicht.
Ich	verstehe	Meyer	nicht.
Warum	kommt	er heute	nicht?
	Kennst	du mich	nicht?

Sentences with a Second Prong

nicht PRECEDES PREDICATE ADJECTIVES

Er	ist	leider	nicht	gesund.
Leider	ist	er	nicht	gesund.
Warum	ist	er denn	nicht	glücklich?
	Ist	sie wirklich	nicht	glücklich?

nicht PRECEDES PREDICATE NOUNS

Sie	ist	doch	nicht	meine Mutter.
Warum	werden	Sie	nicht	Arzt?
	Sind	Sie	nicht	Frau Meyer?

nicht PRECEDES DIRECTIVES—THAT IS, THE ANSWER TO *wohin*-QUESTIONS*

Nächstes Jahr	fahren	wir	nicht	nach Deutschland.
Wir	gehen	sonntags	nicht	ins Kino.
Warum	geht	ihr sonntags	nicht	in die Kirche?

nicht PRECEDES OTHER VERBAL COMPLEMENTS

Morgen abend	bleibe	ich natürlich	nicht	zu Hause.
Warum	bleibst	du morgen abend	nicht	zu Hause?
Warum	fährt	denn der Zug	nicht	ab?
Warum	lernt	sie denn	nicht	fahren?

47 Intonation of nicht

The intonation of **nicht** corresponds to the intonation of English *not:* If the sentence containing **nicht** is an intentional and somewhat curt contradiction to an immediately preceding statement, **nicht** is stressed and functions as the stress point of the sentence.

Sie sind Frau Schmidt, nicht *wahr?*	You are Mrs. Schmidt, *aren't you?*
Nein, ich bin *nicht* Frau Schmidt.	*No,* I am *not* Mrs. Schmidt.

In all other cases, **nicht** is completely unstressed.

Sie sind Frau *Schmidt,* nicht *wahr?*	You are Mrs. *Schmidt, aren't you?*
Nein, ich bin nicht Frau *Schmidt,* ich bin Frau *Döring.*	*No,* I am not Mrs. *Schmidt,* I am Mrs. *Döring.*

48 noch, schon, and mehr

Noch means *still* or *yet* and signifies that a state of affairs continues to exist.

Sie ist noch ein *Kind.*	She is still a *child.*
Er *schläft* noch.	He's still *asleep.*

* Both **wo** and **wohin** correspond to English *where.* **Wo** asks for the place at which an entire action takes place; **wohin** asks for a goal toward which an action is directed and at which it ends.

This **noch** can be emphasized by a preceding or following stressed **immer** (which, when used without **noch**, means *always*).

Sie ist *immer* noch ein Kind.   She is *still* a child.
Sie ist noch *immer* ein Kind.

If a negative state continues to exist, **noch** (**noch immer, immer noch**) precedes **nicht** or **kein.**

Er *schläft* noch nicht.   He isn't *asleep* yet.
Er schläft *immer* noch nicht.   He *still* isn't asleep.
Sie *haben* noch keine Kinder.   They don't *have* any children yet.

NOTE: *Noch* **ein** frequently means *another*.

Trinken Sie *noch* eine Tasse Kaffee?   Would you like another cup of coffee?

Schon signifies that a state of affairs exists already, perhaps earlier than expected. **Schon** is therefore the opposite of **noch nicht** and **noch kein.**

Er ist schon zu Hause.   **Er ist noch nicht zu Hause.**
He's already at home.   He isn't home yet.

Sie haben schon zwei Kinder.   **Sie haben noch keine Kinder.**
They have two children already.   They don't have any children yet.

To express that a state or an action has come to an end, German uses either **kein . . . mehr** (with a noun between **kein** and **mehr**) or **nicht mehr.** In this context, **kein . . . mehr** and **nicht mehr** have the same (temporal!) meaning as *no more* in *He is no more.* The usage of **kein . . . mehr** and **nicht mehr** parallels that of **kein** and **nicht.**

Ich brauche das Geld nicht mehr.   I don't need the money anymore.
Sie ist kein Kind mehr.   She is no longer a child.
Wir wohnen nicht mehr in München.   We don't live in Munich anymore.

German **mehr** and English *more*, either by themselves or together with an immediately following noun, can also have a *quantitative* meaning, which always involves a comparison. This comparison may be merely implied. English *more than* is expressed by **mehr als.**

Er arbeitet mehr als ich.   He works more than I do.
Ich brauche mehr Geld.   I need more money (than I have).
Er hat mehr Geld als ich.   He has more money than I have.
Er hat nicht mehr Geld als ich.   He doesn't have more money than I have.
Hier sind fünf Mark; mehr (Geld) habe   Here are five marks; I don't have any more.
  ich nicht.

49 doch to Answer a Negative Question

If a negative question is answered in the affirmative, **doch** with a strong stress is used instead of **ja.**

| Fährst du nicht nach Köln? | *Doch,* natürlich fahre ich nach Köln. |
| Fährst du nicht nach Köln? | *Doch,* aber nicht *heute.* |

Doch is also used to contradict a negative statement with an affirmative statement.

| Ich bin doch kein Kind mehr. | *Doch,* du *bist* noch ein Kind. |

50 Professional Status

Certain nouns, such as **Arzt, Schriftsteller, Soldat, Student,** and **Studentin,** can be used to express legal or professional status, and in this function they are used without any article.

It is perfectly normal to say:

Wir brauchen einen Arzt.   We need a doctor.

However, the question *What is your profession?* can only be answered by:

Ich bin Arzt.
Mein Sohn wird Arzt.

If these sentences are negated, either **kein** or **nicht** may be used.

Ich bin kein Arzt

or

Ich bin nicht Arzt.

51 Infinitives with and without zu

The infinitive of a verb is not merely used as a dictionary entry. Both in English and in German, infinitives are frequently used in connection with other verbs. The infinitive is used sometimes with, and sometimes without, *to* or **zu.**

Infinitive with zu

Er hat nichts zu tun.	He has nothing to do.
Er scheint zu schlafen.	He seems to be asleep.
Warum brauchst du heute nicht zu arbeiten?	Why don't you have to work today?

Infinitive without zu

Er kann arbeiten.	He can work.
Du mußt kommen.	You must come.
Soll ich gehen?	Shall I go?

52 Modal Auxiliaries

The most important verbs used with a following infinitive without **zu** are the modal auxiliaries, or simply the modals.

They usually express, by themselves, not a specific action, but an attitude toward the action expressed by the infinitive. Thus English *shalt* and *must* in *Thou shalt not steal* and *I must go home* view the action expressed by *steal* and *go home* as forbidden or necessary.

These modals are conjugated irregularly both in English and in German: *he must,* not *he musts;* **er kann,** not **er kannt.**

The English modals are incomplete: they have, for instance, no infinitive and no compound tenses. The German system, though grammatically complete, has peculiarities of its own.

NOTE:

1. When **müssen** is negated, it is usually stressed and expresses the absence of a compelling necessity. The text in the picture above,

> **Gute Bücher *müss*en nicht teuer sein**

means

> Good books don't *have* to be expensive.

However, the far more common negation of **müssen** is with **nicht brauchen zu,** which expresses the idea that there is no need to do something. Compare the following two sentences:

> **Nein, ich *muß* heute nicht nach München fahren.**
> No, I don't *have* to go to Munich today.

> **Nein, ich brauche heute *nicht* nach München zu fahren.**
> No, I *don't* need to go to Munich today.

2. English *must not* (*mustn't*) is expressed by **nicht dürfen.**

Security during illness—Modern illness protection need not be expensive.

53 The Six German Modals and Their Meaning

It is definitely unwise to attempt to equate each form of a modal with a corresponding English modal. Instead, you should master the basic meaning of each modal.

können to be able to		
Ich kann lesen.	I can read.	} *expresses ability*
müssen to have to		
Ich muß nach Hause gehen.	I have to go home.	} *expresses necessity*
dürfen to be allowed to		
Ich darf hierbleiben.	I have permission to stay here.	} *expresses permission*
Das darfst du nicht tun.	You mustn't do that.	
mögen would like to		
Ich möchte hierbleiben.	I would like to stay here.	} *expresses desire*
wollen to want to		
Ich will ins Kino gehen.	I intend to go to the movies	} *expresses intention*
sollen to be (supposed) to		
Ich soll nach Bonn fahren.	I am (supposed) to go to Bonn.	*expresses imposed obligation; in questions it may express a suggestion*
Sollen wir ins Theater gehen?	Shall we go to the theater?	

54 The Forms of the German Modals

	KÖNNEN	**WOLLEN**	**MÜSSEN**	**MÖGEN***	**SOLLEN**	**DÜRFEN**
ich	kann	will	muß	möchte	soll	darf
du	kannst	willst	mußt	möchtest	sollst	darfst
er sie es	kann	will	muß	möchte	soll	darf
wir	können	wollen	müssen	möchten	sollen	dürfen
ihr	könnt	wollt	müßt	möchtet	sollt	dürft
sie	können	wollen	müssen	möchten	sollen	dürfen
Sie	können	wollen	müssen	möchten	sollen	dürfen

* These forms of **mögen** will be explained in Unit 9.

55 Position of Dependent Infinitives

When infinitives like **arbeiten** or **zu arbeiten** depend on modals or on verbs like **brauchen**, they form a second prong, follow the inner field, and are preceded by **nicht.**

MODAL IN FIRST PRONG, INFINITIVE IN SECOND PRONG

FRONT FIELD	1ST PRONG	INNER FIELD	NICHT	2ND PRONG
muß				
Er	arbeitet	heute		

Er	muß	heute	arbeiten.
Er	soll	heute	arbeiten.
Er	darf	heute	arbeiten.
Er	scheint	heute	zu arbeiten.

Questions are treated in the same way.

Warum	mußt	du heute	arbeiten?
Warum	willst	du heute	arbeiten?
	Arbeitet	er heute?	
	Muß	er heute	arbeiten?
	Kann	er heute	arbeiten?

The procedure is the same if **nicht** stands at the end of the inner field.

Er	möchte	heute	nicht	arbeiten.
Er	kann	heute	nicht	arbeiten.
Er	braucht	heute	nicht	zu arbeiten.
Er	scheint	heute	nicht	zu arbeiten.
Warum	will	er denn heute	nicht	arbeiten?
Warum	braucht	er denn heute	nicht	zu arbeiten?

56 The Two-Box Second Prong

If a simple verb like **arbeiten** is pushed out of the slot for the first prong by a modal, it moves into the slot for the second prong. But what happens if the

Er will heute ins Kino gehen.

verb displaced by the modal or by an auxiliary such as **brauchen** and **scheinen** is a compound verb with some complement already filling the slot for the second prong? The second prong has two boxes, so to speak, and the infinitive dependent on an auxiliary verb always goes into the second box, whereas all complements go into the first box. The following diagram shows what happens:

FRONT FIELD	1ST PRONG	INNER FIELD	1ST BOX	2ND BOX
Er	geht	heute	ins Kino.	

A modal comes in and pushes **gehen** into the second box.

Er	will	heute	ins Kino	gehen.

This two-box second-prong pattern, in which the verbal complement precedes the infinitive without **zu**, is used so frequently in German that German dictionaries list many compound verbs, especially if the complement is a preposition or an adverb, in the form in which they appear in this two-box sequence (see 31). Thus **fahre zurück** in **Ich fahre morgen zurück** is listed under **zurückfahren**, because it occurs so frequently in such sentences as **Ich will morgen zurückfahren.**

If an infinitive with **zu** is required with compound verbs like **zurückfahren,** this **zu** is inserted between complement and infinitive, and the whole thing is written as one word.

> **Er braucht nicht zurückzufahren.**
> **Er braucht das Licht nicht auszumachen.**

But if complement and infinitive are not written as one word, **zu** remains separate as well.

> **Er braucht nicht nach München zu fahren.**

57 Replacement or Omission of the Dependent Infinitive

An infinitive can be replaced by **das,** if the verb was mentioned in the sentence immediately preceding.

> **Sie arbeiten heute? Dürfen Sie das?**

The infinitives **gehen, fahren,** and others, if clearly understood, are frequently omitted. Compare English *He wants out.*

> **Ich muß nach Hause.**   (**gehen** omitted)
> **Ich will heute nach Köln.**   (**fahren** omitted)
> **Du brauchst nicht zu arbeiten, wenn**
> ** du nicht willst.**   (**arbeiten** omitted)

58 Contrast Intonation

Imagine the following situation: Mr. and Mrs. Baker have had a serious traffic accident. A friend calls the hospital and asks, "How are Mr. and Mrs. Baker?" The doctor answers, "Mrs. Baker is alive." Can this be the answer to the question "How are Mr. *and* Mrs. Baker?" It can be, but only if the doctor uses the intonation pattern

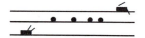

Mrs. Ba-ker is a-live

By using this intonation pattern, the doctor clearly implies that Mr. Baker is dead. A German doctor, in the same situation, will answer:

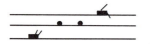

Frau Me-yer lebt

No German will fail to register the implication that Herr Meyer is dead.

This "contrast-intonation" pattern is not the same pattern as in sentences

with two stressed syllables such as

Sie wohnt noch im-mer in Köln

Contrast intonation is characterized by the fact that the first stressed syllable, usually standing in the front field, has a rising pitch starting on level 1, and the second stressed syllable has a falling pitch starting on level 3.

CONTRAST INTONATION

Geld hat sie

IMPLICATION

A-ber in-tel-li-gent ist sie nicht
(contrast intonation)

or

A-ber sie ist nicht in-tel-li-gent
(normal intonation)

59 Word Order under Contrast Intonation

Under contrast intonation, the second prong frequently appears in the front field. The two sentences

 and

Sie ist in-tel-li-gent   **In-tel-li-gent ist sie**

are not interchangeable. The first one is a remark of praise, the second is a sophisticated insult. Likewise,

 and

Er ist nicht zu Hau-se   **Zu Hau-se ist er nicht**

are not interchangeable; for only the second contains some implication like "Let's try to reach him somewhere else!"

Under contrast intonation, **kein** is replaced by (**ein**) . . . **nicht.**

Meyer ist kein _Dummkopf._
Ein _Dummkopf_ ist Meyer _nicht._

Ich habe kein *Geld.*
Geld habe ich *nicht*   or   *Geld* *habe* ich nicht.

Observe that contrast intonation is not the same as contradiction intonation.
If speaker A asserts:

Erika ist intelli*gen*t

Speaker B can contradict him bluntly and say:

Nein, sie ist *nicht* intelligent. (contradiction)

Speaker B could also say:

Ja, intelli*gen*t *ist* sie.   Yes, she is *intelligent* all right.
                                                        (But!) (Contrast!)

60 The Imperative

The English imperative is identical with the infinitive. One can say *Be my
guest* no matter whether one calls the person addressed *Jack* or *Dr. Able.*
German distinguishes between the **du**-form, the **ihr**-form, and the **Sie**-form
of the imperative. At this point, we introduce only the **Sie**-form, which looks
like the infinitive plus an immediately following **Sie: Kommen Sie! Gehen
Sie! Sehen Sie!** The imperative of **sein** is **Seien Sie!**

Imperatives, like yes-or-no questions, have verb-first position; they are distinguished by intonation.

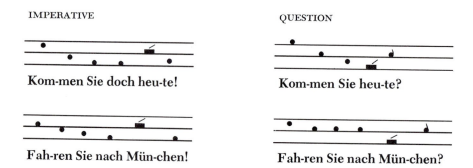

IMPERATIVE   QUESTION

Kom-men Sie doch heu-te!   Kom-men Sie heu-te?

Fah-ren Sie nach Mün-chen!   Fah-ren Sie nach Mün-chen?

In a polite request, the stress point of an imperative sentence is placed on
level 2, as in the examples above. If **bitte** (*please*) is used, it must be placed
either at the very beginning or after the unstressed elements following the
first prong.

Bitte besuchen Sie uns doch!
Besuchen Sie uns doch bitte!

If the stress point is raised to level 3, the request, in spite of the use of **bitte**, is changed into a command.

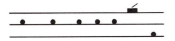

Kom-men Sie bit-te heu-te!

Exercises

A. Express in German.

1. He is intelligent, isn't he?
2. He lives in Vienna, doesn't he?
3. She has a house in Cologne, doesn't she?
4. You are a doctor, aren't you?
5. They have a son, don't they?

SEE ANALYSIS 42 (p. 63)

B. Transform the following sentences by substituting **kein** for **nicht ein**. Say each pair of sentences aloud to practice the shift in intonation. Do not stress **kein**, but the inflected verb.

> **Ich kenne hier nicht *einen* Menschen.**
> **Ich *kenne* hier keinen Menschen.**

1. Er hat auch nicht einen Freund.
2. Wir haben hier nicht einen Arzt.
3. Heute abend fährt auch nicht ein Zug nach Garmisch-Partenkirchen.

SEE ANALYSIS 43 (p. 64)

C. Negate the following sentences by using **kein.** Do not stress **kein.**

1. Das ist Wasser.
2. Haben Sie einen Wagen?
3. Sie hat eine Tochter.
4. Brauchst du Geld?
5. Trinken Sie Kaffee, Frau Meyer?

SEE ANALYSIS 44–45 (pp. 64-65)

D. Negate the following sentences by using **nicht;** use **noch nicht** and **nicht mehr** only where necessary.

1. Du bist doch meine Mutter.
2. Er liebt mich aber.
3. Sie wohnen noch in Düsseldorf.
4. Ihr seid intelligent.
5. Er ist schon zu Hause.

SEE ANALYSIS 46–48 (pp. 65-68)

E. Write replies to the following negative statements or questions by using **doch.**

> **Wohnt er nicht mehr in München?**
> **Doch, er wohnt immer noch in München.**

1. Ich bin doch kein Kind mehr.
2. Fährst du heute nicht nach Stuttgart?
3. Sind Sie heute abend nicht allein?
4. Haben wir keine Butter mehr?
5. Lebt denn Tante Amalie nicht mehr?

SEE ANALYSIS 49 (pp. 68-69)

F. For each of the following sentences, invent a preceding sentence with contrast intonation.

> —————————————, und *ich* bleibe zu *Hause.*
> *Du* kannst ins *Kino* gehen, und *ich* bleibe zu *Hause.*

SEE
ANALYSIS
58–59

(pp. 74-76)

1. —————————————, und *ich* muß *ar*beiten.
2. —————————————, aber intelli*gent* ist er *nicht.*
3. —————————————, aber eine *Toch*ter *ha*ben sie nicht.
4. —————————————, aber ihr *Freund hat* Geld.
5. —————————————, aber *ich* studiere *Deutsch.*
6. —————————————, aber *ar*beiten *will* er nicht.

G. Express in German.

1. I do not know one single person (human being) here.
2. Would you still like to live in Berlin, Erika?
3. I know he is not home yet.
4. Money is not everything, but can one be happy without money?
5. We do not intend to buy a house yet.
6. I know she can't be happy.
7. He is not permitted to drink wine.
8. Can't he drink coffee either?
9. We are supposed to go to America next year.

Vocabulary

als	than	das Ei, –er	egg
der Arzt, ¨e	physician, doctor	erst	first; not until; only
bald	soon	erst dann	not until (only)
beginnen	to begin		then
bei (*with dat.*)	at; at the home of;	essen (du ißt, er ißt)	to eat
	near	etwas	something; somewhat
bei dem Regen	in this rain	Euro′pa	Europe
besuchen	to visit	frei	free
bitte	please	gegen (*with acc.*)	against
der Bruder, ¨	brother	die Gewähr	guarantee
darum	for that reason	das Glas, ¨er	glass
denn	for (*conj.*)	ein Glas Wasser	a glass of water
dürfen	(*see* 52 *ff.*)	das Glück	happiness; luck
die Ecke, –n	corner	hassen	to hate
viereckig	square	heiraten	to marry
egoi′stisch	egoistic, selfish	hören	to hear

immer	always
immer noch, noch immer	still
die Intelligenz'	intelligence, intellect
Ita'lien	Italy
italie'nisch	Italian
der Instinkt'	instinct
instinktiv'	instinctive(ly)
die Jugend	(time of) youth
kaum	hardly
kennenlernen	to meet, to become acquainted with
der Klatsch	gossip
das Klavier, –e	piano
am Klavier	at the piano
können	(see 52 ff.)
kosten	to cost
der Krieg, –e	war
lassen (du läßt, er läßt)	to let, to leave
leben	to be alive, to live
die Liebe	love
man (acc.: einen)	one (indefinite pron.)
die Mark	mark
zwei Mark	two marks
mehr	more
mehr als	more than
nicht mehr	no longer
kein Kind mehr	no longer a child
meist	most
meistens	in most cases
die meisten Tische	most tables
mögen	(see 52 ff.)
das Muse'um, die Muse'en	museum
müssen	(see 52 ff.)
nehmen (du nimmst, er nimmt)	to take
oft	often
ohne (with acc.)	without
ohne mich	without me
prima	wonderful (colloquial)
rauchen	to smoke
scheinen	to seem; to shine
er scheint zu schlafen	he seems to be asleep
schlafen (du schläfst, er schläft)	to sleep
der Schriftsteller, –	writer, author
sehen (du siehst, er sieht)	to see
sehr	very
sehr oft	very often
sollen	(see 52 ff.)
der Soldat', –en	soldier
der Sommer, –	summer
diesen Sommer	this summer
sprechen (du sprichst, er spricht)	to talk
die Tante, –n	aunt
die Tasse, –n	cup
eine Tasse Kaffee	a cup of coffee
das Taxi, –s or die Taxe, –n	taxi
das Thea'ter, –	theater
das Tier, –e	animal
der Tisch, –e	table, desk
die Tragik	tragedy
die Uhr, –en	clock, watch
es ist sechs Uhr	it is six o'clock
Wieviel Uhr ist es?	What time is it?
Um wieviel Uhr?	At what time?
die Vernunft	reason (intellectual power)
das Volk, ⸚er	people
der Volkswagen, –	VW
wahr	true
das Wasser	water
der Wein, –e	wine
wenn	whenever; if; when
wiedersehen	to see again
auf Wiedersehen	good-by
Wieviel?	How much?
wirklich	real; really
wollen	(see 52 ff.)
zehn	ten
die Zeit, –en	time
zwingen	to force
zwischen	between

17. Sept.

14 Uhr

Auto- u. Solo-
Moto-Cross

ROTTENEGG

Das Rennen findet bei jeder Witterung statt

Orbis Druck, 4053 Held

Unit 4 The Dative —Prepositions with Dative and Accusative—Word Order in the Inner Field— The Perfect—Time Phrases

Patterns

[1] The Dative of the Personal Pronouns

This pattern drill contains all the dative forms of the personal pronouns. After memorizing these pronouns, follow the system used in this drill and recite these sentences until you can do them automatically.

SEE
ANALYSIS
61–62

(pp. 93-95)

Heute helfe ich *dir*, und morgen hilfst du *mir*.
Heute helfe ich *ihm*, und morgen hilft er *mir*.
Heute helfe ich *ihr*, und morgen hilft sie *mir*.
Heute helfe ich *euch*, und morgen helft ihr *mir*.
Heute helfe ich *ihnen*, und morgen helfen sie *mir*.

Heute hilfst du *mir*, und morgen helfe ich *dir*.
Heute hilfst du *ihm*, und morgen hilft er *dir*.
Heute hilfst du *ihr*, und morgen hilft sie *dir*.
Heute hilfst du *uns*, und morgen helfen wir *dir*.
Heute hilfst du *ihnen*, und morgen helfen sie *dir*.

Heute helfen wir *dir*, und morgen hilfst du *uns*.
Heute helfen wir *ihm*, und morgen hilft er *uns*.
Heute helfen wir *ihr*, und morgen hilft sie *uns*.
Heute helfen wir *euch*, und morgen helft ihr *uns*.
Heute helfen wir *ihnen*, und morgen helfen sie *uns*.

[2] The Dative with **glauben** and **helfen**

Follow the instructions for [1]. Do not change intonation.

SEE
ANALYSIS
61–62

(pp. 93-95)

Wenn du mir nicht *glaubst*, kann ich dir nicht *hel*fen.
Wenn er mir nicht *glaubt*, kann ich ihm nicht *hel*fen.
Wenn sie mir nicht *glaubt*, kann ich ihr nicht *hel*fen.
Wenn sie mir nicht *glauben*, kann ich ihnen nicht *hel*fen.

Rottenegg in Austria: The race will take place in any weather.

Wenn du uns nicht *glaubst*, können wir dir nicht *hel*fen.
Wenn er uns nicht *glaubt*, können wir ihm nicht *hel*fen.
Wenn sie uns nicht *glaubt*, können wir ihr nicht *hel*fen.
Wenn ihr uns nicht *glaubt*, können wir euch nicht *hel*fen.
Wenn Sie uns nicht *glau*ben, können wir Ihnen nicht *hel*fen.

[3] The Dative with **danken**

Follow the instructions for [1]. Do not change intonation.

SEE
ANALYSIS
61–62

(pp. 93-95)

Ich *weiß*, du hilfst mir *gern*. Aber wie kann ich dir *dan*ken?
Ich *weiß*, er hilft mir *gern*. Aber wie kann ich ihm *dan*ken?
Ich *weiß*, sie hilft mir *gern*. Aber wie kann ich ihr *dan*ken?
Ich *weiß*, ihr helft mir *gern*. Aber wie kann ich euch *dan*ken?
Ich *weiß*, sie helfen mir *gern*. Aber wie kann ich ihnen *dan*ken?

[4] The Dative with **antworten**

Follow the instructions for [1]. Do not change intonation.

SEE
ANALYSIS
61–66

(pp. 93-95)

Na*tür*lich kannst du mich fragen! Aber ich brauche dir nicht zu *ant*worten!
Na*tür*lich kann er mich fragen! Aber ich brauche ihm nicht zu *ant*worten!
Na*tür*lich kann sie mich fragen! Aber ich brauche ihr nicht zu *ant*worten!
Na*tür*lich könnt ihr mich fragen! Aber ich brauche euch nicht zu *ant*worten!
Na*tür*lich können sie mich fragen! Aber ich brauche ihnen nicht zu *ant*worten!

[5] The Dative with **gehören;** Replacement of **er, sie, es** by **der, die, das**

Practice these pairs of sentences until you can produce the second
sentence orally when you hear the first.

SEE
ANALYSIS
61–62, 77

(pp. 93-95,
114)

Das ist mein Wagen. Der gehört mir.
Das ist deine Uhr. Die gehört dir.
Das ist sein Auto. Das gehört ihm.
Das ist ihr Hut. Der gehört ihr.

Das ist unsere Zeitung. Die gehört uns.
Das ist euer Haus. Das gehört euch.
Das ist Ihr Hund. Der gehört Ihnen.

Das sind meine Zeitungen. Die gehören mir.
Das sind deine Häuser. Die gehören dir.
Das sind seine Hüte. Die gehören ihm.

Das sind unsere Zeitungen. Die gehören uns.
Das sind eure Häuser? Die gehören euch?
Das sind ihre Hüte. Die gehören ihnen.
Das sind Ihre Blumen. Die gehören Ihnen.

After you have mastered the pattern above, be prepared to produce
orally **Das ist mein Wagen** when you hear **Der Wagen gehört mir.**

[6] The Dative with **gehören**

Formulate similar questions and answers. Do not place the word
containing the answer in the front field. Be prepared to do this
orally in class.

		SEE ANALYSIS 61–62, 77 (pp. 93-95, 114)
Wem	gehört das *Haus* da?	
Das	gehört Frau *Schulz*.	
Wem	gehören denn diese *Häus*er hier?	
Das da	gehört *mir*.	
So? Das	gehört *dir?*	
Frau *Schmidt* sagt, das Auto	gehört *ihr*.	
Nein, es	gehört *uns*.	
	Gehört dieses Auto *euch?*	
Nein, es	gehört Frau *Ber*tram.	
Was? Dieses Auto	gehört *Ih*nen, Frau Bertram?	

[7] Variations; Plural Verb Forms after **es** and **das**

Practice these sentences until, when hearing one, you can produce
the other four.

Das Haus gehört dem *Vater*.—Das Haus gehört meinem *Vater*.—Das Haus gehört *ihm*.—
Es ist *sein* Haus.—Das ist *sein* Haus.

Der Wagen gehört der *Tante*.—Er gehört meiner *Tante*.—Er gehört *ihr*.—Es ist *ihr*
Wagen.—Das ist *ihr* Wagen.

Die Bücher gehören den *Kindern*.—Sie gehören unseren *Kindern*.—Sie gehören *ihn*en.—
Es sind *ih*re Bücher.—Das sind *ih*re Bücher.

SEE
ANALYSIS
61–62,
77–78
(pp. 93-95,
114)

[8] Adjectives with the Dative

Form variations by changing the pronouns.

		SEE ANALYSIS 64 (pp. 96-97)
Das ist interessant.	That's interesting.	
Das ist mir interessant.	I think that's interesting.	
Er ist böse.	He is angry.	
Er ist mir böse.	He is angry with me.	
Sie ist zu jung.	She is too young.	
Sie ist mir zu jung.	She is too young as far as I'm concerned.	
Ist Ihnen das recht, Frau Meyer?	Is that all right with you, Mrs. Meyer?	
Natürlich ist mir das recht.	Of course that's all right with me.	
Ist das Ihrem Mann recht, Frau Meyer?	Is that all right with your husband, Mrs. Meyer?	
Natürlich ist ihm das recht.	Of course that's all right with him.	

[9] Prepositions with the Accusative

Form variations of your own, but do not replace nouns by pronouns.

SEE
ANALYSIS
65
(p. 97)

Wir müssen	durch	die Stadt fahren.
Herr Lenz arbeitet	für	meinen Vater.
Hast du etwas	gegen	mich?
Ich muß	ohne	ihn fahren.
Ich kann	ohne	dich nicht leben.

[10] Prepositions with the Dative

SEE
ANALYSIS
66
(pp. 97-98)

Woher *kommst* du?   Aus dem *Kino!*
                                 Aus der *Stadt!*

Wir sind *alle* hier   außer meinem *Vater.*
                                 außer *ihm.*
                                 außer *Ihn*en, Herr Lenz.

Hans ist heute   bei seinem *Vater.*
                                 bei seiner *Mut*ter.
                                 bei *uns.*

Mit wem gehst du ins Kino?   Mit Frau *Hoff*mann!
                                 Mit *ihr!*
                                 Mit *der?*

Wann wollt *ihr* denn heiraten?   Nach dem *Kriege!*
Er fährt   nach Österreich.
                                 nach *Hause.*
                                 nach Amerika.

Ich komme heute sehr spät nach *Hause.*—*Wann?*—Um *neun.*
Wie *spät* ist es jetzt?—*Zehn* nach *sechs.*

Seit wann bist *du* denn hier?   Seit einer *Stunde!*
                                 Seit drei *Wochen!*
                                 Seit einem *Jahr!*

Von wem hast du das *Buch?*   Von meinem *Bruder!*
                                 Von meiner *Tante!*
                                 Ich habe es von meinem *Vater!*

Halt! Zu den Zügen nach Deutschland nur durch die Zollhalle

Attention: Voyageurs à destination vers Allemagne, passage obligatoire par la halle de douane

Attention: To trains for Germany only through the customs

Wohin gehst du? Zum Postamt.

Wohin *gehst* du?

Zu meinem *Vater!*
Zu *ihm!*
Zur Universi*tät!*
Zu meiner *Tante!*
Zum *Essen!*

[11] Word Order in the Inner Field

Study the following sentences and observe the word order. Note that
if you answer with a complete sentence, the element containing the
answer always stands at the end of the inner field unless the verb
itself is the answer.

Ich gebe meiner Frau eine *Uhr.*
Ich gebe ihr eine *Uhr.*
Ich gebe die Uhr meiner *Frau.*
Ich gebe sie meiner *Frau.*
Ich gebe ihr die *Uhr.*
Ich *gebe* sie ihr.

Was willst du denn deiner Mutter *schic*ken?
Ich glaube, ich schicke ihr *Blu*men.
Was willst du denn mit diesen *Blu*men hier machen?
Die schicke ich meiner *Mut*ter.
Ich glaube, ich schicke sie meiner *Mut*ter.
Ich glaube, ich schicke diese Blumen meiner *Mut*ter.

Fritz möchte seiner Freundin ein *Buch* schicken.
Was will Fritz seiner Freundin schicken?
Ein *Buch!*
Er will ihr ein *Buch* schicken!
Wem will Fritz das Buch schicken?
Seiner *Freun*din!
Er will das Buch seiner *Freun*din schicken.
Er will es seiner *Freun*din schicken.

SEE
ANALYSIS
67

(pp. 98-100)

Warum will Fritz seiner Freundin denn ein *Buch* schicken?
Warum will er seiner Freundin denn ein *Buch* schicken?
Warum will er ihr denn ein *Buch* schicken?
Willst du das Buch deiner *Freun*din schicken?
Willst du es deiner *Freun*din schicken?
Willst du es ihr *schic*ken?
Willst du deiner Freundin ein *Buch* schicken?
Willst du ihr ein *Buch* schicken?
Nein, ich will ihr *Geld* schicken.
Wann willst du ihr das Geld denn *schic*ken?
Wann willst du es ihr denn *schic*ken?

[12] The Perfect

Read these sentences aloud to get used to this pattern, in which the
participle appears at the end of the sentence.

SEE
ANALYSIS
68–72
(pp. 101-105)

FRONT FIELD	1ST PRONG	INNER FIELD	NICHT	1ST BOX	2ND BOX
A. Auxiliary: haben					
Ich	habe	Physik			studiert.
Was	haben	Sie			studiert?
Ich	habe	ihren Vater	nicht		gekannt.
Er	hat	sie	nie		geliebt.
Wir	haben	Frau Meyer			gesehen.
Wir	haben	Sie	nicht		verstanden.
Warum	haben	Sie mich	nicht		verstanden?
Ich	habe	gestern			arbeiten müssen.
Ich	habe	gestern	nicht		zu arbeiten brauchen.
Er	hat	noch nie			arbeiten wollen.
Ich	habe	ihn leider	nicht		besuchen dürfen.
Ich	habe	gestern	nicht	zu Hause	bleiben wollen.
B. Auxiliary: sein					
Er	ist	heute morgen			gestorben.
Wir	sind	gestern abend			gekommen.
Der Zug	ist	schon		ab-	gefahren.
Warum	seid	ihr heute		zu Hause	geblieben?
Sie	ist	schon		nach Hause	gegangen.
Meyer	ist	schon immer		ein Idiot	gewesen.

Wer hat denn gestern Tante Amalie zum *Bahn*hof gebracht?
Wer hat denn Tante Amalie *ges*tern zum Bahnhof gebracht?
Wer hat sie denn gestern zum *Bahn*hof gebracht?
Warum hast *du* sie denn nicht zum Bahnhof gebracht?

Herr Kunz hat seiner Frau in Frankfurt ein *Auto* gekauft.
Er hat seiner Frau das Auto in *Frank*furt gekauft.
Er hat ihr das Auto in *Frank*furt gekauft.
Er hat es ihr in *Frank*furt gekauft.
Nein, in Ber*lin* hat er es ihr *nicht* gekauft.

[13] The Perfect: Point-of-Time Phrases

The following conversational sentences contain time expressions
which denote a date or a point in time. Observe that English always
uses the past tense.

Meyer ist heute morgen nach Österreich gefahren?—*Nein,* er ist schon *gestern* gefahren.

Did Meyer go to *Austria* this morning?— *No,* he went *yesterday.*

SEE ANALYSIS 72–73

(pp. 104-106)

Kennen Sie Frau *Leh*mann?—Ja, die habe ich vor einem Jahr in *Mün*chen kennengelernt.

Do you know Mrs. *Lehmann?*—Yes, I met (was introduced to) her a year ago in *Munich.*

Was habt *ihr* denn gestern abend gemacht? *Wir* sind gestern abend ins *Kino* gegangen.

What did *you* do last night? *We* went to the *movies* last night.

Sie wollen nach *Wien* fahren? *Da* kommen Sie zu *spät.* Der Zug nach Wien ist schon vor einer *Stunde* abgefahren.

You want to go to *Vienna?* Then you are too *late.* The train to Vienna *left* an *hour* ago.

Nun bist du also endlich in Ober*ammergau, Tante Amalie. Hast du heute nacht gut ge*schlafen?—Ich habe über*haupt* nicht geschlafen. Der Wirt hat seine *Kuh* di*rekt* unter meinem *Zimmer.* Und die Kuh hat die *ganze* Nacht ge*muht.* Außer*dem* habe ich gestern abend zuviel *Kaf*fee getrunken.

So you're finally in *Oberammergau,* Aunt *Amalie.* Did you *sleep* well last night? —I wasn't able to sleep at *all.* The landlord keeps his *cow directly* under my *room.* And the cow *mooed all* night. *Besides,* I had too much *coffee* last night.

[14] The Perfect: Frequency Phrases

Note the difference between closed-end and open-end frequency phrases.

closed-end: **Washington hat nie gelogen.**
open-end: **Fritzchen Müller hat noch nie gelogen.**

Meine Eltern wohnen in Hannover, und das ist ziemlich weit von hier. Sie haben uns dieses Jahr erst *ein*mal besucht, und wir haben sie noch nie besucht. Wir haben

My parents live in Hanover, and that is rather far from here. They have visited us only once this year, and we haven't ever visited them. We have no car, you

SEE ANALYSIS 74

(pp. 106-108)

nämlich keinen Wagen. Mein Vater hat auch keinen Wagen. Er hat nie fahren gelernt. Und er meint, jetzt ist er zu alt.

know. My father also doesn't have a car. He never *did* learn to drive. And now he thinks he is too old.

Sind Sie und Ihre Frau schon einmal in die Schweiz gefahren, Herr Kruse?—Nein, bis jetzt noch nicht.

Have you and your wife ever gone to Switzerland, Mr. Kruse?—No, so far we haven't.

Letztes Jahr sind wir nur dreimal in die Oper gegangen.

Last year we went to the opera only three times.

So, deine Mutter will uns schon wieder besuchen? Aber Inge! Sie hat uns dieses Jahr doch schon dreimal besucht.—Sie hat uns nicht *schon* dreimal besucht. Sie hat uns *erst* dreimal besucht.

So your mother wants to visit us again? But Inge, she's already visited us three times.—She has not visited us *already* three times; she has visited us *only* three times.

Wie oft sind Sie letztes Jahr nach Frankfurt geflogen?—Nicht *ein*mal. (Nur *zwei*mal.)

How often did you fly to Frankfurt last year?—Not once. (Only twice.)

Wie oft sind Sie dieses Jahr schon nach Frankfurt geflogen?—Noch gar nicht. (Schon zweimal; Erst zweimal.)

How often have you flown to Frankfurt this year?—Not at all yet. (Twice already; Only twice.)

So? Fritz studiert jetzt Mathematik? Er hat doch immer Arzt werden wollen.

So Fritz is studying math now? Didn't he always want to become a doctor?

Natürlich studiert Fritz Medizin. Er hat doch schon immer Arzt werden wollen.

Of course Fritz is studying medicine. He has always wanted to be a doctor.

[15] The Perfect: Stretch-of-Time Phrases

The following sentences contain stretch-of-time phrases. Note the difference between "all-past" and "up-to-now" situations.

SEE
ANALYSIS
75
(pp. 108-113)

Kennen Sie Zürich?—Ja, ich habe zwei Jahre lang in Zürich *gewohnt,* vor dem *Kriege.*

Do you know *Zürich?*—Yes, I *lived* in Zurich for two years before the *war.*

Hast du Erika schon besucht?—*Ja,* aber erst *ge*stern. Ich habe lange nicht gewußt, wo sie *wohnt.*

Have you seen *Erika?*—*Yes,* but only *yesterday.* I didn't know for a long time where she is *living.*

Ich bin damals Athe*ist* gewesen und habe *lange* nicht an Gott ge*glaubt.* Aber *heute weiß* ich: ohne *Gott* kann man nicht *leben.*

At that time, I was an *atheist,* and for a *long* time I did not *believe* in God. But *now* I *know:* One cannot *live* without *God!*

Wie geht's denn Herrn *Meyer?*—Oh, *jetzt* geht's ihm wieder *gut.* Aber *letzt*es Jahr ist er monatelang *krank* gewesen und hat *lange* nicht *ar*beiten können.

How is Mr. *Meyer?*—Oh, *now* he's *all right* again. But *last* year he was *sick* for *months,* and for *quite* some time he wasn't able to *work.*

Ich *weiß*, Erika wohnt seit drei Wochen hier in *Köln*, aber bis *heute* habe ich sie noch *nicht* besuchen können. Ich habe *wirk*lich noch keine *Zeit* gehabt, sie zu be*su*chen.

I *know* Erika has been living here in *Cologne* for three weeks. But up to *now* I have not yet been able to *visit* her. I *really* haven't had the *time* yet to *visit* her.

Na*tür*lich muß mein Sohn in Tübingen viel *ar*beiten. Und warum auch *nicht! Ich* habe *auch* vier Jahre in *Tübingen* studiert, und *ich* habe *auch* arbeiten müssen.

Of *course* my son has to *work* hard in Tübingen. And why *not!* I, *too*, went to the University of *Tübingen* for four years, and *I, too*, had to work hard.

Ist Schmidt ge*sund* aus Afrika zurückgekommen?—*Nein*, seine Frau hat *jahre*lang auf ihn ge*war*tet. Aber *letz*tes Jahr hat sie gehört, daß er nicht mehr *lebt*.

Did Schmidt get home *safe* from Africa?—No, his wife *waited* for him for *years*, but *last* year she heard that he is no longer *alive*.

Seit wann wohnt denn seine Frau schon bei ihrer *Toch*ter?—Oh, schon *lange*, schon seit *vier* oder fünf *Jah*ren.

Since when has his wife been living with her *daughter*?—Oh, for *quite* some time, it must be *four* or *five years* by now.

Wo ist denn *Ihr* Sohn, Frau Meyer?—*Mein* Sohn ist seit Anfang Mai in *Hei*delberg. Er studiert Medi*zin*.

And where is *your* son, Mrs. Meyer?—*My* son has been in *Heidelberg* since the beginning of May. He is studying *medicine*.

Wie lange sitzt du denn schon hier und *war*test?—Seit einer *Stunde!*

How long have you been sitting here *waiting*?—For an *hour!*

Nein, hier hat es gestern *nicht* geregnet. Hier hat es schon *wochen*lang nicht mehr geregnet. Wir warten schon *lange* auf *Re*gen.

No, it did not rain *here* yesterday. It hasn't rained here for *weeks*. We have been waiting for rain for quite some *time*.

Conversation

I

HERR LORENZ: So, jetzt muß ich aber *wirk*lich gehen, Herr Kunz.

HERR KUNZ: Aber wa*rum* denn? Es ist doch erst fünf *Uhr*.

HERR LORENZ: *Ja*, aber ich will nach dem Essen noch mit meiner Frau ins *Ki*no.

HERR KUNZ: Mit dem *Wa*gen sind Sie doch in zehn Mi*nu*ten zu Hause.

HERR LORENZ: Mit dem *Wa*gen, *ja*. Ich *ha*be aber heute keinen Wagen.

HERR KUNZ: Sie haben keinen *Wa*gen? Bei *dem Re*gen?

HERR LORENZ: Nein, den *Wa*gen hat heute meine *Frau*. Bei dem Regen hat sie nicht mit dem *Zug* in die Stadt fahren wollen.

HERR KUNZ: Aha, also sind *Sie* mit dem Zug gefahren.

TAXI-FUNK
Berlin e.G.m.b.H.
66 00 22
Berlin 61
Mehringdamm 107

**TAG
UND
NACHT
BEREIT**

66 00 22

Vorbestellung
jederzeit

Willst du mit dem Taxi ins Museum, Tante Amalie?   Die Nummer ist sechs-sechs, null-null, zwo-zwo.

II

FRAU KUNZ: Herr Lorenz, glauben Sie, Ihre Frau ist schon aus der Stadt zurück?
HERR LORENZ: Natürlich, Sie hat doch den Wagen.
FRAU KUNZ: Dann rufen Sie sie doch an; sie soll mit dem Wagen zu uns kommen. Ich
                habe Ihre Frau schon so lange nicht gesehen.
HERR LORENZ: Das ist eine Idee.
FRAU KUNZ: Natürlich, und Sie können mit meinem Mann noch ein Glas Bier trinken.
HERR LORENZ: Vielen Dank, Frau Kunz. Und meine Frau rufe ich sofort an.
FRAU KUNZ: Darf ich mit Ihrer Frau sprechen, Herr Lorenz?
HERR LORENZ: Aber natürlich.

III

FRAU KUNZ: Frau Lorenz? Guten Abend, hier ist Gertrud Kunz.
FRAU LORENZ: Ah, Frau Kunz, guten Abend. Wie geht's Ihnen denn?
FRAU KUNZ: Danke, mir geht's gut. Ihnen hoffentlich auch.
FRAU LORENZ: Danke, ja. Ich komme gerade aus der Stadt,—es hat ja so geregnet.
FRAU KUNZ: Ja, hier regnet es immer noch.
FRAU LORENZ: Gottseidank bin ich heute mit dem Wagen gefahren, und mein Mann ist
                mit dem Zug in die Stadt gefahren.
FRAU KUNZ: Ich weiß. Ihr Mann ist hier bei uns. Er hat seit zwei Uhr mit meinem Mann
                hier gearbeitet. Aber jetzt sind sie fertig.
FRAU LORENZ: Das ist gut. Dann kann ich doch mit dem Wagen kommen und ihn abholen.
FRAU KUNZ: Ich höre, Sie wollen heute abend noch ins Kino.
FRAU LORENZ: Ja, nach dem Essen.
FRAU KUNZ: Hören Sie, Frau Lorenz, können Sie nicht zum Essen zu uns kommen?
FRAU LORENZ: Aber gerne, vielen Dank, Frau Kunz. Ich habe Sie ja schon so lange nicht
                gesehen.
FRAU KUNZ: Ja, und wenn es Ihnen recht ist, können wir nach dem Essen alle vier ins
                Kino gehen.

Reading

Viel Lärm um nichts?

Kapitel Eins: A News Item

New York Star. International Edition. Paris, April 30—According to
a report from Konstanz, Germany, the famous German novelist
Johannes Schmidt-Ingelheim has been missing since April 8.
Schmidt-Ingelheim had gone to Africa to collect material for a new ₅
novel which is to deal with the fate of General Rommel, the famous
commander of the German Afrika Korps in World War II. In a
letter from Cairo, dated April 8, Schmidt-Ingelheim promised to call
his wife on April 12, her birthday, from Casablanca. Since then he
has not been heard from. Schmidt-Ingelheim's novel *Wie das Gesetz* ₁₀
es befahl (*As the Law Demanded*) is the literary sensation of the
year. Even here in Paris, critics praise his objectivity and the
penetrating realism of the scenes dealing with the battle on the
Normandy beaches. Everybody here feels that this book was written
by a man who, "as the law demanded," did his best as a soldier, ₁₅
but who nevertheless remained a human being. Just a few weeks
ago Schmidt-Ingelheim was awarded the *Grand Prix Littéraire de
l'Europe.*

Viel Lärm um nichts the German translation of *Much Ado about Nothing*

Kapitel Zwei: Frau Schmidt-Ingelheim am Telefon

Hier Frau Schmidt-*I*ngelheim! . . .   ₂₀
*Meh*rens?—*Bit*te, ich kann Sie nicht ver*st*ehen. . . .

Ach *so*, Behrens, B wie *Ber*ta. . . .
Und Sie sind ein Freund von meinem *Mann*, Herr Behrens? . . .

Ach *so*, Sie haben den Artikel im *New York Star* gelesen. Und *Sie*
sind von der *Bild*-Zeitung? . . .   ₂₅

Nein, nein, ich bin *nicht* mit meinem Mann nach *Kairo* gefahren.
Er hat mir nur aus Kairo ge*schrie*ben! „Ich fahre morgen nach
Casa*blanc*a", hat er geschrieben. . . .

Nein, nein, nicht mit einer *Jacht!* Mit der *Luft*hansa! . . .

So, Sie kennen Herrn Thistlethwaite? Ja, Herr Thistlethwaite ist ein ₃₀
Freund von meinem Mann. . . .

Und Sie sagen, Herr Thistlethwaite hat am 9. April [am *neun*ten
April] auf seiner Jacht in Alexandria von *den* Ingelheims geredet? . . .

„Die *I*ngelheims sind auf meiner Jacht", hat er gesagt? . . .

Nein, da haben Sie Herrn Thistlethwaite nicht richtig ver*stan*den. Ich *sage* Ihnen doch, ich bin *nicht* mit meinem Mann nach Ägypten gefahren. Ich bin zu *Hause* geblieben. . . .

Nein, unsere Tochter ist es *auch* nicht gewesen. Unsere *Toch*ter ist doch erst *acht*. Wir haben ja erst vor *neun* Jahren ge*hei*ratet, in 5 Berlin! . . .

Bin ich *glück*lich mit Johannes? Aber na*tür*lich bin ich *glück*lich! . . .

Warum *Kä*the nicht glücklich mit ihm gewesen ist? Aber wo haben *Sie* denn von *Kä*the gehört? . . .

So, so, die *Zei*tung weiß alles! *Ja*, mein Mann hat von seiner ersten 10 Frau eine *Toch*ter. Erika heißt sie. . . .

Nein, sie muß jetzt *zwan*zig sein. Ich *ken*ne sie nicht. Ich habe sie noch *nie* gesehen. . . .

Ja, mein Mann redet *viel* von seiner *Toch*ter. Aber be*sucht* hat sie uns noch *nie*. . . .   15

Na*tür*lich möchte ich die Erika *ken*nenlernen. Aber sie *darf* uns nicht be*su*chen, die Mutter *will* das nicht. . . .

Nein, die Tochter ist *nicht* mit ihrem Vater nach Alexandria gefahren. . . .

Was die Tochter *tut?* Ich *glau*be, sie studiert Archäologie.—Aber 20 hier kommt der *Brief*träger. Vielleicht bringt er einen Brief von meinem *Mann*. . . .

Gut, Sie rufen mich später wieder *an*.

(Fortsetzung folgt—To be continued)

ersten first (disregard the ending **–en**)

PETER OTTO CHOTJEWITZ

Peter Otto Chotjewitz (born 1934 in Berlin) is another contemporary writer who joined Günter Bruno Fuchs in playing the "titmouse fiddle."

Reisen

ich
bin mit dem Zug nach Ulm gefahren
ich bin
mit dem Zug nach Ulm gefahren
ich bin mit   5
dem Zug nach Ulm gefahren
ich bin mit dem
Zug nach Ulm gefahren

ich bin mit dem Zug
nach Ulm gefahren   10
ich bin mit dem Zug nach Ulm
gefahren
ich bin mit dem Zug nach Ulm gefahren

nun bin ich in Ulm:
was soll ich hier?   15

From: G. B. Fuchs, *Die Meisengeige: Zeitgenössische Nonsensverse* (Munich: Carl Hanser Verlag, 1964).

Analysis

61 The Dative Case

The term "case" was explained in **24.** There are four cases in German: nominative, genitive, dative, and accusative.

In this unit, the dative case is introduced. The dative is the case of the indirect object, or—to use the German term—of the dative object. This dative object answers the question *To whom—**Wem?** It is usually a person.

She gave the money to Charlie.
She gave the money to him.
To whom did she give it?—To Charlie, to him.

Note that whenever you have a genuine dative object in English, you can, by rearranging the sentence, force the form with *to* to appear or to disappear.

She gave him the book.
She gave the book to him.

The *him* in *She gave him the book* is therefore syntactically not the same kind of *him* as that in

She loves him

for only the first *him* can be changed into a *to him*. The *him* which can be replaced by *to him* corresponds to the German dative. Note also that the *to* in

He took Charlie to the station

cannot be eliminated, since *to the station* is not an object but a directive. It is important that you remember this distinction when dealing with the German dative (indirect) object, which *never* uses the preposition *zu*.

The Forms of the Dative Case

INTERROGATIVE PRONOUNS

NOM.	wer	who
DAT.	*wem*	to whom
ACC.	wen	whom

NOTE: The interrogative pronouns **wer, wem,** and **wen** have the same endings as the corresponding forms of the masculine definite article **der, dem, den.**

der-WORDS

	MASC.	FEM.	NEUT.	PLURAL
NOM.	der	die	das	die
DAT.	*dem*	*der*	*dem*	*den*
ACC.	den	die	das	die

ein-WORDS

	MASC.	FEM.	NEUT.	PLURAL
NOM.	kein	keine	kein	keine
DAT.	*keinem*	*keiner*	*keinem*	*keinen*
ACC.	keinen	keine	kein	keine

NOTE: There is no difference between the dative endings of the **ein**-words and those of the **der**-words.

PERSONAL PRONOUNS

SINGULAR	NOM.	ich	du	er	sie	es	Sie
	DAT.	*mir*	*dir*	*ihm*	*ihr*	*ihm*	*Ihnen*
	ACC.	mich	dich	ihn	sie	es	Sie
PLURAL	NOM.	wir	ihr		sie		Sie
	DAT.	*uns*	*euch*		*ihnen*		*Ihnen*
	ACC.	uns	euch		sie		Sie

NOUNS

In the singular, nouns have no special ending for the dative. Occasionally, masculine and neuter nouns of one syllable use **-e** (**dem Manne**), but this ending is obsolescent and no longer required, except in such idiomatic expressions as **zu Hause** or **nach Hause.**

A number of masculine German nouns have the ending **-en** in all cases except the nominative singular—e.g., **der Student, dem Studenten, den Studenten,** plural **die Studenten; der Mensch, dem Menschen, den Menschen,** plural **die Menschen.**

The noun **Herr** is declined as follows:

SINGULAR	NOM.	**der Herr**
	DAT.	**dem Herrn**
	ACC.	**den Herrn**
PLURAL	NOM.	**die Herren**
	DAT.	**den Herren**
	ACC.	**die Herren**

In the dative plural, all German nouns must end in **-n,** except those foreign words the plural of which ends in **-s.** If the nominative plural already ends in **-n,** no additional **-n** is required.

NOM. SING.	NOM. PLURAL	DAT. PLURAL
der Mann	**die Männer**	**den Männern**
die Frau	**die Frauen**	**den Frauen**
die Freundin	**die Freundinnen**	**den Freundinnen**
das Auto	**die Autos**	**den Autos**

NOTE: Nouns ending in **-in** double the **-n** in the plural in order to keep the **-i-** short: **die Freundin, die Freundinnen.**

62 Verbs with Only a Dative Object

For a speaker of English, the *him* in

> They helped him

is clearly a direct object. For a native German, the verb **helfen** means *to give help to.* For this reason, **helfen,** and a number of other verbs, take a dative object, *not* an accusative object, in German.

We are introducing three of these verbs in this unit. They are

gehören	to belong to (ownership)
helfen	to help, give help to
danken	to thank, give thanks to

Note that of the corresponding English verbs, only *belong* must be used with the preposition *to.* You can only say *The book belongs to me,* not *The book belongs me.* English, unlike German, does not distinguish between ownership and membership. German **gehören zu** expresses membership only.

Der Hund gehört uns.	The dog belongs to us.
Maria gehört zu uns.	Mary is one of us, belongs to our group.

The indispensable *to* (when *to belong to* expresses ownership) is one important case where an English verb cannot get rid of the *to,* and where German nevertheless cannot use **zu.**

63 Verbs Governing the Dative and Accusative

In English there are a number of verbs that can be used with both an indirect and a direct object.

Mr. Jones gave his wife a hat.

The German sentence

Er schenkt seiner Frau einen Hut

has the same structure.

The most important verbs in this group are

geben	to give
schenken	to give (a present)
bringen	to bring, to take
zeigen	to show
glauben	to believe
sagen	to tell, to say
antworten	to (give an) answer (to)

NOTE:

1. The English phrases *to take something to somebody* and *to take somebody home* are expressed in German by using **bringen.**

| **Er bringt ihr eine Tasse Kaffee.** | He is taking her a cup of coffee. |
| **Er bringt sie nach Hause.** | He is taking her home. |

2. **Glauben** sometimes takes only a dative object and sometimes only an accusative object.

| **Ich glaube dir.** | I believe you. |
| **Das glaube ich nicht.** | I don't believe that. |

But, unlike English, German can combine these two sentences into one.

| **Das glaube ich dir nicht.** | I don't believe what you say. |

Observe that the dative object represents the person and the accusative object represents the facts.

3. **Antworten** and **sagen** can also be used with two objects.

| **Was hat er dir geantwortet?** | What answer did he give you? |
| **Was hat er dir gesagt?** | What did he tell you? |

But

| **Was hat er dich gefragt?** | What did he ask you? |

64 Adjectives Governing the Dative

Certain adjectives like **interessant, böse,** and **recht,** as well as most adjectives preceded by **zu,** can be used with the dative to point out the person for whom the grammatical subject has the quality denoted by the adjective.

Das ist interessant.	That's interesting.
Das ist mir interessant.	I think that's interesting.
Er ist böse.	He is angry.
Er ist mir böse.	He is angry with me.
Sie ist zu jung.	She is too young.
Sie ist mir zu jung.	She is too young as far as I'm concerned.

65 Prepositions Governing the Accusative

A small group of prepositions is *always* used with the accusative. This group includes: **durch** (*through*), **für** (*for*), **gegen** (*against*), and **ohne** (*without*).

66 Prepositions Governing the Dative

Some prepositions are *always* used with the dative case. All the important prepositions of this group are introduced in this unit: **aus** (*out of*), **außer** (*except*), **bei** (see note 2 below), **mit** (*with*), **nach** (*after*), **seit** (*since*), **von** (*from*), **zu** (*to*).

NOTE:

1. A third group of prepositions, which includes **in** and **vor,** is used with either dative or accusative. These prepositions will be introduced in Unit 7.

2. **Bei** does not normally correspond to English *by;* it expresses the idea of close proximity, and frequently means *at the house of.*

Er wohnt in Potsdam bei Berlin.	He lives in Potsdam near Berlin.
Er wohnt bei seiner Tante.	He is living with his aunt.

3. Some prepositions are normally contracted with the following article into a single word, as long as the article is not stressed (see **77**).

von dem	**Ich komme vom Bahnhof.**	I am coming from the station.
zu dem	**Ich gehe zum Bahnhof.**	I am on my way to the station.
zu der	**Ich gehe zur Universität.**	I am on my way to the university.
durch das	**Er geht durchs Haus.**	He is going through the house.
für das	**Er hat kein Geld fürs Kino.**	He has no money for the movies.
bei dem	**Meine Frau ist beim Arzt.**	My wife is at the doctor's.

But

Bei *dem* Regen kommt er nicht.	He won't come in *this* rain.

4. **Nach** is used to indicate time.

Nach dem Abendessen gehen wir ins Kino.	After supper, we'll go to the movies.
Er kommt nach acht Uhr.	He will arrive after eight o'clock.

Nach indicates *place* if a geographical proper name is mentioned:

> Er geht nach Amerika
> > nach Deutschland
> > nach Bayern
> > nach Berlin

and in the idiom:

> Er geht nach Hause.

5. If no geographical proper name is used, **zu** is normally used to express direction.

Er geht zum Bahnhof.	He goes to the station.
Er geht zur Universität.	He is walking to the university.

Zu must be used with persons:

Er geht zu Karl	He goes to Karl
Ich gehe zu meinem Vater	I go to my father

and in the idiom:

Er ist zu Hause.	He is at home.

67 Word Order within the Inner Field

Word order within the inner field is governed by *one* principle: The various elements are arranged in the order of increasing news value. The following rules govern most normal situations and are therefore safe to use.

The Position of the Subject

If a pronoun subject like **er, sie,** or **wir** stands in the inner field, it follows the verb immediately.

Gestern hat er es ihm gesagt.	He told it to him yesterday.

Since nouns generally have more news value than pronouns, noun subjects in the inner field are usually preceded by pronoun objects.*

> **Heute ge*hört* ihm das Haus.**

Accusative Pronouns Precede Dative Pronouns

Accusative personal pronouns always precede dative personal pronouns.

Warum will er es ihm nicht sagen?	Why doesn't he want to tell him that?

---

* However, **Heute gehört das Haus *ihm*** is also possible, if there is a strong stress on **ihm**.

Leider kann ich es Ihnen nicht schenken.	Unfortunately, I can't give it to you.
Ich habe es ihm geschickt.	I have sent it to him.

Pronoun objects stand at the beginning of the inner field and can be preceded only by a subject.

Heute gehört es *ihm*.
Heute gehört das Haus *ihm*.

Nouns and Pronouns

Nouns have more news value than pronouns. A noun object therefore follows a pronoun object.

Ich habe es meinem Vater schon gesagt.	I've already told it to my father.
Ich kaufe mir morgen einen Hut.	I am going to buy myself a hat tomorrow.

Dative and Accusative Nouns

Nouns preceded by definite articles usually refer to something already known or mentioned before. Nouns preceded by indefinite articles (**ein Buch,** plural **Bücher**), on the other hand, usually introduce something not mentioned before—something, therefore, of news value.

Since the sequence of elements in the inner field is determined by increasing news value, noun objects preceded by definite articles are usually placed before nouns preceded by indefinite articles.

Ich habe dem Studenten ein *Buch* gegeben.
Ich habe das Buch einem Stu*denten* gegeben.

If both nouns are preceded by a definite article, the sequence is also determined by news value. In the sentence

Hast du dem Kind die Medi*zin* gegeben?

the topic under discussion is the child; in the sentence

Hast du die Medizin dem *Kind* gegeben?

the question is raised of what has happened to the medicine.

Time Phrases

The position of time phrases in the inner field is again determined by news value, but they must precede **ein**-objects, which are position-fixed at the end of the inner field.

Ich habe ihm gestern das *Buch* gegeben.
Ich habe ihm das Buch *gestern* gegeben.
Ich habe ihm *gestern* ein Buch gegeben.

Several time phrases follow each other in the order of greater specificity.

> **Er ist gestern morgen um 10 Uhr 5 gestorben.**   He died at 10:05 yesterday morning.
>
> **Er ist gestern abend um neun nach München gefahren.**   Last evening at nine he went to Munich.

Place Phrases

Sentences of the type

> **Ich kaufe mir morgen in Berlin einen Hut**

are so frequent that one can say: *Usually, place follows time.*

On the whole, place phrases which are neither directives (which belong in the second prong) nor used in connection with a preceding time phrase are comparatively rare. Their position within the inner field depends on their news value.

> **Ich habe meine Frau in der Schule kennengelernt.**   I met my wife in school. (when the topic "wives" is under discussion)
>
> **Ich habe in der Schule meine Frau kennengelernt.**   (when the topic "school" is under discussion)

Summary: The following variations show some of the possible positions of elements in the inner field. Note particularly how pronouns (no news value) are position-fixed at the beginning of the inner field and **ein**-nouns (always news value) are position-fixed at the end of the inner field. The elements in between are interchangeable (except for the time-place sequence); their sequence depends largely on increasing news value. Continue the table below by adding other possible arrangements of the same basic sentence (see also Exercise F, p. 116).

FRONT FIELD	1ST PRONG	INNER FIELD				NICHT	2ND PRONG
		Subject	Pos.-Fixed Pronouns	Interchangeable Elements	Pos.-Fixed ein-Nouns		
Hans	hat			seinem Freund das Buch gestern			gegeben.
Hans	hat			gestern seinem Freund das Buch			gegeben.
Er	hat			das Buch seinem Freund gestern		nicht	gegeben.
Er	hat		es	seinem Freund gestern			gegeben.
Er	hat		es	gestern seinem Freund			gegeben.
Er	hat		ihm	gestern das Buch		nicht	gegeben.
Gestern	hat	Hans		seinem Freund in der Schule	ein Buch		gegeben.
Er	hat		ihm	gestern in der Schule das Buch			gegeben.
Hans	hat		es ihm	gestern		nicht	gegeben.
Seinem Freund	hat	Hans		gestern in der Schule	ein Buch		gegeben.
Er	hat			gestern das Buch	einem Freund		gegeben.
Gestern	hat	er	es	in der Schule seinem Freund			gegeben.
Gestern	hat	er	es ihm				gegeben.
In der Schule	hat	Hans		seinem Freund das Buch		nicht	gegeben.
In der Schule	hat	er	es	seinem Freund		nicht	gegeben.
In der Schule	hat	er	es ihm	gestern		nicht	gegeben.
Gestern	hat	er	ihm		ein Buch		gegeben.

68 The German Perfect

By now you have become accustomed to the fact that German does not have as many verb forms as English. English *I see, I am seeing,* and *I do see* are all expressed in German by **ich sehe.**

This is also true in regard to the past tenses. While English has the forms

PAST	I did	PRESENT PERFECT	I have done
	I was doing		I have been doing

German must get along with

PAST	**Ich tat**	PERFECT	**Ich habe getan**

69 Formation of the German Participle

German verbs form their participles in either a *regular* or an *irregular* way.

Regular Verbs

All regular verbs place the unchanged stem in the frame
    ge———t
Thus the participle of **lieben** is **geliebt,** the participle of **glauben** is **geglaubt.**

All verbs with the **ge**———**t** frame are called *weak* verbs.

INFINITIVE	STEM	PARTICIPLE
hassen	hass-	gehaßt
machen	mach-	gemacht
regnen	regn-	geregnet
sagen	sag-	gesagt
wohnen	wohn-	gewohnt

The **ge-** prefix is never stressed. Since the **-t** of the frame must be audible, verbs like **heiraten** insert **-e-** before the **-t.**

INFINITIVE	STEM	PARTICIPLE
arbeiten	arbeit-	gearbeitet
heiraten	heirat-	geheiratet

A participle cannot have more than one unstressed prefix. Therefore all verbs formed with the unstressed prefixes **be-, emp-, ent-, er-, ge-, ver-,** and **zer-** form their participle without the **ge-** prefix. Verbs ending in **-ieren,** like **studieren,** which always begin with at least one unstressed syllable, also form their participles without **ge-.**

INFINITIVE	PARTICIPLE
gehören	gehört
studieren	studiert
telefonieren	telefoniert

Irregular Verbs

Most irregular verbs place either the unchanged stem, or a changed form of the stem, or even an entirely different stem in the frame

     ge———en

Thus the participle of **bleiben** is **geblieben,** that of **fahren** is **gefahren,** and that of **sein** is **gewesen.** Verbs using the frame **ge———en** are called *strong* verbs. Since the type of change in these strong verbs is as unpredictable as English *sing, sang, sung* versus *sting, stung, stung,* we will list all strong verbs together with weak verbs that have irregular forms in the tables of "Strong and Irregular Verbs" at the end of Unit 5 and all subsequent units.

The irregular verbs are used with such great frequency in everyday German that you should memorize the participles together with their auxiliaries. The participles of verbs introduced in Units 1–3 are:

INFINITIVE	PARTICIPLE	INFINITIVE	PARTICIPLE
beginnen	hat begonnen	scheinen	hat geschienen
bleiben	ist geblieben	schlafen	hat geschlafen
denken	hat gedacht	schreiben	hat geschrieben
essen	hat gegessen	sehen	hat gesehen
fahren	ist gefahren	sein	ist gewesen
gehen	ist gegangen	sprechen	hat gesprochen
haben	hat gehabt	trinken	hat getrunken
heißen	hat geheißen	tun	hat getan
kennen	hat gekannt	verstehen	hat verstanden
kommen	ist gekommen	werden	ist geworden
lassen	hat gelassen	wissen	hat gewußt
lesen	hat gelesen	zwingen	hat gezwungen
lügen	hat gelogen		

Modal Auxiliaries

Whenever the modal auxiliaries and **brauchen** are used with a dependent infinitive, their participles are identical with their infinitives. These forms are often referred to as "double infinitives."

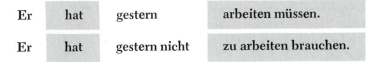

| Er | hat | gestern | arbeiten müssen. |
| Er | hat | gestern nicht | zu arbeiten brauchen. |

If the modals are used without a dependent infinitive, their participles are "normal"; that is, **gemußt, gewollt, gekonnt, gesollt, gedurft, gebraucht.**

  Das habe ich nicht gewollt.   This is not what I intended.

70 The Use of **sein** and **haben** as Auxiliaries

Certain English verbs used to form their compound tenses with *to be.* Thus older editions of the King James version of the Bible, translated in the seventeenth century, had *Christ is risen.* But now even the Bible translations have changed from *Christ is risen* to *Christ has risen,* so that *to have* is today the only auxiliary still used. In contrast, the use of **sein** as an auxiliary is still very common in German.

The German verbs using **sein** instead of **haben** are all intransitive; that is, they do not govern an accusative object. Usually, though not in the case of **sein** and **bleiben,** they indicate a change in the position or the condition of the grammatical subject. If no such change is involved, even intransitive verbs use **haben.**

> **Er hat gelogen.**   He has told a lie.

The choice between **haben** and **sein** has nothing to do with the difference between weak and strong verbs. Even weak verbs like **verreisen** (*to go on a trip*) (participle: **verreist**) take **sein** because a change in the location of the subject is involved.

> **Er ist gestern verreist.**   He went on a trip yesterday.

71 Position of the Participle

The participle has a reserved "slot": the second box of the second prong. This means that it is preceded by **nicht** and by the verbal complements (if any) in the first box.

FRONT FIELD	1ST PRONG	INNER FIELD	NICHT	1ST BOX	2ND BOX
Er	kommt	heute.			
Er	ist	gestern	nicht		gekommen.
Der Zug	fährt		noch nicht	ab.	
Der Zug	ist		noch nicht	ab-	gefahren.
Sie	ist	leider	nicht	glücklich.	
Sie	ist	leider	nie	glücklich	gewesen.
Ich	bleibe	natürlich	nicht	zu Hause.	
Ich	bin	natürlich	nicht	zu Hause	geblieben.

NOTE: Verb complements like **aus, ab,** and **wieder** are written with the participle as one word: **abgefahren, ausgemacht, wiedergekommen.**

When a modal is used with an infinitive, the participle of the modal (which looks like an infinitive) goes into the second box behind the dependent infinitive.

FRONT FIELD	1ST PRONG	INNER FIELD	NICHT	1ST BOX	2ND BOX
Ich	muß	morgen		nach Köln	fahren.
Ich	habe	gestern	nicht	nach Köln	zu fahren brauchen.

72 The Use of the German Perfect

Take a look at the following English and German sentences and compare the verb tenses:

1. **Ich glaube, er wohnt in Berlin.**
   (present)

   I think he lives in Berlin.
   (present)

2. **Nein, er wohnt jetzt in Berlin.**
   (present)

   No, he is now living in Berlin.
   (present progressive)

3. **Mein Vater hat nie in Berlin gewohnt.**
   (perfect)

   My (late) father never lived in Berlin.
   (past)

4. **Vor drei Jahren habe ich noch in Berlin gewohnt.**   (perfect)

   Three years ago I was still living in Berlin.
   (past progressive)

5. **Haben Sie schon einmal in Berlin gewohnt?**   (perfect)

   Have you ever lived in Berlin?
   (present perfect)

6. **Wir wohnen seit Jahren in Berlin.**
   (present)

   We have been living in Berlin for years.
   (perfect progressive)

You can see that in conversational sentences of this type English uses six different tenses where German can get along with two, the present and the perfect.

Leaving out the German future (which will be introduced later), it can be stated that German, which has no progressive forms at all, has only four major tenses: the present, the perfect, the past, and the pluperfect. The past and the pluperfect are the major tenses for story telling. The present and the perfect are the set used for conversation. For this reason we introduce the perfect first, and then, in Unit 5, the past and the pluperfect.

In conversational situations the present is used to refer to what is happening at the moment of speaking or what will happen later. The perfect is used to refer to what happened prior to the moment of speaking. This is why **er wohnt** and **wir wohnen,** in sentences 1, 2, and 6 above, mean *he lives, he is living,* and *we have been living.* The wording of 6 is most alien to native speakers of English. However, you will agree that the sentence *Fritz has been living in Berlin since 1960* implies that Fritz is living in Berlin at the moment of speaking. So German, which uses the present to refer to everything that is happening at the moment of speaking or later, remains consistent by using the present tense: **Fritz wohnt seit 1960 in Berlin.** Similarly, **hat gewohnt,** in sentences 3, 4, and 5 above, means *lived, was living,* and *has lived,* for in all these cases the verbs refer to something that happened prior to the moment of speaking. You should acquire the habit of expressing *all* actions which happened before the moment of speaking by using the perfect.

This means that the important difference in English between

> Last winter we went to the opera three times

and

> This winter we have gone to the opera three times

cannot be expressed in German by changing tenses, because in German both sentences have to use the frame

Wir sind . . . in die Oper gegangen.

73 Point-of-Time Phrases

A time phrase like *on July 15* clearly refers to a specific point in time. But sometimes, even phrases like *last year* which look like stretch-of-time phrases, that is, phrases which express the duration of an event, denote a pointlike date rather than a stretch. Of course, it can be taken for granted that last year had at least 365 days. However, when you say:

> **Letztes Jahr sind wir nach Deutschland**   Last year we went to Germany
> **gefahren**

you do not mean that it took you all year to get to Germany. The time phrase **letztes Jahr** does not measure the length of **fahren.** What you do mean is: At some point in the course of last year, you took a boat or a plane to Germany.

Point-of-time phrases present no syntactical problems. They refer to a point prior to the moment of speaking (**gestern abend**), or to the moment of speaking (**jetzt**), or to a point following the moment of speaking (**nächstes Jahr**). If a point prior to the moment of speaking is involved, the perfect is used. If the moment of speaking or a point following the moment of speaking is involved, one uses the present tense.

> **Er ist gestern abend nach Köln gefahren.**
> **Er ist jetzt in Köln.**
> **Er fährt nächstes Jahr nach Köln.**

All English and German point-of-time phrases are either adverbs, prepositional phrases, or time nouns like **Sonntag** used without a preposition. Some of these are:

ADVERBS   gestern, heute, morgen, heute morgen, gestern abend, jetzt

PREPOSITIONAL PHRASES   **nach einem Jahr** (*after one year*), **um drei Uhr** (*at three o'clock*), **vor einem Jahr** (*a year ago*)

TIME NOUNS   Sonntag, nächsten Sonntag, dieses Jahr, letztes Jahr, nächstes Jahr

NOTE:

1. Time nouns used without a preposition show the accusative case (**näch-sten Sonntag**). If a preposition is used, this preposition determines the case: **nach einem Jahr** (**nach** always governs the dative); **für einen Monat** (**für** always governs the accusative).

2. Phrases with **vor** (plus dative) may be misleading to the beginner. German **vor** is not equivalent to English *for;* **vor** means *in front of.* Therefore, **vor einem Jahr** means "at a point just in front of one year," or, simply, *a year ago.*

3. Time phrases with **in** (plus dative) pose no problem. German **in einer Stunde** means either *within one hour,* or *in one hour.* If it is a future hour, use the present.

> **Ich fliege in einer Stunde nach Frank-**   I'll be on my way to Frankfurt in one hour.
> **furt.**

If it is a past hour, use the German perfect.

> **Wir sind in sechs Stunden nach Frank-**   We completed the flight to Frankfurt within
> **furt geflogen.**   six hours.

74 Scanning the Past: Frequency Phrases

Quite frequently, a speaker will look back into the past. He will let his mind roam along the time-line that stretches from some point in the past toward the moment of speaking; he will scan this line point by point and then count the number of times that a certain event happened or did not happen. To describe what his memory reveals, he will make use of such frequency terms as *often, three times,* and *never.*

For instance: If you remember three nights at the opera last season and three nights, so far, during the current season, you might actually come up with the two statements already mentioned in **72.**

> Last winter we went to the opera   **Letzten Winter sind wir dreimal in**
> three times.   **die Oper gegangen.**

> This winter we have gone to the   **Diesen Winter sind wir schon**
> opera three times.   **dreimal in die Oper gegangen.**

Observe the change of verbal tenses in English: It is *went* (past tense) in the first statement and *have gone* (present perfect) in the second statement. German, on the other hand, keeps the perfect **sind gegangen.** Instead, the frequency phrase changes from **dreimal** to **schon dreimal.** Why?

As long as you are counting the number of times you were at the opera *last* season, you are scanning a time-line which reaches from the beginning to the end of that season. But last year's season clearly closed prior to the moment of speaking. You are therefore scanning a *closed-end* time-line.

If, on the other hand, you are counting the number of times you have been at the opera during the *current* season, you are scanning a line which reaches into the moment of speaking and beyond. The current season has not ended yet. You are therefore scanning an *open-end* time-line.

All native speakers of English seem to know, consciously or subconsciously, the difference between scanning a closed-end time-line and scanning an open-end time-line. For all of them invariably obey the following rule: When scanning a closed-end time-line (last year's opera season) they use past tense forms like *went*. But when scanning an open-end time-line (the current opera season) they use present perfect forms like *have gone*. Vice versa: The use of the past tense signifies that the speaker is thinking of a closed-end time-line, and the use of the present perfect signifies that the speaker is thinking of an open-end time-line.

This is why any native American, when he talks about the legendary veracity of the first American president, will invariably say:

> Washington never told a lie.

It is the past tense *told* which contains the signal: "I am talking about Washington's life, which is, as you know, a closed-end time-line."

In contrast, a German cannot choose between two verbal tenses. To talk about any event which happened or did not happen before the moment of speaking, he can only use the perfect. But he must choose between a closed-end frequency phrase (like **nie**) and an open-end frequency phrase (like **noch nie**).

Meyer wohnt jetzt in Berlin. Drei Jahre hat er in München gewohnt. Aber er hat mich nie besucht.	Meyer is now living in Berlin. For three years, he lived in Munich. But he never called on me. (Meyer's residence in Munich is a closed-end time-line.)
Meyer wohnt jetzt hier in München. Aber er hat mich noch nie besucht.	Meyer is now living here in Munich. But he has never called on me yet. (Meyer's residence in Munich is an open-end time-line.)

IMPORTANT FREQUENCY TERMS

CLOSED-END TERMS (GERMAN PERFECT, ENGLISH PAST)		OPEN-END TERMS (GERMAN PERFECT, ENGLISH PRESENT PERFECT)	
not once			
nicht *ein*mal	not (even) once	**noch gar nicht**	not at all
nie	never	**noch nicht** *ein*mal	not once
		noch nie	never yet
once			
je?	ever?	**schon einmal**	once so far
mal, einmal	once	*schon* einmal	once before
nur *ein*mal	just once	**erst** *ein*mal	only once so far

CLOSED-END TERMS		OPEN-END TERMS	
(GERMAN PERFECT, ENGLISH PAST)		(GERMAN PERFECT, ENGLISH PRESENT PERFECT)	

more often

oft	often	**schon oft**	often
öfters	several times	**schon öfters**	several times
dreimal	three times	**schon dreimal**	three times so far
nur dreimal	only three times	**erst dreimal**	only three times so far

at all times

immer	always	**schon immer**	always

NOTE: There is a neat difference between **nur dreimal, schon dreimal,** and **erst dreimal.** The **nur** adds to the simple **dreimal** the flavor "and that was all." The **schon** adds not only the open-end meaning but sometimes the notion "and that is more than expected." The **erst** adds the expectation "I hope that was merely the first three times."

Now try to find out what the following sentences mean:

> **Ich habe noch nie geraucht.**
> **Bist du schon mal ins Museum gegangen?**
> **Ich habe sie nie kennengelernt.**
> **Ich habe sie noch nicht kennengelernt.**
> **Ich bin auch einmal jung gewesen.**
> **Sie ist noch nie glücklich gewesen.**
> **Ich habe schon oft im Hotel Berlin gegessen.**
> **Wir haben auch oft im Hotel Berlin gegessen.**
> **So ist es schon immer gewesen.**

75 Stretch-of-Time Phrases

Some English time phrases like *for three years* clearly denote a stretch rather than a point of time. For a German learning English, such phrases are difficult to handle. The trouble with them is that they do not, by their own strength, contain any hint as to where the end point of the stretch is located. The location of the end point depends entirely on the verbal tense used.

If you use the past tense, the end point precedes the moment of speaking.

> For three years he *was not able* to drive. (He is driving again.)

If you use the present perfect, the time stretches into (and perhaps beyond) the moment of speaking.

> He *has not been able* to drive for three years. (He cannot drive at the moment of speaking.)

If you use the present tense, the three-year period will definitely end at some time after the moment of speaking.

> The judge was hard on him. He *can't* drive for three years.

German, which has only two tenses reserved for conversation, cannot fix the end point of time stretches by using three tenses. To make up for this deficiency, German has invented an ingenious and, to native English speakers, a totally alien system for locating the end point of stretches of time: German uses two distinct sets of stretch-of-time phrases.

One set—for lack of a better name, let us call them up-to-now phrases—is used to refer to periods of time which begin somewhere in the past and continue up to (and perhaps beyond) the moment of speaking. Such up-to-now phrases always start with **schon** or **seit. Schon** without **seit** is followed by the accusative, **seit** and **schon seit** are followed by the dative. Take the phrase **ein Monat.** Used as an up-to-now phrase, it becomes

	schon einen Monat	
Wir wohnen	**seit einem Monat**	**in München.**
	schon seit einem Monat	

Whereas English *since* can only be followed by a point-of-time phrase (*since Monday*—**seit Montag**), German **seit** can also be followed by a noun expressing a stretch-of-time (**seit drei Jahren**—*for these last three years*).

A second set—let us call them end-in-past-or-future phrases—refers to stretches of time which end *either* in the past (when used with the perfect) *or* in the future (when used with the present tense). These phrases do *not* start with **schon** or **seit.**

UP-TO-NOW	END-IN-PAST-OR-FUTURE	
schon lange	**lange**	for a long time
seit langem		
schon seit langem		
	noch lange	for a long time thereafter
seitdem		ever since
schon drei Jahre	**drei Jahre**	for three years
seit drei Jahren		
schon seit drei Jahren		
schon tagelang	**tagelang**	for days
schon wochenlang	**wochenlang**	for weeks
schon jahrelang	**jahrelang**	for years

Let us see how this system works.

How to Express What Was but Is No Longer

Ich habe lange an Gott geglaubt.
Ich habe lange nicht an Gott geglaubt.

Both sentences are misleading to English-speaking people. They know that **lange** means *for a long time,* and they believe that **habe geglaubt** means *have believed.* So they "translate" the first sentence by *I have believed in God for a long time.* And that's exactly what this sentence does *not* mean. German **habe geglaubt** denotes a past act of believing. How long did this act last? Well, **lange!** But **lange** is an end-in-past-or-future phrase. In connection with the perfect it refers to a period which came to an end before the moment of speaking. The sentence means *For a long time I believed in God,* that is, the speaker once believed in God, but at some point in the past had a change of heart, stopped believing in God, and is consequently now an atheist.

In the second sentence, **habe nicht geglaubt** refers to a past act of not believing. How long did this disbelief last? Again, **lange,** that is, for a long period which came to an end in the past. The speaker no longer "disbelieves" that God exists. He now believes. He is a theist.

German phrases like **noch zwei Minuten** or **noch lange** are also end-in-past-or-future phrases. Remember that **noch** basically means *still* and expresses continuation. **Noch lange** therefore means "continued for quite a while longer."

Meyers sind um zehn Uhr nach Hause gegangen.	The Meyers went home at ten.
Aber Schmidts sind *noch lange* geblieben.	But the Schmidts stayed for quite a while longer.

Now try to figure out what is meant by:

Ich habe lange auf ihn gewartet.	(Is the speaker still waiting?)
Ich habe lange nicht arbeiten können.	(Is the speaker still unable to work?)
Er hat zwei Jahre nicht fahren dürfen.	(Is he permitted to drive again?)
Wie lange hat sie in Bonn gewohnt?	(Is she still living in Bonn?)
Ich habe drei Jahre in Bonn gewohnt.	(Is the speaker living in Bonn?)
Meyer hat noch drei Jahre gelebt.	(Is Meyer still alive?)
Meyers sind noch lange geblieben.	(Are they still there?)

How to Express What Has Been and Still Is

(or What Has Not Been and Still Is Not)

Wir wohnen schon seit drei Jahren in München.
Seit drei Jahren wohnen wir nicht mehr in München.

Both sentences use the present tense. The first sentence describes a positive action (**wohnen**) which is still going on; the second sentence describes the absence of an action (**nicht mehr wohnen**) which is still in effect at the moment of speaking. **Seit drei Jahren** is an up-to-now phrase denoting a stretch of time which started three years ago and continues up to (and

beyond) the moment of speaking. The English phrase corresponding to
seit drei Jahren is *these last three years* or *for three years*. The first sentence
therefore means *These last three years we have been living in Munich* or
We have been living in Munich for three years. Note that *these last three
years* is actually an English up-to-now phrase, whereas *for three years* can
be either an up-to-now or an end-in-past-or-future phrase.

The second sentence contains **nicht mehr** (*no longer*). It can be translated
clumsily by *During these last three years we have not been living in Munich
anymore*, or, better, *We left Munich three years ago*.

Remember: If you want to express what *has been* and still *is* (or what *has
not been* and still *is not*), use the present tense and an up-to-now phrase
starting with **schon** or **seit**.

Now figure out what is meant by:

> **Er kann seit drei Jahren nicht arbeiten.**
> **Ich kenne Herrn Meyer schon seit Jahren.**
> **Das weiß ich schon lange.**
> **Wie lange wartest du denn schon?**

How to Express What Will End after the Moment of Speaking

> **Wir bleiben zwei Tage in München.**
> **Keinen Kaffee mehr, bitte. Sonst schlafe ich die ganze Nacht nicht.**

Both sentences show the present tense. **Zwei Tage** and **die ganze Nacht**
(containing no **schon** or **seit**) are end-in-past-or-future phrases which, when
used with a present tense, refer to a stretch of time which will end in the
future. It makes really no difference whether the speaker already is in
Munich or whether he intends to go to Munich. What is important is that
the end of the **zwei Tage** must follow the moment of speaking. The first sentence means *We shall stay in Munich for two days* or *We are staying in
Munich for two days*.

If used together with the present tense, **die ganze Nacht** must also refer to
a period of time which will end in the future. The sentence means *Or else I
won't be able to sleep all night*.

What is meant by:

> **Wie lange kannst du hier bleiben?**
> **Ich kann nicht lange bleiben.**
> **Gut, ich warte eine Stunde, aber nicht länger.**
> **Das kann noch lange dauern.**
> **Wir bleiben zwei Jahre in Deutschland.**
> **Wir bleiben noch zwei Jahre in Deutschland.**

Darauf haben Sie schon lange gewartet: Eine Suppe für den großen Hunger.

How to Express What Had Been Going On, and Then Broke Off at the Very Moment of Speaking

Ich habe schon lange auf dich gewartet.

The sentence contains the up-to-now **schon lange** denoting a stretch of time reaching up to the moment of speaking. This time the up-to-now phrase is used with the perfect. The use of the perfect means that the verbal activity (**warten**) is no longer going on at the moment of speaking. The two ideas, "reaching up to the moment of speaking (**schon lange**)" and "no longer going on at the moment of speaking (the perfect tense)," add up to the notion "ending just at the moment of speaking."

The sentence means *I have been waiting for you for a long time*. The anxiously awaited husband has just arrived. The waiting is over.

Perhaps you can now understand the following "true-to-life" report: Mrs. Meyer is expecting a baby. The Meyers have two boys; now they want a girl. Two months before the blessed event they say:

Wir wünschen uns schon lange ein Mädchen.

They use the present tense to make it clear that they do desire a girl at the moment of speaking. They use the up-to-now phrase **schon lange** to make it clear that the desire is not new. They have had it for a long time, they still have it, and they will continue to have it until they have a girl. The sentence means *We've been wanting a girl for a long time*.

Two months later a smiling nurse shows the father the new baby. It is, indeed, a girl, and she says:

Darauf (*for this event*) **haben Sie schon lange gewartet.**

She uses the perfect **haben gewartet** to indicate that the waiting is now a thing of the past. She uses the up-to-now phrase **schon lange** to indicate that the waiting continued right up to the moment of speaking before it stopped and did become a thing of the past. The sentence means *This is just what you've been waiting for all this time.*

But maybe the new baby is another boy. What then? Well, they try again. After five boys in a row, they give up. Years later, when the five boys come home to help their parents celebrate their wedding anniversary, Mrs. Meyer says wistfully:

Wir haben uns ja lange ein Mädchen gewünscht.

She again uses the perfect to indicate that the hoping and waiting for a girl is a thing of the past. But now she uses the end-in-past-or-future phrase **lange,** which, when used with the perfect, means that the period of hoping came to an end at some time before the moment of speaking. The third sentence means *For a long time we wanted a girl.*

76 für-Phrases

It is one thing to say *I want to rest for a few minutes* and another to say *I want to sit down for a few minutes.* English *to rest* is one of those "stretchable" verbs (the technical term is "durative") which have no end built into them, and *for a few minutes,* used in connection with such a verb, actually measures the length of the verbal activity. In contrast, *to sit down* is a "punctual" verb (the technical term is "perfective") that does have an end built in. The phrase *for a few minutes,* if used together with *to sit down,* does not measure the length of sitting down. The few minutes start when the act of sitting down has been completed.

German **für**-phrases like **für eine Woche** should only be used in connection with "punctual" verbs like **nach Rom fahren,** because the **fahren** automatically ends in Rome. It is idiomatic to say:

Ich fahre morgen für eine Woche nach Rom.
Er ist gestern für eine Woche nach Rom gefahren.
Er hat München für immer verlassen.

It would not be idiomatic to say:

Beware!   [Ich will für zwei Jahre in Köln studieren.]   DO NOT USE!
Americanism! [Ich habe für zwei Jahre in Köln studiert.]

One can only say:

Ich will zwei Jahre in Köln studieren.
Ich habe zwei Jahre in Köln studiert.

In other words, if a stretch of time is "filled out" by an uninterrupted activity (a durative verb like **studieren** and **wohnen**), it is not safe to use a **für**-phrase.

77 Replacement of er, sie, es by der, die, das

In informal but perfectly acceptable German, nouns and names are frequently replaced by **der, die, das** instead of by **er, sie, es.** When used in this function, **der, die,** and **das** are not articles, but demonstrative pronouns, and the dative plural is **denen,** not **den.** These demonstrative pronouns may be stressed or unstressed.

Wem gehört denn der *W*agen?	**Der Wagen gehört *mir*.**
	Er gehört *mir*.
	Der gehört *mir*.
Wo hast du denn den *Hut* gekauft?	**Den habe ich in *Mün*chen gekauft.**
Wo hast du denn *den* gekauft?	***Den* habe ich in *Mün*chen gekauft, aber *den* hier habe ich in Ber*lin* gekauft.**
Kennen Sie Frau Dr. Walter?	**Ja, die habe ich in Ber*lin* kennengelernt.**
	Ja, mit *der* gehe ich heute abend ins Theater.

Note that if stressed, these demonstrative pronouns may mean *this one* and *that one*.

For the time being, do not use either the personal pronouns or the demonstrative pronouns after a preposition unless they refer to persons.

78 es and das, Followed by Plural Verb Forms

A daughter recognizing that a certain lady on the TV screen is her mother can say:

It's my mother!
That's my mother!

This impersonal *it* or *that* is used in sentences identifying somebody or something for the first time. *She is my mother,* on the other hand, is used when *she* has already been talked about and a further statement is being made about her. German makes the same distinction.

Es ist meine Mutter!
Das ist meine Mutter!

But

Kennen Sie Frau Bertram?
Natürlich! Sie ist meine Mutter!

In contrast to English *it* and *that*, German **es** and **das** are followed by plural verb forms when the identifying nouns are in the plural.

Es sind die Kinder.	It's the children.
Das sind die Kinder.	That's the children.

Exercises

A. Give negative answers to the following questions.

1. Bist du glücklich mit ihm?
2. Wohnt ihr noch in Freiburg?
3. Mußt du denn morgen nach Augsburg fahren?
4. Hast du noch Geld?
5. Redet Frau Müller noch immer soviel?
6. Ist Erika intelligent?
7. Geht Fritz schon in die Schule?
8. Lebt Meyer noch?
9. Brauchst du *auch* einen Hut? (Use contrast intonation.)
10. Brauchst du auch einen *Hut?* (Use contrast intonation.)

B. Replace the dative or accusative pronouns in italics by the proper form of the nouns in parentheses.

1. Ich will *es* nicht lesen. (Buch)
2. Kennst du *ihn?* (mein Vater)
3. Ich kann *ihn* schon sehen. (Zug)
4. Kennt er *sie?* (deine Frau)
5. Tante Amalie will mit *ihr* nach Spanien fahren. (unsere Tochter)
6. Die Uhr gehört *ihr.* (meine Frau)
7. Liebt sie *ihn* denn nicht? (ihr Mann)
8. Liebt er *sie* denn nicht? (seine Frau)
9. Ich will nicht für *ihn* arbeiten. (Herr Meyer)
10. Bei *der* möchte ich nicht wohnen. (deine Tante)

C. Express the following sentences in German. This is not meant to be a translation exercise; the English sentences should "trigger" their German equivalents. Practice the sentences orally until you can produce them without hesitation. Only then should you try to write them down.

1. That is my house.
2. It (the house) belongs to me.
3. It (the house) belongs to you?
4. Yes, to me.
5. This house belongs to Hans.
6. It (the house) belongs to him.
7. It (the house) belongs to her.
8. The car belongs to her.
9. It (the car) belongs to her.
10. It is her car.

D. Replace nouns and names by personal pronouns.

> **Ich fahre mit meinem Freund Fritz.**
> **Ich fahre mit ihm.**

1. Er wohnt bei seiner Tante.
2. Er will zu seinem Vater.
3. Er hilft seiner Mutter.
4. Er hilft seiner Freundin.
5. Er hilft seinem Freund.
6. Er kommt von seinem Freund Hans.
7. Er arbeitet für seinen Bruder.
8. Er arbeitet heute ohne seinen Freund.
9. Außer Erika sind wir alle hier.
10. Bei meiner Tante bin ich gern.

E. Complete the following sentences by using either **nach, zu,** or **bei.**

SEE
ANALYSIS
66
(pp. 97-98)

1. Ich gehe ——————— Bahnhof.
2. Er wohnt ——————— seiner Tante.
3. Wir gehen ——————— Meyers.
4. Sie sind ——————— Hans.
5. Wir fahren ——————— Europa.
6. Wir fahren ——————— Universität.
7. Wir fahren ——————— Hotel.
8. Wir fahren ——————— Wien.
9. Man spricht nicht ——————— Essen.
10. Oskar wohnt ——————— Schmidts.

F. In the following sentences, the inner field is left empty. Fill the inner field with each of the several series of words by rearranging them in the correct word order.

SEE
ANALYSIS
67
(pp. 98-100)

1. Ich habe ——————————— geschenkt.
   - (a) es, gestern, ihm
   - (b) das Buch, gestern, ihm
   - (c) ein Buch, gestern, meinem Vater
   - (d) es, gestern, meinem Vater

2. Willst du ——————————— schenken?
   - (a) einen Hund, deiner Freundin
   - (b) den Hund, deiner Freundin
   - (c) deiner Freundin, ihn
   - (d) einen Hund, ihr
   - (e) ihn, ihr

3. Wollen Sie ——————————— schicken?
   - (a) Ihrem Vater, das Buch
   - (b) ein Buch, ihm (Ihrem Vater)
   - (c) es, ihm
   - (d) Ihrem Vater, es
   - (e) das Buch, ihm

4. Ich habe ——————————— mitgebracht.
   - (a) ein Buch, meiner Freundin, aus Berlin
   - (b) aus Berlin, ein Buch, ihr
   - (c) das Buch, ihr, aus Berlin
   - (d) ihr, es, aus Berlin

5. Darf ich ——————————— ins Haus schicken, Herr Doktor?
   - (a) morgen, Ihnen, den Wein
   - (b) die Blumen, morgen, Ihrer Frau
   - (c) sie (die Blumen), ihr (Ihrer Frau), morgen
   - (d) sie (die Blumen), morgen, Ihrer Frau
   - (e) Blumen, Ihrer Frau, morgen
   - (f) Blumen, ihr, morgen
   - (g) die Blumen, ihr, morgen

G. Restate the following sentences by using the perfect tense.

1. Er arbeitet auch sonntags.
2. Sie bleibt Sonntag zu Hause.
3. Wieviel Geld brauchst du?
4. Inge fährt heute nach Mannheim.
5. Ich gehe mit Tante Amalie ins Museum.
6. Außer mir glaubt dir das kein Mensch.
7. Wir haben in Nürnberg ein Haus.
8. Seine Kinder hassen ihn.
9. Ihr Mann kommt zurück.
10. Ich kenne ihn.
11. Das Wasser kocht schon.
12. Er kommt heute spät nach Hause.
13. Was sagt er denn?—Nichts! Er lacht!
14. Bei Meyer lerne ich nichts.
15. Liebt sie ihren Mann denn nicht?
16. Was machst du denn Sonntag?
17. Regnet es in Bremen?
18. Er studiert Medizin.
19. Ich verstehe ihn nicht.
20. Er wird Arzt.
21. Das wissen wir nicht.
22. Wo wohnt ihr denn?
23. Zahlst du für den Wein?
24. Wann rufst du sie an?
25. Du antwortest ihm?
26. Wann machst du das Licht aus?

27. Ich bringe Erika nach Hause.
28. Natürlich danke ich ihm.
29. Dich frage ich nicht.
30. Warum gibst du mir kein Geld?
31. Dieses Haus gehört meinem Vater.
32. Warum helft ihr ihm denn nicht?
33. Ich kaufe mir eine Zeitung.

34. Er will nicht arbeiten.
35. Ich rauche nie.
36. Mein Mann redet wieder viel zuviel.
37. Was schenkst du ihr denn?
38. Wem schicken Sie denn das Buch?
39. Er schreibt mir nicht.
40. Wo sitzt sie denn?

H. Complete the following sentences.

1. Wir haben das Haus gesehen, aber gekauft (haben wir es nicht).
2. Seine Freundin ist intelligent, aber interessant _____.
3. Ich gehe oft ins Theater, aber ins Kino _____.
4. Er hat den Professor gehört, aber verstanden _____.
5. Ich fahre mit dir nach Innsbruck, aber nach Casablanca _____.

SEE
ANALYSIS
58–59

(pp. 74-76)

I. In order to test your understanding of time phrases, place each of the sentences below into one of the following categories:

a. having come to an end in the past
b. reaching from the past into the moment of speaking
c. ending at the moment of speaking
d. definitely ending in the future

1. Wir bleiben *noch ein Jahr* in Köln.
2. Wir sind *noch ein Jahr* in Deutschland geblieben.
3. Sie hat *zwei Jahre* auf Hans gewartet.
4. Sie wartet *seit zwei Jahren* auf Hans.
5. Meine Mutter hat uns *erst zweimal* besucht.
6. Ich habe ihn *oft* besucht.
7. *Wie lange* wartest du denn *schon?*
8. *Wie lange* hast du denn *schon* gewartet?
9. Ich warte *eine Stunde.*
10. *Wie lange* hast du denn gewartet?

11. Wir wünschen uns *schon lange* einen Sohn.
12. Wir haben uns *lange* einen Sohn gewünscht.
13. Das habe ich dir *schon lange* sagen wollen.
14. Er hat doch *immer* Arzt werden wollen.
15. Er hat doch *schon immer* Arzt werden wollen.
16. Ich kann *nur zwei Stunden* bleiben.
17. George Washington hat *nie* gelogen?
18. So einen Mantel habe ich mir *schon lange* gewünscht.

SEE
ANALYSIS
72–75

(pp. 104-113)

J. Express in German.

1. He gave his girl friend a watch.
2. He gave the watch to his girl friend.
3. He gave it (the watch) to her.
4. He is coming from the movies.
5. Are you living with your aunt, Erika?
6. Were you living with your aunt at that time?
7. Why did you come home so late?
8. Meyer bought a car in Stuttgart.

9. Meyer bought a house (which stands) in Konstanz.
10. (While) in Konstanz, he bought a house.
11. For a long time I did not know that.
12. I have known that for a long time.
13. Last year I didn't smoke one (single) cigarette. But now I smoke ten each (*accusative*) day.
14. Since the beginning of May I have not smoked one (single) cigarette.
15. I did not smoke for two years.
16. Two years ago, I smoked too much.
17. You are still smoking too much.
18. Yes, I believe in God. But for a long time I did not believe in God.
19. Meyer died three years ago.
20. Meyer died a year ago.

Vocabulary

abholen	to pick up, to call for
ach so!	oh, I see!
acht	eight
Ägyp'ten	Egypt
alt	old
anfangen (fängt an, hat angefangen)	to begin, to start
der Anfang, ⁔e	beginning, start
anrufen (hat angerufen)	to call up (on the telephone)
antworten (*with dat. of person*)	to answer
der April'	April
aus	out of; from
aus Köln	from Cologne
außer	besides, except for
außerdem	moreover
der Bahnhof, die Bahnhöfe	railway station
zum Bahnhof	to the station
im Bahnhof	within the station
am Bahnhof	at the station
Bayern	Bavaria
befehlen (befiehlt, hat befohlen) (*with dat. of person*)	to command, to order
bei (*with dat.*)	at, with near
bei Schmidts	at the Smiths'
das Bild, ‒er	picture

bis	until, up until; up to, as far as
bis gestern	until yesterday
bis Köln	as far as Cologne
bis zum Winter	(up) until winter
bis zum Bahnhof	as far as the station
zwei bis drei	two to three
die Blume, ‒n	flower
böse	mad, angry at; bad, evil
der Brief, ‒e	letter
der Briefträger, ‒	mailman
bringen (hat gebracht)	to bring
ich bringe dich nach Hause	I'll take you home
damals	at that time
danken (*with dat. of person*)	to thank
danke!	thank you, thanks!
vielen Dank!	thank you very much!
durch (*with acc.*)	through
einmal (*colloquial:* mal)	once, at some time
zweimal	twice
dreimal	three times
viermal, etc.	four times, etc.
noch *nicht* einmal	not even
auch nicht *ein*mal	not once

die Eltern (*pl.*)	parents
endlich	finally
das Essen	meal
beim Essen	while eating
beim Abendessen	at supper
fragen	to ask
die Frage, –n	question
ganz	entire(ly)
die ganze Nacht	all night
den ganzen Tag	all day
gar kein	none at all
gar nicht	not at all
geben (gibt, hat gegeben)	to give
gehören (*with dat. of person*)	to belong to (property)
gehören zu	to belong to (membership)
gerade	just; straight
ich esse gerade	I am eating just now
gern(e)	gladly
ich esse gerne	I like to eat
ich möchte gerne etwas essen	I'd like to eat something
ich habe ihn gern	I like him
das Gesetz, –e	law
gestern	yesterday
glauben an (*with acc.*)	to believe in
helfen (hilft, hat geholfen) (*with dat. of person*)	to help
das Hotel, –s	hotel
der Hut, ⸚e	hat
die Idee', die Ide'en	idea
je, jemals	ever
jung	young
kochen	to cook, to boil
die Kuh, ⸚e	cow
lachen	to laugh
lang	long
lange	for a long time
jahrelang	for years
fünf Jahre lang	for five years
letzt	last
letzten Mai	last May
letztes Jahr	last year
letzte Woche	last week
der Mai	May
meinen	to say, to think
die Minu'te, –n	minute
der Mo'nat, –e	month
der Montag, –e	Monday
muhen	to moo
die Nacht, ⸚e	night
heute nacht	this coming night; last night
but gestern abend	last night (before going to bed), yesterday evening
neun	nine
die Oper, –n	opera
recht	right
rechts	to the right
das ist mir recht	that's all right with me
du hast recht	you are right
reden	to talk, to speak
schenken	to give (as a present)
schicken	to send
schreiben (hat geschrieben)	to write
die Schule, –n	school
seit (*with dat.*)	since
seitdem	since that time (*adv.*)
seit langem	for a long time
seit Anfang Mai	since the beginning of May
sieben	seven
sitzen (hat gesessen)	to sit
sonst	otherwise, at other times
die Stadt, ⸚e	city
sterben (stirbt, ist gestorben)	to die
die Stunde, –n	hour
der Tag, –e	day
das Telefon, –e	telephone
am Telefon	on the telephone
telefonieren mit	to talk on the phone with
überhaupt	anyway; at all
die Universität, –en	university
verreisen	to go on a trip
vielleicht	perhaps
vor	before; in front of; ago
vor einem Jahr	a year ago
warten auf (*with acc.*)	to wait for
weit	far away
der Wirt, –e	innkeeper
die Woche, –n	week
Woher?	From where?
wünschen	to wish
ziemlich	rather, quite
ziemlich weit	quite far
zwanzig	twenty

Unit 5
Numbers—The Past—The Pluperfect—
Verb-Last Position—Open Conditions—
um . . . zu—mit—Word Formation

Patterns

[1] Cardinal Numbers

Learn the numbers; then go through the drills as indicated.

Null, eins, zwei, drei, vier, fünf, sechs, sieben, acht, neun, zehn, elf, zwölf, dreizehn, vierzehn, fünfzehn, sechzehn, siebzehn, achtzehn, neunzehn, zwanzig.

SEE
ANALYSIS
79

(p. 131)

eins und eins ist zwei	eins plus eins ist zwei
eins und zwei ist . . .	eins plus zwei ist . . .
eins . . .	eins . . .
zwanzig weniger eins ist neunzehn	zwanzig minus eins ist neunzehn
neunzehn weniger eins . . .	zwanzig minus zwei ist . . .
achtzehn . . .	zwanzig . . .
Wieviel Uhr ist es?	Es ist zehn Uhr dreizehn.
Wie spät ist es?	Es ist zehn Uhr dreizehn.
Wann kommt der Zug an?	Um sechs Uhr siebzehn.
Um wieviel Uhr kommt der Zug an?	Um sechs Uhr siebzehn.
Wann fährt der Zug ab?	Um sieben Uhr sechzehn.
Um wieviel Uhr fährt der Zug ab?	Um sieben Uhr sechzehn.
Wann fängt das Theater an?	Um acht Uhr fünfzehn.

[2] Past Tense of Weak Verbs

In order to practice the forms of the past tense, vary these sentences by substituting the subjects in parentheses.

SEE
ANALYSIS
80–81, 84

(pp. 131-133,
134-136)

Leider glaubte sie mir nicht.	Unfortunately, she did not believe me. (you)
Nach dem Krieg heiratete er ein Mädchen aus Kiel.	After the war he married a girl from Kiel. (I)

Billerbeck's beds are as different as people.

Damals brauchte ich nicht so oft nach Bremen zu fahren.

At that time I didn't have to go to Bremen so often. (we)

Die Tochter lachte gerade wie ihr Vater.

The daughter laughed just like her father. (the daughters)

Wir machten damals oft Reisen.

At that time we often went on trips. (I)

Vor dem Krieg lebte Ingelheim in Berlin.

Before the war Ingelheim lived in Berlin. (we)

Rosemarie studierte damals in Göttingen.

At that time Rosemarie studied in Göttingen. (Rosemarie and I)

[3] The Past Forms of the Modals

Vary these sentences by substituting the subjects in parentheses.

SEE
ANALYSIS
85
(p. 136)

Ich konnte gestern leider nicht kommen; ich mußte zu Hause bleiben.

Unfortunately, I couldn't come yesterday; I had to stay home. (we)

Er wollte nicht mit Tante Amalie ins Museum gehen.

He didn't want to go to the museum with Aunt Amalie. (I)

Warum wolltest du denn nicht ins Theater gehen?

Why didn't you want to go to the theater? (they)

Warum mußtet ihr denn nach Mannheim fahren?

Why did you have to go to Mannheim? (you, sing.)

Hans sollte mir helfen, aber er wollte nicht.

Hans was supposed to help me, but he didn't want to. (Hans and Inge)

Wir wollten mitgehen, aber wir durften nicht.

We wanted to go along, but we weren't allowed to. (they)

[4] Past Tense of haben

Form your own variations.

SEE
ANALYSIS
85
(p. 136)

Ich fahre *heu*te nach Berchtesgaden; *ges*tern hatte ich keine *Zeit.*

I am going to Berchtesgaden today; yesterday I didn't have time.

Warum *hat*test du denn keine Zeit?

Why didn't you have any time?

Herr Lenz hatte *auch* keine Zeit. Wir hatten *alle* zu viel zu tun.

Mr. Lenz had no time either. We all had too much to do.

Was, ihr hattet keine *Zeit?*

What, you had no time?

Sie hatten *alle* zu viel zu tun.

They all had too much to do.

Hatten Sie gestern *auch* so viel zu tun, Herr Lohmann?

Did you also have so much to do yesterday, Mr. Lohmann?

[5] Past Tense of sein

SEE
ANALYSIS
85
(p. 136)

Form your own variations.

Herr Lenz ist heute in Saar*brück*en.— *Ges*tern war er in *Trier.*

Mr. Lenz is in Saarbrücken today.—Yesterday he was in Trier.

Wo warst *du* gestern, Inge?—*Ich* war in *Frank*furt.

Where were you yesterday, Inge?—I was in Frankfurt.

Ist Fritz heute *auch* hier?—Nein, er war *ge*stern hier; *heute* ist er in *Frank*furt.

Is Fritz here too today?—No, he was here yesterday; today he is in Frankfurt.

Wir waren gestern *auch* in Frankfurt.—Wo wart *ihr* gestern?

We were in Frankfurt, too, yesterday.— Where were you yesterday?

Wo waren *Sie* denn, Herr Lenz?

Where were you, Mr. Lenz?

[6] Past Tense of Strong Verbs

Vary these sentences by substituting the subjects and objects in parentheses.

Ich rief sie damals jede Woche an.	I called her every week then. (she, me)	SEE ANALYSIS 82 (pp. 133-134)
Ich bekam jede Woche drei Briefe von ihr.	I got three letters from her every week. (she, me)	
Sonntags blieb er immer zu Hause.	On Sundays he always stayed home. (they)	
Damals brachte ich sie jeden Abend nach Hause.	At that time, I took her home every night. (he, me)	
Sie luden uns oft zum Essen ein.	They often invited us to dinner. (we, them)	
Wir aßen damals oft im Regina.	We often ate at the Regina then. (I)	
Er fuhr jeden Sommer in die Alpen.	He went to the Alps every summer. (we)	
Wir fanden ihn in der Regina-Bar.	We found him in the Regina Bar. (they)	
Ich gab ihm jede Woche zwanzig Mark.	I gave him twenty marks every week. (we, them)	
Sonntags gingen wir nie ins Kino.	On Sundays we never went to the movies. (he)	
Wir halfen ihm damals oft bei seiner Arbeit.	We often helped him with his work. (they, us)	
Damals hieß sie noch Schmidt.	At that time, her name was still Schmidt. (my)	
Ich kannte sie gut.	I knew her well. (we, him)	
Er kam immer spät nach Hause.	He always came home late. (they)	
Wir ließen unsere Kinder zu Hause.	We left our children at home. (they)	
Er lief nach Hause.	He ran home. (she)	
Ich dachte damals oft an sie.	I often thought of her then. (we, them)	
Er schien mich nicht zu kennen.	He didn't seem to know me. (they, us)	
Er schlief oft bis elf.	He often slept until eleven o'clock. (I)	
Sie schrieb ihm jede Woche drei Briefe.	She wrote him three letters every week. (he, her)	
Ich saß im Garten und las ein Buch.	I was sitting in the garden reading a book. (he)	
Von Irmgard sprach er nie.	He never talked about Irmgard. (she)	
Er stand vor dem Kino und wartete auf mich.	He was standing in front of the movie house waiting for me. (she)	
Leider trank er.	Unfortunately he drank. (she)	

Und dann tat er jahrelang gar nichts.	Then he didn't do a thing for years. (she)
Er starb drei Jahre später.	He died three years later. (she)
Jeden Sommer verschwand er für eine Woche.	Every summer he disappeared for a week (they)
Sie verstand ihn einfach nicht.	She simply didn't understand him. (he, her)
Sie wurde Ärztin.	She became a doctor. (he)
Sie wußte nichts von seiner Reise.	She didn't know anything about his trip. (we, your)

[7] Two Past Forms in One Sentence

Read these sentences carefully and note their narrative character.

SEE
ANALYSIS
80–83

(pp. 131-134)

Er kaufte ein Buch und schenkte es seiner Freundin.	He bought a book and gave it to his friend.
Peter kam um zehn Uhr aus dem Theater und fuhr nach Hause.	At ten o'clock, Peter got out of the theater and drove home.
Werner ging mit Ursula ins Kino; dann brachte er sie nach Hause.	Werner went to the movies with Ursula; then he took her home.
Herr Kunz trank ein Glas Wein und las die Zeitung.	Mr. Kunz drank a glass of wine and read the paper.
In Hamburg regnete es, aber in Casablanca schien die Sonne.	It was raining in Hamburg, but in Casablanca the sun was shining.

[8] Verb-Last Position in Dependent Clauses

By leaving out the main clauses, change the dependent clauses
into assertions or questions.

SEE
ANALYSIS
89–95

(pp. 137-143)

Ich weiß, daß er Geld   hat.
Ich weiß, daß er Geld   hatte.
Ich weiß, daß er Geld   gehabt hat.

Ich weiß nicht, ob Fritz mit dem Auto zum Bahnhof   fährt.
Ich wußte, daß er immer mit dem Auto zur Arbeit   fuhr.
Ich glaube nicht, daß er mit dem Auto zum Bahnhof   gefahren ist.

Ich möchte, daß du morgen vernünftig   bist.
Ich hoffe, daß du gestern vernünftig   warst.
Ich weiß, daß du immer vernünftig   gewesen bist.

Wissen Sie, ob Meyers hier   wohnen?
Wir wußten, daß Meyers da   wohnten.
Wie soll ich wissen, wo Meyers   gewohnt haben?

Weiß er, daß er dir helfen   soll?
Er wußte, daß er mir helfen   sollte.

[9] The Pluperfect

Form your own variations.

Als ich ihn kennenlernte, war er gerade aus Afrika zurückgekommen.	When I met him, he had just come back from Africa.	**SEE ANALYSIS 87–88**
Er bekam die Gelbsucht, weil er zuviel gegessen hatte.	He got jaundice because he had eaten too much.	(p. 137)
Wir wußten nicht, daß er Soldat geworden war.	We didn't know that he had become a soldier.	
Er war zwei Jahre lang in Norwegen gewesen, als man ihn an die Westfront schickte.	He had been in Norway for two years when he was sent to the western front.	
Als ich Hans nach dem Krieg wiedersah, war er Schriftsteller geworden.	When I saw Hans again after the war, he had become a writer.	

[10] Open Conditions

Reverse the order of conditions and conclusions.

> **Wenn es morgen nicht regnet, können wir arbeiten.**
> **Wir können morgen nur arbeiten, wenn es nicht regnet.**

Wenn ich kann, komme ich.	Ich _____, wenn _____.	**SEE ANALYSIS 96**
Ich fahre nur nach Casablanca, wenn du auch fährst.	Wenn du _____, _____ auch.	
Wenn Herr Büttner schon hier ist, schicken Sie ihn zu mir.	Schicken Sie ____, wenn er ____.	(pp. 143-144)
Wenn du kein Geld hast, helfe ich dir gerne.	Ich helfe _____, _____.	
Ich trinke nie Wein, wenn ich Auto fahren muß.	Wenn ich _____, _____.	

[11] um ... zu

Inge fuhr nach Frankfurt, um ins Theater zu gehen.
Er fuhr nach Kairo, um dort einen Roman zu schreiben.
Sie ging ins Theater, um *Hamlet* zu sehen.
Er studierte Englisch, um Shakespeare lesen zu können.
Herr Lenz ging in die Stadt, um seiner Frau ein Buch zu kaufen.
Um nach Casablanca fahren zu können, muß man viel Geld haben.
Um eine Frau verstehen zu können, muß man sie lieben.

SEE ANALYSIS 97

(pp. 144-145)

VARIATIONS

After studying **97**, replace the **weil**-clauses and **wenn**-clauses by **um ... zu**-clauses.

Wenn Gudrun ins Theater gehen wollte, mußte sie immer nach Salzburg fahren.
Um _____ zu können, mußte _____.

Salzburg Hauptbahnhof.

Wenn man in Baden-Baden wohnen will, muß man viel Geld haben.

Um _____ zu können, muß _____.

Er lernt Deutsch, weil er Nietzsche lesen will.

Er lernt Deutsch, um _____ zu können.

Herr Köhler ist in die Stadt gefahren, weil er seiner Frau ein Buch kaufen will.

Herr Köhler ist in die Stadt gefahren, um _____ zu kaufen.

Conversation

FRAU AUMÜLLER:	Weißt du, ob Gerhard und Margret das Haus hier in Bonn ge*kauft* haben?
FRAU BRÜCKNER:	Das *weiß* ich nicht; aber warum *fragst* du?
FRAU AUMÜLLER:	Weil *wir* es gerne kaufen möchten, wenn Gerhard und Margret es nicht wollen.
FRAU BRÜCKNER:	Das ist mir *neu*. Ich denke, ihr wollt ein Haus in *Köln* kaufen.
FRAU AUMÜLLER:	Das *woll*ten wir auch. Gestern sind wir nach *Köln* gefahren und haben das Haus noch einmal ge*sehen*. Es war wirklich *sehr* schön.
FRAU BRÜCKNER:	Aber ge*kauft* habt ihr es *nicht*? War es denn zu *teuer*?
FRAU AUMÜLLER:	Nein, zu *teuer* war es *nicht*, aber wir wollen doch lieber hier in *Bonn* bleiben.—Übrigens habe ich in Köln einen *Hut* gekauft.
FRAU BRÜCKNER:	*Wirk*lich? Den mußt du mir *zeig*en.

Reading

Viel Lärm um nichts?

Kapitel Drei: Ein Interview mit Schmidt-Ingelheim

REPORTER: Wie lange sind Sie schon in Kairo, Herr Schmidt-Ingelheim?

SCHMIDT-INGELHEIM: Seit vierzehn Tagen*—seit Anfang April.

REPORTER: Und wie lange wollen Sie noch hierbleiben?

SCHMIDT-INGELHEIM: Das kann ich Ihnen noch nicht sagen; ich wollte noch zwei, drei 5 Wochen hier arbeiten, aber gerade hat mich ein Freund angerufen und wollte wissen, ob ich mit nach Casablanca fahren will. Er hat eine Jacht, wissen Sie, und weil ich schon lange nicht mehr auf einem Schiff gewesen bin, dachte ich, ich fahre vielleicht mit.

REPORTER: Das kann nur Mr. Thistlethwaite gewesen sein, oder? 10

SCHMIDT-INGELHEIM: Sie haben recht—aber wie wußten Sie denn, . . . ?

REPORTER: Ich habe ihn vor drei oder vier Wochen zufällig kennengelernt und habe ihn seitdem zwei- oder dreimal besucht. Von ihm weiß ich auch, daß Sie hier sind. Er hat viel von Ihnen und von Ihrer Frau gesprochen—wie schön Ihre Frau ist, und wie intelligent—und er 15 hat mir auch erzählt, daß Sie wieder an einem Roman arbeiten.

SCHMIDT-INGELHEIM: Ja, mein Roman! Um diesen Roman zu schreiben, bin ich nach Kairo gekommen, wissen Sie—ich mußte ein paar† Wochen allein sein, um arbeiten zu können. Und außerdem wollte ich Afrika wiedersehen, —der Roman hat viel mit Afrika zu tun. 20

REPORTER: Es ist also wieder ein Kriegsroman, Herr Schmidt-Ingelheim?

SCHMIDT-INGELHEIM: Ja, ja,—*Ende bei Karthago* heißt er. Ich arbeite jetzt schon seit zwei Jahren an diesem Roman, aber wissen Sie, wenn man immer so zu Hause sitzt, dann . . .

REPORTER: Das kann ich gut verstehen, Herr Schmidt-Ingelheim.—Sie mußten 25 eine Reise machen; Sie mußten nach Afrika kommen, um über ihren Roman nachdenken zu können; Sie mußten einmal verschwinden . . .

SCHMIDT-INGELHEIM: Richtig! Kein Telefon, kein Briefträger, keine Reporter—verstehen Sie, ich möchte wirklich einmal verschwinden, spurlos verschwinden. Nur so für vierzehn Tage oder drei Wochen. Aber so ist das Leben 30 leider nicht. Und der Briefträger kommt auch; heute morgen zum Beispiel habe ich einen Brief von meiner Tochter bekommen—sie

---

* **vierzehn Tage** in German, the usual way of expressing *two weeks*.
† **ein paar** a few.

schreibt, daß sie seit drei Wochen mit einer Gruppe von Archäologen in Ägypten ist und zufällig in der Zeitung gelesen hat, daß ich in Kairo bin.

REPORTER: Ihre Tochter? Das habe ich nicht gewußt, daß Sie eine Tochter haben.   5

SCHMIDT-INGELHEIM: Oh, doch,—von meiner ersten* Frau; sie wird Ende Mai zwanzig und studiert in Mainz Archäologie. Ich habe sie seit zehn Jahren nicht gesehen.

REPORTER: Das ist ja interessant.—Aber ich möchte Sie noch etwas fragen, Herr Ingelheim. Ihr Roman—können Sie mir nicht noch etwas von 10 Ihrem Roman erzählen?

SCHMIDT-INGELHEIM: Möchte ich ja gern, aber ich muß jetzt wirklich gehen. Meine Tochter erwartet mich zum Frühstück. Ich bin neugierig, ob wir uns wiedererkennen.

Kapitel Vier: Ein Brief an Frau Schmidt-Ingelheim   15

KATHARINA SCHMIDT   *65 Mainz/Rhein/Riedbachstraße 4*

                                                                               den 12. Mai

Sehr geehrte Frau Schmidt-Ingelheim!

Gerade habe ich in der† Zeitung gelesen, daß Ihr Mann seit drei Wochen in Afrika spurlos verschwunden ist.   20

Ich weiß, was Sie durchmachen. Mein Mann war auch einmal drei Wochen spurlos verschwunden. Aber wenn Sie diesen Brief bekommen, ist Hans vielleicht schon wieder zu Hause und sagt Ihnen beim Frühstück: „Ohne deinen Kaffee, Ingrid, wäre das Leben nur halb so schön.“   25

Woher ich weiß, daß er das sagt? Ich bin Frau Schmidt Nummer eins, und ich glaube, Sie sind Frau Schmidt Nummer zwei oder drei. Ich weiß nicht, wie oft Hans geheiratet hat, und ich möchte es auch nicht wissen. Ich möchte aber, daß Sie warten, bis Hans wiederkommt, und daß er nicht mehr in die Zeitung kommt. Sie 30 brauchen nicht zu fürchten, daß ihm etwas passiert ist. Ihrem Hans passiert nie etwas; ich kenne ihn. Ich habe ihn einmal geliebt, wissen Sie; und oft, wenn ich sehe, wie seine Tochter mit einem Lachen in den Augen zum Frühstück kommt, gerade wie früher ihr Vater, dann frage ich mich, ob ich ihn nicht vielleicht doch noch 35 liebe.

Sehr geehrte standard form of address: literally "very honored Mrs. Schmidt-Ingelheim"

wäre would be

* **ersten** first.
† The use of dative or accusative after prepositions like **an** and **in** will be discussed in Unit 7.

Nein, passiert ist ihm nichts. Wie habe ich Angst gehabt, als er
1939 Soldat wurde. Damals wußte ich noch nicht, daß ich keine
Angst zu haben brauchte. Man schickte ihn in ein Städtchen hinter
der Westfront, und da hat er ein Jahr lang Brieftauben gefüttert.
Gerade als es 1940 im Westen gefährlich wurde, schickte man ihn 5
nach Hause, weil er Hepatitis bekam.

Wir heirateten.

Hans hatte aber keine Hepatitis. Er hatte nur Gelbsucht, weil er
zu gut gegessen und zu viel getrunken hatte; und so wurde er 1941
wieder Soldat. Man schickte ihn, wieder mit Brieftauben, nach 10
Norwegen. Seine Briefe sprachen im Sommer vom Fischen, und im
Winter vom Schilaufen. Bei Kriegsende war er zufällig in Ingelheim,
und die Amerikaner nahmen ihn gefangen. Jetzt bekam er wirklich
Hepatitis, und man schickte ihn nach Hause. Dreiundzwanzig
Schüler haben 1931 mit ihm das Abitur gemacht. Von den drei- 15
undzwanzig leben heute noch sechs, und ihm allein ist im Krieg
nichts passiert.

Hans wurde Schriftsteller. Seinen Kriegsroman *Wie das Gesetz es
befahl* habe ich auf der Maschine geschrieben. Er machte damals oft
Reisen, ohne mich, und wohin, weiß ich nicht. Ich habe ihn auch 20
nie gefragt. Er mußte, so sagte er, zwei oder drei Wochen allein sein,
um seine Romane schreiben zu können. Aber er kam immer wieder,
mit seinem Lachen in den Augen, und trank seinen Kaffee, wie man
Rheinwein trinkt. Aber dann passierte ihm doch etwas. Als er von
einer Reise zurückkam, sagte er beim Frühstück: „Ohne deinen 25

1939: neunzehnhun-
dertneunundddreißig

1940: neunzehnhun-
dertvierzig

die Gelbsucht jaun-
dice
1941: neunzehnhun-
derteinundvierzig

1931: neunzehnhun-
derteinunddreißig
Abitur comprehen-
sive examination at
the end of German
secondary school

Kaffee, Gisela, wäre das Leben nur halb so schön." Ich weiß nicht,
wer Gisela war, aber ich fuhr mit meiner Tochter zu meiner Mutter.

Noch einmal, sehr geehrte Frau Schmidt, Ihrem Hans ist nichts
passiert. Ich weiß, er lebt und ist gesund. Seit Sie geheiratet haben,
war er wohl noch nie so lange „spurlos verschwunden". Ich gratu- 5
liere Ihnen; Sie müssen interessant sein, interessanter als ich. Aber
wenn er wieder zu Hause ist, dann fragen Sie ihn doch beim
Frühstück: „Wie war Giselas Kaffee? Oder hieß sie diesmal nicht
Gisela?" Vielleicht verschwindet er dann drei Wochen mit Ihnen.
Auf keinen Fall aber dürfen Sie mit Ihren Kindern zu Ihrer Mutter 10 **Auf ... Fall** under
fahren. Ich habe damals einen Fehler gemacht; ich hoffe, Sie machen   no circumstances
diesen Fehler nicht.

Ihre
Katharina Schmidt

P.S.   Meine Tochter ist übrigens seit drei Wochen mit einer Gruppe 15
von Archäologen in Ägypten. Ich hoffe, sie erfährt nicht, daß ihr
Vater in Kairo ist.

Kapitel Fünf: Frau Schmidt-Ingelheim wieder am Telefon

Ah, Herr Behrens; gut, daß Sie wieder anrufen. Wissen Sie was?
Der Briefträger hatte wirklich zwei Briefe von meinem Mann. Und 20
seine Tochter, die Erika, war *doch* in Kairo. . . .

Nein, Johannes wußte es auch nicht. Sie studiert doch Archäologie
und war gerade in Ägypten, und zufällig war sie in Kairo, als mein
Mann in Kairo war. Die Welt ist doch wirklich klein, nicht? . . .

Und diese Männer! Er hatte mir geschrieben, daß er nicht mit der 25
Lufthansa nach Casablanca wollte. Thistlethwaite hatte ihn und
seine Tochter eingeladen, mit ihm auf seiner Jacht nach Casablanca
zu fahren. Und dann nimmt der Mann den Brief mit aufs Schiff, und
gefunden hat er ihn erst in Casablanca im Hotel. . . .

Nein, nein, alles ist O.K.; ich fahre morgen nach Zürich und hole 30
ihn ab. . . .

Ja, so sind die Männer, aber ich bin ja so glücklich, daß er gesund
ist. . . .

Ja, mit dem Nekrolog müssen Sie jetzt natürlich noch warten. . . .

Natürlich, ich sage ihm morgen, daß Sie angerufen haben. Ich 35
danke Ihnen, Herr Behrens. Auf Wiederhören!

Analysis

79 Cardinal Numbers

The numbers from 0 to 20 are:

null	sieben	vierzehn
eins	acht	fünfzehn
zwei	neun	sechzehn
drei	zehn	siebzehn
vier	elf	achtzehn
fünf	zwölf	neunzehn
sechs	dreizehn	zwanzig

Note the difference in spelling:

sech*s*	but	sechzehn
sieb*en*	but	siebzehn

One can say either

zwei und zwei ist vier   or   **zwei plus zwei ist vier**

and

vier weniger zwei ist zwei   or   **vier minus zwei ist zwei**

Plus and **minus** are mathematical terms; **und** and **weniger** are used in non-mathematical everyday language.

80 The Past Tense of Weak Verbs

Just as the present-tense form **ich gehe** may mean both *I go* and *I am going*, the past-tense form **ich ging** may mean both *I went* and *I was going;* in other words, German does not have progressive forms in any tense.

It was pointed out in Unit 4 that weak verbs form their participles by prefixing **ge-** and adding **-t** to the stem, whereas strong verbs form their participles by prefixing **ge-** and adding **-en** to the stem.

WEAK	STRONG
lieben, geliebt	bleiben, geblieben
lachen, gelacht	lesen, gelesen
kennen, gekannt	sein, gewesen

There is also a difference in the way weak and strong verbs form the past tense.

Weak verbs form the past tense by adding a personal ending starting with -t-
to the unchanged (or only slightly changed) stem.

INFINITIVE	STEM	PERSONAL ENDING	PAST TENSE
lieben	lieb-	-te	ich liebte
		-test	du liebtest
		-te	er liebte
		-ten	wir liebten
		-tet	ihr liebtet
		-ten	sie liebten

Thousands of verbs follow the pattern of **lieben** without any deviation.
Some deviations are regular and will be discussed in the next paragraph.
The few irregular deviations will be found in the tables of irregular verbs
which, from now on, will follow the vocabulary of each unit.

81 Regular Deviations in the Past of Weak Verbs

Three slight deviations will not appear in the tables of irregular verbs:

Modals

The modals lose the umlaut found in the infinitive.

dürfen	ich durfte
können	ich konnte
müssen	ich mußte
sollen	ich sollte
wollen	ich wollte

We will not use, for a while, the past-tense forms belonging to **ich möchte**.
Note the difference between **ich konnte** (*I was able to*) and **ich kannte** (*I
knew*).

Verbs with an -e- before the Ending -te

The endings -te, -test, -te, -ten, -tet, and -ten must be clearly audible. Therefore, verbs with a stem ending in -d or -t, like **arbeiten** and **reden**, insert an
-e- between the stem and the ending.

ich arbeitete	wir arbeiteten
du arbeitetest	ihr arbeitetet
er arbeitete	sie arbeiteten

ich redete	wir redeten
du redetest	ihr redetet
er redete	sie redeten

In order to make sure that the second syllable starts with the same consonant as it does in the infinitive, an **-e-** before the ending **-t** is also found in the past forms of verbs like **regnen, atmen** (*to breathe*), and **rechnen** (*to figure, to calculate*).

es regnete
er atmete
er rechnete

The Verb **haben**

ich hatte	wir hatten
du hattest	ihr hattet
er hatte	sie hatten

NOTE: In the past tense, the third person singular of a weak verb *never* ends in **-t**.

82 Past Tense of Strong Verbs

To form the past, strong verbs add the following endings to the changed stem:

ich:	—	wir:	-en
du:	-st	ihr:	-t
er:	—	sie:	-en

The change in the stem is unpredictable, and the best way to master these forms is to memorize them as they appear in the tables of irregular verbs.

INFINITIVE	CHANGED STEM	PERSONAL ENDING	PAST TENSE
		-	ich ging
		-st	du gingst
		-	er ging
gehen	ging-	-en	wir gingen
		-t	ihr gingt
		-en	sie gingen

Like the weak verbs whose stems end in **-d** or **-t**, strong verbs ending in **-d** or **-t** insert an **-e-** between the stem and the ending in the **du**-form and the

ihr-form.

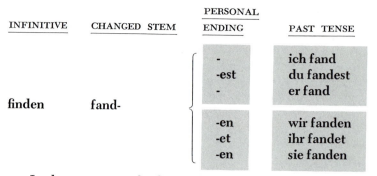

INFINITIVE	CHANGED STEM	PERSONAL ENDING	PAST TENSE
		-	ich fand
		-est	du fandest
		-	er fand
finden	fand-		
		-en	wir fanden
		-et	ihr fandet
		-en	sie fanden

NOTE: In the past tense, the first and third persons singular of a strong verb *never* have an ending.

83 The Principal Parts of Strong and Irregular Weak Verbs

One can form all the tenses of an English verb like *to sing* if one knows the three forms

sing   sang   sung

These three forms are called the *principal parts* of *to sing*.

In learning German you must learn two additional forms:

1. The **er**-form of verbs like **fahren**—that is, of strong verbs with a vowel change in the second and third persons singular. (Weak verbs never change their stem vowel in the present tense.)

2. The auxiliary (**haben** or **sein**) used to form the perfect.

Thus the principal parts of **kennen, schreiben,** and **fahren,** arranged in the traditional way, are:

kennen	kannte	hat gekannt	kennt
schreiben	schrieb	hat geschrieben	schreibt
fahren	fuhr	ist gefahren	fährt

The verb **kennen** is a weak verb. However, it changes the vowel in the past and in the perfect in an unpredictable way and therefore appears in the table of irregular verbs.

84 The Difference between the Past and the Perfect

In conversational situations, German uses only the perfect to refer to actions that were completed before the moment of speaking. Now that you will start memorizing

schlafen   schlief   hat geschlafen   schläft

you will be tempted to use **er schlief** when you should use **er hat geschlafen.**

Thus, when Aunt Amalie shows up for breakfast in the morning, you should not ask her:

[Schliefst du heute nacht gut, Tante Amalie?]

You can only ask her:

Hast du heute nacht gut geschlafen, Tante Amalie?

She, too, will use the perfect and answer:

Nein, heute nacht habe ich nicht gut geschlafen.

Compare also:

A: Wohnt Dr. Müller noch hier in der Beethovenstraße?

B: Nein, leider nicht. Dr. Müller ist vor einem Jahr gestorben, und seine Frau ist mit den Kindern nach München gezogen.

Not

[Dr. Müller starb vor einem Jahr, und seine Frau zog nach München.]

As long as you are having a two-way conversation with someone, you must refer to all things which preceded the moment of speaking by using the perfect. However, if two-way conversation is suspended while you start retelling the events of the past as you see them, then conversation changes to narration, and you must use the simple past to enumerate, step by step, those events, and *only* those events, which are part of the progressing story.

Wir wohnten damals in Bonn, in der Beethovenstraße. Uns gegenüber wohnte ein Arzt, ein Dr. Müller, mit seiner Familie. Eines Tages hörten wir, daß Dr. Müller mit Hepatitis im Krankenhaus lag. Er starb kurz vor Weihnachten, und seine Frau zog im Januar mit den Kindern nach München. Seitdem haben wir nichts mehr von Frau Dr. Müller gehört.

Compare also:

Hans wurde Schriftsteller. Seinen Kriegsroman *Wie das Gesetz es befahl* habe ich auf der Maschine geschrieben. Er machte damals oft Reisen, ohne mich, und wohin, weiß ich nicht. Ich habe ihn auch nie gefragt. Er mußte, so sagte er, zwei oder drei Wochen allein sein, um seine Romane schreiben zu können. Aber er kam immer wieder, mit seinem Lachen in den Augen, und trank seinen Kaffee, wie man Rheinwein trinkt. Aber dann passierte ihm doch etwas. Als er von einer Reise zurückkam, sagte er beim Frühstück: „Ohne deinen Kaffee, Gisela, wäre das Leben nur halb so schön." Ich weiß nicht, wer Gisela war, aber ich fuhr mit meiner Tochter zu meiner Mutter.

Most of the verb forms in this passage are past-tense forms. These forms narrate, step by step, the events of the story. The perfect forms **habe ich auf der Maschine geschrieben** and **Ich habe ihn auch nie gefragt** are parenthetical remarks which interrupt the story. The two present forms **ich**

weiß nicht refer to the time of writing the letter, not to what the author knew while the past was going on. Such shifts from the narrative past to a present or to a perfect are quite normal. The present or perfect forms in such cases interrupt the story and re-establish a connection with the present.

85 The Use of the Past Tense of **haben, sein,** and the Modals

What has been said about the difference between the past and the perfect is not applicable to the modals, to **sein,** and sometimes to **haben.**

In most cases, the forms

ich bin gewesen	are replaced by	**ich war**
ich habe arbeiten müssen		**ich mußte arbeiten**
ich habe arbeiten können		**ich konnte arbeiten**
ich habe arbeiten dürfen		**ich durfte arbeiten**
Meyer hat mir helfen sollen		**Meyer sollte mir helfen**
Meyer hat mir helfen wollen		**Meyer wollte mir helfen**
Der Zug hat um zwei ankommen sollen		**Der Zug sollte um zwei ankommen**

It is not exactly wrong to use the perfect. One *does* hear it, especially in connection with such open-end phrases as **noch nie, schon oft,** or **erst zweimal.**

> **Ich bin noch nie in Paris gewesen.**
> **Ich bin erst zweimal in Paris gewesen.**
> **Wir haben schon oft sonntags arbeiten müssen.**

But one also hears:

> **Ich war noch nie in Paris.**
> **Ich war erst zweimal in Paris.**
> **Wir mußten schon oft sonntags arbeiten.**

Compare also:

> **Ich konnte gestern nicht kommen. Meine Mutter war krank, und da bin ich zu Hause geblieben.**
> (**bleiben** is not a modal)

86 The Use of the Past in Dependent Clauses

Frequently a perfect form in the main clause is accompanied by a past form in the dependent clause (see **89–94**). This is virtually obligatory in **als**-clauses and in all other clauses which fix the time of an event or describe the circumstances that brought the event about.

Ich habe bis elf gewartet. Aber als er dann immer noch nicht kam, bin ich ins Bett gegangen.	I waited until eleven. But when he still did not come, I went to bed.

NOTE: If the action of the dependent clause occurs while the action of the main clause is in progress, the past tense may be used in both clauses.

Als ich meine Frau kennenlernte, wohnte sie in München.

87 The Formation of the Pluperfect

The German pluperfect is formed by combining the simple past of **haben** or **sein** with the participle of the main verb. Verbs which use **sein** for the perfect, like

bleiben   **blieb**   **ist geblieben**   **bleibt**

also form their pluperfect with **sein: ich war geblieben** (*I had stayed*). Verbs which, like

schreiben   **schrieb**   **hat geschrieben**   **schreibt**

use **haben** for the perfect, also use **haben** for the pluperfect: **ich hatte geschrieben** (*I had written*).

88 The Use of the Pluperfect

Like the English past perfect, the German pluperfect is the tense used to describe events or situations which precede events or situations that occurred in the past.

Hans hatte die Gelbsucht, weil er monatelang zu gut gegessen und zu viel getrunken hatte.	Hans had jaundice, because for months he had been eating and drinking too much.
Es war Abend geworden, und es regnete.	Night had come and it was raining.

When the sentence

Erich wohnt jetzt schon drei Jahre in München, ist aber noch nie ins Theater gegangen

becomes part of a narrative, it will appear as

Erich wohnte damals schon drei Jahre in München, war aber noch nie ins Theater gegangen.

The up-to-now situation of the first sentence has become an up-to-then situation in the second sentence.

89 Dependent Clauses

Dependent clauses are syntactical units of main clauses. They can function as any part of the main clause: as subject, predicate noun, object, adverb, and so forth.

SUBJECT	*The winner* gets the prize.
	Whoever wins gets the prize.
PREDICATE NOUN	This is not *the expected result*.
	This is not *what I had expected*.
OBJECT	I'll never know *your thoughts*.
	I'll never know *what you think*.
ADVERB	He met John *during his stay in New York*.
	He met John *while he stayed in New York*.

Dependent clauses are usually introduced by a connecting word: a subordinating conjunction (*while, because, if,* etc.), a relative pronoun (*who, whom, what,* etc.), or an interrogative pronoun (*who, what, when, why,* etc.).

After certain introductory phrases containing a verb of thought, the connecting word can be left out.

> I am sure (that) he'll come.

If the connecting word is left out, we speak of *unintroduced* dependent clauses.

In English, the word order in both introduced and unintroduced dependent clauses is usually the same as the word order of a main clause.

> She took him to the airport.
> I know she took him to the airport.
> I know that she took him to the airport.

In German, *only unintroduced dependent clauses have the same structure as main clauses*. We have had many examples of this type.

> **Meyer arbeitet heute in Bonn.**
> **Ich glaube, Meyer arbeitet heute in Bonn.**

All unintroduced dependent clauses in German have verb-second position. They normally start with the subject, and the introductory main clause is never negated. If the main clause is negated, a major change takes place which has no parallel in English (see **90**).

90 Verb-Last Position

You are by now very familiar with the fact that in all main clauses the first prong (the inflected verb) is the second structural unit, while the second prong (infinitives, participles, and all complements) stands at the end, unless there is an end field.

This two-prong principle disappears in introduced dependent clauses. *In all introduced dependent clauses, the finite verb (the first prong) appears be-*

hind the second prong, and the normal slot for the first prong remains empty.
We therefore speak of *verb-last position.*

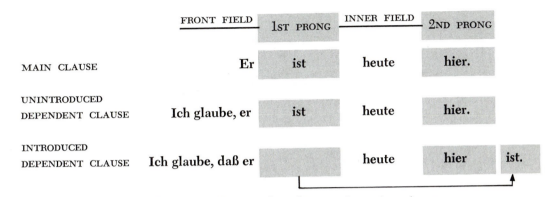

	FRONT FIELD	1ST PRONG	INNER FIELD	2ND PRONG	
MAIN CLAUSE	Er	ist	heute	hier.	
UNINTRODUCED DEPENDENT CLAUSE	Ich glaube, er	ist	heute	hier.	
INTRODUCED DEPENDENT CLAUSE	Ich glaube, daß er		heute	hier	ist.

Note that the sequence of elements following the subject **er** is a mirror image
of the sequence of elements in the corresponding English sentence; that is,
if the German sequence is 1–2–3, the English sequence will be 3–2–1.

	1	2	3
, daß er	heute	hier	ist
that he	is	here	today
	3	2	1

Here are some further examples of this mirror image principle, which holds
for a great many English and German sentences and explains, for example,
why the German sequence of time-place corresponds to the English sequence
of place-time.

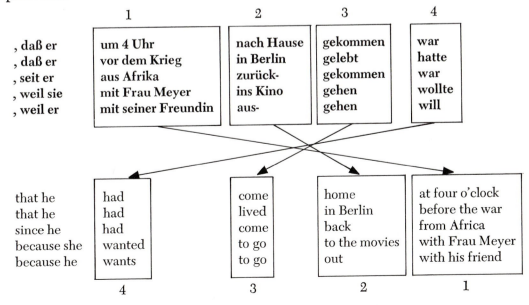

	1	2	3	4
, daß er	um 4 Uhr	nach Hause	gekommen	war
, daß er	vor dem Krieg	in Berlin	gelebt	hatte
, seit er	aus Afrika	zurück-	gekommen	war
, weil sie	mit Frau Meyer	ins Kino	gehen	wollte
, weil er	mit seiner Freundin	aus-	gehen	will

	4	3	2	1
that he	had	come	home	at four o'clock
that he	had	lived	in Berlin	before the war
since he	had	come	back	from Africa
because she	wanted	to go	to the movies	with Frau Meyer
because he	wants	to go	out	with his friend

Try to find other examples in the patterns and exercises.

NOTE: Verbal complements like an, aus, ab, and any others that are written as one word with an infinitive, must also be connected in verb-last position.

>   **Die Laternen gehen an.—Wenn die Laternen angehen, . . .**
>   **Er macht das Licht aus.—Daß er das Licht ausmacht, . . .**
>   **Er lernte sie in Bonn kennen.—Als er sie in Bonn kennenlernte, . . .**

All introduced dependent clauses follow this pattern of verb-last position. In this unit, the following groups of connecting words are used:

Subordinating Conjunctions

Ich weiß,	*daß*	er seit drei Wochen	verschwunden	*ist.*
Er will erst schreiben,	*wenn*	er wieder	zu Hause	*ist.*
Ich mußte warten,	*bis*	Herr Behrens mich	angerufen	*hatte.*
Er schrieb erst,	*als*	er von seiner Reise	zurückgekommen	*war.*
Er blieb zu Hause,	*weil*	er nicht	ins Kino gehen	*wollte.*
Er redet nicht viel,	*seit*	er aus Afrika	zurückgekommen	*ist.*

Interrogative Conjunctions

Sie wußte nicht mehr,	*wer*	ihr das Buch	gegeben	*hatte.*
Ich weiß nicht,	*was*	er in Norwegen	gemacht	*hat.*
Wissen Sie,	*wo*	er bei Kriegsende		*war?*
Wissen Sie,	*warum*	er	nach Paris gefahren	*ist?*

The examples with interrogative conjunctions show: Any German word question can be changed into a dependent clause by changing word order.

>   **Wann ist er nach Hause gekommen?**
>   **Ich weiß nicht, wann er nach Hause gekommen ist.**

91 wenn and wann

Observe the difference between

>   **So viel wie gestern abend redet Meyer nur, wenn er zuviel getrunken hat.**

and

>   **Weißt du, wann Meyer gestern nach Hause gegangen ist?**

Both **wenn** and **wann** frequently correspond to English *when*. But German **wann** *is an interrogative and means only "at what time."* Conversely: Every English *when* which can be replaced by *at what time* must be expressed by German **wann.**

92 The Conjunction **ob**

Any German yes-or-no question can be changed into a dependent clause by moving the verb to the end and introducing the clause with the subordinating conjunction **ob.**

Hat Meyer Geld?
Weißt du, ob Meyer Geld hat?

Hat sie geheiratet?
Weißt du, ob sie geheiratet hat?

NOTE: In English, yes-or-no questions can be changed into dependent clauses by using either *whether* or *if.*

	Is he here?
Do you know whether	he is here?
Do you know if	he is here?

Every English *if* which can be replaced by *whether* must be expressed by **ob** in German. This **ob** cannot be replaced by **wenn.**

93 Dependent Clauses in the Front Field

In all the above examples, the dependent clause follows the main clause. *If the dependent clause precedes the main clause, it is considered the first element of the main clause; that is, it occupies the front field of the main clause—and must therefore be followed by the first prong of the main clause* to conform to the principle of verb-second position. This means that, separated by a comma, the finite verb of the main clause immediately follows the finite verb of the dependent clause.

In Hamburg	bin	ich jeden Abend	ins Kino	gegangen.
Als ich in Hamburg war,	bin	ich jeden Abend	ins Kino	gegangen.

Frequently, especially after **wenn**-clauses, the dependent clause—that is, the first element of the main clause—is repeated and summed up at the beginning of the main clause by either **dann** or **so.** This **dann** or **so** immediately precedes the first prong—that is, the second element of the main clause.

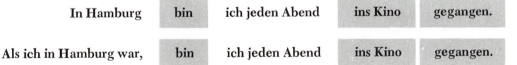

Wenn ich seine Tochter sehe,
    1

           dann | *weiß ich, daß ich ihn immer noch liebe.*
           1a   2

English uses a similar construction in such sentences as

Well, if you won't sell, then there's nothing more to be said.

94 Position of the Subject in Dependent Clauses

In most dependent clauses, the subject follows the connecting word. (See all the above examples.) However, a noun subject may be preceded by pronoun objects.

Ich weiß, daß *Herr Meyer seiner Frau* einen Sportwagen geschenkt hat.
Ich weiß, daß *Herr Meyer ihr* einen Sportwagen geschenkt hat.
Ich weiß, daß *ihr Herr Meyer* einen Sportwagen geschenkt hat.

In order to increase the news value of a noun subject, it may be moved toward the end of the inner field. Thus, in the following sentences, the news value is shifted from the time element to the subject:

Ich kann nicht glauben, daß *die Laternen* hier schon um vier Uhr angehen.
Ich kann nicht glauben, daß hier schon um vier Uhr *die Laternen* angehen.

95 Intonation of Dependent Clauses

It was pointed out in Unit 1 that when a German assertion sinks down at the end to level 1 of the three intonation levels, as it does in

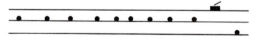

Wir blei-ben heu-te na-tür-lich zu Hau-se

the fall to level 1 means "this is the end of the sentence."

Whenever an assertion is followed by a dependent clause, the speaker has several possibilities.

1. He may want to indicate that everything important has already been said in the main clause. In that case the entire dependent clause may have level-1 intonation, and the preceding main clause shows the usual 2–3–1 intonation pattern.

Ich war schon ins Bett ge-gang-en, als er nach Hau-se kam

2. He may pack *all* the news value into the dependent clause and speak the preceding main clause entirely on level 2.

Ich war doch schon hier, als er kam

3. He may want to distribute the news value over the main clause and the dependent clause by placing (at least) *one* stressed syllable in the main clause and (at least) *one* stressed syllable in the dependent clause.

Er will war-ten   , bis du kommst

The intonation patterns in (1) and (2) contain nothing new (they simply represent a "long-breath" variation of **Es regnet**), but the intonation pattern under (3) illustrates a new principle:

The main clause and the dependent clause are usually separated by a slight pause; and at the end of the main clause the pitch of the unstressed syllables does not sink to level 1 (which would signal the end of the sentence), but is spoken on level 3. This lack of a drop in pitch is a signal meaning: "This is not the end of the sentence; wait for the next clause."

The high-pitch last-syllable intonation is also characteristic for dependent clauses which precede a main clause.

Wenn es mor-gen reg-net , blei-ben wir zu Hau-se

96 Open Conditions

A condition is an event or a situation without which another event or situation cannot take place. Thus, in the statement *If the weather is good tomorrow, we can go to the beach,* good weather is the prerequisite for the trip to the beach. The *if*-clause (the grammatical "condition") does not indicate whether or not the weather will be good; it simply states that unless the weather is good, the second part of the statement (the grammatical "conclusion") will not become a reality.

Similarly, if someone says, *I haven't seen my old teacher for years. If he is still alive, he was fifty years old last Monday,* this means that the speaker does not know whether the teacher is still alive, and that consequently he doesn't know whether the teacher was able to celebrate his fiftieth birthday. *The question as to the reality of the facts is left open.* However, this question *is not left open* if someone says, *If my teacher were still alive, he would have turned fifty last Monday.* The speaker now implies that the teacher is dead. In other words: The situation described in the condition is known to be unreal and to exist only in the speaker's thought and imagination.

The difference in meaning between *if he is alive* and *if he were alive* depends entirely on verb forms. The *is* leaves the question of the actual facts open; the *were* expresses the unreality of the situation imagined.

Wenn es in Europa regnet…

…scheint im Libanon die Sonne

From now on, we shall use the terms "open conditions" and "irreal" or "contrary-to-fact conditions" to indicate whether the question of the facts is open or whether these facts are contrary to reality and merely assumed in imagination.

In Unit 5, only open conditions are introduced. Irreal conditions, which require the use of the subjunctive, will be discussed in Unit 6. German *if*-clauses are introduced by the subordinating conjunction **wenn.** As dependent clauses, they require verb-last position.

> **Wenn Else kommen kann, gehe ich mit ihr ins Museum.**
> **Wenn ihm nichts passiert ist, muß er schon zu Hause sein.**
> **Ich schenke dir den Roman gern, wenn du ihn haben möchtest.**
> **Wenn Sie diesen Brief bekommen, müssen Sie mir sofort antworten.**
> **Ich habe keine Angst, wenn mein Mann nach Afrika fährt.**

NOTE: Without context, some of these sentences, especially the last two, are ambiguous, since **wenn** means both *when* and *if*. Thus the last sentence may mean

> I won't be afraid if my husband goes to Africa

or

> I am not afraid when my husband goes to Africa.

97 um … zu

We have introduced a number of situations in which an infinitive must be used with the preposition **zu.**

> **Er braucht heute nicht zu arbeiten.**
> **Er scheint zu glauben, daß Meyer intelligent ist.**

There is another type of infinitive construction, as, for example, in the English sentence

> We eat to stay alive

which can be expanded into

> We eat in order to stay alive.

Whenever this English expansion is possible, German *must* introduce the infinitive phrase with the preposition **um**.

> **Wir essen, um zu leben.**

This construction with **um . . . zu** must be separated from the main clause by a comma. When it is expanded by other syntactical units, **um** stands at the beginning and the infinitive stands at the end of the phrase.

> **Er fuhr nach Kairo,** *um* **dort einen Roman** *zu schreiben.*
> **Sie ging nach Mainz,** *um* **dort Archäologie** *zu studieren.*
> *Um* **das Haus kaufen** *zu können,* **braucht er Geld.**

Usually, the **um . . . zu** phrase occupies either the end field or the front field.

NOTE: If the **um . . . zu** clause follows the main clause, it can be replaced by a clause of the type **weil . . . er will** (**wollte**); if it precedes the main clause, it can be replaced by an open condition.

> **Er braucht Geld, um nach Berlin zu fahren.**
> **Er braucht Geld, weil er nach Berlin fahren will.**

> **Um nach Berlin fahren zu können, braucht man Geld.**
> **Wenn man nach Berlin fahren will, braucht man Geld.**

98 mit as a Verbal Complement

The preposition **mit** is frequently used as a verbal complement, meaning *along*. It forms the second prong of the predicate.

> **Rosemarie geht** *auch* **mit.**   Rosemarie is coming along too.

If the sentence is negated, **mit** is preceded by **nicht**.

> **Rosemarie geht diesmal leider nicht mit.**

Mit is often used with, and always precedes, directives.

> **Sie geht wieder mit nach Deutschland.**

Mit alone can never occupy the front field.

> IMPOSSIBLE: [**Mit geht sie diesmal nicht.**]

If used with an infinitive, **mit** and the infinitive are written as one word.

> **Sie möchte wieder mitgehen.**

If the sentence contains a prepositional phrase with **mit**, the verbal complement **mit** is not used.

> **Ich gehe mit ihr nach Deutschland.**

99 Word Formation

The native speaker of any language not only has an active and a passive vocabulary at his disposal, but also knows how to construct new words from known stems. Thus, by adding the suffix *-ing* to the stem of *love*, English derives the form *loving;* by adding the suffix *-er*, English forms the agent noun *lover*, and by adding the prefix *be-* plus the suffix *-ed*, the adjective *beloved* is formed. The suffix *-er* can not only be added to the stem *lov-;* it also appears in *worker, reader, listener, drinker, driver*, and many other agent nouns. The suffix *-er* is a very important part of our active vocabulary. We know how to use it, we know its semantic function, and anyone who doesn't know how to use the suffix *-er* cannot use English properly.

In German, even more frequently than in English, prefixes and suffixes are used to form derivatives. It is therefore important to learn when and how to apply the German prefixes and suffixes. From now on we shall present a section on word formation in most units.

100 The Suffixes -chen and -lein

These suffixes are added to nouns to form diminutive nouns, all of which are neuter. Thus the nouns **Vater, Mutter, Bruder, Haus, Stadt,** and **Mann** are the base for the diminutives

Väterchen	**Väterlein**
Mütterchen	**Mütterlein**
Brüderchen	**Brüderlein**
Häuschen	**Häuslein**
Städtchen	**Städtlein**
Männchen	**Männlein**

Diminutives umlaut the stem vowel and remain unchanged in the plural. The suffix **-chen** is standard, **-lein** is rather poetic.

Some nouns drop their ending before adding the diminutive.

die Tasse	**das Täßchen**
der Garten	**das Gärtchen**

If added to nouns referring to persons, diminutives express either smallness or affection; if added to nouns designating things, they express either smallness or polite "belittling."

ein Täßchen Kaffee	**ein Städtchen**
ein Gläschen Wein	**ein Häuschen**

NOTE: The noun **Fräulein** now means *Miss;* the nouns **Männchen** and **Weibchen** are zoological terms meaning the male and the female (of the species).

101 The Suffix -er

The German suffix **-er** corresponds to the English suffixes *-er* and *-or*. It is added to verb stems to form agent nouns, which denote the person or instrument that performs the action implied.

denken	**der Denker**	the thinker
lesen	**der Leser**	the reader
zeigen	**der Zeiger**	the hand (of a clock)

In some cases, the agent noun shows a vowel change from **a** to **ä**.

schlafen	**der Schläfer**	the sleeper (sleeping person)

If agent nouns refer to human beings, the suffix **-in** is added to the suffix **-er** to form feminine agent nouns.

lesen	**der Leser, –**	**die Leserin, –nen**

NOTE: The suffix **-in** may also be added to other nouns.

der Student,–en	**die Studentin, –nen**
der Freund, –e	**die Freundin, –nen**

102 Infinitives as Neuter Nouns

German infinitives can be used as neuter nouns.

mit einem Lachen	with a laugh
Das Leben ist schön.	Life is beautiful.

These neuter nouns denote the activity expressed by the verb. **Beim (bei dem)**, followed by such a verbal noun, always means "in the process (or act) of" or "while."

beim Fahren	in the act of driving
beim Essen	while eating
beim Trinken	while drinking

103 Compound Nouns

Both in English and in German two nouns can be combined to form a compound noun. For example, *house* and *dog* can form two combinations— *house dog* and *doghouse*, a house dog being a kind of dog and a doghouse being a kind of house. The second part of the compound is always the basic form, which is modified by the first part. For this reason, German compounds derive their gender from the second part. Thus:

das Haus	**der Hund**	**der Haushund**
der Hund	**das Haus**	**das Hundehaus**

Other examples found in Unit 5 include:

der Krieg	der Roman	der Kriegsroman
der Brief	die Taube	die Brieftaube
der Brief	der Träger	der Briefträger
der Westen	die Front	die Westfront
der Rhein	der Wein	der Rheinwein

NOTE: In many such compounds, a letter is inserted between the two parts —for example, **Kriegsroman, Damenhut, Liebesbrief**. While there are some historical grammatical explanations for these formations, there are no general rules. It is best, therefore, to memorize these compounds as they occur.

Exercises

A. Read the following problems.

SEE
ANALYSIS
79

(p. 131)

$2 + 4 = 6$	$1 + 14 = 15$	$19 - 12 = 7$
$12 + 4 = 16$	$9 + 11 = 20$	$16 - 10 = 6$
$7 + 3 = 10$	$18 + 1 = 19$	$8 - 5 = 3$
$7 + 10 = 17$	$16 + 2 = 18$	$20 - 3 = 17$
$5 + 8 = 13$	$17 + 2 = 19$	$11 - 11 = 0$

B. The following is an excerpt from a railroad timetable. Form questions and statements using the information given.

> **Wann fährt der Zug nach München in Köln ab?—Um 2 Uhr.**
> **Der Zug kommt um 8 Uhr 16 in Ulm an.**
> **Wie lange ist der Zug in Frankfurt?—12 Minuten.**

SEE
ANALYSIS
79

(p. 131)

Köln	ab	2.00		München	ab	1.20
Bonn	an	2.18		Ulm	an	4.04
	ab	2.20			ab	4.05
Frankfurt	an	4.15		Stuttgart	an	5.08
	ab	4.20			ab	5.14
Heidelberg	an	5.12		Heidelberg	an	8.02
	ab	5.17			ab	8.06
Stuttgart	an	7.01		Frankfurt	an	9.08
	ab	7.06			ab	9.20
Ulm	an	8.16		Bonn	an	11.17
	ab	8.17			ab	11.20
München	an	10.03		Köln	an	12.00

C. This exercise is meant as a quick drill of the present, past, and perfect forms of weak verbs. Transform according to the following pattern:

antworten — er antwortet, er antwortete, er hat geantwortet

arbeiten	— ich	heiraten	— wir	
brauchen	— wir	hoffen	— ich	
danken	— er	kochen	— sie	
fragen	— sie	lachen	— er	
gehören	— es	leben	— wir	
glauben	— du	lernen	— wir	
hassen	— er	lieben	— ich	

SEE ANALYSIS 80–81 (pp. 131-133)

D. Restate the following sentences in the past tense. In each sentence, add **damals**, as in the following example:

Erika studiert in München.
Erika studierte damals in München.

1. Hans hat nie Hunger.
2. Er besucht seinen Vater in Nürnberg.
3. Wir kaufen ein Haus in Bayreuth.
4. Dieses Haus gehört meinem Vater.
5. Er antwortet mir nicht.
6. Ist deine Mutter nicht in Dortmund?
7. Wir können leider nicht kommen.
8. Ich will ihm die Stadt zeigen.
9. Er soll zu Hause bleiben.
10. Ich darf es ihm nicht sagen.
11. Wir müssen leider nach Hause fahren.
12. Er braucht nicht zu arbeiten.

SEE ANALYSIS 80–85 (pp. 131-136)

E. Form the present, past, and perfect. All verbs in this exercise are irregular.

bleiben — wir bleiben, wir blieben, wir sind geblieben

anfangen	— ich	kennen	— ich	sitzen	— wir
anrufen	— er	kommen	— wir	sprechen	— ich
bringen	— er	lassen	— er	sterben	— er
essen	— er	lesen	— er	trinken	— wir
fahren	— du	scheinen	— es	tun	— ich
geben	— er	schlafen	— er	verstehen	— er
gehen	— wir	schreiben	— ich	werden	— er
helfen	— er	sehen	— er	wissen	— du
heißen	— sie	sein	— ihr		

SEE ANALYSIS 83 (p. 134)

F. Restate the following sentences in the past tense.

1. Kurt geht zum Bahnhof.
2. Er versteht Professor Hansen sehr gut.
3. Georg hört mich nicht.
4. Jutta hilft mir bei der Arbeit.
5. Ingelheim antwortet nicht.

SEE ANALYSIS 80–85 (pp. 131-136)

6. Herr Bergmann kommt um 9 Uhr aus dem Kino.
7. Herr Lenz fährt mit seinem Freund durch die Stadt.
8. Ich sehe meine Mutter in Freiburg.
9. Er trinkt keinen Wein.
10. Ich hole ihn in Tübingen ab.
11. Er bekommt jeden Tag einen Brief von seiner Freundin.
12. Hans lädt mich oft zum Essen ein.
13. Er denkt lange nach.
14. So etwas passiert nicht oft.
15. Hans und Inge stehen vor dem Theater.

G. Transform the ten sentences of this exercise according to the following pattern:

> **Er wohnt in Berlin.**
> **a. Ich glaube, er wohnt in Berlin.**
> **b. Ich glaube nicht, daß er in Berlin wohnt.**
> **c. Ich möchte wissen, ob er in Berlin wohnt.**

SEE
ANALYSIS
89–90

(pp. 137-140)

1. Ernst Wagner studiert Mathematik.
2. Der Wagen gehört Frau Körner.
3. Sie kann sie sehen.
4. Er will mir die Stadt zeigen.
5. Frau Lenz geht mit Frau Hoffmann ins Kino.
6. Er muß heute nach Düsseldorf.
7. Hans will ohne Inge ins Theater gehen.
8. Herr Meyer hat zu viel Wein getrunken.
9. Sie sind gestern in Berlin gewesen.
10. Er hat in Innsbruck einen Freund besucht.

H. Ask correct questions for the following answers. Your questions should ask for the italicized parts of the answers.

> **Er geht *heute abend* ins Kino.**
> **Wann geht er ins Kino?**

Then restate the question, starting with **Ich möchte wissen.**

> **Ich möchte wissen, wann er ins Kino geht.**

1. Ihr Mann ist *gestern* nach Wien gefahren.
2. Erika war gestern *in Berlin.*
3. Es (das Buch) gehört *meinem Vater.*
4. Er hat ihr *ein Buch* geschenkt.
5. Er heißt *Fritz.*
6. *Mein Vater* hat das gesagt.
7. Er geht *mit Inge* ins Kino.

I. Join the following pairs of sentences to form open conditions. The first sentence should always become the **wenn**-clause.

> **Es regnet morgen. Wir gehen ins Kino.**
> **Wenn es morgen regnet, gehen wir ins Kino.**

1. Du hast Geld. Du kannst ein Haus kaufen.
2. Du hast kein Geld. Du kannst das Haus nicht kaufen.
3. Er studiert Mathematik. Er muß intelligent sein.
4. Nancy ist intelligent. Sie lernt Deutsch.
5. Morgen regnet es nicht. Wir besuchen euch.
6. Ihr wollt ins Kino gehen. Wir gehen mit.
7. Herr Meyer wohnt in Berlin. Ich kann ihn besuchen.
8. Er ist dein Freund. Er hilft dir bestimmt.
9. Du liebst mich. Du fährst nicht nach Casablanca.
10. Man hat kein Geld. Man kann nicht an die Riviera fahren.

SEE
ANALYSIS
96

(pp. 143-144)

J. Of the following pairs of sentences, change the second to an infinitive with **um . . . zu.**

> **Inge fuhr nach Frankfurt. Sie wollte ins Theater gehen.**
> **Inge fuhr nach Frankfurt, um ins Theater zu gehen.**

1. Ingelheim fuhr nach Afrika. Er wollte einen Roman schreiben.
2. Er kam nach Frankfurt. Er wollte seinen Vater besuchen.
3. Seine Tochter ging nach Mainz. Sie wollte Archäologie studieren.
4. John fuhr nach Deutschland. Er wollte Deutsch lernen.
5. Hans ging zum Telefon. Er wollte Inge anrufen.

SEE
ANALYSIS
97

(pp. 144-145)

K. Form diminutives with **-chen** with the following nouns.

1. das Rad	5. das Tier	9. die Stadt
2. das Glas	6. das Bild	10. der Garten
3. der Hund	7. der Brief	11. der Kopf
4. die Tasse	8. der Hut	

SEE
ANALYSIS
100

(p. 146)

L. Try to guess the meaning of the following nouns in **-er.**

1. der Fahrer	6. der Läufer	11. der Lügner
2. der Erzähler	7. der Arbeiter	12. der Besucher
3. der Weinkenner	8. der Anfänger	13. der Hörer
4. der Käufer	9. der Korkzieher	14. der Nichtraucher
5. der Uhrmacher	10. der Redner	

SEE
ANALYSIS
101

(p. 147)

M. Express in German. Where appropriate, defend your choice of the German past or perfect.

1. Are you taking her along?
2. Hans went along to Vienna.
3. Does he want to go along to Berlin, too?
4. At that time the house belonged to my father.
5. I simply couldn't believe it.
6. If you want to, you may go.
7. I don't know where he was.

8. I don't know whether he was in Stuttgart.
9. It is ten after eleven, and I must go home.
10. Today he visited his friend.
11. They went to Berlin today.
12. I bought the book yesterday, but I haven't read it yet.
13. Unfortunately, I didn't understand him.
14. He never needed much money.
15. Why didn't you stay home yesterday, Karl?
16. The train left at 8:11.
17. How am I supposed to know whether he went to Casablanca?
18. I hope I'll never see him again.
19. Whether Meyer really went to Casablanca I cannot tell you. (Use **sagen.**)
20. Why he wanted to go to the movies with Inge, I don't know.
21. If you are home tomorrow, I would like to visit you.
22. I'd like to visit Ingrid, but I don't know whether she is at home.
23. Before the war he was a writer.
24. Then he became a soldier.
25. I married him because I loved him.
26. I didn't meet him at that time, for he was in Norway.
27. I know he is here, but I haven't seen him yet.
28. He had not visited us for years when I accidentally saw him in Heidelberg.
29. I have known her for a long time, but I don't know who she is.
30. When he met her in Berlin she was still a child.
31. He only wants to go if I go too.
32. I'd like to know when he'll come home.
33. If I see him, I'll tell him that you were here and that you wanted to speak with him.
34. I wanted to visit him (in order) to thank him, but unfortunately he wasn't home.
35. I can't visit you tomorrow, because tomorrow I have to be in Munich.

Basic Vocabulary*

achtzehn	eighteen	**ankommen**	to arrive
als	when; than; as	**die Arbeit, –en**	work
als er kam	when he came	**das Auge, –n**	eye
	(single event in the past)	**bekommen**	to get, to receive
		bestimmt	definitely, certainly
die Alpen (*pl.*)	the Alps	**daß** (*conj.*)	that
der Amerikaner, –	American	**denken**	to think
die Angst, ⁓e	fear, anxiety	**diesmal**	this time
Angst haben vor (*with dat.*)	to be afraid of	**dort**	there
		dreizehn	thirteen

* From this unit on, some of the new words introduced in each unit will appear under the heading "Additional Vocabulary." Most of these words appear primarily in the Reading sections and occur less frequently throughout the text than those in the main vocabulary sections.

einfach	easy, simple	das Paar, –e	pair
einladen	to invite	ein paar	a few
das Ende, –n	end	passieren	to happen
erfahren	to learn, to experience	es ist passiert	it has happened
erwarten	to expect	die Reise, –n	trip
erzählen	to relate, to tell	eine Reise machen	to take a trip
die Fami′lie, –n	family	schön	beautiful, pretty;
der Fehler, –	mistake		good, O.K.
finden	to find	der Schüler, –	pupil; student (in a
das Frühstück, –e	breakfast		secondary school)
beim Frühstück	at breakfast	sechzehn	sixteen
frühstücken	to eat breakfast	siebzehn	seventeen
fünfzehn	fifteen	die Sonne, –n	sun
fürchten	to fear	die Spur, –en	trace
gar nichts	nothing at all	spurlos	without a trace
der Garten, ∸	garden	stehen	to stand
gefangennehmen	to capture, to take	die Straße, –n	street
	prisoner	suchen	to look for, to seek, to
gratulieren	to congratulate		search
die Gruppe, –n	group	teuer	expensive
halb	half	über	over
halb so schön	half as beautiful	überall′	everywhere
eine halbe Stunde	half an hour	um . . . zu	in order to
hinter	behind	vernünftig	reasonable
klein	little	verschwinden	to disappear
der Kopf, ∸e	head	verschwunden	lost
die Kopfschmerzen	headache	(adj.)	
(pl.)		vierzehn	fourteen
kurz	short	Weihnachten (pl.)	Christmas
das Lachen	laughter	weil (conj.)	because
laufen	to run	die Welt, –en	world
das Leben, –	life	weniger	minus, less
das Mädchen, –	girl	Auf Wiederhören	good-by (telephone)
nachdenken über	to reflect, to meditate	Auf Wiedersehen	good-by (in person)
	about	wohl	probably; well
neu	new	zeigen	to show
das ist mir neu	that's news to me	ziehen	to move (change resi-
neugierig	curious		dence)
neunzehn	nineteen	nach Köln ziehen	to move to Cologne
null	zero	zwölf	twelve
ob	whether		

Additional Vocabulary

das Abitur′	final comprehensive	die Brieftaube, –n	carrier pigeon
	examination in	durchmachen	to go through, to
	the secondary		suffer
	school	der Fisch, –e	fish
atmen	to breathe	fischen	to fish
das Bett, –en	bed	füttern	to feed

gefährlich	dangerous
die Gelbsucht	jaundice
das Kapi'tel, –	chapter
die Maschi'ne, –n	machine; typewriter
die Mathematik'	mathematics
Norwegen	Norway
rechnen	to calculate, to figure
der Roman', –e	novel

das Schiff, –e	ship, boat
schilaufen	to ski
der Westen	the West
die Westfront	the western front
zufällig	by coincidence, by chance, accidentally

Strong and Irregular Verbs

abfahren, fuhr ab, ist abgefahren, er fährt ab	to depart, to leave
anfangen, fing an, hat angefangen, er fängt an	to begin, to start
angehen, ging an, ist angegangen, er geht an	to go on
ankommen, kam an, ist angekommen, er kommt an	to arrive
anrufen, rief an, hat angerufen, er ruft an	to call up (on the telephone)
ausgehen, ging aus, ist ausgegangen, er geht aus	to go out
befehlen, befahl, hat befohlen, er befiehlt	to order, to command
beginnen, begann, hat begonnen, er beginnt	to begin, to start
bleiben, blieb, ist geblieben, er bleibt	to stay, to remain
bringen, brachte, hat gebracht, er bringt	to bring
denken, dachte, hat gedacht, er denkt	to think
einladen, lud ein, hat eingeladen, er lädt ein	to invite
erfahren, erfuhr, hat erfahren, er erfährt	to find out, to learn
essen, aß, hat gegessen, er ißt	to eat
fahren, fuhr, ist gefahren, er fährt	to drive, to go (by train, boat, car)
finden, fand, hat gefunden, er findet	to find
fliegen, flog, ist geflogen, er fliegt	to fly
geben, gab, hat gegeben, er gibt	to give
gefangennehmen, nahm gefangen, hat gefangengenommen, er nimmt gefangen	to capture, to take prisoner
gehen, ging, ist gegangen, er geht	to go, to walk
haben, hatte, hat gehabt, er hat	to have
heißen, hieß, hat geheißen, er heißt	to be called; to mean
helfen, half, hat geholfen, er hilft	to help
kennen, kannte, hat gekannt, er kennt	to know, to be acquainted with
kommen, kam, ist gekommen, er kommt	to come
lassen, ließ, hat gelassen, er läßt	to let, to leave
laufen, lief, ist gelaufen, er läuft	to run
lesen, las, hat gelesen, er liest	to read
lügen, log, hat gelogen, er lügt	to tell a lie
nachdenken, dachte nach, hat nachgedacht, er denkt nach	to reflect, to meditate
nehmen, nahm, hat genommen, er nimmt	to take, to seize
scheinen, schien, hat geschienen, er scheint	to seem; to shine
schilaufen, lief Schi, ist schigelaufen, er läuft Schi	to ski

schlafen, schlief, hat geschlafen, er schläft	to sleep
schreiben, schrieb, hat geschrieben, er schreibt	to write
sehen, sah, hat gesehen, er sieht	to see
sein, war, ist gewesen, er ist	to be
sitzen, saß, hat gesessen, er sitzt	to sit
sprechen, sprach, hat gesprochen, er spricht	to speak, to talk
stehen, stand, hat gestanden, er steht	to stand
sterben, starb, ist gestorben, er stirbt	to die
trinken, trank, hat getrunken, er trinkt	to drink
tun, tat, hat getan, er tut	to do
verschwinden, verschwand, ist verschwunden, er verschwindet	to disappear
verstehen, verstand, hat verstanden, er versteht	to understand
werden, wurde, ist geworden, er wird	to become
wiedersehen, sah wieder, hat wiedergesehen, er sieht wieder	to see again
wissen, wußte, hat gewußt, er weiß	to know
zwingen, zwang, hat gezwungen, er zwingt	to force

KÜNSTLERISCHE VOLKSHOCHSCHULE

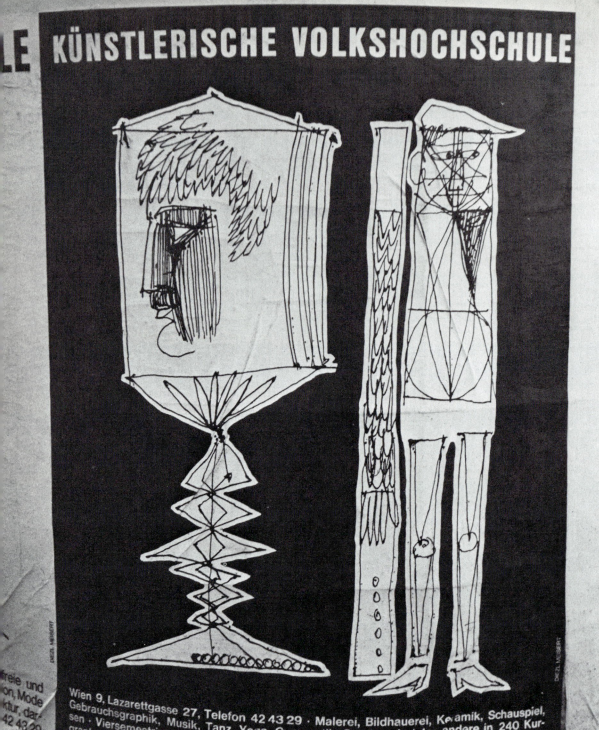

Wien 9, Lazarettgasse 27, Telefon 42 43 29 · Malerei, Bildhauerei, Keramik, Schauspiel, Gebrauchsgraphik, Musik, Tanz, Yoga, Gymnastik, Sport und vieles andere in 240 Kursen · Viersemestrige Lehrgänge mit Zertifikatabschluß: Photoreporter und Pressephotographen, Bau- und Raumgestaltung, Schaufensterdekoration, Kunstgewerbe, bildende und angewandte Kunst, Gebrauchsgraphik, Keramik, Journalistik, Karikatur, Restaurieren

Unit 6 The Future Tense—The Subjunctive

Patterns

[1] The Future Tense

Ich glaube, ich werde sie nie wiedersehen.	I believe I will never see them (her) again.	SEE ANALYSIS 104 (p. 173)
Diesen Sonntag werde ich nie vergessen.	I shall never forget this Sunday.	
Diesen Sonntag werde ich leider nie vergessen können.	Unfortunately, I shall never be able to forget this Sunday.	
Nein, Herr Harms, ich werde es nicht vergessen. Ich werde Sie morgen um 9 Uhr 10 anrufen.	No, Mr. Harms, I shall not forget it. I'll give you a ring at 9:10 tomorrow.	
Gertrud ist schon vor einer Stunde abgefahren, also wird sie jetzt schon lange zu Hause sein.	Gertrude left an hour ago, so she has probably been home for a long time now.	
Ich möchte wissen, warum Peter mich immer noch nicht angerufen hat; ob er mir böse ist?—Warum soll er dir böse sein? Er wird (wohl) noch schlafen.	I'd like to know why Peter hasn't called me up yet. I wonder whether he's mad at me.—Why should he be mad at you? He's probably still asleep.	
Den Helmut habe ich schon wochenlang nicht gesehen. Wo kann der denn nur sein?—Er wird wieder in Essen arbeiten müssen.	I haven't seen Helmut in weeks. Where could he be?—He probably has to work in Essen again.	

[2] Wishes with Past Subjunctive

Ich wollte, ich hätte heute abend nicht so viel *gegessen*. Aber leider *habe* ich zuviel gegessen.	I wish I hadn't *eaten* so much tonight. But unfortunately I *did* eat too much.	SEE ANALYSIS 105–107 (pp. 173–177)
Ich wünschte, Ingelheim hätte gestern abend nicht nur von seinen *Brief*tauben geredet. Von seinen Kriegsromanen hat er *gar* nicht gesprochen.	I wish Ingelheim hadn't just talked about his *carrier* pigeons last night. He didn't talk at *all* about his war novels.	

Poster for adult education on a kiosk in Vienna.

Es wäre nett gewesen, wenn du meinen *Geburts*tag nicht wieder vergessen hättest. Aber natürlich *hast* du ihn wieder vergessen.

It would have been nice if you hadn't forgotten my *birthday* again. But of course you *did* forget it again.

Wenn wir doch nur an die *Ostsee* gefahren wären. Warum *sind* wir eigentlich nicht an die Ostsee gefahren?

If only we had gone to the *Baltic*. Why *didn't* we go to the Baltic?

Wenn wir doch nur zu *Hause* geblieben wären. *Müllers* waren ver*nün*ftig. *Die sind* zu Hause geblieben.

If we had only stayed at *home*. The *Müllers* were *intelligent*. *They did* stay at home.

VARIATIONS

Complete the following wishes, changing from negative to positive, and vice versa.

Mein Mann ist gestern nach Lübeck gefahren. Wenn mein Mann gestern doch nur

_____.

Ich bin leider zu schnell gefahren. Ich wollte, ich _____ nicht so schnell _____.

Ich habe leider meinen Paß verloren. Ich wollte, ich _____ meinen Paß _____.

Leider haben wir das Haus nicht gekauft. Wenn wir das Haus doch nur _____.

Du hast mir nicht genug Geld geschickt. Es wäre gut gewesen, wenn du mir mehr Geld

_____.

Mosers sind gestern abend viel zu lange geblieben. Ich wünschte, Mosers _____ gestern abend nicht so lange _____.

Ich habe meinen Mantel zu Hause gelassen. Ich wollte, ich _____ meinen Mantel

_____.

Du warst gestern leider nicht zu Hause. Ich wollte, du _____ gestern zu Hause

_____.

[3] Irreal **wenn**-Clauses with Past Subjunctive

SEE
ANALYSIS
105–107
(pp. 173-177)

Wenn sie mir ge*schrie*ben hätte, hätte ich ihr *auch* geschrieben.

If she had *written* to me, I would have written to her, *too*.

Na*tür*lich hätte ich ihr geschrieben, wenn sie mir geschrieben hätte.

Of *course* I would have written to her if she had written to me.

Wenn es gestern nicht ge*reg*net hätte, hätten wir in den *Schwarz*wald fahren können. Aber es *hat* geregnet, und wir konnten *nicht* in den Schwarzwald fahren.

If it had not *rained* yesterday, we could have driven to the Black *Forest*. But it *did* rain, and we could *not* drive to the Black Forest.

Nein, wir wären *nicht* so bald nach Hause gefahren, wenn das *Essen* nicht so schlecht gewesen wäre. Und das Essen war wirklich *sehr* schlecht.

No, we *wouldn't* have gone home so soon if the *food* had not been so bad. And the food was really *very* bad.

Wenn Ingelheim nicht von *Gisela* geredet hätte, wäre seine Frau *nicht* zu ihrer Mutter gefahren.

If Ingelheim had not talked about *Gisela*, his wife would *not* have gone to her mother.

VARIATIONS

Change the following pairs of sentences into irreal **wenn**-clauses with irreal conclusions.

Es war neblig, und wir konnten die Berge nicht sehen. Wenn es nicht so neblig _____, _____ wir die Berge _____.

Erika studierte *auch* Germanistik, und so haben wir uns kennengelernt. Wenn Erika nicht *auch* Germanistik _____, _____ wir uns nicht _____.

Ich hatte kein Geld. Ich konnte nicht nach Österreich fahren. Wenn ich Geld _____ _____, _____ ich nach Österreich _____.

[4] Past Subjunctive in Irreal Statements with **gerne, lieber, am liebsten**

Meyers hätten gerne ein *Mäd*chen gehabt, aber jetzt haben sie wieder einen *Jun*gen.

The Meyers would rather have had a *girl*, but now they have another *boy*.

SEE ANALYSIS 105–107
(pp. 173-177)

Ich wäre viel lieber in den *Zoo* gegangen. Aber Tante Amalie wollte ins M*u*seum.

I would much rather have gone to the *zoo*, but Aunt Amalie wanted (to go) to the *museum*.

Wir wären gestern abend am liebsten zu *Hau*se geblieben. Aber Kellers hatten uns Karten für den "*Sommernachtstraum*" geschickt. Und da konnten wir natürlich *nicht* zu Hause bleiben.

We would have liked very much to stay at *home* last night. But the Kellers had sent us tickets for "Midsummer Night's *Dream*." So we *couldn't* stay at home, of course.

VARIATIONS

Change the following factual statements with **leider** into irreal statements of preference.

Helga hat leider nicht geheiratet. Helga _____ natürlich sehr gerne _____.

Letztes Jahr sind wir leider nicht nach Europa gefahren. Letztes Jahr _____ wir gerne _____.

Wir haben gestern abend keinen Wein getrunken. Wir _____ gestern abend gerne einmal eine Flasche Wein _____.

Leider schickte man ihn an die Front. Er _____ viel lieber hinter der Front Brieftauben _____. (**füttern**)

Leider sind wir nicht nach Braunschweig gezogen. Am liebsten _____.

[5] Wishes with **würde**-Forms

SEE
ANALYSIS
108

(pp. 177-179)

Ich wünschte, ihr würdet endlich heiraten. Wie lange wollt ihr denn noch warten?	I wish you'd finally get married. How long do you want to wait anyway?
Es wäre gut, wenn meine Frau endlich fahren lernen würde.	It would be good if my wife would finally learn how to drive.
Ich wollte, wir würden endlich einen Fernseher kaufen.	I wish we'd finally buy a TV.
Wenn Ingelheim doch nur aufhören würde, immer von seinen Brieftauben zu reden.	If Ingelheim would only stop talking about his pigeons all the time.

VARIATIONS

Using the infinitive phrases **einmal zusammen in die Berge fahren, nach München ziehen, nicht schon wieder regnen,** express a wish using **wenn doch nur** phrases.

[6] The **würde**-Form in Irreal Speculations

SEE
ANALYSIS
108

(pp. 177-179)

Professor Schnarf würde *nie* zugeben, daß er *auch* nicht alles weiß.	Professor Schnarf would *never* admit that he doesn't know everything *either*.
Ich würde gerne einmal drei Wochen mit dir verschwinden. Aber haben wir so viel Zeit?	I'd love to disappear with you for three weeks sometime. But do we have that much time?
Am liebsten würde ich ein Mädchen wie Ursula heiraten. Aber leider *ist* sie schon verheiratet.	I'd like nothing better than to marry a girl like Ursula. But unfortunately she's married *already*.
Wir würden ja viel lieber in München wohnen. Aber mein Mann arbeitet ja hier in Augsburg.	We'd much rather live in Munich, but, as you know, my husband works here in Augsburg.

VARIATIONS

Mein Mann arbeitet in Augsburg, aber er _____ viel lieber in München _____.

Mein Mann will, daß ich ihm einen Hut kaufe, aber ich _____ ihm viel lieber einen Mantel _____.

Ich soll immer von meinen Kriegsromanen reden, aber ich _____ viel lieber von meinen Brieftauben _____.

[7] The Present Subjunctive of **haben, sein,** and the Modals in Wishes

SEE
ANALYSIS
109

(pp. 179-181)

Wenn wir doch nur wenigstens *ein* Mädchen hätten.	If only we had at least one girl.

Wenn du doch nur nicht immer so pessimistisch wärst. | If only you weren't always so pessimistic.

Es wäre nett, wenn wir nächstes Jahr wieder nach Tirol fahren könnten. | It would be nice if we could go to the Tyrol again next year.

Ich wollte, Meyer müßte auch jeden Tag acht Stunden arbeiten. | I wish Meyer would have to work eight hours every day, too.

Ich wollte, deine Tochter dürfte uns einmal besuchen. | I wish your daughter could visit us sometime.

VARIATIONS

Change the following factual statements into irreal wishes.

Marie Luise ist leider nicht glücklich. Ich wollte, sie _____ glücklich.

Rückers haben nur zwei Söhne. Ich wünschte, sie _____ auch eine Tochter.

Franz-Josef Rohrmoser hat so viel Geld, daß er nicht zu arbeiten braucht. Es wäre gut, wenn Rohrmoser nicht so viel Geld _____. Dann _____ er *auch* arbeiten.

Meine Frau kann leider nicht fahren. Wenn meine Frau doch nur fahren _____.

[8] Irreal Conditions in the Present Subjunctive of haben, sein, and the Modals

Wenn wir wollten, könnten wir auch jedes Jahr in die Alpen fahren. Aber wir wollen gar nicht. | If we wanted to, we could go to the Alps too every year. But we don't want to.

Wenn ich nicht so allergisch gegen Katzen wäre, hätten wir auch eine Katze. | If I weren't so allergic to cats, we would have a cat, too.

Nein, Dr. Möllenhoff hat mir nicht verboten zu schwimmen. Ich dürfte jeden Tag schwimmen, wenn ich wollte, nur radfahren darf ich nicht. | No, Dr. Möllenhoff did not forbid me to swim. I could swim every day if I wanted to. I just mustn't ride a bike.

Ich wäre *glück*lich, wenn ich jeden Tag in die Stadt fahren müßte. Ich bin viel zu viel allein. | *I* would be *happy* if I had to go to town every day. I am much too much alone.

SEE ANALYSIS 109 (pp. 179-181)

VARIATIONS

Change the following pairs of sentences to irreal conclusions and irreal **wenn**-clauses.

Ich brauche nicht so schwer zu arbeiten wie Meyer. Ich bin sonntags nicht zu müde, im Garten zu arbeiten. Wenn ich so schwer arbeiten _____ wie Meyer, _____ ich sonntags zu müde, im Garten zu arbeiten.

Meine Frau kann gottseidank fahren. Darum haben wir zwei Autos. Wenn meine Frau nicht fahren _____, _____ wir nur ein Auto.

Ich bin nicht unglücklich, denn ich darf wieder schwimmen. Ich _____ unglücklich, wenn ich nicht wieder schwimmen _____.

[9] Irreal Statements with the Present Subjunctive of haben, sein, and the Modals

SEE
ANALYSIS
109

(pp. 179-181)

Du hast recht. Ich sollte nicht so viel rauchen.

You are right. I shouldn't smoke so much.

Du hast recht. Ich müßte jeden Tag eine halbe Stunde schwimmen.

You are right. I ought to swim for half an hour every day.

Wir hätten viel lieber ein Haus mit einer Terrasse. Dann könnten wir im Sommer auf der Terrasse schlafen.

We'd much rather have a house with a terrace. Then we could sleep on the terrace during the summer.

Natürlich könnten wir dieses Haus in der Stadt verkaufen und ein Landhaus kaufen. Aber dann wärst du eine "grüne Witwe" und genau so unglücklich wie deine Freundin.

Of course we could sell this house in the city and buy a country place. But then you'd be a "green widow" and you'd be just as unhappy as your friend.

VARIATIONS

Du _____ (sollen) wirklich jeden Tag eine halbe Stunde schwimmen.

Du _____ (können) ja auch jeden Tag eine halbe Stunde schwimmen.

Du _____ (müssen) jeden Tag mit dem Rad in die Stadt fahren. Dann _____ (sein) du nicht so dick.

Wir _____ (haben) auch gerne ein Auto. Dann _____ (können) wir jedes Wochenende in die Berge fahren.

[10] Wishes with Present Subjunctives of Other Verbs

SEE
ANALYSIS
110

(pp. 181-184)

Ich wünschte, das Haus gehörte uns.

I wish that house belonged to us.

Wäre es nicht nett, wenn das Haus uns gehörte (gehören würde)?

Wouldn't it be nice if that house belonged to us?

Es wäre wirklich sehr nett, wenn Sie uns morgen die Stadt zeigten (zeigen würden).

It would really be very nice if you showed (would show) us the town tomorrow.

Wenn ich doch nur wüßte, ob mein Mann noch lebt.

If I only knew whether my husband is still alive.

Wenn doch nur endlich die Sonne wieder schiene (scheinen würde).

If only the sun would shine again at last.

Ich wünschte, du gingst nicht jeden Abend erst nach zwölf ins Bett (du würdest

I wish you didn't go to bed (as late as) after midnight every night.

nicht jeden Abend erst nach zwölf ins Bett gehen).

[11] Irreal Conditions with Other Verbs

| | | SEE ANALYSIS 110 (pp. 181-184) |

Wenn mein Mann stürbe, müßte ich zu meiner Mutter ziehen.

If my husband died, I'd have to move in with my mother.

Wenn wir keinen Hund und keine Kinder hätten, fänden wir sofort eine Wohnung (würden wir sofort eine Wohnung finden).

If we had no dog and no children, we'd immediately find an apartment.

Wenn du wüßtest, was ich weiß, hättest du auch Angst.

If you knew what I know, you would be afraid too.

VARIATIONS

Du gehst nicht früh genug ins Bett. Du kommst jeden Morgen zu spät.

Wenn du früh genug ins Bett gingst, _____ du nicht jeden Morgen zu spät.
_____ du nicht jeden Morgen zu spät _____.

Wir spielen Freitag abends immer bis zwei Uhr Bridge. Darum fahren wir nicht jeden Samstag in die Berge.

Wenn wir Freitag abends nicht immer so lange Bridge spielten,
_____ wir jeden Samstag in die Berge.
_____ wir jeden Samstag in die Berge _____.

[12] Irreal Statements with Other Verbs

| | | SEE ANALYSIS 110 (pp. 181-184) |

Ich würde Lieselotte sofort heiraten. Aber sie will mich nicht.

I'd marry Lieselotte immediately, but she doesn't want me.

Wen *würde* sie denn heiraten?—Das hat sie mir nicht gesagt.

Whom *would* she marry?—She didn't tell me that.

Es ist wirklich kalt heute abend. *Ich* ließe meinen Mantel *nicht* zu Hause (würde meinen Mantel *nicht* zu Hause lassen).

It's really cold tonight. *I wouldn't* leave my coat at home.

Wenn Kufners ins Kino gehen, lassen sie ihre Kinder einfach allein zu Hause. Wir würden unsere Kinder nie allein lassen.

When the Kufners go to the movies, they just leave their children alone at home. We would never leave our children alone.

Du willst Günter DM 200 für ein Motorrad leihen? Nein, das täte ich nicht (würde ich nicht tun).

You want to lend Günter 200 marks for a motorcycle? No, I wouldn't do that.

Du willst Ulrich anrufen? *Ich* riefe ihn *nicht* an (würde ihn *nicht* anrufen). Ich würde warten, bis *er* anruft.

You want to call Ulrich? I wouldn't do that. I'd wait until *he* calls.

Ich weiß, Meyers wohnen jetzt in Berlin. Wir wohnten natürlich auch lieber in Berlin.

Wollen Sie nicht einmal an die Front, Ingelheim?—Nein, ich würde lieber wieder Brieftauben füttern. Die tun einem nichts.	Would you like to be sent to the front, Ingelheim?—No, I'd rather feed pigeons again. They don't hurt you.
Ich weiß, du gingst viel lieber mit Erika ins Kino (würdest viel lieber mit Erika ins Kino gehen). Und du lädst mich nur ein, weil du sie ärgern willst.	I know you'd much rather take Erika to the movies; and you invite me only because you want to make her angry.
Würdest du es mir wirklich sagen, wenn du es wüßtest?—Ich weiß nicht, ob ich es dir sagen würde.	Would you really tell me (about) it, if you knew it?—I don't know whether I'd tell you.

VARIATIONS

Using both the simple subjunctive and the **würde**-form, formulate some irreal preferential statements, replacing **leider** by **am liebsten.**

Wir fahren nächstes Jahr leider nicht nach Deutschland.
Leider gehen wir heute nicht schwimmen.
Wir spielen leider nicht Golf.
Wir wohnen leider nicht in Freiburg.

[13] **hätte** in Dependent Clauses with "Double Infinitive"

SEE ANALYSIS 112 (pp. 184-185)

Wenn Dora nicht hätte nach München fahren müssen, hätte Schulz sie nie kennengelernt.*	If Dora hadn't had to go to Munich, Schulz would never have met her.
Wenn du nicht hättest kommen können, wäre ich sehr unglücklich gewesen.	If you had not been able to come, I would have been very unhappy.
Wenn er gestern abend nicht hätte zu Hause bleiben müssen, hätte er mit uns ins Kino gehen können.	If he had not had to stay home last night, he could have gone to the movies with us.

VARIATIONS

Wolfgang konnte nicht kommen. Es wäre nett gewesen, wenn ———————

* In irreal **wenn**-clauses, **nicht müssen** is used rather than **nicht brauchen zu.**

PATTERNS

Warum jeder, der im Wirtschaftsleben steht, eine American Express Karte haben sollte

Andrea durfte nicht mitgehen. Es wäre nett gewesen, wenn _____.
Bernhard mußte zu Hause bleiben. Es wäre nett gewesen, wenn _____.
Sie hat nie zu kochen brauchen. Es wäre nett gewesen, wenn sie auch einmal _____.

[14] Polite Requests

Invent variations of your own.

Könnte (Kann) ich noch eine Tasse Kaffee haben?	Could I have another cup of coffee?	SEE ANALYSIS 111 (p. 184)

Guten Abend! Hätten (Haben) Sie vielleicht noch ein Zimmer frei?

Good evening! Do you by any chance still have a room available?

Könnten (können) Sie mir vielleicht sagen, ob die Maschine aus Hamburg schon angekommen ist?

Could you perhaps tell me whether the flight from Hamburg has arrived yet?

Dürfte ich Sie bitten, mir den Wein ins Haus zu schicken?

Could I ask you to deliver the wine to my house?

Guten Morgen! Könnten Sie mir bitte Zimmer 6 geben? Danke schön!

Good morning! Would you connect me with room 6, please? Thank you.

Könnten (Würden) Sie mich morgen um zehn anrufen?

Could you call me up at ten tomorrow?

Ich hätte gerne einen Kriminalroman.

I would like to have a detective story.

Haben Sie noch ein Zimmer frei? Ich hätte gern ein Zimmer mit Bad.

Do you still have a room available? I would like to have a room with bath.

[15] Indirect Discourse: Present and Future Time

Be prepared to change orally all statements in direct discourse to indirect discourse, and vice versa.

Hans sagte: „Mein Vater bleibt noch in Salzburg."
   Hans sagte, sein Vater bliebe noch in Salzburg.
   Hans sagte, sein Vater würde noch in Salzburg bleiben.

SEE ANALYSIS 117 (pp. 186-188)

Frau Lenz sagte: „Ulrike wohnt nicht mehr in Bremen.“
Frau Lenz sagte, du wohntest nicht mehr in Bremen.
Frau Lenz glaubte, du würdest wohl nicht mehr in Bremen wohnen.

Inge sagte: „Erika fährt morgen nach Nürnberg.“
Inge sagte, Erika führe morgen nach Nürnberg.
Inge sagte, Erika würde morgen nach Nürnberg fahren.
Inge sagte, daß Erika morgen nach Nürnberg führe.
Inge sagte, daß Erika morgen nach Nürnberg fahren würde.

Meyer sagte, sein Frau lernte jetzt fahren.
Meyer sagte, er studierte Anthropologie.
Meyer sagte, er wollte seinen Vater besuchen.
Meyer sagte, er müßte morgen arbeiten.
Meyer sagte, er brauchte nicht nach Köln zu fahren.
Meyer sagte, der Film wäre sehr gut.
Meyer sagte, das wäre ihm recht.
Meyer sagte, Erika hätte heute keine Zeit.
Meyer sagte, er ginge mit Inge ins Kino.
Meyer sagte, sie kämen heute sehr spät nach Hause.

[16] Indirect Questions: Present and Future Time

Be prepared to transform orally all direct questions into indirect
questions, and vice versa.

SEE
ANALYSIS
117
(pp. 186-188)

Er fragte: „Ist dein Vater heute abend zu Hause?“
Er fragte, ob mein Vater heute abend zu Hause wäre.
Er fragte: „Wohin geht ihr heute abend zum Essen?“
Er fragte, wohin wir heute abend zum Essen gingen.
Er fragte: „Kommt Fritz morgen?“
Er wollte wissen, ob Fritz morgen käme.

Er fragte, ob ich krank wäre.
Er fragte, ob wir das Haus in Wiesbaden kaufen wollten.
Er fragte, ob er mich zum Bahnhof bringen dürfte.
Er fragte mich, warum ich denn nicht mit nach Bern führe.
Er wollte wissen, ob Maria zu Hause wäre.
Er wollte wissen, warum Hans nicht mitgehen könnte.

[17] Indirect Discourse: Past Time

SEE
ANALYSIS
117
(pp. 186-188)

Be prepared to transform direct statements into indirect statements,
and vice versa.

Er sagte: „Ich arbeitete damals in Hamburg.“
Er sagte, daß er damals in Hamburg gearbeitet hätte.

Er sagte: „Ich habe damals in Hamburg gearbeitet."
Er sagte, daß er damals in Hamburg gearbeitet hätte.
Er sagte: „Ich hatte gerade eine Woche in Hamburg gearbeitet."
Er sagte, daß er gerade eine Woche in Hamburg gearbeitet hätte.

Er sagte, außer Ernst und seiner Frau wäre niemand da gewesen.
Er sagte, kein Mensch hätte ihm geglaubt.
Frau Schmidt sagte, ihr Mann hätte nach Afrika fahren wollen.
Frau Schmidt sagte, Johannes hätte nach Kairo fahren müssen.

[18] Indirect Questions: Past Time

Be prepared to transform direct questions into indirect questions,
and vice versa.

Er fragte: „Warum sind Sie denn gestern nicht nach Graz gefahren?"
Er fragte, warum ich denn gestern nicht nach Graz gefahren wäre.
Er fragte: „Mit wem warst du denn gestern abend im Theater?"
Er wollte wissen, mit wem ich gestern abend im Theater gewesen wäre.

Er wollte wissen, wieviel die Zigarren gekostet hätten.
Er wollte wissen, wie lange ich für die Lufthansa gearbeitet hätte.

SEE
ANALYSIS
117
(pp. 186-188)

Conversation

I

ERIKA: Du Hans, Tante Amalie hat angerufen.

HANS: Was wollte sie denn?

ERIKA: Sie wollte wissen, ob du heute nachmittag mit ihr ins Museum gehen könntest.

HANS: Du hast ihr doch hoffentlich gesagt, ich wäre heute nicht zu Hause.

ERIKA: Nein, ich dachte, du würdest gerne mit ihr gehen.

HANS: Das hättest du nicht tun sollen.

ERIKA: Ja, wenn ich gewußt hätte, daß du nicht willst, dann hätte ich ihr natürlich gesagt, du könntest heute nicht. Aber ich dachte, . . .

HANS: Du solltest nicht immer so viel denken.

II

TANTE AMALIE: Das war wirklich nett von dir, daß du mit mir ins Museum gegangen bist. Und jetzt würde ich gerne noch eine Tasse Kaffee trinken.

HANS: Das ist mir recht. Wo möchtest du denn hin?

TANTE AMALIE: Ich ginge gerne mal ins Café Schneider; da war ich schon lange nicht mehr.

HANS: Gut, und dann könnten wir Erika anrufen. Sie käme sicher auch gerne.

TANTE AMALIE: Ja, und wie wäre es, wenn ihr dann zum Abendessen zu mir kommen würdet?

HANS: Das wäre sehr nett, Tante Amalie, aber ich kann leider nicht; ich habe zu viel zu tun.

TANTE AMALIE: Wenn du nur nicht immer so viel arbeiten müßtest!

HANS: Ja, aber ohne meine Arbeit wäre das Leben nur halb so schön.

III

ERIKA: Na, Hans, wie war's denn?

HANS: Ach, weißt du, Tante Amalie ist ja eigentlich sehr nett. Wenn sie nur nicht immer so viel reden würde.

ERIKA: Dann wäre sie nicht Tante Amalie.

HANS: Weißt du, sie hat mir erzählt, daß sie gestern bei Overhoffs den Museumsdirektor kennengelernt hat. Sie sagte, er wäre sehr interessant und hätte ihr sehr viel über Picasso erzählt.

ERIKA: Nun, wenn sie jetzt den Direktor kennt, brauchst du vielleicht nicht mehr so oft mit ihr ins Museum zu gehen.

HANS: Ja, und wenn sie den Direktor heiraten würde, brauchte ich nie mehr mit ihr ins Museum zu gehen. Dann könnte sie im Museum wohnen.

ERIKA: Hans, das ist nicht sehr nett von dir.

Reading

JOHANNES SCHMIDT-INGELHEIM

Eine unmögliche Geschichte

Dieses Wochenende werde ich nicht vergessen, auch wenn ich noch hundert Jahre leben sollte. Natürlich wird mir kein Mensch glauben, was ich erlebt habe. Aber wahr ist es doch.

eine unmögliche Geschichte an impossible story

Die Geschichte fing Freitag morgen in Tripolis an, das heißt, eigentlich hat sie schon angefangen, als wir noch mit Rommel in 5 Afrika gegen die Amerikaner kämpften.

Mein Schulfreund Hermann Schneider, Erich Karsten und ich wohnten damals in Tripolis bei dem Ägypter Ali und seiner Frau Busuq. Ali war ungefähr sechzig; Busuq war mindestens achtzig. Vor Busuq

hatten wir alle Angst. Wenn wir mit ihr sprachen, hatten wir das
Gefühl: sie sieht dich nicht nur an, sie sieht durch dich durch. Nur
Erich hatte keine Angst vor ihr. Für ihn war diese Frau eine
Königin. Er brachte ihr immer etwas mit, wenn er ins Haus kam, 5
und man sah, es machte ihn glücklich, wenn sie seine Geschenke
annahm.

Einmal, als wir nicht weit von der Stadt an unserem Wagen ar-   **Wir warfen uns zu**
beiteten, erschienen plötzlich ein paar englische Tiefflieger. Wir   **Boden** we threw our-
warfen uns zu Boden, aber nicht schnell genug. Als wir wieder auf- 10 selves on the ground
standen, blieb Erich mit einer Kopfwunde wie tot liegen.

Wir fuhren mit ihm nach Tripolis zurück. Als Busuq Erichs Wunde
sah, befahl sie uns, ihn ins Haus zu bringen. Wir hatten, wie immer,
Angst vor ihr. Darum gehorchten wir und brachten ihn ins Haus.
Wir konnten aber nicht bei ihm bleiben und kamen erst nach 15
vierzehn Tagen wieder zurück. Erich war noch schwach, aber die
Wunde war gottseidank geheilt.

Doch Erich war nicht mehr unser Erich. Er redete nicht mehr so viel
wie früher, und seine Augen schienen sagen zu wollen: Ich weiß
etwas, was ihr nicht wißt. Außerdem sah er oft stundenlang irgend- 20
wohin in die Ferne und war sozusagen einfach nicht da.

Nun, Hermann und ich hatten keine Zeit, Erich zu analysieren. Die
Situation in Afrika war damals schon gefährlich, und wir fragten uns
oft: Wie kommt ihr nur zurück nach Deutschland?

Zwei oder drei Wochen später saßen Hermann und ich in Alis Haus 25
und schrieben Briefe. Erich saß bei uns und war wieder einmal
sozusagen nicht da. Aber plötzlich sah er mich mit seinem Ich-weiß-
etwas-was-du-nicht-weißt Blick an und sagte: „Weißt du, daß deine
Frau dir gerade einen Brief schreibt, um dir zu erzählen, daß deine
Tochter schon bis fünf zählen kann?" Niemand lachte. Ich wußte 30
nicht, was ich denken sollte.

Ungefähr zehn Tage später flog man Hermann und mich nach
Deutschland. Erich blieb in Afrika zurück. Wie lange er noch bei
der Ägypterin gewesen ist, weiß ich nicht. Ich habe ihn erst dieses
Wochenende wiedergesehen.   35

Kurz vor dem Abflug nach Deutschland aber bekam ich damals noch
einen Brief von meiner Frau. Was sie schrieb, machte mich unruhig.
„Es wäre wirklich nett", schrieb sie, „wenn Du* hier wärst. Du
hättest sehen sollen, wie Dein Töchterchen heute morgen an den
Fingern bis fünf gezählt . . . Du, Hans, was ich gerade erlebt habe, 40
ist wirklich unglaublich, und ich muß mich zwingen, ruhig zu

---

* In letters, all pronouns of direct address must be capitalized (**Du, Dich, Dein,
Ihr,** etc.).

bleiben. Ich hatte beim Schreiben plötzlich das Gefühl, daß jemand hinter mir stand. Ich fühlte es. Ich wußte einfach, daß jemand hinter mir stand. Ich saß eine Zeitlang still, dann sprang ich auf. Niemand war im Zimmer. Aber Hans, auf dem Boden waren Fußabdrücke, wie Du sie machst, wenn Du mit Deinen Militärschuhen ₅ nach Hause kommst. Du darfst nicht lachen. Ich weiß, was ich Dir schreibe, kann einfach nicht passieren. Aber es *ist* passiert!—Oder ist es doch nicht passiert? Hans, ich bin einfach zu viel allein."

(Fortsetzung folgt)

BERTOLT BRECHT

Bertolt Brecht (born 1898 in Augsburg) was one of the major figures in German literature during the first half of this century, and also one of the most controversial. Though best known in America for his plays, for example, *Mutter Courage, Der gute Mensch von Sezuan, Der kaukasische Kreidekreis,* he also produced poetry and prose. In 1933, he emigrated from National Socialist Germany, first to Denmark, then to Finland, and then, via Siberia, to the United States. He lived in California until 1948, then returned to East Berlin, where he died in 1956. The following story is from his *Geschichten vom Herrn Keuner.*

This text by Bertolt Brecht is unedited and an exact reprint of the original. The verb forms used are almost entirely in the subjunctive. Two of these subjunctive forms, **sei** and **bestehe,** will be introduced in Unit 7.

Since the text contains some structural patterns and a number of words with which you are not familiar, we have added an English translation.

We advise you to first read the entire text in English from beginning to end. Then reread the English text sentence by sentence and compare each sentence with its German equivalent. Pay no attention to adjective endings; they will be introduced in Unit 10. Finally, you should be able to read the German text with almost complete comprehension.

Wenn die Haifische Menschen wären

„Wenn die Haifische Menschen wären", fragte Herrn K. die kleine Tochter seiner Wirtin, „wären sie dann netter zu den kleinen Fischen?" „Sicher", sagte er. „Wenn die Haifische Menschen wären, würden sie ₅ im Meer für die kleinen Fische gewaltige Kästen bauen lassen, mit allerhand Nahrung drin, sowohl Pflanzen als auch Tierzeug. Sie würden sorgen, daß die Kästen immer frisches Wasser hätten, und sie würden ₁₀

If Sharks Were People

"If sharks were people," the landlady's little daughter asked Mr. K., "would they be nicer to the little fishes?"
"Certainly," he said. "If sharks were people they would have enormous boxes built in the sea for the little fishes with all sorts of things to eat in them, plants as well as animal matter.

They would see to it that the boxes always had fresh water and, in gen-

Bertolt Brecht.

überhaupt allerhand sanitäre Maßnahmen treffen. Wenn zum Beispiel ein Fischlein sich die Flosse verletzen würde, dann würde ihm sogleich ein Verband gemacht, damit es den Haifischen nicht wegstürbe 5 vor der Zeit. Damit die Fischlein nicht trübsinnig würden, gäbe es ab und zu große Wasserfeste; denn lustige Fischlein schmekken besser als trübsinnige. Es gäbe natürlich auch Schulen in den großen Kästen. In 10 diesen Schulen würden die Fischlein lernen, wie man in den Rachen der Haifische schwimmt. Sie würden zum Beispiel Geographie brauchen, damit sie die großen Haifische, die faul irgendwo liegen, finden 15 könnten. Die Hauptsache wäre natürlich die moralische Ausbildung des Fischleins. Sie würden unterrichtet werden, daß es das Größte und Schönste sei, wenn ein Fischlein sich freudig aufopfert, und daß sie alle an 20 die Haifische glauben müßten, vor allem, wenn sie sagten, sie würden für eine schöne Zukunft sorgen. Man würde den Fischlein beibringen, daß diese Zukunft nur gesichert sei, wenn sie Gehorsam lernten. Vor allen 25 niedrigen, materialistischen, egoistischen und marxistischen Neigungen müßten sich die Fischlein hüten und es sofort den Haifischen melden, wenn eines von ihnen solche Neigungen verriete. Wenn die 30 Haifische Menschen wären, würden sie natürlich auch untereinander Kriege führen, um fremde Fischkästen und fremde Fischlein zu erobern. Die Kriege würden sie von

eral, take hygienic measures of all kinds. For instance, if a little fish injured one of its fins, it would be bandaged at once, so that the sharks should not be deprived of it by an untimely death. To prevent the little fishes from growing depressed there would be big water festivals from time to time, for happy little fishes taste better than miserable ones. Of course there would also be schools in the big boxes. In these schools the little fishes would learn how to swim into the sharks' jaws. They would need geography, for example, so that when the big sharks were lazing about somewhere they could find them.

The main thing, of course, would be the moral education of the little fishes. They would be taught that the greatest and finest thing is for a little fish to sacrifice its life gladly, and that they must all believe in the sharks, particularly when they promise a splendid future. They would impress upon the little fishes that this future could only be assured if they learned obedience. The little fishes would have to guard against all base, materialistic, egotistic, and Marxist tendencies, reporting at once to the sharks if any of their number manifested such tendencies.

If sharks were people they would also, naturally, wage wars among themselves, to conquer foreign fish boxes and little foreign fishes. They would let their own little fishes fight these

ihren eigenen Fischlein führen lassen. Sie
würden die Fischlein lehren, daß zwischen
ihnen und den Fischlein der anderen Haifische ein riesiger Unterschied bestehe. Die
Fischlein, würden sie verkünden, sind be- 5
kanntlich stumm, aber sie schweigen in
ganz verschiedenen Sprachen und können
einander daher unmöglich verstehen. Jedem
Fischlein, das im Krieg ein paar andere
Fischlein, feindliche, in anderer Sprache 10
schweigende Fischlein tötete, würden sie
einen kleinen Orden aus Seetang anheften
und den Titel Held verleihen. Wenn die
Haifische Menschen wären, gäbe es bei
ihnen natürlich auch eine Kunst. Es gäbe 15
schöne Bilder, auf denen die Zähne der
Haifische in prächtigen Farben, ihre Rachen
als reine Lustgärten, in denen es sich
prächtig tummeln läßt, dargestellt wären.
Die Theater auf dem Meeresgrund würden 20
zeigen, wie heldenmütige Fischlein begei-
stert in die Haifischrachen schwimmen, und
die Musik wäre so schön, daß die Fischlein
unter ihren Klängen, die Kapelle voran,
träumerisch, und in allerangenehmste Ge- 25
danken eingelullt, in die Haifischrachen
strömten. Auch eine Religion gäbe es ja,
wenn die Haifische Menschen wären. Sie
würden lehren, daß die Fischlein erst im
Bauche der Haifische richtig zu leben 30
begännen. Übrigens würde es auch aufhören, wenn die Haifische Menschen wären,
daß alle Fischlein, wie es jetzt ist, gleich
sind. Einige von ihnen würden Ämter bekommen und über die anderen gesetzt 35
werden. Die ein wenig größeren dürften
sogar die kleineren auffressen. Das wäre für
die Haifische nur angenehm, da sie dann
selber öfter größere Brocken zu fressen be-
kämen. Und die größern, Posten habenden 40
Fischlein würden für die Ordnung unter
den Fischlein sorgen, Lehrer, Offiziere, Ingenieure im Kastenbau usw. werden. Kurz,
es gäbe überhaupt erst eine Kultur im Meer,
wenn die Haifische Menschen wären."

wars. They would teach the little fishes that
there was a vast difference between themselves and the little fishes of other sharks.

Little fishes, they would proclaim, are well
known to be dumb, but they are silent in
quite different languages and therefore cannot possibly understand each other. Each
little fish which killed a few other little
fishes in war—little enemy fishes, dumb in
a different language—would have a little
seaweed medal pinned on it and be awarded
the title of Hero.

     If sharks were people they
would also have art, naturally. There would
be lovely pictures representing sharks' teeth
in glorious colors, their jaws as positive
pleasure grounds in which it would be a joy
to gambol.

     The seabed theaters would show
heroic little fishes swimming rapturously
into sharks' jaws, and the music would be
so beautiful that to its strains the little fishes,
headed by the band, would pour dreamily
into the sharks' jaws, lulled in the most de-
lightful thoughts. There would also be a
religion if sharks were people.

     It would
teach that little fishes only really start to
live inside the bellies of sharks. Moreover,
if sharks were people, not all little fishes
would be equal anymore, as they are now.
Some of them would be given positions and
be set over the others. The slightly bigger
ones would even be allowed to gobble up
the smaller ones. That would give nothing
but pleasure to the sharks, since they would
more often get larger morsels for themselves. And the bigger little fishes, those
holding positions, would be responsible for
keeping order among the little fishes, become teachers, officers, box-building engineers, and so on. In short, the sea would
only start being civilized if sharks were
people."

Analysis

104 The Future

Formation

The German future is formed by using **werden** as an auxiliary in the first prong and any infinitive in the second prong.

ich werde ...sein	ich werde ...haben	ich werde ...fahren
du wirst ...sein	du wirst ...haben	du wirst ...fahren
er wird ...sein	er wird ...haben	er wird ...fahren
wir werden ...sein	wir werden ...haben	wir werden ...fahren
ihr werdet ...sein	ihr werdet ...haben	ihr werdet ...fahren
sie werden ...sein	sie werden ...haben	sie werden ...fahren

Use

Since the present tense can refer to future time, the future tense is comparatively rare. One usually hears

Ich fahre morgen nach Berlin

but it is also perfectly normal to say

Ich werde morgen nach Berlin fahren.

If a sentence contains no time phrase, the future is used more frequently in order to avoid ambiguity.

Ihr werdet ja sehen, wie es ist.   You'll see how it is.

Very frequently, future forms express not futurity but present probability. Such a probability statement often contains adverbs such as **wohl** (*probably*), **sicher** (*certainly*), **vielleicht** (*perhaps*), and **wahrscheinlich** (*probably*).

Es ist jetzt sieben. Inge wird wohl (sicher, wahrscheinlich) schon zu Hause sein.   It's seven o'clock now. Inge is probably at home by now.

105 Indicative and Subjunctive: Definitions

All verbal forms used in Units 1 to 5 referred to facts. That is to say, they were used in a context of reality to express real events (or, occasionally, open conditions).

> **Ich weiß nicht, ob sie an der Riviera wohnen. Aber wenn sie an der Riviera wohnen, müssen sie Geld haben.**
>
> I don't know whether they live on the Riviera. But if they live on the Riviera, they must have money.

All forms used in a context of reality to refer to facts are said to be used in the *indicative* (reality) *mood*.

However, quite frequently, a speaker does not want to talk about facts, but about something which exists only in his thought or in his imagination, in his desires or fears.

All verbal forms used in a context of irreality to talk about contrary-to-fact situations which are merely imagined are said to be used in the *subjunctive* (irreality) *mood*.

INDICATIVE

> **Weißt du, daß Dortmund heute nach-mittag das Spiel *verloren hat?***
>
> Do you know that Dortmund *lost* the game this afternoon?

(Since **verloren hat** and *lost* refer to a past fact, both **verloren hat** and *lost* are indicative forms.)

SUBJUNCTIVE

> **Wäre es nicht schrecklich, wenn sie das Spiel nächsten Samstag auch *ver-lören?***
>
> Wouldn't it be terrible if they *lost* next Saturday's game, too?

(Since **verlören** and *lost* refer to imagined events of the future, both **verlören** and *lost* are subjunctive forms.)

INDICATIVE

> **Wir hörten, daß sie drei Tage im Hotel Regina *gewohnt hatten.***
>
> We heard that they *had stayed* at the Regina for three days.

(Since both **gewohnt hatten** and *had stayed* refer to actual facts of the past, they are indicative (pluperfect) forms.)

SUBJUNCTIVE

> **Wenn sie im Hotel Regina *gewohnt hätten,* hätten wir sie leicht finden können.**
>
> If they *had stayed* at the Regina, we could have found them easily.

(Now both **gewohnt hätten** and *had stayed* refer to a contrary-to-fact situation of the past. Therefore both **gewohnt hätten** and *had stayed* are subjunctive forms.)

The question now is: Do English and German have one set of forms which are all indicative and another set of forms which are all subjunctive?

If you look at the examples above, you can see that this is certainly not the case in English. All English past indicative forms (like *lost*) can also be used as subjunctives referring to present or future time; and all English pluperfect indicative forms (like *had stayed*) can also be used as past subjunctive forms. There are no longer any exceptions.

It is clearly different in German. The form **verloren hat** is indicative only, and **verlören** can only be used as a subjunctive. Similarly **gewohnt hatten** is indicative only, while **gewohnt hätten** is always subjunctive.

What makes things complicated is that not all German indicative forms have different corresponding subjunctive forms; some indicatives can, as in English, also double up as subjunctives. To make things easier for you, we will start with one set of German forms which can never be used in the indicative (reality) mood. This set is known as the *past subjunctive*.

106 The Past Subjunctive

As illustrated by the following tables, the past subjunctive is derived from, but not identical with the pluperfect. If the auxiliary in the indicative is **hatte** in the pluperfect, it is **hätte** in the past subjunctive, and the indicative **war** is changed to **wäre**.

PLUPERFECT INDICATIVE	PAST SUBJUNCTIVE
ich hatte gekauft	ich hätte gekauft
du hattest gekauft	du hättest gekauft
er hatte gekauft	er hätte gekauft
wir hatten gekauft	wir hätten gekauft
ihr hattet gekauft	ihr hättet gekauft
sie hatten gekauft	sie hätten gekauft
ich war gegangen	ich wäre gegangen
du warst gegangen	du wär(e)st gegangen
er war gegangen	er wäre gegangen
wir waren gegangen	wir wären gegangen
ihr wart gegangen	ihr wär(e)t gegangen
sie waren gegangen	sie wären gegangen

PAST SUBJUNCTIVE OF MODALS	
ich hätte ihn besuchen können	I could have visited him
du hättest ihn besuchen können	you could have visited him
er hätte ihn besuchen können	he could have visited him
wir hätten ihn besuchen sollen	we should have visited him
ihr hättet ihn besuchen sollen	you should have visited him
sie hätten ihn besuchen sollen	they should have visited him
ich hätte arbeiten müssen	I would have had to work
du hättest arbeiten müssen	you would have had to work
er hätte arbeiten müssen	he would have had to work
wir hätten nicht zu arbeiten brauchen	we would not have had to work
ihr hättet nicht zu arbeiten brauchen	you would not have had to work
sie hätten nicht zu arbeiten brauchen	they would not have had to work

NOTE: Forms like **hätte können, hätte müssen,** or **hätte brauchen** are structured like **hätte gekauft.** The participles of the modals look like infinitives as long as they follow another infinitive; hence the term "double infinitive," which, strictly speaking, is incorrect because the second infinitive is really a past participle. Observe that the English forms *could have, should have, would have* always start with **hätte** in German.

107 Uses of the Past Subjunctive

The past subjunctive appears with great frequency in the following three constructions:*

CONSTRUCTION 1 Wishes starting with **ich wollte, ich wünschte, es wäre nett, wenn . . . ,** or **wenn ich doch nur . . . .**

If an English speaker starts a sentence with *I wish*, it is a good bet that he will go on with such unintroduced dependent clauses as *you were here* or *we had bought that house.* The corresponding German sentences start with **ich wünschte, ich wollte, es wäre nett (gut, besser, schön), wenn . . . ,** or with **wenn ich doch nur. . . .**

All these German ways of starting to express a wish are fixed and frozen stereotype constructions. Do not use a **daß**-clause after **ich wünschte** and **ich wollte,** and do not leave out the **doch** in **wenn ich doch nur . . . .** If used as indicated, all four ways of starting a wish can only be followed by a subjunctive form.

Ich wünschte, wir hätten vor zwei Jahren ein *Haus* gekauft. Aber leider *haben* wir kein Haus gekauft.	I wish we had bought a house two years ago. But unfortunately we did not buy a house.
Ich wollte, meine Tochter wäre nicht nach Kairo gefahren. Aber sie *ist* gefahren.	I wish my daughter had not gone to Cairo. But she *did* go.
Es wäre nett gewesen, wenn wir gestern abend zu Hause geblieben wären. Mußten wir wirklich zum Oktoberfest gehen?	It would have been nice if we had stayed at home last night. Did we really have to go to the Oktoberfest?

* These same three constructions are used to show the use of the future subjunctive (**würde**-forms) (**108**), the present subjunctive of **sein, haben,** and the modals (**109**), and the present subjunctive of other verbs (**110**). The three constructions are:
1. Wishes starting with **ich wollte, ich wünschte, es wäre nett, wenn . . . ,** or **wenn ich doch nur . . . .**
2. Irreal **wenn**-clauses followed or preceded by irreal conclusions.
3. Irreal statements of preference.

Wenn wir doch nur unser Haus nicht verloren hätten. Aber wir *haben* es verloren.	If only we had not lost our house. But we *did* lose it.

CONSTRUCTION 2 Irreal **wenn**-clauses followed or preceded by irreal conclusions.

In the main clauses (the clauses without *if*), there is no English construction parallel to the German past subjunctive; English has to use constructions with *would have;* in the *if*-clauses, however, English and German are structurally parallel.

Natürlich wären wir zum Künstlerball nach München gefahren, wenn meine Schwester uns eingeladen hätte. Aber sie *hat* uns nicht eingeladen.	Of course we would have gone to Munich for the artists' ball, if my sister had invited us. But she *didn't* invite us.
Wenn Frau Meyer ihren Paß immer in der Handtasche gehabt hätte, hätte sie ihn nicht verloren.	If Mrs. Meyer had always carried her passport in her handbag, she would not have lost it.

CONSTRUCTION 3 Irreal statements of past preference using **gerne** (*with pleasure*), **lieber** (*rather*), or **am liebsten** (*would have liked most of all*).

Note that English again uses the *would have* construction as the equivalent of the German past subjunctive.

Wir wären gestern abend auch gerne ins Ballett gegangen. Aber wir konnten keine Karten bekommen.	We would have also liked to go to the ballet last night. But we couldn't get any tickets.
Wir hätten ja auch lieber in München gewohnt. Aber mit unseren fünf Kindern konnten wir das einfach nicht.	We, too, would have rather lived in Munich. But with our five children we simply couldn't.
Mein Mann hätte am liebsten einen Mercedes gekauft. Aber wir haben die Hypothek auf unserem Haus noch nicht abgezahlt, und da hat er einen VW gekauft.	My husband would have liked most of all to buy a Mercedes. But we have not yet paid off the mortgage on our house. So he bought a VW.

108 The Future Subjunctive: The **würde**-Forms

The future subjunctive, **würde** plus infinitive, corresponds to English *would* plus infinitive. It is derived from the future indicative. These same **würde**-forms also serve as the German "conditional."

FUTURE INDICATIVE	FUTURE SUBJUNCTIVE
ich werde gehen	ich würde gehen
du wirst gehen	du würdest gehen
er wird gehen	er würde gehen
wir werden gehen	wir würden gehen
ihr werdet gehen	ihr würdet gehen
sie werden gehen	sie würden gehen

The difference between the future indicative and the future subjunctive is that the future indicative refers to future facts,

Alle Menschen werden einmal sterben   All men will die someday

and the **würde**-forms refer to future events which the speaker does not expect to happen.

Alle Menschen würden sofort sterben, wenn die Erde in die Sonne fallen sollte.

All men would die immediately, if the earth should ever fall into the sun.

This is an irreal speculation, for the earth is not likely to fall into the sun.

Quite often the **würde**-forms refer to present rather than to future time, especially in irreal conclusions.

Wenn wir Tante Amalies Geld geerbt hätten, würden wir jetzt an der Riviera wohnen.   If we had inherited Aunt Amalie's money, we'd be living on the Riviera now.

The **würde**-forms appear in the same three constructions as the forms of the past subjunctive: wishes, irreal **wenn**-clauses, and irreal statements.

CONSTRUCTION 1   Wishes starting with **ich wollte, ich wünschte, es wäre nett, wenn . . .** , or **wenn ich doch nur. . . .**

Ich wünschte, er würde noch eine Woche hier bleiben. Aber er kann nicht.   I wish he would stay for one more week. But he can't.

Es wäre nett, wenn wir sofort eine Wohnung finden würden.   It would be nice if we were to find an apartment right away.

Wenn Meyers doch nur endlich nach Hause gehen würden. Wie lange wollen sie denn bleiben?   If the Meyers would only go home at last. How long do they intend to stay?

CONSTRUCTION 2   Irreal **wenn**-clauses followed or preceded by irreal conclusions.

Ich würde gerne mitgehen, wenn er mich bitten würde.   I'd be glad to go along if he would ask me.

Wenn er mich bitten würde, würde ich gerne mitgehen.   If he would ask me, I'd be glad to go along.

CONSTRUCTION 3   Irreal statements (speculations), often using **gern, lieber,** and **am liebsten.**

Leider ist es heute etwas neblig. Sonst würden wir von hier aus die Berge sehen können.	Unfortunately, it is a little foggy today; otherwise we'd be able to see the mountains from here.
Nein, wir verkaufen unser Haus nicht. Das würde uns Tante Amalie nie verzeihen. Sie hat es uns doch zu unserer Hochzeit geschenkt.	No, we won't sell our house. Aunt Amalie would never forgive us. She gave it to us as a wedding present, you know.
Nein, ich würde einen Mann wie Karl Müller nie heiraten. Er trinkt doch.	No, I'd never marry a man like Karl Müller. He drinks, you know.
Meyers fahren jedes Jahr zusammen nach Italien. Ich würde auch gerne einmal mit dir nach Italien fahren.	The Meyers go to Italy together every year. I'd like to go to Italy with you sometime, too.

109 The Present Subjunctive of **haben, sein,** and the Modals

The present subjunctive of these verbs is derived from the past indicative. But they clearly refer only to contrary-to-fact situations imagined to exist at the moment of speaking or at some later point.

	INDICATIVE	SUBJUNCTIVE	INDICATIVE	SUBJUNCTIVE	INDICATIVE	SUBJUNCTIVE
ich	war	wäre	hatte	hätte	konnte	könnte
du	warst	wär(e)st	hattest	hättest	konntest	könntest
er	war	wäre	hatte	hätte	konnte	könnte
wir	waren	wären	hatten	hätten	konnten	könnten
ihr	wart	wär(e)t	hattet	hättet	konntet	könntet
sie	waren	wären	hatten	hätten	konnten	könnten

	INDICATIVE	SUBJUNCTIVE	INDICATIVE	SUBJUNCTIVE	INDICATIVE	SUBJUNCTIVE
ich	mußte	müßte	durfte	dürfte	sollte	sollte
du	mußtest	müßtest	durftest	dürftest	solltest	solltest
er	mußte	müßte	durfte	dürfte	sollte	sollte
wir	mußten	müßten	durften	dürften	sollten	sollten
ihr	mußtet	müßtet	durftet	dürftet	solltet	solltet
sie	mußten	müßten	durften	dürften	sollten	sollten

	INDICATIVE	SUBJUNCTIVE
ich	wollte	wollte
du	wolltest	wolltest
er	wollte	wollte
wir	wollten	wollten
ihr	wolltet	wolltet
sie	wollten	wollten

The table shows: With the exception of **wollen** and **sollen,** all these verbs make a sharp distinction between the past indicative and the present subjunctive. The corresponding English forms (*was, had, could, had to, had the permission to, would, should*) make no such distinction at all: The English past indicatives are also used as present subjunctives. The only surviving exception in English is rapidly disappearing in colloquial speech where

If she were a little older, I would like her better

is being replaced by

If she was a little older, I would like her better.

The forms in the table above are the most frequently used of all German subjunctives. They appear in the usual three constructions.

CONSTRUCTION 1   Wishes starting with **ich wollte, ich wünschte, es wäre nett, wenn . . . ,** or **wenn ich doch nur. . . .**

Es wäre nett, wenn du morgen kommen könntest. Aber ich weiß, du kannst nicht.	It would be nice if you could come tomorrow. But I know you can't.
Wir wollten, wir hätten auch eine Tochter. Aber wir haben keine Tochter.	We wish we had a daughter, too, but we don't have a daughter.
Wenn Fritz doch nur nicht so viel trinken wollte.	If only Fritz wouldn't drink so much.
Wenn ich doch nur besser sehen könnte.	If only I could see better.
Wenn Meyers doch nur nicht so viele Kinder hätten.	If only the Meyers didn't have so many children.
Wenn mein Mann doch nur nicht so viel arbeiten müßte.	If only my husband didn't have to work so much.
Wenn wir ihn doch nur endlich besuchen dürften.	If only we could visit him at last.
Wenn meine Frau doch nur gesund wäre.	If only my wife were well.

CONSTRUCTION 2   Irreal **wenn**-clauses followed or preceded by irreal conclusions.

Wenn ich jeden Tag acht Stunden arbeiten müßte, hätte ich auch keine Lust, abends in die Oper zu gehen.	If I had to work eight hours every day, I wouldn't want to go to the opera in the evening either.

Wenn Inge jetzt Frau Dr. Anton Fischer wäre, könnte sie auch nach Frankfurt fahren und einen Sportwagen kaufen.	If Inge were Dr. Anton Fischer's wife now, she could go to Frankfurt too and buy a sports car.
Natürlich dürften Sie keinen Whisky trinken, wenn Sie Hepatitis hätten.	Of course you wouldn't be allowed to drink whisky if you had hepatitis.

CONSTRUCTION 3   Irreal statements of preference.

Du hast recht. Das Essen hier könnte wirklich besser sein.	You are right. The food here really could be better.
Du hast recht. Das Essen hier sollte wirklich besser sein.	You are right. The food here really ought to be better.
Du hast recht. Das Essen hier müßte wirklich besser sein.	You are right. The food here really ought to be better.
Unser VW ist nicht schlecht. Aber wir hätten lieber einen Mercedes.	Our VW is not bad, but we'd rather have a Mercedes.
Leider bin ich Ingenieur. Ich wäre viel lieber Arzt.	Unfortunately I'm an engineer. I'd much rather be a doctor.

110 The Present Subjunctive of Weak and Strong Verbs

Weak verbs (the verbs that place the stem into the frame ge——t to form the participle) use the same form for the past indicative and the present subjunctive. This means that forms like es **regnete, wir wohnten,** or **er heiratete** are, all by themselves, just as ambiguous as *they lost* in the sentences

They lost the game this afternoon.
Wouldn't it be terrible if they lost next Saturday, too.

When used in the indicative (reality) mood, they refer to past facts. When used in the subjunctive (irreality) mood, they change their time reference and refer either to contrary-to-fact present-time situations or to irreal future situations.

PAST INDICATIVE				PRESENT SUBJUNCTIVE			
ich wohnte	I	was	living	wenn ich wohnte	if I	were	living
du wohntest	you	were	living	wenn du wohntest	if you	were	living
er wohnte	he	was	living	wenn er wohnte	if he	were	living
wir wohnten	we	were	living	wenn wir wohnten	if we	were	living
ihr wohntet	you	were	living	wenn ihr wohntet	if you	were	living
sie wohnten	they	were	living	wenn sie wohnten	if they	were	living

Strong verbs (the ones that place a changed stem into the frame **ge____en**)
form the present subjunctive by adding the endings **-e, -est, -e, -en, -et, -en**
to the stem of the past, which is umlauted whenever possible, that is, whenever the vowel of the past tense stem is **a, o,** or **u.** The endings **-est** and **-et**
are often shortened to **-st** and **-t.**

PAST INDICATIVE		PRESENT SUBJUNCTIVE	
ich ging	I went	wenn ich ginge	if I went
du gingst		wenn du gingest, gingst	
er ging		wenn er ginge	
wir gingen		wenn wir gingen	
ihr gingt		wenn ihr ginget, gingt	
sie gingen		wenn sie gingen	
ich fuhr	I went	wenn ich führe	if I went
du fuhrst		wenn du führest, führst	
er fuhr		wenn er führe	
wir fuhren		wenn wir führen	
ihr fuhrt		wenn ihr führet, führt	
sie fuhren		wenn sie führen	

As you can see from this table, the **wir**-form and the plural **sie**-form of non-
umlauted strong forms are again ambiguous. This means that

    Wenn wir nach Hause gingen

can mean either *whenever we went home* or *if we were to go home,* whereas

    Wenn wir nach München führen

can only be a subjunctive, because the past indicative would be **wir fuhren.**

The ambiguity of weak forms like **wir wohnten** and of strong forms like **wir
gingen** is not disturbing at all, as long as they are used in a construction
such as **ich wollte, ich wünschte, es wäre nett, wenn . . . ,** and **wenn ich doch
nur. . . .** These constructions have such a strong flavor of irreality that even
such ambiguous forms as **wir brauchten, wir wohnten,** and **wir gingen**
automatically assume present subjunctive meaning.

Ich wollte, wir brauchten heute nicht zu arbeiten.	I wish we didn't have to work today.
Ich wünschte, wir wohnten in München.	I wish we were living in Munich.
Es wäre nett, wenn wir auch einmal in die Oper gingen.	It would be nice if we, too, went to the opera for a change.
Wenn ich doch nur nicht so schwer zu arbeiten brauchte.	If only I didn't have to work so hard.

The only time that the ambiguity of forms like **es regnete** or **wir gingen** becomes a problem is when one of them appears in a **wenn**-clause and another
one in the following conclusion. Two of them together would be interpreted

as past-tense indicatives. Thus the sentence

Wenn es regnete, gingen wir nach Hause

would mean

Whenever it rained, we went home.

In order to ensure the intended contrary-to-fact subjunctive character of such constructions, the verb in the conclusion must be changed to a **würde**-form. Thus

Wenn es regnete, würden wir nach Hause gehen

can only mean

If it were raining, we would go home.

The use of the **würde**-form is widespread. As far as **haben, sein,** and the modals are concerned, the shorter forms **hätte, wäre, könnte, müßte** are used more frequently than the longer forms **würde haben, würde sein, würde können,** and **würde müssen.** In the case of other strong and weak verbs, one hears the longer forms **würde finden** and **würde wohnen** just as frequently as the shorter forms **fände** and **wohnte.** Only weak forms referring to the future are almost always replaced by the **würde**-form.

The present subjunctive forms described in the table above appear, as usual, in the following three constructions.

CONSTRUCTION 1 Wishes starting with **ich wollte, ich wünschte, es wäre nett, wenn . . . ,** or **wenn ich doch nur. . . .**

Ich wollte, mein Vater kaufte mir ein Auto (würde mir ein Auto kaufen).	I wish my father would buy me a car.
Ich wünschte, wir blieben noch eine Woche hier (wir würden noch eine Woche hier bleiben).	I wish we'd stay here another week.
Es wäre nett, wenn wir sofort eine Wohnung fänden (finden würden).	It would be nice if we found an apartment immediately.
Wenn Meyers doch nur endlich nach Hause gingen (gehen würden).	If the Meyers would only go home at last.

CONSTRUCTION 2 Irreal **wenn**-clauses followed or preceded by irreal conclusions.

Wenn sie mir schriebe, schriebe ich ihr auch (würde ich ihr auch schreiben).	If she wrote to me, I'd write to her, too.
Ich würde auch jedes Jahr nach Europa fahren (führe auch jedes Jahr nach Europa), wenn ich so viel Zeit hätte wie Meyer.	I'd go to Europe every year, too, if I had as much time as Meyer.

CONSTRUCTION 3   Irreal statements of preference using **gerne, lieber,** or **am liebsten.**

Du willst wieder nach Deutschland fahren? Ich führe lieber in die Schweiz (würde lieber in die Schweiz fahren).	You want to go to Germany again? I'd rather go to Switzerland.
Ein Mädchen wie Erika findet man nicht oft. Ich würde sie gerne heiraten.	You don't find a girl like Erika very often. I'd like to marry her.
Nein, ich möchte jetzt keinen Martini. Am liebsten tränke ich eine Tasse Kaffee (würde ich eine Tasse Kaffee trinken).	No, I don't want a Martini now. I'd really like to have a cup of coffee.

111 Polite Requests

In social gatherings, in hotels, stores, and so forth, the **würde**-forms and the present subjunctives are used to express polite requests.

Hätten Sie vielleicht noch ein Zimmer frei?
Ich hätte gerne ein Zimmer mit Bad.
Könnte ich noch eine Tasse Kaffee haben.
Würden Sie mir vielleicht noch eine Tasse Kaffee bringen.

112 Position of **hätte** in Connection with "Double Infinitives"

It was pointed out before that when the modals and **brauchen** are used with a dependent infinitive, the participles look like infinitives.

Ich habe sie noch nicht besuchen können.

As a result, **besuchen können** looks like a double infinitive. If subjunctive sentences like

Er hätte zu Hause bleiben können

or

Er hätte nicht zu Hause bleiben sollen

are changed into dependent clauses which should show verb-last position, the **hätte** does not go to the end, but follows **nicht** and precedes the second prong.

Wenn ich doch nur hätte zu Hause bleiben können.
Es wäre nett gewesen, wenn ich gestern nicht hätte zurückfahren müssen.

NOTE: This exception to the principle of verb-last position occurs also in those rare cases when the indicative is used.

Sie war mir böse, weil ich sie noch nie hatte besuchen können.

113 Irregular Subjunctive Forms

A few verbs form the present subjunctive in an irregular way.

PAST INDICATIVE	PRESENT SUBJUNCTIVE
ich brachte	**ich brächte**
ich kannte	**ich kennte**
ich half	**ich hülfe**
ich starb	**ich stürbe**

114 sollte

German **sollte** is one of the ambiguous forms which can be used either as a past indicative or as a present subjunctive.

Past Indicative

Jedesmal, wenn du mit mir ins Theater gehen solltest, hattest du Kopfschmerzen.

Every time you were supposed (Every time I wanted you) to go to the theater with me, you had a headache.

Wir sollten schon um acht in Köln sein. Jetzt ist es neun, und wir sind immer noch in Bonn.

We were supposed to be in Cologne at eight. Now it is nine, and we are still in Bonn.

Present Subjunctive

In the *if*-clause, the present subjunctive denotes a future possibility which the speaker does not expect to materialize. The conclusion shows the indicative.

Wenn es morgen regnen sollte, bleiben wir zu Hause.

If it should rain tomorrow, we'll stay at home.

In the conclusion, the present subjunctive denotes an as yet unfulfilled obligation. The *if*-clause shows the indicative.

Wenn du kannst, solltest du ihm helfen.
Du solltest nicht soviel essen.

If you can, you should (ought to) help him.
You should not (ought not to) eat so much.

115 eigentlich

Eigentlich is a frequently used sentence adverb which has no equivalent in English. To questions, it gives the flavor of "to come right down to it."

Warum sind wir eigentlich in die Schweiz gefahren?

In assertions, usually containing subjunctives like **sollte, wollte, müßte,** and **dürfte, eigentlich** adds the flavor "but I guess that's out."

Eigentlich sollten wir morgen nach Berlin fahren.
We should go to Berlin tomorrow. (But I guess we won't.)

116 The Position of **nicht** Again

Irreal wishes and irreal **wenn**-clauses frequently follow the pattern: I wish "the whole thing" hadn't happened. One such "whole thing" is described within the brackets of the factual statement

Gestern abend hat Ingelheim [wieder drei Stunden lang nur von seinen Brieftauben geredet].
Last night, Ingelheim [talked again for three hours about nothing but his carrier pigeons].

The "whole thing" was unpleasant. It should not have happened. But it did happen, and nobody can change it. But one can, at least in thought, erase it from the realm of reality. This is done by using a contrary-to-fact subjunctive and by placing a condemning **nicht** right in front of the "whole thing."

Ich wollte, Ingelheim hätte gestern abend nicht [wieder drei Stunden lang nur von seinen Brieftauben geredet].

The **nicht**, in such cases, does not precede the second prong (**geredet**), but the complete description of whatever the speaker considers the "whole thing."

117 The Subjunctive in Indirect Discourse

The English System

When I, the speaker, want to report to one person, my wife for instance, what another person, for instance my father, has just told me over the phone, I can freely choose between two syntactical patterns:

I can use quotation marks and repeat verbatim what my father said. If he said, "Fred, I am sick," I can report, *Father just called and said, "Fred, I am sick."* Such "direct discourse" presents no problems. One simply quotes verbatim what one hears.

I may also use the "indirect discourse" pattern—that is, I may change the original statement into a dependent clause: *Father just called and said he was sick.* In this case the original words *I am sick* change into *he was sick.* If the original is "I was sick last week," I may report: *Father just called and said he had been sick last week.*

The rule governing English indirect discourse is usually formulated as follows: If the opening verb (*said, told, reported, maintained, read*) is in the past tense, then any *present tense* in the words to be reported is normally changed to *past tense* and any *past tense* (simple past, present perfect, past perfect) is normally changed to *past perfect.*

Schematically, this English system can be represented as follows:

	DIRECT DISCOURSE	INDIRECT DISCOURSE
PRESENT TENSE	I am sick.	He said he was sick.
	I have money.	He said he had money.
ANY PAST TENSE	I was sick.	He said he had been sick.
	I have broken my arm.	He said he had broken his arm.
	I had not thought of it.	He said he had not thought of it.

In learning German, you will find it helpful to regard this shift in verb forms not as a shift in tense but as a shift from the indicative to the subjunctive. You will then automatically do what you ought to do: shift from the German indicative to the German subjunctive.

The German System

AFTER AN OPENING VERB IN ONE OF THE PAST TENSES

If the original statement (that is, the statement in quotation marks) referred to the present time, the present subjunctive is used, and such forms as **wohnte** and **liebte** do no have to be replaced by **würde**-forms.

If the original statement referred to the future, one can use either the present subjunctive or the future subjunctive; forms like **heiratete**—that is, weak verbs with a future meaning—are usually replaced by a **würde**-form.

DIRECT DISCOURSE	INDIRECT DISCOURSE
Ich bin krank.	**Er sagte, er wäre krank.**
Ich wohne in München.	**Er sagte, er wohnte in München.**
Ich kann kommen.	**Er sagte, er könnte kommen.**
Ich werde zu Hause bleiben.	**Er sagte, er würde zu Hause bleiben (bliebe zu Hause).**
Ich komme morgen.	**Er sagte, er käme morgen (würde morgen kommen).**
Ich werde sie bestimmt heiraten.	**Er sagte, er würde sie bestimmt heiraten.**
Fährst du morgen nach Köln?	**Er wollte wissen, ob ich morgen nach Köln führe.**

If the original statement was made in any past tense, one shifts to the past subjunctive (**wäre** or **hätte** plus participle).

DIRECT DISCOURSE	INDIRECT DISCOURSE
Ich war krank.	**Er sagte, er wäre krank gewesen.**
Ich bin krank gewesen.	**Er sagte, er wäre krank gewesen.**
Bei uns schien die Sonne.	**Er sagte, bei ihnen hätte die Sonne geschienen.**
Eva ist schon nach Hause gegangen.	**Er sagte, Eva wäre schon nach Hause gegangen.**

If the original statement contained a subjunctive, no change is possible.

DIRECT DISCOURSE	INDIRECT DISCOURSE
Wenn wir Geld hätten, würden wir sofort heiraten.	**Er sagte, wenn sie Geld hätten, würden sie sofort heiraten.**

AFTER AN OPENING VERB IN THE PRESENT TENSE

If the opening verb is in the present tense, a change from indicative to subjunctive is possible though not as frequent in spoken German as in literary German. However, after an **ich**-form in the present tense, the subjunctive is apt to indicate deceit.

DIRECT DISCOURSE	INDIRECT DISCOURSE
Meyer ist intelligent.	**Fritz meint, Meyer ist intelligent.**
	Fritz meint, Meyer wäre intelligent.
	Ich sage, Meyer ist intelligent.
	Ich sage ihm einfach, Meyer wäre intelligent.

NOTE: In the examples above, indirect discourse appears in the form of unintroduced clauses with verb-second position. Occasionally, they are introduced by **daß** and then show verb-last position.

> **Er sagte, daß in Hamburg die Sonne schiene.**

118 The Prefix un-

The prefix **un-** is added to many adjectives and a few nouns to form antonyms.

glücklich	**unglücklich**
interessant	**uninteressant**
vernünftig	**unvernünftig**
das Wissen (knowledge)	**das Unwissen** (ignorance)
das Glück (happiness, good luck)	**das Unglück** (misfortune, accident)

119 The Suffix -lich Added to Nouns

Like the English suffix *-ly*, the German suffix **-lich** is added to nouns. It forms adjectives with the meaning of "having the qualities one associates with things or people of such a nature." The stem vowel of the noun is usually umlauted.

der Freund	friend	**freundlich**	friendly
die Mutter	mother	**mütterlich**	motherly
das Kind	child	**kindlich**	childlike
die Welt	world	**weltlich**	worldly, secular
die Natur	nature	**natürlich**	naturally

120 The Suffixes -bar and -lich Added to Verb Stems

Added to verb stems, **-bar** and **-lich** form passive adjectives corresponding to English adjectives in *-able* and *-ible*.

glauben	to believe	**unglaublich**	unbelievable
brauchen	to use	**brauchbar**	usable
vergessen	to forget	**unvergeßlich**	unforgettable

Some of the adjectives formed by **-lich** have an active meaning. (Compare English *durable*.)

sterben	to die	**sterblich**	mortal, apt to die
vergessen	to forget	**vergeßlich**	forgetful

Exercises

A. Change the following factual statements to irreal wishes. Change from negative to affirmative and vice versa. Start first with **ich wollte**, then with **ich wünschte, es wäre besser gewesen, wenn . . .** , **wenn** (*subject*) **doch nur. . . .**

> **Wir haben das Haus leider nicht gekauft.**
> **Wenn wir das Haus doch nur gekauft hätten.**

SEE
ANALYSIS
106–107

(pp. 175-177)

1. Sie hat mich nicht angerufen.
2. Er ist mit der Lufthansa geflogen. (Place **nicht** in front of **mit.**)
3. Ich habe meinen Mantel zu Hause gelassen. (Place **nicht** in front of **zu Hause.**)
4. Ich bin mit meiner Tochter zu meiner Mutter gefahren. (Place **nicht** in front of **mit.**)
5. Wir konnten das Haus nicht kaufen. (Watch the position of **hätten.**)
6. Ich habe heute abend zuviel Kaffee getrunken. (Replace **zuviel** by **nicht so viel.**)

B. Change the following factual assertions to irreal preferential statements using first **gerne**, then **lieber**, and then **am liebsten**, all three of them replacing **leider**.

> **Wir haben leider das Haus in Köln nicht gekauft.**
> **Wir hätten lieber das Haus in Köln gekauft.**

SEE
ANALYSIS
106–107

(pp. 175-177)

1. Wir sind leider nicht in die Berge gefahren.
2. Wir sind leider nicht in den Zoo gegangen.
3. Ich habe heute morgen leider nicht bis neun geschlafen.
4. Ich bin gestern leider nicht mit meiner Freundin ins Kino gegangen.

C. Change the following pairs of factual statements to irreal conditions.

> **Rosemarie studierte damals in München. Ich habe sie kennengelernt.**
> **Wenn Rosemarie damals nicht in München studiert hätte, hätte ich sie nie kennengelernt.**

SEE
ANALYSIS
106–107

(pp. 175-177)

1. Tante Amalie schickte mir jeden Monat fünfhundert Mark. Ich konnte Medizin studieren.
   Ich _____ nie Medizin studieren _____, wenn Tante Amalie mir nicht _____.

2. Ich habe damals in Nordafrika einen Amerikaner getroffen. Ich bin nach dem Kriege nach Amerika gefahren.
   Ich _____ nach dem Kriege nie _____, wenn ich nicht damals in Nordafrika _____.

3. Ingelheim sprach beim Frühstück von Gisela. Seine Frau fuhr mit ihrer Tochter zu ihrer Mutter.

Wenn Ingelheim nicht beim Frühstück —————, ————— seine Frau nie mit ihrer Tochter —————.

D. Change the following factual statements to irreal wishes. Change from affirmative to negative and from negative to affirmative. Start first with **ich wollte**, then with **ich wünschte**, then with **es wäre nett, wenn . . .** , and finally with **wenn ich doch nur. . . .** Use only **würde**-forms.

> **Du wirst Erika nicht heiraten.**
> **Es wäre nett, wenn du Erika heiraten würdest.**

1. Du redest zu oft von deinen Brieftauben. (Change **zu** to **nicht so.**)
2. Du verschwindest nie drei Wochen mit mir. (Replace **nie** by **auch einmal.**)
3. Wir fahren dieses Wochenende nicht in die Berge.
4. Wir fahren nächstes Jahr nicht wieder nach Deutschland.
5. Hans und Erika heiraten dieses Jahr nicht.

SEE ANALYSIS 108 (pp. 177-179)

E. Replacing **leider** by **gerne**, **lieber**, or **am liebsten**, change the following factual statements to preferential statements using only **würde**-forms. Change from negative to affirmative.

> **Wir fahren leider nächstes Jahr nicht wieder nach Deutschland.**
> **Wir würden am liebsten nächstes Jahr wieder nach Deutschland fahren.**

1. Ich gehe heute abend leider nicht mit Erika ins Kino.
2. Wir wohnen ja leider nicht im Regina.
3. Wir trinken leider nie eine Flasche Wein zusammen. (Replace **nie** by **auch einmal.**)
4. Er kauft leider keinen Mercedes.

SEE ANALYSIS 108 (pp. 177-179)

F. Change the following factual statements to irreal wishes starting first with **ich wollte**, then with **ich wünschte**, then with **es wäre gut, wenn . . .** , and finally with **wenn wir (er) doch nur. . . .** Change from affirmative to negative and vice versa.

> **Mein Mann muß zu schwer arbeiten.**
> **Ich wollte, mein Mann brauchte nicht so schwer zu arbeiten.**
> **Ich wünschte, mein Mann brauchte nicht so schwer zu arbeiten.**
> **Es wäre gut, wenn mein Mann nicht so schwer zu arbeiten brauchte.**
> **Wenn mein Mann doch nur nicht so schwer zu arbeiten brauchte.**

1. Ich habe leider keinen Bruder.
2. Wir sind noch nicht zu Hause. (Replace **noch nicht** by **schon.**)
3. Du bist immer so pessimistisch. (Place **nicht** in front of **immer.**)
4. Wir dürfen ihn heute noch nicht besuchen. (Change **heute noch nicht** to **schon heute.**)
5. Wir müssen zu schwer arbeiten. (Replace **zu** by **nicht so.**)

SEE ANALYSIS 109 (pp. 179-181)

G. Change the following factual statements to irreal statements about what should or could be, but is not. Use the verb in parentheses.

> **Ich trinke zu viel. (sollen)**
> **Ich sollte nicht so viel trinken.**

SEE
ANALYSIS
109

(pp. 179-181)

1. Wir haben kein Auto. (müssen)
2. Wir fahren Sonntag nicht in die Berge. (können)
3. Wir schwimmen nicht jeden Tag eine halbe Stunde. (sollen)
4. Nächstes Jahr heiraten wir noch nicht. (können) (Replace **noch nicht** by **schon.**)

H. Combine the following pairs of sentences to irreal **wenn**-clauses followed or preceded by an irreal conclusion.

> **Wir können nicht heiraten. Du willst nicht heiraten.**
> **Wenn du wolltest, könnten wir heiraten.**

SEE
ANALYSIS
109

(pp. 179-181)

1. Ich bin kein Arzt. Ich kann Ihnen nicht helfen.
2. Wir haben kein Geld. Wir können nicht mit Meyers in die Schweiz fahren.
3. Ich bin nicht glücklich. Du willst immer nur von deinen Brieftauben reden. (Ich
   _____ glücklich, wenn du nicht immer _____.)

I. Using both the short forms, like **führen,** and the long forms, like **würden fahren,** change the following factual statements into irreal wishes, starting first with **ich wollte** or **ich wünschte,** then with **es wäre nett, wenn . . . ,** and finally with **wenn** (*subject*) **doch nur . . . .**

> **Sie wohnen leider nicht mehr hier in Köln.**
> **Wenn sie doch nur noch hier in Köln wohnten.**
> **Wenn sie doch nur noch hier in Köln wohnen würden.**

SEE
ANALYSIS
110

(pp. 181-184)

1. Du fährst leider morgen schon wieder nach Hause. (Place **nicht** in front of **schon.**)
2. Meine Frau ruft mich zu oft im Büro an. (Replace **zu** by **nicht so.**)
3. Unser Sohn telefoniert jeden Abend zwei Stunden mit seiner Freundin. (Place **nicht** in front of **jeden Abend.**)

J. Formulate irreal preferential statements using only **am liebsten** this time. Place this **am liebsten** in the front field. Change from negative to affirmative and vice versa. Use both the short forms and the **würde**-forms.

> **Wir fahren dieses Wochenende leider nicht in die Berge.**
> **Am liebsten führen wir dieses Wochenende in die Berge.**
> **Am liebsten würden wir dieses Wochenende in die Berge fahren.**

1. Ich sitze jetzt leider nicht im Hofbräuhaus und trinke ein Glas Bier.
   (Do not repeat **würde.**)
2. Ich studiere leider nicht Medizin.
3. Nein, im Dezember heiraten wir leider noch nicht. (Place **schon** in front of **Dezember.**)
4. Ich bleibe nicht jeden Tag bis neun im Bett.
5. Ich rauche leider nicht jeden Morgen nach dem Frühstück eine Zigarre.

SEE
ANALYSIS
110
(pp. 181-184)

K. The following sentences contain a dependent clause introduced by **weil.** Changing the **weil**-clause into a **wenn**-clause, transform the sentences into irreal conditions. Use both the short forms and the **würde**-forms in the conclusion.

> Wir wohnen in der Stadt, weil wir keine Kinder haben.
> Wenn wir Kinder hätten, wohnten wir nicht in der Stadt.
> Wenn wir Kinder hätten, würden wir nicht in der Stadt wohnen.

1. Weil ich nicht in München wohne, gehe ich nicht jeden Tag ins Theater.
2. Weil ich nicht soviel Geld wie Meyer habe, kaufen wir kein Landhaus.
3. Weil Frau Meyer Frau Meyer ist, rufe ich sie jetzt nicht an.
4. Weil Meyer nicht Auto fahren kann, fährt er immer mit dem Zug in die Stadt. (Place **nicht** in front of **immer.**)
5. Weil wir einen Hund haben, finden wir keine Wohnung.

SEE
ANALYSIS
109–110
(pp. 179-184)

L. Change the following sentences to indirect discourse, starting with **er sagte, daß.** . . . Change pronouns as appropriate.

1. Meyer wohnt in Köln.
2. Ich brauche kein Geld.
3. Wir arbeiten heute nicht.
4. Ich brauche nicht nach Bonn zu fahren.
5. Ich bleibe heute abend zu Hause.
6. Das kann ich Ihnen nicht glauben.
7. Ich will ihn in Berlin besuchen.
8. Ich möchte mit dir ins Kino gehen.
9. Ich muß Ingelheims Roman lesen.
10. Ich darf mit meinem Vater nach Afrika fahren.

SEE
ANALYSIS
117
(pp. 186-188)

M. Change the following sentences to indirect discourse, starting with **er sagte,** . . . Change pronouns as appropriate.

1. Man hat ihn nach Norwegen geschickt.
2. Leider war sie viel zu intelligent.
3. Leider hatte sie zuviel Geld.
4. Er ist nicht mit uns nach Berlin gefahren.
5. Ich mußte nach Casablanca fliegen.
6. Wir konnten das Haus in Köln nicht kaufen.
7. Ich habe zuviel Kaffee getrunken.
8. Er konnte uns gestern nicht besuchen.
9. Leider mußte ich damals Brieftauben füttern.
10. Den Roman von Ingelheim habe ich noch nicht gelesen.

SEE
ANALYSIS
117
(pp. 186-188)

N. Change the following questions to indirect yes-or-no questions. First start with **ich wüßte gerne, ob** . . . (indicative), and then with **er fragte mich, ob** . . . (subjunctive).

SEE
ANALYSIS
117

(pp. 186-188)

1. Fährt Erika morgen bestimmt nach Berlin?
2. Sind Sie verheiratet?
3. Wohnen Sie in München?
4. Haben Sie noch ein Zimmer frei?
5. Kennst du meine Freundin?
6. Kannst du mich morgen anrufen?

O. Change to direct questions. Change pronouns as appropriate.

1. Er wollte wissen, ob ich nach Berlin kommen könnte.
2. Er wollte wissen, ob mein Vater Schriftsteller wäre.
3. Er wollte wissen, was er mir schenken sollte.
4. Er wollte wissen, ob mein Vater bald nach Hause käme.
5. Er wollte wissen, ob ich ihm vielleicht zwanzig Mark geben könnte.
6. Er wollte wissen, warum ich Angst vor ihm hätte.

P. Change to indirect questions (past time). Start with **er fragte mich,** . . . Change pronouns as appropriate.

SEE
ANALYSIS
117

(pp. 186-188)

1. Waren Sie damals auch Student?
2. Warst du gestern abend in der Universität?
3. Hattest du kein Geld bei dir?
4. Stand da drüben nicht früher ein Hotel?
5. Warum hattest du eigentlich nie Geld?
6. Wie lange war Hans denn in Afrika?
7. Warum konntest du nicht nach Hause kommen?
8. Warum ist Inge nicht mitgegangen?
9. Wen wolltest du denn in Berlin besuchen?
10. Mußtest du gestern abend schon wieder arbeiten?

Q. Change to direct questions.

1. Er fragte, ob viele Leute dagewesen wären.
2. Er fragte, ob ich gestern krank gewesen wäre.
3. Er fragte, ob es wahr wäre, daß es im Winter hier immer so kalt ist.
4. Er fragte, ob ich auch Hepatitis gehabt hätte.
5. Er fragte, wie lange ich in Afrika gewesen wäre.
6. Er fragte, warum ich um neun Uhr noch im Bett gelegen hätte.
7. Er fragte, warum Inge nicht hätte mit nach Italien fahren dürfen.
8. Er fragte, warum Erika gestern abend hätte zu Hause bleiben müssen.
9. Er fragte, warum ich ihr nicht hätte schreiben können.
10. Er fragte, ob sein Sohn nicht hätte zu Hause bleiben können.

R. Express in German.

1. If it began to rain now, we wouldn't be able to work anymore.
2. If it begins to rain now, we can't work anymore.
3. When it began to rain, we couldn't work anymore.
4. I was often unhappy; but when I saw her, I was always happy.

5. I'd like to know whether he is really a writer.
6. I wish he weren't a writer.
7. I don't understand why you always want to eat here.
8. I wish we could always eat here.
9. I wish we'd eat at home tonight.
10. It would have been nice if you had stayed at home.
11. Why did Ingelheim go to Africa alone?
12. It was not against the law.
13. I really should (ought to) invite him, but I have no time.
14. I really should have invited him, but I had no time.
15. Not until yesterday did I hear from him.
16. Not until yesterday did he ask me whether I could go to Bonn with him.
17. She told me she would go to Bonn with me.
18. If only we could go to Bonn again!
19. Thank goodness I've always been healthy.
20. He said he had never been in Berlin.
21. I'd like to have a cup of coffee.
22. When Ingelheim became twenty, he got hepatitis.
23. You should have seen him three years ago.
24. If only she had learned to drive.
25. Has he found the mistake yet?—No, not yet.
26. He told us that Ingelheim had disappeared in Africa without a trace.
27. I shall never be able to forget you.
28. I wish he didn't always forget my birthday.
29. I wish you hadn't forgotten my birthday again.
30. Whenever I needed her, she came immediately.
31. I know Aunt Amalie is unreasonable.
32. In three weeks they saw sixteen cities; now they believe they know Europe.
33. He knows he should have stayed at home.
34. If he hadn't lived in Munich at that time, he would never have met her.

Basic Vocabulary

achtzig	eighty	**der Berg, —e**	mountain
jemanden ärgern	to make somebody angry	**besser**	better
		bitten (um) (*with acc.*)	to ask (for), to request
aufhören	to stop	**dick**	thick; fat
es hört auf zu regnen	it stops raining	**eigentlich**	actually, really
das Bad, ¨er	bath	**erben**	to inherit
baden	to bathe	**erleben**	to experience

erscheinen	to appear	der Nebel	fog
fern	far away, distant	neblig	foggy
die Ferne	distance	nett	nice; friendly
das Fest, –e	celebration, festival	niemand	nobody, no one
der Finger, –	finger	(*dat.*: niemand,	
die Flasche, –n	bottle	niemandem;	
eine Flasche Wein	a bottle of wine	*acc.*: niemand,	
fliegen	to fly	niemanden)	
der Flieger, –	flyer	der Ort, –e	town; place
der Tiefflieger, –	strafing plane	der Vorort, –e	suburb
der Flug, –̈e	flight	der Paß, die Pässe	passport
der Abflug, –̈e	departure	plötzlich	suddenly
der Flughafen, –̈	airport	der Rhein	the Rhine
früh	early	ruhig	quiet, restful
früher	earlier; formerly	unruhig	restless
fühlen	to feel	der Samstag, –e	Saturday
das Gefühl, –e	feeling	samstags	on Saturdays
geboren	born	schenken	to present, to give
ich bin geboren	I was born	das Geschenk, –e	present, gift
die Geburt, –en	birth	schlecht	bad
der Geburtstag, –e	birthday	schnell	fast, rapid
genug	enough	schrecklich	terrible
die Geschichte, –n	story; history	der Schuh, –e	shoe
hundert	hundred	schwach	weak
irgendwo	somewhere (location)	die Schweiz	Switzerland
irgendwohin	somewhere (goal)	schwer	hard; heavy (in
jemand	somebody, someone		weight)
(*dat.*: jemand,		die Schwester, –n	sister
jemandem;		schwimmen	to swim
acc.: jemand,		sechzig	sixty
jemanden)		der See, –n	lake
der Junge, –n	boy	die See (*no pl.*)	ocean, sea
die Karte, –n	map; ticket	seekrank	seasick
die Landkarte, –n	map	sicher	certain, sure; prob-
die Fahrkarte, –n	train ticket		ably
die Katze, –n	cat	spielen	to play
leicht	easy; light (in weight)	springen	to jump
am liebsten	(to like) most of all	aufspringen	to jump up
liegen	to lie (flat); to be	stehen	to stand
	situated	aufstehen	to arise, to get up
dieses Mal	this time	still	quiet, still
noch einmal	once more	die Tasche, –n	pocket; bag
manchmal	sometimes	die Handtasche, –n	handbag
diesmal	this time	tot	dead
jedesmal	every time	ungefähr	approximate(ly), about
zwei mal zwei	two times two	verbieten	to forbid, to prohibit
man	one (*pron.*)	vergessen	to forget
(*dat.*: einem;		verheiratet	married
acc.: einen)		ich bin verheiratet	I am married
der Mantel, –̈	coat, overcoat	verlieren	to lose
mindestens	at least	wahrschein'lich	probably
möglich	possible	wenigstens	at least
der Montag, –e	Monday	werfen	to throw
müde	tired	die Wohnung, –en	apartment

wünschen	to wish	eine Zeitlang	for a while (*not:* for a long time)
zählen	to count		
zahlen	to pay (in restaurant)	das Zimmer, –	room
abzahlen	to pay off	zusammen	together
bezahlen	to pay for something		

Additional Vocabulary

allergisch	allergic	der König, –e	king
annehmen	to accept, to assume, to take on	der Künstler, –	artist
		die Situation', –en*	situation
ansehen	to look at	die Terras'se, –n	terrace
der Blick, –e	look, glance	das Wissen	knowledge
blicken	to look, to glance	die Witwe, –n	widow
der Boden, ‥	ground; floor	die Wunde, –n	wound
der Fußabdruck, ‥e	footprint	das Zentrum, die Zentren	center
gehorchen	to obey		
heilen	to heal	die Zigar're, –n	cigar
die Hypothek', –en	mortgage	der Zoo, –s	zoo
kämpfen	to fight	zu'geben	to admit

* All nouns ending in **-tion** are feminine and are declined like **Situation**; -tion is pronounced like **-tsion** and always stressed.

Strong and Irregular Verbs

annehmen, nahm an, hat angenommen, er nimmt an	to accept; to assume, to take on
ansehen, sah an, hat angesehen, er sieht an	to look at
bitten, bat, hat gebeten, er bittet	to ask for, to request
erscheinen, erschien, ist erschienen, er erscheint	to appear
liegen, lag, hat gelegen, er liegt	to lie (flat); to be situated
springen, sprang, ist gesprungen, er springt	to jump
aufspringen, sprang auf, ist aufgesprungen, er springt auf	to jump up
stehen, stand, hat gestanden, er steht	to stand
aufstehen, stand auf, ist aufgestanden, er steht auf	to get up, to rise, to arise
verbieten, verbot, hat verboten, er verbietet	to forbid
vergessen, vergaß, hat vergessen, er vergißt	to forget
verlieren, verlor, hat verloren, er verliert	to lose
werfen, warf, hat geworfen, er wirft	to throw

Unit 7 Prepositions with Dative or Accusative—
The Genitive Case—**ein**-Words without Nouns—
The Indirect-Discourse Subjunctive

Patterns

[1] Prepositions with either Dative or Accusative

Analyze the use of case after the prepositions. Be prepared to
produce the answers orally in class when you hear the questions.

Wo fahrt *ihr* denn hin?—*Wir* fahren an den *Neck*ar.
  Where are *you* going?—*We* are going to the *Neckar.*

SEE
ANALYSIS
121
(pp. 211-213)

Wo *wart* ihr denn gestern?—Wir waren gestern am *Neck*ar.
  Where *were* you yesterday?—We were at the *Neckar* yesterday.

Wohin ist er denn mit seiner Frau gefahren?—Er ist mit ihr in den Schwarzwald gefahren.
  Where did he go with his wife?—He went to the Black Forest with her.

Wo wohnt er denn?—Er wohnt im Schwarzwald.
  Where does he live?—He lives in the Black Forest.

Wo hat er sie denn hingefahren?—Er hat sie ans Theater gebracht.
  Where did he take her?—He took her to the theater.

Wo hat er denn auf sie gewartet?—Am Theater.
  Where did he wait for her?—At the theater.

Wo hat er denn seinen Hut hingelegt?—Er hat ihn aufs Bett gelegt.
Wo lag denn sein Hut?—Er lag auf dem Bett.

Was hat er denn mit seinem Geld gemacht?—Er hat es auf die Bank gebracht.
Wo hast *du* dein Geld?—*Ich* habe mein Geld *auch* auf der Bank.

Wo hast du den Wagen denn *hin*gestellt?—Hinter das *Haus.*
Wo *steht* denn dein Wagen?—Hinter dem *Haus.*

Was habt *ihr* denn gestern gemacht?—*Wir* sind gestern ins The*a*ter gegangen.
Wo wart ihr denn gestern abend?—Im Theater.

Was haben Sie denn mit meiner Zeitung gemacht?—Ich habe sie neben Ihren Hut gelegt.
Neben meinem Hut liegt sie aber nicht.—Wo kann sie denn sein?

Election poster for the Social Democratic party.

Wie seid ihr nach Deutschland geflogen?—Wir sind nonstop über den Atlantik geflogen.
Und wo habt ihr gefrühstückt?—Über dem Atlantik.

Es regnete, und wir hielten unter der Brücke.
Es regnete, und wir liefen unter die Brücke.

Wo haben Sie Rosemarie denn gesehen?—Vor dem Hotel.
Bringen Sie mir bitte den Wagen?—Ja, ich bringe ihn vor das Hotel.

Ich war schon vor dem Krieg in Afrika.
Vor zehn Jahren stand hier ein Haus.
Sollen wir vor oder nach dem Theater essen?
Vor einem Jahr kam Ingelheim nach Hause.
Ich möchte vor dem Essen noch einen Brief schreiben.

Wo lag denn der Brief?—Er lag zwischen den Zeitungen, und ich konnte ihn nicht finden.

Er konnte den Brief lange nicht finden; seine Frau hatte ihn zwischen die Zeitungen
    gelegt.

[2] Prepositions with the Genitive

SEE
ANALYSIS
125

(pp. 216-219)

Während des Sommers war Schmidt in Tirol.
    During the summer Schmidt was in the Tyrol.

Während der Woche kannst du mich nicht besuchen.
    During the week you can't visit me.

Sie können doch wegen des Regens nicht zu Hause bleiben.
    You can't stay at home because of the rain.

Wir haben trotz des Regens gestern gearbeitet.
    We worked yesterday in spite of the rain.

Wir haben trotz dem Regen gestern gearbeitet.
    We worked yesterday in spite of the rain.

Try to form sentences of your own using **während, wegen,** and **trotz.**

[3] The Attributive Genitive

Rephrase the German sentences by using the elements indicated in
parentheses.

SEE
ANALYSIS
125

(pp. 216-219)

Am Abend ihres Geburtstages ging er mit ihr ins Theater.
    On the evening of her birthday he went to the theater with her.
    (on the evening of his birthday)

Gegen Ende des Jahres kam er aus Afrika zurück.
    Toward the end of the year he came back from Africa.
    (toward the end of the week)

Die Integrität des Menschen ist das Thema dieses Buches.
  The theme of this book is the integrity of man.
  (the intelligence of our children)

Herr Harms ist ein Freund meines Mannes.
  Mr. Harms is a friend of my husband.
  (the son of my friend)

Werners Freundin kenne ich nicht.
  I don't know Werner's girl friend.
  (Ingrid's aunt)

Schmidt-Ingelheims Roman habe ich nicht gelesen.
  I haven't read Schmidt-Ingelheim's novel.
  (father's books)

Hast du Mutters Hut gesehen?
  Have you seen mother's hat?
  (Karl's car)

Den Vater dieses Mädchens kenne ich sehr gut.
  I know this girl's father very well.
  (his friend's mother)

Dr. Thümmel ist ein Schüler meines Mannes.
  Dr. Thümmel is a student of my husband's.
  (a friend of my father's)

Von dem Geld meines Vaters habe ich nie etwas gesehen.
  I've never seen anything of my father's money.
  (my wife's money)

[4] von plus Dative as a Genitive Substitute

Hannelore? Das ist doch die Freundin von Werner Schlosser!
  Hannelore? She's Werner Schlosser's friend, isn't she?
  (Hans Wagner's wife)

Herr Behrens ist ein Freund von meinem Mann.
  Mr. Behrens is a friend of my husband's.
  (Mrs. Behrens; of my wife's)

Herr Behrens ist ein Freund von Johannes.
  Mr. Behrens is a friend of Johannes's.
  (Mrs. Behrens; a friend of Inge's)

Und die Tochter von diesen Leuten willst du heiraten?—Na und?
  And you want to marry the daughter of those people?—Well, so what?
  (the son of that man?)

Renate ist eine von Dieters Freundinnen.
  Renate is one of Dieter's girl friends.
  (Jürgen; Armin's friends)

SEE
ANALYSIS
124–125
(pp. 214-219)

Note the difference in the use of the genitive and of **von** plus dative
in the following sentences. When is the **von**-phrase obligatory?

Ingelheims Kinder sind noch klein.
Die Kinder von Ingelheim sind noch klein.
Die Kinder von Ingelheims sind noch sehr klein.
Ingrids Kinder sind noch sehr klein.
Die Kinder von Ingrid sind noch sehr klein.
Sie war eine Freundin von Overhoffs Frau.
Er war der Vater von dreizehn Kindern.
Ich bin kein Freund von Rheinwein.
Jeder Leser von Kriegsromanen weiß, wer Schmidt-Ingelheim ist.

[5] Special Constructions

SEE
ANALYSIS
125

(pp. 216-219)

Er ist ein Freund von mir.

von _____ (du)
von _____ (er)
von _____ (sie)
von _____ (wir)
von _____ (ihr)
von _____ (Sie)
von _____ (meine Mutter)
von _____ (mein Vater)

Möchten Sie noch eine Tasse Tee?
    Would you like another cup of tea?

Haben Sie schon gewählt?—Ja, ich hätte gerne ein Glas Mosel.
    Have you decided yet?—Yes, I'd like a glass of Moselle.

Meine Frau würde gerne ein Glas Wasser trinken.
    My wife would like to drink a glass of water.

[6] **ein**-Words without Nouns

Form variations of your own.

SEE
ANALYSIS
126

(p. 219)

Ich habe leider kein Buch mitgebracht. Hast du eins bei dir?
    Unfortunately, I didn't bring a book along. Do you have one with you?

Keiner von seinen Freunden hat ihn besucht.
    None of his friends visited him.

Hier ist das Buch von Rolf.—Nein, das ist meins.
    Here is Rolf's book.—No, that's mine.

Mir gehört das Buch nicht; es muß deins sein.
    That book doesn't belong to me. It must be yours.

Wem gehört denn der Porsche? Ist das Ihrer, Frau Kröger?
  Who owns that Porsche? Is it yours, Mrs. Kröger?

Einen Ihrer Romane habe ich gelesen.
  I have read one of your novels.

Einen von Ihren Romanen habe ich gelesen.
  I have read one of your novels.

Eine seiner Töchter studiert jetzt Medizin.
  One of his daughters is studying medicine now.

Eine von seinen Töchtern studiert jetzt Medizin.
  One of his daughters is studying medicine now.

[7] The Indirect-Discourse Subjunctive

After studying these sentences, form statements in indirect discourse
using the assertions printed below the pattern sentences. If possible,
use both forms of the subjunctive.

SEE
ANALYSIS
127
(p. 219)

„Ich bin nur zwei Tage in München.“
Sie sagte, sie wäre nur zwei Tage in München.
Sie sagte, sie sei nur zwei Tage in München.

„Ich habe ein Zimmer im Regina.“
Sie sagte, sie hätte ein Zimmer im Regina.
Sie sagte, sie habe ein Zimmer im Regina.

„Wann bist du denn gestern abend nach Hause gekommen?“
Er fragte mich, wann ich gestern abend nach Hause gekommen wäre.
Er fragte mich, wann ich gestern abend nach Hause gekommen sei.

München, Ludwigstraße von der Feldherrnhalle.

„Ich mußte gestern nach Regensburg fahren."
Er sagte, er hätte gestern nach Regensburg fahren müssen.
Er sagte, er habe gestern nach Regensburg fahren müssen.

„Ihr braucht nicht auf mich zu warten; ich komme erst morgen."
Er sagte, wir brauchten nicht auf ihn zu warten; er käme erst morgen.
Er sagte, wir brauchten nicht auf ihn zu warten; er komme erst morgen.

„Kannst du mit mir frühstücken?"
Er fragte, ob ich mit ihm frühstücken könnte.
Er fragte, ob ich mit ihm frühstücken könne.

„Dann können wir zusammen frühstücken."
Er sagte, wir könnten dann zusammen frühstücken.

VARIATIONS

Transform the following statements into indirect discourse in
accordance with the examples above.

„Er ist schon lange wieder zu Hause."

„Morgen habe ich keine Zeit."

„Ich kann Sie morgen leider nicht besuchen."

„Leider muß ich morgen nach Wiesbaden fahren."

„Fahren *Sie* doch morgen nach Mainz, Herr Rombach."

„Ich darf meinen Mann noch nicht besuchen."

„Ich will nicht studieren."

„Wann fahren Sie nach Essen?"

„Der Mantel ist ganz neu."

„Ich muß mal telefonieren."

Conversation

The following is one continuous conversation in typical, everyday German.
The first two sections may be used for class drill and memorization. The third
section is meant for listening and reading practice. The entire conversation,
as well as an additional section, also appears on tape.

I

TELEFONISTIN: Hotel Regina, guten Morgen.

KLAUS: Guten Morgen. Ich hätte gerne Zimmer 641 (sechseinundvierzig).

TELEFONISTIN: Einen Augenblick, bitte.

II

ROSEMARIE: Ja, bitte?

KLAUS: Rosemarie? Guten Morgen.

ROSEMARIE: Klaus? Guten Morgen. Du hättest aber wirklich nicht so früh anzurufen brauchen. Ich schlafe ja noch.

KLAUS: Das höre ich.

ROSEMARIE: Wieviel Uhr ist es denn? Sieben? Oder ist es schon acht?

KLAUS: Acht? Es ist zwanzig nach zehn.

ROSEMARIE: Nein, das ist nicht möglich—zwanzig nach zehn?

KLAUS: Doch, das *ist* möglich. Wenn es *nicht* schon so spät wäre, hätte ich dich nicht angerufen.

ROSEMARIE: Ja, und wenn wir gestern abend nicht so lange getanzt hätten, wäre ich auch schon lange auf.

KLAUS: Aber wer wollte denn gestern so lange tanzen, du oder ich?

ROSEMARIE: Ich, natürlich. Wenn ich nur zwei Tage in München bin, will ich doch auch etwas sehen.

KLAUS: Na, *so* interessant ist die Regina-Bar ja *auch* nicht!

III

ROSEMARIE: Du, Klaus, wo bist du denn eigentlich? Hier im Hotel?

KLAUS: Nein, ich bin noch zu Hause. Aber wenn du willst, komme ich um elf ins Hotel. Dann können wir zusammen frühstücken. Du könntest natürlich auch auf deinem Zimmer frühstücken, und ich komme erst um zwölf—wie du willst.

ROSEMARIE: Nein, das möchte ich nicht. Wenn ich nur drei Nächte in München bin, will ich mit *dir* frühstücken.

KLAUS: Gut, Rosemarie—ich bin um elf in der Hotelhalle—und es wäre schön, wenn du nicht erst um zwölf kämst: ich habe Hunger, ich bin schon seit acht Uhr auf.

ROSEMARIE: Aber Klaus, du weißt doch, daß du nie auf mich zu warten brauchst. Gestern hast du auch gesagt, daß ich um acht Uhr da sein müßte oder wir kämen nicht mehr in das Restaurant—wie hieß es doch?

KLAUS: Feldherrnkeller.

ROSEMARIE: Ja richtig—wir kämen nicht mehr in den Feldherrnkeller, weil dort immer so viele Leute seien. Na, und wann war ich da? Um zehn vor acht. —Übrigens, Klaus, wie ist denn das Wetter? Ich habe noch nicht aus dem Fenster gesehen, aber es wäre schön, wenn heute die Sonne schiene.

KLAUS: Das Wetter könnte nicht besser sein. Heute morgen sah es ja aus, als ob

es wieder regnen würde—und wenn du nicht hier wärst, hätte es heute bestimmt geregnet.

ROSEMARIE: Vielen Dank für das Kompliment, Klaus. Aber wenn es geregnet hätte, das hätte auch nichts gemacht. Wir hätten ja in ein Museum gehen können. Aber weißt du was? Ich ginge nach dem Frühstück gerne durch die Stadt; ich möchte mir doch einen Mantel kaufen, und es wäre nett, wenn wir das zusammen machen könnten.

KLAUS: Gut—und was machen wir, wenn wir den Mantel gekauft haben?

ROSEMARIE: Dann können wir eine Stunde auf einer Bank in der Sonne sitzen.

KLAUS: Im Hofgarten:* Das wäre prima. Wir gehen eine Stunde in den Hofgarten, und dann gehen wir essen.

* The Royal Gardens, a public park in the center of Munich.

Reading

Eine unmögliche Geschichte (Fortsetzung)

Ich wußte sofort, daß meine Frau diesen Brief an dem Tag geschrieben hatte, als ich mit Erich und Hermann bei Ali gesessen hatte und Erich plötzlich sagte: „Du Hans, deine Frau schreibt dir gerade einen Brief." Aber wie gesagt, ich wußte damals nicht, wo Erich war, und habe ihn erst letzten Freitag in Tripolis wieder- 5 gesehen.

Ich arbeite gerade an meinem Roman *Ende bei Karthago* und war nach Afrika geflogen, um noch einmal die Gegend zu besuchen, wo wir damals gegen die Amerikaner gekämpft haben. Es war darum ganz natürlich, daß ich, sofort nachdem ich in Tripolis angekommen 10 war, zu Busuqs Haus gehen wollte. Es steht tatsächlich noch. Ich wollte gerade mit meiner Leica eine Aufnahme machen (hätte ich

diese Aufnahme doch nur gemacht!), als jemand aus dem Haus
kam. Es war Erich.

Erich, der mich jahrelang immer nur in Uniform gesehen hatte,   **der** (*relative pro-*
erkannte mich nicht. Er sah nur einen Mann mit einer Kamera—   *noun*) who. (Relative
und war auf einmal verschwunden. Verschwunden, sage ich: er ging ₅ pronouns will be dis-
nicht um die Ecke, er ging nicht ins Haus zurück, er war plötzlich cussed in Unit 8.)
einfach nicht mehr da. „Diese Sonne“, dachte ich, „die macht einen
noch ganz verrückt.“ Dann ging ich ins Haus. Ali saß im Garten. Er
war jetzt über achtzig. Er erzählte mir, daß seine Frau kurz nach dem **achtzig** eighty
Ende des Krieges gestorben sei und daß mein Freund Erich ihn jedes ₁₀
Jahr einmal besucht habe. Ja, Erich wäre gerade vor ein paar
Minuten im Haus gewesen und habe ihm, wie jedes Jahr um diese
Zeit, fünf Goldstücke dagelassen. Tatsächlich stand Ali auf, nahm
einen Stein aus der Wand des Hauses, griff in ein Loch hinter dem
Stein und zeigte mir fünf Goldstücke, fünf Zwanzigmarkstücke. ₁₅
„Also war es wirklich Erich, den du gesehen hast und der dann   **den** whom
einfach nicht mehr da war“, sagte ich mir; und plötzlich wußte ich:
hier ist etwas nicht in Ordnung.

Ich ging ins Hotel zurück, um nachzudenken. Im Hotel wartete ein
Brief von Hermann Schneider aus Hamburg auf mich. „Lieber ₂₀   **Lieber Hans** Dear
Hans“, schrieb Hermann, „ich habe Dich zwar seit Ende des Krieges Hans
nicht mehr gesehen, aber ich habe alle Deine Bücher gelesen. Ich
gratuliere Dir zu Deinen Detektivromanen, die ich viel besser finde **die** which
als Deine Kriegsromane. Dein Verleger ist ein Freund von mir und   **der Verleger**
hat mir versprochen, Dir diesen Brief nachzuschicken. Aber da er ₂₅ publisher
mir nicht sagen wollte, wo Du bist, weiß ich nicht, wo und wann
Dich mein Brief erreichen wird. Ich habe eine Bitte an den Detektiv
in Dir.

„Wie Du vielleicht weißt, bin ich in Hamburg Direktor der Hansa-
Bank. In unserer Bank verschwinden seit zehn Jahren jedes Jahr um ₃₀
diese Zeit fünf Zwanzigmarkstücke. Natürlich sind hundert Mark
in Gold nicht viel Geld. Aber es ist doch seltsam, daß jemand in
unserer Bank jedes Jahr fünf Goldstücke stiehlt. Ich will noch nicht
die Polizei anrufen, denn ich habe das Gefühl, ich stehe hier vor
irgendeinem Geheimnis. Ich bitte Dich daher, die Sache zu unter- ₃₅ **irgendein** some kind
suchen. Du könntest ein paar Wochen lang in der Bank ‚arbeiten‘   of
und versuchen, den Dieb zu finden. Mein Privatsekretär ist übrigens
unser Freund Erich Karsten.“

Erich Karsten!

Erich Karsten! Gerade vor einer Stunde war er bei Ali gewesen und ₄₀
hatte ihm, „wie jedes Jahr um diese Zeit“, fünf Goldstücke gegeben.
Und damals hatte er mit seinen Militärschuhen hinter meiner Frau
gestanden und den Brief gelesen.

Es wäre nicht gerade intelligent gewesen, Hermann Schneider von
Tripolis aus anzurufen. Wenn Erich der Dieb war—und er mußte
es sein—durfte er auf keinen Fall wissen, daß ich gerade heute in
Tripolis war, als er Ali fünf Goldstücke ins Haus getragen hatte.

nicht gerade not exactly

Ich nahm daher ein Taxi zum Flughafen, bekam auf der Maschine 5
nach Paris noch einen Platz und rief Hermann Schneider von Paris
aus an. Da ich nicht wußte, ob Erich bei Hermann war oder nicht,
erzählte ich Hermann, ich sei ein paar Tage in der Normandie
gewesen, hätte gerade seinen Brief bekommen und werde gegen
sechs in Hamburg ankommen. Ich gab meinem Freund die Flug- 10
nummer und bat ihn, mich abzuholen. „Natürlich hole ich dich ab",
sagte Hermann. „Ich wohne nicht weit vom Hamburger Flughafen.
Es ist zwar sehr heiß hier in Hamburg, aber gottseidank habe ich
hinter dem Haus ein Schwimmbecken."

Hamburger When city names are used attributively, they have the ending **–er.**

Es war ungefähr sieben Uhr, als wir vor Hermanns Haus hielten. 15
Vor dem Haus stand ein Volkswagen. „Das ist Gerdas Wagen", sagte
Hermann. „Sie hat deine Romane gelesen und wollte dich gerne
kennenlernen; übrigens werden wir nächste Woche heiraten. Ich—"

Hinter dem Haus schrie eine Frau. Sie schrie, daß mir fast das Herz
stillstand. Bevor ich wußte, was geschah, hatte Hermann einen 20
Revolver aus dem Wagen geholt und lief hinter das Haus. Ich folgte
ihm. Am Schwimmbecken stand ein Mädchen, blond, schön und
mit einer Figur, wie man sie sonst nur im Film sieht. Auf dem
Wasser schwamm ein Hut. Sie zitterte, zeigte auf den Hut und
sagte: „Er ist weg—oh, ich hasse diesen Menschen."   25

(Fortsetzung folgt)

Ein Kapitel aus *Tristram Shandy* von Lawrence Sterne

Ever since the eighteenth century, the Germans have shown a lively interest in English
literature. Although cultural exchanges between nations were not as instantaneous as they
are today, when German translations of English and American works follow the original
often within a few months, the German reading public eagerly awaited new publications
even then. One of the novels that became widely known was *Tristram Shandy* by the sati-
rist Lawrence Sterne (1713–1768). Its cast of whimsical characters and their constant play
on words had universal appeal. The following excerpt from the German translation of 1801
will show you that playing around with language is not the exclusive province of gram-
marians. Having wrestled with German verbs for so long now, maybe you will agree with
Mr. Sterne when he says, "I am convinced that there is a North west passage to the intellectual world. . . . The whole entirely depends upon the auxiliary verbs, Mr. Yorick."

The original German translation was printed in *Fraktur,* the traditional German type face
until the 1930s and 40s. See if you can decipher the facsimile of the title page (opposite).

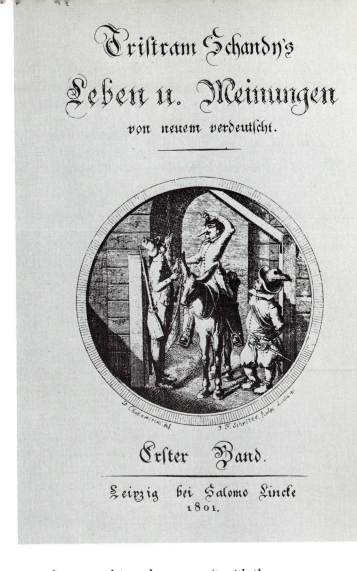

Tristram Schandy's

Leben u. Meinungen

von neuem verdeutscht.

Erster Band.

Leipzig bei Salomo Lincke
1801.

Read the original English first in its entirety, then reread it and compare it with the German.

Chapter XLIII	Dreiundvierzigstes Kapitel
—The whole entirely depends, added my father, in a low voice, upon the auxiliary verbs, Mr. *Yorick.*	—Die ganze Sache, setzte mein Vater mit leiser Stimme hinzu, kommt auf die Auxiliar-Verba an, lieber Yorick.
The verbs auxiliary we are concerned in 5 here, are, *am; was; have; had; do; did; make; made; suffer; shall; should; will; would; can; could; owe; ought; used;* or *is wont.*—And these varied with tenses, *present, past, future,* and conjugated with 10 the verb *see,*—or with these questions	Die Auxiliar-Verba, mit denen wir's hier zu tun haben, sind: *bin, war; habe, hatte; tue, tat; mache, machte; soll, sollte; will, wollte; kann, konnte; muß, mußte; pflege, pflegte.*— Und diese abgeändert durch die Tempora oder Zeiten, die *gegenwärtige, vergangene, zukünftige,* und konjugiert mit dem Zeit-

added to them;—*Is it? Was it? Will it be?*
Would it be? May it be? Might it be? And
these again put negatively, *Is it not? Was it
not? Ought it not?*—Or affirmatively,—*It is;
It was; It ought to be.* Or chronologically,—
Has it been always? Lately? How long ago?
—Or hypothetically,—*If it was? If it was
not?* What would follow?—If the *French*
should beat the *English?* If the *Sun* go out
of the *Zodiac?*

Now, by the right use and application of
these, continued my father, in which a
child's memory should be exercised, there is
no one idea can enter his brain how barren
soever, but a magazine of conceptions and
conclusions may be drawn forth from it.—

Didst thou ever see a white bear? cried my
father, turning his head round to *Trim,* who
stood at the back of his chair:—No, an'
please your honour, replied the corporal.—
But thou couldst discourse about one, *Trim,*
said my father, in case of need?—How is it
possible, brother, quoth my uncle *Toby,* if
the corporal never saw one?—'Tis the fact
I want, replied my father,—and the possibility of it, is as follows.

A white bear! Very well. Have I ever seen
one? Might I ever have seen one? Am I
ever to see one? Ought I ever to have seen
one? Or can I ever see one?

Would I had seen a white bear! (for how
can I imagine it?)

If I should see a white bear, what should I
say? If I should never see a white bear,
what then?

worte *sehen,* oder auch mit diesen beige-
fügten Fragen: *Ist es? war es? wird es sein?
könnt' es sein?* und diese wieder verneinend
gesetzt: *Ist es nicht? war es nicht? müßt' es
nicht?* oder bejahend: *Es ist; es war; es
sollte sein;* oder auch chronologisch: *Ist es
immer gewesen? neuerlich? wie lange her?*
—oder hypothetisch: *Wenn es wäre? wenn
es nicht wäre?* was folgte dann?—Wenn die
Franzosen die Engländer schlügen? Wenn
die Sonne aus dem Tierkreise ginge?

Bei dem richtigen Gebrauch und der ge-
hörigen Anwendung dieser Auxiliaren nun,
fuhr mein Vater fort, in welchen das Ge-
dächtnis eines Kindes fleißig geübt werden
sollte, kann durchaus keine Idee in des
Kindes Kopf kommen, so unfruchtbar sie
auch sein mag, aus welcher sich nicht
ein ganzes Magazin von Begriffen und
Schlüssen herholen ließe. Hat Er schon
einen weißen Bären gesehn? rief mein
Vater, und wandte sich mit dem Gesichte
nach *Trim,* der hinter seinem Stuhle stand.
—Nein, mit Ew. Gnaden Erlaubnis, antwortete der Korporal.—Er könnte aber doch
wohl davon sprechen, *Trim,* sagte mein
Vater, wenns erfordert würde?—Wie ist das
möglich, Bruder, sagte mein Onkel *Toby,*
wenn der Korporal nie einen gesehn hat?—
Das ist's eben, was ich will, erwiderte mein
Vater—und die Möglichkeit erhellet aus
Folgendem:

Ein weißer Bär! Wohl. Hab' ich je einen
gesehn? Hätt' ich je einen sehen können?
Werd' ich je einen zu sehn bekommen?
Müßte ich denn je einen gesehn haben?
Oder kann ich einen zu sehn bekommen?

Ich wollte, ich hätt' einen weißen Bären
gesehn! denn wie kann ich mir ihn sonst
vorstellen?

Wenn ich einen weißen Bären sähe, was
würd' ich sagen? Wenn ich nie einen weißen
Bären sehen sollte, was dann?

If I never have, can, must, or shall see a white bear alive; have I ever seen the skin of one? Did I ever see one painted?—described? Have I never dreamed of one?

Wenn ich nie einen lebendigen weißen Bären gesehen habe, sehn kann, soll, muß, oder werde; hab' ich je seine Haut gesehn? hab' ich je einen abgemalt gesehen?—oder beschrieben?—hat mir nie von einem geträumt?

Did my father, mother, uncle, aunt, brothers or sisters, ever see a white bear? What would they give? How would they behave? How would the white bear have behaved? Is he wild? Tame? Terrible? Rough? Smooth?

Haben mein Vater, Mutter, Onkel, Tante, Brüder oder Schwestern je einen weißen Bären gesehn? was würden sie darum geben? wie würden sie sich dabei gebärden? wie würde der weiße Bär sich benommen haben? Ist er wild? zahm? fürchterlich? rauh? glatt?

—Is the white bear worth seeing?—

—Ist der weiße Bär des Sehens wert?

—Is there no sin in it?—

—Ist nichts Sündliches dabei?—

—Is it better than a black one?

—Ist er besser als ein schwarzer?

Analysis

121 Prepositions with either Dative or Accusative

Nouns or pronouns following the prepositions **aus, außer, bei, mit, nach, seit, von, zu** must always be in the dative case.

> **Ich komme von meiner Tante.**
> **Ich komme von ihr.**

Nouns or pronouns following **durch, für, gegen, ohne** must always be in the accusative.

> **Ich gehe ohne meinen Freund.**
> **Ich gehe ohne ihn.**

In both groups, it is the preposition alone that determines the case of the following noun or pronoun.

There is, however, a group of prepositions which can be used with either dative or accusative, and the case of the noun or pronoun following these prepositions depends on the particular situation.

These prepositions are:

> **an, auf, hinter, in, neben, über, unter, vor, zwischen**

These nine prepositions are used to describe local areas in relation to some fixed point of reference. Thus, the English phrases *under the sofa* and *behind the sofa* describe different areas in relation to the *sofa*.

To a native speaker of English, the phrase *under the sofa* is not ambiguous; it can be used without danger of confusion in such sentences as

> The dog slept under the sofa

and

> The dog crawled under the sofa.

However, the same speaker of English will usually distinguish between *in* and *into* in such sentences as

The dog slept in the house.	The dog ran into the house.
He moved in high circles.	He moved into high circles.
He slipped in his slippers.	He slipped into his slippers.

The areas designated by *into* are the goals toward which the actions of running, moving, and slipping are directed; and in each case, the action stops when that goal has been reached. On the other hand, the area *in the house* is not reached by sleeping there. The dog was in the house when he started to sleep; and the poor fellow who slipped in his slippers had already slipped into his slippers and was in his slippers when he started to slip in his slippers.

A German will argue that the difference between *sleeping in the house* and *running into the house* is exactly parallel to the difference between *sleeping under the sofa* and *crawling under the sofa*.

Germans are very conscious of this difference because their language forces them to distinguish not only between *in*-situations and *into*-situations, but also between the two kinds of *under*-situations. The distinction is made in German not by the use of different prepositions like *in* and *into* but by the use of different cases following one and the same preposition.

If the area described by one of the nine prepositions above functions as the end-point or goal reached by the action (of crawling under the sofa), the noun following this preposition shows the accusative case.

If the area is the place where the entire action (of sleeping under the sofa) goes on from beginning to end, the noun following the preposition shows the dative.

This means that a German will always distinguish between **unter das Sofa** and **unter dem Sofa**.

Der Hund schläft unter dem Sofa.	**Der Hund springt unter das Sofa.**
Der Hund schläft hinter dem Sofa.	**Der Hund springt hinter das Sofa.**
Der Hund schläft auf dem Sofa.	**Der Hund springt auf das Sofa.**

It is important to realize that the distinction between dative and accusative after these nine prepositions is not one of rest versus motion. In both situations there may be motion (*He walked in the garden* and *He walked into the garden*). The determining factor is whether or not, in the course of the verbal action, a border line is crossed by either the subject or the object. If such a border line is crossed, the accusative must be used; if not, the dative must be used. This border line may be real or imagined. Thus, the area **vor dem Haus** does not have a clearly defined border, but there is nevertheless common consent as to the meaning of **vor dem Haus.** If this area **vor dem Haus** is entered in the course of the verbal action, the accusative must be used: **Er fuhr vor das Haus** (*He drove up to the house*). If the entire verbal action takes place within the area **vor dem Haus,** the dative must be used: **Er hielt vor dem Haus** (*He stopped in front of the house*).

On the other hand, after verbs which cannot imply motion, such as **sein** and **bleiben,** the dative is always required with these nine prepositions.

> **Er ist schon im Bett.**
> **Ich bleibe heute im Bett.**

NOTE:

1. The preposition corresponding to English *on* is **auf**, not **an.** German **an** describes an area "leaning against and touching" the point of reference. Thus it is **Frankfurt am Main** and **Köln am Rhein** (cf. *Stratford-on-Avon*). One speaks of a bed which stands **an der Wand** (**an** plus dative) after it has been pushed **an die Wand** (**an** plus accusative).

2. Unless the article is stressed, the following contractions are customary: **an dem = am; an das = ans; in dem = im; in das = ins.** The contractions **aufs, hinterm, übers, unterm** also occur in colloquial German.

3. If used with the accusative, **über** means either *over* with the implication "into the territory across," or it means *via* or *by way of*.

> **Er sprang über *den* Zaun.**   He jumped over the fence (into the neighbor's garden).
>
> **Er ist über *die* Schweiz nach Italien gefahren.**   He went to Italy via Switzerland.

When **über** means *via*, the corresponding interrogative is **wie?**, not **wohin?**

> **Wie seid ihr nach Italien gefahren, über Österreich oder über die Schweiz?**   How did you go to Italy, via Austria or via Switzerland?

but

> **Wohin seid ihr gefahren?**   Where did you go?
> **Nach Italien! Und zwar über die Schweiz!**   To Italy—and by way of Switzerland!

(Note that the article *must* be used with **Schweiz,** but is not used with the names of most other countries.)

4. As you already know, the preposition **vor** frequently means *ago*. If so used, it must be followed by the dative: **vor drei Jahren** (*three years ago*).

122 wo and wohin

The difference between **unter dem Sofa** and **unter das Sofa** reappears in the difference between **wo** and **wohin**. If you ask a **wo**-question, chances are that the answer will contain one of the nine "local area" prepositions with the dative; if you ask a **wohin**-question, chances are that the answer will contain one of those prepositions with the accusative.

> **Wo warst du denn?—In der Stadt.**
> **Wohin willst du denn?—In die Stadt.**

123 The Splitting of **wohin, woher, dahin,** and **daher**

In spoken German, the interrogatives **wohin** (*to which place*) and **woher** (*from which place*) and the demonstratives **dahin** (*to that place*) and **daher** (*from that place*) are usually split in such a way that **hin** and **her** become part of the second prong. They are then treated as if they were complements like **ab** or **an** and thus join a following verb form. Thus, there are two distinct patterns of the types **Wohin . . . gehen** and **Wo . . . hingehen.**

UNSPLIT POSITION	SPLIT POSITION
Wohin *gehst* **du?**	**Wo gehst du** *hin?*
Wohin willst du *gehen?*	**Wo willst du denn** *hingehen?*
Woher *kommst* **du?**	**Wo kommst du** *her?*
Woher ist der Brief ge*kommen?*	**Wo ist denn der Brief** *her*gekommen?
Dahin *will* **ich nicht.**	**Da will ich gar nicht** *hin.*
Daher komme ich *auch.*	**Da komme ich** *auch* **her.**

These "split" forms are very commonly used. When a German unexpectedly meets a friend, he asks:

> **Wo kommst** *du* **denn her?**

not

> **Woher kommst du?**

124 The Genitive Case

The English phrases *John Miller's house* and *the house of John Miller* are interchangeable. Both forms are *possessives* and answer the question *whose?* But *John Miller's* is called a genitive form, and *of John Miller* is a prepositional phrase used as a substitute for that genitive form. Forms like *John's* are normally used when referring to persons or to personifications; phrases with *of* are used in English when referring to things or ideas. It is normal to say *the purpose of the experiment*, not *the experiment's purpose*. Phrases with *of* are much more prevalent than forms with -*'s*.

In this unit the German genitive case is introduced. It is important to recognize from the very beginning two areas where German differs from English:

1. Phrases like *John's father* as well as phrases like *the purpose of the experiment* can be expressed in German by genuine genitive forms—that is, without the use of a preposition. German, in other words, does not make any distinction between persons and things. For example, **das Haus meines Vaters** and **der Titel meines Romans** correspond to *my father's house* and the incorrect *my novel's title.*

2. There is a growing tendency in German, especially in the spoken language, to avoid the genitive and to replace it with a prepositional phrase with **von**, again without any distinction between persons and things. It is very important, therefore, that you memorize thoroughly the patterns demonstrating these constructions, and that you keep in mind the fact that quite often the same English phrase can be expressed in two different ways in German.

ein Freund meines Mannes	or	**ein Freund von meinem Mann**
das Ende dieses Romans	or	**das Ende von diesem Roman**

Forms of the Genitive Case

INTERROGATIVE PRONOUNS

NOM.	**wer**	**was**
GEN.	*wessen*	
DAT.	**wem**	**was**
ACC.	**wen**	**was**

NOTE: **Was** has no genitive of its own. The dative **was** is used only after prepositions governing the dative, for example. **Von** *was* **habt ihr geredet?**

DEFINITE AND INDEFINITE ARTICLES

	MASC.	FEM.	NEUT.	PLURAL
NOM.	**der**	**die**	**das**	**die**
	ein	**eine**	**ein**	**(keine)**
GEN.	*des*	*der*	*des*	*der*
	eines	*einer*	*eines*	*(keiner)*
DAT.	**dem**	**der**	**dem**	**den**
	einem	**einer**	**einem**	**(keinen)**
ACC.	**den**	**die**	**das**	**die**
	einen	**eine**	**ein**	**(keine)**

GENITIVE OF NOUNS

Feminine nouns have the same form throughout the singular; there is no special ending for the genitive.

NOM.	die Frau	die Zeitung
GEN.	der Frau	der Zeitung
DAT.	der Frau	der Zeitung
ACC.	die Frau	die Zeitung

The majority of masculine and neuter nouns add the ending **-es** if their stem consists of one syllable, and **-s** if their stem consists of two or more syllables.

NOM.	der Mann	der Bahnhof	das Buch
GEN.	des Mannes	des Bahnhofs	des Buches
DAT.	dem Mann	dem Bahnhof	dem Buch
ACC.	den Mann	den Bahnhof	das Buch

Some masculine nouns, for example, **der Student, der Mensch, der Polizist'** (*the policeman*) have the ending **-en** in the genitive; this ending **-en** in such nouns occurs in all forms but the nominative singular.

	SINGULAR	PLURAL
NOM.	der Student	die Studenten
GEN.	des Studenten	der Studenten
DAT.	dem Studenten	den Studenten
ACC.	den Studenten	die Studenten

There are a few nouns that are irregular in the singular, for example, **das Herz** (*the heart*).

	SINGULAR	PLURAL
NOM.	das Herz	die Herzen
GEN.	des Herzens	der Herzen
DAT.	dem Herz(en)	den Herzen
ACC.	das Herz	die Herzen

The genitive plural of nouns has the same form as the nominative plural and the accusative plural. Remember that the dative plural of most German nouns ends in **-n** (see **61**).

NOM.	die Männer	die Frauen	die Bücher
GEN.	der Männer	der Frauen	der Bücher
DAT.	den Männern	den Frauen	den Büchern
ACC.	die Männer	die Frauen	die Bücher

125 Use of the Genitive

Prepositions Governing the Genitive

There are a number of prepositions which must be used with the genitive, but only three of these are important at this stage of your studies: **während** (*during*); **wegen** (*because of*); and **trotz** (*in spite of*).

Während des Krieges war Schmidt in Norwegen.
Wegen des Regens bleiben wir zu Hause.
Trotz des Regens fahren wir nach Köln.

With **trotz** and **wegen**, there is a tendency to replace the genitive with the dative, but this is still considered colloquial (**trotz dem Regen**). The compound **trotzdem** (*in spite of that, nevertheless*) has become standard.

We have now introduced all the major German prepositions. Remember that they *must* be used with specific cases. There are four different groups:

WITH THE GENITIVE:	**während, wegen, trotz**
WITH THE DATIVE:	**aus, außer, bei, mit, nach, seit, von, zu**
WITH THE ACCUSATIVE:	**durch, für, gegen, ohne**
WITH EITHER DATIVE OR ACCUSATIVE:	**an, auf, hinter, in, neben, über, unter, vor, zwischen**

The Genitive of Time

Occasionally, the genitive is used to express indefinite time. In contrast to English *one day* (past) and *some day* (future), **eines Tages** can be used for both past and future. Similarly: **eines Morgens, eines Abends,** and, by analogy, **eines Nachts** (and not **einer Nacht**).

The Attributive Genitive

By far the most common occurrence of the genitive is its use as an attribute. It then modifies a noun in the same way that an adjective does.

The government's decision did not come unexpectedly.
(*government's* is an attribute of the subject *the decision*)

The Thurbers expected Joan's cousin to arrive momentarily.
(*Joan's* is an attribute of the direct object *cousin*)

In these sentences, the possessive attributes can be eliminated without impairing the basic structure of the sentence; in other words, even without the attributes, the sentences are complete units of thought.

The decision did not come unexpectedly.
The Thurbers expected (the) cousin momentarily.

In German, the use of the attributive genitive is considered standard in the written language. It is used in two positions:

1. If the genitive form is a proper name, it *precedes* the noun it modifies. The genitive of all proper names ends in **-s.**

Schmidt-Ingelheims Roman war eine Sensation.
Werners Freundin kannte er nicht.
Inges Mutter ist schon hier.

Note that German does not use an apostrophe with this personal genitive.

2. If the genitive form is a common noun, it *follows* the noun it modifies.

Am Abend ihres Geburtstages ging er mit ihr ins Theater.
Die Integrität des Menschen ist das Thema seines Romans.

This means that *the woman's husband* must be rendered by **der Mann der Frau** and *the girl's father* by **der Vater des Mädchens.**

In the spoken language, the situation is far more complicated. While the attributive genitive is still considered standard German by most educated speakers, there is a steady erosion of these forms. The genitive most frequently replaced is the real possessive genitive in such forms as *my father's house* (expressing ownership: *My father owns the house*). The German equivalent is **das Haus meines Vaters,** but the variant **das Haus von meinem Vater** also occurs and is used even by many well-educated Germans.

Von plus dative is always used when the genitive would not be recognizable—that is, primarily in the absence of an article or of a **der-** or **ein-**word.

die Bücher von Studenten	students' books
der Vater von zehn Kindern	the father of ten children
eine Freundin von Müllers Frau	a friend of Müller's wife

With **Freund** and other nouns expressing similar relationships, **von** plus dative is used as the equivalent of the English phrases

He is a friend of mine.	Er ist ein Freund von mir.
He is a friend of Karl's.	Er ist ein Freund von Karl.

The idea *one of* in such sentences as *He is one of my friends* is expressed by **einer (eine, eins) von** (see **130**).

Er ist einer von meinen Freunden.
Sie ist eine von Karls Freundinnen.

In such phrases as *a cup of coffee, a glass of wine, a pound of butter*, where the first noun denotes a measure and the second something measured, the second German noun shows no case.

eine Tasse Kaffee
ein Glas Wein
ein Pfund Butter

If more than one measured unit is involved, only feminine nouns are used in the plural; masculines and neuters retain the singular form.

zwei Tassen Kaffee
zwei Glas Wein
zwei Pfund Butter

Compounding of nouns is another means by which German very frequently expresses the equivalent of English phrases with *of*, for example, *the production of leather goods:* **die Produktion von Lederwaren** or **die Lederwarenproduktion.** English, of course, uses the same device, but usually without spelling the compound as one word: *wheat production, book publishing,* and so forth.

126 ein-Words without Nouns

When **ein**-words are not followed by nouns, their declension is the same as that of the **der**-words. The neuter ending is usually **-s** instead of **-es.** Thus **mein Freund** becomes **meiner; ein Buch** becomes **eins.**

> **Inges Freund heißt Ulrich, und** *meiner* **heißt Werner.**
> **Ich habe leider kein Buch. Hast du** *eins?*
> **Hier steht ein Wagen, und dort steht noch einer.**

127 The Indirect-Discourse Subjunctive

In addition to the forms of the general subjunctive introduced in Unit 6, German has a second set of subjunctive forms which are mainly used in indirect discourse.

The only forms of this set in general use are the following:

PRESENT INDIRECT-DISCOURSE SUBJUNCTIVE

	sein	All other verbs						
		haben	werden	können	wollen	lieben	nehmen	fahren
ich	sei	habe	werde	könne	wolle	liebe	nehme	fahre
du	—	—	—	—	—	—	—	—
er	sei	habe	werde	könne	wolle	liebe	nehme	fahre
wir	seien	—	—	—	—	—	—	—
ihr	—	—	—	—	—	—	—	—
sie	seien	—	—	—	—	—	—	—

PAST INDIRECT-DISCOURSE SUBJUNCTIVE

ich sei gekommen	ich habe gegessen
er sei gekommen	er habe gegessen
wir seien gekommen	————
sie seien gekommen	————

NOTE:

1. The **ich**-form is always identical with the **er**-form.

2. The past indirect-discourse subjunctive replaces the past and the perfect of the indicative.

128 The Use of the Indirect-Discourse Subjunctive

As stated in Unit 6, the forms of the regular subjunctive can *always* be used in indirect discourse. It is not possible to formulate any definite rule stating when the indirect-discourse subjunctive should be used. It simply exists as an alternative preferred by some and almost completely avoided by others. In spoken German, the regular subjunctive is constantly gaining ground. Of the **ich**-forms listed above, the forms of **sein** and the modals are clearly recognizable as subjunctive forms; all other **ich**-forms are indistinguishable from the present-tense indicative (**ich liebe** can be either subjunctive or indicative).

Those who do use the indirect-discourse subjunctive usually follow this rule: The forms not recognizable as subjunctive occur only in indirect questions.

> **Sie fragte mich, ob ich sie liebe.**

In an indirect assertion, the unrecognizable **ich liebe** is replaced by the regular subjunctive **ich liebte.**

> **Ich sagte ihr, daß ich sie liebte.**

To illustrate the range of choice, let us assume that somebody asks the following question:

> **Liebst du mich denn, und findest du mich schön?**

By using the regular subjunctive only, this question could be reported in the form

> **Sie fragte mich, ob ich sie denn liebte und schön fände.**

By using the new set only, one could write:

> **Sie fragte mich, ob ich sie denn liebe und schön finde.**

Most probably, one will find a mixture; thus (in Heinrich Böll, *Ansichten eines Clowns*)

> **Sie fragte mich, ob ich sie denn liebe und schön fände**

is followed, at the end of the same paragraph, by:

> **Ich murmelte [*mumbled*], ja, ja, ich fände sie schön und liebte sie.**

NOTE:

1. If the original statement was made in the regular subjunctive, it cannot be changed.

> **„Es wäre schön, wenn heute die Sonne schiene.“**
> **Er sagte, es wäre schön, wenn heute die Sonne schiene.**

2. To put an imperative into indirect discourse, **sollen** is used.

> **„Seien Sie mir nicht böse.“**
> **Er sagte, ich sollte ihm nicht böse sein.**
> **Er sagte, ich solle ihm nicht böse sein.**

129 Word Formation

The Suffix -ung

The suffix **-ung** is added to many verb stems. It forms feminine nouns, the plural form being **-ungen,** and often corresponds to English *-tion.*

die Einladung	invitation
die Erwartung	expectation
die Erzählung	story, narration
die Hoffnung	hope
die Untersuchung	investigation
die Versuchung	temptation
die Wohnung	living quarters, apartment

The Suffix -ig

The suffix **-ig** may be added to nouns to form adjectives corresponding to English derivatives of the type *stone: stony, cat: catty,* which all express possession of the quality typical of the thing denoted by the noun.

der Stein	**steinig**	stony
der Hunger	**hungrig**	hungry
die Seite	**einseitig**	one-sided

The suffix **-ig** is also added to some time expressions to form adjectives which have no equivalents in English.

die Zeit	**zeitig**	in (good) time
	rechtzeitig	on time, at the right time
das Jahr	**-jährig**	
	dreijährig	three years old, lasting for three years
	ein dreijähriges Kind	a three-year-old child
	eine dreitägige Wanderung	a three-day hike
heute	**heutig**	of today
	die heutige Zeitung	today's paper
jetzt	**jetzig**	of today, present, contemporary
	der jetzige Bürgermeister heißt Böttle	the name of the present mayor is Böttle
damals	**damalig**	then
	der damalige Bürgermeister hieß Meyer	the then mayor's name was Meyer

Note also:

hier	**hiesig**	
	die hiesige Bevölkerung	the local population

The Suffix -los

The suffix **-los** corresponds to English *-less*. It is added to nouns to form adjectives.

das Herz	**herzlos**	heartless
die Arbeit	**arbeitslos**	unemployed
die Zeit	**zeitlos**	timeless

Exercises

A. Read aloud, then write out the numbers.

$$1 + 10 = 11 \qquad\qquad 11 - 4 = 7$$
$$6 + 10 = 16 \qquad\qquad 10 - 2 = 8$$
$$12 + 5 = 17 \qquad\qquad 9 - 0 = 9$$
$$14 + 6 = 20 \qquad\qquad 16 - 6 = 10$$

Es ist jetzt 7 Uhr 20. (7^{20} Uhr)
Es ist jetzt 8 Uhr 19.
Es ist jetzt 9 Uhr 18.
Es ist jetzt 10 Uhr 17.
Es ist jetzt 11 Uhr 16.
Es ist jetzt 12 Uhr 15.

B. Form questions for the following statements, using either **wo** or **wohin**.

SEE
ANALYSIS
122

(p. 214)

1. Ich habe den Tisch an die Wand gestellt.
2. Gestern habe ich im Theater Frau Schönberg gesehen.
3. Ich wollte mir auf dem Bahnhof eine Zeitung kaufen.
4. Im Sommer war er mit Rosemarie an der Mosel.
5. Morgen fährt er mit Rosemarie nach Bonn.
6. Seine Tochter war in Mainz.
7. Meine Frau liest die Zeitung immer im Bett.
8. Zu Hause trinkt Anton immer Tee.
9. Meyer hat uns zum Bahnhof gefahren.

C. Answer the following questions, using in your answers one of the prepositions that can take either the dative or the accusative.

SEE
ANALYSIS
121

(pp. 211-213)

1. Wohin hat er seinen Hut gelegt?
2. Wo hast du sie gesehen?
3. Wo waren Sie während des Krieges, Herr Schmidt?
4. Wo steht denn euer Wagen?
5. Wo geht ihr heute abend hin?

6. Wo wohnen Sie in München, Herr Schneider?
7. Wie seid ihr nach Italien gefahren?
8. Was hast du denn mit meinem Hut getan?
9. Wo hast du heute gefrühstückt?

D. Express in German.

SEE
ANALYSIS
125

(pp. 216-219)

1. He is my friend.
2. He is Karl's friend.
3. He is my sister's friend.
4. He is a friend of my sister's.
5. He is one of my sister's friends.
6. He is my father.
7. He is Ursula's father.
8. He is my wife's father.
9. He is her son.
10. He is Jutta's son.
11. He is my brother's son.
12. Karl is one of my brother's sons.
13. Ernst is one of the sons of Mr. Bertram.
14. Fritz is her friend.
15. Fritz is a friend of hers.
16. Fritz is one of her friends.
17. Her daughters are very intelligent.
18. Ingrid's daughter is also very intelligent.
19. Ingelheim's daughters are intelligent.
20. The Ingelheims' daughters are intelligent.

E. Give appropriate answers to the following questions, using either the genitive or **von** plus dative.

SEE
ANALYSIS
125

(pp. 216-219)

1. Wessen Buch ist das?
2. Mit wessen Wagen sind Sie denn nach Aachen gefahren?
3. Mit wessen Freundin warst du im Theater?
4. Von wessen Roman sprecht ihr denn?
5. Wessen Haus habt ihr gekauft?
6. Wessen Tochter hat er geheiratet?
7. Wessen Freundin ist das?
8. Wessen Vater hast du besucht?
9. Für wessen Haus willst du so viel Geld bezahlen?
10. Durch wessen Freundin hast du ihn kennengelernt?

F. Fill the blanks with appropriate **ein**-words.

SEE
ANALYSIS
126

(p. 219)

1. Ich habe leider kein Buch. Hast du _____?
2. Ich habe meinen Wagen nicht hier, Herr Schnitzler. Wo ist denn _____?
3. Habt ihr schon ein Haus? Nein, wir haben noch _____.

4. Hast du Zeit? Ich habe _____.
5. Das ist _____ von den Büchern, die mein Vater mir geschickt hat.
6. Er ist auch _____ von den Soldaten, die nicht über den Krieg sprechen wollen
7. Ich habe nicht _____ von seinen Büchern gelesen.
8. _____ seiner Romane habe ich mir gekauft.
9. Mein Hut ist das nicht; es muß _____ sein, Frau Kästner.

G. Supply the missing words.

1. Ich habe heute morgen meine Frau _____ Bahnhof gebracht.
2. Woher wissen Sie denn, daß Johannes schon _____ verheiratet war?
3. Mein Mann spricht oft _____ seiner Tochter.
4. In Frankreich war Ingelheim nur während _____ Krieges.
5. Ich habe gerade gelesen, daß Sie _____ drei Wochen in München wohnen.
6. Liegt er immer noch _____ Bett?
7. Von Ingelheims Kriegsroman spricht heute _____ Mensch mehr.
8. Ich bin nicht Soldat geworden, um Brieftauben _____ füttern.
9. Der Arzt glaubte, Ingelheim _____ Hepatitis, aber er _____ nur zu viel getrunken.
10. Ich weiß, daß Anton nach Berlin gefahren _____.
11. Kannst du mir sagen, _____ Ingelheims Kinder haben?
12. Er ist einer _____ Ingelheims Söhnen.
13. Ich möchte wissen, _____ du mich eigentlich geheiratet hast.
14. Können Sie mir sagen, _____ der Zug nach Bamberg fährt?
15. _____ der Krieg anfing, studierte Schmidt in Frankfurt Medizin.
16. Man kann doch nicht im Garten arbeiten, _____ es regnet.
17. Er fragte mich, ob ich heute abend auch ins Konzert _____.
18. Ich wollte, ich _____ dich nie gesehen.
19. Wenn er nicht an die Ostsee gefahren _____, hätte ich ihn nie kennengelernt.
20. Ich habe das Haus nicht kaufen _____.

H. Rewrite Hermann Schneider's letter to Ingelheim (page 207) in indirect discourse, using either the normal subjunctive or, when possible, the indirect-discourse subjunctive.

I. Express in German.

1. We really ought to put (**stellen**) that (little) table between our beds.
2. Do you always have to put your books on the breakfast table?
3. Why can't they lie on the breakfast table?
4. During the war Ingelheim was on the western front.
5. At that time he was happy that he did not have to go to Africa.
6. It is cold tonight; I wish you hadn't forgotten your overcoat.
7. If only that woman hadn't been so unfriendly!
8. If only I hadn't accepted the money!
9. You should have given him more money.
10. I wish I weren't so far away from you.

J. Write a brief paragraph in German containing the following ideas; use the past tense. Do *not* translate the passage; just use it as an outline. Use your own words, but do not attempt to use any construction or any vocabulary that you haven't had yet.

Hermann Schneider drove to the Hansa-Bank at 7 A.M. It was hot, and he would much rather have stayed at home by his swimming pool. But he had to go to the bank, because Karsten had just called to tell him that five gold pieces had disappeared again. Schneider didn't understand why this could happen every year. The thief had to be somebody who worked in the bank, but Schneider did not want to call the police yet. He would rather discuss the matter with Karsten first, he thought.

K. Now write a brief dialogue between Schneider and his fiancée Gerda, taking place in the evening of the same day.

Hermann tells Gerda about the theft of the gold pieces. She wants to know whether he has told Karsten about it, and whether Karsten had any ideas. Yes, he has, and Karsten thought it was somebody who works in the bank, but he was very much against calling the police. Gerda has an idea: What about Hermann's friend Ingelheim? He has written detective stories, and perhaps he can help Hermann. But Hermann hasn't seen Ingelheim since the war and doesn't know where he is. Gerda suggests that he call Ingelheim's publisher, which Hermann promises to do the next morning. Gerda is pleased, because she has wanted to meet Ingelheim for a long time.

L. Try to guess the meaning of the following compounds and derivatives. Disregard adjective endings.

1. ein achtjähriges Mädchen
2. wir haben eine Vorkriegswohnung
3. er arbeitet nur vormittags
4. er ist ein Bergsteiger
5. das Alleinsein ist schwer
6. ruhelos auf und ab gehen
7. kinderlos
8. eine vielköpfige Familie
9. ich bin wunschlos glücklich
10. endlos
11. ein gleichseitiges Dreieck
12. ein vielseitiger Künstler
13. gottlos
14. unfreundlich
15. ein Autounglück
16. Zigaretten sind ungesund
17. schlaflos
18. die Dinosaurier sind ausgestorben
19. ein Mittagsschläfchen halten
20. ein Stückchen Seife
21. ich kann nur ein Stündchen bleiben
22. das Dasein und das Sosein
23. ein Menschenkenner
24. die Tänzerin
25. die Bahnhofshalle
26. unhörbar
27. in unerreichbarer Ferne
28. unbrauchbar
29. eine winterliche Landschaft
30. eine liebliche Gegend
31. du bist herzlich eingeladen
32. die herzliche Einladung
33. böse Erfahrungen machen
34. eine Kurzgeschichte
35. bildlich gesprochen
36. eine Nacherzählung
37. die Menschwerdung Gottes
38. eine ärztliche Untersuchung
39. Einzahlung und Auszahlung
40. eine Anzahlung machen
41. etwas auf Abzahlung kaufen

Basic Vocabulary

auf	on, on top of; up; open
aufsein	to be up (out of bed)
der Augenblick, –e	moment
aussehen	to look, to give the appearance
die Bank, ⸚e	bench
die Bank, –en	bank
bestimmt	definite(ly)
bevor (*conj.*)	before
die Bitte, –n	request
da (*conj.*)	since
daher	therefore; from there, from that place
dahin	there, toward that place
erkennen (an)	to recognize (by)
erreichen	to reach, to attain
der Fall, ⸚e	case; fall
auf jeden Fall	in any case, at any rate
auf keinen Fall	in no case, under no circumstances
fast	almost
das Fenster, –	window
folgen (*with dat.*)	to follow
Frankreich	France
Freitag	Friday
gegen sechs Uhr	around six o'clock
geschehen	to happen, to occur
halten	to hold; to stop
heiß	hot
her	toward the speaker (in the sense of "hither")
herauskommen	to come out
herkommen	to come here
das Herz, –en (*gen.*: des Herzens; *dat.*: dem Herzen)	heart
hin	away from the speaker
hineingehen	to go in
hinfahren	to go there
der Hof, ⸚e	(royal) court; courtyard
der Hofgarten	the Royal Gardens
der Bahnhof, ⸚e	railroad station

holen	to get, to fetch
irgendein	some kind of
jahrelang	for years
legen	to lay, to place (flat)
die Leute (*pl.*)	people
es macht nichts	it doesn't matter
möglich	possible
unmöglich	impossible; (*sentence adv.*) not possibly
na! (*interj.*)	well
nachdem' (*conj.*)	after
nachschicken	to forward (mail)
die Ordnung	order
in Ordnung	in order, all right, O.K.
der Platz, ⸚e	place, seat
die Polizei' (*no pl.*)	police
der Polizist', –en	policeman
die Sache, –n	thing, matter
schwimmen	to swim
das Schwimmbecken, –	swimming pool
selten	rare, seldom
seltsam	strange, peculiar
stehlen	to steal
stellen	to place, to put (upright)
das Stück, –e	piece
das Goldstück, –e	gold coin
tanzen	to dance
tatsächlich	actual(ly)
der Tee	tea
tragen	to carry; to wear
trotz (*with gen. or dat.*)	in spite of
unter	under
verrückt	crazy
versprechen	to promise
von (Paris) aus	from (Paris)
wählen	to choose; to dial
während (*with gen.*)	during
die Wand, ⸚e	wall
weg	away
wegen (*with gen. or dat.*)	because of
zwar	to be sure

Additional Vocabulary

die Aufnahme, –n	picture, photo	der Keller, –	cellar
die Brücke, –n	bridge	das Loch, –er	hole
der Dieb, –e	thief	schreien	to cry, to scream
die Gegend, –en	area	der Sekretär, –e	secretary (male)
geheim	secret	die Sekretärin, –nen	secretary (female)
das Geheimnis, –se	secret	der Stein, –e	stone
das Gold	gold	untersuchen	to investigate
greifen	to grasp, to reach out (for something)	der Verleger, –	publisher
		wie gesagt	as I said
die Halle, –n	hall, lobby	zittern	to tremble

Strong and Irregular Verbs

bekommen, bekam, hat bekommen, er bekommt	to get, to receive
erkennen, erkannte, hat erkannt, er erkennt	to recognize
geschehen, geschah, ist geschehen, es geschieht	to happen, occur
greifen, griff, hat gegriffen, er greift	to grasp
halten, hielt, hat gehalten, er hält	to hold, stop
schreien, schrie, hat geschrie(e)n, er schreit	to scream, cry out
schwimmen, schwamm, ist geschwommen, er schwimmt	to swim
stehlen, stahl, hat gestohlen, er stiehlt	to steal
tragen, trug, hat getragen, er trägt	to carry
versprechen, versprach, hat versprochen, er verspricht	to promise

3.–10. SEPT. 1972
LEIPZIGER MESSE
DEUTSCHE DEMOKRATISCHE REPUBLIK

Unit 8 Relative Pronouns—**wann, ob, als, wenn**—**gar**—**da**-Compounds—**wo**-Compounds—Prepositional Objects

Patterns

[1] Definite Relative Pronouns

After studying Analysis **130**, analyze carefully the relative clauses contained in these sentences.

SEE ANALYSIS 130 (pp. 242-243)

Mein Vater, der nicht studiert hatte, konnte nicht verstehen, warum ich Schriftsteller werden wollte.
> My father, who had not gone to the university, could not understand why I wanted to become a writer.

Sein Vater, dessen Frau aus Moskau kam, sprach gut Russisch.
> His father, whose wife came from Moscow, spoke Russian well.

Seine Frau, deren Vater aus Leningrad kam, sprach gut Russisch.
> His wife, whose father came from Leningrad, spoke Russian well.

Kennen Sie meinen Freund Rombach?—Meinen Sie den Rombach, dem das Corona-Hotel gehört?
> Do you know my friend Rombach?—Do you mean the Rombach to whom the Corona Hotel belongs?

Ist das der Hut, den dir dein Mann aus Paris mitgebracht hat?
> Is that the hat your husband brought you from Paris?

Habe ich dir schon die Omega gezeigt, die ich in Zürich gekauft habe?
> Have I shown you the Omega (that) I bought in Zurich?

Das Essen, das wir hier bekommen, ist so gut, daß wir noch eine Woche bleiben wollen.
> The food we get here is so good that we want to stay another week.

Ich wußte natürlich, woher die Goldstücke kamen, die bei Ali in einem Loch in der Wand lagen.
> I knew, of course, where the gold pieces came from that were lying in a hole in the wall at Ali's.

Auch Sie sollten einmal nach Leipzig fahren.

Ich wollte Ali und Busuq wiedersehen, deren Gast ich während des Krieges gewesen war.
I wanted to see Ali and Busuq again, whose guest I had been during the war.

Ist das der Wagen, mit dem du nach Sylt gefahren bist?
Is that the car you went to Sylt in?

Hermann, durch den ich meine Frau kennengelernt habe, ist jetzt Bankdirektor in Hamburg.
Hermann, through whom I met my wife, is now director of a bank in Hamburg.

Wer waren denn die drei Herren, Marie-Louise, mit denen ich Sie gestern abend gesehen habe?
Who were the three gentlemen with whom I saw you last night, Marie-Louise?

Wer sind eigentlich diese Schäufeles, von denen du immer redest?
Who are those Schäufeles, anyway, that you always talk about?

Ihre Kinder, für die sie so schwer gearbeitet hat, wollen heute nichts mehr von ihr wissen.
Today her children, for whom she worked so hard, don't want to have anything to do with her anymore.

Der Mann, ohne dessen Hilfe ich heute nicht Arzt wäre, ist Professor Bornemann.
The man without whose help I wouldn't be a doctor today is Professor Bornemann.

SEE
ANALYSIS
130

(pp. 242-243)

[2] Indefinite Relative Pronouns

Wer Geld hat, hat auch Freunde.
Wer Geld hat, der hat auch Freunde.
(He) who has money has friends, too.

Was Schellenberger gestern abend zu erzählen hatte, war wirklich nicht viel.
Was Schellenberger gestern abend zu erzählen hatte, das war wirklich nicht viel.
What Schellenberger had to say last night really wasn't very much.

Herr Gruber hat mich zum Essen eingeladen, was ich sehr nett finde.
Mr. Gruber has invited me to dinner, which I think is very nice.

Ich habe leider nicht alles verstanden, was sie gesagt hat.
Unfortunately, I did not understand everything she said.

Professor Bodenstein hat wirklich nichts gesagt, was ich nicht schon wußte.
Professor Bodenstein really didn't say anything that I didn't already know.

Ich habe dieses Wochenende in Afrika etwas erlebt, was man eigentlich nicht erleben kann.
This weekend I experienced something in Africa that one really cannot experience.

[3] wann

SEE
ANALYSIS
131

(pp. 244-245)

Form other questions with **wann** and transform them into dependent clauses.

„Wann ist Wolfgang denn gestern abend nach Hause gekommen?"
Wolfgang, Vater möchte wissen, wann du gestern abend nach Hause gekommen bist.

„Wann will Heidi denn heiraten?"
Ich weiß nicht, wann sie heiraten will.

[4] ob

Form other yes-or-no questions and transform them into dependent
clauses.

„Fährst du nach Bern?"
Mutter will wissen, ob du nach Bern fährst.

SEE
ANALYSIS
131

(pp. 244-245)

„War Erich wirklich in Tripolis?"
Ich habe nie erfahren können, ob Erich wirklich in Tripolis war.

[5] als ob, als wenn, als

Form parallel examples. Be prepared to produce orally **Er tut, als ob
er schliefe** when you hear **Er schläft.**

Er tut, als ob er schliefe. Er tut, als schliefe er.	He acts as if he were asleep.
Er tat, als ob er schliefe. Er tat, als schliefe er.	He acted as if he were asleep.
Er tut, als ob er geschlafen hätte. Er tut, als hätte er geschlafen.	He acts as if he had been asleep.
Er tat, als ob er geschlafen hätte. Er tat, als hätte er geschlafen.	He acted as if he had been asleep.
Er tat, als wenn er schliefe.	He acted as if he were asleep.
Er tat, als wenn er geschlafen hätte.	He acted as if he had been asleep.
Gerda sah aus, als wäre sie krank.	Gerda looked as if she were sick.

SEE
ANALYSIS
131

(pp. 244-245)

[6] als with the Comparative

Form parallel sentences with **besser als** and **mehr als.**

Du bist auch nicht besser als er.	You are no better than he is.
Das ist besser als nichts.	That is better than nothing.
In Berlin wohnen mehr Menschen als in Unterzwingenbach.	More people live in Berlin than in Unterzwingenbach.
Frau Behrens hat in Baden-Baden mehr Geld verloren, als sie wollte.	Mrs. Behrens lost more money in Baden-Baden than she intended to.
Er wußte bestimmt mehr, als er uns gesagt hat.	I'm sure he knew more than he told us.

SEE
ANALYSIS
131

(pp. 244-245)

[7] The Conjunction als

SEE
ANALYSIS
131

(pp. 244-245)

Als Ingelheim ins Hotel kam, wartete ein Brief auf ihn.
Als wir in Tripolis waren, wohnten wir bei Ali und Busuq.
Hermann und ich saßen bei Ali, als Erich von meiner Frau sprach.
Wir wollten gerade ins Haus gehen, als eine Frau laut schrie.

[8] wenn

Form parallel sentences with **wenn,** in the meaning of both *if* and
whenever.

SEE
ANALYSIS
131

(pp. 244-245)

Wenn es morgen regnet, bleiben wir zu Hause.
Wenn er schon hier wäre, könnten wir ihn besuchen.
Wenn er damals hier gewesen wäre, hätten wir ihn besuchen können.
Wenn der Sommer kam, fuhren unsere Eltern immer mit uns an die Nordsee.
Jedesmal, wenn Tante Amalie uns besuchte, mußte ich mit ihr ins Museum gehen.
Wenn ich in München bin, gehe ich abends immer ins Theater.

[9] gar nicht, gar kein, gar nichts

Study these sentences carefully. Note that whenever **gar** is stressed,
it denies an immediately preceding idea. Be prepared to form your
own examples.

SEE
ANALYSIS
132

(pp. 245-246)

Meyer ist gar nicht *dumm;* er weiß immer, was er will.
    Meyer isn't at all stupid; he always knows what he wants.

Was, Heidi will heiraten? Das habe ich gar nicht ge*wu*ßt.
    What? Heidi wants to get married? I didn't have any idea of that.

Er spricht so leise, daß man ihn gar nicht ver*ste*hen kann.
    He speaks so softly that you can't understand him at all.

Wie hast du denn geschlafen?—Ich habe *gar* nicht geschlafen.
    How did you sleep?—I didn't sleep at all.

Was habt ihr denn heute gelernt?—*Gar* nichts, wir haben nur gespielt.
    What did you learn today?—Nothing at all, we only played.

Ingelheim *war* gar kein General; er war nur Leutnant.
    Ingelheim wasn't a general at all; he was only a lieutenant.

[10] da-Compounds with Unstressed da-

Wo ist denn mein Kugelschreiber?—Ich schreibe gerade damit.
  Where is my ballpoint pen?—I'm writing with it.

Wir haben *auch* ein Haus mit einer Garage dahinter.
  We, too, have a house with a garage behind it.

Das ist die Marienkirche, und in dem Haus da*neben* hat früher mein Bruder gewohnt.
  That's St. Mary's, and my brother used to live in the house next to it.

Haben Sie Ingelheims Roman gelesen?—Nur den Anfang davon.
  Have you read Ingelheim's novel?—Only the beginning of it.

SEE
ANALYSIS
133, 135

(pp. 246-247, 248)

[11] Stressed da-Compounds; Split da-Compounds;
der hier, der da

Be prepared to produce orally the statements containing da-compounds when you hear the initial statements.

Den Kugelschreiber kannst du zurückbringen.
*Da*mit (mit *dem*) kann ich nicht schreiben.
Da kann ich nicht mit schreiben.
Der Kugelschreiber hier ist mir zu schwer. Darf ich mal *den* da versuchen?

In die *O*per brauchst du mit Tante Amalie *nicht* zu gehen.
*Da*bei schläft sie immer ein.
Da schläft sie immer bei *ein*.
Sonntag im Kino ist sie *auch* eingeschlafen.—Aber im Gloria-Palast läuft heute abend ein Hitchcock-Film. Bei *dem* (*da*bei) schläft sie be*stimmt* nicht ein.

SEE
ANALYSIS
134–136

(pp. 247-249)

[12] wo-Compounds

Wofür brauchst du denn so viel Geld? Was willst du denn kaufen?
  What do you need so much money for? What do you want to buy?

Für was brauchst du denn das Geld?
  What do you need the money for?

Ich weiß nicht, wofür er das Geld ausgegeben hat.
  I don't know what he spent the money for.

War der Briefträger immer noch nicht da?—Warum fragst du denn schon wieder? Auf was (worauf) wartest du denn eigentlich, auf einen Brief von deiner Freundin?
  Hasn't the mailman been here yet?—Why are you asking again? What are you waiting for anyway, a letter from your girl friend?

SEE
ANALYSIS
138

(p. 249)

[13] Prepositional Objects

After memorizing these verbs with their prepositions, form variations
of your own.

SEE
ANALYSIS
139–141
(pp. 249-253)

Angst haben vor

Hast du Angst vor ihm?—Nein, nicht vor ihm, aber vor seiner Intelligenz.
   Are you afraid of him?—No, not of him, but of his intelligence.

antworten auf

Sie hat immer noch nicht auf meinen Brief geantwortet.
   She still hasn't answered my letter.

bitten um

Dürfte ich Sie um eine Tasse Kaffee bitten?
   Could I ask you for a cup of coffee?

danken für

Ich hätte ihm natürlich schon längst für die Blumen danken sollen.
   Of course I should have thanked him for the flowers long ago.

denken an and **nachdenken über**

Weißt du, daß ich noch oft an unsre Reise denke?
   Do you know that I still think often about our trip?
Über *dies*es Problem habe ich *auch* schon nachgedacht.
   I've thought about this problem, too.

einladen zu

Darf ich Sie zu einem Glas Wein einladen?
   May I invite you to (have) a glass of wine (with me)?

fragen nach

Hat jemand nach mir gefragt?—Du kannst dir doch denken, daß sie alle nach dir gefragt
      haben.
   Did anybody ask about me?—Don't you know that they all asked about you?

gehören zu

Diese Schlüssel gehören zu unserem VW.
   These keys belong to our VW.
Weißt du, daß Meyer jetzt zur Antivivisektionsliga gehört?
   Do you know that Meyer belongs to the Anti-Vivisection League now?

glauben an

Ein Athe*ist* glaubt nicht an Gott.
   An atheist doesn't believe in God.

halten von, halten für

Was halten Sie von Biedermann? Ich halte ihn für sehr intelligent.—Ich nicht, ich halte ihn
      gar nicht für intelligent.
   What do you think of Biedermann? I think he is very intelligent.—I don't; I don't think
      he's intelligent at all.

hoffen auf

Ich weiß, ihr Touristen hofft, daß morgen wieder die Sonne scheint. Aber die Leute *hier* hoffen auf *Regen.*

    I know you tourists hope that the sun is going to shine again tomorrow. But the people here are hoping for rain.

hören von

Seit dem Krieg habe ich nichts mehr von Franz Schuster gehört.

    Since the war, I haven't heard anything from Franz Schuster (of Franz Schuster, about Franz Schuster).

lachen über

Ich lache gar nicht über dich; ich lache nur über deinen Akzent.

    But I'm not laughing at you; I'm only laughing at your accent.

reagieren auf

Wie reagieren denn Ihre Leser auf diesen Kriegsroman?

    How do your readers react to this war novel?

Wie hat er denn auf dich reagiert?

    How did he react to you?

sein für, sein gegen

Wer nicht für mich ist, ist gegen mich.

    Whoever is not for me, is against me.

sprechen von

Von seiner Frau hat er nicht gesprochen.

    He didn't talk about his wife.

Ich weiß nicht, warum er nie von seinen Romanen spricht.

    I don't know why he never talks about his novels.

sprechen über

Heute abend spricht Professor Leid über Psychoanalyse.

    Tonight Professor Leid will speak about psychoanalysis.

verstehen von

Du weißt doch, daß ich nichts von Archäologie verstehe.

    You know, don't you, that I know nothing about archaeology.

warten auf

Wie lange wartest du denn schon auf Andreas?

    How long have you been waiting for Andreas?

Wartet ihr schon lange auf mich?

    Have you been waiting for me for a long time?

Wir warten schon zwei Stunden auf dich.

    We've been waiting for you for two hours.

wissen von

Leider weiß ich gar nichts von Ingelheim.

    Unfortunately I know nothing about Ingelheim.

Was weißt *du* denn von den Kämpfen in der Normandie?

    What do *you* know about the fighting in Normandy?

Conversation

Snatches of Conversation Overheard
by the Hat-Check Girl at the Regina Bar

FRAUENSTIMME 1: Und als er dann endlich erschienen ist, habe ich gesagt: „Jetzt hättest du aber wirklich nicht mehr zu kommen brauchen." Und weißt du, was er mir darauf geantwortet hat? Ich hätte ja nicht auf ihn zu warten brauchen!

FRAUENSTIMME 2: Na so was! Wenn er *mir* das gesagt hätte, dann hätte ich ihm aber . . .

FRAU A: Wer? Der mit dem Hut? Das soll Schmidt-Ingelheim sein?

FRAU B: Nein, nicht *der. Der* da, mit dem Mantel über dem Arm.

FRAU A: Glaubst du wirklich, daß er das ist?

FRAU B: Ganz bestimmt. Gestern war doch sein Bild in der Zeitung. Er ist gerade aus Afrika zurückgekommen.

FRAU A: *Der* sieht aber gut aus, den möchte ich kennenlernen.

FRAU B: Du, ob das wohl seine Frau ist, die da neben ihm steht?

FRAU A: Nein, bestimmt nicht, die ist doch viel zu jung für ihn;—vielleicht seine Tochter.

MANN: . . . mir viel zu heiß war! Im Theater ist es mir immer zu heiß, und dann auch noch Wagner. Da schläft man ja bei ein. Fünf Stunden hab' ich da gesessen, und am liebsten wär' ich schon nach zehn Minuten aufgestanden und nach Hause gegangen. Acht Stunden im Büro sitzen und dann noch Wagner! Nee, da mach' ich nicht mehr mit. Das nächste Mal bleibe ich zu Hause und lese meine Zeitung.

FRAU:	Von mir aus kannst du ruhig zu Hause bleiben. Dann gehe ich eben allein. Ach, ich liebe doch Wagner so sehr . . .
MÄDCHEN A:	Niemand weiß etwas davon—kein Mensch. Außer dir habe ich das noch niemandem erzählt, und du mußt mir versprechen, daß du mit keinem darüber redest, auch mit Fritz nicht.
MÄDCHEN B:	Natürlich nicht! Mit wem könnte ich über so etwas reden? Du kennst mich doch. Übrigens, weißt du, daß die Erika den Hans jetzt *doch* heiraten will?
MÄDCHEN A:	Ach was! Wirklich? Das hätte ich nicht gedacht.
MÄDCHEN B:	Ja, doch! Sie hat mir's gestern erzählt, es soll aber noch niemand etwas davon wissen.
MÄNNERSTIMME 1:	. . . bei Dinkel, sagst du?
MÄNNERSTIMME 2:	Ja, bei Dinkel, bei der Seifenfirma. Da ist er jetzt Reklamechef.
MÄNNERSTIMME 1:	Das hätte ich von dem Fritz nicht erwartet. Da hat er aber Glück gehabt.
MÄNNERSTIMME 2:	Du kennst doch den Reklametext, der jetzt überall in den Zeitungen steht?
MÄNNERSTIMME 1:	Du meinst: „DEO-Seife riecht gut. Aber das ist nicht wichtig"?
MÄNNERSTIMME 2·	Genau. „Wichtig ist nur, daß *Sie nicht* riechen." Das hat Fritz geschrieben.
MÄNNERSTIMME 1:	So was Blödes. Aber er war ja schon immer . . .

Reading

Eine unmögliche Geschichte (Schluß)

„Wer ist weg?" fragte Hermann. „Herr Karsten", antwortete das Mädchen. Hermann führte sie zu einem der Gartenstühle, versuchte, ganz ruhig zu sein, und sagte: „Gerda, dies ist mein Freund Schmidt-Ingelheim. Ich habe ihn gerade am Flugplatz abgeholt", und als sie nicht auf seine Worte reagierte, sagte er: „Gerda, könntest du dich 5 zwingen, mir und Hans jetzt zu erzählen, was hier geschehen ist?"

Es dauerte doch noch ein paar Minuten, bis Gerda ruhig sprechen konnte. Dann erzählte sie: „Ich bin kurz nach fünf mit meiner Mutter hier angekommen. Wir sahen, daß du noch nicht zurück warst. Mutter ist spazierengegangen, und ich wollte schwimmen, 10

bis du kamst. Als ich ins Wasser sprang, war niemand hier, das weiß ich bestimmt. Aber als ich aus dem Wasser wollte, stand Herr Karsten oben und hielt mir die Hand hin, um mir zu helfen. Ich erschrak, schrie laut und sprang zurück. Herr Karsten fiel ins Wasser. Als ich auf dieser Seite aus dem Wasser kam, war Herr 5 Karsten weg. Aber da schwimmt sein Hut."

hielt ... hin held out his hand

Hermann, dem ich auf dem Weg vom Flughafen erzählt hatte, was in Tripolis geschehen war, sah mich an, dann ging er ins Wohnzimmer, holte ein Telefon, stellte es auf den Gartentisch beim Schwimmbecken, wählte eine Nummer und wartete. Gerda und ich 10 hörten, wie es am anderen Ende klingelte. Dann gab mir Hermann den Hörer. „Hier Karsten", sagte eine Männerstimme. Und obwohl ich seit dem Kriege nicht mit Erich gesprochen hatte, erkannte ich seine Stimme sofort. Ich log und sagte ihm, ich riefe vom Flughafen aus an. 15

Ich hätte gehofft, Hermann könnte mich abholen, er sei aber nirgends zu sehen, und zu Hause sei er auch nicht. „Er wollte dich auch abholen", sagte Erich, „aber vielleicht ist er nicht so schnell durch die Stadt gekommen, wie er wollte. Ich rufe ihn trotzdem sofort noch einmal an und sage ihm, daß du da bist. Aber er ist 20 bestimmt nicht mehr zu Hause."

Einen Augenblick später klingelte das Telefon. Wir antworteten nicht. „Wie weit ist es von hier bis zu Erichs Wohnung?" fragte ich Hermann. „Mit dem Wagen mindestens eine Stunde", war die Antwort. Ich sagte nichts, auch Gerda schwieg; aber ich glaube, 25 sie fühlte, daß Hermann und ich mehr wußten, als wir sagten.

Endlich meinte Hermann: „Gerda, die Geschichte, die du uns da erzählt hast, ist einfach unmöglich. Wem der Hut auf dem Wasser gehört, weiß ich nicht. Aber Erich kann er nicht gehören, Erich kann nicht hier gewesen sein. Wenn er hier gewesen wäre, könnte er 30 jetzt nicht zu Hause sein. Weißt du was, wir warten, bis deine Mutter zurückkommt, und dann fahre ich euch beide in meinem Wagen nach Hamburg zurück. Hans kann mit deinem VW hinter uns herfahren."

hinter uns herfahren follow us

Es war schon ungefähr neun, als wir Gerda und ihrer Mutter gute 35 Nacht sagten. Gerda hatte versprochen, ein Bad zu nehmen, eine

Tasse Tee mit Kognak zu trinken und dann ins Bett zu gehen. Um   **um halb zehn** _at half_
halb zehn saßen wir bei Hermann, tranken einen Whisky und re-   _past nine_
deten von den Fußabdrücken hinter dem Stuhl meiner Frau, von
den fünf Goldstücken hinter dem Stein in Alis Haus und von Erichs
Hut in Hermanns Schwimmbecken. Wir versuchten, etwas zu er- 5
klären, was man einfach nicht erklären kann.

Da klingelte das Telefon; Hermann nahm den Hörer ab. Lange
sagte er nichts, und ich wußte nicht, mit wem er sprach. „Wir
kommen sofort, Gerda", sagte er dann, legte den Hörer auf und
sprang auf. „Aber so etwas ist doch einfach unmöglich!" rief er. 10
„Was ist unmöglich?" fragte ich und versuchte, ruhig zu bleiben.
Das Telefon klingelte wieder. Diesmal ging ich in Hermanns Ar-
beitszimmer, wo noch ein Telefon stand, und hörte mit.

„Hier ist Elisabeth Meyer", hörte ich eine Frauenstimme sagen. „Bei
mir in der Wohnung wohnt ein Herr Karsten. Soviel ich weiß, ist 15
er Ihr Privatsekretär. Herr Direktor, Ihrem Sekretär muß irgendetwas passiert sein. Er ist heute noch gar nicht weggewesen. Seit
dem Frühstück sitzt er auf seinem Zimmer. Vor ein paar Minuten
habe ich an seine Tür geklopft, um ihn zu fragen, ob er nicht etwas
essen wollte. Während ich klopfte, hörte ich einen lauten Schrei, 20
und dann war es still im Zimmer. Ich habe die Polizei schon angerufen, aber es wäre vielleicht gut, wenn Sie auch kämen. Er ist
doch ein Freund von Ihnen." „Ich komme sofort, Frau Meyer", sagte
Hermann und legte auf. Dann sagte er zu mir: „Hans, das ist zum
Verrücktwerden. Du mußt sofort zu Gerda fahren. Die zwei Frauen 25
dürfen heute abend nicht allein in ihrer Wohnung sein. Du kannst
meinen Wagen nehmen, und ich fahre mit einer Taxe zu Erichs
Wohnung. Ich sehe dich dann später bei Gerda. Sie soll dir erzählen,
was dort passiert ist." „O.K.", sagte ich. Dann liefen wir aus dem
Haus.   30

Gerda und ihre Mutter waren erstaunt, mich allein zu sehen.
„Hermann ist zu Erich gefahren", sagte ich. „Erichs Wirtin hat ihn   **vor einer halben**
vor einer halben Stunde laut schreien hören, und sie meint, ihm sei   **Stunde** _half an hour_
etwas passiert."   _ago_

„Aber Erich war doch vor einer halben Stunde hier", sagte Gerda. 35
„Hat Ihnen Hermann denn nichts davon erzählt?"—„Unmöglich!
Wie kann er vor einer halben Stunde hier gewesen sein, wenn er
vor einer halben Stunde in seinem Zimmer laut geschrien hat?
Gerda, ich glaube, Sie hätten keinen Kognak trinken sollen."

Aber Gerda lachte nicht. „Hans, Sie wissen mehr als Sie sagen", 40
meinte sie, und dann erzählte sie mir, was passiert war. „Nachdem
Sie beide heute abend weggegangen waren, nahm ich, wie ich versprochen hatte, ein Bad. Als ich nach zehn Minuten aus der Badewanne stieg, stand plötzlich der Karsten wieder vor mir. Wie er ins

Badezimmer gekommen ist, weiß ich nicht. Niemand hat geklingelt,
und meine Mutter hat niemand hereingelassen. Auch durch den
Garten kann er nicht gekommen sein, sonst hätte bestimmt der Hund
gebellt. Fitzi schläft nämlich auf der Terrasse, wissen Sie. Aber
trotzdem stand Karsten in der Badezimmertür und fragte: ‚Wo 5
haben Sie meinen Hut?‘ Ich wurde wütend, nahm meinen Schuh
und schlug ihm damit auf den Kopf. Und dann war er plötzlich weg,
gerade wie heute nachmittag im Schwimmbecken. Und mein Schuh
ist auch weg.“—„Ich glaube, wir sollten jetzt wirklich eine Tasse
Tee mit Kognak trinken“, sagte ich zu den Frauen, „oder noch 10
besser einen Kognak ohne Tee.“ Dann warteten wir auf Hermann.
Es war schon eins, als er kam. „Eine unglaubliche Geschichte“, fing
er an, „einfach unmöglich. Als ich vor Erichs Wohnung hielt, war
die Polizei gerade angekommen. ‚Aber ich sage Ihnen doch, er hat
laut geschrien‘, hörte ich die Wirtin sagen, ‚gerade als ich an die 15
Tür klopfte, um ihn zu fragen, ob ich ihm etwas zu essen bringen
könnte. Als er mir dann nicht antwortete, habe ich Sie sofort angerufen, und ich habe hier vor der Tür gestanden, bis Sie kamen.‘—
Es dauerte fast zehn Minuten, bis die Polizisten endlich die Tür
aufmachen konnten. Dann gingen wir alle ins Zimmer. Erich war 20
weg; kein Mensch war im Zimmer, aber auf dem Tisch stand eine
Tasse Kaffee, der noch warm war. Die Polizisten wußten nicht, was
sie von der Sache halten sollten. Ich konnte ihnen nicht helfen, denn
wenn ich ihnen erzählt hätte, was seit gestern geschehen ist, hätten
sie bestimmt gedacht, ich wäre verrückt.“   25

Ich wäre nicht erstaunt gewesen, wenn Gerda jetzt hysterisch geworden wäre, aber sie blieb ruhig, erzählte noch einmal, daß Erich
in der Tür zum Badezimmer gestanden und sie nach seinem Hut
gefragt habe, daß sie ihm mit einem Schuh auf den Kopf geschlagen
hätte, und daß Erich plötzlich einfach nicht mehr dagewesen sei.   30

Hermann, die zwei Frauen und ich redeten, bis es Tag wurde.

Dann frühstückten wir zusammen—Gerdas Kaffee war übrigens unglaublich gut—und fuhren nach Hause.

Gestern abend waren Gerda und ihre Mutter wieder bei uns. Wir
saßen gerade beim Abendessen, als das Telefon klingelte. Ich hörte 35
wieder mit. Es war die Polizei, aber nicht die Hamburger Polizei.
Es war Interpol in Tripolis. Vor dem Haus eines Ägypters habe*
man am Morgen einen Mann gefunden, tot und mit einer Wunde
im Kopf. Die Untersuchung durch die Polizei hätte bis jetzt zu
nichts geführt. Einen Paß habe der Mann nicht gehabt; in seiner 40
Tasche wäre ein Brief gewesen, adressiert an Hermann, aber

---

* Note that the use of the subjunctive is sufficient to indicate indirect discourse;
no introductory statement such as **Man sagte uns, . . .** is necessary.

außer hundert Mark wäre in dem Brief nichts gewesen. Niemand wisse, wer der Mann sei; in keinem der Hotels in Tripolis kenne man ihn, und so sei nur die eine Spur da, die zu Hermann führe, und ob er wüßte, wer der Mann sein könnte. Übrigens habe man neben ihm—wie seltsam—einen Damenschuh gefunden, und sonst ₅ gar nichts.

Hermann zitterte. „Das könnte mein Privatsekretär Erich Karsten sein", sagte er, „er ist seit gestern abend spurlos verschwunden. Ich werde sofort die Polizei hier in Hamburg anrufen." Dann legte er auf.   ₁₀

Heute nachmittag fliege ich nach Hause. Meine Frau holt mich, wie immer, am Flughafen ab.

Aber was soll ich ihr erzählen?

Erich Kästner

Erich Kästner (born 1899 in Dresden) is best known in the United States for his children's story *Emil und die Detektive* (1929). He wrote, especially in the late 1920s and 30s, a large number of humorous and satirical poems, one of which is the following "Sachliche Romanze" (1929). Because of his bitter social criticism, much of which was directed against German militaristic tendencies, he was forbidden to write by the Nazis, and his books were burned in 1933. He stayed in Germany, however, and, after World War II, wrote for the American-sponsored *Neue Zeitung* in Munich from 1945–48. He refers to his poetry, most of which is written in the same matter-of-fact style as the "Sachliche Romanze" as *Gebrauchslyrik* ("utility poetry").

Sachliche Romanze

Als sie einander acht Jahre kannten
(und man darf sagen: sie kannten sich gut),
kam ihre Liebe plötzlich abhanden.
Wie andern Leuten ein Stock oder Hut.

Sie waren traurig, betrugen sich heiter,   ₅
versuchten Küsse, als ob nichts sei,
und sahen sich an und wußten nicht weiter.
Da weinte sie schließlich. Und er stand dabei.

Vom Fenster aus konnte man Schiffen winken.
Er sagte, es wäre schon Viertel nach Vier   ₁₀
und Zeit, irgendwo Kaffee zu trinken.
Nebenan übte ein Mensch Klavier.

sachlich matter-of-fact
abhanden kommen to get lost
der Stock, ⸚e walking stick, cane

traurig sad
betrugen sich heiter acted cheerful
der Kuß, Küsse kiss
sich each other
weinen to cry
winken to wave at

nebenan next door
üben to practice

Sie gingen ins kleinste Café am Ort
und rührten in ihren Tassen.
Am Abend saßen sie noch immer dort.   15
Sie saßen allein, und sie sprachen kein Wort
und konnten es einfach nicht fassen.

rühren   to stir

fassen   to comprehend

Analysis

130 Relative Pronouns

The Definite Relative Pronoun

The German relative pronouns are **der, die, das.** Their forms are the same as those of the definite article, except that the singular genitive and the plural genitive and dative add the ending **-en.** This **-en** necessitates doubling the **-s** in the masculine and neuter forms in order to keep the preceding **-e-** short.

	MASC.	FEM.	NEUT.	PLURAL
NOM.	der	die	das	die
GEN.	dessen	deren	dessen	deren
DAT.	dem	der	dem	denen
ACC.	den	die	das	die

Relative pronouns must agree in gender and number with their antecedent; but their case depends on their function within the relative clause. *The German relative pronouns are never omitted.* All relative clauses are thus introduced dependent clauses and therefore have verb-last position.

Kennst du den Mann, *der* **gestern hier war?**
Do you know the man who was here yesterday?
Kennst du die Frau, *die* **gestern hier war?**
Kennst du das Mädchen, *das* **gestern hier war?**

Sein Vater, *dessen* **Frau aus Leningrad kam, sprach gut Russisch.**
His father, whose wife came from Leningrad, spoke Russian well.
Seine Frau, *deren* **Vater aus Leningrad kam, sprach gut Russisch.**

Wer war denn der Junge, mit *dem* **ich dich gestern gesehen habe?**
Who was the boy I saw you with (with whom I saw you) yesterday?
Wer war denn die Dame, mit *der* **ich dich gestern gesehen habe?**
Wer war denn das Mädchen, mit *dem* **ich dich gestern gesehen habe?**

Der Junge, *den* **du gestern gesehen hast, ist mein Sohn.**
The boy (whom) you saw yesterday, is my son.

Die Dame, *die* **du gestern gesehen hast, ist meine Tante.**
Das Mädchen, *das* **du gestern gesehen hast, ist meine Schwester.**

Kennst du die Leute, *die* **gestern hier waren?**
Do you know the people who were here yesterday?

Wer waren denn die Mädchen, mit *denen* **ich dich gestern gesehen habe?**
Who were the girls I saw you with (with whom I saw you) yesterday?

Die Mädchen, *die* **du gesehen hast, waren meine Schwestern.**
The girls (whom) you saw were my sisters.

Relative clauses do not always follow their antecedents immediately. If only the second prong is needed to complete the main clause, this clause is not interrupted by a relative clause.

Ich wollte Hermann Schneider besuchen, mit dem ich während des Krieges in Afrika gewesen war.
I wanted to visit Hermann Schneider, with whom I had been in Africa during the war.

Not

[Ich wollte Hermann Schneider, mit dem ich während des Krieges in Afrika gewesen war, besuchen.]

The Indefinite Relative Pronoun

The German indefinite relative pronouns are **wer** and **was.** They are always used if there is no antecedent.

Wer **Geld hat, hat auch Freunde.**
Whoever (He who) has money has friends, too.

Wer **nicht für mich ist, ist gegen mich.**
Whoever is not for me is against me.

Was **er zu erzählen hatte, war nicht viel.**
What he had to tell was not much.

Was er zu erzählen hatte, das war nicht viel.
Wer Geld hat, der hat auch Freunde.
Wer mich liebt, den liebe ich auch.

In the last three examples, **das, der,** and **den** repeat the relative clause.

Was is also used to refer to an entire clause or to **alles, nichts,** or **etwas.**

Hans hat mich zum Essen eingeladen, was ich sehr nett finde.
Ich habe nicht alles verstanden, was er gesagt hat.
Er hat nichts gesagt, was ich nicht schon wußte.
Ich habe etwas erlebt, was man eigentlich nicht erleben kann.

131 wann, ob, als, wenn

Wann is an interrogative, meaning *when*. It can only be used in situations where English *when* can be replaced by *at what time*. **Wann** is used:

1. To introduce a question.

> **Wann fährst du nach Köln?**
> When (at what time) are you going to Cologne?

2. As an interrogative conjunction when a **wann**-question is changed into a dependent clause.

> **Mutter will wissen, wann du nach Köln fährst.**
> Mother wants to know when (at what time) you are going to Cologne.

Ob is a conjunction used to change a yes-or-no question into a dependent clause. **Ob** means *whether,* and it must be used whenever *whether* could be used in the corresponding English sentence.

> **Fährst du nach Berlin?**
> **Mutter will wissen, ob du nach Berlin fährst.**

Als is used in the following ways:

1. As a particle in comparisons, it means *than* and is used only to compare what is *not* equal. Comparison of adjectives will be discussed in Unit 11.

> **Er trinkt mehr als du.**   He drinks more than you (drink).
> **Ich habe nicht mehr als hundert Mark.**   I don't have more than a hundred marks.

2. As a conjunction, **als** means *when* and introduces dependent clauses referring to *one single event or situation in the past*. English *when* has a much wider usage: It corresponds to German **als** only if it can be replaced by *at the time when* followed by a past tense.

> **Als mein Mann noch lebte, gingen wir oft ins Theater.**
> When (at the time when) my husband was still alive, we often went to
>   the theater.

3. **Als** may be the short version of **als ob** or **als wenn**, both meaning *as if*. When so used, **als** or **als ob** is followed either by the general subjunctive or, less frequently, by the indirect-discourse subjunctive.

If **als** is equivalent to **als ob** (**als wenn**), the verb of the dependent clause follows immediately after **als**.

> **Er tat, als ob er schliefe.**   He acted as if he were asleep.
> **Er tat, als schliefe er.**
> **Er tat, als schlafe er.**

> **Er tat, als wenn er alles wüßte.**   He acted as if he knew everything.
> **Er tat, als wüßte er alles.**

Wenn is troublesome because it introduces both conditional and time clauses.

1. In conditional clauses, **wenn** always corresponds to English *if;* and any *if*

which cannot be replaced by *whether* must be rendered by **wenn.**

2. In time clauses, **wenn** basically means *whenever* and presents no difficulties as long as it is used with this meaning.

3. Trouble arises because English *when* is apt to be a source of interference. English *when* is used as an interrogative and then corresponds to German **wann.** English *when* can also be a time conjunction meaning "at the time when." In this latter function, *when* corresponds to **als** if the clause refers to one single event in the past, and it corresponds to **wenn** if the clause refers to present or future time. The following table summarizes the situation:

	IF (condition)	IF (whether)	WHEN- EVER	WHEN (interrog.) (at what time)	WHEN (conj.) (at the time when)
PAST	wenn	ob	wenn	wann	als
PRESENT	wenn	ob	wenn	wann	wenn
FUTURE	wenn	ob	wenn	wann	wenn

NOTE: You can eliminate all interference caused by your own speech habits if you realize that:

(a) In the sentence *I'd like to know when he came home, when* is an interrogative replaceable by *at what time; when* therefore corresponds to German **wann.**

> **Ich möchte wissen, wann er nach Hause gekommen ist.**

(b) In *When my husband was still alive, we often went to the theater, when* is replaceable by *at the time when; when* therefore corresponds to German **als,** because it refers to a single event or situation in the past.

> **Als mein Mann noch lebte, sind wir oft ins Theater gegangen.**

(c) In *When he comes home from the war, we will get married, when* is also replaceable by *at the time when.* But this time it refers to the future and corresponds to German **wenn.**

> **Wenn er aus dem Krieg nach Hause kommt, heiraten wir.**

Since **wenn** also corresponds to English *if,* this last German sentence is ambiguous; only the context makes the meaning clear. There are no linguistic means in German of distinguishing between *when* and *if* as long as **wenn** refers to the future.

132 gar nicht, gar kein, gar nichts

The particle **gar** is used in connection with a following **nicht, kein,** or **nichts** either to add the idea "contrary to expectation" or to strengthen the negative particle in the same way in which *at all* strengthens the *not* in *not at all.*

> **Meyer ist gar nicht so dumm, wie du denkst.**
> Meyer isn't as stupid as you think.

Ich habe heute nacht gar nicht geschlafen.
I didn't sleep at all last night.

Ingelheim war gar kein General; er war nur Leutnant.
Ingelheim wasn't a general at all, he was only a lieutenant.

**Ich dachte, er würde mir wenigstens Blumen mitbringen; aber er hat
   mir gar nichts mitgebracht.**
I thought he would at least bring me flowers; but he didn't bring me
   anything at all.

Nicht, kein, and **nichts** after **gar** are never stressed.

133 da-Compounds with an Unstressed da-

You should by now be thoroughly familiar with the forms of the so-called
personal pronouns.

	SINGULAR			PLURAL
NOM.	er	sie	es	sie
DAT.	ihm	ihr	ihm	ihnen
ACC.	ihn	sie	es	sie

All these pronouns can be used to replace *any* noun, not just nouns referring
to persons. If a noun like **der Wagen** is replaced by a pronoun, the masculine
der Wagen is replaced by **er, ihm, ihn.**

Er (der Wagen) ist sechs Jahre alt.	It is six years old.
Das sieht man ihm nicht an.	It doesn't look it.
Ich habe ihn auch immer gut gepflegt.	I've always taken good care of it.

One would expect this system to be carried through consistently so that,
thinking of **der Wagen,** you could say:

[**Ich will mit ihm nach Paris fahren.**]

Unfortunately, this is not the case. After a preposition, all pronouns are
strictly *personal* pronouns, that is, they can only refer to persons and not to
things. The **mit ihm** in the sentence above can therefore refer to your friend,
but not to your car.

If **mit meinem Wagen** is to be replaced by something comparable to *with it,*
all nouns referring to things (and all the pronouns you are tempted to use)
become **da-,** preceding and compounded with the preposition (cf. English
thereby). Thus

mit meinem Wagen

becomes

damit

This **da-** is a substitute for any noun which does not refer to persons. There is no longer any difference between masculine, feminine, and neuter; no difference between dative and accusative; and no difference between singular and plural. Thus the questions

Was soll *ich* **denn**	**mit dem Schlüssel?** **mit der Uhr?** **mit dem Buch?** **mit den Büchern?**

all become

Was soll *ich* **denn**	**damit?**

Similarly, the questions

Was hast du denn	**für diesen Wein** **für diese Uhr** **für dieses Haus** **für diese Blumen**	**be***zahlt?*

all become

Was hast du denn	**dafür**	**be***zahlt?*

The **da-** in the examples above is unstressed just as the corresponding articles and the nouns are unstressed. The preposition is usually unstressed, too, but occasionally it may become the stress point of the sentence.

> **Ich habe nichts da***ge***gen, aber ich bin auch nicht da***für***.**

134 da-Compounds with Stressed da-

As long as *unstressed* nouns and pronouns denoting things are replaced after prepositions, you have no choice but to replace them with a **da-**compound. However, if *stressed* nouns and pronouns denoting things and preceded by a preposition are to be replaced, you have a choice. You can use either the stressed demonstrative pronoun *after* the preposition or a stressed **da-** *preceding* the preposition.

Thus

Was soll ich denn	**mit** *dem* **Schlüssel?** **mit** *der* **Uhr?** **mit** *dem* **Buch?** **mit** *den* **Büchern?**	or	**mit dem** *Schlüssel?* **mit der** *Uhr?* **mit dem** *Buch?* **mit den** *Büchern?*

may become either

	mit *dem?*
Was soll ich denn	mit *der?*
	mit *dem?*
	mit *denen?*

or

| Was soll ich denn | *da*mit? |

In assertions, **da**-compounds with a stressed **da**- usually occupy the front field and carry contrast intonation.

Was soll ich denn mit *dem* **Hut?** *Da***mit gehe ich** *nicht* **in die Kirche.**
So, Jutta hat ge*hei***ratet?** *Davon* **habe ich nichts ge***wußt***.**

NOTE:

1. The second example above shows that **da**-compounds are used not only to refer to things, but also to refer to entire sentences.

Davon (daß Jutta geheiratet hat) habe ich nichts gewußt.

2. Do not replace directives like **ins Haus, zum Bahnhof, nach Berlin** with **da**-compounds. Such directives are sometimes replaced by **hin** or **dahin**.

Mußt du zum Bahnhof? Ich bringe dich gerne *hin***.**
Ich soll nach Kairo fahren? Nein, *da***hin fahre ich nicht.**
Sie fahren nach Berlin? Da möchte ich *auch* **gerne mal hinfahren.**

135 Table of **da**-Compounds

If the preposition starts with a vowel, **dar**- is used instead of **da**-.

dadurch	dabei	dahinter
dafür	damit	daneben
dagegen	danach	daran
	daraus	darauf
	davon	darin
	dazu	darüber
		darunter
		davor
		dazwischen

Note that **ohne, außer, seit,** and the prepositions governing the genitive (**während, wegen, trotz**) do not form **da**-compounds. **Außer** forms **außerdem** (*besides*), **seit** forms **seitdem** (*since then*, conj. *since*), and **trotz** forms **trotzdem** (*in spite of that, nevertheless*).

136 Split da-Compounds

In the spoken language, da-compounds may be split. The da- (stressed or unstressed) then stands in the front field, and the preposition becomes the first part of the second prong. This pattern, however, is quite colloquial.

*Da*mit	war	mein Mann *gar* nicht		zufrieden.
Da	war	mein Mann *gar* nicht	mit	zufrieden.

If the preposition begins with a vowel, **daraus** does not become **da . . . aus**, but **da . . . draus; daran**: **da . . . dran; darauf**: **da . . . drauf**; and so on.

137 der hier and der da

In spoken German, the contrast *this one: that one* is expressed by **der hier** (or **dieser hier**): **der da** (or **dieser da**).

Dieses Haus hier möchte ich nicht, aber das da hätte ich gerne.
Dieser Kugelschreiber hier ist mir zu schwer. Mit dem kann ich nicht schreiben. Kann ich den da mal versuchen?
Die hier (diese Uhr hier) kostet mir zu viel. Darf ich die da mal sehen?

138 wo-Compounds

If the question word **was** is preceded by a preposition, it may be replaced by **wo** (**wor-** in front of vowels) compounded with and followed by the preposition in question. One may ask:

An was glaubst du?   or   Woran glaubst du?
An was denkst du?   or   Woran denkst du?
Auf was wartest du?   or   Worauf wartest du?

Also the indefinite relative pronoun **was** may be replaced by **wo-**.

Ich möchte wissen, auf was du noch wartest.
Ich möchte wissen, worauf du noch wartest.

139 Prepositional Objects

It was pointed out in Unit 2 that prepositions can be used by themselves as verbal complements. They are then joined to a following infinitive and appear in a dictionary under the preposition.

Du mußt das Licht ausmachen.   You have to turn off the light.

We now introduce a number of semantic units which consist of a verb plus a whole prepositional phrase rather than of a verb and just a preposition.

We are not thinking of time phrases like **vor einem Jahr,** of directives like **ins Kino,** or of place phrases like **zu Hause.** To be sure, directives and phrases like **zu Hause** are second-prong complements; however, **zu Hause bleiben, im Bett bleiben,** and **bei Schmidts bleiben** are not separate dictionary entries; they are examples of the use of **bleiben,** which when used without such complements is almost as devoid of independent meaning as **sein.**

What we are thinking of is the type of prepositional phrase occurring in such sentences as

> She waited for him
> She waited on him

where *to wait for somebody* and *to wait on somebody* are clearly separate dictionary entries: A woman may be willing to wait *for* a man, but that does not necessarily mean that she is also willing to wait *on* him. The phrase *on him* forces a meaning on the verb *to wait* which is clearly different from the meaning of the same verb in *to wait for somebody.*

> She waited on him   means   She served him.
> She waited for him   means   She expected him.

Now, if we call *him* the object of *expected,* we can call *on him* or *for him* the object of *waited.* We call phrases like *on him* and *for him,* when they occur in such semantic units as *to wait on somebody* and *to wait for somebody,* prepositional objects.

Both English and German have literally hundreds of such fixed combinations of verbs plus prepositional objects. Unfortunately, however, the prepositions used with the German verbs hardly ever correspond to the prepositions used with the English verbs. Compare the following sentences:

Ich bin *in* sie verliebt.	I'm in love *with* her.
Ich bin *mit* ihr verlobt.	I'm engaged *to* her.
Ich warte *auf* sie.	I'm waiting *for* her.
Ich lache *über* sie.	I'm laughing *at* her.
Ich glaube *an* sie.	I believe *in* her.
Ich habe Angst *vor* ihr.	I'm afraid *of* her.
Ich bin stolz *auf* sie.	I'm proud *of* her.

Note that the prepositional objects sometimes belong to such compound verbs as **Angst haben** or **stolz sein.**

140 Frequent Prepositional Objects

Memorize the following verbs with their prepositions:

Angst haben vor (*dat.*)	to be afraid of
antworten auf (*acc.*)	to reply to (something)
bitten um (*acc.*)	to ask for (something)
danken für (*acc.*)	to thank (someone) for
denken an (*acc.*)	to think of, to remember
nachdenken über (*acc.*)	to think, meditate about
einladen zu (*dat.*)	to invite to
fragen nach (*dat.*)	to ask about, inquire about
gehören zu (*dat.*)	to be part or a member of, to belong to
glauben an (*acc.*)	to believe in
halten von (*dat.*)	to have an opinion about; to think (highly, a great deal, not much, etc.) of (somebody or something)
halten für (*acc.*)	to think that something (or somebody) is (something)
hoffen auf (*acc.*)	to hope for, to trust in, to look forward to
hören von (*dat.*)	to hear from somebody or about something
lachen über (*acc.*)	to laugh about
jemanden auslachen	to laugh at (make fun of) somebody
reagieren auf (*acc.*)	to react to (something or somebody)
sein für or **sein gegen** (*acc.*)	to be for or against
sprechen von (*dat.*)	to talk of, to mention
sprechen über (*acc.*)	to talk in detail about a topic
verstehen von (*dat.*)	to understand about
warten auf (*acc.*)	to wait for
wissen von (*dat.*)	to know about

NOTE: A number of these prepositional objects use the prepositions **an, auf, über**. In all cases listed, **an, auf,** and **über** are used with the accusative, even though these phrases are not directives answering the question **wohin.** There are a few cases where the dative *must* be used—for example, with **Angst haben vor.** From now on, the correct case will be indicated in the vocabulary. The importance of using the correct case can be seen in the following:

   Ich warte auf *die* **Straßenbahn**

means

   I am waiting for the streetcar

whereas

   Ich warte auf *der* **Straßenbahn**

could only mean

   I am waiting on top of the streetcar.

141 The Syntax of Prepositional Objects

<u>Preposition plus Noun or Personal Pronoun</u>

The prepositional object constitutes the second prong. Under contrast intonation, it can be placed in the front field.

Ich warte auf sie.
Auf Fritz brauchst du heute abend nicht zu warten.
An meinen Geburtstag hast du natürlich nicht gedacht.

<u>Replacement of Nouns and Pronouns by Demonstratives</u>

The stressed demonstratives used to replace nouns or names usually occur in the front field.

Erika? Von der hat kein Mensch gesprochen.
Erika? Auf die brauchst du nicht zu warten.

Meyers? Von denen haben wir lange nichts gehört.
Meyers? Auf die brauchst du nicht zu warten.

Das ist ein *Wein!* Mit *dem* werden Sie be*stimmt* zufrieden sein! Gegen *den* kann auch ein *Kenner* nichts sagen.

<u>Prepositional **da**-Compounds</u>

The **da**-compounds with an unstressed **da**- appear in the first box of the second prong. The compounds with a stressed **da**- appear in the front field, with contrast intonation.

*Da*ran *glaube* ich nicht.
Ich *glaube* noch nicht daran.

*Da*rauf kann ich nicht *war*ten.
Ich hoffe, ich brauche nicht darauf zu *war*ten.

<u>Prepositional **wo**-Compounds</u>

Like all questions, questions introduced by a **wo**-compound can be changed into dependent clauses.

Auf was wartet er denn?
Worauf wartet er denn?

Ich weiß nicht, auf was er wartet.
Ich weiß nicht, worauf er wartet.

da-Compounds with an Anticipatory Function

The prepositional object may be replaced by a dependent clause or an infinitive phrase. If this is the case, a **da**-compound anticipating or repeating this dependent clause frequently appears in the main clause.

Ich habe gar nicht daran gedacht, daß du ja auch in Köln wohnst.	It had slipped my mind that you too live in Cologne.

or

Daran, daß du ja auch in Köln wohnst, habe ich gar nicht gedacht.

or

Daran habe ich gar nicht gedacht, daß du ja auch in Köln wohnst.	
Ich möchte Ihnen noch einmal dafür danken, daß Sie gekommen sind.	I would like to thank you once more (for the fact that you came) for your coming.
Ich hoffe immer noch darauf, sie wiederzusehen.	I still hope to see her again.

These anticipatory **da**-compounds are especially frequent if the ideas contained in the dependent clause or in the infinitive phrase have been expressed before in some form and are not news either for the speaker or for the listener.

142 Word Formation: Feminine Nouns Ending in -in

Masculine nouns denoting persons (and a few animals), especially agent nouns in **-er**, form corresponding feminines ending in **-in** (plural **-innen**).

der Freund	**die Freundin**
der Lehrer	**die Lehrerin**
der Student	**die Studentin**

Exercises

A. Each of the following incomplete sentences contains a blank for a relative pronoun. Fill in the correct forms.

1. das Haus, aus _____ er kam
2. die Betten, zwischen _____ der Tisch stand
3. der Blick, mit _____ er mich ansah

SEE ANALYSIS 130 (pp. 242-243)

4. die vielen Aufnahmen, _____ ich von ihm gemacht habe
5. die Leute, _____ zu uns kamen
6. der Herr, nach _____ Sie fragen
7. der Materialismus, gegen _____ wir kämpfen
8. das Haus, in _____ wir wohnen
9. das Theater, vor _____ ich sie treffen wollte
10. die Familie, bei _____ du wohnst
11. das Haus, vor _____ wir unseren Wagen stellten
12. seine Frau, _____ Vater in Berlin Architekt war
13. meine Bücher, ohne _____ ich nicht leben kann
14. der Zug, mit _____ du fahren willst
15. die Blicke, _____ sie mir zuwarf
16. die Ecke, an _____ er stand
17. die Stadt, von _____ wir sprachen
18. ihr Mann, _____ Vater in Berlin Architekt war
19. die zwei Fußabdrücke, _____ wir neben dem Haus fanden

B. Join the following pairs of sentences by changing one of them into a relative clause.

SEE
ANALYSIS
130
(pp. 242-243)

1. Werners Vater sprach gut Englisch. Er hatte lange in Amerika gelebt.
2. Werners Vater sprach gut Englisch. Seine Frau kam aus London.
3. Ich habe dich gestern abend im Theater mit einem jungen Mann gesehen. Wer war denn der junge Mann?
4. In Mainz besuchte ich meinen Freund Emil. Ich bin mit ihm in die Schule gegangen.
5. Ich fuhr nach Hamburg, um Hermann wiederzusehen. Während des Krieges war ich mit Hermann in Afrika.
6. Wer ist denn eigentlich dieser Schmidt? Du redest schon seit Tagen von ihm.
7. Der Brief lag vor ihr auf dem Tisch. Ihr Mann hatte ihn aus Kairo geschickt.
8. Ich kann diese Vase doch nicht wegwerfen. Tante Amalie hat sie mir geschickt.

C. Restate the following sentences by starting with **Er sah aus, als ob . . .** and **Er sah aus, als. . . .**

SEE
ANALYSIS
131
(pp. 244-245)

1. Er hat die Gelbsucht.
2. Er hat nicht gut geschlafen.
3. Er hat viel erlebt.
4. Er ist unglücklich.
5. Er war krank.

D. Restate the following sentences in the past tense. Note that with the change from present tense to past tense, **wenn** must be in some cases changed to **als**.

SEE
ANALYSIS
131
(pp. 244-245)

1. Wir können erst ins Theater gehen, wenn Else kommt.
2. Jedesmal, wenn Tante Amalie hier ist, muß ich mich zwingen, nett zu ihr zu sein.
3. Wenn mein Zug in München ankommt, bist du schon lange zu Hause.
4. Wenn meine Wohnung groß genug wäre, könnte ich auch fünfundzwanzig Leute einladen.
5. Wenn Hans geht, gehe ich auch.

E. In the following sentences, supply **als, als ob, ob, wann,** or **wenn.**

1. Ich weiß, jemand hat hinter mir gestanden, _____ ich den Brief schrieb.
2. _____ ich gewußt hätte, daß sie nicht schwimmen konnte, wäre ich natürlich nicht mit ihr fischen gegangen.
3. Können Sie mir sagen, _____ der Zug aus Kiel ankommt?
4. Können Sie mir sagen, _____ der Zug aus Kiel schon angekommen ist?
5. Ich wußte nicht, _____ Erich mich erkannt hatte; jedenfalls tat er, _____ hätte er mich nicht gesehen.
6. Ich bin so müde. _____ ich nur endlich einmal lange schlafen könnte!
7. Ich bin nicht sicher, _____ ich das Geschenk annehmen soll oder nicht.
8. Was? Tante Amalie will uns schon wieder besuchen? _____ kommt sie denn?
9. Aber Inge, du tust ja, _____ *du* immer mit ihr ins Museum gehen müßtest.
10. Du weißt doch, ich komme erst um 7 Uhr nach Hause. _____ soll ich denn essen, _____ das Theater schon um 7 Uhr 30 anfängt?

SEE
ANALYSIS
131
(pp. 244-245)

F. Read the following sentences and supply either **nicht** or **nichts,** or the correct form of **kein.**

1. Ich habe seit gestern morgen gar _____ gegessen.
2. Daß du in Italien warst, habe ich gar _____ gewußt.
3. Hast du denn mit deiner neuen Kamera noch gar _____ Aufnahmen gemacht?
4. Es ist doch dumm, daß er uns gar _____ geschrieben hat, wann er ankommt.
5. Aber der Hund hat doch gar _____ gebellt.

SEE
ANALYSIS
132
(pp. 245-246)

G. Fill in each blank by using a form of the demonstrative **der, die, das.**

1. Sollen Inge und Gerda auch kommen?—Nein, _____ brauchst du nicht einzuladen; _____ können zu Hause bleiben; mit _____ will ich nichts mehr zu tun haben.
2. Kennen Sie _____ Friedrich Bertram?—Aber natürlich; mit _____ war ich doch in Mainz auf der Schule.
3. Diese Schuhe hier möchten Sie also doch nicht, gnädige Frau?—Nein, ich nehme lieber _____ da.
4. Nein, Maria; mit _____ Hut kannst du nicht nach Paris fahren. _____ läßt du besser zu Hause.—Aber Paul, _____ kommt doch aus Paris. _____ hast du mir doch letztes Jahr aus Paris mitgebracht.
5. Dieser Kaffee ist aber gut. Wo hast du _____ denn gekauft?— _____ hat mein Mann gekauft.—Dein Mann? Versteht _____ was von Kaffee?

H. In the following sentences, substitute a **da**-compound for the italicized prepositional phrases.

1. Der Garten *hinter dem Haus* braucht viel Wasser.
2. *Mit dem Hut* kannst du nicht in die Stadt gehen.
3. Und *vor dem Wohnzimmer* ist eine grosse Terrasse.
4. Er hat viel Geld *für das Haus* bezahlt.
5. Aber den Namen *unter dem Bild* kann ich nicht lesen.

SEE
ANALYSIS
133–135
(pp. 246-248)

I. In the following sentences, substitute for the prepositional phrase in the front field (a) a stressed **da**-compound and (b) the preposition plus demonstrative article.

> **Für *den* Wein hast du zuviel bezahlt.**
> (a) *Da*für hast du zuviel bezahlt.
> (b) **Für *den* hast du zuviel bezahlt.**

SEE
ANALYSIS
134

(pp. 247-248)

1. Mit *dem* Wagen fahre ich nicht.
2. Mit *dies*em Hut kann ich nichts anfangen.
3. In *dies*em Bett kann ich nicht schlafen.
4. Für *den* Wagen bezahle ich keine zweitausend Mark.
5. Mit *mein*er Leica kann ich auch bei Nacht Aufnahmen machen.

J. Write down the questions to which the following sentences would be the answers. Start each question with (a) a **wo**-compound and (b) the preposition plus **was**.

> **Meine Tochter hat Angst vor der Schule.**
> (a) **Wovor hat sie denn Angst?**
> (b) **Vor was hat sie denn Angst?**

SEE
ANALYSIS
138

(p. 249)

1. Wir warten auf schönes Wetter.
2. Ich brauche das Geld für einen neuen Wagen.
3. Wir haben gerade von dem neuen Film gesprochen.
4. Ich denke gerade daran, daß Vater morgen Geburtstag hat.
5. Ich habe ihn an seiner Stimme erkannt.

K. Read the following sentences aloud and supply the missing prepositions.

SEE
ANALYSIS
139–141

(pp. 249-253)

1. Ich glaube ＿＿＿＿＿＿ Gott.
2. Wir haben ＿＿＿＿＿＿ unserer Reise gesprochen.
3. Denkst du auch noch ＿＿＿＿＿＿ mich?
4. Hast du schon ＿＿＿＿＿＿ den Brief geantwortet?
5. Hast du auch nicht vergessen, ihn ＿＿＿＿＿＿ seiner Frau zu fragen?
6. Ich danke Ihnen ＿＿＿＿＿＿ Ihre Hilfe.
7. Meyer hat mich ＿＿＿＿＿＿ einem Glas Wein eingeladen.
8. Dürfte ich Sie ＿＿＿＿＿＿ eine Zigarette bitten?
9. Er spricht nie ＿＿＿＿＿＿ seiner Frau.
10. ＿＿＿＿＿＿ wen warten Sie denn?

L. Read the following sentences aloud and supply the missing articles or possessives.

SEE
ANALYSIS
139–141

(pp. 249-253)

1. Wir warten auf ＿＿＿＿＿＿ Zug aus Hannover.
2. Wir warten auf ＿＿＿＿＿＿ Bahnhof.
3. Meyer hat Angst vor ＿＿＿＿＿＿ Frau.
4. Ingelheim hat viel über ＿＿＿＿＿＿ Krieg geschrieben.

5. Kurt stand an _____ Ecke und wartete auf _____ Freundin.
6. Ich muß in _____ Universität über _____ Krieg zwischen Rom und Karthago sprechen.
7. Ich halte nicht viel von _____ Film.
8. Wir hoffen sehr auf _____ Mitarbeit Ihres Mannes, Frau Becker.
9. Frau Doktor, als Sie an die Tür kamen, habe ich Sie für _____ Tochter gehalten.
10. Sie hat den ganzen Abend nicht von _____ Mann gesprochen.

M. Using the verbs in parentheses, form main clauses containing a **da**-compound anticipating the dependent clause.

> (schon lange nachdenken), wo ich dieses Jahr hinfahren soll.
> Ich denke schon lange darüber nach, wo ich dieses Jahr hinfahren soll.

1. (sehr hoffen), daß er morgen kommen kann.
2. (gerade sprechen), daß er im Sommer nach Italien fahren will.
3. (warten), daß mein Mann endlich nach Hause kommt.
4. (nicht viel halten), daß meine Tochter Psychologie studieren will.
5. (wohl bitten dürfen), daß Sie um acht Uhr im Büro sind.

SEE ANALYSIS 141 (pp. 252-253)

N. Expand the prepositional objects in the following sentences into dependent clauses.

> Ich warte auf einen Brief von ihr.
> Ich warte darauf, daß sie mir schreibt.

1. Ich möchte Ihnen noch einmal für Ihre Hilfe danken.
2. An seinen Geburtstag gestern habe ich gar nicht gedacht.
3. Wir sind sehr unglücklich über die Heirat unserer Tochter.
4. Lacht sie immer noch über seinen Akzent?

SEE ANALYSIS 141 (pp. 252-253)

O. Expand the prepositional objects in the following sentences into infinitive phrases.

> Erika denkt gar nicht an eine Italienreise.
> Erika denkt gar nicht daran, nach Italien zu fahren.

1. Darf ich Sie zu einem Glas Wein einladen, Herr Rohrmoser?
2. Ich habe meinen Freund um Ingelheims Romane gebeten.
3. Hoffst du immer noch auf ein Wiedersehen mit ihr?
4. Ich hoffe auf ein Wiedersehen mit Ihnen.
5. Ich habe wochenlang auf einen Brief von ihr gewartet.

SEE ANALYSIS 141 (pp. 252-253)

P. Read the following sentences starting with each of the italicized words and rearrange the syntax accordingly.

SEE ANALYSIS 141 (pp. 252-253)

1. Daran, *daß* wir heute vor zehn Jahren geheiratet haben, hast *du natürlich* nicht gedacht.

2. Natürlich bin *ich* nicht *glücklich darüber, daß* Heidi so jung heiraten will.
3. Mir hat *er gestern* nichts *davon* gesagt, *daß* er bald heiraten will.

Q. Express in German.

1. Not until yesterday did he ask me whether I wanted to marry him.
2. The man with whom Mrs. Ingelheim is talking is called Behrens.
3. If the walls in this room could talk, we would never have to read a novel again.
4. Hans wanted to know whether I could pick him up at the station.
5. When did you pick him up?
6. Can you tell me when you picked him up? (indicative)
7. When I arrived, she was not there yet.
8. He acted as if the house belonged to him.
9. He looked as if he hadn't slept well.
10. You know him better than her, don't you?
11. That was more than I had expected.
12. If it hadn't been so hot in Africa, we would not have flown back to Germany.
13. That was a moment I shall not forget.
14. The man I saw in front of the house was Erich.
15. Behind the stone was a hole in which Ali had five goldpieces.
16. He said that he had seen nothing at all.
17. If I'm not there at three o'clock, you'll simply have to wait for me.
18. When I knocked at the door, Erich didn't answer.
19. And this is a picture of our house.—And where is your swimming pool?—That's behind it.
20. In front of the house stood a Mercedes; next to it stood a Volkswagen.

Basic Vocabulary

der Arm, –e	arm	**der Gast, ¨e**	guest
auflegen	to put down (the receiver)	**halten für**	to consider
		halten von	to have an opinion about; to think (highly, a great deal, not much, etc.) of
aufmachen	to open		
ausgeben	to spend (money)		
beide	both		
blöde	stupid		
so was **Blödes**	what a stupid thing	**die Hand, ¨e**	hand
dauern	to last, to take (time)	**die Hilfe**	help
dreißig	thirty	**irgendetwas**	something, anything
dumm	stupid, dumb	**klingeln**	to ring (said of a bell)
einschlafen	to fall asleep	**klopfen**	to knock
erklären	to explain	**anklopfen**	to knock at the door
erschrecken	to be frightened	**längst, schon längst**	for a long time (by now); a long time ago
erstaunt	astonished		
fallen	to fall, to drop		
führen	to lead, to guide	**laut**	loud

leise	soft, without noise	schlagen	to beat, to hit
der Mittag, —e	noon	der Schluß, ÷e	end, conclusion
der Nachmittag, —e	afternoon	der Schlüssel, –	key
na so was	(expression of aston-	schweigen	to be silent, to say
	ishment) You		nothing
	don't mean it!	die Seife	soap
	What do you	die Seite, —n	page; side
	think of that!	so etwas (so was)	something like this
der Name, —n	name	soviel (conj.)	as far as
(gen.: des Namens;		spazierengehen	to go for a walk
dat.: dem Namen;		steigen	to climb
acc.: den Namen)		die Stimme, —n	voice
nee (colloquial) =	no	stolz (auf)	proud (of)
nein		die Straßenbahn, —en	streetcar
nirgends	nowhere	der Stuhl, ÷e	chair
oben	up (above); upstairs;	trotzdem	in spite of that;
	on top		nevertheless
obwohl'	although	die Tür, —en	door
pflegen	to take care of	verliebt	in love
das Problem', —e	problem	verlobt	engaged
reagieren auf	to react to	von (mir) aus	as far as (I am)
die Reklame, —n	advertising		concerned
ruhig	quiet, calm; (sentence	warm	warm
	adv.) it won't	der Weg, —e	way, path
	bother me, I'll stay	wichtig	important
	calm about it	zufrie'den	satisfied, content
russisch	Russian		

Additional Vocabulary

die Adresse, —n	address	der Kugelschreiber, –	ballpoint pen
adressieren	to address	der Leutnant, —s	lieutenant
die Badewanne, —n	bathtub	mitmachen	to go along, to
bellen	to bark		cooperate
der General', ÷e	general	die O'per, —n	opera; opera house
der Hörer, –	(telephone) receiver;	der Schrei, —e	scream
	listener	die Vase, —n	vase
die Kugel, —n	ball; globe	wütend	mad, angry

Strong and Irregular Verbs

einschlafen, schlief ein, ist eingeschlafen, er schläft ein	to fall asleep
erschrecken, erschrak, ist erschrocken, er erschrickt	to be frightened
fallen, fiel, ist gefallen, er fällt	to fall
schlagen, schlug, hat geschlagen, er schlägt	to beat, hit
schweigen, schwieg, hat geschwiegen, er schweigt	to be silent, say nothing
spazierengehen, ging spazieren, ist spazierengegangen, er geht spazieren	to go for a walk
steigen, stieg, ist gestiegen, er steigt	to climb

Unit 9 Negation—Present and Past Infinitives—Subjective and Objective Use of Modals—Reflexive Pronouns—Contrary-to-Fact Conditions without **wenn**

Patterns

[1] Position of **nicht**

Study these sentences carefully and determine how much of each sentence is negated by **nicht**.

Aber du kannst doch nicht den ganzen Tag schlafen!
　　But you can't sleep all day!
　　(Question: Was kannst du nicht tun? Answer: Den ganzen Tag schlafen.)

SEE
ANALYSIS
46

(pp. 65-67)

Warum denn nicht? Ich habe die ganze Nacht nicht geschlafen.
　　Why not? I didn't sleep all night.
　　(Question: Was hast du die ganze Nacht nicht getan? Answer: Geschlafen.)

Meyer war krank und hat lange nicht arbeiten können.
　　Meyer was sick, and for a long time he couldn't work.

Heute haben wir nicht lange arbeiten können.
　　Today we couldn't work very long.

Du brauchst nicht auf dem Sofa zu schlafen. Wir haben ein Bett für dich.
　　You don't have to sleep on the sofa. We have a bed for you.

Ich kann in diesem Bett einfach nicht schlafen. Es ist zu kurz.
　　I simply can't sleep in this bed. It is too short.

Geschlafen habe ich. Aber ich habe nicht gut geschlafen.

Ingelheim war in Kairo. Aber! War er allein in Kairo, oder war er nicht allein in Kairo?

[2] nicht A, sondern B

Ich wartete nicht auf Inge. Ich wartete auf Erika.
Ich wartete damals nicht auf Inge, sondern auf Erika.
Ich habe nicht auf Inge, sondern auf Erika gewartet.
Ich habe nicht auf Inge gewartet, sondern auf Erika.
Nicht auf Inge, sondern auf Erika habe ich gewartet.

SEE
ANALYSIS
143

(p. 280)

Der Wein ist gut hier in Gumpoldskirchen.

Du weißt doch, daß ich nicht auf Inge, sondern auf Erika gewartet habe.

Er ist gestern nicht nach Ber*lin*, sondern nach *Ham*burg gefahren.
Du weißt doch, daß ich nicht auf Inge gewartet habe, sondern auf Erika.

Er ist nicht *gest*ern, sondern erst *heu*te nach Berlin gefahren.
Er ist nicht *gest*ern nach Berlin gefahren, sondern erst *heu*te.
Er ist gestern nicht nach Ber*lin* gefahren, sondern nach *Ham*burg.

Wir sind gestern nicht nach Hamburg ge*flo*gen, sondern ge*fah*ren.

Inge ist nicht nur schön, sondern auch intelligent.
Weißt du, daß Inge nicht nur schön, sondern auch intelligent ist?
Weißt du, daß Inge nicht nur schön ist, sondern auch intelligent?

[3] Numbers from 1 to 100

SEE
ANALYSIS
144

(p. 280)

zwanzig, einundzwanzig, zweiundzwanzig, dreiundzwanzig, vierundzwanzig, fünfundzwanzig, sechsundzwanzig, siebenundzwanzig, achtundzwanzig, neunundzwanzig, dreißig,
einunddreißig, zweiunddreißig, vierzig, dreiundvierzig, vierundvierzig, fünfundvierzig,
fünfzig, fünfundfünfzig, sechsundfünfzig, sechzig, sechsundsechzig, siebenundsechzig,
siebzig, siebenundsiebzig, achtundsiebzig, achtzig, achtundachtzig, neunundachtzig, neun-
zig, hundert (einhundert)

ein mal zwei ist zwei	hundert (geteilt) durch zehn ist zehn
zwei mal zwei ist vier	neunzig (geteilt) durch zehn ist neun
drei mal zwei ist sechs	achtzig (geteilt) durch zehn ist acht
vier mal zwei ist acht	siebzig (geteilt) durch zehn ist sieben
fünf mal zwei ist zehn	sechzig (geteilt) durch zehn ist sechs

[4] Past Infinitives

SEE
ANALYSIS
145

(p. 281)

Er scheint zu schlafen.
Er scheint gut geschlafen zu haben.

Er schien in Paris zu sein.
Er schien in Paris gewesen zu sein.

Sie scheint Geld zu haben.
Sie scheint Geld gehabt zu haben.

Meyer schien sehr glücklich zu sein.
Meyer scheint sehr glücklich gewesen zu sein.

Wer Arzt werden will, muß sechs Jahre studieren.
Wer Arzt ist, muß sechs Jahre studiert haben.

Ich muß um sechs Uhr meine Brieftauben füttern.
Ich muß um sechs Uhr meine Brieftauben gefüttert haben.

[5] müssen

Read these sentences carefully and determine whether **müssen**
is used objectively or subjectively.

SEE
ANALYSIS
146
(pp. 281-288)

Jetzt habe ich keine Zeit. Ich muß erst die Kinder in die Schule schicken.
  I have no time now. I have to send the children off to school first.

Sie sagte, sie hätte keine Zeit. Sie müßte erst die Kinder in die Schule schicken.
  She said she didn't have time. She had to send the children off to school first.

Sie sagte, sie hätte erst die Kinder in die Schule schicken müssen.
  She said she had had to send the children off to school first.

Diesen Brief habe ich heute von einem Herrn Brandt bekommen. Er muß Amerikaner
  sein. Er schreibt: „Gestern ich war in Berlin und habe gekauft Ihren Roman."
  I got this letter from a Mr. Brandt today. He must be an American. He writes, "Yesterday I was in Berlin and bought your novel."

Ich hörte sofort, daß Herr Brandt trotz seines Namens Amerikaner sein mußte, denn er
  sagte: „Morgen ich kann nicht kommen, weil ich muß fahren nach Berlin."
  I heard immediately that Mr. Brandt had to be an American in spite of his name, for
  he said, "Tomorrow I can't come because I have to go to Berlin."

Sie ist doch in Stuttgart aufs Gymnasium gegangen. Sie muß also Englisch können und
  Faulkner gelesen haben.
  But she went to the Gymnasium in Stuttgart. So she must know English and must have
  read Faulkner.

Wir sind gestern nicht nach Hamburg
geflogen, sondern gefahren.

Tante Amalie muß schon wieder im
Museum gewesen sein.

Sie ist doch in Stuttgart aufs Gymnasium gegangen. Sie müßte eigentlich Englisch können
und Faulkner gelesen haben.
But she went to the Gymnasium in Stuttgart. So she ought to know English and ought
to have read Faulkner.

VARIATIONS

Following the pattern of the examples below, answer the questions
by using a subjective form of **müssen**; try to support your
conclusion with a sentence starting with **denn**.

(a) **Ist sie wirklich schon achtzehn?**
Sie muß achtzehn sein, denn sie will nächste Woche heiraten.

(b) **Waren Meyers wirklich an der Riviera?**
Sie müssen an der Riviera gewesen sein, denn sie sind so braun wie Kaffee.

Hat Meyer wirklich so viel Geld?
Ist Inge wirklich intelligent?
War Ingelheim schon einmal verheiratet?
Woher wußtest du, daß er Amerikaner war?

[6] wollen

Study these sentences carefully and determine whether **wollen** is
used subjectively or objectively; then follow the instructions below.

SEE
ANALYSIS
146
(pp. 281-288)

Tante Amalie will uns nächste Woche besuchen.
Tante Amalie wants to visit us next week.

Ich habe dich noch nie gebeten, mir zu helfen. Und jetzt, wo ich dich brauche, sagst du
nein. Und du willst mein Freund sein!
I have never asked you to help me, and now that I need you, you say no. And you
claim to be my friend!

Er will in Wien studiert haben? Das glaube ich nicht.
He says he studied in Vienna? I don't believe that.

Hast du nicht gesagt, du wolltest morgen nach Zürich fahren?
  Didn't you say you wanted to go to Zurich tomorrow?

Als Ingelheim den Preis bekam, wollte natürlich jeder seinen Roman schon gelesen haben.
  Ich hatte ihn *wirk*lich gelesen.—So?—Und ich wollte, ich hätte ihn *nicht* gelesen.
  When Ingelheim got the prize, everybody pretended to have read his novel already,
  of course. *I* really *had* read it.—Really?—And I wish I *hadn't* read it.

VARIATIONS

Change the following sentences according to the pattern of the
example.

> **Er behauptet, ein Freund des Direktors zu sein.**
> **Er will ein Freund des Direktors sein.**

Er behauptet, ein Freund des Direktors gewesen zu sein.
Er behauptete, ein Freund des Direktors zu sein.
Er behauptete, ein Freund des Direktors gewesen zu sein.
Er behauptet, ein Haus an der Riviera zu haben.
Er behauptet, ein Haus an der Riviera gehabt zu haben.
Er behauptete, ein Haus an der Riviera zu haben.
Er behauptete, ein Haus an der Riviera gehabt zu haben.

[7] sollen

Reread Analysis 114; then read the following sentences carefully
and decide which express "hearsay about the grammatical
subject." Then follow the instructions below.

SEE
ANALYSIS
146
(pp. 281-288)

Du sollst nicht stehlen.
  Thou shalt not steal.

Wir sollen morgen um acht auf dem Bahnhof sein.
  We are supposed to be at the station at eight tomorrow.

Er sagte, wir sollten morgen um acht Uhr auf dem Bahnhof sein.
  He said we were to be at the station at eight tomorrow.

Ich weiß, ich sollte nicht soviel rauchen.
  I know I shouldn't smoke so much.

Das werde ich nie vergessen! Und wenn ich hundert Jahre alt werden sollte!
  I'll never forget that, even if I should live to be a hundred.

Die Brücke sollte schon letztes Jahr fertig sein, aber sie ist immer noch nicht fertig.
  The bridge was supposed (was rumored) to be finished last year, but it still isn't finished.

Damals suchte IBM zwanzig Ingenieure. Alle sollten Deutsch können und mindestens vier
　　Semester Elektronik studiert haben.
　　At that time, IBM was looking for twenty engineers. They all were supposed to know
　　　German and to have had at least four semesters of electronics.

Wo ist denn der Erich?—Der soll schon wieder an der Riviera sein.
　　Where is Erich?—Supposedly he is on the Riviera again.

Hast du etwas von Dietlinde gehört?—Die soll im Juni geheiratet haben. Ihr Mann soll
　　Ingenieur sein.
　　Have you heard anything about Dietlinde?—I've heard that she got married last June.
　　　I understand her husband is an engineer.

VARIATIONS

Change the following sentences according to the pattern of
the example.

> **Ich höre, Meyer wohnt in Berlin.—Meyer soll in Berlin wohnen.**

Ich höre, er ist schon wieder in Tirol.　　　　　　Er _____ schon wieder in Tirol _____.
Ich höre, er ist noch nie in Afrika gewesen.　　　Er _____ noch nie in Afrika _____
　　　　　　　　　　　　　　　　　　　　　　　　_____.

Ich höre, seine Frau war krank.　　　　　　　　Seine Frau _____ krank _____ _____.
Ich höre, Erika hat geheiratet.　　　　　　　　Erika _____ geheiratet _____.
Ich höre, er muß schon wieder nach Ame-　　　Er _____ schon wieder nach Amerika
　　rika fahren.　　　　　　　　　　　　　　　_____ müssen.

[8] mögen

Acquaint yourself with the indicative use of **mögen,** both as a
nonmodal and as a subjective modal. Then follow the instructions
below.

SEE
ANALYSIS
146

(pp. 281-288)

Ingelheims Romane sind ja ganz gut, aber als Mensch mag ich ihn gar nicht.
　　Ingelheim's novels aren't bad, but as a person I don't care for him at all.

Ich mochte ihn schon nicht, als wir während des Krieges in Afrika waren.
　　I disliked him already when we were in Africa during the war.

Meine Frau hat ihn auch nie gemocht.
　　My wife never liked him either.

Danke, Schweinefleisch mag ich nicht; ich esse lieber ein Steak.
　　Thanks, I don't care for pork; I'd rather have a steak.

Wie alt ist seine Tochter eigentlich?—Oh, ich weiß nicht. Sie mag achtzehn oder neun-
　　zehn sein.
　　How old is his daughter?—Oh, I don't know, maybe eighteen or nineteen.

Er mochte damals etwa dreißig sein.
   At that time, he was probably about thirty.

Was mag ihm nur passiert sein?
   I wonder what has happened to him?

Er mag gedacht haben, ich hätte ihn nicht gesehen.
   He may have thought that I hadn't seen him.

VARIATIONS

Change the following sentences according to the pattern of the
example.

Ich glaube, sie ist etwa zwanzig.—Sie mag etwa zwanzig sein.

Ich glaube, sie war zwanzig.—Sie _____ zwanzig _____.
Ich glaube, sie war damals etwa zwanzig.— Sie _____ damals etwa zwanzig _____ _____.
Ich glaube, er hat mich nicht gesehen.—Er _____ mich nicht _____ _____.
Ich glaube, das ist Zufall.—Das _____ Zufall _____.
Ich glaube, das war Zufall.—Das _____ Zufall _____ _____.

[9] können

Read the following sentences and determine whether **können** is
used objectively (ability) or subjectively (inference); then
follow the instructions below.

SEE
ANALYSIS
146
(pp. 281-288)

Klaus ist krank und kann leider nicht kommen.
   Klaus is sick and unfortunately can't come.

Heute ist ja schon Donnerstag. Bis Samstag kann ich den Roman nicht gelesen haben.
   But today is Thursday already. I can't possibly have read the novel by Saturday.

Intelligent kann sie nicht sein. Wenn sie intelligent wäre, würde sie nicht für Meyer
   arbeiten.
   She can't be intelligent. If she were intelligent, she wouldn't work for Meyer.

Sie war fast noch ein Kind und konnte nicht älter sein als siebzehn.
   She was still almost a child and couldn't have been any older than seventeen.

Wenn Meyer kein Geld hätte, könnte er keinen Mercedes 300 fahren.
   If Meyer didn't have any money, he couldn't drive a Mercedes 300.

Seine Frau sagte, er sei krank und könne leider nicht kommen.
   His wife said he was sick and unfortunately wouldn't be able to come.

Könnte ich vielleicht ein Zimmer mit Bad haben?
   Could I have a room with bath?

Und der Herr, der mich sprechen wollte, hat nicht gesagt, wie er heißt? Wer kann das nur
    gewesen sein? Er sprach mit einem Akzent, sagen Sie? Hm, das könnte Mr. Taylor
    gewesen sein.
    And the gentleman who wanted to talk to me didn't tell you his name? Who could that
        have been? You say he had an accent? Hm, that could have been Mr. Taylor.

Ich glaube, wir sollten heute im Garten arbeiten. Morgen könnte es regnen.
    I think we should work in the garden today. It could (might) rain tomorrow.

Meyer hätte fliehen können, aber er wollte nicht.
Wahrscheinlich ist er noch im Lande, aber er könnte natürlich auch geflohen sein.

Natürlich hätte er das Geld stehlen können, aber er ist doch kein Dieb.
Sie können doch gar nicht wissen, ob ihm das Geld wirklich gehört; er könnte es ja auch
    gestohlen haben.

VARIATIONS

Change the following sentences according to the pattern of the
example.

> **Ist er schon hier?**
> **Nein, er kann noch nicht hier sein. Es ist doch erst acht.**

Ist sie schon verheiratet?
Nein, _____. Sie ist doch erst sechzehn.

War er gestern abend im Kino?
Nein, _____. Er war gestern abend bei Meyers.

Bist du sicher, daß es Erich war?
Nein, sicher bin ich nicht, aber _____.

[10] dürfen

Study the use of **dürfen** in these sentences and determine whether
it is used objectively or subjectively.

SEE
ANALYSIS
146
(pp. 281-288)

Darf ich heute abend ins Kino gehen, Mutti?
Kann ich heute abend ins Kino gehen, Mutti?
    May I go to the movies tonight, Mom?

Ich fragte sie, ob ich sie nach Hause bringen dürfte.
    I asked her whether I could (might) take her home.

Rauchen darf man hier leider nicht.
    Unfortunately smoking is not permitted here.

Sie dürfen nicht mehr so viel Kaffee trinken, Frau Emmerich.
    You mustn't (shouldn't) drink so much coffee anymore, Mrs. Emmerich.

Wann ist er denn weggefahren?—Vor zwei Stunden.—Dann dürfte er jetzt schon in
  Frankfurt sein.
    When did he leave?—Two hours ago.—Then we can assume that he is in
    Frankfurt by now.

Ich möchte wissen, wer mich gestern abend um elf noch angerufen hat.—Das dürfte
  Erich gewesen sein; der ruft doch immer so spät an.
    I wonder who called me last night at eleven.—I suppose that was Erich; he always
    calls that late, doesn't he?

[11] Reflexive Pronouns, **selbst, selber**

Ich habe mich schon gebadet.
Hast du dich schon gebadet?
Er hat sich schon gebadet.
Wir haben uns schon gebadet.
Habt ihr euch schon gebadet?
Sie haben sich schon gebadet.

Er hat mir ein Auto gekauft.
Er hat sich ein Auto gekauft.

Sie haben uns ein Haus gebaut.
Sie haben sich ein Haus gebaut.

Er konnte es mir einfach nicht erklären.
Er konnte es sich einfach nicht erklären.

Ich halte ihn für dumm, aber er hält sich für sehr intelligent.

Zuerst hat er nur Landschaften gemalt. Dann hat er monatelang seine Frau und seine
  Kinder gemalt, und jetzt malt er nur noch sich *selbst* (*sel*ber).

Hat er den Porsche für *sich* gekauft oder für seine *Frau?*

Er hat nicht nur von seiner *Frau* geredet, sondern auch von *sich.*—Wirklich? Mir hat er
  noch *nie* etwas von sich *selbst* erzählt.

Bis jetzt haben wir immer nur an unsere *Kin*der gedacht. Aber jetzt müssen wir endlich an
  uns *selbst* denken.

Fritz ist doch erst *vier!* Kann er sich wirklich schon *sel*ber baden?

Warum soll *ich* denn das Buch für dich lesen? Kannst du's nicht *sel*ber lesen?

VARIATIONS

> **Er hat sich ein Auto gekauft.—Ich habe mir ein Auto gekauft.**

Er hat sich schon gebadet?—Du _____?
Er hat sich schon gebadet?—Ihr _____?
Sie haben sich ein Haus gebaut.—Wir _____.

SEE
ANALYSIS
147
(pp. 288-290)

Using the phrase **ein Haus bauen,** form sentences, with and without modals, negative and affirmative, using dative reflexive pronouns.

[12] Contrary-to-Fact Conditions without **wenn**

SEE
ANALYSIS
148

(p. 290)

Wäre Ingelheim nicht Soldat gewesen, so hätte er keine Kriegsromane schreiben können.
    If Ingelheim hadn't been a soldier, he couldn't have written war novels.

Hätte Erich seinen Hut nicht verloren, so hätte niemand geglaubt, was Gerda erzählte.
    If Erich hadn't lost his hat, nobody would have believed what Gerda was saying.

Hätten wir uns dieses Wochenendhaus nicht gekauft, dann könnten wir jetzt jeden Sommer nach Italien fahren.
    If we hadn't bought this weekend house, we could go to Italy every summer now.

Hättest du mir doch nur geschrieben, daß du Geld brauchtest! Du weißt doch, daß ich dir gerne geholfen hätte.
    If only you had written that you needed money! You know that I would have been glad to help you.

Hätte ich doch nur gewußt, daß Monika krank war! Ich hätte sie gerne besucht.
    Had I only known that Monika was sick! I would have been glad to visit her.

VARIATIONS

Transform the following sentences into wishes.

> **Er hat meine Freundin nicht eingeladen.**
> **Wenn er nur meine *Freun*din eingeladen hätte!**
> **Wenn er meine Freundin nur *ein*geladen hätte!**
> **Hätte er doch nur meine *Freun*din eingeladen!**
> **Hätte er meine Freundin doch nur *ein*geladen!**

Guten Morgen! Was möchten Sie gern zum Frühstück, bitte?

Portion Kaffee — Nescafé — Tee — Schokolade mit Butter, Konfitüre, Marmelade, Honig, Brot, Brötchen, Hörnchen, Zwieback   3,50

Eierspeisen

1 weichgekochtes Ei	—,60
2 Eier im Glas	1,20
2 Stück Rühreier oder Spiegeleier	1,50
2 Spiegeleier mit Schinken oder Speck	2,50

Diverses

Käse nach Wahl	1,50
Porridge mit Sahne und Zucker	1,50
Cornflakes mit Sahne oder Milch	1,50
Joghurt mit Zucker	1,—

Kleine Fleischbeilage

Wurstaufschnitt	1,50
Spezial-Frühstücksteller (unser Titelfoto)	1,50
Gekochter Schinken	1,80
Roher Räucherschinken	2,—
Roastbeef	2,—

Fruchtsäfte und Früchte

Orangensaft, frisch gepreßt	1,50
Grapefruitsaft	1,25
Tomatensaft	1,25
Karottensaft, frisch	1,50
Frische halbe Pampelmuse	1,—
Geeiste Melone	nach Jahreszeit
Gemischtes Kompott oder Backpflaumen mit Sahne	2,—
Frisches Obst	zum Tagespreis

15 % Etage · Etagenaufschlag pro Person DM 0,50 · 10 % Service

Er war gestern nicht hier.
Er ist mit seiner Frau nach Kärnten gefahren.
Er hat meiner Frau Blumen geschickt.

Reading

Woher wußten Sie denn, daß ich Amerikanerin bin?

Ich weiß, mein Deutsch ist gut und fast akzentfrei; und wenn ich
nach Deutschland fahre, glaubt man oft, daß ich in Deutschland
geboren bin. Aber letztes Jahr habe ich gelernt, daß man mehr als
die Sprache können muß, wenn man nicht will, daß jeder sofort
weiß, daß man Amerikaner ist.   5

Ich war mit meinem Mann in Hamburg, und wir wohnten in den
Vier Jahreszeiten. Morgens im Frühstückszimmer saßen wir kaum   **Vier Jahreszeiten**
an unserem Tisch, als der Kellner kam und uns fragte: "And what   Four Seasons
would you like for breakfast?" Woher wußte er, daß wir Amerikaner
waren?   10

Mein Kleid hatte ich am Tage vorher in Hamburg gekauft; ich hatte
keinen Lippenstift an, und meine Dauerwelle hatte ich mir in Köln   **der Lippenstift, –e**
machen lassen. Außerdem las mein Mann eine Hamburger Zeitung.   lipstick
Und trotzdem sagte der Kellner: "What would you like for break-   **die Dauerwelle** per-
fast?" Ich war neugierig und fragte: „Herr Ober, woher wissen   15   manent
Sie, daß wir Amerikaner sind?"   **neugierig** curious

„Wenn man seit dreißig Jahren Kellner ist, dann sieht man das
sofort, gnädige Frau", sagte er auf Deutsch. „Als Sie Platz nahmen,

Good morning! What would you like for breakfast, please?		Small meat supplements	
		Sausages cold meat	1,30
		Assorted cold meat	1,50
Coffee — Nescafé — tea — chocolate		Boiled ham	1,80
compl. with butter, jam, marmelade, honey,		Smoked ham	2,—
rolls, recent-rolls, bread, biscuits	3,50	Roastbeef	2,—
Egg - dishes		**Fruit and fruit-juices**	
1 soft boiled egg	—,60	Orange juice, fresh	1,50
2 boiled eggs in a glass	1,20	Grapefruit juice	1,25
Scrambled eggs or fried eggs	1,50	Tomato juice	1,25
2 fried eggs with ham or bacon	2,50	Carrots juice, fresh	1,50
		Fresh half grapefruit	1,—
Sundries		Mixed fruits or stewed prunes with cream	2,—
Assorted cheese	1,30	Fresh fruit	price of day
Porridge with cream and sugar	1,50		
Cornflakes with cream or milk	1,50		
Yoghurt with sugar	1,—	15% room-service · room-tax per person DM 0,50 · 10% service	

hat Ihnen Ihr Mann den Stuhl gehalten,—und das tut man in Deutschland nicht. Und als ich an Ihren Tisch kam, habe ich sofort gesehen, daß Sie Ihren Ring an der linken Hand tragen,—und das tut man in Deutschland nur, solange man verlobt ist."

„Und woher wußten Sie, daß wir verheiratet sind?"   5

„Gnädige Frau, das darf ich Ihnen wirklich nicht sagen."

„Das brauchen Sie auch nicht", sagte mein Mann, der bis jetzt hinter seiner Zeitung gesessen und nichts gesagt hatte. Er grinste, faltete die Zeitung zusammen, gab sie dem Kellner und sagte: „Herr Ober, Sie sind ein Menschenkenner.—Also: zwei Orangen- 10 saft, Spiegeleier mit Schinken, Toast und Kaffee."

"In other words, an American breakfast," sagte der Ober und verschwand.

grinsen to grin
zusammenfalten to fold
der Saft juice
Spiegelei fried egg, sunny side up
der Schinken ham

Aus deutschen Zeitungen

The following passages appeared in recent issues of German newspapers. They have been slightly modified, but are typical of the kind of German you will find in newspapers.

Scotland Yard untersucht Bombenanschlag*

London (dpa). Ein Spezialteam von Kriminalisten Scotland Yards untersucht seit gestern intensiv die Ursachen der Explosion, die am Vorabend die Wohnung des Industrieministers zerstört hatte. Der

der Anschlag, ‥e attack
dpa = Deutsche Presse Agentur

* The reading selections of this unit contain a number of adjectives with endings. Disregard these endings for the time being; they will be discussed in Unit 10.

Leiter des Teams ist anonym; man kennt ihn nur als „Commander X", den Spezialisten für die Jagd auf Bombenattentäter. Bis jetzt fehlt von den Tätern jede Spur.

die Jagd hunt, chase
der Attentäter, – assassin

Fill in the blanks after rereading the passage.

1. Scotland Yard _____ die Ursachen einer Explosion.
2. Eine Bombe hatte die _____ eines Ministers zerstört.
3. Man weiß nicht, wie der _____ des Teams heißt.
4. Man _____ ihn nur als „Commander X".
5. Commander X ist ein _____ für die Jagd auf Bombenattentäter.
6. Von den Tätern _____ noch jede Spur.

Nötig wie innere Reformen

Baden-Baden (dpa). Die Entwicklungshilfe ist nach der Meinung des Bundesministers für wirtschaftliche Zusammenarbeit genau so nötig und wichtig wie innere Reformen in der Bundesrepublik. In einem Interview des Südwestfunks erklärte der Minister gestern, Entwicklungshilfe sei genau so eine Investition in die gemeinsame Zukunft wie die Investitionen in Schulen und Universitäten. Der Minister sagte, die Entwicklungshilfe solle von jetzt an vor allem für solche Projekte zur Verfügung stehen, die den Aufschwung von ganzen Landstrichen in die Wege leiten können. Außerdem will der Minister mehr als bisher Familienplanungsprogramme fördern.

wirtschaftlich economic
die Investition, –en investment
gemeinsam common
vor allem above all
zur Verfügung stehen to be available
der Aufschwung upswing, improvement
der Landstrich, –e region
in die Wege leiten to initiate
fördern to further

German "journalese" contains a large number of compound nouns. Analyze the following:

die Entwicklungshilfe	**die Entwicklung**	development
	die Hilfe	aid
der Bundesminister	**der Bund**	federation
	der Minister	minister
die Bundesrepublik	**der Bund**	federation
	die Republik	republic
die Zusammenarbeit	**zusammen**	together
	die Arbeit	work
der Südwestfunk	**der Südwesten**	southwest
	der (Rund) funk	radio
das Familienplanungsprogramm	**die Familie**	family
	die Planung	planning
	das Programm	program

Sonntag auf der Autobahn relativ störungsfrei

Hamburg (dpa/AP). Der Verkehr auf den Autobahnen und Fern-
straßen der Bundesrepublik war am Sonntag zwar lebhaft und
dicht, aber im allgemeinen störungsfrei, während am Samstag die
Rückreisewelle des Ferienverkehrs von Süden nach Norden noch
einmal sehr intensiv gewesen war.   5

Der starke Rückreiseverkehr, den die Polizei von Nordrhein-Westfalen für dieses Wochenende erwartet hatte, da dort am Montag
die Schule wieder beginnt, blieb aus. Am Sonntagmittag war der
Verkehr normal; nur auf der Autobahn Frankfurt-Köln gab es
infolge eines Unfalls bei Limburg noch einmal einen Verkehrsstau. 10

Auf den Autobahnen in Bayern und Hessen war der Verkehr dicht,
aber relativ reibungslos. In Rheinland-Pfalz, Saarland, Niedersachsen
und in Norddeutschland war es am Sonntag ruhig. Fünf Tote und
zwei Schwerverletzte gab es bei einem Verkehrsunfall auf der
Bundesstraße 80 in der Nähe von Gertenbach (Kreis Witzenhausen). 15
Beim Überholen eines Traktors stieß ein Personenwagen mit einem
Kleinbus aus Göttingen zusammen. Dabei kamen zwei zehnjährige
Kinder und drei Erwachsene ums Leben.

Ein glückliches Ende nahm am Samstagvormittag ein Zwischenfall
auf der Autobahn Köln-Aachen, wo ein Autofahrer die Gegenfahr- 20
bahn befuhr. Die Polizei warnte über den Rundfunk alle Benutzer
der Autobahn, konnte aber den „Linksfahrer" erst nach 15 km zum
Halten bringen. Der Fahrer hatte die falsche Einfahrt benutzt.

lebhaft lively
die Welle, –n wave

blieb aus did not
materialize
infolge (*with gen.*)
as a consequence of
der Stau back-up
Hessen Hesse
reibungslos smooth
Rheinland-Pfalz
Rhineland-Palatinate
Niedersachsen
Lower Saxony
überholen to pass
zusammenstoßen to
collide
ums Leben kommen
to be fatally injured
der Zwischenfall, ¨-e
incident
die Fahrbahn, –en
lane
falsch wrong, false

Complete the following sentences.

1. Am Sonntag war der Verkehr relativ störungsfrei, aber am Samstag

   _____.

2. Der Verkehr war so intensiv, weil viele Leute _____

   _____.

3. Viele reisten nach Nordrhein-Westfalen zurück, denn dort _____

   _____.

4. Der Unfall auf der Bundesstraße 80 passierte, weil _____

   _____.

5. Der Zwischenfall auf der Autobahn Köln-Aachen nahm wahrscheinlich deshalb ein glückliches Ende, weil die Polizei _____

   _____.

6. Der Bericht nennt den Autofahrer einen „Linksfahrer", weil er

   _____.

7. Der Autofahrer fuhr auf der Gegenfahrbahn, weil er _____

   _____.

Wall-Street im Aufschwung

Das New Yorker Finanzzentrum Wall Street hatte am Montag den
erfolgreichsten Tag seiner Geschichte. Die New Yorker Aktienbörse
erreichte mit dem Umsatz von 31,730 Mill. einen absoluten Rekord.
Der Dow-Jones Durchschnittswert für 30 repräsentative Industrie-
papiere stieg um 32,93 Punkte auf 888,95.

die Aktienbörse, –n
stock exchange
der Umsatz   volume
(of exchange)
5 Mill. = Millionen

Erdölleitung wieder in Betrieb

Das Leck in der Pipeline Marseille-Karlsruhe in der Nähe des Dorfes
Chateauneuf-en-Galoire ist repariert. Wie die Erdölvertriebsorgan-
isation am Dienstag meldete, ist damit die Zufuhr nach Ostfrank-
reich und Südwestdeutschland gesichert.

das Erdöl   petroleum
das Leck   leak
vertreiben   to
distribute
melden   to announce
die Zufuhr   supply

Warnsignal: Vorsicht Betrunkener (dpa)

Auf einer Straße bei Heiningen (Kreis Göppingen) fand die Polizei
am Mittwoch zwei Warndreiecke, zwischen denen ein Betrunkener
schlief. Ein Autofahrer mit Sinn für Humor wollte den Betrunkenen,
der auf der Straße seinen Rausch ausschlief, nicht wecken, sondern
stellte vor und hinter dem alkoholisierten Hindernis einfach die
Warnzeichen auf. Die Autos kurvten so lange um den gut markierten
Straßen-Schläfer herum, bis die Polizei kam und den Betrunkenen
und die Warndreiecke einsammelte.

betrunken   drunk

der Rausch   stupor
5 das Hindernis, –se
obstacle

einsammeln   to
collect

Retell the story from the point of view of the **Autofahrer;** *begin as
follows:*

Gestern ist mir etwas Komisches passiert. Ich fuhr auf der Straße
nach Heiningen. . . .

Sport: Fünfmal Gold am Wochenende

Helsinki (stz). Die zwei letzten Tage der Leichtathletik-Europa-
meisterschaften waren ein Triumph für die Mannschaft aus der
Bundesrepublik. Nach vier Tagen des Wartens auf eine Goldmedaille
gab es am Wochenende fünf Siege. Der Weltrekordler Uwe Beyer
(Mainz) gewann am Samstag das Hammerwerfen mit 72,36 m; die
Weitsprungweltrekordlerin Heide Rosendahl (Leverkusen) gewann
den Fünfkampf mit 5299 Punkten und Ingrid Mickler (Mainz) den
Weitsprung mit 6,76 m. Am Schlußtag kamen noch zwei Staffeler-
folge dazu. Die Sprinterinnen Elfgard Schüttenhelm, Inge Helten,
Annagret Irrgand und Ingrid Mickler gewannen die 4 x 100 m Staffel
in der Europarekordzeit von 43,3 Sekunden. Die 4 x 400 m Staffel

die Leichtathletik
track
die Meisterschaft
championship
die Mannschaft, –en
5 team
der Fünfkampf
pentathlon

die Staffel   relay

der Männer kam mit Horst Schloeske, Thomas Jordan, Martin Jellinghaus und Hermann Koehler in 3:02,9 Minuten ins Ziel.

das Ziel   finish line

A typical radio program reproduced as it appeared in a daily newspaper.

NDR   Norddeutscher Rundfunk
WDR   Westdeutscher Rundfunk

Mittelwelle   middle wave = AM
UKW Ultrakurzwelle   ultra shortwave = FM

NDR/WDR • Mittelwelle

Nachrichten: 6.00, 7.00, 8.00, 9.00, 10.00, 11.00, 12.00, 13.00, 14.00, 15.00, 16.00, 17.00, 18.00, 19.00, 22.00, 23.00, 24.00
Kommentar: 6.05, 7.05, 13.10, 19.10, 22.10

6.00 Wetter **6.10** Mit Musik in den Tag **6.55** Andacht
7.10 Kleine Melodie
8.10 Musikalisches Mosaik
9.05 Opernkonzert: Ouvertüre zu „Die diebische Elster" (Rossini). Aus „Der Bajazzo" (Leoncavallo). Aus „Die lustigen Weiber von Windsor" (Nicolai)
10.05 Mein Vater ist der Staat. 3. Verwahranstalten ohne Alternativen zur Verwahrlosung. Untersuchung über Heimerziehung. Von Ruth Herrmann
12.05 Landfunk **12.15** Musik zur Mittagspause **12.50** Presseschau
13.15 Opernkonzert. Alexander Borodin: „Fürst Igor". Peter Tschaikowski: „Pique Dame". Nikolai Rimski-Korsakow: „Sadko", „Schneeflöckchen"
14.05 Musik für Kammerorchester. Luigi Boccherini: Sinfonie A-Dur op. 1 Nr. 3. Jan Adam Fransek Mica: Concertino notturno in Es-Dur für Violine, Viola, Oboe, zwei Hörner, Fagott und Streicher u. a.
15.05 Wir lesen vor: Die Geschichte des Pandesowna (3). Aus dem Buch „Die Handschrift von Saragossa". Von Jan Potocki **15.30** Vetter Michel. Niederdeutsche Volksliederkantate (Kneip)
16.05 Virtuose Solisten. Camille Saint-Saens: Havanaise für Violine und Orchester u. a. **16.30** Kinderfunk. Bilderbuchgeschichten und Informationen für Eltern. Auswahl Sybil Gräfin Schönfeld. Es liest Eduard Marks
17.05 Aus der Welt der Arbeit **17.30** Musik zum Feierabend — Volkstümliche Melodien — Aus dem NDR-Tanzstudio
18.30 Echo des Tages
19.25 Auf ein Wort **19.30** Kammerkonzert. Dag Wirén: Serenade für Streicher op. 11. Claude

NDR • UKW (2. Programm)

Nachrichten: 6.30, 7.30, 8.30, 9.30, 10.30, 11.30, 12.30, 13.30, 14.30, 15.30, 16.30, 17.30, 18.30, 19.30, 21.30, 22.30, 23.30
Umschau: 17.35
Kommentar: 18.25

6.00 Marktrundschau **6.05** Plattdeutsche Morgenansprache **6.10** Vorschau **6.15** Tanzmusik **6.30** Musik für junge Leute
7.00 Wirtschaft — aktuell **7.30** Popmusik und Schlager
8.00 Hör mal 'n beten to! — Popmusik und Schlager **8.35** Andacht **8.40** Leichte Musik (St)
9.00 NDR 2 von neun bis halb eins: Musik und Informationen; dazwischen: **9.00** Musik — Veranstaltungskalender **9.30** Regionale Meldungen — Musik **10.00** Taschenbücher und Krimis — Musik **11.00** Aus Arbeit und Wirtschaft — Musik **12.00** Verkehrsnotizen — Musik
12.30 Kurier am Mittag
13.30 Tanz- und Unterhaltungsmusik (St)
14.30 Musik für junge Leute
15.00 Glückwünsche und Musik **15.35** Niederdeutsche Chronik: Urlaub in Hamburg? Die Großstadt als Erholungsort
16.00 NDR-Swing-Time **16.35** Der 5-Uhr-Club. Am Mikrofon: Monika Jetter
18.35 Die klingende Drehscheibe (St)
19.35 Budapester Magazin. Bericht über kulturelle Ereignisse
20.00 Zu Gast bei anderen Sendern (St) **20.45** Wolfgang Sauers Musikmagazin
21.35 Dabei fällt mir ein . . . Uniformen. Gedanken von Frank Freytag **21.45** Tanzmusik (St)
22.15 Sport aktuell **22.30** Still im Aug' erglänzt die Träne. Lieder, die zu Herzen geh'n. Zusammengestellt von Harro Torneck **22.45** Vokal — instrumental — international, präsentiert von Walter Richard Langer
23.30 Berichte von heute
0.00 Vorschau. Anschließend: Intermezzo mit dem Orchester Ted Heath und Glen Campbell, Gesang **0.10** Musik bis zum frühen Morgen

Franz Kafka.

FRANZ KAFKA

Franz Kafka (born 1883 in Prague), though most of his works were published posthumously, was one of the most influential prose writers of this century. Among his best-known works are the novels *Der Prozeß* (The Trial) and *Das Schloß* (The Castle) and such stories as *Das Urteil* (The Judgment), *Die Verwandlung* (Metamorphosis), and *Der Landarzt* (The Country Doctor). He died in 1924. The short piece below was written around 1920–22.

Heimkehr

Ich bin zurückgekehrt, ich habe den Flur durchschritten und blicke mich um. Es ist meines Vaters alter Hof. Die Pfütze in der Mitte. Altes, unbrauchbares Gerät, ineinanderverfahren, verstellt den Weg zur Bodentreppe. Die Katze lauert auf dem Geländer. Ein zerrissenes Tuch, einmal im Spiel um eine Stange gewunden, hebt sich im Wind. Ich bin angekommen. Wer wird mich empfangen? Wer wartet hinter der Tür der Küche? Rauch kommt aus dem Schornstein, der Kaffee zum Abendessen wird gekocht. Ist dir heimlich, fühlst du dich zu Hause? Ich weiß es nicht, ich bin sehr unsicher. Meines Vaters Haus ist es, aber kalt steht Stück neben Stück, als wäre jedes mit seinen eigenen Angelegenheiten beschäftigt, die ich teils vergessen habe, teils niemals kannte. Was kann ich ihnen nützen, was bin ich ihnen und sei ich auch des Vaters, des alten Landwirts Sohn. Und ich wage nicht, an der Küchentür zu klopfen, nur von der Ferne horche ich, nur von der Ferne horche ich stehend, nicht so, daß ich als

Homecoming

I have returned, I have crossed the entranceway and am looking around. It is my father's old place. The puddle in the middle. Old, unusable equipment, shoved into a heap, bars the way to the stairway to the loft. The cat lies in wait on the railing. A torn cloth, wound around a stake once at play, rises in the wind. I have arrived. Who will receive me? Who is waiting behind the kitchen door? Smoke comes from the chimney, coffee for supper is being made. Do you feel at home? I don't know, I am very unsure. My father's house it is, but coldly piece stands by piece, as if each were occupied with its own affairs which partly I have forgotten, partly never knew. Of what use can I be to them, what am I to them, even if I am my father's, the old farmer's, son. And I dare not knock at the kitchen door, only from the distance I listen, only from the distance I listen, standing, not in such a way that I could be surprised as an eavesdropper. And because I listen from a distance, I hear nothing, only the soft ring

Horcher überrascht werden könnte. Und weil ich von der Ferne horche, erhorche ich nichts, nur einen leichten Uhrenschlag höre ich oder glaube ihn vielleicht nur zu hören, herüber aus den Kindertagen. Was sonst in der Küche geschieht, ist das Geheimnis der dort Sitzenden, das sie vor mir wahren. Je länger man vor der Tür zögert, desto fremder wird man. Wie wäre es, wenn jetzt jemand die Tür öffnete und mich etwas fragte. Wäre ich dann nicht selbst wie einer, der sein Geheimnis wahren will.

of a clock do I hear, or perhaps I only imagine hearing it, from the days of my childhood. What else happens in the kitchen is the secret of those sitting there, which they keep from me. The longer you hesitate in front of the door, the more of a stranger you become. How would it be if someone opened the door now and asked me something. Would I then myself not be like one who wants to keep his secret.

AUS DER BIBEL

Das Gleichnis vom verlornen Sohn

Aus dem Evangelium nach Lukas 15: 11–32

The Parable of the Prodigal Son

From The Gospel According to Luke 15: 11–32

[11] Er sprach aber: Ein Mann hatte zwei Söhne. [12] Und der jüngere von ihnen sagte zum Vater: Vater, gib mir den Teil des Vermögens, der mir zukommt! Der aber verteilte seine Habe unter sie. [13] Und nicht viele Tage darnach nahm der jüngere Sohn alles mit sich und zog hinweg in ein fernes Land, und dort vergeudete er sein Vermögen durch ein zügelloses Leben. [14] Nachdem er aber alles durchgebracht hatte, kam eine gewaltige Hungersnot über jenes Land, und er fing an, Mangel zu leiden. [15] Und er ging hin und hängte sich an einen der Bürger jenes Landes; der schickte ihn auf seine Felder, Schweine zu hüten. [16] Und er begehrte, seinen Bauch mit den Schoten zu füllen, die die Schweine fraßen: und niemand gab sie ihm. [17] Da ging er in sich und sprach: Wie viele Tagelöhner meines Vaters haben Brot im Überfluß, ich aber komme hier vor Hunger um! [18] Ich will mich aufmachen und zu meinem Vater gehen und zu ihm sagen: Vater, ich habe gesündigt gegen

[11] Again he said: 'There was once a man who had two sons; [12] and the younger said to his father, "Father, give me my share of the property." So he divided his estate between them. [13] A few days later the younger son turned the whole of his share into cash and left home for a distant country, where he squandered it in reckless living. [14] He had spent it all, when a severe famine fell upon that country and he began to feel the pinch. [15] So he went and attached himself to one of the local landowners, who sent him on to his farm to mind the pigs. [16] He would have been glad to fill his belly with the pods that the pigs were eating; and no one gave him anything. [17] Then he came to his senses and said, "How many of my father's paid servants have more food than they can eat, and here am I, starving to death! [18] I will set off and go to my father, and say to him, 'Father, I have sinned, against God and against you; [19] I am no longer fit to be called your son; treat me as

den Himmel und vor dir; ¹⁹ ich bin nicht mehr wert, dein Sohn zu heißen; stelle mich wie einen deiner Tagelöhner! ²⁰ Und er machte sich auf und ging zu seinem Vater. Als er aber noch fern war, sah ihn sein Vater und fühlte Erbarmen, lief hin, fiel ihm um den Hals und küßte ihn. ²¹ Der Sohn aber sprach zu ihm: Vater, ich habe gesündigt gegen den Himmel und vor dir; ich bin nicht mehr wert, dein Sohn zu heißen. ²² Doch der Vater sagte zu seinen Knechten: Bringet schnell das beste Kleid heraus und ziehet es ihm an und gebet ihm einen Ring an die Hand und Schuhe an die Füße, ²³ und holet das gemästete Kalb, schlachtet es und lasset uns essen und fröhlich sein! ²⁴ Denn dieser mein Sohn war tot und ist wieder lebendig geworden, er war verloren und ist wiedergefunden worden. Und sie fingen an, fröhlich zu sein.

²⁵ Sein älterer Sohn aber war auf dem Felde; und als er kam und sich dem Hause näherte, hörte er Musik und Reigentanz. ²⁶ Und er rief einen der Knechte herbei und erkundigte sich, was das sei. ²⁷ Der aber sagte ihm: Dein Bruder ist gekommen, und dein Vater hat das gemästete Kalb geschlachtet, weil er ihn gesund wiedererhalten hat. ²⁸ Da wurde er zornig und wollte nicht hineingehen. Doch sein Vater kam heraus und redete ihm zu. ²⁹ Er aber antwortete und sagte zum Vater: Siehe, so viele Jahre diene ich dir und habe nie ein Gebot von dir übertreten; und mir hast du nie einen Bock gegeben, damit ich mit meinen Freunden fröhlich wäre. ³⁰ Nun aber dieser dein Sohn gekommen ist, der deine Habe mit Dirnen aufgezehrt hat, hast du ihm das gemästete Kalb geschlachtet. ³¹ Da sagte er zu ihm: Kind, du bist allezeit bei mir, und alles, was mein ist, ist dein. ³² Du solltest aber fröhlich sein und dich freuen; denn dieser dein Bruder war tot und ist lebendig geworden, und war verloren und ist wiedergefunden worden.

one of your paid servants.' " ²⁰ So he set out for his father's house. But while he was still a long way off his father saw him, and his heart went out to him. He ran to meet him, flung his arms round him, and kissed him. ²¹ The son said, "Father, I have sinned, against God and against you; I am no longer fit to be called your son." ²² But the father said to his servants, "Quick! fetch a robe, my best one, and put it on him; put a ring on his finger and shoes on his feet. ²³ Bring the fatted calf and kill it, and let us have a feast to celebrate the day. ²⁴ For this son of mine was dead and has come back to life; he was lost and is found." And the festivities began.

²⁵ 'Now the elder son was out on the farm; and on his way back, as he approached the house, he heard music and dancing. ²⁶ He called one of the servants and asked what it meant. ²⁷ The servant told him, "Your brother has come home, and your father has killed the fatted calf because he has him back safe and sound." ²⁸ But he was angry and refused to go in. His father came out and pleaded with him; ²⁹ but he retorted, "You know how I have slaved for you all these years; I never once disobeyed your orders; and you never gave me so much as a kid, for a feast with my friends. ³⁰ But now that this son of yours turns up, after running through your money with his women, you kill the fatted calf for him." ³¹ "My boy," said the father, "you are always with me, and everything I have is yours. ³² How could we help celebrating this happy day? Your brother here was dead and has come back to life, was lost and is found."

Analysis

143 nicht..., sondern...

The English pattern "not A, but B," which occurs in such sentences as

> You are not my friend, but my enemy

is expressed in German by **nicht A, sondern B.**

> **Das war nicht gestern, sondern vorgestern.**
> That was not yesterday, but the day before yesterday.

Such sentences use contrast intonation. The element introduced by **nicht** (or **kein**) has a rising stress (╱), and the element introduced by **sondern** has a falling stress (╲). The **nicht** (or **kein**) and the **sondern** are normally unstressed.

The element introduced by **sondern** can either stand behind the second prong in the end field, or it can follow immediately upon the **nicht A–** element.

> **Ich war nicht gestern in Berlin, sondern vorgestern.**
> **Ich war nicht gestern, sondern vorgestern in Berlin.**

144 Numbers from 1 to 100

The German system is quite similar to English. From 0 to 12, each number has its own name; from 13 on, and with the exception of 100, the numbers are either compounded or are derived from the basic set 1–9. Note that from 21 to 29, 31 to 39, and so on, German reverses the English pattern: *twenty-one* becomes **einundzwanzig.**

null		**zwanzig**	
eins		**einundzwanzig**	
zwei		**zweiundzwanzig**	*zwanzig*
drei	**dreizehn**	**dreiundzwanzig**	*dreißig*
vier	**vierzehn**	**vierundzwanzig**	**vierzig**
fünf	**fünfzehn**	**fünfundzwanzig**	**fünfzig**
sechs	*sechzehn*	**sechsundzwanzig**	*sechzig*
sieben	*siebzehn*	**siebenundzwanzig**	*siebzig*
acht	**achtzehn**	**achtundzwanzig**	**achtzig**
neun	**neunzehn**	**neunundzwanzig**	**neunzig**
zehn			**(ein)hundert**
elf			
zwölf			

Particular attention must be paid to the spelling and pronunciation of the italicized numbers in the table.

145 Present and Past Infinitives

In any sentence containing an infinitive, there is always a time relation between this infinitive and the inflected verb. Consider the sentences

Er scheint zu schlafen.	He seems to be asleep.
Er schien zu schlafen.	He seemed to be asleep.

In both sentences the infinitive (**schlafen**) refers to the same time as the inflected verbs (**scheint** and **schien**).

If the infinitives, compared to the time of the inflected verb, refer to the same time, they are called present infinitives, *even if* (as in **er schien zu schlafen**) both the inflected verb and the infinitive refer to past time compared to the moment of speaking. Up to now, only such present infinitives have been used in this book.

The situation is quite different in sentences such as

Er scheint gut geschlafen zu haben.	He seems to have slept well.
Er schien gut geschlafen zu haben.	He seemed to have slept well.

Here the infinitive **geschlafen zu haben** (*to have slept*) refers to a point in time which precedes the time of the inflected verb. The compound infinitives used in such cases are called past infinitives.

In German past infinitives, the participle (**geschlafen**) precedes the infinitive of the auxiliary, which is always either **haben** or **sein**. The **zu** stands between the participle and **sein** or **haben**. **Zu** is, of course, not used after modals.

PRESENT INFINITIVE	PAST INFINITIVE
schlafen	geschlafen (zu) haben
sein	gewesen (zu) sein
essen	gegessen (zu) haben
abfahren	abgefahren (zu) sein
kennenlernen	kennengelernt (zu) haben
glücklich sein	glücklich gewesen (zu) sein.

146 The Subjective Use of Modals

In such sentences as

Alle Menschen müssen sterben	All humans must die
Ich muß morgen arbeiten	I must (have to) work tomorrow

both English *must* and German **müssen** express an unavoidable necessity which compels the grammatical subject (sometimes the speaker himself) to do something no matter whether the subject likes it or not. The speaker reports this compelling necessity objectively as something belonging to the realm of facts. He is using *must* and **müssen** *objectively.*

The situation is quite different when, walking around the block, I see Meyer proudly displaying a brand-new expensive sports car and make the remark

Hm! Meyer must have money.   **Hm! Meyer muß Geld haben.**

I do not mean, in this case, that Meyer is compelled to have money whether he likes it or not. What I do mean is "Looking at the visible facts, I cannot help but arrive at the conclusion that Meyer has money." The modals *must* and **muß** still express necessity, but the necessity involved is the psychological necessity of the speaker's judgment—which might be wrong. The speaker is now using *must* and **muß** *subjectively.*

The subjective use of German modals is quite frequently parallel to English usage, and you could easily have handled a sentence like

Wer kann das sein?—Das könnte Meyer sein!
Who can that be?—That could be Meyer!

Nevertheless, we have tried to avoid the subjective use of German modals until now. First of all, subjective modals (both in English and in German) are frequently followed by a past infinitive, and past infinitives are used for the first time in this unit. Second, the subjective use of modals in German is not *entirely* parallel to English. There are important differences. We shall therefore have to look systematically into the use of all modals again.

Since subjective modals involve judgments and inferences rather than facts, the speaker expresses this judgment *either* as valid for the moment of speaking *or* (in storytelling) as valid in the past. He therefore uses only two tenses: the present tense and the simple past.

EXAMPLE:

PRES. INDICATIVE	kann	muß
PRES. SUBJUNCTIVE	könnte	müßte
PAST INDICATIVE	konnte	mußte
PAST SUBJUNCTIVE	hätte . . . können	hätte . . . müssen

In most cases, the subjunctive of modals used subjectively does not express irreality, but simply a toned-down and more tentative subjective judgment.

müssen

The present indicative sentence

Er muß schon angekommen sein   He must have arrived by now

expresses an inference and therefore is an example of the subjective use of **müssen.** The sentence can be changed to a subjunctive sentence with **müßte** to express the same inference in a more tentative way.

Er müßte eigentlich schon hier sein.   He ought to be here by now.

In English, *ought* expresses the idea of the subjunctive **müßte.**

Eine Reise um die Welt muß nicht ein Vermögen kosten und nicht ewig dauern.

wollen

When used objectively, **wollen** attributes to the grammatical subject a definite intention.

Fritz will Arzt werden.   Fritz wants to become a doctor.

If, in the opinion of the speaker, the grammatical subject aims not at being or doing something, but merely at making others believe that he is something or has done something, then intention turns into pretension and claim; and the speaker, changing the meaning of **wollen,** uses it subjectively with the meaning *to claim.*

Er will Arzt sein und in Wien studiert haben.
He claims to be a doctor and to have studied in Vienna.
(But there is something about him which makes me suspicious.)

Sometimes, it is only context, not structure, that will show whether **wollen** has the objective meaning *to intend* or the subjective meaning *to claim.* Thus

Sie wollen alle dabei gewesen sein

may mean, subjectively:

They all claim to have been there.

It may also mean, objectively:

They all want to have been there.
(They all want to be able to say, "I was there.")

sollen

Both German **sollen** and English *to be supposed to* may be used objectively as well as subjectively.

When used objectively, these verbs refer to a plan of operation or pattern of behavior not made or prescribed by the speaker. Thus, if a traveling companion tells you:

Wir sollen morgen früh alle um acht in der Hotelhalle sein
All of us are supposed to be in the lobby at eight tomorrow morning

his use of **sollen** implies that the plan of operation was not made by him. He read what was posted on the bulletin board or he just heard about it from somebody else. The sentence may therefore contain at least an element of hearsay.

This element of hearsay may become the predominant meaning of both **sollen** and *to be supposed to*. If it does, they are used subjectively.

Erika soll geheiratet haben. Ihr Mann soll Zahnarzt sein.
Erika is supposed to have married. I understand her husband is a dentist.

Meyer soll Geld haben.
Meyer is said to have money. (It is common gossip.)

Now the speaker does not report a new plan of operation. He simply tells that he has heard something which, in his judgment, may or may not be just hearsay.

Again, it is frequently only context that will show whether **sollen** is used objectively or subjectively. Thus

Meyer soll jeden Tag eine halbe Stunde schwimmen

may either refer to hearsay or to what the doctor prescribed. In colloquial German, the "hearsay" **sollen** does not appear in the subjunctive.

mögen

Up to this point, we have used only the forms **ich möchte, du möchtest,** and so on. But although these **möchte**-forms are the ones used most frequently, **mögen,** like the other modals, has a complete set of forms.

PRESENT INDICATIVE	PRESENT SUBJUNCTIVE
ich mag	ich möchte
du magst	du möchtest
er mag	er möchte
wir mögen	wir möchten
ihr mögt	ihr möchtet
sie mögen	sie möchten

PAST INDICATIVE	PAST SUBJUNCTIVE		
ich mochte	ich hätte . . . (infinitive)		mögen
du mochtest	du hättest	”	”
er mochte	er hätte	”	”
wir mochten	wir hätten	”	”
ihr mochtet	ihr hättet	”	”
sie mochten	sie hätten	”	”

PERFECT WITH DEPENDENT INFINITIVE	PERFECT WITHOUT INFINITIVE
ich habe . . . mögen	ich habe gemocht
du hast . . . mögen	du hast gemocht
etc.	etc.

The verb **mögen** can be used without a following infinitive. If so used, it means *to like* and takes an accusative object.

Sie mag ihn nicht.	She doesn't like him.
Wir mögen kein Schweinefleisch.	We don't like pork.
Wir mochten ihn nicht.	We did not like him.
Ich habe sie nie gemocht.	I never liked her.

When used as a modal—that is, with a dependent infinitive, **mögen** has an objective and a subjective meaning.

Used objectively, **mögen** plus infinitive expresses the fact that the grammatical subject has a desire. This use, for all practical purposes, is restricted to the **möchte**-forms.

When used subjectively, as in **Das mag sein** (*That may be*), **mögen** means *may* and denotes that the speaker presents his statement with the reservation that what he reports "may be" the case. As a matter of fact, **Mag sein!**, used as a sentence by itself, does mean *Maybe!*

This subjective use of **mögen** occurs quite frequently in modern literature. The present indicative **mag** denotes a present possibility, and **mochte**, the past indicative, a past possibility. The use of the past infinitive is frequent. The following examples are taken from modern literature:

Man mag es nicht glauben wollen.	You may not want to believe it.
Das mag einer der Punkte gewesen sein.	That may have been one of the points.
Das mochte wirklich Zufall gewesen sein.	Perhaps that was really a coincidence.
Er mag geglaubt haben, ich verstände ihn.	He may have thought that I understood him.

können

When used objectively, **können** expresses either the ability of the grammatical subject to do something, or the availability of facilities to do it.

Leider konnte sie nicht schwimmen.
Unfortunately she couldn't (was not able to) swim.

Man kann heute nonstop von Frankfurt nach Los Angeles fliegen.
Today you can fly nonstop from Frankfurt to Los Angeles.

When used subjectively, **können** expresses a possibility inferred by the speaker on the basis of observable facts. English expresses such inferred possibility by using *can* or *may* in the present, and *could* or *might* in the past or in the subjunctive.

Das kann nicht Frau Müller sein; die ist doch heute in München.
That can't be Mrs. Müller; she is in Munich today, you know.

However, the almost complete parallelism between *can, could,* and **können** is disturbed by an irritating exception. The sentence

Ist Meyer noch hier? Ich kann ihn nicht finden!—Er kann schon nach Hause gegangen sein
Is Meyer still here? I can't find him!—He may have gone home already

is another proof that both English and German modals can be used objectively as well as subjectively. German **kann ihn nicht finden** and English *can't find him* clearly express, objectively, that is, without including any judgment or inference by the speaker, ability or, in this case, absence of ability. But **kann nach Hause gegangen sein** and *may have gone home* have nothing to do with ability (as in **kann finden**) or permission (as in *may I go home*). **Meyer kann nach Hause gegangen sein** and *Meyer may have gone home* mean: "I, the speaker, think it is possible that Meyer has gone home."

The present tense indicatives **kann** and *may* can be replaced by the present subjunctives **könnte** and *might*.

Meyer könnte schon nach Hause gegangen sein.
Meyer might have gone home already.

Now the speaker expresses his judgment more tentatively and politely. But the change from **kann** to **könnte** and from *may* to *might* does not involve (as in the change from *I am* to *if I were*) a change from reality to irreality, only a change from a somewhat blunt statement to a more tentative and polite statement.

German **könnte** and English *might* are present-tense forms referring to the moment of speaking. In connection with a past infinitive, they express a possibility, *to be reckoned with at the moment of speaking*, that Meyer has done something previous to the moment of speaking.

Unfortunately the sentence

Meyer might have gone home

can also appear as

Meyer could have gone home.

This last sentence, although you might not realize it at first, is highly ambiguous and an irritating source of interference for students of German. The reason is this: The past tense reality statement

Meyer konnte fliehen

Meyer could (was able to)   escape   (and he did escape)

can be changed, as you learned in Unit 6, to the irreal contrary-to-fact statement

Meyer hätte fliehen können, aber er wollte nicht.

Meyer would have been able to escape, but he did not want to.

We are now no longer talking about the present-time possibility, to be reckoned with at the moment of speaking, we are now talking about Meyer's past ability (not used by him) *to do* something at the time that the chance was good.

The irreal sentence

Meyer would have been able to escape

expresses this idea objectively and without ambiguity. For some reason, the same idea can also be expressed by the pattern

Meyer could have escaped

which, however, may also mean, subjectively:

We must reckon right now with the possibility that Meyer has escaped.

Meyer könnte geflohen sein.

German forces its speakers to distinguish sharply between these two patterns:

1. Present subjunctive **könnte** plus past infinitive: **könnte geflohen sein.** (present possibility, existing at the moment of speaking, that somebody *has done* something).

2. Past subjunctive **hätte können** plus present infinitive: **hätte fliehen können** (an unused past opportunity for somebody *to do* something while the chance was good).

Remember that both **könnte geflohen sein** and **hätte fliehen können** may be expressed by English *could have escaped*.

dürfen

Of the six modals, **dürfen** has the lowest frequency. When used objectively, **dürfen** means *may* or *to be permitted*. Since nobody wants to be bossy or be bossed around, **dürfen**, like **erlauben**, is not used very often. Even a child prefers

Kann ich heute abend ins Kino gehen?

to the obedient

Darf ich heute abend ins Kino gehen?

The real "live" use of **dürfen** therefore tends to be restricted to situations where a regulation, or just common sense and not a person giving permission, is involved.

Hier dürfen wir nicht parken.	We cannot (mustn't) park here.
Ich darf abends keinen Kaffee mehr trinken.	I must not drink coffee at night anymore.

The only subjective use of **dürfen** is syntactically extremely restricted. You will occasionally hear:

Erika dürfte jetzt schon in Frankfurt sein.

Erika is probably already in Frankfurt by now. (She took a train from Munich.)

Do not attempt to form sentences of this type yourself. To express probability, use the sentence adverb **wahrscheinlich** (*probably*) and say:

Erika schläft wahrscheinlich noch

not

[Erika dürfte noch schlafen.]

scheinen

German **scheinen**, if used with the meaning *to seem* is followed by an infinitive with **zu** (and is therefore, strictly speaking, not a modal). But we mention it here because it behaves like a subjective modal and can be used in only two tenses, present and past. It can be followed by either a present or a past infinitive.

Er scheint zu schlafen.
Er scheint gut geschlafen zu haben.
Er schien zu schlafen.
Er schien gut geschlafen zu haben.

147 Reflexive Pronouns, selbst, selber

Very often, the subject and the object of a verb are one and the same person or thing.

He hurt himself.
I bought myself a car.

In all these cases, English uses reflexive pronouns for the object. The use of *myself* rather than *me* is linguistic luxury. *I bought me a car* is just as clear as *I bought myself a car.* This is the reason why German does not use special reflexive pronouns for the first and second persons:

Ich habe mich verletzt.	I hurt myself.
Du hast dich verletzt.	You hurt yourself.
Wir haben uns verletzt.	We hurt ourselves.
Ihr habt euch verletzt.	You hurt yourselves.
Ich habe mir ein Auto gekauft.	I bought myself a car.
Du hast dir ein Auto gekauft.	You bought yourself a car.
Wir haben uns ein Auto gekauft.	We bought ourselves a car.
Ihr habt euch ein Auto gekauft.	You bought yourselves a car.

Whereas the distinction between *I hurt me* and *I hurt myself* is luxury, the distinction between the nonreflexive *him* and the reflexive *himself* in the third person may be the difference between murder and suicide.

He killed him.	He killed himself.

However, one single reflexive pronoun for all third persons will do. In German this third-person reflexive is **sich.** This **sich** serves both as a dative and as an accusative, both as a singular and as a plural.

Er hat sie verletzt.	He hurt her.
Sie hat ihn verletzt.	She hurt him.
Er hat sich verletzt.	He hurt himself.
Sie hat sich verletzt.	She hurt herself.
Sie haben sie verletzt.	They hurt her.
Sie haben ihn verletzt.	They hurt him.
Sie haben sich verletzt.	They hurt themselves.
Er hat ihr ein Auto gekauft.	He bought her a car.
Sie hat ihm ein Auto gekauft.	She bought him a car.
Er hat sich ein Auto gekauft.	He bought himself a car.
Sie hat sich ein Auto gekauft.	She bought herself a car.
Sie haben ihr ein Auto gekauft.	They bought her a car.
Sie haben ihm ein Auto gekauft.	They bought him a car.
Sie haben sich ein Auto gekauft.	They bought themselves a car.

English reflexive pronouns are either stressed or unstressed.

I almost *killed* myself.	I must also think of my*self.*

If you want to stress a German reflexive, you can either stress the reflexive pronoun (**mich,** for instance), or you can imitate English and add (but as a separate word) a stressed and undeclinable **selbst** or **selber.**

Ich muß auch mal an *mich* denken.	I must think of my*self,* too.
Ich muß auch mal an mich *selbst* denken.	I must think of my*self,* too.

Ich muß auch mal an mich *sel*ber   I must think of my*self*, too.
denken.

When stressed, English reflexive pronouns frequently assume the meaning
"without help."

Do it your*self!*

You can express the same idea in German by using the undeclinable **selber,**
which, in this case, becomes a verbal complement.

Fritz ist doch schon fünf. Er kann sich jetzt schon *sel*ber **anziehen.**
After all, Fritz is five now. He can get dressed by him*self* now.

As long as this **selber** belongs to the subject, it can be used even without a
reflexive pronoun.

Das kann ich morgen *sel*ber **machen.**   I can do it my*self* tomorrow.

148 Contrary-to-Fact Conditions without wenn

In contrary-to-fact conditions, the conjunction **wenn** may be omitted. In
contemporary German, and particularly in the spoken language, this pattern
occurs almost exclusively in past time.

**Wenn Ingelheim nicht Soldat gewesen wäre, hätte er keine Kriegs-
romane schreiben können.**
**Wäre Ingelheim nicht Soldat gewesen, dann hätte er keine Kriegs-
romane schreiben können.**

The clause with the omitted **wenn** always shows verb-first position and
usually precedes the conclusion. The conclusion is usually introduced by
dann or **so.**

If the condition stands alone to express a wish or desire, the **wenn** can also be
omitted, but again primarily in past time.

Wenn er mir nur geschrieben hätte!
Hätte er mir doch nur geschrieben!

NOTE: These wishful **wenn-**clauses are independent syntactical units and
almost always contain a **nur** or **doch nur** or a **wenigstens.** Like all sentence
adverbs, this **nur** or **wenigstens** shifts position as follows: The elements
preceding *nur, doch nur,* or *wenigstens* are unstressed and include all those
things which have already been talked about; the elements following *nur,
doch nur,* or *wenigstens* are all news items.

Ich wollte ja studieren. Wenn ich nur das Geld dazu gehabt hätte!
Jetzt habe ich das Geld. Wenn ich das Geld nur früher gehabt hätte!

149 ja

The most obvious use of **ja,** of course, is to answer a question. Frequently, however, it is used in the same position and with the same affirmative function, even if there is no question or previous conversation. Similar to English *well,* this ja can precede any reaction.

Ja, das ist aber schön, daß ihr doch noch gekommen seid.	Well, how nice that you came after all.
Ja, was machen wir denn jetzt?	Well, what are we going to do now?

As an unstressed sentence adverb, **ja** occurs very frequently. It has two functions:

1. The speaker wants to express the idea that the facts asserted are well known and accepted by both speaker and listener.

Bei uns regnet es im Sommer ja sehr oft.	As you know, we have lots of rain during the summer.
Wir müssen ja alle einmal sterben.	We've all got to die, you know.

2. In sentences spoken with emphatic stress, **ja** heightens the emotional flavor.

Das ist ja *himm*lisch.
Ich *komm*e ja schon.
Ich bin ja *so* glücklich.
Das ist ja nicht *mög*lich.

When used as a sentence adverb, **ja** follows items of no news value and precedes items with news value, unless the verb itself is stressed.

150 Word Formation: Adverbs in **-erweise**

These sentence adverbs are formed from adjectives and express a judgment.

glücklicherweise	fortunately, it is fortunate that
möglicherweise	possibly, it is possible that
normalerweise	normally, as a rule, it is normal that

151 Word Formation: Adverbs in **-ens**

The following derivatives are frequently used:

frühestens	at the earliest	**nächstens**	in the near future
spätestens	at the latest	**mindestens**	at least
höchstens	at most	**wenigstens**	at least
meistens	in most cases, mostly		

Exercises

A. Without changing word order, negate the following sentences by using **nicht** in two different positions.

SEE
ANALYSIS
46

(pp. 65-67)

1. Ich möchte mit Rosemarie ins Theater gehen.
2. Meyer hat lange arbeiten können.
3. Ich bin oft ins Kino gegangen.
4. Ich kann aber auf dem Sofa schlafen.
5. Sie wollte aber den Meyer heiraten.

B. Using the **nicht A, sondern B** pattern, combine the following pairs of sentences.

> Wir fahren nicht im Juli nach Berlin. Wir fahren im August.
> (a) Wir fahren nicht im Juli, sondern im August nach Berlin.
> (b) Wir fahren nicht im Juli nach Berlin, sondern im August.

SEE
ANALYSIS
143

(p. 280)

1. Ich habe nicht meine Mutter besucht. Ich habe meinen Vater besucht.
2. Er hat nicht acht Stunden gearbeitet. Er hat nur zwei Stunden gearbeitet.
3. Gestern abend hat Erich keinen Wein getrunken. Er hat nur Bier getrunken.
4. Er hat mir kein Buch geschenkt. Er hat mir einen Hut geschenkt.

SEE
ANALYSIS
144

(p. 280)

C. Read and write down the following:

1, 2, 3, 7, 11, 13, 17, 19, 23, 31, 37, 41, 43, 47,

53, 59, 61, 67, 71, 73, 79, 83, 87, 89, 93, 97.

D. In the following sentences, change the present infinitives to past infinitives.

> Maria muß schon aufstehen.
> Maria muß schon aufgestanden sein.

SEE
ANALYSIS
145

(p. 281)

1. Meyer muß nach Berlin fahren.
2. Er scheint sehr freundlich zu sein.
3. Mein Vater scheint sehr viel von ihm zu halten.
4. Sie kann doch nicht schon wieder spazierengehen.
5. Ihr Mann muß sehr viel Geld haben.

E. Change the following sentences, all containing objective modals, from present indicative to present subjunctive and add **eigentlich** in the place indicated by /. Then translate these sentences into English.

1. Ich soll / um sechs Uhr zu Hause sein.
2. Hans muß / hierbleiben.
3. Wir müssen heute abend / schon wieder ausgehen.
4. Wir können / auch einmal ins Theater gehen.
5. Ich kann ja / auch mit *Inge* spazierengehen.

F. Connect the following pairs of sentences by means of the words in parentheses. Which of the connecting words are adverbs, which are coordinating conjunctions, and which are subordinating conjunctions?

1. Ich habe nichts davon gewußt. Er hat mir nicht geschrieben. (weil)
2. Er stand lange vor der Tür. Er klopfte endlich an. (dann)
3. Er wollte nicht mit Professor Müller sprechen. Er hatte Angst vor ihm. (denn)
4. Er war krank. Ich konnte ihn nicht besuchen. (daher)
5. Ich konnte ihn nicht besuchen. Er war krank. (da)
6. Ich rief von Paris aus an. Erich sollte nicht wissen, daß ich in Afrika gewesen war. (weil)
7. Er fuhr sofort nach Hamburg. Er hatte meinen Brief bekommen. (nachdem)
8. Sollen wir ins Kino gehen? Sollen wir zu Hause bleiben? (oder)
9. Tante Amalie kommt morgen. Wir gehen bestimmt wieder ins Museum. (Wenn . . . , dann)
10. Erich hat die Goldstücke gestohlen. Ich kann es nicht glauben. (Daß . . . , das)
11. Ich habe Erich nicht mehr gesehen. Wir waren zusammen in Afrika. (seit)
12. Ich war mit Erich zusammen in Afrika. Ich habe ihn nicht mehr gesehen. (seitdem)
13. Er ist nicht mit ins Kino gegangen. Er hat seiner Frau einen Brief geschrieben. (sondern)
14. Der Meyer will mich heiraten. Ich kann nur lachen. (Daß . . . , darüber)
15. Er hätte eigentlich um zehn nach Hause gehen sollen. Er blieb bis elf. (trotzdem)
16. Er blieb bis elf. Er sollte um zehn zu Hause sein. (obwohl)
17. Ich habe ihn lange gesucht. Ich habe ihn nicht finden können. (aber)
18. Er hat mir nicht geschrieben. Ich habe ihm auch nicht mehr geschrieben. (darum)
19. Gestern bei Meyers habe ich eine Frau kennengelernt. Ihr Mann soll Arabisch sprechen. (deren)

G. Change the following sentences in two ways: (a) Change the modal to the perfect; (b) keep the modal in the present and change the infinitive to a past infinitive. Then translate the two resulting sentences so as to show the difference in meaning.

Er soll um acht Uhr zu Hause sein.	
(a) **Er hat um acht Uhr zu Hause sein sollen.**	He had to be at home at eight.
(b) **Er soll um acht Uhr zu Hause gewesen sein.**	He is said to have been at home at eight.

1. Er kann nicht in Berlin arbeiten.
2. Ingelheim muß Soldat werden.
3. Ingeborg muß heiraten.
4. Meyer will ein Haus an der Riviera kaufen.
5. Ingelheim soll Arabisch lernen.

SEE ANALYSIS 146 (pp. 281-288)

H. By using the proper forms of modals, express in one sentence each of the following ideas.

1. There is a rumor that five gold pieces have disappeared.
2. Ingelheim claims that he fought in Africa.

SEE
ANALYSIS
146

(pp. 281-288)

3. I came to the conclusion that he was living in Berlin.
4. I have arrived at the conclusion that he had been in America.
5. You should have gone to Berlin two years ago.
6. There was a rumor that she had gone to Berlin.
7. It is possible that he is still here.
8. It is not possible that he was in Berlin.
9. It has never been possible for him to go to Berlin.
10. He tries to give the impression that he was a friend of my father's.

I. Change the following sentences from the past indicative to the past subjunctive. Add **eigentlich** in the place indicated by /.

> **Ich mußte gestern nach Berlin fahren.**
> **Ich hätte gestern eigentlich nach Berlin fahren müssen.**

1. Ich sollte gestern / meine Mutter besuchen.
2. Ich durfte es Ihnen / nicht sagen.
3. Ich brauchte / gar nichts zu sagen.
4. Ich konnte damals / auch nach Casablanca fliegen.
5. Mir konntest du das ja / erzählen.

J. In the following sentences, change the modals from indicative to subjunctive.

1. Er kann, wenn er will.
2. Ich konnte auch mitgehen.
3. Ich muß auch einmal nach Italien fahren.
4. Ich mußte gestern zu Hause bleiben.
5. Sie sollen nicht so viel rauchen.
6. Sein Sohn sollte in Heidelberg studieren.

K. The following sentences contain a dependent clause introduced by **weil.** By changing the **weil**-clause, first into a conditional clause with **wenn** and then without **wenn,** transform the sentences into contrary-to-fact conditions. Start all sentences with the conditional clause.

> **Weil er krank war, konnte er nicht arbeiten.**
> **(a) Wenn er nicht krank gewesen wäre, hätte er arbeiten können.**
> **(b) Wäre er nicht krank gewesen, dann hätte er arbeiten können.**

SEE
ANALYSIS
148

(p. 290)

1. Weil ich nicht so viel Geld hatte wie Meyer, konnte ich nicht an der Riviera wohnen.
2. Weil es mir in Hamburg zu kalt war, bin ich nach Afrika gefahren.
3. Er kam spät nach Hause, weil er ins Kino gegangen war.
4. Er hat sie geheiratet, weil sie Geld hatte.
5. Weil das Essen so schlecht war, fuhren wir nach Hause.

L. Change the following statements to wishes contrary to fact, using either **doch nur** or **doch nur nicht** and starting with **wenn** and then without **wenn**. (Like **eigentlich, doch nur** follows the pronouns and elements of no news value.)

> **Er ist nach Italien gefahren.**
> (a) **Wenn er doch nur nicht nach Italien gefahren wäre.**
> (b) **Wäre er doch nur nicht nach Italien gefahren.**

1. Er kam so oft.
2. Er hat mir nicht geschrieben, daß er Geld braucht.
3. Sie hat mir gesagt, daß sie Thusnelda heißt.
4. Die Desdemona konnte ich leider nicht spielen.
5. Ich habe nicht gewußt, daß du auch in Berlin warst.

SEE
ANALYSIS
148

(p. 290)

M. Express in German.

1. He must have waited for me for three hours.
2. He had to wait for me for three hours.
3. He can't have slept long. I called him up at seven o'clock, but I couldn't reach him anymore.
4. Had he sent the letter to me, I could have answered him immediately.
5. His letter must have arrived when I had already gone to Munich.
6. What you claim to have experienced cannot have happened.
7. He has always wanted to go to Africa.
8. He cannot have been in Africa.
9. Erich must have recognized me.
10. Erika seems to have arrived already.
11. I don't think much of him.
12. I often think of you.
13. He ought to have arrived an hour ago.
14. Dr. Schmidt was at the Meyers' too; you must have met him there.
15. It could not have been Erich, for I knew that Erich had gone to the airport to pick up Ingelheim.
16. Could I have another cup of coffee, please?
17. Could you work in the garden yesterday?
18. Of course we could have gone to the movies, but we didn't want to.
19. She claims to be thirty; she looks as if she were thirty-five; but she is said to be forty.
20. She may have thought that Erich wanted to help her.

Basic Vocabulary

allgemein	common	das Kleid, –er	dress
im allgemeinen	usually; generally	das Land, ¨er	land; country
anziehen	to dress	die Landschaft, –en	landscape
ich ziehe mich an	I am getting dressed	der Landstrich, –e	region
		leiten	to lead
arabisch	Arabic	der Leiter, –	leader, director
baden	to bathe	die Leitung, –en	power line, gas line
ich bade mich	I take a bath	link–	left
bauen	to build	links	to the left
behaupten	to maintain, claim	die Lippe, –n	lip
das Beispiel, –e	example	der Lippenstift, –e	lipstick
benutzen	to use	malen	to paint
das Bett, –en	bed	die Meinung, –en	opinion
bisher	up to now	Mittwoch	Wednesday
braun	brown	möglicherweise	possibly
das Brot, –e	bread	nah(e)	near
dabei	at the scene; in the process	nächstens	in the near future
		in der Nähe von	in the neighborhood of
dicht	thick, dense		
Dienstag	Tuesday	normalerweise	normally
Donnerstag	Thursday	parken	to park
das Dorf, ¨er	village	der Preis, –e	price; prize
der Erfolg, –e	success	der Punkt, –e	point
erfolgreich	successful	der Ring, –e	ring
etwa	about; by any chance	die Regierung, –en	government
falten	to fold	die Bundes-regierung, –en	federal government
fehlen	to be missing		
das Feld, –er	field	schneiden	to cut
die Ferien (pl.)	vacation	der Schnitt, –e	cut
fertig	ready; complete	der Durchschnitt, –e	average
das Fleisch	flesh; meat	im Durchschnitt	on the average
fliehen	to flee, to escape	der Schinken, –	ham
froh	glad	schlachten	to butcher, slaughter
fröhlich	gay, glad	das Schwein, –e	pig
frühestens	at the earliest	das Schweinefleisch	pork
genau	exact(ly)	selbst, selber	self (see 147)
gewinnen	to win	(indeclinable)	
glücklicherweise	fortunately	siebzig	seventy
gnädige Frau	(formal way of addressing a married woman)	der Sieg, –e	victory
		das Sofa, –s	sofa
		solch	such
das Gymnasium, die Gymnasien	German secondary school	sondern (nicht A, sondern B)	but (not A but B)
der Himmel, –	sky, heaven	spätestens	at the latest
himmlisch	heavenly	die Sprache, –n	language
Juli	July	der Süden	south
der Kellner, –	waiter	teilen	to divide
der Oberkellner, –	headwaiter	verteilen	to distribute
Herr Ober	(usual way of addressing a waiter)	geteilt durch	divided by
		die Ursache, –n	cause
		der Unfall, ¨e	accident

der Verkehr	traffic
(jemanden) verletzen	to hurt (somebody)
vorgestern	day before yesterday
vorher (*adv.*)	before, earlier
wachsen	to grow
erwachsen	grown up
während (*conj.*)	while
wecken	to awaken
der Wecker, –	alarm clock
die Welle, –n	wave
die Dauerwelle, –n	permanent

der Wert, –e	worth; value
der Zahn, ⸚e	tooth
das Zeichen, –	sign
zerstören	to destroy
der Zufall, ⸚e	accident; chance
zufällig	accidentally; by chance
die Zukunft	future
zusammen	together

Additional Vocabulary

der Ingenieur, –e	engineer
das Kalb, ⸚er	calf
der Lohn, ⸚e	wage(s)
die Sünde, –n	sin
sündig	sinful

vergeuden	to squander
das Vermögen, –	fortune
der Zorn	anger

Strong and Irregular Verbs

anziehen, zog an, hat angezogen, er zieht an	to dress
fliehen, floh, ist geflohen, er flieht	to flee, escape
gewinnen, gewann, hat gewonnen, er gewinnt	to win
schneiden, schnitt, hat geschnitten, er schneidet	to cut
wachsen, wuchs, ist gewachsen, er wächst	to grow

Schaubuden-Graphik

Ausstellung der Puppentheater-Sammlung
im Münchner Stadtmuseum   Aug./Sept. 1970

Unit 10 Adjectives

Patterns

[1] Attributive Adjectives, Nominative Singular

Read the analysis first; then try to visualize the slots while you read these examples.

		SEE ANALYSIS 153 (pp. 316-319)

Der neue Direktor hieß Bodenstein.　The name of the new director was Bodenstein.

Ein junger Mann wartete auf ihn.　A young man was waiting for him.
Die junge Frau hieß Petra.　The young woman's name was Petra.
Eine junge Frau stand neben ihm.　A young woman was standing next to him.
Das kleine Mädchen hieß auch Petra.　The little girl's name was also Petra.
Petra war noch ein kleines Mädchen, als ich sie kennenlernte.　Petra was still a little girl when I met her.

Mein lieber Vater!　My dear Father: (Salutation)
Meine liebe Mutter!　My dear Mother:
Mein liebes Kind!　My dear Child:
Lieber Vater!　Dear Father:
Liebe Mutter!　Dear Mother:
Liebes Kind!　Dear Child:
Das ist wirklich ein guter Wein!　That is really a good wine!
Guter Wein ist teuer.　Good wine is expensive.
Klare Fleischsuppe ist eine Spezialität unseres Hauses.　Clear broth is a specialty of the house.

Eine gute Suppe gehört zu jeder Mahlzeit.　A good soup belongs with every meal.
Unsere italienische Gemüsesuppe ist auch nicht schlecht.　Our Italian vegetable soup isn't bad either.

Frisches Obst ist immer gut.　Fresh fruit is always good.
Das italienische Obst ist nicht mehr so teuer wie früher.　Italian fruit is no longer as expensive as it used to be.
Ich empfehle Ihnen Dortmunder Union; das ist ein gutes Bier.　I recommend Dortmunder Union; that's a good beer.

VARIATIONS

Der Mann war sehr alt. Es war ein sehr _____ Mann.

Sie ist intelligent. Sie ist ein _____ Mädchen.

Bei schlechtem Wetter können Sie in ein gutes Museum gehen.

299

Der Wein ist wirklich gut. Das ist wirklich ein _____ Wein.

Sie ist immer noch schön. Sie ist immer noch eine _____ Frau.

Das Wasser ist aber kalt. Das ist aber _____ Wasser.

Das Bier hier ist gut. Das ist wirklich ein _____ Bier.

So klein ist eure Barbara nicht mehr. Sie ist kein _____ Kind mehr.

Gestern war es kalt. Gestern war ein _____ Tag.

[2] Attributive Adjectives, Accusative Singular

SEE
ANALYSIS
153
(pp. 316-319)

Hast du den alten Mann gesehen?	Did you see the old man?
Nein, einen alten Mann habe ich nicht gesehen.	No, I haven't seen an old man.
Ich kenne die junge Dame leider nicht.	I don't know the young lady, unfortunately.
Ich habe das junge Mädchen lange nicht gesehen.	I haven't seen the young girl for a long time.
Schmidts haben gestern ein kleines Mädchen bekommen.	The Schmidts had a little girl yesterday.
Nehmen Sie ein heißes Bad und gehen Sie früh ins Bett.	Take a hot bath and go to bed early.

VARIATIONS

Gestern war das Wetter schlecht. Gestern hatten wir _____ Wetter.

Gestern war es kalt. Gestern hatten wir einen _____ Tag.

Der Wein war gut. Wir haben einen _____ Wein getrunken.

Das Bier ist wirklich gut. Wo habt ihr denn dieses _____ Bier gekauft?

Meyers Frau ist jung. Meyer hat eine _____ Frau.

[3] Attributive Adjectives, Dative Singular

SEE
ANALYSIS
153
(pp. 316-319)

Mit *dem* alten Wagen fahre ich aber nicht an den Bodensee.	I won't drive to the Lake of Constance with *that* old car.
Was soll ich denn mit einem alten Wagen?	What am I supposed to do with an old car?
Wir wohnten damals in einer kleinen Stadt.	At that time we lived in a small town.
Wir wohnten damals in einem kleinen Städtchen an der Elbe.	We then lived in a small town on the Elbe River.
Ingrid ist aus guter Familie.	Ingrid comes from a good family.

VARIATIONS

Gibt es hier warmes Wasser?—Ja, wir haben nur Zimmer mit _____ Wasser.

Das Haus ist alt. Wir wohnen in einem _____ Haus.

Die Stadt ist klein. Wir wohnen in einer _____ Stadt.

Das Wetter ist schlecht. Bei dem _____ Wetter bleibe ich zu Hause.

Seit wann ist Inge denn blond?—Sie meint, mit _____ Haar sieht sie besser aus.

[4] Attributive Adjectives, Genitive Singular

Während des letzten Krieges mußte Ingelheim Brieftauben füttern.

During the last war, Ingelheim had to feed carrier pigeons.

Ingrid war die Tochter eines bekannten Architekten in Berlin.

Ingrid was the daughter of a well-known architect in Berlin.

Der Besuch der alten Dame ist ein Stück von Dürrenmatt.

The Visit of the Old Lady is a play by Dürrenmatt.

Wegen des schlechten Wetters konnten wir in Frankfurt nicht landen.

Because of the bad weather we couldn't land in Frankfurt.

SEE ANALYSIS 153 (pp. 316-319)

VARIATIONS

Die Reise war lang, aber trotz der _____ Reise war ich gar nicht müde.

Ein intelligenter Mann raucht PRIVAT. PRIVAT, die Zigarette des _____ Mannes.

Denken Sie modern? Der Preis eines _____ Hauses ist nicht so hoch, wie Sie denken.

[5] Attributive Adjectives, Plural

Die jungen Leute gehen ins Kino.

The young people go to the movies.

Unsere deutschen Freunde wohnen in Freiburg.

Our German friends live in Freiburg.

Liebe Eltern!

Dear Parents:

Petra ist die Mutter der beiden Kinder.

Petra is the mother of the two children.

Eines der kleinen Mädchen hieß Petra.

One of the little girls was called Petra.

Was halten Sie von den italienischen Autos?

What do you think of the Italian cars?

Für seine neuen Brieftauben hat Ingelheim viel Geld bezahlt.

Ingelheim paid a lot of money for his new carrier pigeons.

Niemand liest seine letzten Romane.

Nobody reads his last novels.

Er brachte ihr rote Rosen.

He brought her red roses.

Sie hat zwei intelligente Kinder.

She has two intelligent children.

SEE ANALYSIS 153 (pp. 316-319)

VARIATIONS

Meyers Kinder sind intelligent. Meyer hat _____ Kinder.

Rot ist meine Lieblingsfarbe; daher bringt er mir immer _____ Rosen.

Ich habe Freunde in Amerika. Ich fliege morgen zu meinen _____ Freunden.

Sie kennen doch Amerika, nicht wahr? Was halten Sie denn von den _____ Schulen?

[6] Series of Attributive Adjectives

SEE
ANALYSIS
153

(pp. 316-319)

Der blonde junge Mann da drüben heißt Kleinholz.

The name of the blond young man over there is Kleinholz.

Zuerst kam ein blonder junger Mann aus dem Zoll.

First a blond young man came out of customs.

Die blonde junge Dame ist seine Frau.

The blonde young lady is his wife.

Zuerst kam eine blonde junge Dame aus dem Zoll.

First a blonde young lady came out of customs.

Das kleine blonde Mädchen hieß Petra.

The name of the blonde little girl was Petra.

Vor dem Haus saß ein blondes kleines Mädchen.

A blonde little girl was sitting in front of the house.

Die Eltern des netten jungen Mannes kamen aus Leipzig.

The parents of the nice young man came from Leipzig.

Mit deinem alten grauen Mantel kannst du dich in Berlin nicht sehen lassen.

With your old gray coat you can't let yourself be seen in Berlin.

Ich nehme an, Sie kennen den netten jungen Mann da drüben.

I assume you know the nice young man over there.

Die hellen, kurzen Sommernächte Norwegens hat er nie vergessen können.

He has never been able to forget the bright, short summer nights of Norway.

Helle kurze Sommernächte wie in Norwegen gibt es in Afrika nicht.

In Africa, there are no bright, short summer nights as in Norway.

Mit seinen langen, sentimentalen Romanen hat er viel Geld verdient.

He has made a lot of money with his long, sentimental novels.

Wir haben nur Zimmer mit fließendem warmen und kalten Wasser.

We have only rooms with running hot and cold water.

VARIATIONS

Insert the adjectives **neu** and **automatisch** in the following sentences.

Ich wollte, ich hätte eine Waschmaschine.
Der Preis einer Waschmaschine ist gar nicht so hoch.
Die Preise unserer Waschmaschinen sind gar nicht so hoch.
Mit dieser Waschmaschine ist Ihre Frau bestimmt zufrieden.
Ist das eure Waschmaschine?
Diese Waschmaschinen sind gar nicht teuer.
Waschmaschinen sind gar nicht teuer.
Wir können nur noch Waschmaschinen verkaufen.

[7] der-Words

SEE
ANALYSIS
155

(p. 321)

Bei diesem schlechten Wetter bleibe ich zu Hause.

In this bad weather I'll stay home.

Welche deutschen Städte haben Sie denn gesehen?

Which German cities did you see?

Jeder junge Mensch sollte einmal ein Jahr lang im Ausland leben.

Every young person ought to live abroad for a year.

Von hier aus fährt jede halbe Stunde ein Zug nach Stuttgart.

From here, a train goes to Stuttgart every half hour.

Dort haben wir schon manchen schönen Tag verbracht.

We've spent many a beautiful day there.

Mancher von den jungen Soldaten wußte gar nicht, wofür er kämpfte.

Many a young soldier didn't know at all what he was fighting for.

VARIATIONS

Express in German.

Who is this young man?

Which young man? (*nom.*)

Who are these young men?

Which young men?

In which hotel does he live?

He always lives in this old hotel.

These old hotels are not expensive.

Every good hotel should have a garage.

[8] solcher, solch, so

So einen guten Freund finde ich so bald nicht wieder.

Such a good friend I will not find again soon.

Wie kann ein so intelligenter Mensch nur so blöd sein!

How can a man who is that intelligent be so stupid!

Für einen so alten Wagen bekommst du bestimmt keine tausend Mark.

I'm sure you won't get a thousand marks for a car as old as that.

Für solch einen Wagen muß man mindestens zwanzigtausend Mark bezahlen.

For such a (fancy) car you'll have to pay at least twenty thousand marks.

Ich wußte gar nicht, daß er noch so kleine Kinder hat.

I didn't know that his children are still that little.

Solche Kinder wie die möchte ich auch haben.

I'd like to have children like that too.

SEE
ANALYSIS
156

(pp. 321-322)

Using such combinations as **gute Freundin, schönes Haus, hübsche Kinder,** form your own variations.

[9] all, ganz

Alles Gute zum neuen Jahr wünscht Dir Deine Luise.

All good wishes for the New Year. Yours, Louise.

SEE
ANALYSIS
157

(pp. 322-323)

Was hilft ihm jetzt all sein schönes Geld? Er muß doch sterben.	What good does all his lovely money do him now? He's got to die anyway.
Was hilft ihm denn jetzt das ganze Geld?	What good does all that money do him now?
Was sollen wir denn mit all dem Brot?	What are we going to do with all that bread?
Ich habe alle meine alten Freunde besucht.	I visited all my old friends.
All meine Freunde sind Ärzte.	All my friends are doctors.
Ich habe alle seine Romane gelesen.	I have read all his novels.
Ich habe seine Romane alle gelesen.	I have read all his novels.
Kannst du für uns alle *Kar*ten kaufen?	Can you buy tickets for all of us?
Kannst du Karten für uns *al*le kaufen?	Can you buy tickets for all of us?
Ich habe alle Karten gekauft, die noch zu haben waren.	I've bought all the tickets that were still to be had.
Alle guten Karten waren schon ausverkauft.	All the good tickets were sold out already.
Das Geld ist alle.	The money is all gone.
Der Wein ist alle.	The wine is all gone.
Wir alle sind dir dankbar.	We are all grateful to you.
Wir sind dir alle dankbar.	We are all grateful to you.
Er hat den ganzen Tag auf mich gewartet.	He waited for me all day.
Fritzchen hat einen ganzen Apfel gegessen.	Fritzchen has eaten a whole apple.
Sie war ganz allein.	She was all alone.
Wie geht's dir denn?—Danke, ganz gut.	How are you?—Thanks, pretty well.
Wir sind durch ganz Österreich gefahren.	We drove through all of Austria.

Form variations of your own on all but the first two examples above.

[10] Adjectives Used as Nouns

SEE
ANALYSIS
158

(pp. 323-324)

In dem Zimmer lag ein Toter.	A dead man was lying in the room.
Die Polizei fand einen Toten im Zimmer.	The police found a dead man in the room.
Kein Mensch wußte, wer der Tote war.	Nobody knew who the dead man was.
Wer ist denn die Blonde da drüben?	Who is the blonde over there?
Der junge Deutsche auf Zimmer Eins ist erst gestern angekommen.	The young German in room 1 arrived only yesterday.
Auf Zimmer Eins wohnt ein junger Deutscher.	A young German lives in room 1.
John wohnt mit einem jungen Deutschen auf Zimmer Eins.	John lives in room 1 with a young German.
Den jungen Deutschen habe ich noch nicht kennengelernt.	I haven't met the young German yet.
Auf Zimmer Eins wohnen zwei junge Deutsche.	Two young Germans are living in room 1.

Die beiden jungen Deutschen habe ich noch nicht kennengelernt.	I haven't met the two young Germans yet.
Er spricht ein gutes Deutsch.	He speaks good German.
Sie haben recht, er spricht wirklich gut Deutsch.	You are right, he really does speak German well.
Auf Wiedersehen, und alles Gute.	Good-by and good luck.
Er hat viel Gutes getan.	He has done much good.
Könnte ich noch etwas Warmes zu essen bekommen?	Could I still get something hot to eat?
Ich habe gestern etwas sehr Schönes erlebt.	Yesterday I experienced something very beautiful.
Ich hoffe, ich habe nichts Wichtiges vergessen.	I hope I haven't forgotten anything important.

By changing gender, number, or case, form variations on all
those examples above that refer to persons.

[11] Participles Used as Adjectives and Nouns

SEE ANALYSIS 159 (pp. 324-325)

Es war nicht leicht, in einer zerstörten Stadt zu leben.	It was not easy to live in a destroyed city.
Er kam mit einem gebrochenen Bein vom Schilaufen zurück.	He returned from skiing with a broken leg.
Sie kam mit gebrochenem Herzen vom Schilaufen zurück.	She returned from skiing with a broken heart.
Er war bei uns immer ein gern gesehener Gast.	He was always a welcome guest at our house. (Literally: he was a gladly seen guest.)
Erich Merkle ist ein guter Bekannter von uns.	Erich Merkle is a close acquaintance of ours.
Frau Merkle ist eine gute Bekannte von meiner Frau.	Mrs. Merkle is a close acquaintance of my wife's.
Haben Sie Bekannte hier in der Stadt?	Do you have acquaintances here in town?
Haben Sie Verwandte in Westfalen?	Do you have relatives in Westphalia?
Otto Müller ist ein Verwandter von mir.	Otto Müller is a relative of mine.
Heidi ist eine entfernte Verwandte von mir.	Heidi is a distant relative of mine.
Das ist der amerikanische Gesandte.	That is the American ambassador.
Sein Vater war ein hoher Beamter bei der Bundesregierung.	His father was a high official in the federal government.
Alle deutschen Lehrer sind Beamte.	All German teachers are civil servants.
Hier auf der Post arbeiten über hundert Beamtinnen.	More than a hundred women civil servants work here at the post office.
Auch Frau Meyer ist eine Beamtin.	Mrs. Meyer is a civil servant too.

Form variations of your own.

[12] -d Adjectives

SEE
ANALYSIS
160

(p. 325)

Wer war denn der gut aussehende junge   Who was the good-looking young man last
Mann gestern abend?   night?

Er hatte so ein gewinnendes Lächeln.   He had such a winning smile.

Alles um sich her vergessend, saßen sie mit   Forgetting everything around them, they
klopfendem Herzen unter der blühenden   sat under the blooming linden tree, with
Linde; und ihre vielsagenden Blicke aus   their hearts pounding, and the meaning-
leuchtenden Augen sagten mehr als ihre   ful glances of their shining eyes said
zurückhaltenden Worte.   more than their reserved words.
              (from Schmidt-Ingelheim,
        Die Frau mit dem Flamingo, p. 97)

[13] derselbe

SEE
ANALYSIS
161

(p. 326)

Ist das derselbe Wein, den wir gestern   Is that the same wine that we drank last
abend getrunken haben?   night?
Wir wohnen in demselben Hotel, in dem   We are staying in the same hotel in which
Fürstenbergs gewohnt haben.   the Fürstenbergs stayed.
Seit Jahren trägt sie jeden Sonntag dasselbe   For years she's been wearing the same dress
Kleid.   every Sunday.
Wir saßen gestern mit Fürstenbergs am   Yesterday we sat at the same table with
selben Tisch.   the Fürstenbergs.

Form variations of your own.

[14] was für

SEE
ANALYSIS
162

(p. 326)

Was ist denn das für ein Wagen?
Was für ein Wagen ist das?   } What kind of car is that?

Was hast du dir denn für einen Wagen
gekauft?
Was für einen Wagen hast du dir denn   } What kind of car did you buy?
gekauft?

Mit was für einem Wagen bist du denn   What kind of car did you go in?
gefahren?

Ich muß noch immer daran denken, was   I still remember what wonderful days we
für wunderbare Tage wir an der Ostsee   spent at the Baltic Sea.
verbracht haben.

Ich muß noch immer daran denken, was   I still remember what an unforgettable day
für einen unvergeßlichen Tag wir an der   we spent by the Mosel.
Mosel verbracht haben.

PATTERNS

Was ist denn das für ein Wagen?

Hast du gesehen, was für einen unmöglichen Hut die Anita schon wieder auf hat?	Did you see what an impossible hat Anita has on again?
Weißt du noch, mit was für einem unmöglichen Hut sie damals im Theater war?	Do you remember with what an impossible hat she came to the theater?

By changing nouns, form variations on each of the examples above.

[15] viel, wenig

Meyer hat viel Geld.	Meyer has a lot of money.	**SEE ANALYSIS 163**
Ja, aber das viele Geld macht ihn auch nicht glücklich.	Yes, but all that money doesn't make him happy either.	(pp. 327-328)
Sein vieles Geld macht ihn nicht glücklich.	All his money doesn't make him happy.	

. . . was für einen unvergeßlichen
Tag wir an der Mosel verbracht
haben.

Heute ist Sonntag, und viele Leute fahren heute spazieren.

Today is Sunday, and many people go for a ride today.

Was haben Sie denn während der vielen langen Winternächte in Norwegen gemacht?

What did you do during the many long winter nights in Norway?

Ich habe viel zu wenig Geld, um jedes Jahr in die Schweiz fahren zu können.

I have far too little money to be able to go to Switzerland every year.

Mit dem wenigen Geld, das du mir schickst, kann ich nicht viel kaufen.

With the little money you send me I can't buy much.

Wir haben dieses Wochenende nur wenige Gäste im Hause. Bei dem Wetter bleiben die Leute zu Hause.

We have only a few guests here this weekend. In this weather, people stay at home.

VARIATIONS

Insert the correct form of **viel**.

Ich habe nicht _____ Geld.

Was tut sie denn mit ihrem _____ Geld?

Wie _____ Kinder habt ihr denn?

Wie _____ Bier habt ihr denn getrunken?

Was machst du denn jetzt mit deinen _____ Büchern?

Er hat schon immer _____ gelesen.

[16] ander-

SEE
ANALYSIS
164
(p. 328)

So geht das nicht; das mußt du anders machen.

It won't work that way; you'll have to do it differently.

Aber Erich, du bist ja ganz anders als früher.

But Erich, you are so different from the way you used to be.

Erich soll ein ganz anderer Mensch geworden sein.

Erich supposedly has become a completely different person.

Er spricht von nichts anderem als von seiner Amerikareise.

He talks about nothing (else) but his trip to America.

Den einen Herrn kannte ich, aber wer war denn der andere?

One of the gentlemen I knew, but who was the other one?

Den anderen Herrn kenne ich auch nicht.

I don't know the other gentleman either.

Das muß jemand anders gewesen sein.

That must have been somebody else.

Das kann niemand anders gewesen sein als Meyer.

That can have been nobody (else) but Meyer.

Anderen hat er geholfen; sich selbst kann er nicht helfen.

Others he has helped; himself he cannot help.

VARIATIONS

Insert the correct form of **ander-**.

Es war ganz ――――――, als ich gedacht
    hatte.

Dieses Buch war es nicht; es war ein
    ――――――.

Wer waren denn die ―――――― Herren?

Ich habe leider keinen ―――――― Mantel.

Sie wohnen in einem ―――――― Hotel.

Alle ―――――― gingen nach Hause.

Ich war es nicht; es war jemand ――――――.

Ich hätte lieber etwas ――――――.

[17] ein paar, einige, mehrere

„In ein paar Tagen bin ich wieder hier",
    hatte er gesagt. Aber dann wurden aus
    den paar Tagen ein paar Jahre.

"I'll be back in a few days," he had said.
    But then the few days turned into a few
    years.

SEE
ANALYSIS
165

(pp. 328-329)

Es waren nur ein paar Leute da.

Only a few people were there.

Mit den paar Mark kannst du doch nicht
    nach Davos fahren.

You can't go to Davos with those few marks.

Ein paar schöne Tage haben wir ja gehabt,
    aber die meiste Zeit hat es geregnet.

We did have a few nice days, but most of
    the time it rained.

Ich hätte gerne ein paar kleine Würstchen
    zum Frühstück.

I'd like to have a few sausages for break-
    fast.

Bringen Sie mir doch bitte ein Paar Würst-
    chen.

Could I have a couple of sausages (frank-
    furters), please?

Ich habe nur zwei Paar gute Schuhe mitge-
    bracht.

I've only brought two pairs of good shoes.

Anton und Emma waren ein schönes Paar.

Anton and Emma were a lovely couple.

Einige von unseren Lesern möchten wissen,
    ob Ingelheim noch in Konstanz wohnt.

Some of our readers would like to know
    whether Ingelheim still lives in Con-
    stance.

Wir kamen durch mehrere alte Dörfer.

We came through several old villages.

Wie weit geht der amerikanische
Einfluß? Aufgenommen in einer
bayerischen Kleinstadt.

Im Löwen kann man für ein paar Mark gut essen.	At the Lion Inn one can eat well for a few marks.
Ich habe auch schon einige Male da gegessen.	I've eaten there several times, too.
Letzte Woche habe ich mehrere Male im Löwen gegessen.	Last week I ate at the Lion several times.

Form variations of your own.

Reading

Ankunft in Deutschland

Wir wollen annehmen, daß Sie während der Nacht über den Atlantik geflogen sind und morgens auf dem Rhein-Main Flughafen bei Frankfurt ankommen, vielleicht nach einer Zwischenlandung in Paris oder London.

Wenn Sie nonstop fliegen, ist die Flugzeit von New York etwa 5 sieben Stunden, von Chicago neun Stunden und von San Franzisko etwa dreizehn Stunden. Dazu kommt aber der Zeitunterschied zwischen Amerika und Europa. Wenn Sie in New York abfliegen, ist es vielleicht 7 P.M. EST, und wenn Sie in Frankfurt ankommen, ist es 7 Uhr MEZ. MEZ heißt Mitteleuropäische Zeit. Wenn es in 10 Frankfurt Mitternacht ist, ist es in New York erst 7 Uhr abends. Das heißt, Sie kommen in Frankfurt um 2 Uhr nachts an, aber in Frankfurt ist es dann schon 7 Uhr morgens.

Vielleicht bleiben Sie oft bis zwei Uhr morgens auf, aber es ist doch spät und eigentlich Zeit, schlafen zu gehen. Aber die Nacht ist vor- 15 bei, für immer verloren. Sie haben im Flugzeug ein amerikanisches Dinner gegessen, von acht bis zehn Uhr abends, und dann tat man, als käme jetzt eine lange Nacht. Alle Lichter gingen aus, und weil es dunkel war, haben Sie versucht zu schlafen. Vielleicht haben Sie auch eine Stunde geschlafen, aber dann hielt Ihnen die Stewardess 20 plötzlich ein Glas Orangensaft unter die Nase und tat, als ob es **der Saft, ⁻e** juice sechs Uhr morgens wäre.

Und jetzt landen Sie also in Frankfurt. „Bitte anschnallen", lesen **anschnallen** to fasten Sie über Ihrem Sitz und „Nicht rauchen", und über den Laut- the seat belt sprecher hören Sie: „Wir möchten Sie bitten sitzenzubleiben, bis 25 die Maschine völlig zum Stillstand gekommen ist." Gottseidank wie- **völlig** completely derholt die Stewardess das auf Englisch: „Please remain seated until the plane has come to a complete stop."

Dann hält die Maschine, aber vom Flugzeug zum Empfangsgebäude ist es mindestens eine halbe Meile,—nein, Sie denken jetzt schon ganz europäisch und sagen zu Ihrer netten Nachbarin: „Das ist ja fast ein Kilometer! Müssen wir denn jetzt dahin laufen?" „Nein, nein", lacht die Nachbarin, die gerade ein Jahr als Austauschstudentin in Amerika studiert hat, „da kommen schon die Busse."

Auf vielen europäischen Flughäfen holen Busse die Fluggäste direkt am Flugzeug ab und bringen sie zum Empfangsgebäude. Man hat dann nur noch ein paar Meter zu gehen und ist schon an der Paßkontrolle. Die Formalitäten sind schnell erledigt; der Beamte sieht Ihren Paß kaum an. Dann kommt der Zoll. Die deutsche Studentin ist vor Ihnen an der Reihe. „Haben Sie etwas zu verzollen?" „Nein, gar nichts." „Dann machen Sie doch bitte einmal Ihren Koffer auf." Eine halbe Minute, und die Studentin ist fertig; sie hatte wirklich nichts zu verzollen. Jetzt kommen Sie an die Reihe. Der Zollbeamte sieht schon, daß Sie Amerikaner sind. (Die meisten Amerikaner in Europa sehen aus, als ob sie Amerikaner wären.) „Anything to declare?" fragt er. „Coffee, tea, cigarettes?" Aber weil Sie nicht rauchen und auch keinen Kaffee trinken, können Sie ruhig sagen: „Nein, gar nichts." „O.K.," sagt der Beamte, „danke schön", und dann sagt er noch: „Viel Spaß", was so viel heißt wie „Have fun."

Dann gehen Sie durch eine große Glastür, und da steht Ihre Kusine Emma und sagt: „Da bist du ja endlich." Und Sie sind froh, daß Sie eine Kusine Emma haben, die jetzt alles für Sie tun wird, weil sie ein praktisches Mädchen ist und weiß, daß man um drei Uhr morgens sehr müde ist.

Aber nicht alle haben eine Emma.

Wenn Sie nun keine Kusine in Frankfurt haben, dann haben Sie noch viel zu tun, bevor Sie sich schlafen legen können. Zunächst brauchen Sie deutsches Geld. Sie gehen also zu einer Wechselstube. Solche Wechselstuben gibt es auf allen deutschen Flughäfen und in den großen Bahnhöfen. Es dauert nicht lange, und Sie haben

der Empfang, ⸚e reception; **das Gebäude, –** building

5 **der Austausch** exchange

10 **erledigen** to take care of, to settle

verzollen to pay duty on

15

20 **der Spaß** fun, pleasure

25

30 **die Stube, –n** room; **wechseln** to change, exchange

Flug	Flight	nach Flugplan scheduled	Abflugzeit expected	Ausgang Gate
PA	744	1520	1545	B8
PA	001	1530		B7
LH	023	1600		B2
BE	1964	1715		
SK	636	1830		

PAA 744 1520
BERLIN-TEMPELHOF
WARTERAUM - WAITING ROOM B

statt Ihres amerikanischen Reiseschecks deutsches Bargeld in der Hand.

das Bargeld cash

Es gibt nun drei Möglichkeiten: Erstens—und das ist die vernünftigste Möglichkeit—Sie haben schon von Amerika aus in Frankfurt ein Zimmer bestellt und schlafen sich zunächst aus. Zweitens: Sie ₅ wollen vielleicht mit der Bahn weiterfahren, sagen wir nach Koblenz, weil Sie am nächsten Tag mit dem Schiff den Rhein hinunter fahren wollen. Drittens, wenn *Ihre* Kusine Emma in *München* wohnt, dann müssen Sie natürlich noch am gleichen Tag nach München weiterfliegen. ₁₀

die Bahn = Eisenbahn
sagen wir let's say

Sie gehen also zum Lufthansaschalter und geben einer der jungen Damen Ihren Flugschein.

der Schalter, – ticket window, counter
der Schein, –e ticket

„Ich komme gerade aus New York und möchte nach München weiterfliegen."

„Haben Sie schon einen Platz gebucht?" ₁₅

„Ja, für heute nachmittag."

„Das ist Flug Nummer 604, Abflug 13.45 Uhr (dreizehn Uhr fünfundvierzig), Ankunft in München um 14.30 Uhr. Warteraum B bitte,—der Flug wird um 13.15 Uhr aufgerufen."

der Raum, –̈e room

Die junge Dame wiegt Ihren Koffer, dann gibt sie Ihnen Ihr Ticket ₂₀ zurück, und Sie können nun in aller Ruhe etwas essen, eine Zeitung lesen (vielleicht die *Frankfurter Rundschau,* die *Frankfurter Allgemeine* oder einen Artikel im *Spiegel*) und die Leute beobachten. Um halb zwei gehen Sie zum Ausgang B 6, dann fahren Sie wieder mit dem Bus zum Flugzeug, und pünktlich um dreiviertel zwei ₂₅ startet Ihre Maschine zum Flug nach München.

pünktlich prompt(ly), punctual(ly)
dreiviertel zwei a quarter of two

Der Wolf und die sieben Geißlein*

Es war einmal eine alte Geiß, die hatte sieben junge Geißlein, und **eine alte Geiß** an old
hatte sie lieb, wie eine Mutter ihre Kinder lieb hat. Eines Tages goat
wollte sie in den Wald gehen und etwas zu essen holen. Da rief
sie alle sieben ins Haus und sprach: „Liebe Kinder, ich will in den
Wald. Wenn der Wolf kommt, dürft ihr ihn nicht ins Haus lassen. 5
Wenn er hereinkommt, so frißt er euch alle. Der Bösewicht verstellt **Der Bösewicht . . . oft**
sich oft, aber an seiner Stimme und an seinen schwarzen Füßen the rascal often dis-
werdet ihr ihn gleich erkennen." Die Geißlein sagten: „Liebe guises himself
Mutter, du brauchst keine Angst zu haben." Da meckerte die Alte **meckern** to bleat
und ging in den Wald. 10

Es dauerte nicht lange, so klopfte jemand an die Haustür und rief:
„Macht auf, ihr lieben Kinder, eure Mutter ist da und hat jedem
von euch etwas mitgebracht." Aber die Geißlein hörten an der
Stimme, daß es der Wolf war. „Wir machen nicht auf", riefen sie,
„du bist nicht unsere Mutter, die hat eine feine und liebliche 15
Stimme, aber deine Stimme ist rauh; du bist der Wolf." Da ging der **rauh** rough
Wolf fort und kaufte ein Stück Kreide; die aß er und machte damit **damit** with it
seine Stimme fein. Dann kam er zurück, klopfte an die Haustür und
rief: „Macht auf, ihr lieben Kinder, eure Mutter ist da und hat
jedem von euch etwas mitgebracht." Aber der Wolf hatte seinen 20
schwarzen Fuß in das Fenster gelegt; das sahen die Kinder und
riefen: „Wir machen nicht auf, unsere Mutter hat keinen schwarzen
Fuß, wie du; du bist der Wolf." Da lief der Wolf zu einem Bäcker
und sprach: „Ich habe etwas an meinem Fuß, kannst du etwas Teig
auf meinen Fuß streichen?" Und als der Bäcker den Teig auf seinen 25 **der Teig** dough
Fuß gestrichen hatte, so lief er zum Müller und sprach: „Kannst du

---

* This story is taken, with very few changes, from the famous collection of fairy
tales by the brothers Grimm. The German of these fairy tales is highly sophisticated and yet of classic simplicity. Every German child grows up with Grimm.
The standard introduction to German fairy tales, **Es war einmal . . .** , corresponds to the English *Once upon a time, there was . . . .*

etwas Mehl auf meinen Fuß streuen?" Der Müller dachte: „Der   streuen sprinkle
Wolf will einen betrügen", und wollte es nicht tun; aber der Wolf   betrügen deceive
sprach: „Wenn du es nicht tust, so fresse ich dich." Da bekam der
Müller Angst und machte ihm den Fuß weiß. Ja, so sind die
Menschen.*   5

Nun ging der Bösewicht wieder zu der Haustür, klopfte an und
sprach: „Macht auf, Kinder, euer liebes Mütterchen ist zurück und
hat jedem von euch etwas aus dem Wald mitgebracht." Die Geißlein
riefen: „Du mußt uns erst deinen Fuß zeigen, sonst wissen wir
nicht, ob du unser liebes Mütterchen bist." Da legte er den Fuß 10
ins Fenster, und als sie sahen, daß er weiß war, so glaubten sie,
es wäre alles wahr, was er sagte, und machten die Tür auf. Wer
aber hereinkam, das war der Wolf.

Da bekamen sie alle Angst. Das eine sprang unter den Tisch, das
zweite ins Bett, das dritte in den Ofen, das vierte in die Küche, das 15
fünfte in den Schrank, das sechste unter die Waschschüssel, das   die Waschschüssel
siebte in den Kasten der Wanduhr. Aber der Wolf fand sie alle und   washbowl
fraß sie eins nach dem andern; nur das jüngste in dem Uhrkasten
fand er nicht. Als der Wolf die Sechs gefressen hatte, ging er fort,
legte sich draußen vor dem Haus unter einen Baum und fing an 20
zu schlafen.

Es dauerte nicht lange, da kam die alte Geiß aus dem Wald wieder
nach Hause. Ach, was mußte sie da sehen! Die Haustür stand auf,
Tisch, Stühle und Bänke waren umgeworfen. Sie suchte ihre Kinder,
aber sie konnte sie nicht finden. Sie rief sie alle bei Namen, aber 25
niemand antwortete. Endlich, als sie an das jüngste kam, da rief
eine feine Stimme: „Liebe Mutter, ich bin im Uhrkasten." Sie holte
es heraus, und es erzählte ihr, daß der Wolf gekommen wäre und
die anderen alle gefressen hätte. Da könnt ihr denken, wie sie über
ihre armen Kinder geweint hat.*   30

Endlich ging sie hinaus, und das jüngste Geißlein lief mit. Als sie
vor das Haus kam, so lag da der Wolf unter dem Baum und
schnarchte, daß die Äste zitterten. „Ach Gott", dachte sie, „vielleicht
leben meine Kinder doch noch." Da mußte das Geißlein ins Haus
laufen und Schere, Nadel und Zwirn holen. Dann schnitt sie dem 35 Schere, ... Zwirn
Bösewicht den Bauch auf, und kaum hatte sie einen Schnitt getan,   scissors, needle, and
so steckte schon ein Geißlein den Kopf heraus, und als sie weiter   thread
schnitt, so sprangen sie alle sechs heraus, und waren noch alle am
Leben. Das war eine Freude! Die Alte aber sagte: „Jetzt wollen
wir Steine suchen, mit denen füllen wir dem Bösewicht den Bauch, 40
solange er noch schläft." Da brachten die sieben Geißlein Steine

---

* Observe the change of tense: this sentence is not part of the story.

herbei und steckten sie ihm in den Bauch. Dann nähte ihn die Alte wieder zu.

Als der Wolf endlich ausgeschlafen hatte, stand er auf, und weil ihn die Steine in seinem Bauch durstig machten, so wollte er zu einem Brunnen gehen und trinken. Als er aber an den Brunnen kam 5 und trinken wollte, da zogen ihn die Steine in den Brunnen hinein, und er mußte ertrinken. Als die sieben Geißlein das sahen, da kamen sie herbeigelaufen, riefen laut: „Der Wolf ist tot! der Wolf ist tot!" und lachten und tanzten mit ihrer Mutter um den Brunnen.

da . . . herbeigelaufen they came running

ERICH KÄSTNER

Die Entwicklung der Menschheit

Einst haben die Kerls auf den Bäumen gehockt,
behaart und mit böser Visage.
Dann hat man sie aus dem Urwald gelockt
und die Welt asphaltiert und aufgestockt,
bis zur dreißigsten Etage.   5

Da saßen sie nun, den Flöhen entflohn,
in zentralgeheizten Räumen.
Da sitzen sie nun am Telefon.
Und es herrscht noch genau derselbe Ton
wie seinerzeit auf den Bäumen.   10

Sie hören weit. Sie sehen fern.
Sie sind mit dem Weltall in Fühlung.
Sie putzen die Zähne. Sie atmen modern.
Die Erde ist ein gebildeter Stern
mit sehr viel Wasserspülung.   15

Sie schießen die Briefschaften durch ein Rohr.
Sie jagen und züchten Mikroben.
Sie versehn die Natur mit allem Komfort.
Sie fliegen steil in den Himmel empor
und bleiben zwei Wochen oben.   20

Was ihre Verdauung übrigläßt,
das verarbeiten sie zu Watte.
Sie spalten Atome. Sie heilen Inzest.
Und sie stellen durch Stiluntersuchungen fest,
daß Cäsar Plattfüße hatte.   25

der Kerl, –s guy
hocken to squat
der Urwald, ¨er jungle
locken to lure
aufstocken to build up
die Etage, –n floor
der Floh, ¨e flea
entfliehen to flee from
heizen to heat
der Raum, ¨e room
herrschen to prevail
seinerzeit formerly
das Weltall universe
putzen to brush
die Erde earth
der Stern, –e star
gebildet educated
die Wasserspülung toilet flushing
schießen to shoot
die Briefschaften mail
das Rohr, –e pipe
jagen hunt
züchten breed
versehen to supply
steil steep
der Himmel sky
empor up
die Verdauung digestion
übriglassen leave over
verarbeiten transform
die Watte cotton
spalten to split
feststellen to ascertain
die Untersuchung, –en investigation
der Plattfuß, ¨e flat foot

So haben sie mit dem Kopf und dem Mund
den Fortschritt der Menschheit geschaffen.
Doch davon mal abgesehen und
bei Lichte betrachtet sind sie im Grund
noch immer die alten Affen.   30

(1932)

der Mund, ⸚er   mouth
der Fortschritt   progress
schaffen   to create
die Menschheit   mankind
absehen von   to disregard
betrachten   to look
im Grund   basically
der Affe, –n   ape

Analysis

152 Predicate Adjectives and Adverbs

Most English adjectives can be transformed into adverbs by adding the
suffix *-ly*, for example, *high, highly; beautiful, beautifully;* for some others,
there is a separate adverbial form, for example, *good, well;* and only a few
have the same form both as adjectives and as adverbs, for example, *fast.*

In German, there is no distinction between the predicate adjective and the
adverb.

Seine Frau soll sehr *schön* sein.
His wife is supposed to be very *beautiful.*

Sie soll auch sehr *schön* singen können.
Supposedly she can also sing very *beautifully.*

153 Strong (Primary) and Weak (Secondary) Adjective Endings

Up to now, we have used only predicate adjectives. Predicate adjectives are
verbal complements. They constitute the second prong and never have any
ending.

Meyer war wochenlang krank.

Attributive adjectives are used much more frequently than predicate adjectives. Attributive adjectives belong to a following noun and they indicate
their affiliation with this noun by having an ending which depends on the
case, gender, and number of that noun. Observe, for instance, how the endings of **intelligent** in the following sentences change with the gender of the
noun used.

Wir haben einen intelligenten Sohn.
Wir haben eine   intelligente   Tochter.
Wir haben ein   intelligentes Kind.

The endings of attributive adjectives are the bane of German grammar. They are a bothersome anachronism, and you will sympathize with Mark Twain, who said he would rather decline two glasses of German beer than one German adjective.

The trouble is that attributive adjectives use not just one set of endings but two: a set of primary (or *strong*) endings and a set of secondary (or *weak*) endings.

The strong endings are the endings of the **der**-words. Because these endings are unstressed (as in **jeder, jede, jedes**), the long **-ie** of **die** becomes **-e** and the **-as** of **das** becomes **-es.** The complete set of strong endings follows:

der-WORD ENDINGS (ALL STRONG)

	MASC.	FEM.	NEUT.	PLURAL
NOM.	-er	-e	-es	-e
GEN.	-es	-er	-es	-er
DAT.	-em	-er	-em	-en
ACC.	-en	-e	-es	-e

You are also familiar with the endings shown by **ein**-words (**ein, kein, mein,** etc.).

ein-WORD ENDINGS (EITHER ZERO OR STRONG)

	MASC.	FEM.	NEUT.	PLURAL
NOM.	—	-e	—	-e
GEN.	-es	-er	-es	-er
DAT.	-em	-er	-em	-en
ACC.	-en	-e	—	-e

With the exception of the three cases in which **ein**-words have no ending at all, all **ein**-words use the same strong endings as the **der**-words.

We now introduce you to a new set of endings: the weak or secondary endings. There are only two weak endings, **-e** and **-en.** They are distributed as follows:

WEAK ENDINGS

	MASC.	FEM.	NEUT.	PLURAL
NOM.	-e	-e	-e	-en
GEN.	-en	-en	-en	-en
DAT.	-en	-en	-en	-en
ACC.	-en	-e	-e	-en

Note that only the masculine singular distinguishes between nominative and accusative. Observe also that the five **-e** endings are arranged like the Big Dipper.

Attributive adjectives use both strong and weak endings. The trick is to learn (and to overlearn until you can do it automatically) when to use a strong ending and when to use a weak ending.

To help you master strong and weak endings, we provide a table on the opposite page.

You *must* observe the following three rules. Study these rules before you proceed to the sentences in the table. The table has four slots, marked 0, 1, 2, and 3 respectively. The zero-slot is reserved for the three endingless forms of the **ein**-words; the 3-slot is reserved for the noun that follows the adjective; slots 1 and 2 are reserved for the adjective that precedes the noun. The last column in the table indicates which rule applies to the particular sentence.

RULE 1   If no strong ending (on a **der**-word or **ein**-word) precedes the adjective, the adjective itself takes a strong ending and is placed in slot 1.

RULE 2   If slot 1 is occupied either by a **der**-word or by one of the **ein**-words *with* an ending, the adjective goes into slot 2 and takes a weak ending.

RULE 3   If a second adjective follows the first, it takes the same ending (either strong or weak) as the first. In other words, the first adjective in front of a noun determines the endings of all other adjectives preceding that noun.

You can add a second adjective to each sentence in the table, and it will take the same ending as the first. For example:

> **dieser intelligente junge Mann**
> **dieses intelligente junge Mädchen**
> **ein intelligenter junger Mann**
> **ein intelligentes junges Mädchen**

These three rules are easy to learn. However, it will take time and lots of practice to acquire the facility to apply them automatically. We seriously urge you to memorize the thirty-five sentences in the table so that you can recite them without using a wrong ending.

To sum up: Slot 1 *must be filled* as long as there is a word that can take a strong ending. If there is no word that *has* to take strong endings (like **der**), the adjective "moves forward" and takes strong endings.

		SLOT 0 NO ENDING	SLOT 1 STRONG ENDING	SLOT 2 WEAK ENDING	SLOT 3 NOUN		RULE TO BE APPLIED
1	NOM. SING.	Dies (das) ist		guter	Kaffee.		1
2		Dies (das) ist		gute	Butter.		1
3		Dies (das) ist		gutes	Bier.		1
4	NOM. SING.	Das (dies) ist	ein	guter	Kaffee.		1
5		Das (dies) ist		eine	gute	Suppe.	2
6		Das (dies) ist	ein	gutes	Bier.		1
7	NOM. SING.			Der	junge	Mann	blieb zu Hause.	2
8				Die	junge	Dame	blieb zu Hause.	2
9				Das	kleine	Kind	blieb zu Hause.	2
10	GEN. SING.	Ich bin die Frau		eines	intelligenten	Mannes.	2
11		Ich bin der Mann		einer	intelligenten	Frau.	2
12		Sie ist die Mutter		eines	intelligenten	Kindes.	2
13	DAT. SING.	Bei		dichtem		Nebel	bleiben wir zu Hause.	1
14		Bei		großer		Hitze	bleiben wir zu Hause.	1
15		Bei		schlechtem		Wetter	bleiben wir zu Hause.	1
16	DAT. SING.	Mit		dem	alten	Wagen	fahre ich nicht.	2
17		Mit		der	alten	Kutsche	fahre ich nicht.	2
18		Mit		dem	alten	Auto	fahre ich nicht.	2
19	ACC. SING.	Gegen		hohen		Blutdruck	nehmen Sie Vitalin.	1
20		Gegen		große		Nervosität	nehmen Sie Vitalin.	1
21		Gegen		hohes		Fieber	nehmen Sie Vitalin.	1
22	ACC. SING.	Siehst du		den	jungen	Mann	da drüben?	2
23		Ich sehe		keinen	jungen	Mann.		2
24		Siehst du		die	junge	Frau	da drüben?	2
25		Ich sehe		keine	junge	Frau.		2
26		Siehst du		das	kleine	Mädchen	da drüben?	2
27		Ich sehe	kein	kleines		Mädchen.		1
28	NOM. PL. ALL GENDERS			Gute		Menschen	lügen nicht.	1
29				Die	guten	Menschen	lügen nicht.	2
30	GEN PL.	Die Eltern		intelligenter		Kinder	sind meistens auch intelligent.	1
31		Die Eltern		dieser	intelligenten	Kinder	sind auch intelligent.	2
32	DAT. PL.	Die Eltern von		intelligenten		Kindern	sind meistens auch intelligent.	1
33		Die Eltern von		diesen	intelligenten	Kindern	sind auch intelligent.	2
34	ACC. PL.	Wir haben		gute		Kinder.		1
35		Wir haben		unsere	guten	Kinder.		2

154 Adjective Endings: Variants

1. In the dative masculine and neuter, the sequence **-em -en** is so ingrained that of two or more adjectives not preceded by an **ein**-word or **der**-word only the first tends to take the strong ending **-em.**

	SLOT 0	SLOT 1	SLOT 2	SLOT 3
Bei		diesem	nebligen kalten	Wetter
Bei		nebligem	kalten	Wetter

2. In the genitive masculine and neuter, with adjectives not preceded by a **der**-word or an **ein**-word, the strong endings have been replaced by weak endings. These forms, however, do not, as a rule, occur in the spoken language.

	SLOT 0	SLOT 1	SLOT 2	SLOT 3
Trotz			starken	Nebels
Trotz			schlechten	Wetters

The spoken language prefers the regular pattern with the dative.

	SLOT 0	SLOT 1	SLOT 2	SLOT 3
Trotz		starkem		Nebel
Trotz		schlechtem		Wetter

3. Adjectives ending in **-el** and **-er** drop the **-e-** if an attributive ending is added.

Das Zimmer war dunkel.	The room was dark.
Sie saßen in einem dunklen Zimmer.	They sat in a dark room.
Die Zimmer hier sind aber sehr teuer.	The rooms here are very expensive.
Wir wohnten in einem teuren Zimmer.	We lived in an expensive room.

4. The adjective **hoch** drops the **-ch**-sound if an ending is added and substitutes a silent **-h-.**

Der Baum war sehr hoch.	The tree was very tall.
Vor dem Haus stand ein hoher Baum.	A tall tree stood in front of the house.

155 der-Words

The following are declined like the definite article; that is, they take strong endings:

dieser   this
jeder   each, every
welcher   which, what
mancher   many a; *plural:* some

(a) The neuter singular **dieses** may be used without an ending (**dies**) in the nominative and accusative.

Dies Buch hier ist wirklich gut.

In sentences identifying or introducing persons or objects, **dies** must be used.

Gerda, dies ist mein Freund Hans.
Und dies, meine Damen und Herren, war das Schlafzimmer des Königs.

(b) **Jeder** has no plural forms. The plural of **jeder Mensch** is **alle Menschen.**

(c) **Welcher** is normally used as an interrogative: **in welcher Stadt?** (*in which (what) city?*).

156 so, solch

In the singular, both **so ein** and **ein so** are usually followed by adjectives.

Sie ist doch so ein intelligentes Mädchen.	She is such an intelligent girl.
Ein so intelligentes Mädchen findet sicher eine gute Stellung.	A girl who is that intelligent will certainly find a good job.

In the plural, **so** is immediately followed by an adjective.

Ich wußte gar nicht, daß er noch so kleine Kinder hat.

I didn't know that his children are still so little.

It is advisable to use **solch** only with a strong ending and without a following adjective; it then means "such a degree of" or "that kind of" (cf. English *with such force*).

Warum hast du denn immer solche Angst? (so große Angst?)

Why are you always so afraid?

Mit solchen Menschen will ich nichts zu tun haben.

I don't want to have anything to do with that kind of people.

157 all, ganz

All is used with or without endings. When there is an ending, it is always strong.

SINGULAR

(a) Forms with an ending are not used very frequently. They occur, immediately followed by a noun, in stereotyped phrases.

Ich wünsche dir alles Gute

and in proverbial expressions:

Aller Anfang ist schwer.

(b) If used without an ending, **all** must be followed by a **der**-word or a possessive adjective.

all das schöne Geld
all mein Geld

Such phrases express bulk quantity, and **all** can be replaced by the attributive adjective **ganz**.

das ganze schöne Geld
mein ganzes Geld

PLURAL

(a) **All** with an ending is the plural of **jeder** and means "every single one of them"; it precedes nouns and follows pronouns.

Alle meine Brüder sind im Krieg gefallen.
Wir alle haben ihn gestern besucht.

In the spoken language, it is usually separated from its noun or pronoun and placed in the inner field preceding the first item of news value.

Meine Brüder sind im Krieg alle gefallen.
Wir haben ihn gestern alle besucht.
Gestern haben wir ihn alle besucht.

(b) **All** without an ending refers again to bulk quantity and means "the whole bunch of them." Again, it must be followed by a **der-** or an **ein-**word.

Ich habe all meine Bücher verloren.

Again, this "bulk" meaning of **all** can be replaced by the attributive adjective **ganz**.

Ich habe meine ganzen Bücher verloren.

NOTE: **Alle** may be used predicatively to mean *all gone* in the sense of "there isn't any left."

Das Geld ist alle.
Der Wein ist alle.

Ganz, if not used as a replacement for **all**, is used in the following ways:

(a) As an attributive adjective meaning *whole* or *entire*.

Er hat den ganzen Tag auf mich ge-wartet.	He waited for me all day.

(b) As an adverb, meaning *completely*, modifying an adjective.

Sie war ganz allein.	She was all alone.

(c) As an *unstressed* adverb, meaning *quite* or *rather*, modifying such "praising" adjectives as **gut, glücklich, intelligent.**

Das Wetter war ja ganz gut, aber es hätte besser sein können.	The weather wasn't bad, but it could have been better.

Do not thank your hostess by saying **Das Essen war ganz gut.** This would mean that the food wasn't bad, but certainly nothing to rave about.

(d) Without an ending and preceding geographical names. It then means *all of.*

Wir sind durch ganz Deutschland gefahren.

158 Adjectives Used as Nouns

In such English phrases as

the idle rich	*Gentlemen Prefer Blondes*
he helped the poor	*The Naked and the Dead*

the adjectives *rich, poor, blonde, naked,* and *dead* are used as plural nouns. In German, many more adjectives can be used as nouns than in English, and, unlike English, they very often occur in the singular. <u>If so used, they are capitalized</u>, but are otherwise treated like attributive <u>adjectives;</u> thus, **der reiche Mann** becomes **der Reiche.**

SLOT 0	SLOT 1	SLOT 2	SLOT 3	
	der	**Reiche**		the rich man
	die	**Alte**		the old woman
	das	**Gute**		the good
mein	**Alter**			my old man
	die	**Armen**		the poor
	der	**Tote**		the dead man
	die	**Tote**		the dead woman
	die	**Toten**		the dead
ein	**Toter**			a dead man

When an adjective follows **nichts, etwas, viel,** as in English *nothing new* or *something important,* the German adjective is capitalized and has a strong neuter singular ending.

> **Es gibt leider nichts Neues.**
> **Ich habe etwas Wichtiges vergessen.**
> **Das führt zu nichts Gutem.**
> **Er hat viel Gutes getan.**

NOTE: Of all nouns indicating nationality, **Deutsch** is the only one declined like an adjective.

> **der Deutsche**   the German (man)
> **die Deutsche**   the German (woman)

159 Participles Used as Adjectives and Nouns

In German, as in English, participles can be used as attributive adjectives.

SLOT 0	SLOT 1	SLOT 2	SLOT 3	
	die	**zerstörte**	**Stadt**	the destroyed city
	eine	**zerstörte**	**Stadt**	a destroyed city
	zerstörte		**Städte**	destroyed cities
ein	**gestohlenes**		**Goldstück**	a stolen gold coin
	das	**gestohlene**	**Goldstück**	the stolen gold coin
mein	**geliebter**		**Sohn**	my beloved son

Both German and English can use participles as plural nouns.

die Verwundeten the wounded
die Besiegten the conquered

Unlike English, however, German can also use participles as singular nouns.

SLOT 0	SLOT 1	SLOT 2	SLOT 3
ein	**der**	**Verwundete**	
	Verwundeter		
	der	**Gekreuzigte**＊	
	der	**Erwählte**†	
	die	**Betrogene**‡	

Similarly:

der Bekannte acquaintance—from: **bekannt sein** to be (well) known
die Bekannte
der Verwandte relative—from: **verwandt sein** to be related
die Verwandte
der Beamte official, civil servant—from: **das Amt** office
  (originally: **der Beamtete** one who is given an office)

but

die Beamt*in*

160 -d Adjectives

In principle, any German verb can form an adjective corresponding to English adjectives in -*ing* simply by adding the suffix **-d** to the infinitive. These **-d** derivatives can be used safely only as attributive adjectives. Both the English -*ing*-form and the German **-d**-form are often referred to as "present participles."

	SLOT 0	SLOT 1	SLOT 2	SLOT 3
		das	**lachende**	**Kind**
mit	**ein**	**lachendes**		**Kind**
		klopfendem		**Herzen**
		ihre	**leuchtenden**	**Augen**

＊ The crucified one (Christ).
† The chosen one (title of Thomas Mann's novel *The Holy Sinner*).
‡ The deceived one (title of Thomas Mann's novel *The Black Swan*).

161 derselbe

There are two German adjectives to express English *the same:* **der gleiche** and **derselbe.** The forms of **derselbe** are written as one word unless the article is contracted with a preposition. Both **der-** and **selb-** must be declined.

> **Ist das derselbe Wein wie gestern?**
> **Ist das der gleiche Wein wie gestern?**
> **Wir trinken heute wieder denselben Wein wie gestern.**
> **Wir wohnen in derselben Stadt.**
> **Wir wohnen im selben Hotel.**
> **Wir wohnen im gleichen Hotel.**
> **Wir wohnen in demselben Hotel.**

Strictly speaking, **der gleiche** expresses similarity (the same kind), and **derselbe** expresses identity (the very same). However, this distinction is rapidly disappearing.

162 was für

There is no English structural equivalent for the very frequently used construction with **was für.** The **für** in this fixed phrase does not have any influence on the case of the following adjective or noun. **Was für** means *what kind of* or *what.*

In the nominative and accusative, **was** occupies the front field; **für** plus the noun or pronoun may either follow the **was** immediately or stand in the inner field, usually right before the second prong.

> *Was für ein Wagen* ist denn das da drüben?
> *Was* ist denn das *für ein Wagen* da drüben?*
> *Was* ist denn das da drüben *für ein Wagen?*
>
> *Was für einen Wagen* hast du dir denn gekauft?
> *Was* hast du dir denn *für einen Wagen* gekauft?
>
> *Was für Bücher* hast du mir denn mitgebracht?
> *Was* hast du mir denn *für Bücher* mitgebracht?

In the dative, the **was für** construction cannot be split. Nor can it be split if it is preceded by a preposition.

> *Was für einem Mann* gehört denn der Wagen?
> *Mit was für einem Wagen* bist du denn gefahren?
> *Durch was für Dörfer* seid ihr denn gefahren?
> *Auf was für einen Mann* wartest du denn?

---

* da drüben is end field; remember the sentence **Das Bier ist gut hier in München.**

163 viel, wenig

Viel (*much;* plural: *many*) and wenig (*little;* plural: *few*) have the same characteristics. Their use is in a state of flux, but it is safe to use them in the following ways.

(a) In the singular, viel and wenig express bulk and áre usually used without endings.

> Wieviel Fisch habt ihr gegessen? (wieviel—one word)
> Wir haben damals viel Fisch und wenig Fleisch gegessen.

Adjectives used after these endingless forms have strong endings.

> Ich habe noch viel deutsches Geld.
> Ich habe nur noch wenig deutsches Geld.

After definite articles, viel and wenig, still indicating bulk, take normal adjective endings.

> das viele Geld
> mit dem wenigen Geld

NOTE: Vielen Dank (*thank you very much*) is an exception.

(b) In the plural, viele means *many* and wenige *few*. They are treated as attributive adjectives.

	SLOT 1	SLOT 2	SLOT 3
mit	viele junge die wenigen	vielen jungen	Leute Leute Worten

(c) Viel and wenig may be used as adverbs preceding comparatives.

> Er war viel älter als sie.
> Er war nur wenig älter als sie.
> Er hatte viel mehr Geld als ich.

Viel must not be confused with the adverb sehr (*very*), which sometimes corresponds to an English *very much*.

Ich habe sie sehr geliebt.	I loved her very much.
Ich ginge sehr gerne mit nach Köln.	I'd like very much to go along to Cologne.
Er war sehr krank.	He was very sick.
Die Amerikaner essen sehr viel Fleisch.	Americans eat very much meat.
Ich war sehr dagegen.	I was very much against it.
Es waren sehr viele Leute dort.	There were very many people there.

English *very* usually precedes *much, many,* or some other adjective or adverb. German **sehr,** on the other hand, is an independent adverb and does not have to be followed by anything.

> **Sie liebte ihn sehr.**

164 ander-

Ander- means *other, different,* or *else.* If used attributively or after **etwas** or **nichts,** it takes the same endings as any other attributive adjective and is often preceded by **ganz.**

> **Das eine Buch kenne ich, aber das andere habe ich noch nicht gelesen.**
> **Erika kenne ich ja, aber wer war denn die andere Dame?**
> **Dieser Herr war es nicht, es muß ein anderer gewesen sein.**
> **Das ist natürlich etwas anderes.** (*something else*)
> **Das ist etwas ganz anderes.** (*something quite different*)

NOTE: For some unfathomable reason, no form of **ander-** is capitalized.

If **ander-** is used as an adverb or a predicate adjective, it always has the form **anders.**

> **Ich hätte das ganz anders gemacht.**   I would have done that quite differently.
> **Er ist anders, als er früher war.**   He is different than he used to be.

Note also the following frequently used phrases:

> **Das kann nicht mein Bruder gewesen sein, das muß *jemand anders*** (*somebody else*) **gewesen sein.**
> **Das kann *niemand anders*** (*nobody else*) **gewesen sein als Anton Meyer.**

165 mehrere, einige, ein paar

All three of these terms mean "more than two, but not many."

Mehrere and **einige** are never used with an article, as is possible with English *the several states.* They therefore take strong endings.

Mehrere means *several,* **einige** and **ein paar** mean *a few* or *some.*

SLOT 0	SLOT 1	SLOT 2	SLOT 3
	mehrere junge		Leute
	einige deutsche		Bücher
ein paar	junge		Leute
ein paar	deutsche		Bücher

Do not confuse **wenige**, meaning *few* in the sense of *not many*, with **ein paar**, meaning *a few* in the sense of *some*.

> **Wenige Menschen wußten, wer er wirklich war.**
> **Ein paar Menschen wußten, wer er wirklich war.**
> **Bring mir doch bitte ein paar Zigaretten mit.**
> **Ich komme in ein paar Minuten.**
> **Er wollte in Berlin ein paar Freunde besuchen.**
> **Er ist ein paar Tage in Berlin gewesen.**
> **Wir haben ein paar schöne Tage an der Riviera verbracht.**

After the definite article, **ein paar** becomes **paar**.

> **Die paar schönen Tage an der Riviera waren viel zu kurz.**

Note the difference between **ein paar** (*a few*) and **ein Paar** (*a pair, a couple*):

> **Wir aßen Suppe mit ein paar Würstchen.**
> **Wir aßen Suppe mit einem Paar Würstchen.**
> **Anton und Emma waren ein schönes Paar.**

166 Word Formation: Nouns Derived from Weak Verbs

The stem of some weak verbs appears as a noun of action—that is, a noun denoting the activity expressed by the verb. Feel free to use the nouns listed, but do not try to invent your own—they may not exist. Most of these nouns are masculine, but there are also a few feminines and neuters.

antworten	die Antwort, –en	das war eine gute Antwort
baden	das Bad, ⸚er	ein heißes Bad
besuchen	der Besuch, –e	Der Besuch der alten Dame (*Dürrenmatt*)
blicken	der Blick, –e	ein vielsagender Blick
danken	der Dank (*no pl.*)	vielen Dank
fragen	die Frage, –n	das kommt nicht in Frage (*that's out of the question*)
glauben	der Glaube, *gen.* des Glaubens (*no pl.*)	Glaube, Hoffnung, Liebe
grüßen	der Gruß, ⸚e	viele Grüße aus den Bergen
hassen	der Haß (*no pl.*)	Ohne Liebe kein Haß (*Ingelheim*)
heiraten	die Heirat, –en	ich bin gegen diese Heirat
kaufen	der Kauf, ⸚e	ein guter Kauf
küssen	der Kuß, die Küsse	mit Gruß und Kuß, Dein Julius
lieben	die Liebe (*no pl.*)	Liebe macht blind

reden	die Rede, –n	er hielt eine lange Rede
suchen	die Suche (*no pl.*)	die Suche nach dem Dieb
tanzen	der Tanz, ⸚e	der Tanz um das goldene Kalb
versuchen	der Versuch, –e	ein chemischer Versuch
wünschen	der Wunsch, ⸚e	alle guten Wünsche zum Neuen Jahr

The most common nouns of action are the feminine nouns in **-ung** (see **129**).

167 Word Formation: Nouns Derived from Strong Verbs

Theoretically, any one of the various forms of the stem of a strong verb can occur as a noun denoting the action of the verb, or the result of such action, or the thing used for such action.

Action: **der Schlaf** sleep

Result of action: **der Fund** the find

Thing used for action: **der Sitz** the seat

Again, it is safe to use the nouns listed, but do not invent your own. Note that of the nouns ending in **-t** and **-e,** most are feminine.

abfahren	die Abfahrt, –en	departure
anfangen	der Anfang, ⸚e	beginning
ankommen	die Ankunft, ⸚e	arrival
annehmen	die Annahme, –n	reception; assumption
anrufen	der Anruf, –e	phone call
ansehen	die Ansicht, –en	view; sight
ausgeben	die Ausgabe, –n	expense; delivery
aufnehmen	die Aufnahme, –n	reception; photograph
ausgehen	der Ausgang, ⸚e	exit
aussehen	die Aussicht, –en	expectation; view
befehlen	der Befehl, –e	order, command
beginnen	der Beginn (*no pl.*)	beginning
bitten	die Bitte, –n	request
brechen	der Bruch, ⸚e	break, fracture; fraction
fahren	die Fahrt, –en	drive, trip
fallen	der Fall, ⸚e	fall; case
geben	die Gabe, –n	gift
	das Gift, –e	poison
	die Mitgift (*no pl.*)	dowry
gehen	der Gang, ⸚e	gait; corridor; gear (in a motor)
gewinnen	der Gewinn, –e	profit, gain
greifen	der Griff, –e	handle; grasp
helfen	die Hilfe, –n	help

lesen (to read; to gather)	die Weinlese, –n „Spätlese"	grape harvest a wine made from overripe grapes
liegen	die Lage, –n	situation
raten	der Rat, ⸚e	advice
scheinen	der Schein (*no pl.*) der (Geld) schein, –e	appearance; light bank note
schlafen	der Schlaf (*no pl.*)	sleep
schlagen	der Schlag, ⸚e	strike, stroke, hit
schneiden	der Schnitt, –e	cut
schreiben	die Schrift, –en die Heilige Schrift	(hand)writing Bible, Holy Writ
sehen	das Gesicht, –er	face
sitzen	der Sitz, –e	seat
sprechen	die Sprache, –n	language, speech
springen	der Sprung, ⸚e	jump
stehen	der Stand, ⸚e	stand
trinken	das Getränk, –e	beverage
tun	die Tat, –en die Tatsache, –n	deed (actual) fact
verbieten	das Verbot, –e	prohibition
verlieren	der Verlust, –e	loss
verstehen	der Verstand (*no pl.*)	reason, intelligence
ziehen	der Zug, ⸚e	train

Exercises

A. Insert the adjectives given in parentheses into the following sentences.

1. Meyer ist mit einer Frau verheiratet. (sehr intelligent)
2. Eine Frau ist sie *nicht.* (intelli*gent*)
3. Er ist dumm, aber er hat eine Frau geheiratet. (intelligent)
4. Sie ist dumm, aber sie hat einen Mann geheiratet. (intelligent)
5. Er ist ein Mensch. (intelligent)
6. Wer *ist* denn der Mann, von dem ihr da sprecht? (intelligent)
7. Sie ist ein Kind. (intelligent)
8. Wer *ist* denn das Mädchen, von dem ihr da sprecht? (intelligent)
9. Von einem Mädchen hätte ich das nicht erwartet. (so intelligent)
10. Mein Sohn hat ein Mädchen geheiratet. (intelligent)
11. Meyers haben drei Kinder. (intelligent)
12. Frauen wissen immer, was sie wollen. (intelligent)
13. Mit Studenten kann man gut arbeiten. (intelligent)

SEE
ANALYSIS
153
(pp. 316-319)

14. Was machen Sie denn mit den Kindern in Ihrer Schule? (intelli*gent*)
15. Sie ist mit einem Mann verheiratet. (intelligent)

B. Restate the following sentences, leaving out the italicized **der-** or **ein-**words.

SEE
ANALYSIS
153
(pp. 316-319)

1. *Jeder* gute Wein ist teuer.
2. *Alle* intelligenten Frauen wissen, was sie wollen.
3. Das ist wirklich *ein* guter Wein.
4. *Dieses* deutsche Bier ist sehr gut.
5. *Mein* lieber Vater!
6. *Das* frische Obst ist jetzt zu teuer.
7. Bei *dem* starken Regen fahre ich nicht in die Stadt.

C. Place the word in parentheses in front of the adjective.

SEE
ANALYSIS
153
(pp. 316-319)

1. Für intelligente Kinder tun wir viel zu wenig. (unsere)
2. Automatische Uhren sind teuer. (diese)
3. Nach kurzer Pause fuhren wir weiter. (einer)
4. Beide Kinder gingen damals schon in die Schule. (seine)
5. Westfälischer Schinken ist eine Spezialität unseres Hauses. (dieser)

D. Restate the following sentences by changing the italicized nouns to the singular and by making the corresponding changes in the **der-**words and adjectives.

SEE
ANALYSIS
153
(pp. 316-319)

1. Siehst du *die jungen Mädchen* da drüben?
2. Woher hast du denn *die schönen Bücher*?
3. *Diese neuen Maschinen* fliegen tausend Kilometer in der Stunde.
4. Wir fragten *die jungen Männer,* wo sie herkämen.
5. *Die kleinen Dörfer* lagen im Schwarzwald.

E. Restate the following sentences by changing the nouns to the singular. Change the adjective ending as required and place an **ein-**word before the adjective.

SEE
ANALYSIS
153
(pp. 316-319)

1. Ich habe Verwandte in Frankfurt.
2. Bei uns wohnen jetzt amerikanische Studenten.
3. Vor ihm saßen zwei blonde Mädchen.
4. Er rauchte österreichische Zigaretten.
5. Meyers sind gute Freunde von mir.

F. In the following sentences, insert an appropriate **der-** or **ein-**word (if necessary) and the correct form of the adjective in parentheses.

1. Mit _____ _____ Roman hat er viel Geld verdient. (letzt)
2. Wir wohnen in _____ _____ Haus. (neu)

SEE
ANALYSIS
153

(pp. 316-319)

3. Gestern abend habe ich _____ _____ Professor kennengelernt. (deutsch)
4. Ich freue mich auf _____ Sonntag. (nächst)
5. Mein Mann ist gerade von _____ _____ Reise zurückgekommen. (lang)
6. Mit _____ _____ Schreibmaschine kann ich nicht schreiben. (alt)
7. Wann soll _____ _____ Brücke denn fertig sein? (neu)
8. Mit _____ _____ Mantel kannst du nicht nach Paris fahren. (alt)
9. Bist du mit _____ _____ Sekretärin zufrieden? (neu)
10. Die Mutter _____ _____ Kinder hieß Alexandra. (beide)
11. Ich möchte ein Zimmer mit _____ Wasser. (fließend)
12. Haben Sie etwas _____ gehört? (neu)
13. Er hat viel _____ getan. (gut)
14. Er hat zwei _____ Romane geschrieben. (gut)

G. Express in German.

1. We have two small children.
2. He lived with his old mother.
3. I hope you'll marry an intelligent woman.
4. She wrote him a long letter.
5. She never read his long letters.
6. Good coffee is very expensive.
7. He is an old friend of mine.
8. She is a good friend of mine.
9. Is that the new hotel?
10. Last week I was in Berlin.
11. Last Monday I was in Berlin.
12. I am living with my German relatives.
13. I have a German aunt.
14. Do you know that we have a new director?
15. Dear Hans!
16. Our dear old Aunt Amalie died last week.
17. In which hotel did you live?
18. She really is a very interesting woman.
19. In this city we don't have one single good hotel.
20. We all went to the movies last night.
21. I have read all his novels.
22. This is really a good wine.
23. My old friends are all dead.
24. All my old friends are dead.
25. She has married a young German.
26. He married a young German.
27. In the room above me lives a young German (man).
28. I have forgotten something very important.
29. Today I experienced something very beautiful.
30. When a man is thirty-nine, he is no longer a young man in the eyes of a young girl.

H. Change singular nouns in the following sentences to plurals.

SEE
ANALYSIS
153
(pp. 316-319)

1. Was für einen herrlichen Tag wir gehabt haben!
2. Was für ein Buch möchtest du denn gerne haben?
3. Was für eine schöne Tochter Sie haben!
4. Was ist denn das für ein Haus?

I. Change the plural nouns in the following sentences to singulars.

1. Was für schöne Kinder sind das!
2. Was müssen das für Menschen sein!
3. Was für schöne Tage waren das!
4. Was für interessante Kleider die Anita anhat!

J. Insert the words italicized in the first sentence as adjectives into the second sentence.

SEE
ANALYSIS
153
(pp. 316-319)

1. Der Wind hatte die Brücke *zerstört*. Wir konnten nicht über die _____ Brücke fahren.
2. Dieses Wasser ist *kalt*. Trinken Sie gerne _____ Wasser?
3. Erich hatte fünf Goldstücke *gestohlen*. Mit den _____ Goldstücken fuhr er nach Afrika.
4. Die Maschine aus London ist gerade *gelandet*. Die gerade _____ Maschine hat 35 Minuten Verspätung.

K. Change the italicized inflected form of the verb into a **-d** adjective and insert it into the second sentence.

SEE
ANALYSIS
153
(pp. 316-319)

1. Der *sieht* aber gut *aus*. Er ist ein gut _____ junger Mann.
2. Die Linden *blühten* noch; sie saßen unter einer _____ Linde.
3. Das Kind *schlief*, als er abfuhr. Er sah noch einmal auf das _____ Kind und fuhr dann ab.
4. Die Kinder *spielten* auf der Straße, aber der alte Mann sah die _____ Kinder nicht.

L. Construct a conversation between yourself and your cousin Emma, who has come to pick you up at the Frankfurt Airport. This is not an exercise in translation, but you should nevertheless follow the English outline. Use your imagination, but avoid using patterns that you are not thoroughly familiar with. Be prepared to produce a similar conversation orally in class.

Emma, of course, wants to know how you are, how the flight was, whether you are tired, and whether you would like to have breakfast before driving into town. You try to figure out what time it is in New York and you talk a bit about time differences. When Emma mentions MEZ, you are puzzled because you've never heard the term. Emma explains. Then you decide that you are really tired and ought to get to your hotel. She wants to know whether you have ordered a room, which, of course, you have done. Emma thinks it might be a good idea to call the hotel to be sure that you have the room. Since you have never made a phone call in Germany, you ask her whether she would please do that for you. While she telephones, you want to get some German money. She asks you to come to the exit in ten minutes, and she will get her car in the meantime.

Now, here is your first sentence: Emma: „Da bist du ja endlich."

Basic Vocabulary

ander–	other
eins nach dem anderen	one after the other
anders	different (*see* **164**)
arm	poor
ausschlafen	to get enough sleep
ich schlafe mich aus	I'll get enough sleep
der Baum, ⁀e	tree
das Bein, –e	leg
bekannt	well known
der Bekannte, –n	acquaintance (*see* **159**)
beobachten	to observe
bestellen	to order
blühen	to bloom, to blossom
das Blut	blood
der Blutdruck	blood pressure
brechen	to break
buchen	to reserve (a seat)
der Bus, –se	bus
da drüben	over there
dankbar	grateful, thankful
derselbe	the same (*see* **161**)
draußen	outside
dunkel	dark
der Durst	thirst
durstig	thirsty
einige	some, several, a few
die Eisenbahn, –en	railroad
die Autobahn	(name of German freeways)
die Fahrbahn, –en	lane
die Bahn	(short for) railroad or streetcar
entfernt	distant
erstens	first (ly)
zweitens	second (ly)
drittens, etc.	third (ly), etc.
ertrinken	to drown
Euro'pa	Europe
europä'isch	European
fein	fine
das Fenster, –	window
das Fieber	fever
fließen	to flow
das Flugzeug, –e	airplane
fortgehen	to go away
fressen	to eat (said of an animal)
die Freude, –n	joy
frisch	fresh
der Fuß, ⁀e	foot
das Gemüse, –	vegetable
gleich	(*adj.*) same, like, equal; (*time adv.*) immediately, presently
grau	gray
grüßen	to greet
der Gruß, ⁀e	greeting
das Haar, –e	hair
heiß	hot
hell	bright
hereinkommen	to come in
herum'	around
hinunter	down
den Rhein hinunter	down the Rhine
die Hitze	heat
hoch	high
der Januar	January
die Kreide	chalk
die Küche, –n	kitchen
die Kutsche, –n	coach, jalopy
landen	to land
lehren	to teach
der Lehrer	teacher
lieb	dear
liebhaben	to love
lieblich	lovely
der Liebling, –e	darling, favorite
mancher	many a (*see* **155**)
mehrere	several

Mitternacht	midnight	stecken	to stick; to put
modern'	modern	die Suppe, –n	soup
die Möglichkeit, –en	possibility	tausend	thousand
der Nachbar, –n	neighbor	der Unterschied, –e	difference
die Nase, –n	nose	verbringen	to spend (time)
der Ofen, ∺	stove, oven	verdienen	to earn
Österreich	Austria	verkaufen	to sell
die Pause, –n	pause, intermission	die Verspätung, –en	delay
die Post	mail; post office	Verspätung haben	to be late, not on
raten	to advise; to guess		schedule
der Rat, ∺e	advice, counsel;	verwandt	related
	council	der Verwandte, –n	relative (see 159)
das Rathaus, ∺er	city hall, town hall	verwunden	to wound
rechtzeitig	on time	vorbei	gone, past
reich	rich	der Wald, ∺er	woods, forest
die Reihe, –n	row; series	was für	what kind of (see 162)
ich bin an der	it's my turn	waschen	to wash
Reihe		weinen	to weep, cry
ich komme an die	I'm next	weiß	white
Reihe		welcher	which
die Rose, –n	rose	wenig	little (see 163)
rot	red	werfen	to throw
rufen	to call	umwerfen	to knock over
die Ruhe (no pl.)	rest, quietness	wiederho'len	to repeat
in aller Ruhe	at leisure	wiegen	to weigh
der Saft, ∺e	juice	wunderbar	wonderful, marvelous
der Schrank, ∺e	cupboard	der Wunsch, ∺e	wish
schwarz	black	die Wurst, ∺e	sausage
sentimental'	sentimental	das Würstchen, –	sausage
solange (conj.)	as long as	ziehen	to pull; to move
solcher	such (see 156)	der Zoll, ∺e	customs; duty
stark	strong; heavy (as	zunächst	first, first of all
	rain, wind, etc.)		

Additional Vocabulary

der Apfel, ∺	apple	die Farbe, –n	color
der Ast, ∺e	branch	die Lieblingsfarbe	favorite color
das Ausland	foreign countries	der Fluggast, ∺e	airplane passenger
er lebt im Ausland	he lives abroad	der Flugschein, –e	airplane ticket
backen	to bake	füllen	to fill
der Bäcker, –	baker	die Geiß, –en	goat
der Bauch, ∺e	stomach, belly	der Gesandte, –n	ambassador, envoy
der Beamte, –n	civil servant, (govern-	herbei	here, hither
	ment) official	der Kasten, ∺	chest, box
		der Koffer, –	suitcase
(gen.: des Beamten;		die Kusi'ne, –n	(female) cousin
dat.: dem Beamten)		leuchten	to shine
die Beamtin, –nen	official (female)	die Mahlzeit, –en	meal
der Brunnen, –	well, fountain	das Mehl	flour
empfehlen	to recommend		

die Meile, –n	mile	**schnarchen**	to snore
der Müller, –	miller	**streichen**	to spread (as paint), stroke
nähen	to sew		
das Obst (*no pl.*)	fruit	**der Wolf, ̈-e**	wolf

Strong and Irregular Verbs

ausgeben, gab aus, hat ausgegeben, er gibt aus	to spend
ausschlafen, schlief aus, hat ausgeschlafen, er schläft aus	to get enough sleep
brechen, brach, hat gebrochen, er bricht	to break
ertrinken, ertrank, ist ertrunken, er ertrinkt	to drown
fließen, floß, ist geflossen, er fließt	to flow
fortgehen, ging fort, ist fortgegangen, er geht fort	to go away
fressen, fraß, hat gefressen, er frißt	to eat (said of animals)
hereinkommen, kam herein, ist hereingekommen, er kommt herein	to come in
raten, riet, hat geraten, er rät	to advise; to guess
rufen, rief, hat gerufen, er ruft	to call
streichen, strich, hat gestrichen, er streicht	to spread (as paint), stroke
verbringen, verbrachte, hat verbracht, er verbringt	to spend (time)
wiegen, wog, hat gewogen, er wiegt	to weigh
ziehen, zog, hat gezogen, er zieht	to pull, move

Für alle unter 21
durch 21 Länder
Europas mit
INTER-RAIL 72

Auskünfte in Bahnhöfen und Reisebüros

Österreichische Verkehrswerbung Gesellschaft m. b. H., 1090 Wien — „BP 341 b" – Druck: Elbemühl

Unit 11 Infinitive Constructions—**hin** and **her**—Comparison of Adjectives—The Rhetorical **nicht**—Numbers

Patterns

[1] **lernen** plus Infinitive

Observe the position of the dependent infinitives; then complete
the variations below.

Ingelheim kannte ich schon vor dem Kriege, aber seine Frau lernte ich erst kennen, als er
    mit ihr nach München zog.
Ingelheim kenne ich schon lange, aber seine Frau habe ich leider noch nicht kennenge-
    lernt. Ich möchte sie gerne kennenlernen.
Ali war sehr intelligent, aber er hatte nie lesen gelernt.
Viele Kinder lernen schon mit fünf Jahren lesen.
Bevor Sie nach Kalifornien gehen, müssen Sie unbedingt Auto fahren lernen.
Es wäre besser, wenn Sie Auto fahren gelernt hätten.
    It would be better if you had learned to drive.

SEE
ANALYSIS
169

(pp. 363-369)

VARIATIONS

Complete the following sentences by using the infinitives in
parentheses. Use more than one tense if possible.

Es wäre besser, wenn sie _____ (kochen lernen).
Ich möchte wissen, ob sie _____ (kochen lernen).
Ich dachte, du _____ (schwimmen lernen).
Sie soll tatsächlich _____ (Auto fahren lernen).
Ich hoffe, daß er hier jemanden _____ (kennenlernen).

[2] **bleiben** plus Infinitive

Observe again the position of the dependent infinitives; then
complete the variations below.

Bitte bleiben Sie doch sitzen, Herr Schmidt.
    Please stay seated (don't get up).

SEE
ANALYSIS
169

(pp. 363-369)

Auch wenn Sie nicht Auto fahren gelernt haben, brauchen Sie nicht zu Hause zu bleiben.

339

Warum hat sie denn den Meyer geheiratet? Um nicht sitzenzubleiben?—Ja, weil sie nicht
    sitzenbleiben wollte.
      Why did she marry Meyer? In order not to become an old maid?—Yes, because she
      didn't want to become an old maid.

Du brauchst noch nicht aufzustehen; du kannst noch liegen bleiben.
      You don't have to get up yet; you can still stay in bed.

Wem gehört denn das Buch da?—Das weiß ich nicht; es ist gestern abend hier liegenge-
    blieben.
      To whom does that book belong?—I don't know; it was left here last night.

Meine Uhr ist gestern abend plötzlich stehengeblieben.
      My watch suddenly stopped last night.

Bitte gehen Sie weiter; Sie dürfen hier nicht stehenbleiben.
      Please go on, you mustn't stop here.

VARIATIONS

Complete the following sentences, using the infinitives in parentheses.
Use more than one tense, if possible.

Bitte ——————, Herr Vollmer (sitzen bleiben).
Ich hoffe, meine Uhr —————— (stehenbleiben).
Ich glaube, meine Uhr —————— (stehenbleiben).
Ich dachte, meine Uhr —————— (stehenbleiben).
Er kommt heute nicht zum Frühstück. Er —————— (liegen bleiben).

[3] gehen and fahren plus Infinitive

Observe again the position of the dependent infinitives; then
complete the variations that follow.

SEE
ANALYSIS
169
(pp. 363-369)

Wie wäre es, wenn wir jetzt essen gingen?
Andreas ist auch schon essen gegangen.
Können wir bald essen gehen?
Du brauchst doch nicht schon wieder essen zu gehen; du hast doch gerade erst gefrüh-
    stückt.
Wie wär's denn, wenn wir Sonntag baden gingen?
Was habt ihr denn heute gemacht?—Erst sind wir schwimmen gegangen, und dann sind
    wir spazierengefahren.

VARIATIONS

Complete the following sentences by using the infinitives in
parentheses. Use more than one tense, if possible.

Es wäre nett, wenn wir morgen —————— (schwimmen gehen).
Er soll jeden Tag mit Erika —————— (schwimmen gehen).

Ist Hans schon im Bett?—Ja, er _____ (schlafen gehen).
Ich wollte, wir _____ (schlafen gehen).

[4] hören and sehen plus Infinitive

Observe how **hören** and **sehen** behave like modals in these sentences.
Then follow the instructions below.

SEE
ANALYSIS
169

(pp. 363-369)

Ich hörte ihn gestern abend nach Hause kommen.	I heard him come home last night.
Ich habe ihn gestern abend nach Hause kommen hören.	
Ich habe gehört, wie er gestern abend nach Hause kam.	
Wir sahen sie in Berlin die Desdemona spielen.	We saw her play Desdemona in Berlin.
Wir haben sie die Desdemona spielen sehen.	We've seen her play Desdemona.

VARIATIONS

Form sentences with the following phrases, using modals, subjunctives, and various tenses.

Emma einmal (noch nie) lachen sehen
den Kleinen schreien hören
die Maria nach Hause kommen hören

[5] lassen (to leave)

SEE
ANALYSIS
169

(pp. 363-369)

Heute regnet es bestimmt nicht. Deinen Regenmantel kannst du zu Hause lassen.
    I'm sure it won't rain today. You can leave your raincoat at home.

Heute regnet es bestimmt nicht. Du hättest deinen Mantel zu Hause lassen können.
    I'm sure it won't rain today. You could have left your raincoat at home.

Bitte lassen Sie mich jetzt allein.	Please leave me alone now.
Ich wollte, er ließe mich in Ruhe.	I wish he'd leave me alone (in peace).

Express in German.

I've left my coat at home.
I wish I hadn't left it at home.
Why do you always leave your coat at home?

Jetzt habe ich schon wieder meinen Mantel im Hotel hängenlassen.
    Now I've left my coat at the hotel again.

Und wo ist deine Handtasche?—Die habe ich bei Tante Amalie auf dem Tisch stehen-
  lassen.
  Where is your bag?—I left it on the table at Aunt Amalie's.

Und deine Handschuhe hast du wohl auch irgendwo liegenlassen?
  And I suppose you left your gloves somewhere too?

Express in German (note that the infinitives **hängen, liegen, stehen**
behave like prefixes and do not change).

I hope you won't leave your coat in the hotel again.
I have left my gloves at Aunt Amalie's.
You can't leave your car in front of the hotel.

[6] lassen (to cause, either by permission or request, somebody to do something)

SEE
ANALYSIS
169
(pp. 363-369)

(a) The inner field contains only the accusative noun or pronoun which functions as the
subject of the following infinitive.

Ich lasse dich nicht nach Berlin fahren.
  I will not let you go to Berlin alone.

Ich habe ihn doch nach Berlin fahren lassen.
  I let him go to Berlin after all.

Ich wollte, ich hätte ihn nicht nach Berlin fahren lassen.
  I wish I had not let him go to Berlin.

Du kannst mich doch nicht ohne Geld nach Berlin fahren lassen.
  You certainly cannot let me go to Berlin without money.

Ich hätte ihn nicht allein nach Berlin fahren lassen sollen.
  I should not have permitted him to go to Berlin alone.

Warum darf ich denn nicht allein ins Kino gehen? Müllers lassen ihre Tochter auch allein
  ins Kino gehen.
  Why can't I go to the movies alone? The Müllers also let their daughter go to the movies
  alone.

Meyer mußte gestern den Arzt kommen lassen.
  (Literally: Meyer had to let the doctor come yesterday.)
  Meyer had to call the doctor yesterday.

Express in German.

Why don't you let me study medicine?
I wish you would let me study medicine.
I wish we had let him study medicine.
We can't let him study medicine.

We shouldn't have let her study medicine.
We shall let her study medicine.

(b) The inner field contains the accusative subject of the dependent infinitive. This subject is followed by an accusative object. Both subject and object (in that order!) precede
the infinitive.

SEE
ANALYSIS
169

(pp. 363-369)

Lassen Sie mich das mal sehen!
　　Let me see that!

Lassen Sie mich doch erst meinen Kaffee trinken!
　　Let me first drink my coffee!

Er will die Briefe heute abend zu Hause tippen. Sollen wir ihn die Schreibmaschine mit
　　nach Hause nehmen lassen?
　　Shall we let him take the typewriter home?

Lassen Sie den Meyer diese Arbeit machen.
　　Let Meyer do that work.

Express in German.

Shall we let Fritz wash the car?
Why don't you let me wash the car, father?
Could you let me finish reading this letter? (Use **zu Ende lesen.**)

(c) The subject of the dependent infinitive is suppressed. Some trained or professional
person (waiter, barber, mechanic, physician) is implied. Only the accusative object of the
dependent infinitive precedes.

SEE
ANALYSIS
169

(pp. 363-369)

Wir lassen gerade unser Dach reparieren.
　　(Literally: We are just letting [somebody] repair our roof.)
　　We are just having our roof repaired.

Wir müssen unser Auto reparieren lassen.
Wir haben den Motor noch nie reparieren lassen müssen.
Mein Freund Egon muß sich operieren lassen.

Express in German.

We should have (somebody) paint (**anstreichen**) our house.
Why don't you have an operation (let [somebody] operate on you)?

(d) The subject of the infinitive is suppressed. The accusative object in front of that infinitive is preceded by a personal dative (reflexive or nonreflexive) denoting the person for
whose benefit some other person is doing something.

SEE
ANALYSIS
169

(pp. 363-369)

Ich habe ihm ein Telegramm schicken lassen.
　　I had (my secretary) send him a telegram.
　　(I had a telegram sent to him.)

Ich habe ihm sagen lassen, daß er mich morgen anrufen soll.
> I had (somebody) tell him that he should give me a ring tomorrow.
> (I sent word to him to give me a ring tomorrow.)

Frau Lenz hat sich schon wieder einen Mantel machen lassen.
> Mrs. Lenz again had (somebody) make her a coat.
> (Mrs. Lenz has had another coat made.)

Meyer tut, was er will. Er läßt sich nie etwas sagen.
> Meyer does what he wants to. He never permits (anybody) to tell him anything.
> (He never listens to anybody.)

Ich lasse mir eine Tasse Kaffee aufs Zimmer bringen.
> I request that (somebody) bring me a cup of coffee to my room.
> (I have a cup of coffee brought to my room.)

Warum hat sie sich das Frühstück denn nicht aufs Zimmer bringen lassen?
> Why didn't she have her breakfast sent to her room?
> (Literally: Why didn't she tell somebody to send her the breakfast to the room?)

Wo hast du dir die Haare schneiden lassen?
> Where did you get your hair cut?

Express in German (using the phrase **sich die Haare schneiden lassen**).

I must get a haircut today.
I got a haircut yesterday.
Why didn't you get a haircut today?
Yes, I'll get a haircut tomorrow.

SEE
ANALYSIS
169

(pp. 363-369)

(e) The subject of the infinitive is expressed by a prepositional **von**-phrase. This **von**-phrase is preceded by a personal dative and followed (or preceded) by an accusative object.

Ich lasse mir immer die Haare von meiner Frau schneiden.
> I always let my wife cut my hair.

Wir lassen uns von Overhoff ein Haus bauen.
> We are having Overhoff build us a house.

Wir lassen unseren Kindern von Overhoff ein Haus bauen.
> We are having Overhoff build a house for our children.

François? Nein, von dem lasse ich mir nie wieder die Haare schneiden.
> François? No, I'll never have my hair cut again by him.

Früher haben wir uns immer die Brötchen vom Bäcker ins Haus schicken lassen.
> We used to have the baker deliver our breakfast rolls.

Express in German.

I always have him cut my hair.
I'll never have him make me a coat again.
Why don't you let François cut your hair?

(f) The dependent infinitive is preceded by a **von**-phrase subject, which itself is preceded by an accusative object.

SEE
ANALYSIS
169

(pp. 363-369)

Ich lasse meine Frau von Dr. Meinecke operieren.
   I shall ask Dr. Meinecke to operate on my wife.

Petra läßt sich von ihrem Mann verwöhnen.
   Petra lets her husband spoil her.

Ich ließe mich auch gerne von dir verwöhnen!
   I would like it, if you spoiled me too!

Erika läßt sich von keinem küssen.
   Erika does not let anybody kiss her.

Express in German.

I won't have Dr. Meinecke operate on me.
Did you let him take you home?

[7] brauchen, scheinen, haben, sein

Observe the use of infinitives with **zu** depending on these verbs.

Du brauchst nicht auf mich zu warten; ich komme heute spät nach Hause.
   You don't need to wait for me; I'll come home late today.

SEE
ANALYSIS
169

(pp. 363-369)

Du hättest nicht auf mich zu warten brauchen.
   You needn't have waited for me.

Es scheint zu regnen.
Er scheint zu schlafen.
Er scheint nicht zu Hause zu sein.

Er scheint schon abgefahren zu sein.
Er scheint heute nicht arbeiten zu müssen.

Ich kann leider nicht mitgehen; ich habe noch etwas zu tun.
    I'm sorry, but I can't come along; I still have something to do.

Ich hatte den ganzen Tag nichts zu tun.
    I didn't have anything to do all day.

Wenn ich nicht so viel zu tun gehabt hätte, hätte ich dir gerne geholfen.
    If I hadn't had so much to do, I would gladly have helped you.

Nur um etwas zu tun zu haben, ging er jeden Abend ins Kino.
    Just to have something to do, he went to the movies every night.

Da ist nichts zu machen.
    There's nothing to be done (about it).

Hans war einfach nicht zu finden.
    Hans was simply not to be found.

Professor Mertens ist immer gut zu verstehen.
    Professor Mertens is always easy to understand.

Er soll gut zu verstehen gewesen sein.
    He is supposed to have been easy to understand. (I hear he was easy to understand.)

VARIATIONS

Express in German.

Don't you have anything to do?   It would be nice if I had nothing to do today.
Don't you have anything to say?   I wish I had something to do today.
Why does he never have anything to say?   He seems to have nothing to do today.

[8] End-Field Infinitives (The Group **anfangen**)

In the following sentences, note that the clause to which the
infinitive belongs has to be completed before the infinitive phrase
can be started. Then complete the variations below.

SEE
ANALYSIS
170

(pp. 369-371)

Es fing an zu regnen.
Als es anfing zu regnen, gingen wir nach Hause.
Es hat angefangen zu regnen.
Es fing an, sehr stark zu regnen.
Als es anfing, sehr stark zu regnen, gingen wir nach Hause.
Kannst du nicht endlich aufhören zu arbeiten?
Weil ich vergessen hatte, ihm zu schreiben, kam er nicht zum Bahnhof.
Hast du denn nicht versucht, sie anzurufen?

VARIATIONS

Change the following sentences to infinitive clauses and use the verbs
in parentheses to form introductory clauses.

> **Es regnet nicht mehr. (aufhören)**
> **Es hat aufgehört zu regnen.**

Er will in Davos gewesen sein. (behaupten)
Ich habe ihr nicht geschrieben. (vergessen)
Meyer will seiner Frau ein Auto schenken. (versprechen)
Ich möchte sie bald wiedersehen. (hoffen)
Ich wollte dich gestern abend anrufen. (versuchen)

[9] End-Field Infinitives (The Group **befehlen**)

Observe the identity of the personal dative and the unmentioned
subject of the end-field infinitive. Then complete the variations.

SEE
ANALYSIS
170

(pp. 369-371)

Er schlug mir vor, an die Nordsee zu fahren.
> He suggested that I go to the North Sea.

Wenn Sie mir nicht vorgeschlagen hätten, an die Nordsee zu fahren, hätte ich meinen
Mann nie kennengelernt.
> If you hadn't suggested that I go to the North Sea, I would never have met my husband.

Ich rate dir, nicht mehr so viel zu rauchen.
> I advise you not to smoke so much anymore.

Wir erlauben unseren Kindern nicht, jede Woche zweimal ins Kino zu gehen.
> We don't allow our children to go to the movies twice a week.

In Deutschland ist es verboten, im Kino zu rauchen.
> In Germany it is forbidden to smoke in the movie theater.

Niemand kann mir befehlen, einen Mann zu heiraten, den ich nicht liebe.
> Nobody can order me to marry a man I don't love.

VARIATIONS

Change the following sentences to infinitive clauses and use the
verbs in parentheses to form introductory clauses. Use **Er** and the
perfect tense throughout.

> **Fahren Sie doch mal an die See. (raten)**
> **Er hat mir geraten, einmal an die See zu fahren.**

Trinken Sie jeden Abend vor dem Schlafengehen ein Glas Wein. (empfehlen)
Bleiben Sie morgen zu Hause. (erlauben)
Ich wünsche nicht, daß Sie mit meiner Tochter ins Theater gehen. (verbieten)
Fahren Sie doch mit mir nach München. (vorschlagen)

[10] End-Field Infinitives after Adjectives

After studying these sentences, complete the variations.

SEE
ANALYSIS
170

(pp. 369-371)

Inge war froh, ihren Mann wiederzusehen.
  Inge was glad to see her husband again.

Ich wußte, Inge wäre froh gewesen, ihren Mann wiederzusehen.
  I knew Inge would have been glad to see her husband again.

Ich bin immer bereit gewesen, ihm zu helfen.
  I have always been ready to help him.

Ich war sehr erstaunt, Erich aus dem Haus des Ägypters kommen zu sehen.
  I was very astonished to see Erich come out of the Egyptian's house.

VARIATIONS

Change the following sentences to infinitive clauses. Use the
subjects of these sentences and the adjectives in parentheses to form
introductory clauses.

Inge sah ihren Mann wieder. (froh)
Inge war froh, ihren Mann wiederzusehen.

Gottseidank sind wir wieder zu Hause. (glücklich)
Erich half uns immer. (bereit)
Ich sah ihn letztes Wochenende in Hamburg wieder. (erstaunt)

[11] End-Field Infinitives after **da**-Compounds

Note that the subject of the inflected verb is also the unmentioned
subject of the infinitive.

SEE
ANALYSIS
170

(pp. 369-371)

Ich denke nicht daran, mit Inge schwimmen zu gehen.
Du weißt doch, daß ich gar nicht daran denke, mit Inge schwimmen zu gehen.
Ich habe ja gar nicht daran gedacht, mit Inge schwimmen zu gehen.
Ich hätte nie daran gedacht, mit Inge schwimmen zu gehen.

Form similar sentences with **Angst haben vor, jemanden bitten
um, hoffen auf.**

[12] End-Field Infinitives with **um . . . zu,
ohne . . . zu, statt . . . zu**

SEE
ANALYSIS
171

(pp. 371-372)

Note how the German construction changes if the subject of the
infinitive is not also the subject of the inflected verb.

Wir bleiben heute zu Hause, um endlich einmal arbeiten zu können.
  We're going to stay at home today in order to get some work done finally.

Wir bleiben heute zu Hause, damit mein Mann endlich einmal arbeiten kann.
> We're going to stay at home today in order that my husband can finally get some work
> done (so that my husband can finally get some work done).

Ohne auch nur einen Augenblick nachzudenken, lief Hermann hinter das Haus.
> Without a moment's thought, Hermann ran behind the house.

Mit Meyer kann man nie sprechen, ohne daß seine Frau dabei ist.
> You can never talk to Meyer without his wife being there too.

Hast du schon wieder die ganze Nacht gelesen, statt zu schlafen?
> Have you read all night again instead of going to sleep?

Statt daß man *Mey*er nach Berlin geschickt hätte, muß *ich* schon wieder fahren.
> Instead of their having sent Meyer to Berlin (which they should have done and didn't),
> I have to go again.

[13] hin and her

Be prepared to produce orally the sentences on the left when you
hear the sentences on the right, and vice versa.

Ich fahre sofort hin.	Er kommt sofort her.	**SEE**
Kannst du hinfahren?	Kannst du herkommen?	**ANALYSIS**
Ich bin sofort hingefahren.	Er ist sofort hergekommen.	**172**
Ich brauche nicht hinzufahren.	Er braucht nicht herzukommen.	(pp. 372-375)
Wer hat dich denn dahingebracht?	Wer hat dich denn hierhergebracht?	
Wie bist du denn dahingekommen?	Wie bist du denn hierhergekommen?	
Sie fahren nach Tirol? Dahin fahre ich auch.	Sie kommen aus Tirol? Daher komme ich auch.	

VARIATIONS

Form variations with the following pattern:

> **Den kenne ich noch von früher her.**
> (Literally: I've known him from an earlier time on.)

von der Schule	von der Tanzstunde
vom Kriege	von München

Form variations of the following situations with **vorher** and **nachher**:

> **Gestern abend waren wir im Theater. Vorher haben wir im Regina gegessen, und
> nachher waren wir bei Schmidts.**

Letzten Mittwoch war ich in Salzburg.
Um sieben haben wir zu Abend gegessen.
Morgen mittag besuche ich Tante Amalie.

Memorize the following sentences.

Weißt du was? Rosemarie hat vorhin angerufen.
Ich war vorhin bei Schmidts.
Diese Uhr hier ist hin,—die ist kaputt.
Meine Ruh' ist hin, mein Herz ist schwer. (Goethe)

Be prepared to produce the sentences on the left when you hear the
sentences on the right, and vice versa.

Wohin gehst du denn?	Wo gehst du denn hin?
Woher kommst du denn?	Wo kommst du denn her?
Wohin ist er denn gegangen?	Wo ist er denn hingegangen?
Woher ist er denn gekommen?	Wo ist er denn hergekommen?
Dahin gehe ich auch.	Da gehe ich auch hin.
Daher komme ich auch.	Da komme ich auch her.

In the following examples, note the difference in meaning between
the forms with **hin-** and **her-** and the forms without **hin-** and **her-**.

Die Titanic ist untergegangen.
  The Titanic sank.

Die Sonne geht unter.
  The sun sets.

Wo seid ihr denn untergekommen?
  Where did you find a place to stay?

Das Licht ist ausgegangen.
  The light went out.

Die Sonne geht auf.
  The sun rises.

Ich gehe ins Eßzimmer hinunter.
  I'm going down to the dining room.

Er kommt sofort herunter.
  He'll be down in a minute.

Ist er schon heruntergekommen?
  Has he come down yet?

Er ist gerade hinausgegangen.
  He just went out.

Herr Doktor Schmidt ist schon hinaufge-
  gangen.
  Dr. Schmidt has already gone up.

Ich konnte ihn nicht mehr einholen.
  I couldn't catch up with him anymore.

Mit zweihundert Mark im Monat kann ich
  nicht auskommen.
  I can't get along on two hundred marks
  a month.

Hast du die Zeitung schon hereingeholt?
  Have you brought the paper in yet?

Ich habe ihn noch nicht herauskommen
  sehen.
  I haven't seen him come out yet.

Note the "prepositional brackets" in the following sentences.

Er kam aus dem Haus heraus.
Er ging ins Haus hinein.
Wir fahren durch den Panamakanal hindurch.
Wir stiegen auf den Berg hinauf.
Er sprang über den Zaun hinüber.

[14] Comparative Forms of Adjectives

Be prepared to produce orally the sentences on the right when
you hear the sentences on the left.

SEE
ANALYSIS
173

(pp. 375-378)

Sie ist so alt wie ich.
Hier ist es so kalt wie in Hamburg.
Leider ist sie nicht so jung wie er.
Hier ist es nicht so warm wie bei euch.
Die Alpen sind nicht so hoch wie die Sierras.
Ingelheim ist nicht ganz so interessant wie
    Thomas Mann.
Du bist doch nicht so groß wie ich.
Das Bier hier ist wirklich gut.

Sie ist älter als ich.
Hier ist es kälter als in Hamburg.
Leider ist er jünger als sie.
Bei euch ist es viel wärmer als bei uns.
Die Sierras sind höher als die Alpen.
Thomas Mann ist etwas interessanter als
    Ingelheim.
Doch, ich bin größer als du.
Ja, aber das Bier in München ist noch
    besser.

Tante Dorothea redet genau so viel wie
    Tante Amalie.
Hier ist das frische Obst nicht so teuer wie
    bei uns.
Inges Haar war schon immer so dunkel wie
    meins.
Möchtest du dir gern den Faustfilm anse-
hen?

Nee, nee, die redet noch mehr als Tante
    Amalie, noch viel mehr.
Bei uns ist das Obst viel teurer als bei euch.

Aber seit sie vierzig ist, wird es immer
    dunkler.
Nein, ich ginge viel lieber in einen Wild-
    westfilm.

Form similar pairs with the following adjectives.

schnell, schneller	hart, härter	oft, öfter
freundlich, freundlicher	kurz, kürzer	stark, stärker
arm, ärmer	lang, länger	nah, näher

[15] Superlative Forms of Adjectives

Read the following sentences and complete the variations.

SEE
ANALYSIS
173

(pp. 375-378)

Die Frau mit dem Flamingo ist sein bester Roman.
Ich halte *Die Frau mit dem Flamingo* für _____.

Monika ist die interessanteste Frau, die ich kenne.
Von allen Frauen, die ich kenne, ist sie die _____.

Im Dezember sind die Tage am kürzesten.
Der 21. Dezember ist der _____ Tag des Jahres.

In dieser Show sehen Sie Giganto, den stärksten Mann der Welt.
Giganto ist von allen Männern der _____.

Was ist Ingelheims bester Roman?
Mir gefällt *Die Frau mit dem Flamingo* am _____.

Hier ist es ja das ganze Jahr sehr schön, aber im Mai ist es hier doch am _____.

Spieglein, Spieglein an der Wand,
wer ist die Schönste im ganzen Land?
Frau Königin, Ihr* seid die Schönste hier,
    aber Schneewittchen hinter den Bergen,
    bei den sieben Zwergen,
    ist noch tausendmal schöner als Ihr.

[16] Comparatives and Superlatives: Advertising Slogans

You can find advertisements like these in German magazines.

SEE
ANALYSIS
173

(pp. 375-378)

Sie können natürlich mehr Geld ausgeben, aber es ist nicht sicher, ob Sie einen besseren
    Waschautomaten bekommen.

Gesünder und darum besser ist ein Cottona-Hemd.

Sie sollten nicht weniger für ihr Geld verlangen.

Sie sollten mehr verlangen: Ein VW ist der beste Kauf.

Cinzano on the rocks: der beste Anfang einer guten Sache.

In der ganzen Welt kennt man den Namen Pall Mall als Garantie für teuerste Tabake. Die
    Pall Mall Filter ist eine mild-aromatische Blendcigarette im King-Size-Format. 20 Pall
    Mall Filter kosten DM 2,30.

Was trinken Sie am liebsten, wenn Sie mit Ihrer Frau abends fernsehen? Natürlich
    Löwenbräu.

Wie gern essen wir ein Steak. Noch lieber ist es uns mit einem Schuß Ketchup. Am liebsten
    essen wir es aber mit Thomy's Tomaten-Ketchup. Es gehört zu den neun Thomy's
    Delikatessen.

Statt für jeden etwas, etwas Besonderes für alle: Triumpf, die beste Schreibmaschine.

Jede moderne Frau weiß, wie man sich interessanter macht. Die interessantesten Frauen
    tragen Elastiform.

[17] The Rhetorical nicht

SEE
ANALYSIS
174

(p. 378)

Haben Sie einen *Bru*der?	Do you have a brother?
Haben Sie keinen *Bru*der?	Don't you have a brother?
Haben Sie nicht *ei*nen *Bru*der?	Don't you have a single brother?
Haben Sie nicht einen *Bru*der?	You have a brother, haven't you?

Habe ich nicht einen intelligenten Sohn?

Ist sie nicht ein hübsches Mädchen?

Warst du nicht gestern abend mit Inge im Kino?

Haben Sie nicht früher bei der Hansa-Bank gearbeitet?

Bin ich nicht schon immer dagegen gewesen?

Hat nicht unsere Partei seit Jahren immer wieder bewiesen, daß sie allein den Weg weiß
    in eine bessere Zukunft?

* **Ihr** is an obsolete polite form now replaced by **Sie**.

Change the following statements into rhetorical questions.

Sie haben ihn schon vor dem Krieg kennengelernt, nicht wahr?
Seine Tochter hat den Fritz Müller geheiratet, nicht wahr?
Sie haben schon immer einmal nach Amerika fahren wollen, nicht wahr?

[18] Numbers

Read aloud and observe stress:

SEE ANALYSIS 175 (pp. 379-380)

100	*hund*ert	100	*einh*undert
101	hundert*eins*	200	*zwei*hundert
102	hundert*zwei*	300	*drei*hundert
110	hundert*zehn*	900	*neun*hundert
120	hundert*zwan*zig	1.000	*taus*end
121	hundert*einund*zwanzig		
122	hundert*zweiund*zwanzig	7.839	*sieben*tausend*acht*hundert*neun*und*drei*ßig
198	hundert*acht*und*neun*zig	1.000.000	eine Milli*on*
199	hundert*neun*und*neun*zig	2.000.000	zwei Milli*on*en
200	*zwei*hundert	1.000.000.000	eine Milli*ar*de (one billion)

Ich brauche zweihundert*ein*undvierzig *Mark*.
In unserer Stadt wohnen jetzt über *drei*hunderttausend *Men*schen.
Unsere Bibliothek hat mehrere Milli*on*en *Mark* gekostet.
„Und Noah lebte nach der Flut *drei*hundertund*fünf*zig Jahre; alle Tage Noahs waren
   *neun*hundertund*fünf*zig Jahre, und er *starb*."
   0,7 *null* komma *sie*ben
   0,17 *null* komma *sieb*zehn (*null* komma *eins* *sie*ben)
3,14159 *drei* komma *eins* *vier* *eins* *fünf* *neun*

Read the following numbers.

758	75,8	7,58	2,718282	232.493,00	232,493

DM   4,20 vier Mark zwanzig
DM 121,00 hunderteinundzwanzig Mark
DM 100,21 hundert Mark einundzwanzig
DM   0,75 fünfundsiebzig Pfennig
  $ 1.477,00 vierzehnhundertsiebenundsiebzig Dollar
           eintausendvierhundertsiebenundsiebzig Dollar
  $ 18,37 achtzehn Dollar siebenunddreißig

Am ersten und zweiten Februar waren wir in Berlin, am dritten und vierten in Hamburg
   und vom fünften bis zum zehnten in Bonn.
Berlin, den 1.2.1970 (den ersten Februar 1970)
Hamburg, 8.9.71 (den achten September 1971)

Read the following dates.

13.1.27	7.7.29	18.6.1962
8.2.25	20.8.54	22.2.1732
25.10.04	1.9.39	7.12.1941

Heinrich I. (Heinrich der Erste)
Friedrich Wilhelm IV. (Friedrich Wilhelm der Vierte)
Er war ein Sohn Friedrichs II. (Er war ein Sohn Friedrichs des Zweiten.)

Read the following.

Leo XIII. (1887–1903) (1887 bis 1903)
Pius X. (1903–1914)
Benedict XV. (1914–1922)
Pius XI. (1922–1939)
Pius XII. (1939–1958)
Johannes XXIII. (1958–1963) (der Dreiundzwanzigste)

Und hier, meine Damen und Herren, sehen Sie ein Bild von Herzog August III., der, wie
 Sie wissen, der Vater Sigismunds II. war. Seine Frau Mechthild, eine Tochter Augusts
 V. von Niederlohe-Schroffenstein, soll die schönste Frau ihrer Zeit gewesen sein.

Nein, nach Italien fahren will ich nicht. Erstens habe ich kein Geld, zweitens habe ich
 keine Lust, drittens mag ich Meyers nicht und viertens ist meine Frau dagegen.

Nein, soviel kann ich nicht essen. Die Hälfte davon ist mehr als genug.

Hat Tante Amalie schon ihr Testament gemacht?—Ja, und ein Drittel von ihrem Geld
 bekommt das Museum.

Seine Frau erhielt zwei Drittel seines Vermögens, und das dritte Drittel ging an seine
 beiden Söhne.

Ich hätte gerne ein halbes Pfund Butter.
Geben Sie mir bitte ein viertel Pfund Schinken.

Read aloud:

$\frac{1}{2}$ $\frac{1}{3}$ $\frac{2}{7}$ $\frac{6}{8}$ $\frac{5}{12}$

[19] Time

SEE
ANALYSIS
176

(p. 380)

11.00 Uhr	elf Uhr	11.35 Uhr	fünf nach halb zwölf
11.05 Uhr	fünf nach elf	11.40 Uhr	zehn nach halb zwölf
11.10 Uhr	zehn nach elf	11.45 Uhr	dreiviertel zwölf; viertel vor zwölf
11.15 Uhr	viertel nach elf; viertel zwölf	11.50 Uhr	zehn vor zwölf
11.20 Uhr	zwanzig nach elf	11.55 Uhr	fünf vor zwölf
11.25 Uhr	fünf vor halb zwölf	12.00 Uhr	zwölf Uhr
11.30 Uhr	halb zwölf		

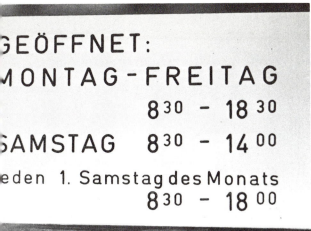

Read aloud and, where possible, in several ways:

9.05 (Uhr)	4.25 (Uhr)	12.45 (Uhr)
9.15	7.45	1.30
10.30	7.57	21.45

Reading

Eisenbahnterminologie

Es ist nicht leicht, einen deutschen Fahrplan zu lesen. Die folgende Tabelle (siehe Seite 357) ist eine Seite aus einem deutschen Kursbuch, und wir wollen versuchen, einen Zug von Frankfurt nach Koblenz zu finden.

Zunächst suchen wir Frankfurt (Zeile 11) und Koblenz (Zeile 23). 5 *Hbf.* steht für Hauptbahnhof. Der erste Zug hat die Nummer D 1269,

der Fahrplan, ∺e
timetable
die Tabelle, –n table
das Kursbuch, ∺er
complete book of time-tables **die Zeile, –n** line

das Haupt, ∺er head;
Haupt– (in compounds) main

d.h. es ist ein D-Zug oder Schnellzug, der nur auf größeren Bahnhöfen hält. Dieser Zug kommt um 13.57 Uhr in Koblenz an, aber er fährt nicht über Frankfurt, sondern direkt von Mannheim nach Mainz. Auch der nächste Zug, D 463, aus Basel in der Schweiz, fährt nicht über Frankfurt. Jetzt kommt ein Eilzug (E 721), ab 5 Frankfurt Hbf. um 12.32 Uhr und an Koblenz um 14.27 Uhr.

d.h. = das heißt that is (i.e.)

eilen to hurry

Eilzüge halten öfter als Schnellzüge, aber nur Personenzüge halten auf allen Bahnhöfen. Außerdem gibt es noch F-Züge, d.h. Fernschnellzüge und TEE (Trans-Europ-Express)–Züge. TEE- und F-Züge haben nur 1. Klasse, alle anderen Züge haben 1. und 2. 10 Klasse. Fahrkarten für die 1. Klasse kosten 12 Pf. pro km, für die 2. Klasse 8 Pf./km. Außerdem gibt es Rückfahrkarten mit 10 bis 40% (Prozent) Ermäßigung. In F-Zügen und D-Zügen bezahlt man zum Fahrpreis noch einen besonderen Zuschlag von 2 bis 4 Mark.

Europ shortened form of **Europa**
die Ermäßigung, –en reduction, reduced price
der Zuschlag, ⸚e surcharge

Zurück zum Fahrplan: Die nächsten beiden Züge sind wieder Eilzüge (E 590 und E 297), aber der erste fährt von Bingerbrück aus nach Saarbrücken, der zweite fährt rechtsrheinisch, d.h. auf der östlichen Seite des Rheins, und Koblenz liegt auf der westlichen Rheinseite, wo die Mosel in den Rhein mündet. Der D 203 (von München nach Dortmund) fährt nicht über Frankfurt, aber der 20 D 1114, ab Frankfurt um 14 Uhr, hat in Mainz Anschluß an diesen Zug. Allerdings muß man dabei umsteigen und hat zwischen den beiden Zügen nur acht Minuten Zeit.

münden to flow into

der Anschluß, ⸚e connection
umsteigen to change (trains)

Der letzte Zug auf unserem Fahrplan ist die beste Verbindung von Frankfurt nach Koblenz und auch der interessanteste Zug. Es ist der 25 Hellas-Expreß, und er kommt aus Athen.

die Verbindung, –en connection
Hellas Greece

Fahrkarten bekommt man am Fahrkartenschalter. Man sagt: „Eine Fahrkarte erster Klasse nach Koblenz", oder als alter Eisenbahnfahrer: „Einmal erster Koblenz."

AUS DEM FAHRPLAN DER BUNDESBAHN

10 KARLSRUHE und FRANKFURT (Main)—KÖLN—DORTMUND°

	Station		D1269	D463	E721	E590	E297	D203	D1114	D455
1	München Hbf.	ab	....	....	....	....	....	9.00	....	8.42
2	Stuttgart Hbf.	ab	....	....	....	....	....	11.55		
3	Basel Bad. Bf.	ab	....	9.18	....	....	....			
	ZUG NR.		**D1269**	**D463**	**E721**	**E590**	**E297**	**D203**	**D1114**	**D455**
4	Karlsruhe Hbf.	ab	11.30	11.36	....	....				von Athen
5	Heidelberg Hbf.				....	....		13.15	....	
6	Mannheim Hbf.		12.06	12.13	....	....		13.34	....	
7	Ludwigshafen (Rh.)				....	....		13.50		
8	Worms Hbf.	ab			....	....				
9	Nürnberg Hbf.	ab				....			....	10.59
10	Würzburg Hbf.	ab			10.09	....			....	12.10
11	Frankfurt Hbf.	ab			12.32	12.42	13.14		14.00	14.04
12	Rüsselsheim				12.51	13.01				
13	Mainz Hbf.	ab	12.53	13.03	13.07	13.17		14.37	14.29	
14	Mainz-Kastel	ab	von Freiburg		von Hof		13.40		an	
15	Wiesbaden Hbf.						13.55		....	14.42
16	Eltville						14.07			
17	Rüdesheim (Rh.)						14.20			15.06
18	Niederlahnstein	ab					15.10			Hellas-Express
19	Bingen (Rhein)	ab	13.12		13.30	13.41			....	
20	Bingerbrück				13.33	13.43		14.58	....	
21	St. Goar				13.57				....	
22	Boppard		13.40		14.10		nach Saarbrücken		....	
23	Koblenz Hbf.		13.57	14.03	14.27			15.40	....	15.57
24	Andernach				14.40				....	
25	Remagen				14.58				....	
26	Bad Godesberg				15.08				....	
27	Bonn	an	14.35	14.40	15.14			16.17	....	16.34
28	Neuwied	ab					15.29		....	
29	Linz (Rhein)						15.48		....	
30	Königswinter					....	16.01		....	
31	Beuel					....	16.09		....	
32	Troisdorf					....	16.16		....	
33	KÖLN Hbf.	an	15.00	15.05	15.41	....	16.35	16.40	....	17.00
34	Aachen Hbf.	an	....	....	....	....		....	....	....
35	Mönchengladb. Hbf.	an	....	....	....	....	17.38	....	....	....
36	Krefeld Hbf.	an	....	....	....	....		....	....	....
	ZUG NR.					**E441**			**E315**	
37	Köln Hbf.	ab	15.05	15.10	15.47	16.13	....	16.45	16.48	17.10
38	Solingen-Ohligs	an	15.23			16.38			17.15	
39	Wuppertal-Elberf.	an	15.38			16.55			17.32	
40	Hagen	an	16.03			17.20			18.03	
41	Münster (Westf.)	ab	....							

° Abbreviations

Hbf.—Hauptbahnhof	Nr.—Nummer	Mönchengladb.—Mönchengladbach
Bf.—Bahnhof	Rh.—am Rhein	Elberf.—Elberfeld
Bad. Bf.—Badischer Bahnhof	St. Goar—Sankt Goar	Westf.—Westfalen

Nicht öffnen, bevor der Zug hält

Zu

Offen

„Einfach oder hin und zurück?"

„Einfach, bitte. Und einen D-Zug-Zuschlag."

„So, mein Herr, das macht 17,88 und 2 Mark für den Zuschlag: 19 Mark 88, bitte."

In Deutschland kann man nicht ohne Fahrkarte auf den Bahnsteig, 5 sondern man muß zuerst durch die Sperre, wo ein Eisenbahnbeamter die Fahrkarte locht. Der Zug soll um 13.47 auf Gleis 12 ankommen, aber kurz vorher hört man über den Lautsprecher: „Der Schnellzug aus München, planmäßige Ankunft 13.47 Uhr, hat voraussichtlich 30 Minuten Verspätung." Aber es dauert etwas länger als eine halbe 10 Stunde, und um halb drei heißt es endlich: „Der verspätete Schnellzug aus München läuft soeben auf Gleis 12 ein. Bitte von der Bahnsteigkante zurücktreten." Der Zug ist nicht stark besetzt, und es ist leicht, in einem Nichtraucherabteil erster Klasse einen Fensterplatz zu bekommen. Der Zug hat eine elektrische Lokomotive; in großen 15 Teilen Deutschlands ist die Eisenbahn elektrifiziert, aber man sieht auch Diesellokomotiven und noch Dampflokomotiven. Der Zug hat Wagen erster und zweiter Klasse; in jedem Wagen gibt es zwölf Abteile mit je sechs Sitzplätzen. In den meisten D-Zügen kann man sich einen Platz reservieren lassen. Außerdem hat der Zug einen 20 Postwagen, einen Gepäckwagen und einen Speisewagen, aber keinen Schlafwagen, denn er kommt schon um 19.06 in Dortmund an, fährt also nicht mehr über Nacht.

einfach (here) one way
hin und zurück round trip

der Bahnsteig, –e platform
die Sperre, –n gate
das Gleis, –e track
planmäßig scheduled, according to plan
voraussichtlich probably
Verspätung haben to be late (not on schedule)
heißt es it is announced
die Kante, –n the edge
das Abteil, –e compartment
der Dampf steam
je (here) each, apiece
das Gepäck baggage
speisen to dine

PETER BICHSEL

Peter Bichsel (born 1935 in Luzern) is a Swiss writer whose short stories, though simple in vocabulary and syntax, are highly sophisticated images of the human condition. They are sometimes tragicomic, often witty, and always poignant and touching.

Ein Tisch ist ein Tisch

Ich will von einem alten Mann erzählen, von einem Mann, der kein Wort mehr sagt, ein müdes Gesicht hat, zu müd zum Lächeln und zu müd, um böse zu sein. Er wohnt in einer kleinen Stadt, am Ende

der Straße oder nahe der Kreuzung. Es lohnt sich fast nicht, ihn zu
beschreiben, kaum etwas unterscheidet ihn von andern. Er trägt
einen grauen Hut, graue Hosen, einen grauen Rock und im Winter
den langen grauen Mantel, und er hat einen dünnen Hals, dessen
Haut trocken und runzelig ist, die weißen Hemdkragen sind ihm ₅
viel zu weit.

Im obersten Stock des Hauses hat er sein Zimmer, vielleicht war er
verheiratet und hatte Kinder, vielleicht wohnte er früher in einer
andern Stadt. Bestimmt war er einmal ein Kind, aber das war zu
einer Zeit, wo die Kinder wie Erwachsene angezogen waren. Man ₁₀
sieht sie so im Fotoalbum der Großmutter. In seinem Zimmer sind
zwei Stühle, ein Tisch, ein Teppich, ein Bett und ein Schrank. Auf
einem kleinen Tisch steht ein Wecker, daneben liegen alte Zeitungen
und das Fotoalbum, an der Wand hängen ein Spiegel und ein Bild.

Der alte Mann machte morgens einen Spaziergang und nachmittags ₁₅
einen Spaziergang, sprach ein paar Worte mit seinem Nachbarn,
und abends saß er an seinem Tisch.

Das änderte sich nie, auch sonntags war das so. Und wenn der
Mann am Tisch saß, hörte er den Wecker ticken, immer den Wecker
ticken.   ₂₀

Dann gab es einmal einen besonderen Tag, einen Tag mit Sonne,
nicht zu heiß, nicht zu kalt, mit Vogelgezwitscher, mit freundlichen
Leuten, mit Kindern, die spielten—und das Besondere war, daß
das alles dem Mann plötzlich gefiel.

Er lächelte.   ₂₅

„Jetzt wird sich alles ändern", dachte er. Er öffnete den obersten
Hemdknopf, nahm den Hut in die Hand, beschleunigte seinen
Gang, wippte sogar beim Gehen in den Knien und freute sich. Er
kam in seine Straße, nickte den Kindern zu, ging vor sein Haus, stieg
die Treppe hoch, nahm die Schlüssel aus der Tasche und schloß ₃₀
sein Zimmer auf.

Aber im Zimmer war alles gleich, ein Tisch, zwei Stühle, ein Bett.
Und wie er sich hinsetzte, hörte er wieder das Ticken. Und alle
Freude war vorbei, denn nichts hatte sich geändert.

Und den Mann überkam eine große Wut.   ₃₅

Er sah im Spiegel sein Gesicht rot anlaufen, sah, wie er die Augen
zukniff; dann verkrampfte er seine Hände zu Fäusten, hob sie und
schlug mit ihnen auf die Tischplatte, erst nur einen Schlag, dann
noch einen, und dann begann er auf den Tisch zu trommeln und
schrie dazu immer wieder: ₄₀

„Es muß sich ändern, es muß sich ändern!"

---

die Kreuzung, –en intersection
es lohnt sich nicht it doesn't pay
unterscheiden to distinguish
der Hals, ⸚e neck
die Haut, ⸚e skin
runzelig shriveled up
der Hemdkragen, – shirt collar
im obersten Stock on the top floor

der Teppich, –e rug

das Vogelgezwitscher twittering of birds

der Knopf, ⸚e button
beschleunigen to accelerate
in den Knien wippen to walk with a spring
zunicken (*with dat.*) to nod at

die Wut anger
rot anlaufen to turn red
zukneifen to squeeze shut
verkrampfen to tighten
die Faust, ⸚e fist
trommeln to drum

Und er hörte den Wecker nicht mehr. Dann begannen seine Hände
zu schmerzen, seine Stimme versagte, dann hörte er den Wecker
wieder, und nichts änderte sich.

„Immer derselbe Tisch", sagte der Mann, „dieselben Stühle, das
Bett, das Bild. Und dem Tisch sage ich Tisch, dem Bild sage ich 5
Bild, das Bett heißt Bett, und den Stuhl nennt man Stuhl. Warum
denn eigentlich? Die Franzosen sagen dem Bett ‚li‘, dem Tisch
‚tabl‘, nennen das Bild ‚tablo‘ und den Stuhl ‚schäs‘, und sie
verstehen sich. Und die Chinesen verstehen sich auch."

„Weshalb heißt das Bett nicht Bild", dachte der Mann und lächelte, 10
dann lachte er, lachte, bis die Nachbarn an die Wand klopften und
„Ruhe" riefen.

„Jetzt ändert es sich", rief er, und er sagte von nun an dem Bett
„Bild".

„Ich bin müde, ich will ins Bild", sagte er, und morgens blieb er oft 15
lange im Bild liegen und überlegte, wie er nun dem Stuhl sagen
wolle, und er nannte den Stuhl „Wecker".

Er stand also auf, zog sich an, setzte sich auf den Wecker und
stützte die Arme auf den Tisch. Aber der Tisch hieß jetzt nicht
mehr Tisch, er hieß jetzt Teppich. Am Morgen verließ also der 20
Mann das Bild, zog sich an, setzte sich an den Teppich auf den
Wecker und überlegte, wem er wie sagen könnte.

> Dem Bett sagte er Bild.
> Dem Tisch sagte er Teppich.
> Dem Stuhl sagte er Wecker.
> Der Zeitung sagte er Bett.   25
> Dem Spiegel sagte er Stuhl.
> Dem Wecker sagte er Fotoalbum.
> Dem Schrank sagte er Zeitung.
> Dem Teppich sagte er Schrank.
> Dem Bild sagte er Tisch.   30
> Und dem Fotoalbum sagte er Spiegel.

Also:

Am Morgen blieb der alte Mann lange im Bild liegen, um neun
läutete das Fotoalbum, der Mann stand auf und stellte sich auf den 35
Schrank, damit er nicht an die Füße fror, dann nahm er seine Kleider
aus der Zeitung, zog sich an, schaute in den Stuhl an der Wand,
setzte sich dann auf den Wecker an den Teppich und blätterte den
Spiegel durch, bis er den Tisch seiner Mutter fand.

Der Mann fand das lustig, und er übte den ganzen Tag und prägte 40
sich die neuen Wörter ein. Jetzt wurde alles umbenannt: Er war

---

schmerzen to hurt
versagen to fail

die Franzosen the French
French: lit bed
    table table
    tableau picture
    chaise chair
die Chinesen the Chinese

überle'gen to meditate

stützen to put

läuten to ring

blättern to page, leaf through
sich etwas einprägen to memorize something
wurde umbenannt was renamed

jetzt kein Mann mehr, sondern ein Fuß, und der Fuß war ein Morgen und der Morgen ein Mann.

Jetzt könnt ihr die Geschichte selbst weiterschreiben. Und dann könnt ihr, so wie es der Mann machte, auch die anderen Wörter austauschen: 5

> läuten heißt stellen,
> frieren heißt schauen,
> liegen heißt läuten,
> stehen heißt frieren,
> stellen heißt blättern. 10

So daß es dann heißt:

Am Mann blieb der alte Fuß lange im Bild läuten, um neun stellte das Fotoalbum, der Fuß fror auf und blätterte sich auf den Schrank, damit er nicht an die Morgen schaute.

Der alte Mann kaufte sich blaue Schulhefte und schrieb sie mit den 15 neuen Wörtern voll, und er hatte viel zu tun damit, und man sah ihn nur noch selten auf der Straße.

blau blue
das Heft, –e notebook

Dann lernte er für alle Dinge die neuen Bezeichnungen und vergaß dabei mehr und mehr die richtigen. Er hatte jetzt eine neue Sprache, die ihm ganz allein gehörte. 20

die Bezeichnung, –en designation

Hie und da träumte er schon in der neuen Sprache, und dann übersetzte er die Lieder aus seiner Schulzeit in seine Sprache, und er sang sie leise vor sich hin.

hie und da now and then
träumen dream
überset'zen to translate

Aber bald fiel ihm auch das Übersetzen schwer, er hatte seine alte Sprache fast vergessen, und er mußte die richtigen Wörter in seinen 25 blauen Heften suchen. Und es machte ihm Angst, mit den Leuten zu sprechen. Er mußte lange nachdenken, wie die Leute zu den Dingen sagen.

das Lied, –er song
vor sich hin to himself
schwerfallen to prove difficult

> Seinem Bild sagen die Leute Bett.
> Seinem Teppich sagen die Leute Tisch. 30
> Seinem Wecker sagen die Leute Stuhl.
> Seinem Bett sagen die Leute Zeitung.
> Seinem Stuhl sagen die Leute Spiegel.
> Seinem Fotoalbum sagen die Leute Wecker.
> Seiner Zeitung sagen die Leute Schrank. 35
> Seinem Schrank sagen die Leute Teppich.
> Seinem Tisch sagen die Leute Bild.
> Seinem Spiegel sagen die Leute Fotoalbum.

Und es kam so weit, daß der Mann lachen mußte, wenn er die Leute reden hörte. 40

Er mußte lachen, wenn er hörte, wie jemand sagte:

„Gehen Sie morgen auch zum Fußballspiel?" Oder wenn jemand sagte: „Jetzt regnet es schon zwei Monate lang." Oder wenn jemand sagte: „Ich habe einen Onkel in Amerika."

Er mußte lachen, weil er all das nicht verstand.

Aber eine lustige Geschichte ist das nicht. Sie hat traurig ange-   5 **lustig**   funny
fangen und hört traurig auf.   **traurig** sad

Der alte Mann im grauen Mantel konnte die Leute nicht mehr verstehen, das war nicht so schlimm.

Viel schlimmer war, sie konnten ihn nicht mehr verstehen.

Und deshalb sagte er nichts mehr.   10

Er schwieg,
sprach nur noch mit sich selbst,
grüßte nicht einmal mehr.

Analysis

168 The Position of Dependent Infinitives

The two German sentences

    Er brauchte sie heute nicht anzurufen.   He did not have to call her up today.
    Er versprach, sie heute nicht anzurufen.   He promised not to call her up today.

seem to have the same structure, but they don't. After **brauchte**, there is no pause, but after **versprach**, the speaker stops for a split second before he goes on to **sie heute nicht anzurufen.** The pause creates the impression that the infinitive phrase which follows is something like a dependent clause —an "infinitive clause." If the two sentences above are changed from the past tense to the perfect, the second one shows a syntactical pattern we have tried to avoid until now.

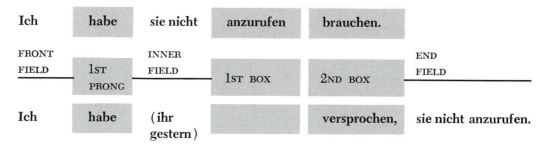

This diagram shows: The infinitive depending on **brauchen** stands in the first box of the second prong, but if this same infinitive depends on **versprechen** it stands in the end field, together with the syntactical units that belong to it.

The difference between the old pattern and the new one is just as striking if we change from verb-second to verb-last position.

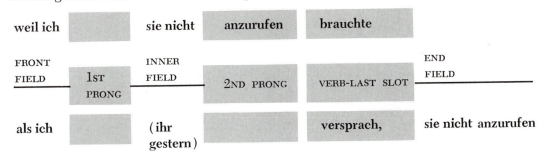

The diagram shows again: The infinitive depending on **versprechen** stands in the end field. *This end field cannot be started until the preceding clause has been completed.*

In the following paragraphs we shall discuss which infinitives belong in the second prong and which belong in the end field.

169 Second-Prong Infinitives

The most important group of verbs that are used with an infinitive in the second prong are the modals and **brauchen** (see **69**). Though **brauchen** has a dependent infinitive with **zu**, it behaves like the modals: the participle following the infinitive is **brauchen,** not **gebraucht.**

> **Ich habe sie heute nicht anrufen können.**
> **Ich habe sie heute nicht anzurufen brauchen.**

However, the modals and **brauchen** are not the only verbs that are used with a second-prong infinitive. There are others, of which some govern an infinitive with **zu** and some an infinitive without **zu.**

Second-Prong Infinitives without **zu**

LERNEN

The infinitives depending on **lernen** all take the second-prong position of **kennen** in **kennenlernen,** but only **kennenlernen** is spelled as one word.

lesen lernen	gehen lernen
schreiben lernen	fahren lernen
kochen lernen	Auto fahren lernen

Sie lernt jetzt fahren.	, weil sie jetzt fahren lernt.
Sie hat schon kochen gelernt.	, weil sie schon kochen gelernt hat.
Ich habe sie schon kennengelernt.	, weil ich sie schon kennengelernt habe.

NOTE: Though **lernen** is used with an infinitive without **zu,** it does not behave like a modal. If it did, **kochen gelernt hat** in the example above would have to be replaced by [hat kochen lernen].

BLEIBEN

The infinitives used most frequently with **bleiben** are **liegen, stehen,** and **sitzen.** As long as **liegen** means literally *lying,* **sitzen** *sitting,* and **stehen** *standing,* they are written separately.

Dieser Baum kann hier stehen bleiben.	This tree can stay here.
Du brauchst noch nicht aufzustehen, du kannst noch etwas liegen bleiben.	You don't have to get up yet; you can stay in bed for a while.
In Deutschland dürfen die Herren sitzen bleiben, wenn die Dame des Hauses ins Wohnzimmer kommt.	In Germany, the gentlemen may stay seated when the lady of the house comes into the living room.

Usually, however, these combinations are used with nonliteral meanings and are spelled as one word. **Stehenbleiben** then means *to stop,* **liegenbleiben** means *to be left behind (forgotten),* and **sitzenbleiben** means *not to find a husband* or *not to be promoted into the next higher class in school.*

Der Hut ist gestern abend hier liegengeblieben.

Meine Uhr ist gestern abend stehengeblieben.

Kein Mädchen möchte gerne sitzenbleiben.

Fritz ist schon wieder sitzengeblieben.

GEHEN AND FAHREN

German **gehen** is frequently used with an infinitive which denotes some routine activity like **essen, schlafen, baden, schilaufen,** and others.

Wir gehen jetzt essen.

Wir wollen morgen schwimmen gehen.

Wir gehen jetzt schlafen.

Er ist schon schlafen gegangen.

Wir wollen morgen schilaufen gehen.

The verb **spazieren** can mean *to promenade.* Today it is mostly used in **spazierenfahren** (*to go for a ride*) and in **spazierengehen** (*to go for a walk*).

Wir sind gestern spazierengefahren.

Wir sind gestern spazierengegangen.

Warum gehen wir nicht etwas spazieren?

Observe again that **gehen** and **fahren** do not behave like modals. If they did, **gegangen** and **gefahren** in the above examples would have to be replaced by **gehen** and **fahren.**

HÖREN AND SEHEN

In the English sentence *I heard him come, him* is the object of the governing verb *heard* and at the same time the subject of the infinitive *come*. The corresponding German sentence **Ich hörte ihn kommen** shows the same relation: the **ihn** is at the same time the object of **hörte** and the subject of **kommen**. In both languages, the dependent infinitive is used without *to* or **zu**.

When used in this pattern, **hören** and **sehen** do behave like modals: their past participles are **hören** and **sehen**, not **gehört** and **gesehen**.

> **Ich habe ihn nie nach Hause kommen hören.**
> **Ich habe ihn kommen sehen.**
> **Das habe ich kommen sehen.**

LASSEN

The verb **lassen** is one of the most frequently used German verbs. It occurs with two different basic meanings: (1) *to leave* and (2) *to cause*.

1. **lassen** *to leave* (*behind*)
> **Ich habe meinen Mantel zu Hause gelassen.**
> **Ich hätte meinen Mantel nicht zu Hause lassen sollen.**

In combination with **hängen, liegen, stehen** (used like **kennen** in **kennenlernen**), **lassen** also means *to leave*. In this case the participle is either **lassen** or **gelassen,** but we advise you to use only **lassen.**

> **Ich habe meinen Mantel zu Hause hängenlassen.**
> **Ich habe mein Buch zu Hause liegenlassen.**
> **Ich habe meinen Schirm** (*umbrella*) **zu Hause stehenlassen.**

2. **lassen** *to cause*

Many languages have a special set of verbs to express the idea "to cause something to happen." One such causative verb is English *to fell a tree* and German **einen Baum fällen,** both meaning "to make a tree fall." But the old method of deriving *to fell* and **fällen** from *to fall* and **fallen** by changing the vowel is now obsolete. Instead, colloquial English expresses the idea of causation by using a variety of auxiliary verbs all followed by either the infinitive or the participle of some other verb.

> Mother makes me brush my teeth every morning.
> She let us go to the movies last night.
> They had Smith build them a house.
> They had their house built by Smith.
> I got him to change his mind.

German, for all practical purposes, has only one "live" causative verb: **lassen.**

When used as a causative, **lassen** behaves like a modal, that is, the participle is **lassen,** not **gelassen;** it is always used with a dependent infinitive of some other verb; it always expresses the idea that the grammatical subject of **lassen** causes somebody to do something. If the subject of the dependent infinitive is mentioned (which is not always the case) it appears in the accusative, as in

    Ich sehe ihn kommen   I see him come

which expresses the two ideas

    Ich sehe ihn

and

    Er kommt

so that **ihn,** as mentioned above, is the direct object of **sehen** and at the same time the subject of **kommen.** Unfortunately, some of the constructions found with **lassen** are totally alien to English and cannot be imitated in English. The following constructions appear regularly. We will describe each of them, and we advise you to memorize each sentence printed in a shaded box.

(a) The inner field contains only the subject of the dependent infinitive, but note that this subject now appears in the accusative. The form **lassen** itself can be the participle used in the perfect. It can also be the infinitive depending on a modal.

Wir lassen ihn gehen. (subject of **gehen: ihn**)	We'll let him go.

Wir haben ihn gehen lassen. (**lassen** is participle)	We've let him go.
Wir müssen ihn gehen lassen. (**lassen** is infinitive)	We have to let him go.
Wir haben ihn gehen lassen müssen. (**müssen** is participle; **gehen** and **lassen** are infinitives)	We had to let him go.
Wir wollen morgen den Arzt kommen **lassen.** (**lassen** is infinitive)	Tomorrow we intend to call the doctor.

(b) The inner field again contains the subject of the dependent infinitive (again in the accusative), but this time followed by an accusative object of that infinitive. So you have two accusatives, one the subject and one the object, both preceding the infinitive.

Lassen Sie mich erst meinen Kaffee trinken. (subject of **trinken: mich;** object of **trinken: meinen Kaffee**)	Let me first drink my coffee.

Lassen Sie mich den Wagen schnell waschen, wenn Sie Zeit haben, Herr Doktor.
Let me quickly wash your car, if you have the time, Doctor.

Er will die Briefe heute abend zu Hause schreiben. Sollen wir ihn die Schreibmaschine mit nach Hause nehmen lassen?
He wants to write the letters at home tonight. Shall we let him take the typewriter home?

Please observe that in English constructions of this type, the subject precedes and the object follows the infinitive. That is the difference between *He wanted his daughter to eat* and *He wanted to eat his daughter.* In German, both the subject and the object (in that order) precede the infinitive.

Mein Mann läßt mich keinen Mercedes kaufen.
   (**mich** is subject and **keinen Mercedes** is object of **kaufen**)

(c) The subject of the infinitive depending on **lassen** is suppressed. Some trained or professional person (physician, mechanic, roofer, waiter, etc.) is implied as the subject. The dependent infinitive is preceded by its direct object.

Wir lassen unseren Wagen waschen.	We have (somebody) wash our car.

Wir haben unseren Wagen waschen lassen. — We had (somebody) wash our car.

Wir müssen unseren Wagen waschen lassen. — We must let (somebody) wash our car.

Wir haben unseren Wagen schon wieder waschen lassen müssen. (subject of **waschen** suppressed, **waschen** depends on the infinitive **lassen**; **müssen** is participle) — We had to have our car washed again.

(d) The subject of the dependent infinitive is again suppressed. The accusative object of the infinitive precedes again. But this time the accusative object is itself preceded by a personal dative (often reflexive) denoting the person for whose benefit some other person (not mentioned) is doing something.

Ich lasse ihm ein Haus bauen.	I have (someone) build him a house.
Ich lasse mir ein Haus bauen.	I have (someone) build me a house.

Sie hat sich eine Perücke machen lassen.
She had (somebody) make her a wig.
(She had a wig made.)

Wir lassen ihr Blumen ins Krankenhaus schicken.
We are requesting (the florist) to send her flowers to the hospital.

Könnten Sie mir eine Tasse Kaffee aufs Zimmer bringen lassen?
Could you have (somebody) bring me a cup of coffee to my room?

Ich muß mir die Haare schneiden lassen.
I must have (somebody) cut my hair.

Please observe that the use of possessive adjectives is avoided in this construction.

(e) The suppressed subject of the infinitive is reintroduced in the form of a prepositional **von**-phrase. In this highly frequent construction the infinitive is preceded by a personal dative, a **von**-phrase subject, and an accusative object:

Wir lassen   uns   von Meyer   ein Haus   bauen!

We have Meyer build us a house.

or by a personal dative, an accusative object, and a **von**-phrase subject:

Wir lassen   uns   das Haus   von Meyer   bauen.

We have our house built by Meyer.

The difference between the two sequences depends on news value.

Ich lasse mir immer die Haare von meiner Frau schneiden.
I always have my wife cut my hair.

Er läßt sich von niemandem etwas sagen.
He won't let anybody tell him anything.

(f) The infinitive is preceded by a **von**-phrase subject. This subject is preceded by an accusative object, frequently a reflexive.

Ich lasse mein Kind nicht von Dr. Meyer operieren.
I won't let my child be operated on by Dr. Meyer.

Ich lasse mich von meiner Frau ver-   I let my wife spoil me.
wöhnen.

Sie läßt sich von ihrem Mann ver-   She lets her husband spoil her.
wöhnen.

Note that you can turn all the sentences mentioned in (c) above into sentences such as these simply by adding a **von**-phrase subject. In most of the sentences mentioned you can interpret **lassen** either as permission or as request. Thus, in the last shaded sentence, it is not just a question of giving written consent to an operation, but of asking Dr. Meyer to do it for a fee.

Second-Prong Infinitives with **zu**

SCHEINEN

The verb **scheinen,** when meaning *to seem,* is used, like **brauchen,** with a second-prong infinitive. It behaves like a subjective modal and occurs only in the present and in the past.

> **Er scheint zu schlafen.**
> **Er schien nicht gut geschlafen zu haben.**

HABEN

The verb **haben** must be mentioned in this context because it is frequently followed by an infinitive with **zu** which *looks* like a second-prong infinitive. Actually, these infinitives usually follow **etwas, nichts, viel,** and **wenig.** The following combinations are used like one single object of **haben:**

etwas zu tun	etwas zu essen
nichts zu tun	nichts zu essen
viel zu tun	viel zu essen
wenig zu tun	wenig zu essen

> **Wenn ich nur nicht soviel zu tun hätte!**
> **Gestern hatten wir kaum etwas zu tun.**
> **Hast du etwas zu trinken im Hause?**

This same construction is frequently found after verbs like **mitbringen** and **kaufen.**

> **Kannst du mir etwas zu lesen mitbringen?**
> **Kannst du mir etwas zu lesen kaufen?**

SEIN

The verb **sein** can be used with a second-prong infinitive provided that the subject of **sein** is the same as the object of the infinitive. English uses this construction in sentences like

> He was easy to find.   **Er war leicht zu finden.**

The English use of the passive infinitive after *to be* cannot be imitated in German.

> He was not to be found.   **Er war nicht zu finden.**

170 End-Field Infinitives

As can be seen from the following examples, the word order of the elements (objects, time phrases, place phrases, etc.) belonging to an end-field infinitive is the same as that found in the inner field preceding a second-prong infinitive.

Ich brauche   **ihn heute nicht**   **anzurufen.**

Ich habe versprochen,   **ihn heute nicht**   **anzurufen.**

All elements in the main clause preceding the infinitive clause take their usual position.

FRONT FIELD	1ST PRONG	INNER FIELD	2ND PRONG	END FIELD
Ich	**habe**	ihr leider	**versprochen,**	sie heute nicht anzurufen.

As long as only the infinitive with **zu** occupies the end field, it is not separated by a comma.

Es fing an zu regnen.

In all other cases a comma is necessary, not only to indicate the pause which separates such infinitive clauses from the preceding part of the sentence, but also to avoid ambiguity.

Er behauptet schon wieder, in Paris gewesen zu sein.
Er behauptet, schon wieder in Paris gewesen zu sein.

The Group anfangen

The following verbs are frequently used with end-field infinitives:

anfangen	to begin
aufhören	to stop, cease
behaupten	to claim
hoffen	to hope
vergessen	to forget
versprechen	to promise
versuchen	to try

In the sentence

Ich habe ihr gestern versprochen, sie heute anzurufen

the subject of **versprechen** is the same as the subject of the end-field infinitive.

The Group **befehlen**

The following verbs all take a personal *dative object* which is the same as the subject of the infinitive clause that follows it.

befehlen	to give an order to somebody
empfehlen	to make a recommendation to somebody
erlauben	to give permission to somebody
helfen	to give help to someone in doing something
raten	to give somebody advice
verbieten	to forbid someone to do something
vorschlagen	to make a suggestion to somebody

Mein Arzt riet mir, einmal an die See zu fahren.

Darf ich Ihnen vorschlagen, einmal einen Mosel zu versuchen?

The End-Field Infinitive after Predicate Adjectives

The following predicate adjectives are frequently used with end-field infinitives:

bereit	ready		**froh**	glad
erstaunt	astonished		**schön**	nice
glücklich	happy			

Sie wissen doch, daß ich immer bereit gewesen bin, Ihrem Mann zu helfen.

Warum sind Sie denn so erstaunt, mich hier zu sehen?

Inge war froh, ihren Mann endlich wiedersehen zu dürfen.

Replacement of Prepositional Objects

Verbs which take a prepositional object frequently replace this complement with a **da**-compound which anticipates an infinitive phrase in the end field (see **141**).

Ich denke ja gar nicht daran,

Du weißt doch, daß ich gar nicht daran denke,

Ich habe ja nie daran gedacht,

Du weißt doch, daß ich nie daran gedacht habe,

} **den Meyer zu heiraten.**

171 um . . . zu, ohne . . . zu, statt . . . zu

We have already used infinitives with **um . . . zu** in the end-field position. The same construction is possible with **ohne . . . zu** and **statt** (**anstatt**) **. . .**

zu. All of these infinitives appear most frequently in either end-field or front-field position.

> **Er fuhr nach Afrika, um dort einen Roman zu schreiben.**
> **Er fuhr nach München, ohne seine Frau mitzunehmen.**
> **Er fuhr nach Afrika, statt zu Hause zu bleiben.**
> **Statt zu Hause zu bleiben, fuhr er nach Afrika.**

English uses an infinitive as the equivalent of the **um . . . zu** forms (*in order to write a novel*), but for the **ohne . . . zu** and **statt . . . zu** forms, English must use the gerund (*without taking his wife along; instead of staying at home*).

In the above examples, the subject of the infinitive clause is the same as the subject of the main clause. If there is a different subject, the infinitive constructions must be replaced by dependent clauses.

um . . . zu	damit
ohne . . . zu	ohne daß
statt . . . zu	statt daß

> **Wir bleiben zu Hause, um endlich einmal arbeiten zu können.**
> **Wir bleiben zu Hause, damit mein Mann endlich einmal arbeiten kann.**

172 hin and her

Hin and **her** are both directional adverbs denoting motion. **Hin** indicates motion away from the speaker or the speaker's position, **her** refers to motion toward the speaker.

hin and her as Verbal Complements

Hin and **her** can both be used by themselves as complements of certain verbs denoting various methods of traveling or change of location.

Thus a person told to visit his father immediately might say:

> **Ich fahre (gehe, reise) sofort hin**

or he might say:

> **Ich werde sofort hinfahren.**
> **Ich bin sofort hingefahren.**
> **Ich brauche nicht sofort hinzufahren.**
> **Ich weiß nicht, ob ich sofort hinfahren kann.**

The father might say:

> **Mein Sohn ist sofort hergekommen.**
> **Kannst du sofort herkommen?**

hin and her with Adverbs of Place and of Time

Since **hin** implies no specific goal and since **her** implies no specific point of origin, they are frequently found after more specific terms like **da, dort, hier,** and after prepositional phrases expressing goal or origin.

> Wer hat dich denn hierhergebracht?
> Du willst sofort zum Flughafen? Wer bringt dich denn dahin?
> Im nächsten Dorf gibt es ein Hotel? Wie weit ist es denn bis dahin?—
>   Zehn Kilometer. Wir kommen gerade daher (dorther, von dorther).

Her may also be used with a temporal meaning.

> Das ist ein alter Freund von mir. Den kenne ich noch *von der Schule her.*
> Den kenne ich noch *von früher her.*
> Gestern abend waren wir im Theater. *Vor*her haben wir im Regina gegessen, und *nach*her waren wir bei Schmidts.

Hin may be used as a predicate adjective meaning *gone* or *beyond repair.*

> Alles ist hin.

Vorhin is an adverb of time meaning *just a little while ago.*

> Vorhin hat Rosemarie angerufen.

hin and her Following wo

In many cases, the use of **her** and **hin** stems from the "splitting" of **wohin** and **woher.**

> Wohin *gehst* du denn?
> Wo gehst du denn *hin?*
> Wo willst du denn *hin?*
> Wo ist er denn *hin*gegangen?
> Wo *du* hingehst, da will ich *auch* hin.
> Woher *kommen* Sie denn?
> Wo kommen *Sie* denn her?
> Wo kann *der* denn hergekommen sein?
> Wo hast du denn den neuen *Mantel* her?

The unseparated **wohin** and **woher** are today slightly literary in character. They *may* be used in conversation, but the separated forms are heard much more frequently.

hin and her Preceding Another Verbal Prefix

Certain English compound verbs have developed special meanings which are apt to trap a foreigner. It is, for instance, a surprise to a German-speaking person to find out that *he threw in the towel* cannot always be replaced by *he threw the towel in.*

In German, the verbal prefixes **ein-, unter-, auf-,** and **aus-,** if used without **hin-** or **her-,** are apt to develop nonliteral meanings. To express a strictly *spatial* meaning **hinein-** or **herein-, hinunter-** or **herunter-, hinauf-** or **herauf-, hinaus-** or **heraus-** must be used.

For example, **untergehen** may mean not only *to sink,* but also *to come to an end, to vanish, to perish.* Note the difference between

> **Die Inkakultur ging unter**   The Inca civilization vanished

and

> **Er ist schon hinuntergegangen.**   He has already gone down.

Compare also:

> **Das Licht ging aus.**   The light went out.
> **Wir sind ausgegangen.**   We went out (theater, restaurant, etc.).
> **Wir sind hinausgegangen.**   We went out (of a room).

There are no definite rules governing the use of **hin-** and **her-** in these cases, but in general it can be said that verbs with **hin-** and **her-** in the complement have a strictly spatial meaning, whereas verbs with the simple complements **ein-, unter-, auf-,** and **aus-** tend to have figurative meanings.

> **Kommst du mit dem Geld aus?**
> Can you get along with the money you have?

> **Er kam heraus.**
> He came out (of a room).

> **Ich konnte mit meinem VW den Mercedes nicht einholen.**
> With my VW I could not catch up with the Mercedes.

> **Hast du die Zeitung schon hereingeholt?**
> Have you brought the paper in yet?

> **Die Sonne ging auf.**
> The sun rose.

> **Wollen Sie bitte in den zweiten Stock hinaufgehen?**
> Would you please go up to the third floor?

> **Wir haben Sie im Hotel Zeppelin untergebracht.**
> We've put you up at the Hotel Zeppelin.

> **Ihre Koffer habe ich schon hinunterbringen lassen.**
> I've already had your suitcases taken down.

hin and her in "Prepositional Brackets"

The sentence

> **Wir fuhren durch den Panamakanal**

expresses the idea

We went through the Panama Canal.

In order to strengthen the feeling of spatial motion, the preposition **durch** can be reinforced by adding the verbal complement **hindurch**.

Wir fuhren *durch* **den Panamakanal** *hindurch.*

This **durch . . . hindurch** acts as a prepositional bracket enclosing the noun. Other frequently used brackets are:

Er kam *aus* **dem Haus** *heraus.*
Er ging *in* **das Haus** *hinein.*
Er stieg *auf* **den Turm** (*tower*) *hinauf.*

Frequently **her,** without a preposition, forms the second bracket; it then expresses continuous motion.

Er lief hinter mir her.
Er lief neben mir her.
Er lief vor mir her.

This tendency to "bracket" is so strong in German that it is found even in such syntactical units as **von Berlin aus** (*from Berlin*); **von da an** (*from then on*); **von mir aus** (*as far as I'm concerned*).

173 Comparison of Adjectives and Adverbs

Forms of the Comparative and the Superlative

Both German adjectives and adverbs form their comparative and superlative forms by adding **-er** and **-(e)st** to the stem, parallel to the English pattern in *fast, fast-er, fast-est.*

schnell, schneller, schnellst-

The English patterns *interesting, more interesting, most interesting,* and *quickly, more quickly, most quickly* are not possible in German.

interessant, interessanter, interessantest-

Helena Rubinstein
macht Sie schöner

The **-e-** in the superlative forms is added whenever the **-st-** ending alone would be hard to pronounce—for example, **weitest-, ältest-, kürzest-.** An exception is the superlative form of **groß.**

>   **groß, größer, größt-**

Many monosyllabic adjectives add an umlaut in both the comparative and superlative.

alt, älter, ältest-	old
arm, ärmer, ärmst-	poor
hart, härter, härtest-	hard
jung, jünger, jüngst-	young
kalt, kälter, kältest-	cold
kurz, kürzer, kürzest-	short
lang, länger, längst-	long
oft, öfter, öftest-	often
schwarz, schwärzer, schwärzest-	black
stark, stärker, stärkst-	strong

Adjectives ending in **-el** and **-er** lose the **-e-** in the comparative.

>   **dunkel, dunkler, dunkelst-**
>   **teuer, teurer, teuerst-**

The adjective **hoch** replaces the **-ch** by a silent **-h-** in the comparative:

>   **hoch, höher, höchst-**

and the adjective **nah** changes the silent **-h** to a **-ch-** in the superlative.

>   **nah, näher, nächst-**

Gut and **viel** have irregular forms:

>   **gut, besser, best-**
>   **viel, mehr, meist-**

and the adverb **gern,** which has no comparative and superlative forms of its own, substitutes the forms of the adjective **lieb.**

>   **gern, lieber, liebst-**

Superlatives cannot be used without an ending; therefore the superlative forms above are followed by hyphens.

Use of Comparison

In comparisons implying equality, **so . . . wie** is used.

>   **Er ist so alt wie ich.**
>   **Er ist nicht so alt wie ich.**
>   **Er ist so schnell gekommen, wie er nur kommen konnte.**

If the comparison expresses inequality, the comparative form of the adjective is used, followed by **als.**

> **Er ist älter als ich.**
> **Er kann nicht älter sein als ich.**
> **Er ist älter, als ich dachte.**

As *attributive adjectives,* comparative and superlative forms are treated like any other adjective; that is, they add normal adjective endings to the **-er** and **-st** suffixes:

> **Einen interessanteren Roman habe ich nie gelesen.**
> **Ein interessanteres Buch habe ich nie gelesen.**
> **Heute ist der längste Tag des Jahres.**

As *adverbs,* comparative forms do not take an ending, and superlative forms always use the pattern **am** (adjective) **-sten.**

> **Mit deinem Mercedes kommen wir bestimmt schneller nach München als mit meinem VW-Bus.**
> **Können Sie mir sagen, wie ich am schnellsten zum Flughafen komme?**
> **Da nehmen Sie am besten ein Taxi.**

As *predicate adjectives,* comparative forms do not take an ending. Superlatives use attributive forms preceded by an article if a noun can be supplied; otherwise they follow the **am** (adjective) **-sten** pattern.

> **Meyers finde ich ja ganz nett, aber Schmidts sind doch netter.**
> **Von seinen drei Töchtern ist Ingrid zwar die intelligenteste, aber nicht die schönste (Tochter).**
> **Ich reise ja sehr gerne, aber zu Hause ist es doch am schönsten.**

Some Special Forms

1. A few comparatives are used with reference to their opposites. For example,

> **Wir haben längere Zeit in Berlin gewohnt**

means: we did not live there a long time, but longer than a short time. Similarly, **eine ältere Dame** (*an elderly lady*) does not mean that the lady is old, but that she is no longer young.

2. To express a high degree of a certain quality, German can use **höchst** as the equivalent of English *most.* Observe the degrees:

Das war ganz interessant.	(quite *interesting*)
Das war interessant.	(*interesting*)
Das war sehr interessant.	(*very* interesting)
Das war aber höchst interessant.	(*most* interesting)

3. Where English repeats the comparative to indicate an increase in degree, German uses **immer** with the comparative.

It was getting warmer and warmer.   **Es wurde immer wärmer.**

174 The Rhetorical **nicht**

If a speaker asks for a positive confirmation of a statement he makes, he adds *don't you?*, *aren't you?*, *haven't you?* and so on, in English and **nicht?** or **nicht wahr?** in German.

Du warst doch gestern abend mit Inge im Kino, nicht?
You and Inge were at the movies last night, weren't you?

This rhetorical **nicht** can be moved toward the front of the inner field if the statement is transformed into a rhetorical question. The normal question

Warst du gestern abend mit Inge im Kino?

thus becomes the rhetorical

Warst du nicht gestern abend mit Inge im *Kino*?

This rhetorical **nicht** appears only in yes-or-no questions. It is never stressed; it is always followed by the stress point of the sentence; and if followed by **ein,** it cannot be replaced by **kein.** An affirmative answer to such rhetorical questions can be either **Ja** or **Doch.** However, even though the speaker always expects a confirmation, the answer can, of course, also be **Nein.**

Haben Sie nicht einen Bruder?   You have a brother, don't you?
Answer: *Ja, Doch,* or *Nein.*

Haben Sie keinen Bruder?   Don't you *have* a brother?
Answer: *Doch* or *Nein,* but never *Ja.*

Haben Sie einen Bruder?   Do you have a brother?
Answer: *Ja* or *Nein,* but never *Doch.*

Further examples:

Warum hast du denn den *Meyer* nicht besucht?
(Real question; stress point precedes *nicht.*)

Hast du den Meyer letzte Woche *nicht* besucht?
(Real question; *nicht* is stressed.)

Hast du nicht letzte Woche den *Meyer* besucht?
(Rhetorical question; stress point follows unstressed *nicht.*)

175 Numbers over 100; Decimals; Ordinal Numbers; Fractions

100	hundert (einhundert)	600	sechshundert
101	hunderteins	1.000	tausend (eintausend)
102	hundertzwei	7.625	siebentausendsechshundertfünfundzwanzig
110	hundertzehn	1.000.000	eine Million
121	hunderteinundzwanzig	2.000.000	zwei Millionen
200	zweihundert	1.000.000.000	eine Milliarde (*one billion*)

Note that German uses periods where English uses commas: 2.325.641. Conversely, in *decimal numbers,* German uses commas where English uses periods.

0,3	null komma drei
12,17	zwölf komma siebzehn
6,5342	sechs komma fünf drei vier zwei

German *ordinal numbers* are attributive adjectives.

der erste	der neunzehnte
der zweite	der zwanzig*ste*
der *dritte*	der einundzwanzig*ste*
der vierte	der dreißig*ste*
der fünfte	etc.
der sechste	
der siebte	
etc.	

To make a figure indicate an ordinal number, German uses a period.

der 4. Juli   the Fourth of July

NOTE:

Heinrich I. (Heinrich der Erste)
Friedrich Wilhelm IV. (Friedrich Wilhelm der Vierte)
Er war ein Sohn Friedrichs II. (Friedrichs des Zweiten)

Series are expressed as follows:

1. erstens		5. fünftens
2. zweitens		6. sechstens
3. drittens		7. siebtens
4. viertens		etc.

„Erstens bin ich zu alt, und zweitens bin ich zu müde."

Fractions:

die Hälfte, –n	das Sechstel, –
das Drittel, –	das Siebtel, –
das Viertel, –	etc.
das Fünftel, –	

Halb can be inflected.

> **Ich hätte gerne ein halbes Pfund Butter.**

All other fractions are uninflected.

> **Ich hätte gerne ein viertel Pfund Butter.**
>
> ½   **ein halb**   ¾   **drei viertel**
> ⅓   **ein drittel**   ⅞   **sieben achtel**

176 Time

In *colloquial* German, the following terms are used to tell time.

8.00 Uhr	acht Uhr	8.30 Uhr	halb neun
8.05 Uhr	fünf nach acht	8.35 Uhr	fünf nach halb neun
8.10 Uhr	zehn nach acht	8.40 Uhr	zehn nach halb neun
8.15 Uhr	viertel nach acht	8.45 Uhr	dreiviertel neun; viertel vor neun
8.20 Uhr	zwanzig nach acht	8.50 Uhr	zehn vor neun
8.25 Uhr	fünf vor halb neun	8.55 Uhr	fünf vor neun

In a railway station or an airport, the following pattern is used:

0.10 Uhr	null Uhr zehn (12:10 A.M.)	20.05 Uhr	zwanzig Uhr fünf (8:05 P.M.)
8.05 Uhr	acht Uhr fünf (8:05 A.M.)	24.00 Uhr	vierundzwanzig Uhr (midnight)

177 Word Formation: Nouns Derived from Adjectives

German, like English, has a number of suffixes which can be used to derive nouns from adjectives.

The Suffix -e

A number of adjectives may be changed into feminine nouns by adding the suffix -e and by umlauting when possible. These nouns correspond in meaning to English nouns in *-th* (*strong, strength; long, length*), *-ness* (*weak, weakness; great, greatness*), or *-ty* (*brief, brevity*).

breit	die Breite	breadth
groß	die Größe	greatness; size
hart	die Härte	hardness
heiß	die Hitze	heat
hoch	die Höhe	height
kalt	die Kälte	cold(ness) *
kurz	die Kürze	shortness, brevity

* But *cold* in the medical sense: **die Erkältung.**

lang	die Länge	length
nah	die Nähe	nearness, proximity
schwach	die Schwäche	weakness
stark	die Stärke	strength
still	die Stille	peacefulness, calm, quiet
warm	die Wärme	warmth

The Suffixes -heit, -keit, -igkeit

Many feminine abstract nouns, also corresponding to English derivatives in
-ity and *-ness,* can be formed by adding one of these three suffixes; they form
their plurals in **-en.** Feel free to use the nouns listed, but do not try to invent
your own: they may not exist. Of high frequency are the formations in **-keit**
added to derivatives in **-bar, -ig,** and **-lich,** and formations in **-igkeit** added
to **-los.**

	dunkel	die Dunkelheit	darkness
	frei	die Freiheit	freedom
	gesund	die Gesundheit	health
	krank	die Krankheit	sickness
	möglich	die Möglichkeit	possibility
	müde	die Müdigkeit	tiredness
	neu	die Neuheit	newness, novelty
		die Neuigkeit	news
	schön	die Schönheit	beauty
	sicher	die Sicherheit	security
	vergangen	die Vergangenheit	past
	wahr	die Wahrheit	truth
	wahrscheinlich	die Wahrscheinlichkeit	probability
	wirklich	die Wirklichkeit	reality
	zufrieden	die Zufriedenheit	contentment
	unfähig	die Unfähigkeit	inability
	unzufrieden	die Unzufriedenheit	discontent
	unsicher	die Unsicherheit	insecurity
der Freund, –e	freundlich	die Freundlichkeit	friendliness
der Hof, ⸚e	höflich	die Höflichkeit	politeness
der Mensch, –en	menschlich	die Menschlichkeit	humaneness
die Sache, –n	sachlich	die Sachlichkeit	objectivity,
(thing, fact, cause)	(objective)		matter-of-factness
sterben	sterblich	die Sterblichkeit	mortality
	unsterblich	die Unsterblichkeit	immortality
die Hoffnung	hoffnungslos	die Hoffnungslosigkeit	hopelessness
der Schlaf	schlaflos	die Schlaflosigkeit	sleeplessness, insomnia
der Dank	dankbar	die Dankbarkeit	gratitude

halten	haltbar	die Haltbarkeit	durability
(to last, to hold up)	(durable)		
teilen	teilbar	die Teilbarkeit	divisibility
(to divide)	(divisible)		
	unteilbar	die Unteilbarkeit	indivisibility
	(indivisible)		

Note the following special cases:

die Kindheit	childhood
die Menschheit	mankind
die Flüssigkeit	liquid
die Seltenheit	rarity
die Einheit	unit, unity
die Einigkeit	accord, being of one mind, unity
einig	in agreement, in accord
vereinigt	united
die Vereinigten Staaten	the United States
einsam	lonely
die Einsamkeit	loneliness, solitude
einzeln	single (apart from the rest)
die Einzelheit	detail
einzig	single, unique, sole
einfach	simple
die Einfachheit	simplicity

Exercises

A. Express in German. All German sentences must contain a form of **lassen.**

SEE
ANALYSIS
169
(pp. 363-369)

1. That leaves me cold.
2. Why didn't you leave your books at home?
3. I don't want to let him take me home. (Use reflexive pronoun plus **von ihm.**)
4. He has his letters written by his wife. (Use reflexive pronoun plus **von seiner Frau.**)
5. You shouldn't let him go to Africa.
6. I must get myself a haircut.
7. Why don't you have your hair cut?
8. He went downtown to get a haircut.
9. She has left her coat here again.
10. You should leave her in peace.
11. We are having a house built in Cologne. (Use reflexive pronoun.)
12. We want to have Overbeck build us a house. (Use reflexive pronoun plus **von Over-beck.**)
13. I wish we had had Overbeck build us a house. (Use reflexive pronoun plus **von Over-beck.**)

B. Restate the following sentences in the perfect.

1. Ich blieb oft vor Alis Haus stehen.
2. Er riet mir, an die Nordsee zu fahren.
3. Wir ließen gestern abend den Arzt kommen.
4. Er braucht *doch* nicht nach Berlin zu fahren.
5. Wir dachten damals daran, nach Köln zu ziehen.
6. Um sechs Uhr gingen wir essen.
7. Der Müller war einfach nicht zu verstehen.
8. Gegen Abend fing es dann an zu regnen.
9. Er lief aus dem Haus, ohne ein Wort zu sagen.

SEE
ANALYSIS
168–170

(pp. 362-371)

C. Transform the following pairs of sentences into sentences with **ohne . . . zu** or **statt . . . zu.** Note that the negation disappears in the infinitive phrase.

> **Er fuhr nach Afrika. Er nahm seine Frau nicht mit.—ohne**
> **Er fuhr nach Afrika, ohne seine Frau mitzunehmen.**

1. Er fuhr nach Afrika. Er blieb nicht zu Hause.—statt
2. Er schrieb ihr einen Brief. Er rief sie nicht an.—statt
3. Er war in Berlin. Er hat mich nicht besucht.—ohne
4. Er kaufte sich einen Wagen. Er hatte nicht das Geld dafür.—ohne

SEE
ANALYSIS
171

(pp. 371-372)

D. Express in German.

1. Where is your coat?—Oh, I left it (hanging) at the Meyers.
2. Perhaps you should try once more to call him.
3. This chair you must leave (standing) in the living room.
4. Now the apartment is in order again at last.—No, you have forgotten to put the chairs back into the living room.
5. He finally had to promise his wife not to go to Africa again.
6. He suggested that my wife should go to the North Sea this year.

E. Change to comparatives.

> **Ich bin nicht so alt wie er. Er ist älter als ich.**

1. Unser Haus ist nicht so groß wie eures.
2. Bei uns ist es nicht so kalt wie bei euch.
3. Glas ist nicht so hart wie ein Diamant.
4. Der Weg war nicht so lang wie ich dachte. (Use **kurz.**)
5. Ich gehe nicht so oft ins Theater wie du.
6. Amerikanisches Bier ist nicht so stark wie deutsches Bier.
7. Von Köln bis Bonn ist es nicht so weit wie von Frankfurt bis Bonn.
8. Ich kann nicht so viel essen wie du.

SEE
ANALYSIS
173

(pp. 375-378)

9. Bier trinke ich nicht so gerne wie Wein.
10. Ich finde ihn nicht so interessant wie seine Frau.

F. Change the adjectives to superlatives.

SEE
ANALYSIS
173
(pp. 375-378)

1. Hans hat viel getrunken.
2. München ist eine schöne Stadt.
3. In München gibt es gutes Bier.
4. Im Dezember sind die Tage kurz.
5. Im Juni sind die Tage lang.
6. Der 21. Juni ist ein langer Tag.
7. Giganto ist ein starker Mann.
8. Ich wäre jetzt gern in Deutschland.
9. In Alaska ist das Obst teuer.

G. Read aloud.

21   32   43   54   65   76   87   98   109   120
213   324   435   546   657   768   801
1.003   1.011   1.021   1.248   1.349   1.492
14.395   128.473   847.666   3.492.716
0,3   7,43   421,7   3.746,4519
DM 0,25   DM 7,50   DM 300,00   DM 16.500,00   DM 1.000.000.000
$\frac{2}{3}$ $\frac{3}{4}$ $\frac{7}{8}$ $\frac{15}{16}$ $\frac{19}{20}$

H. Try to guess the meaning of the following compounds and derivatives.

1. der Telefonanruf
2. der Gastarbeiter
3. auf baldiges Wiedersehen
4. der Besuch der alten Dame
5. das sogenannte Böse
6. eine achtstellige Zahl
7. eine alte Handschrift aus dem fünf-
   zehnten Jahrhundert
8. ein Bilderbuch
9. ich kann es nicht mit Bestimmtheit sagen
10. wir haben eine Dreizimmerwohnung
11. die Zusammenarbeit
12. Reden ist Silber, Schweigen ist Gold
13. ein eintüriges Badezimmer
14. du stehst mir im Wege
15. mit größter Zufriedenheit
16. das Zwischendeck eines Schiffes
17. nur ein Wunschbild
18. in Wirklichkeit war es anders
19. weitblickend
20. wir hatten in diesem Monat viele Aus-
    gaben
21. Gepäckannahme
22. Gepäckausgabe
23. ein weitgereister Mann
24. die Handschuhe
25. die Krankenpflegerin
26. die Natürlichkeit
27. Meyers sind sehr gastfreundlich
28. handgearbeitet
29. das Rädchen
30. mein Fahrrad
31. er ist ein Tunichtgut
32. die Wanduhr
33. ich trinke auf deine Gesundheit
34. er kennt keine Müdigkeit
35. bei Beginn des Konzertes
36. eine große Frage
37. jemandem einen Befehl geben
38. eine dreitägige Konferenz
39. wir sehen uns täglich
40. die Jungsozialisten
41. der damalige Bürgermeister
42. das ist gesetzlich verboten
43. Professorenphilosophie für Philosophie-
    professoren

44. die Schönheitskönigin
45. das macht ein guter Arbeiter mit Leichtigkeit
46. wir werden in Kürze bei euch sein
47. für Meyer sind tausend Mark eine Kleinigkeit

48. die Weimarer Republik hatte eine Hunderttausendmannarmee
49. die Haltestelle der Straßenbahn
50. jede Tür hat einen Griff

I. Imagine that you have a cousin, Hildegard, who lives in Munich and knows no English. You want to visit her during your stay in Germany, so you decide to write her a letter while on the train to Koblenz. For lack of anything profound to say (owing to your lack of that kind of German), you tell her about your adventures at the Frankfurt railroad station.

The envelope, incidentally, would be addressed as follows:

> Fräulein
> Hildegard Pfeilguth
> 8 München 13
> Tengstraße 40

After duly addressing her as "Liebe Hildegard!" you tell her that you arrived in Frankfurt after a good flight. Because you wanted to go to Koblenz on the same day, you took a taxi to the station. Then you describe what happened to you until the Hellas-Express finally started moving.

You sign off by writing: Viele herzliche Grüße
>   Dein John

Basic Vocabulary

abfahren	to depart, to take off	das Dach, ⸚er	roof
allerdings	however	damit' (*conj.*)	so that
sich ändern	to change	deshalb	therefore, for that
es ändert sich	things are changing		reason
sich anziehen	to get dressed	der Dezember	December
aufgehen	to rise (sun, moon);	der Dollar, –s	dollar
	to open	zwanzig Dollar	twenty dollars
aufschließen	to unlock	der Dritte	the third (of a series)
zuschließen	to lock	das Drittel, –	the third (fraction)
auskommen (mit)	to get along (with)	dünn	thin
bereit	ready	einholen	to catch up with
beschreiben	to describe	erhalten	to receive
besetzen	to occupy	erlauben	to permit
besetzt	busy (telephone)	der Februar	February
besonder–	special	fernsehen	to watch TV
besonders (*adv.*)	especially	sich freuen	to be glad
beweisen	to prove	ich freue mich	I am glad
die Bibliothek', –en	library	frieren	to freeze; to be cold
das Brötchen, –	hard roll	ich friere	I am cold

es gibt	there is (are) available
gefallen (*with dat.*)	to please
das gefällt mir	I like that
das Gesicht, –er	face
die Hälfte, –n	half
der Handschuh, –e	glove
hart	hard
Haupt–	main
der Hauptbahnhof, ¨-e	the main station
hin	away (from the speaker); all gone
sich hinsetzen	to sit down
ich setze mich hin	I'll sit down
die Hose, –n	trousers, pants
hübsch	pretty
irgendwo	somewhere
die Karte, –n	map, ticket
die Rückfahrkarte, –n	round-trip ticket
die Landkarte, –n	map
die Klasse, –n	class
das Knie, – (pl. pronounced with two syllables, **Kni-e**, the -e serving as ending)	knee
das Komma, –s	comma
lächeln	to smile
die Lust	pleasure
Lust haben zu	to want to
lustig	funny, cheerful
die Milliarde, –n	billion
die Million, –en	million
der Motor', –en	motor
nachher	afterward
der Norden	the north
die Nordsee	the North Sea
nördlich	northern
der Osten	the east
östlich	eastern
der Süden	the south
südlich	southern
der Westen	the west
westlich	western
ohne ... zu (*plus inf.*)	without (doing)
jemanden operieren	to operate on somebody
der Pfennig, –e	penny
reparieren	to repair
richtig	correct, right
der Rock, ¨-e	jacket, coat; skirt

der Schlag, ¨-e	beat, stroke
schlimm	bad, disagreeable
schießen	to shoot
der Schuß, ¨-e	shot
die Schreibmaschine, –n	typewriter
sich setzen	to sit down
ich setze mich	I'll sit down
der Spiegel, –	mirror
statt (anstatt) ... zu (*with inf.*)	instead of (doing)
stehenbleiben	to stop
der Teil, –e	part
das Telegramm, –e	telegram
das Testament, –e	testament; last will
tippen	to type
die Treppe, –n	staircase
trocken	dry
üben	to practice
unbedingt	by all means
unterbringen	to find living quarters (for somebody)
untergehen	to go down; to perish
unterkommen	to find living quarters (for oneself)
verlangen	to demand
versuchen	to try
jemanden verwöhnen	to spoil somebody (by being too good to him)
voll	full, filled
von ... her	from (an earlier time); from (the direction of)
vorhin	a while ago
vorschlagen	to suggest
der Vorschlag, ¨-e	suggestion
weshalb	for what reason; why

Additional Vocabulary

die Flut, –en	flood		reservieren	to reserve
der Herzog, ⸚e	duke		der Schalter, –	(ticket) window
lochen	to punch (ticket)		der Tabak, –e	tobacco
die Lokomoti′ve, –n	locomotive		der Zaun, ⸚e	fence
die Partei′, –en	party (political)		die Zeile, –n	line (of print)
Prozent′, –e	per cent			

Strong and Irregular Verbs

abfahren, fuhr ab, ist abgefahren, er fährt ab	to depart, to take off
sich anziehen, zog sich an, hat sich angezogen, er zieht sich an	to get dressed
aufgehen, ging auf, ist aufgegangen, er geht auf	to rise (sun, moon); to open
aufschließen, schloß auf, hat aufgeschlossen, er schließt auf	to unlock
auskommen, kam aus, ist ausgekommen, er kommt aus	to get along
beschreiben, beschrieb, hat beschrieben, er beschreibt	to describe
beweisen, bewies, hat bewiesen, er beweist	to prove
erhalten, erhielt, hat erhalten, er erhält	to receive
fernsehen, sah fern, hat ferngesehen, er sieht fern	to watch TV
frieren, fror, hat gefroren, er friert	to freeze; to be cold
gefallen (*with dat.*), gefiel, hat gefallen, er gefällt	to please
schießen, schoß, hat geschossen, er schießt	to shoot
stehenbleiben, blieb stehen, ist stehengeblieben, er bleibt stehen	to stop
unterbringen, brachte unter, hat untergebracht, er bringt unter	to find living quarters (for someone)
untergehen, ging unter, ist untergegangen, er geht unter	to go down; to perish
unterkommen, kam unter, ist untergekommen, er kommt unter	to find living quarters (for oneself)
vorschlagen, schlug vor, hat vorgeschlagen, er schlägt vor	to suggest

126.
cann
statter
volks
fest

25.9.-6.10.1971

mit
Landwirtschaftlichem
Hauptfest
25.9.-3.10.1971

Großfeuerwerk
Mittwoch, 29.9.,
21.30 Uhr

Stuttgart
Deutschland
Germany
Allemagne

Unit 12 Reflexive Verbs—Imperatives

Patterns

[1] selbst and selber Emphasizing a Noun or Pronoun

Das weiß ich *selbst*.

Ihrer Frau geht es also wieder gut—und wie geht es Ihnen *selbst?*

Ich wollte eigentlich meine Sekretärin nach Berlin schicken; aber ich fahre doch besser *sel*ber hin.

Ich habe nicht mit Meyers Frau gesprochen; ich habe mit ihm *selbst* gesprochen.

Meine Frau hat nicht mit ihm gesprochen; ich habe *selbst* mit ihm gesprochen.

SEE
ANALYSIS
178
(pp. 411-412)

VARIATIONS

Insert **selbst** or **selber** in the appropriate place in the second
clause of each sentence.

Das kann ich erst glauben, wenn ich es gesehen habe.

Nein, das hat mir nicht seine Sekretärin gesagt, das habe ich von ihm gehört.

Seine Frau ist ja ganz nett, aber mit Meyer will ich nichts zu tun haben.

[2] Special Cases of selbst and selber

*Da*bei brauchst du mir nicht zu helfen; das kann ich *sel*ber machen.

Was, du mußt den Kleinen immer noch *füt*tern? Kann der sich denn noch nicht *sel*ber füttern?

Muß *ich* denn jeden Morgen zuerst aufstehen? Kannst du dir das Frühstück nicht mal *sel*ber machen?

SEE
ANALYSIS
179
(p. 412)

VARIATIONS

To each of the following sentences, add another one containing
selber in the meaning of *without help*.

> **Du brauchst doch die Kinder nicht zu baden.**
> **Die können sich doch selber baden.**

Danke, du brauchst mir den Koffer nicht zu tragen.

Du brauchst doch den Kaffee nicht zu kochen.

Warum soll *ich* denn deiner Frau schreiben?

Er *selbst* ist ja ganz *nett;* aber mit seiner *Mut*ter könnte ich nicht *le*ben.

Andere hat er ge*rett*et, aber sich *selbst kann* er nicht retten.

Uns schickt Vater jeden Sonntag in die *Kirche,* aber er *sel*ber bleibt zu *Hause* und liest die Zeitung.

VARIATIONS

To each of the following sentences add a contrasting statement containing **selbst**.

> **Ihre *Mutter* hat *viel* Geld; aber sie *selbst* hat *kein* Geld.**

Mein *Mann* ist schon *oft* in Paris gewesen.

Uns schickt Vater jeden Sommer an die *Nord*see.

Ihre *Schwes*tern haben alle ge*hei*ratet.

Ich habe *sel*ber kein Geld.

Ich habe *auch* kein Geld.

Ich kann dir nicht helfen; ich habe *sel*ber viel zu tun.

VARIATIONS

To each of the following sentences add a statement containing **selber** meaning **auch**.

Wir können euch kein Geld schicken. Wir haben _____.

Ich bin gar nicht erstaunt, daß Sie meinen Mann nicht verstehen. Ich kann _____

_____.

Er hat immer gelacht, wenn ich Detektivromane gelesen habe; und jetzt _____

_____.

[3] **selbst, sogar, auch** meaning *even*

Selbst (sogar, auch) *das* ist ihm zu viel.

Selbst (sogar, auch) Herrn Dr. Müller, der sonst immer da ist, konnte ich diesmal nicht sprechen; der war auch in Berlin.

In Berlin sprechen selbst (sogar, auch) kleine Kinder Deutsch.

Selbst (sogar, auch) von seiner Frau läßt er sich nichts sagen.

SEE
ANALYSIS
180
(p. 413)

VARIATIONS

Restate the following sentences, starting with **selbst**.

> **Seiner Frau hat er auch nichts davon gesagt.**
> **Selbst (sogar, auch) seiner Frau hat er nichts davon gesagt.**

In Rom hat es heute *auch* geschneit.

Mein Vater raucht *auch* nicht mehr.

Tante Amalie will *auch* nicht mehr ins Museum.

[4] Reciprocal Pronouns

Note the use of **sich, einander,** and **gegenseitig.**

Hat er sie zuerst geküßt oder hat sie ihn zuerst geküßt?—Das weiß ich nicht. Aber es ist sicher, daß sie sich geküßt haben.

„Sie fühlten sich zueinander hingezogen. Sie schauten sich in die Augen; ihre Lippen trafen sich, und ihre Herzen hatten einander gefunden." (Ingelheim)

So, ihr wollt beide ein Wochenendhaus bauen? Wenn ihr euch gegenseitig helft, dann ist das gar nicht so schwer.

Im Sommer hat er ihr das erste Mal geschrieben, und seitdem schreiben sie sich jede Woche zweimal, und mindestens einmal im Monat rufen sie sich an.

Heute abend gehe ich mit ihr ins Theater.—Wo triffst du sie denn?—Wir treffen uns am Bahnhof.

SEE
ANALYSIS
181
(p. 413)

[5] Occasional Reflexives

entschuldigen: sich entschuldigen: entschuldigt sein; verzeihen
to excuse: to excuse oneself: to be excused; to pardon

SEE
ANALYSIS
182
(p. 413)

Ich glaube, Sie sitzen auf meinem Platz.
   I think you're sitting in my seat.

Oh, entschuldigen Sie, Sie haben recht.
   Excuse me, you're right.

Oh, Entschuldigung, Sie haben recht.
   Excuse me, you're right.

Oh, ich bitte um Verzeihung.
   I'm sorry. *or* I beg your pardon.

Oh, verzeihen Sie!
   I beg your pardon.

Oh, ich bitte um Entschuldigung.   Oh, Verzeihung!
　　Excuse me.   　　I'm sorry.

Entschuldigen Sie mich einen Augenblick; ich muß mal eben telefonieren.

Entschuldigen Sie, gnädige Frau, daß ich so spät komme.—Sie brauchen sich gar nicht
　　zu entschuldigen, bei dem Regen ist das ja kein Wunder.

Sie kommen allein, Edgar?—Meine Frau läßt sich entschuldigen; sie hat sich erkältet und
　　wollte lieber zu Hause bleiben.

Ich kann ja vieles verstehen; aber daß du mich am Frühstückstisch mit Gisela anredest,
　　das ist nicht zu entschuldigen.

Meyer kommt nicht; er ist entschuldigt, er mußte nach Berlin.

[6] Transitional Reflexives

SEE
ANALYSIS
183–184
(pp. 414-416)

sich verlieben in (with acc.)**: verliebt sein in** (with acc.)
to fall in love with: to be in love with

Er ist verliebt.
In wen hat er sich denn diesmal verliebt?
Er soll sich in seine Lehrerin verliebt haben.
Er soll in seine Lehrerin verliebt sein.
Mit einem verliebten jungen Mann ist nichts Vernünftiges anzufangen.

sich verloben mit: verlobt sein mit
to become engaged to: to be engaged to

Ich höre, die Emma soll sich verlobt haben.
Ich dachte, sie wäre schon lange verlobt. Wer ist denn ihr Verlobter?
Darf ich Ihnen meine Verlobte vorstellen, gnädige Frau?
Ich gratuliere dir zu deiner Verlobung, Deine Emma ist wirklich ein nettes Mädchen.

heiraten: sich verheiraten: verheiratet sein mit
to marry: to get married: to be married to

Ich höre, Sie haben sich verlobt. Wann wollen Sie denn heiraten?
Die jüngste Tochter soll sich auch schon verheiratet haben.
Mit wem ist sie denn verheiratet?
Wann heiratest *du* denn, Monika?—Ich muß erst jemanden *finden*, der mich heiraten will.
Sie soll schon dreimal verheiratet gewesen sein.
Ich brauche eine neue Sekretärin; eine verheiratete wäre mir lieber als eine unverheiratete.

sich scheiden lassen von: geschieden sein
to get a divorce from: to be divorced

Kurz nach dem Krieg ließ sich seine erste Frau von ihm scheiden.
Eine geschiedene Frau hat oft ein schweres Leben.
Anton und Emma waren einmal verheiratet; jetzt sind sie geschieden.

sich umziehen: umgezogen sein
to change (clothes): to have changed (clothes)

Ich muß mich noch umziehen, bevor wir ins Theater gehen.
Ich brauche mich nicht umzuziehen, ich bin schon umgezogen.

But note: **umziehen, zog um, ist umgezogen** *to move*
Ich höre, Sie sind umgezogen.—Ja, wir wohnen jetzt in der Ingelheimer Straße.

sich anziehen: angezogen sein
to get dressed: to be dressed

Hast du den Kleinen schon angezogen?
Der kann sich jetzt schon selbst anziehen; den brauche ich nicht mehr anzuziehen.
Er ist schon angezogen; er hat sich selber angezogen.

sich ausziehen: ausgezogen sein
to get undressed: to be undressed

Als er nach Hause kam, zog er sich schnell aus und legte sich ins Bett.
Heute abend bin ich zu müde, um noch ins Kino zu gehen. Ich bin schon ausgezogen und
    möchte mich nicht noch einmal anziehen.

sich ausruhen: ausgeruht sein
to take a rest: to be rested

Du hast in der letzten Zeit viel zu viel gearbeitet; du solltest dich endlich einmal ausruhen.
Ich habe heute morgen bis zehn geschlafen und bin ganz ausgeruht.
Nach vier Wochen an der Riviera sollte er sich eigentlich gut ausgeruht haben.

sich ausschlafen: ausgeschlafen sein
to get enough sleep: to have had enough sleep

Nächsten Sonntag kann ich mich endlich einmal ausschlafen.
Warum stehst du denn heute so früh auf?—Ich konnte nicht mehr schlafen. Ich bin aus-
    geschlafen.

sich erholen: erholt sein
to get a rest (to recover one's strength): to be recovered

Du bist so überarbeitet. Du solltest einmal irgendwohin fahren und dich ein bißchen er-
    holen.
Ich war vier Wochen an der See und habe mich gut erholt.
Als er aus dem Schwarzwald zurückkam, war er gut erholt.

sich rasieren: rasiert sein
to shave: to have shaved, to be shaved

Natürlich mußt du dich noch einmal rasieren, bevor wir zu Erdmanns gehen.
Aber ich habe mich doch heute schon einmal rasiert.

Wenn du nicht rasiert bist, kannst du in diesem Hotel unmöglich ins Frühstückszimmer gehen.

sich aufregen über (with acc.): **aufgeregt sein**
to get excited (upset) about: to be excited (upset)

Frau Meyer hat über tausend Mark im Kasino verloren, und Meyer hat sich furchtbar darüber aufgeregt.
Warum ist Meyer denn so aufgeregt?—Weil seine Frau schon wieder tausend Mark verloren hat.
Meyer soll furchtbar aufgeregt gewesen sein.
Meyer soll sich furchtbar aufgeregt haben.

sich beruhigen: beruhigt sein
to calm down: to be calmed down

Natürlich ist Meyer sehr aufgeregt, aber wie ich ihn kenne, wird er sich auch wieder beruhigen.
Seine Frau hat ihm versprochen, nie wieder ins Kasino zu gehen.—Na ja, dann kann er ja beruhigt sein.

sich entschließen zu: entschlossen sein zu
to make up one's mind to: to have made up one's mind, to be determined

Lieber Johannes, ich habe mich dazu entschlossen, mich von dir scheiden zu lassen.
Ich bin fest entschlossen, mich von dir scheiden zu lassen.

sich erkälten: erkältet sein
to catch a cold: to have a cold

Bei Niedermeyers gestern abend war es so kalt, daß ich mich erkältet habe.
Hannelore ist auch erkältet. War die auch bei Niedermeyers?

sich gewöhnen an (with acc.): **gewöhnt sein an** (with acc.)
to get accustomed (used) to: to be accustomed (used) to

An das Klima hier in Kairo kann ich mich einfach nicht gewöhnen.
An das Klima bin ich jetzt ganz gewöhnt.

sich überzeugen von: überzeugt sein von
to become convinced of: to be convinced of

Ich habe ihm lange nicht geglaubt, aber jetzt habe ich mich davon überzeugen müssen, daß er recht hat.
Ich bin fest davon überzeugt, daß er recht hat.

sich verändern: verändert sein
to change: to have changed, to be changed

Ich habe ihn fast nicht erkannt, so sehr hat er sich verändert.
Seit dem Tod seiner Frau ist er ganz verändert.

sich vorbereiten auf (with acc.): **vorbereitet sein auf** (with acc.)
to prepare for: to be prepared for

Er macht morgen sein Examen.—Hat er sich auch gut darauf vorbereitet?
Ist er auch gut darauf vorbereitet?

öffnen: sich öffnen: geöffnet sein
to open: to be open

Ich habe die Tür geöffnet.
„Die Natur ist ein Buch mit sieben Siegeln (*seals*), das sich nur dem öffnet, der darin zu
    lesen versteht."
Es ist nur dem geöffnet, der es versteht, darin zu lesen.

schließen: sich schließen: geschlossen sein
to close: to be closed

Ich habe die Tür geschlossen.
Und hinter ihm schloß sich das Tor.
Das Tor war noch geschlossen, als wir ankamen.

VARIATIONS

Change the following actions into states.

Sie hat sich in ihren Lehrer verliebt.
Sie hat sich mit ihm verlobt.
Sie soll ihn geheiratet haben.
Sie hat sich scheiden lassen.

Hast du dich schon angezogen?
Meyer soll sich furchtbar darüber
    aufgeregt haben.
Ich hoffe, du hast dich gut ausgeruht.

Change the following states into action; use the perfect.

An das Klima bin ich schon gewöhnt.
Ich bin davon überzeugt, daß sie gut
    küssen kann.

Mein Mann ist wirklich überarbeitet.
Ist er schon wieder nicht rasiert?

[7] sich setzen, sich stellen, sich legen

sitzen; setzen: sich setzen

SEE ANALYSIS 185 (pp. 416-417)

Wer sitzt denn da bei euch am Tisch?—Den kenne ich auch nicht. Der hat sich einfach
    an unseren Tisch gesetzt.
Nein, unter *diesen* Brief setze ich meinen Namen *nicht*.
Ich wollte mich gerade in die erste Reihe setzen, als ich sah, daß Frau Meier da saß; und
    da habe ich mich in die letzte Reihe gesetzt.

stehen; stellen: sich stellen

Wer steht denn da bei Frau Schmidt? Ist das nicht Dr. Gerhardt?
Diese amerikanischen Cocktailparties machen mich wirklich müde. Ich habe stunden-
    lang stehen müssen und war froh, als ich mich endlich setzen konnte.
Ich habe den Wein auf den Tisch gestellt.

Bitte, gnädige Frau, wie wäre es, wenn Sie sich hier auf diesen Stuhl setzten? Und Sie stellen sich links neben Ihre Frau, Herr Doktor. Und der Kleine kann rechts von Ihrer Frau stehen.—So, und jetzt bitte recht freundlich!

In der Zeitung steht, daß Ingelheim spurlos verschwunden ist.—Auf welcher Seite steht das denn?

liegen; legen: sich legen

Ich hatte mich gerade ins Bett gelegt, als Erich anrief. „Liegst' du etwa schon im Bett?" sagte er.

Ich lag noch nicht lange im Bett, als Erich anrief. „Hast du dich etwa schon ins Bett gelegt?" sagte er.

Wo hast du denn mein Buch hingelegt?—Ich habe es auf deinen Schreibtisch gelegt. Liegt es denn nicht mehr dort?

Köln liegt am Rhein. Wolframs-Eschenbach liegt in der Nähe von Nürnberg.

VARIATIONS

Ich habe den Wein auf den Tisch _____.
Der Wein _____ auf dem Tisch.

Ich habe die Kleine schon in ihren Stuhl _____.
Die Kleine _____ schon in ihrem Stuhl.

Ich habe den Kleinen schon ins Bett _____.
Der Kleine _____ schon im Bett.

Warum hast du dich noch nicht ins Bett _____?
Warum _____ du noch nicht im Bett?

Warum hast du dich denn in die letzte Reihe _____?
Warum _____ Reihe?

[8] Nontransitional Reflexives

SEE
ANALYSIS
186

(p. 417)

jemanden langweilen: sich langweilen: gelangweilt sein
to bore somebody: to be bored: to be bored

Meine Damen und Herren, ich hoffe, ich langweile Sie nicht, aber der Oedipuskomplex ist wirklich ein sehr wichtiges Problem.
Meine Damen und Herren, ich sehe, Sie langweilen sich.
Meine Damen und Herren, ich sehe, Sie sind gelangweilt.

sich bemühen: bemüht sein
to try hard

Gnädige Frau, wir haben uns sehr bemüht, ein Zimmer für Sie zu finden, aber wir haben nichts finden können.
Er behauptet, daß er mich liebt, und er ist sehr bemüht (er bemüht sich sehr), Mama davon zu überzeugen.

jemanden interessieren: sich interessieren für: interessiert sein an (with dat.)
to interest somebody: to be interested in: to be interested in (*acquiring or doing*)

Picasso interessiert mich nicht.
Interessieren Sie sich nicht für moderne Tänze?
An einem Chronometer bin ich nicht interessiert.

jemanden ärgern: sich ärgern über (mandatory reflexive; with acc.)
to annoy somebody: to be annoyed with (*by*)

Der Meyer ist wirklich ein Dummkopf. Ich habe mich gestern abend furchtbar über ihn
    geärgert.
Es ärgert mich, daß Meyer immer zu spät kommt.
Ich ärgere mich auch immer darüber, daß er so spät kommt.

jemanden erinnern an (with acc.): **sich erinnern an** (with acc.)
to remind somebody: to remember

Du mußt mich morgen unbedingt daran erinnern, daß ich den Mehrens anrufen muß.
Ihre Frau hat gerade angerufen; sie wollte Sie daran erinnern, daß Sie heute abend Gäste
    haben.—Oh das erinnert mich, ich muß noch Zigarren kaufen; Dr. Mehrens raucht
    keine Zigaretten.
Ich bin Renate Pfeiffer, Herr Professor. Sie erinnern sich sicher nicht mehr an mich,
    aber ich war vor zwanzig Jahren in Ihrem Faust-Seminar.
Oh doch, ich erinnere mich sehr gut an Sie, Fräulein Wilke. Sie kamen immer zehn
    Minuten zu spät.
Daran kann ich mich aber nicht mehr erinnern, Herr Professor.

sich freuen auf (mandatory reflexive; with acc.)
to look forward to

Du kommst doch auch nächsten Samstag zu unserer Party?—Ja, ich freue mich schon
    darauf.

WIR FREUEN UNS AUF
IHREN BESUCH
GEÖFFNET
MO. - FR. 8 - 16ʰ 30

Also, lieber Herr Raschke, wir erwarten Sie am Freitag gegen vier; wir freuen uns sehr auf Ihren Besuch.

sich freuen über (mandatory reflexive; with acc.)
to be pleased with

Und vielen Dank für die Blumen; ich habe mich sehr darüber gefreut.
Vater hat sich sehr darüber gefreut, daß du seinen Geburtstag nicht vergessen hast. Er hat sich sehr über den Wein gefreut.

sich wundern über (mandatory reflexive; with acc.)
to be amazed (surprised) at

Ich habe mich doch gestern abend über den Fritz gewundert. Daß der gar nichts getrunken hat! Früher hat er immer zu viel getrunken.

sich verlassen auf (mandatory reflexive; with acc.)
to rely on

Wenn du den Nolte nach Berlin geschickt hast, kannst du beruhigt sein. Auf den kann man sich verlassen.
Kann ich mich darauf verlassen, daß du um fünf zu Hause bist?

etwas bewegen: sich bewegen
to move something: to move, to be in motion

Ich konnte meine Hand nicht bewegen.
Der Mond bewegt sich um die Erde, und die Erde bewegt sich um die Sonne.
Ich war so müde; ich konnte mich kaum bewegen.

sich eilen: sich beeilen
to hurry

Ich brauche mindestens eine halbe Stunde, um mich umzuziehen.—Kannst du dich nicht mal ein bißchen beeilen (eilen)?
Eilt euch, Kinder, der Vater wartet schon.

sich verfahren: sich verlaufen
to lose one's way driving: to lose one's way walking

Natürlich brauchen wir eine Straßenkarte, sonst verfahren wir uns wieder.
In München kann man sich leicht verlaufen.—Wieso denn? Ich habe mich in München noch nie verlaufen.

NOTE: Do not use **sich vergehen,** which means *to commit a crime.*

etwas umdrehen: sich umdrehen
to turn something around: to turn around

Ich kann den Schlüssel nicht umdrehen, das Schloß muß kaputt sein.
Sie hat sich nach mir umgedreht.

VARIATIONS

Complete the following sentences.

sich ärgern

Hast du _____ heute im Büro wieder _____ müssen?
Über _____ hast du _____ denn heute _____?
Ja, heute habe ich _____ über Meyer geärgert.
Ich glaube, du bist nicht glücklich, wenn du dich nicht _____ kannst.

sich freuen

Ich habe mich sehr _____ gefreut, daß sie gekommen ist. (Use **da**-compound.)
Ich freue mich sehr _____, daß sie morgen kommt. (Use **da**-compound.)

sich verfahren

Wo bleibt er denn? Ob er sich schon wieder _____ hat?
Ich brauche keine Straßenkarte; ich _____ mich nie.

sich umdrehen

Als er mich sah, hat er sich sofort _____.
Aber Anton, du brauchst dich doch nicht immer _____, wenn ein hübsches Mädchen vorbeigeht.

[9] Dative Reflexives

ich stelle mich vor: ich stelle mir vor
to introduce (socially): to imagine

SEE
ANALYSIS
187
(p. 417)

Darf ich mich vorstellen? Ich bin Dr. Ingelheim.
Gnädige Frau, darf ich Ihnen Herrn Dr. Ingelheim vorstellen?
Ich kann mir nicht vorstellen, daß Ingelheim ein guter Soldat gewesen ist.
Ich hatte mir das alles viel leichter vorgestellt.

sich etwas einbilden: eingebildet sein
to imagine (erroneously): to be conceited

Das stimmt doch gar nicht; das bildest du dir nur ein.
Und er hat sich eingebildet, ich wollte ihn heiraten.
Den Erich heirate ich nicht; der ist mir viel zu eingebildet.

sich etwas denken
to imagine something

Du kannst dir gar nicht denken, wie ich mich darauf freue, Dich endlich wiederzusehen.
Ich habe mir gar nichts dabei gedacht, als ich sie fragte, wie es ihrem Mann ginge. Wie konnte ich denn wissen, daß sie geschieden ist?

sich etwas überlegen
to meditate about something

Ich überlege mir oft, ob es nicht besser wäre, wenn wir nach Heidelberg zögen.
Wie wäre es, wenn Sie auch in die Stadt zögen?—Das muß ich mir erst noch überlegen.

sich etwas ansehen: sich etwas anschauen
to look at something

Ich wollte mir den Hitchcock Film eigentlich gar nicht ansehen; aber du kennst ja Tante
    Amalie. Sie interessiert sich nur noch für Hitchcock und Picasso.
Schau dir das an! Da kommt Edith Maschke mit ihrem neuen Freund.—Die hat sich ja
    ganz verändert! Seit wann ist sie denn blond?

VARIATIONS

Complete the following sentences.

Petra freut sich _____ Weihnachten.
Das kann ich _____ nicht vorstellen.
Ich habe _____ noch nicht vorgestellt; ich bin Hans Ingelheim.
Ich kann _____ gar nicht denken, was er _____ dabei gedacht hat.
Das solltest du _____ gut überlegen.
Er soll _____ eingebildet haben, ich wollte _____ heiraten.
Was kann er _____ nur dabei gedacht _____?
Habt ihr _____ schon überlegt, welchen Film _____ euch anschauen
    wollt?

[10] Household Reflexives

SEE
ANALYSIS
188

(pp. 417-418)

Ich putze mir die Zähne.	I am brushing my teeth.
Sie schneidet sich die Haare selber.	She cuts her own hair.
Wo kann man sich hier die Haare schneiden lassen?	Where can you get your hair cut here?
Wir machen uns das Frühstück selber.	We fix our own breakfast.
Willst du dir nicht die Schuhe putzen?	Don't you want to polish your shoes?
Kinder, habt ihr euch schon die Hände gewaschen?	Children, have you washed your hands yet?
Er hat sich den Arm gebrochen.	He broke his arm.
Er hat sich in den Finger geschnitten.	He cut his finger.

[11] Impersonal Reflexives

SEE
ANALYSIS
189

(p. 418)

Es stellte sich heraus, daß Erich das Geld gestohlen hatte.
Es erwies sich, daß das Problem *so* nicht zu lösen war.
Es zeigte sich, daß auch die Elektronen sich um ihre Achse drehen.

PATTERNS

Hol Dir
den Frühling ins Haus...

Worum handelt es sich denn eigentlich?
Es handelt sich um ein wichtiges Problem.
Mein Vater hat mit Diamanten gehandelt.
Wovon handelt dieser Roman denn?
Ich hatte keine Zeit, darüber nachzudenken; ich mußte sofort handeln.

[12] Imperative, du-Form

SEE
ANALYSIS
190–193

(pp. 419-424)

Ruf mich bitte *nicht* vor *acht* an!
Bitte ruf mich *nicht* vor *acht* an!
Aber bitte ruf mich *nicht* vor *acht* an!
Aber ruf mich bitte *nicht* vor *acht* an!
Ruf mich aber bitte *nicht* vor *acht* an!
Aber ruf mich *nicht* vor *acht* an, bitte!

Bitte bring mir doch etwas zu *lesen* mit!
Bring mir doch bitte etwas zu *lesen* mit!
Bring mir doch etwas zu *lesen* mit, *bitte*!
Fahr doch mit uns in den *Schwarz*wald!
Sei mir nicht böse, aber ich muß jetzt gehen.
Sei doch nicht so nervös!

Ruf sie doch noch einmal *an*. Vielleicht ist sie jetzt zu *Hause*.
Bitte ruf sie doch noch einmal *an!*
Ruf sie doch noch mal *an*, bitte!
Bitte sei doch so gut und fahr mich mal eben in die Stadt.
Rede doch nicht so dumm, Anton; du verstehst ja doch nichts davon.
Tu nicht so, als ob du mich nicht gehört hättest.
Sei so gut, Klaus, und trag mir mal meinen Mantel.
Fritzchen, nimm die Finger aus dem Mund!
Lauf doch nicht so schnell, Hans, ich kann ja gar nicht mitkommen.
Fürchte dich nicht; denn ich bin bei dir.

Steh *du* doch mal zuerst auf.
Rede *du* mal mit Meyer, du kennst ihn doch besser als ich.
Bleib *du* doch wenigstens vernünftig.

VARIATIONS

Change the following sentences into **du**-form imperatives; use
doch, doch mal, or **mal** where appropriate.

Ich bringe dir ein Glas Wasser.   Ich gebe dir das Buch morgen.
Ich gehe in den Garten.   Ich nehme mir eine Taxe.
Ich besuche euch in München.   Ich sehe mal nach, ob Meyer schon da ist.

[13] Imperative, **ihr**-Form

SEE
ANALYSIS
190–193

(pp. 419-424)

Kinder, vergeßt nicht, euch die Hände zu waschen.
Bitte vergeßt nicht, euch die Hände zu waschen.
Vergeßt bitte nicht, euch die Hände zu waschen.
Es war schön, daß ihr kommen konntet; besucht uns bald mal wieder.
Seid mir nicht böse. Aber ich muß jetzt wirklich nach Hause.
Also auf Wiedersehen. Und ruft uns an, wenn ihr nach Hause kommt.
Während der Woche haben wir nicht viel Zeit. Aber besucht uns doch mal an einem
    Sonntag!
Geht *ihr* ruhig ins Theater. Ich muß noch arbeiten.
Warum ich sonntags immer zu Hause bleibe? Arbeitet *ihr* einmal jeden Tag zehn
    Stunden, dann wißt ihr warum.

VARIATIONS

Change to **ihr**-form imperatives.

Wir kommen bald wieder.   Wir bringen euch ein paar Blumen mit.
Wir geben doch nicht so viel Geld aus.   Wir lassen uns das Frühstück aufs Zimmer
Wir trinken doch nicht so viel Kaffee.   bringen.
Wir sind euch nicht böse.   Wir bleiben noch ein bißchen hier.

[14] Imperative, **wir**-Form

SEE
ANALYSIS
190–193

(pp. 419-424)

Wo sollen wir denn essen, Rosemarie?—Gehen wir doch mal ins Regina, Klaus, da waren
    wir schon so lange nicht mehr.
Müssen wir denn heute schon wieder zu Müllers?—Natürlich müssen wir.—Also schön,
    fahren wir wieder zu Müllers.
Was, schon wieder Fisch, Maria?—Aber Karl, Fisch ist doch jetzt so billig.—Also gut,
    essen wir wieder Fisch.

VARIATIONS

Change to the **wir**-form, starting with **Schön, ...**

Ich möchte nach München fahren.
Schön, fahren wir doch nach München.

Ich möchte zu Hause bleiben.
Ich möchte heute im Hotel Berlin essen.
Ich möchte heute schwimmen gehen.

[15] Imperative, **Sie**-Form

Bitte, Fräulein, geben Sie mir Zimmer 641.

Seien Sie herzlich gegrüßt von Ihrem Hans Meyer.

Seien Sie vorsichtig, Herr Professor, und überarbeiten Sie sich nicht.

Bitte glauben Sie mir, ich habe alles getan, was ich tun konnte.

Entschuldigen Sie bitte, gnädige Frau; Ihr Ferngespräch nach Hamburg ist da.

Es gibt keine bessere Kamera. Fragen Sie Ihren Fotohändler.

Informieren Sie sich in unserem großen Photo-Katalog.

Lassen Sie sich unser neuestes Modell zeigen.

Wenn Ihnen die starken Zigaretten zu stark und die leichten zu leicht sind, so rauchen Sie PRIVAT, die Zigarette des Mannes von Format.*

Freude am Leben! Wundervolle Urlaubstage, in farbigen Kodakbildern! Und natürlich MARTINI† „on the rocks". Machen Sie Ihren Gästen eine Freude, mit MARTINI, Schluck für Schluck.

SEE
ANALYSIS
190–193
(pp. 419-424)

* **Ein Mann von Format** a man of distinction.
† This does not mean what you think it means. It means vermouth (distilled by Martini) on the rocks.

Und natürlich Martini
„on the rocks".

[16] Impersonal Imperative

SEE
ANALYSIS
190–193

(pp. 419-424)

Alles aussteigen.
Einsteigen bitte.
Bitte einsteigen.
Nicht öffnen, bevor der Zug hält.
Langsam fahren.
Nicht rauchen.
Bitte anschnallen.
Nicht mit dem Fahrer sprechen.
Eintreten ohne zu klingeln.
Nicht stören.
Bitte an der Kasse zahlen.
Nach rechts einordnen.

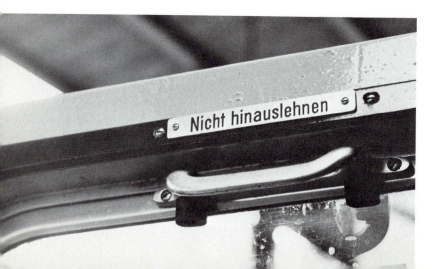

Reading

Ein Wort über deutsche Hotels

Wie überall in der Welt, gibt es in Deutschland teure und billige
Hotels, große und kleine, gute und weniger gute. In den Großstädten
gibt es internationale Hotels, in denen man so komfortabel wohnen
kann wie in internationalen Hotels der ganzen Welt. Im Berlin
Hilton oder im Hotel Berlin, im Frankfurter Hof oder im Hotel **5**
Intercontinental in Frankfurt, im Hotel Vier Jahreszeiten in Hamburg und im Hotel Vier Jahreszeiten in München brauchen Sie kein
Deutsch zu können, um sich Ihr Frühstück aufs Zimmer bringen zu
lassen oder um einen Luftpostbrief nach Chicago aufzugeben. Wenn
Sie aber in einem kleineren Hotel wohnen wollen oder in einer **10**
Pension, oder wenn Sie in einer Kleinstadt oder auf dem Land in
einem Dorfgasthof ein Zimmer haben wollen, dann ist das schon
etwas anderes. Sie können dann natürlich mit den Händen reden,
aber besser ist es doch, wenn Sie Deutsch sprechen. Doch dazu
brauchen Sie ein bißchen Hotel-Jargon. **15**

Wir wollen annehmen, daß Sie in Koblenz übernachten wollen, denn
dorthin haben wir Sie ja mit dem Hellas-Express geschickt. In
Koblenz gibt es etwa 30 Hotels und 25 Gasthöfe und Pensionen. Es
ist nicht immer ganz einfach, den Unterschied zwischen einem Hotel
und einem Gasthof zu sehen. Hotels sind größer als Gasthöfe, und **20**
Gasthöfe sind kleiner als Hotels. (Aber das ist natürlich keine Defi-
nition.) Das größte Hotel in Koblenz hat 120 Betten, der kleinste
Gasthof hat 5 oder 6 Betten. Eine Pension ist etwas, was es in
Amerika nicht gibt. Die meisten Pensionen sind Privathäuser, in
denen man, ganz ähnlich wie in Gasthöfen, übernachten kann und **25**
in denen man Frühstück bekommt. Zum Gasthof gehört noch eine
Gaststätte, ein Restaurant (oft ähnlich wie in England die *neigh-
borhood pubs*), wo man abends hingeht, um ein Glas Wein oder

die Jahreszeit, –en **5**
season

einen Brief aufgeben
10 to mail a letter

die Pension, –en
tourist home
der Gasthof, ̈-e inn

15 der Jargon' pro-
nounced as in French

ein Bier zu trinken. Die „Gaststätten" heißen in vielen Gegenden Deutschlands „Wirtschaften" oder „Wirtshäuser". Auf dem Land haben solche Gasthäuser oft Namen wie „Zum Löwen", „Zum Ochsen", „Zum Goldenen Lamm", „Zum Deutschen Kaiser".

der Löwe, –n lion
der Ochse, –n ox
das Lamm, ̈er lamb

Außer den Hotels, Gasthöfen und Pensionen gibt es in Koblenz auch ₅ eine Jugendherberge mit 540 Betten und einen Campingplatz für etwa 1000 Personen, aber da Sie Ihre erste Nacht in Deutschland weder in einer Jugendherberge noch auf einem Campingplatz verbringen wollen, so gehen Sie in eines der besseren Hotels. In Ihrem Hotelführer haben Sie eins gefunden: Zimmerpreis DM 22,00–26,00, ₁₀ Frühstück DM 3,00, Halbpension DM 30,00–35,00, Vollpension DM 35,00–40,00, und dann heißt es unter „Comfort": *Flw B PB Z G P L T.* Das alles verstehen Sie natürlich erst, wenn Sie unten auf der Seite lesen: T—Zimmertelefon, L—Lift (das normale deutsche Wort für *Lift* ist *Aufzug*), P—Parkplatz, G—Garage (das interes- ₁₅ siert Sie nicht, denn Sie sind ja nicht mit Ihrem eigenen Wagen gekommen), Z—Zentralheizung, PB—Privatbad (von den dreißig Hotels haben nur siebzehn Zimmer mit Bad, und von den Gasthöfen nur drei), B—Bad (das heißt, es gibt ein oder mehrere Bäder, aber diese Bäder gehören nicht zum Zimmer, und man bezahlt zwei ₂₀ oder drei Mark extra dafür), Flw—ganzjährig fließendes warmes Wasser. Vollpension heißt, daß man alle Mahlzeiten im Hotel ißt, bei Halbpension ißt man nur eine Mahlzeit im Hause (entweder Mittag- oder Abendessen). Frühstück ist in vielen deutschen Hotels obligatorisch; d.h., man muß dafür bezahlen, ob man frühstückt oder ₂₅ nicht. Zum Standard-Frühstück in Deutschland gehören Brötchen, Butter, Marmelade und Kaffee oder Tee.

die Jugendherberge, –n youth hostel

der Aufzug, ̈e elevator

das Brötchen, – (hard) roll
die Marmelade, –n any kind of jam
der Gepäckträger, – porter

So, jetzt haben Sie Ihren Reiseführer lange genug studiert; Sie geben dem Gepäckträger, der Ihre Koffer vor den Bahnhof getragen hat,

eine Mark Trinkgeld und nehmen ein Taxi zum Hotel. Der Mann, der Ihnen am Hotel mit Ihrem Gepäck hilft, ist aber kein Gepäckträger, sondern ein Hausdiener. Er bringt Ihre Koffer zum Empfang, und der Mann, der Sie dort empfängt, ist der Portier (oder in manchen größeren Hotels der Empfangschef). 5

Es folgt ein imaginäres Gespräch zwischen Ihnen und dem Portier.

„Ich habe für heute nacht ein Zimmer bestellt."
„Auf welchen Namen, bitte?"
„Ray, aus New York."
„Einen Augenblick, bitte,—und würden Sie inzwischen schon das 10 Anmeldeformular ausfüllen?"
„Sie wollten ein Zimmer mit Bad, Mr. Ray? Leider habe ich nur ein Zimmer mit Dusche, wenn Sie nichts dagegen haben?"
„Das ist mir schon recht. Wie teuer ist denn das Zimmer?"
„26 Mark, plus 15% Bedienung; die Mehrwertsteuer ist eingeschlos- 15 sen."
„Gut. Und gibt es ein Telefon auf dem Zimmer? Ich muß nämlich noch ein paar Ferngespräche führen."
„Aber sicher. Rufen Sie nur die Zentrale an; die Telefonistin verbindet Sie dann. So, hier ist Ihr Schlüssel,—Zimmer 318. Der Aufzug 20 ist hier drüben links, bitte. Das Gepäck lasse ich Ihnen nach oben bringen."

Es gibt keinen Liftboy, sondern es ist ein Aufzug mit Selbstbedienung. Im dritten Stock gehen Sie einen langen Korridor hinunter und suchen Zimmer 318. Nach Zimmer 315 kommt eine Tür 25 mit „H", dann eine mit „D" und dann kommt erst 316. (Statt H und D finden Sie vielleicht auch nur eine Tür mit „00".) Zimmer 318 ist

---

das Trinkgeld, –er tip
der Hausdiener, – bellhop
der Portier, –s desk clerk
der Empfangschef, –s head clerk

anmelden to register;
das Formular, –e form
ausfüllen to fill out

die Dusche, –n shower

bedienen to wait on, serve; **die Bedienung** service charge
die Mehrwertsteuer value added tax
ein Ferngespräch führen to make a long-distance call
die Zentrale, –n switchboard

ganz nett, vielleicht ein bißchen altmodisch, aber doch komfortabel. Am interessantesten finden Sie das Federbett, aber wir müssen Sie warnen: Solche Federbetten sind für die meisten Amerikaner erstens zu warm und zweitens zu kurz; wenn man unter einem Federbett schläft, hat man entweder kalte Füße oder kalte Schultern. Sie 5 klingeln also dem Zimmermädchen und bitten sie, Ihnen statt des Federbettes eine Wolldecke zu bringen. Dann wollen Sie telefonieren; zuerst Köln, und dann Ihre Freundin Barbara, die in Augustdorf bei Detmold wohnt.

die Feder, –n feather
warnen to warn

die Wolle wool

Ferngespräche

Sie nehmen also den Hörer ab, und dann hören Sie die Stimme der Telefonistin: „Zentrale."
„Ja, Fräulein, ich hätte gerne Köln, 20 37 88 (zwo-null, drei-sieben, acht-acht)."
Am Telephon sagt man immer „zwo" statt „zwei." 5
„Köln, 20 37 88—bitte legen Sie wieder auf; ich rufe Sie zurück."
Nach zwei Minuten klingelt das Telefon.
„Die Nummer ist leider besetzt. Soll ich es in ein paar Minuten noch einmal versuchen?"
„Ja, bitte." 10
Fünf Minuten später klingelt es wieder.
„Ihr Gespräch nach Köln. Einen Augenblick, bitte; ich verbinde."
Dann hören Sie am anderen Ende eine Frauenstimme: „Hier bei Doktor Fischer", und weil die Stimme „*bei* Doktor Fischer" sagt, wissen Sie, daß das das Dienstmädchen sein muß. Sie sagen also: 15
„Kann ich bitte Herrn Doktor Fischer sprechen?"
„Darf ich Sie um Ihren Namen bitten?"

(den Hörer) auflegen to put down the receiver

das Dienstmädchen, – maid

„John Ray,—aus New York.“

„Einen Augenblick, bitte, Herr Reh.“

Ihr Gespräch mit Herrn Fischer ist natürlich Ihre Privatsache, und wir wollen es hier nicht abdrucken. Aber nachdem das Gespräch zu Ende ist, sprechen Sie wieder mit der Telefonistin, denn Sie wollen ja Ihre Freundin Barbara auch noch anrufen.   **abdrucken**   to print

„Sagen Sie, Fräulein, kennen Sie Augustdorf bei Detmold?“

„Nein, nie davon gehört; das muß irgendein Dorf sein.“

„Ich hatte den Namen auch noch nie gehört, aber so klein kann es nicht sein, denn die Telefonnummer ist eine Meile lang.“   10 **die Meile, –n**   mile

„Was ist denn die Nummer?“

„05237258.“

„Nein, nein“, lacht die Telefonistin. (Lacht sie über Ihren amerikanischen Akzent oder darüber, daß Sie über deutsche Telefonnummern nicht Bescheid wissen?) „Da haben Sie die Vorwahlnummer mit dazu genommen. Augustdorf ist bestimmt ein Dorf, denn die Nummer ist 258. Die Vorwahl ist 05237. Ihre Kölner Nummer ist mit der Vorwahlnummer noch länger. Köln hat die Vorwahl 0221; das heißt, die Nummer, die ich vorhin gewählt habe, war 0221203788.“   15 **Bescheid wissen**   to know, be informed
    die Vorwahlnummer, –n   area code
    20

“Das wußte ich nicht—unsere amerikanischen Vorwahlnummern haben nur drei Zahlen. Aber versuchen Sie doch jetzt mal Augustdorf.“

„Gut,—und bleiben Sie doch bitte gleich am Apparat.“ Aber Sie haben kein Glück. Die Nummer ist zwar nicht besetzt, aber es antwortet auch niemand. „Da meldet sich leider niemand“, sagt die Telefonistin. „Soll ich es später noch mal versuchen?“   **am Apparat**   on the line
    25
    sich melden   to answer (the phone)

„Nein danke. Ich möchte mir jetzt erst einmal ein bißchen die Stadt ansehen.“

„Dann können Sie es ja von der Post aus noch mal versuchen.“   30

„Gute Idee. Ich will sowieso noch einen Brief aufgeben. Vielen Dank, Fräulein.“

BERTOLT BRECHT

Freundschaftsdienste

Good Turns

Als Beispiel für die richtige Art, Freunden einen Dienst zu erweisen, gab Herr K. folgende Geschichte zum besten. „Zu einem alten Araber kamen drei junge Leute und sagten ihm: ‚Unser Vater ist gestorben. Er

As an example of how to do friends a good turn Mr. K. obliged with the following story. "Three young men came to an old Arab and said: 'Our father has died. He has left us seventeen camels and stipulated in

hat uns siebzehn Kamele hinterlassen und im Testament verfügt, daß der Älteste die Hälfte, der zweite ein Drittel und der Jüngste ein Neuntel der Kamele bekommen soll. Jetzt können wir uns über die Teilung [5] nicht einigen; übernimm du die Entscheidung!' Der Araber dachte nach und sagte: ‚Wie ich es sehe, habt ihr, um gut teilen zu können, ein Kamel zu wenig. Ich habe selbst nur ein einziges Kamel, aber es steht [10] euch zur Verfügung. Nehmt es und teilt dann, und bringt mir nur, was übrigbleibt.' Sie bedankten sich für diesen Freundschaftsdienst, nahmen das Kamel mit und teilten die achtzehn Kamele nun so, daß [15] der Älteste die Hälfte, das sind neun, der Zweite ein Drittel, das sind sechs, und der Jüngste ein Neuntel, das sind zwei Kamele bekam. Zu ihrem Erstaunen blieb, als sie ihre Kamele zur Seite geführt hatten, ein [20] Kamel übrig. Dieses brachten sie, ihren Dank erneuernd, ihrem alten Freund zurück.“

Herr K. nannte diesen Freundschaftsdienst richtig, weil er keine besonderen Opfer [25] verlangte.

his will that the eldest should have half, the second a third, and the youngest a ninth of the camels. Now we can't agree among ourselves on the division: you decide the matter.' The Arab thought about it and said: 'As I see it, you have one camel too few to share them out properly. I've only got one camel myself, but it's at your disposal. Take it and share them out, and [10] give me back only what's left over.'

They thanked him for this good turn, took the camel with them, and then divided the eighteen camels in such a way that the [15] eldest got half—that is, nine—the second a third—that is, six—and the youngest a ninth—that is, two—of the camels.

To their amazement when they had each led their [20] camels aside, there was one over. This they took back to their old friend with renewed thanks.”

Mr. K. called this the right sort of good turn, since it demanded no special sacrifice.

ERICH KÄSTNER

Das Eisenbahngleichnis

Wir sitzen alle im gleichen Zug
und reisen quer durch die Zeit.
Wir sehen hinaus. Wir sahen genug.
Wir fahren alle im gleichen Zug.
Und keiner weiß, wie weit.   [5]

Ein Nachbar schläft, ein andrer klagt,
ein dritter redet viel.
Stationen werden angesagt.
Der Zug, der durch die Jahre jagt,
kommt niemals an sein Ziel.   [10]

das Gleichnis, –se parable

quer durch straight across

klagen to complain

jagen to rush

das Ziel, –e destination

Wir packen aus. Wir packen ein.
Wir finden keinen Sinn.
Wo werden wir wohl morgen sein?
Der Schaffner schaut zur Tür herein
und lächelt vor sich hin.   15

auspacken to unpack
einpacken to pack
der Sinn sense

der Schaffner, –
conductor

Auch er weiß nicht, wohin er will.
Er schweigt und geht hinaus.
Da heult die Zugsirene schrill!
Der Zug fährt langsam und hält still.
Die Toten steigen aus.   20

heulen to howl

Ein Kind steigt aus. Die Mutter schreit.
Die Toten stehen stumm
am Bahnsteig der Vergangenheit.
Der Zug fährt weiter, er jagt durch die Zeit,
und niemand weiß, warum.   25

stumm silent
die Vergangenheit
past

Die I. Klasse ist fast leer.
Ein feister Herr sitzt stolz
im roten Plüsch und atmet schwer.
Er ist allein und spürt das sehr.
Die Mehrheit sitzt auf Holz.   30

feist fat
stolz proud
spüren to feel

die Mehrheit majority
das Holz wood

Wir reisen alle im gleichen Zug
zur Gegenwart in spe.
Wir sehen hinaus. Wir sahen genug.
Wir sitzen alle im gleichen Zug
und viele im falschen Coupé.   35
                                    (1932)

Gegenwart in spe
present-in-the-future
falsch wrong
das Coupé, –s train
compartment

Analysis

178 Emphatic Pronouns

The English reflexive pronouns *myself, yourself, himself,* and so on, sometimes merely repeat, for emphasis, a preceding noun or pronoun. When so
used, they carry the main syntactical stress, but nevertheless they are not
independent syntactical units.

He said it him*self.*
They did it them*selves.*

German cannot repeat a preceding noun or pronoun. Instead, German uses the strongly stressed particles **selbst** or **selber** to emphasize these nouns or pronouns. **Selbst** and **selber** are interchangeable. They always follow the word to be emphasized, either immediately or at the end of the inner field.

Das weiß ich *selbst*.	I know that my*self*.
So! Ihrer Frau geht's gut. Und wie geht's Ihnen *selbst*?	So your wife is fine. And how are you your*self*?
Ich fahre morgen *selbst* nach Berlin.	I am going to Berlin my*self* tomorrow.
Das war der Direktor *selber*.	That was the boss him*self*.

179 Special Cases of **selbst** and **selber**

1. As pointed out, when **selber** is used at the end of the inner field, it frequently assumes the meaning "without help" or "others don't have to."

Du könntest dir das Frühstück auch einmal *selber* machen.	You really could get your *own* breakfast for a change.
Das kann ich doch *selber* machen.	I can do that *myself*.

2. If **selbst** (or **selber**) appears in the front field, contrast intonation is used, and a contrast with others, of whom the opposite statement is true, is implied.

> Sie *selbst* hat kein Geld; aber ihre *Mut*ter hat *viel* Geld.
> Er *selb*er bleibt zu *Hau*se: *uns* schickt er in die *Kir*che.
> Sich *selbst* kann er nicht retten; *an*dere hat er ge*rettet*.

3. If **selbst** (or **selber**) appears in the inner field, it may also be a substitute for **auch** and express the notion "just like others."

> Ich bin *selber* arm, so arm wie du.
> Ich bin *selbst* nicht glücklich, ich bin so unglücklich wie ihr.

180 selbst, sogar, and auch meaning *even*

Selbst, sogar, and **auch,** without stress, may form a syntactical unit with an immediately following stressed word. If so used, they mean *even.*

> **Selbst (sogar, auch)** *das* **ist ihm zu viel.**
>
> **Er** *will* **einfach nicht, und solange jemand nicht** *will,* **kann ihm selbst (sogar, auch)** *Gott* **nicht helfen.**

Compare:

> **Der brave Mann denkt an sich** *selbst* **zu***letzt.* (Schiller)
> A brave man thinks of himself last.

> **Der brave Mann denkt an** *sich,* **selbst zu***letzt.*
> A brave man thinks of himself, even at the very end.

181 Reciprocal Pronouns

Normally, the reflexive plural pronouns can also be used as reciprocal pronouns, and it is not necessary to make a distinction. No one will misunderstand **Sie küßten sich.** This can only mean *They kissed each other,* not *They kissed themselves.*

If it is desirable to express reciprocity, **einander** and **gegenseitig** can be used. **Einander** is literary and replaces the reflexive; **gegenseitig** follows the reflexive.

> **Es waren zwei Königskinder, die hatten einander so lieb.***
> **Wenn ihr euch nicht gegenseitig helft, dann werdet ihr nie fertig.**

182 Occasional Reflexive Verbs

As long as it makes sense, all verbs which take an accusative object are occasionally used with a reflexive object. One such verb, **malen,** was introduced in Unit 9. German **malen** can be used with an accusative noun, with a nonreflexive accusative pronoun, or with an accusative reflexive pronoun.

Ich have zuerst meinen Mann gemalt.	I first painted my husband.
Ich habe zuerst ihn gemalt.	I first painted him.
Und dann habe ich mich gemalt.	And then I painted myself.

Verbs like **malen** are called *occasional* reflexives. They present no syntactical problem. A frequently used verb of this type is **entschuldigen** (see Patterns, pp. 391–392).

---

* First two lines of a folk song.

183 Mandatory Reflexive Verbs

We now introduce an entirely different group of reflexive verbs: the *mandatory* reflexives. These mandatory reflexives can never be used without a reflexive pronoun. The only verb of this type frequently used in colloquial English is *to enjoy oneself*. When used nonreflexively as in *I enjoyed that steak last night*, *to enjoy* means "to derive pleasure from." But the reflexive *to enjoy oneself* means "to have fun." The pronoun *myself*, in this case, is not an object parallel to *that steak*. It is no object at all, but simply a part of the verbal pattern which cannot be left out and which cannot be used together with a noun object. You could not possibly say:

[Thanks for a wonderful evening, Ann. I enjoyed myself and your steaks.]

German has many mandatory reflexive verbs. All of them must be used with a reflexive pronoun, usually the accusatives **mich, dich, uns, euch,** and **sich,** which function (just as the *myself* in *I enjoyed myself*) not as objects but merely as irreplaceable parts of the verbal pattern. Take **sich erkälten** as an example:

Ich habe mich erkältet.	I have caught a cold.
Du hast dich erkältet.	You have caught a cold.
Er hat sich erkältet.	He has caught a cold.
Sie hat sich erkältet.	She has caught a cold.
Wir haben uns erkältet.	We have caught a cold.
Ihr habt euch erkältet.	You have caught a cold.
Sie haben sich erkältet.	They have caught a cold.
Haben Sie sich erkältet, Herr Meyer?	Have you caught a cold, Mr. Meyer?

184 Transitional Reflexives

Some of the occasional reflexives denote a transition of the subject from one state or condition to a new state or condition. Take English *to hurt somebody* and German **jemanden verletzen** as an example. Both can be used with a reflexive pronoun.

Ich habe mich verletzt.   I hurt myself.

When used reflexively, **sich verletzen** and *to hurt oneself* indicate that the subject experiences a change of condition. The new condition is expressed by using a form of **sein** or of *to be* plus the participle **verletzt** or *hurt*.

Ich bin verletzt.   I am hurt.

The participles **verletzt** and *hurt*, in this case, take on the function of predicate adjectives. You must admit that the difference between *I hurt myself* and *I am hurt* (just as the difference between **Ich habe mich verletzt** and **Ich bin verletzt**) is, linguistically speaking, a rather efficient way of expressing the difference between an event and the new state or condition resulting from that event.

German uses the same system also with mandatory reflexives, if they express a transition of the subject from one condition to a new condition. Take again **sich erkälten** as an example.

The reflexive pattern **Ich habe mich erkältet** denotes the event of catching a cold. The new condition or state resulting from that event is expressed by

    Ich bin erkältet.

The infinitive of **Ich bin erkältet** is, of course, **erkältet sein.** It has a complete set of forms, all expressing a state rather than an event.

INFINITIVES	**erkältet sein**	to have a cold
	erkältet gewesen sein	to have had a cold
PRESENT TENSE	**ich bin erkältet**	I have a cold
PAST TENSE	**ich war erkältet**	I had a cold
PERFECT	**ich bin erkältet gewesen**	I have had a cold

The pattern of expressing the difference between an event (**sich erkälten**) and the state resulting from it (**erkältet sein**) is used consistently with all transitional reflexive verbs. See the list in Patterns [6] (pp. 392–395).

Of course, you might argue that it doesn't make much difference whether you say

Ich habe mich erkältet	I caught a cold
Ich habe mich verliebt	I fell in love

or

Ich bin erkältet.	I have a cold.
Ich bin verliebt.	I am in love.

Correct. That's why the speaker has a free choice to express the facts by either pattern. Nevertheless, the sentences

Ich habe mich erkältet	I caught a cold
Ich habe mich verliebt	I fell in love

express an event, whereas the sentences

Ich bin erkältet	I have a cold
Ich bin verliebt	I am in love

express a state. The difference becomes apparent when you use a time phrase.

Compare:

Ich habe mich vor zwei Jahren in Erika verliebt. Two years ago, I fell in love with Erika.	(event, past or perfect tense, point-of-time phrase)
Ich bin seit zwei Jahren in Erika verliebt. I have been in love with Erika for two years.	(present tense in German, present perfect in English, stretch-of-time phrase)

By the way, the participles of transitional reflexives are also used as attributive adjectives. They then take the usual strong or weak endings.

ein verliebter junger Mann
die verliebte junge Dame
mit einem verletzten Finger

NOTE: Reflexives like **sich öffnen**, which denote the transition of an object into a new state without reference to any agent, frequently correspond to English intransitive verbs.

Die Tür öffnete sich.	The door opened. (process)
Die Tür ist geöffnet.	The door is open. (state)
Ich habe die Tür geöffnet.	I opened the door. (action)

185 sich setzen, sich stellen, sich legen

The verbs **sitzen, stehen,** and **liegen** describe a state, not an event. They are intransitive—that is, they cannot take an accusative object—and they are strong verbs.

sitzen, saß, hat gesessen, er sitzt
stehen, stand, hat gestanden, er steht
liegen, lag, hat gelegen, er liegt

Anton und Emma saßen auf der Bank vor dem Haus.
Das Haus stand am Rhein.
Auf dem Tisch lag ein Buch.

The weak reflexive verbs **sich setzen, sich stellen,** and **sich legen** describe the action leading to the state of **sitzen, stehen,** and **liegen.**

Er hat sich auf die Bank gesetzt;	**jetzt sitzt er auf der Bank.**
Er hat sich vor die Haustür gestellt;	**jetzt steht er vor der Tür.**
Er hat sich ins Bett gelegt;	**jetzt liegt er im Bett.**

Note the principal parts of the English equivalents.

INTRANSITIVE	TRANSITIVE
sit, sat, sat	set, set, set
lie, lay, lain	lay, laid, laid

When the weak verbs **setzen, stellen,** and **legen** are used with a nonreflexive accusative object, they also describe an action, again leading to the state of **sitzen, stehen,** and **liegen.**

Sie hat das Kind auf die Bank gesetzt.	**Das Kind sitzt auf der Bank.**
Er hat die Flasche auf den Tisch gestellt.	**Die Flasche steht auf dem Tisch.**
Er hat das Buch auf den Tisch gelegt.	**Das Buch liegt auf dem Tisch.**

NOTE: If a prepositional phrase is used with these verbs, (sich) setzen, (sich) stellen, (sich) legen require the accusative (auf die Bank) and sitzen, stehen, liegen require the dative (auf der Bank).

186 Nontransitional Reflexives

We now introduce a number of high-frequency reflexives which do not denote a transition of the subject from one state or condition to a new state or condition. Most of them denote a continuous activity. One of these is **sich bemühen** (*to try hard, to be after something*). It can also be used in the nonreflexive pattern **bemüht sein.** Both patterns express continuous action, and the following two sentences are completely synonymous.

> **Ich bemühe mich seit einem Monat, eine bessere Stellung zu finden.**
> **Ich bin seit einem Monat bemüht, eine bessere Stellung zu finden.**

> For a month, I have been trying hard to find a better position.

One of the two patterns is therefore superfluous. This is the reason why most of the nontransitional reflexives do not even use nonreflexive patterns like **bemüht sein.** See the list of these reflexives in Patterns [8] (pp. 396–399).

187 Dative Reflexives

Some reflexives use the datives **mir, dir, sich, uns, euch** combined with an impersonal "something" expressed either by a noun or by a dependent clause.

sich etwas überlegen	to think over the pros and cons of a proposition
sich etwas ansehen	to look at something
sich etwas anschauen	
sich etwas vorstellen	to imagine something (as real)
sich etwas denken	to imagine something, to have something in mind
sich etwas einbilden	to imagine something as real which isn't

But

eingebildet sein	to be conceited

188 Household Reflexives

The verbs we call *household* reflexives all take dative pronouns and follow the pattern

> **Ich wasche mir die Hände.**   I'm washing my hands.

In German you do not say [meine Hände], but you wash "the" hands, and you do it "to yourself." Similarly:

Ich putze mir die Zähne.	I am brushing my teeth.
Sie schneidet sich die Haare selber.	She cuts her own hair.
Du putzt dir die Schuhe.	You are polishing your shoes.
Wir machen uns das Frühstück selber.	We make our own breakfast.
Warum kocht ihr euch nicht ein Ei?	Why don't you boil yourselves an egg?
Er hat sich den Arm gebrochen.	He broke his arm.
Ich habe mir in den Finger geschnitten.	I cut my finger.

189 Impersonal Reflexives

Some reflexives are used with the impersonal subject **es.**

Es zeigte sich, daß . . .	It became apparent that . . .
Es stellte sich heraus, daß . . .	It turned out that . . .
Es erwies sich, daß . . .	It was proved that . . .

Es handelte sich um . . .	It was a matter of, we were dealing with . . .
Es handelt sich um Geld.	It is a matter of money.
Es handelt sich hier um eine wichtige Sache.	
We are dealing here with an important problem.	

But note:

Er handelt *mit* Bananen.
He sells bananas; he is in the banana business.

Sein neuer Roman handelt *von* den Kämpfen in der Normandie.
His new novel deals with the battles in Normandy.

Wir haben lange genug geredet. Jetzt müssen wir handeln.
We've talked long enough; now we must act.

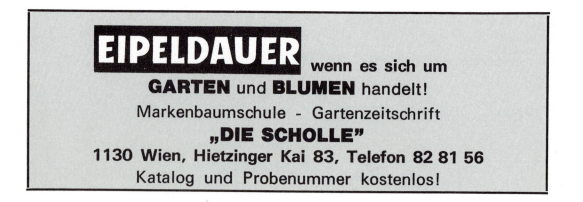

190 The Forms of the Imperative

The imperative is that form of a verb which is used for the expression of a command or a request. The following forms occur:

Weak Verbs

du-FORM	sag(e)	rede	antworte	entschuldige
ihr-FORM	sagt	redet	antwortet	entschuldigt
wir-FORM	sagen wir	reden wir	antworten wir	entschuldigen wir
Sie-FORM	sagen Sie	reden Sie	antworten Sie	entschuldigen Sie
IMPERSONAL FORM	identical with infinitive			

The **Sie**-form was introduced in Unit 3. Of the personal forms, only the **du**-form is not identical with the corresponding forms of the present indicative. The impersonal form is the infinitive used with imperative force.

In principle, the ending **-e** of the **du**-form is optional. However, verbs whose stems end in **-d** (**reden**) or **-t** (**antworten**) or in the suffix **-ig** (**entschuldigen**) are not usually used without the **-e** ending.

Strong Verbs

du-FORM	geh(e)	frag(e)	finde	gib	lauf
ihr-FORM	geht	fragt	findet	gebt	lauft
wir-FORM	gehen wir	fragen wir	finden wir	geben wir	laufen wir
Sie-FORM	gehen Sie	fragen Sie	finden Sie	geben Sie	laufen Sie
IMPERSONAL FORM	identical with infinitive				

du-FORM	nimm	sieh	sei	fahre	werde
ihr-FORM	nehmt	seht	seid	fahrt	werdet
wir-FORM	nehmen wir	sehen wir	seien wir	fahren wir	werden wir
Sie-FORM	nehmen Sie	sehen Sie	seien Sie	fahren Sie	werden Sie
IMPERSONAL FORM	identical with infinitive				

Again, only the **du**-form is not identical with the present indicative. The change of vowel from **a** to **ä** (**ich fahre, du fährst**), from **au** to **äu** (**ich laufe, du läufst**), and from **o** to **ö** (**stoßen, du stößt**) does not occur in the imperative. However, the change from **e** to **ie** or **i** (**ich gebe, du gibst; ich**

sehe, du siehst) must be observed. These changed-vowel forms never show the ending **-e** in the **du**-form. The **du**-form **werde** is irregular, as are the forms of **sein**. In principle, the ending **-e** of the **du**-form is again optional.

191 The Use of the Various Forms of the Imperative

The Use of the du-Form

The **du**-form is used when the persons involved say **du** to each other. It is also used in advertisements.

> **Bring mir bitte Zigaretten mit,**
> **Bring mir doch bitte Zigaretten mit,** } **wenn du in die Stadt fährst!**
> **Bitte bring mir Zigaretten mit,**
>
> **Mach mal Pause, trink Coca-Cola!**

This form can be used together with a **du** immediately following the imperative. This **du** always establishes a contrast between the person addressed and someone else.

> **Steh *du* doch mal zuerst auf!** (wife to husband; she usually gets up first)
> **Rede *du* mal mit Meyer!** (wife to husband; she has talked with Meyer already)

This pattern is sometimes expressed in English by "Why don't *you* . . ."

The ihr-Form

Like the **du**-form, the **ihr**-form is used between persons who say **du** to each other.

> **Kinder, vergeßt nicht,**
> **Kinder, bitte vergeßt nicht,** } **daß ihr um zehn zu Hause sein sollt.**
> **Kinder, vergeßt bitte nicht,**

The use of **ihr** is parallel to the use of **du** with the **du**-form.

> ***Geht* ihr schon! *Ich* komme *später*.**
> **Versucht *ihr* doch mal, mit Meyer zu reden. *Mir* glaubt er nicht.**

The wir-Form

The **wir**-form can only be used if the speaker includes himself among the persons addressed.

> **Wo wollen wir denn essen? Im Regina? Gut, fahren wir ins Regina!**

The English equivalent is *Let's* (*go*).

The Sie-Form

The **Sie**-form is used (with or without **bitte**) between persons who say **Sie** to each other.

> **(Bitte) bringen Sie mir noch ein Glas Wein.**

In advertising it is used without **bitte**.

> **Versuchen Sie SUNIL. Sie werden bestimmt zufrieden sein.**

The Impersonal Form

The impersonal form is the infinitive used to express a request. It is used to give instructions to the public. It therefore appears on traffic signs, at airports, in planes, in railroad stations, and so on. It is also used in advertis-

ing and in modern cookbooks, without exclamation marks.

Alles aussteigen.
Bitte aussteigen.
Aussteigen bitte.
Nicht öffnen, bevor der Zug hält.
Langsam fahren.
Nicht rauchen.
Bitte anschnallen.
Nicht benutzen, während der Zug hält.

192 The Intonation of Imperatives

The imperative as a command is distinguished from the imperative as a polite request by level of intonation.

The imperative expressing a command follows the usual 2–3–1 assertion pattern; that is, the intonation curve goes up to level 3 and then sinks to level 1.

Geh an die *Arbeit*!

Rede nicht so viel!

Steh *du* doch mal zu*erst* auf!

Bringen Sie mir doch mal die *Speise*-karte. (Implication: don't be so inattentive.)

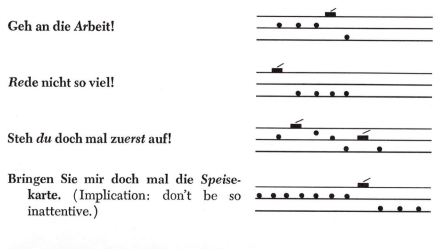

In a polite request using imperative forms, the unstressed syllables preceding the stress point are usually arranged in a downward trend toward level 1, and then the first stressed syllable is raised only to level 2, not to level 3.

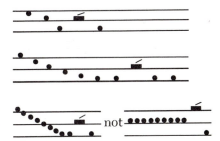

Sei mir nicht *böse*!

Bitte bring mir etwas zu *lesen* mit!

Geben Sie mir doch mal etwas zu *trinken*. (Request by patient, not order to nurse.)

Bleib ruhig im *Bett!* (Why don't you stay in bed! Not: Be quiet in bed!)

Bringen Sie mir doch mal die *Speise*karte. (Would you be so kind as to bring me the menu?)

How to express commands and requests is not so much a question of grammatical correctness as of correct social behavior. Nobody likes to be ordered around, and nobody wants to gain the reputation of being bossy. You are therefore advised to express requests either by questions or by those forms of the imperative which are marked by intonation as requests.

193 The Syntax of the Imperative

The personal forms of the imperative begin the sentence and can be preceded only by **bitte.**

> **Bring mir etwas zu lesen mit!**
> **Bitte bring mir etwas zu lesen mit!**
> **Bring mir bitte etwas zu lesen mit!**
> **Bring mir etwas zu lesen mit, bitte!**

Since the impersonal imperatives are infinitives, they stand at the end of the imperative phrase.

> **Langsam fahren!**
> **Hinten einsteigen!**
> **Bitte die Türen schließen!**
> **Bitte von der Bahnsteigkante zurücktreten!**

When imperatives are negated, **nicht** stands, as usual, at the end of the

inner field. Since the impersonal imperative is an infinitive, it must always follow the **nicht.** Thus the sentence

Man darf nicht mit dem Fahrer sprechen

becomes the impersonal imperative

Nicht mit dem Fahrer sprechen!

Bitte fahr morgen nicht nach Berlin!
Sei doch nicht so ungeduldig!
Warte heute nicht auf mich!
Vergiß mich nicht!
Bitte ruf mich morgen nicht an!
Nicht hinauslehnen.

Any imperative constitutes direct discourse. In order to report, by indirect discourse, that a request was made or a command given, **sollen** is used.

IMPERATIVE
Fahren Sie doch einmal an die See.

INDIRECT DISCOURSE
Der Arzt meinte, ich solle (sollte) doch einmal an die Nordsee fahren.
Der Arzt meinte, er solle (sollte) doch einmal an die Nordsee fahren.
Der Arzt meinte, wir sollten doch einmal an die Nordsee fahren.

194 doch einmal, doch mal

When **einmal** or the shorter **mal** is used in assertions and requests, it may mean *once, for once,* or *for a change.*

Ich will dieses Jahr nicht an die Nordsee. Ich möchte mal in die Berge fahren.
I don't want to go to the North Sea this year. I'd like to go to the mountains for a change.

Steh *du* doch mal zuerst auf.
Why don't you get up first for a change?

Very often, however, the short **mal** loses its literal meaning and expresses simply a note of casualness.

Ich geh' mal in die Stadt.
Ich muß mal telefonieren.

In requests, this casual **mal** is usually preceded by an unstressed **doch.**

Mach uns doch mal eine Tasse Kaffee.   How about fixing us a cup of coffee?

Noch (ein)mal and **doch noch (ein)mal** always mean *once more* or *again.*

Ruf sie doch noch mal an.   Call her up again.

195 eben and gerade

If **eben** is used with a full lexical meaning, it means either *flat, even,* or *just (a while ago).*

ebenes (flaches) Land	flat land
die Ebene, –n	the plain
die Norddeutsche Tiefebene	the North German Plain
Er ist eben gekommen.	He just came.

Eben can also be used as a sentence adverb meaning "it won't take long; I hope you won't mind the interruption." In this function, it minimizes the significance of the action, and for this reason is frequently used in connection with the casual **mal.** As a sentence adverb, **eben** is never stressed.

Ich muß mal eben in die Stadt.
I've got to run downtown for a minute. (Nothing important; I'll be right back.)

Entschuldigst du mich einen Augenblick? Ich muß mal eben telefonieren.
Will you excuse me for a minute? I just want to make a quick phone call.

If **gerade** is used with full lexical meaning, it means *straight.*

eine gerade Linie   a straight line

In connection with numbers, one speaks of **gerade Zahlen** and **ungerade Zahlen** (*even and odd numbers*). It can also mean *just then* or *just now* (see **eben** above).

Er ist gerade (eben) gekommen.   He just came.

Ich war gerade (eben) nach Hause gekommen, als das Telefon klingelte.

196 ruhig

German **ruhig** can be used either as an adjective or as a sentence adverb. As an adjective, it means *calm, quiet.*

> **Sei ruhig.**   Be quiet.

> **Nun sei mal ganz ruhig, Gerda, und versuche, uns zu erzählen, was passiert ist.**

If used as a sentence adverb, **ruhig** denotes that the speaker will remain "quiet" and has no objections.

> **Bleib du ruhig im Bett; ich frühstücke im Flughafen.**
> Don't bother to get up for me; I'll have breakfast at the airport.

> **Ihr könnt ruhig laut sein, Kinder, ich will jetzt *doch* nicht schlafen.**
> I won't mind your being loud; I don't want to sleep now anyway.

Exercises

A. In the following sentences, insert **selbst** or **selber** in as many places as possible and translate the resulting sentences into English. The number of possibilities is indicated in parentheses.

1. Erika fährt nicht. (4)
2. Ich wollte, ich könnte einmal mit Meyer reden. (4)
3. Warum denkst du eigentlich nie an dich? (1)
4. Meyer geht jeden Sonntag in die Kirche. (3)
5. Ich habe Angst gehabt. (3)
6. Mit Erika könnte ich, wenn nötig, ins Museum gehen. (5)

B. Restate the following sentences by using the subject indicated in parentheses. Be sure to distinguish between dative and accusative reflexives.

1. Natürlich haben sie sich schon einmal geküßt. (wir)
2. Kann er sich schon selber anziehen? (du)
3. Und dann sah er sich im Spiegel. (ich)
4. Ich muß mir morgen eine Wohnung suchen. (wir) (ihr)
5. Das können sie sich nicht kaufen. (ich) (du) (er) (Erika)
6. Sie trafen sich am Bahnhof. (wir)
7. Du mußt auch einmal an dich selbst denken. (Sie)
8. Kannst du dir das Frühstück nicht einmal selber machen? (er)
9. Sie hat sich in ihn verliebt. (er)
10. Hat er sich schon umgezogen? (du)

C. Restate the following sentences by using the corresponding perfect of the reflexive.

1. Ich bin gut ausgeruht.
2. Er ist schon rasiert.
3. Er ist seit einer Woche mit meiner Schwester verlobt.
4. Er ist in Rosemarie verliebt.
5. Ich bin schwer erkältet.

SEE
ANALYSIS
183–184

(pp. 414-416)

D. Restate the following sentences by replacing the reflexives with a form of **sein** plus participle.

1. Mit wem hat er sich denn verlobt?
2. Warum hat er sich denn so aufgeregt?
3. Hat Hans sich vorbereitet?
4. Hast du dich schon wieder erkältet?
5. Ich habe mich entschlossen, das Haus zu kaufen.

SEE
ANALYSIS
183–184

(pp. 414-416)

E. In the following sentences, fill in the blanks by using the correct form of **setzen, sitzen; stellen, stehen; legen, liegen.**

1. Als ich nach Hause kam, _____ meine Frau schon im Bett.
2. Als ich nach Hause kam, hatte meine Frau sich schon ins Bett _____.
3. Hast du die Schuhe schon vor die Tür _____?
4. Meine Frau geht nur dann ins Theater, wenn sie in der ersten Reihe _____ kann.
5. Ich hatte einen guten Platz. Aber dann _____ sich der dicke Meyer vor mich, und ich konnte nichts mehr sehen.
6. Gestern im Theater habe ich neben Rosemarie _____.
7. Heute möchte ich eigentlich gern im Garten _____.
8. Ich habe deinen Mantel aufs Bett _____.
9. Der Zug war so voll, daß ich keinen Sitzplatz finden konnte, und ich mußte von Köln bis nach Frankfurt _____.
10. Wir haben den Tisch jetzt an die Wand _____.

SEE
ANALYSIS
185

(pp. 416-417)

F. In the following sentences, replace the transitives **setzen, stellen, legen** or the reflexives **sich setzen, sich stellen, sich legen** with the intransitives **sitzen, stehen, liegen,** or vice versa. Observe the difference in tense and, in some cases, the change of subject; remember also that you have to change case in the prepositional phrase.

| **Sie liegt schon im Bett.** | **Sie hat sich schon ins Bett gelegt.** |

1. Er hat sich neben sie gesetzt.
2. Wir saßen in der ersten Reihe.
3. Sie sitzen alle im Garten.
4. Warum hast du dich denn noch nicht ins Bett gelegt?
5. Er muß sich schon ins Bett gelegt haben.
6. Sie hatte sich direkt neben die Tür gestellt.
7. Er stand am Fenster.
8. Er hat das Buch auf den Nachttisch gelegt.

SEE
ANALYSIS
185

(pp. 416-417)

9. Ich habe meine Schuhe vor die Tür gestellt.
10. Er saß schon am Frühstückstisch.
11. Vor ihm stand eine Tasse Kaffee. (New subject: Ingrid)
12. Er legte die Bibel vor sich auf den Tisch.
13. Wo hast du denn meinen Hut hingelegt?
14. Wo sitzt denn deine Frau? (Start new question with **Wo** and use **sich hinsetzen.**)
15. Wo steht denn mein Wagen? (Start question with **Wohin**; new subject: **du.**)

G. Express in German by using a reflexive verb.

1. Why don't you go to bed?
2. Did you shave this morning?
3. They got engaged.
4. They got a divorce.
5. Can't Fritzchen take a bath by himself now?
6. You ought to change before Aunt Amalie comes.
7. I broke my arm and I can't undress my*self*.
8. Have you had enough sleep?
9. Did you have a good rest?
10. He always gets so excited.
11. Did she finally calm down?

SEE
ANALYSIS
190–193

(pp. 419-424)

H. By placing **bitte** in the front field, inner field, and end field, repeat the following sentences three times.

1. Sei doch nicht so aufgeregt!
2. Laß mich in Ruhe!
3. Sprechen Sie etwas lauter!
4. Ruf mich nicht vor acht an!
5. Komm nicht wieder erst um zwei nach Hause!

SEE
ANALYSIS
190–194

(pp. 419-425)

I. Change the following sentences to imperative sentences, using **doch mal** in the inner field.

1. Könntest du uns eine Tasse Kaffee machen?
2. Würdest du mir etwas zu lesen mitbringen?
3. Könnten Sie uns an einem Sonntag besuchen?
4. Muß *ich* denn immer das Licht ausmachen?
5. Ich rate Ihnen, an die See zu fahren, gnädige Frau.

SEE
ANALYSIS
190–193

(pp. 419-424)

J. Change the following complaints into imperatives. Use **doch bitte** in the inner field.

1. Du rauchst zuviel.
2. Du gibst zuviel Geld aus.
3. Du bist immer so unfreundlich.
4. Können Sie mir kein Zimmer mit Bad geben?
5. Kannst du nicht mal vernünftig sein?

K. Change the following imperatives to the **du**-form and the **ihr**-form. Use **du** and **ihr** only when **Sie** is italicized.

1. Seien Sie doch nicht so aufgeregt!
2. Stehen Sie doch morgen etwas früher auf!

3. Bringen Sie mir ruhig noch eine Tasse Kaffee!
4. Gehen *Sie* doch mal mit Tante Amalie ins Museum!
5. Sprechen Sie ruhig lauter!
6. Gute Nacht, schlafen Sie gut.
7. Ich weiß, dies ist kein schönes Zimmer. Aber finden Sie hier mal ein besseres!
8. Denken Sie mal, wen ich gestern getroffen habe!
9. Fahren Sie doch mal eben zur Post.
10. Verbieten Sie ihm doch einfach, daß er Sie zu Hause anruft.
11. Schlagen *Sie* mir mal etwas vor.
12. Bringen Sie die Bücher bitte in die Bibliothek zurück.
13. Nehmen Sie uns doch bitte mit.
14. Schreien Sie doch nicht so laut!
15. Schwimmen *Sie* doch mal über den Rhein!

SEE
ANALYSIS
190–193
(pp. 419-424)

L. Change the following imperatives to indirect discourse, starting with **Er sagte,** . . .
Use both forms of the subjunctive where possible.

1. Fahren Sie doch mal an die See.
2. Sei nicht so unfreundlich.
3. Schicken Sie mir den Brief nach.
4. Geht doch mit ins Theater.
5. Seid vorsichtig, und macht dem Wolf nicht die Tür auf.

SEE
ANALYSIS
193
(pp. 423-424)

M. Express the following sentences in German. These sentences all contain reflexives. Do not use **sein** plus participle.

1. Are you still interested in her?
2. Think of yourself for a change.
3. I was really mad at him last night.
4. She fell in love with her teacher.
5. We have never been so bored.
6. I've bought myself a new coat.
7. They want to get a divorce.
8. May I introduce myself?
9. Just imagine: after twenty years he still remembered me.
10. I know she has nothing against you; you just imagine that.
11. I am looking forward to seeing her again.
12. We want to have a look at Meyer's new house.
13. I haven't changed yet, and I still have to shave.
14. Hurry up!
15. Don't get so excited.
16. Has she calmed down again?
17. I simply can't get used to his Russian accent.
18. Did you lose your way again? (hiking) (driving)
19. It turned out that Erich wasn't the thief at all.
20. We are dealing with people, gentlemen, and not with machines.

N. Composition.

After you have spent your first night in a German hotel, you decide to write to your cousin Hildegard again. This time, describe what happened to you after your arrival in Koblenz; how you took a taxi to your hotel, and how surprised you were at the difference between this German hotel and American hotels. Tell her what an American motel is like; are there any motels in Germany at all? Then tell her that you have tried to call your friend Barbara, but haven't been able to reach her yet. You will try again and you hope that you'll be able to visit her. Ask Hildegard to write to you in Augustdorf and to let you know whether it is all right with her if you come to Munich in about two weeks.

Restrict yourself to the vocabulary and to the patterns you know. The reading selections of Units 10–12 should provide you with all you need; review them before you start writing.

Basic Vocabulary

Note that, in this vocabulary, all reflexives are listed not only in infinitive form, but also in the **ich**-form, to indicate whether the reflexive pronoun is dative or accusative. It is advisable to memorize the **ich**-forms rather than the infinitives.

ähnlich	similar	sich ausruhen	to rest
ändern	to change (something)	ich ruhe mich aus	I am resting
sich ändern	to change	ausgeruht sein	to be rested
das Wetter ändert sich	the weather changes	aussteigen	to get out (of a vehicle)
sich verändern	to change	einsteigen	to get into (a vehicle)
ich habe mich verändert	I have changed	sich ausziehen	to get undressed
sich etwas anschauen	to look at something	ich ziehe mich aus	I am getting undressed
ich schaue mir etwas an	I look at something	ausgezogen sein	to be undressed
sich etwas ansehen	to look at something	sich bemühen	to try hard
ich sehe mir etwas an	I look at something	ich bemühe mich	I am trying hard
ärgern	to make angry	sich beruhigen	to calm down; stop worrying
sich ärgern über (*with acc.*)	to be angry (mad) at	ich beruhige mich	I'll calm down
ich ärgere mich über ihn	I am mad at him	beruhigt sein	to be calmed down; to not worry any- more
aufgeben	to mail (a letter)	bewegen	to move (something)
sich aufregen über (*with acc.*)	to get excited about	sich bewegen	to move
ich rege mich über . . . auf	I get excited about	die Erde bewegt sich	the earth moves
aufgeregt sein	to be excited	ich kann mich nicht bewegen	I can't move

billig	inexpensive; cheap
ein bißchen	a bit, a little
die Decke, –n	ceiling; cover, blanket
sich etwas denken	to imagine
ich kann mir denken	I can imagine
Deutsch können	to have a mastery of, to know, German
dorthin	to this place; there
drehen	to turn
sich drehen	to turn
sich umdrehen	to turn around
ich drehe mich um	I turn around
sich eilen, sich beeilen	to hurry
ich eile mich, ich beeile mich	I am hurrying
einander	each other
sich einbilden	to imagine
ich bilde mir ein	I imagine
eingebildet sein	to be conceited
empfangen	to receive
der Empfang, –̈e	reception
sich entschließen	to make up one's mind
ich entschließe mich	I make up my mind
entschlossen sein	to be determined
entschuldigen	to excuse
sich entschuldigen	to apologize
ich entschuldige mich	I apologize
entschuldigt sein	to be excused
die Erde	the earth
sich erholen	to get a rest; to recover one's strength
erholt sein	to be well rested (recovered)
erinnern an (with acc.)	to remind somebody of
sich erinnern an	to remember
ich erinnere mich an ihn	I remember him
sich erkälten	to catch a cold
ich erkälte mich	I am catching a cold
erkältet sein	to have a cold
sich erweisen	to turn out; to show
es erweist sich	it turns out; it shows
sich freuen auf (with acc.)	to look forward to
ich freue mich auf ihn	I look forward to (seeing) him
sich freuen über (with acc.)	to be glad about
ich freue mich darüber	I am glad about it
der Führer, –	guide, leader
furchtbar	terrible
das Gasthaus, –̈er	inn, restaurant
der Gasthof, –̈e	inn, restaurant
gegenseitig	each other; mutual
sich gewöhnen an (with acc.)	to get used to
ich gewöhne mich an sie	I am getting used to her
gewöhnt sein an	to be used to
die Großstadt, –̈e	large city, metropolis
die Kleinstadt, –̈e	small town
handeln	to act
sich handeln um (with acc.)	to be a matter of
es handelt sich um	it is a matter of
handeln mit	to deal in (commercial)
handeln von	to deal with (subject matter)
der Händler, –	merchant; dealer
sich herausstellen	to become apparent
es stellt sich heraus	it becomes apparent
hinten (adv.)	in the back
sich interessieren für (with acc.)	to be interested in
ich interessiere mich für ihn	I am interested in him
interessiert sein an (with dat.)	to like to acquire; to show an interest in
inzwischen	meanwhile, in the meantime
das Land, –̈er	country
auf dem Land	in the country
langweilen	to bore
sich langweilen	to be bored
ich langweile mich	I am bored
gelangweilt sein	to be bored
langweilig	boring
sich legen	to lie down
ich lege mich	I lie down
sich hinauslehnen	to lean out
ich lehne mich hinaus	I lean out
lösen	to solve
die Luft, –̈e	air
die Luftpost	airmail
der Mund, –̈er	mouth
mündlich	oral
nämlich	namely; that is to say
öffnen	to open (a door)
die Tür öffnet sich	the door opens

putzen	to clean
sich rasieren	to shave
ich rasiere mich	I am shaving
rasiert sein	to be shaved
retten	to save (from destruction)
schauen	to look, to gaze
sich scheiden lassen von	to get a divorce from
ich lasse mich von . . . scheiden	I am getting a divorce from . . .
geschieden sein	to be divorced
schließen	to close
die Tür schließt sich	the door closes
geschlossen sein	to be closed
schneien	to snow
der Schnee	snow
selbst, selber (indeclinable)	self (see 179); even (see 180)
setzen	to seat; to put
sich setzen	to sit down
ich setze mich	I sit down
sogar	even (see 180)
sowieso	anyhow, anyway
speisen	to eat (formal term)
die Speisekarte, –n	menu
stimmen	to be correct
das stimmt nicht	that's wrong
der Stock	floor (of a building)
im ersten Stock	on the second (!) floor
stören	to disturb
der Tanz, ⸚e	dance
der Tod, –e	death
das Tor, –e	gate
treffen	to meet
überall	everywhere
sich etwas überlegen	to meditate about something
ich überlege mir etwas	I am meditating about something
übernachten	to spend the night
sich umziehen	to change clothes
ich ziehe mich um	I change clothes
umgezogen sein	to have changed clothes
umziehen	to change residence, to move
umgezogen sein	to have changed residence, to have moved
verbinden	to combine; to connect (telephone)
sich verfahren	to lose one's way (driving)
ich verfahre mich	I lose my way (driving)
sich verlassen auf (with acc.)	to rely on
ich verlasse mich auf dich	I rely on you
sich verlaufen	to lose one's way (walking)
ich verlaufe mich	I lose my way (walking)
sich verlieben in (with acc.)	to fall in love with
ich verliebe mich in ihn	I am falling in love with him
verliebt sein in	to be in love with
sich verloben mit	to get engaged to
ich verlobe mich mit ihr	I get engaged to her
verlobt sein mit	to be engaged to
der Verlobte, –n	fiancé
mein Verlobter	my fiancé
verzeihen	to pardon, to excuse
die Verzeihung	pardon
sich vorbereiten auf (with acc.)	to prepare for
ich bereite mich auf . . . vor	I prepare for
vorbereitet sein auf	to be prepared for
vorstellen	to introduce (socially); to imagine
ich stelle ihn vor	I introduce him
ich stelle mich vor	I introduce myself
sich etwas vorstellen	to imagine something
ich stelle mir etwas vor	I imagine something
die Weihnachten (old pl.)	Christmas
das Wunder, –	miracle
wundervoll, wunderbar	wonderful
sich wundern über (with acc.)	to be amazed at (not: "to wonder")
ich wundere mich über	I am amazed at
die Zahl, –en	number

Additional Vocabulary

altmodisch	old-fashioned	das Gespräch, –e	conversation
anreden mit	to address by	heizen	to heat
sich anschnallen	to fasten one's seatbelt	die Heizung, –en	heating system, radiator
ich schnalle mich an	I fasten my seatbelt		
anzeigen	to announce	die Zentralheizung	central heating
der Aufzug, ⸚e	elevator	die Kasse, –n	cash register; cash box
bedienen	to serve; to wait on	das Klima	climate
die Bedienung	service	nervös'	nervous
die Selbstbedienung	self-service	obligato'risch	obligatory
sich einordnen	to get into the correct lane; to merge	schlucken	to swallow
		der Schluck	sip
ich ordne mich ein	I get into the correct lane	die Schulter, –n	shoulder
		der Schwarzwald	Black Forest
sich erkundigen	to inquire	der Urlaub	furlough, vacation
ich erkundige mich	I inquire	vor allem	above all
die Geduld	patience	die Vorsicht	caution
geduldig	patient	vorsichtig	cautious
das Gepäck	baggage		

Strong and Irregular Verbs

sich ansehen, sah sich an, hat sich angesehen, er sieht sich an	to look at
aufgeben, gab auf, hat aufgegeben, er gibt auf	to mail (a letter)
aussteigen, stieg aus, ist ausgestiegen, er steigt aus	to get out of (a vehicle)
einsteigen, stieg ein, ist eingestiegen, er steigt ein	to get into (a vehicle)
sich ausziehen, zog sich aus, hat sich ausgezogen, er zieht sich aus	to get undressed
empfangen, empfing, hat empfangen, er empfängt	to receive
sich entschließen, entschloß sich, hat sich entschlossen, er entschließt sich	to make up one's mind
schließen, schloß, hat geschlossen, er schließt	to close
treffen, traf, hat getroffen, er trifft	to meet
sich umziehen, zog sich um, hat sich umgezogen, er zieht sich um	to change clothes
verbinden, verband, hat verbunden, er verbindet	to combine; to connect (telephone)
sich verfahren, verfuhr sich, hat sich verfahren, er verfährt sich	to lose one's way (driving)
sich verlassen, verließ sich, hat sich verlassen, er verläßt sich	to rely
sich verlaufen, verlief sich, hat sich verlaufen, er verläuft sich	to lose one's way (walking)
verzeihen, verzieh, hat verziehen, er verzeiht	to forgive

Unit 13 The Passive—**es** in the
Front Field—Pre-Noun Inserts

Patterns

[1] The Active Voice of Transitive and Intransitive Verbs;
Actional and Statal Forms of the Passive

This is a presentation of basic forms. Study these examples *after*
you have read **197–199**.

SEE
ANALYSIS
197–199
(pp. 447-449)

PRESENT

INTRANSITIVE	Kochen die Kartoffeln schon?
TRANSITIVE	Mutter kocht jeden Tag Kartoffeln.
ACTIONAL PASSIVE	Bei uns werden jeden Tag Kartoffeln gekocht.
STATAL PASSIVE	Sind die Kartoffeln schon gekocht?

PAST

INTRANSITIVE	Als ich nach Hause kam, standen die Kartoffeln schon auf dem Herd und kochten.
TRANSITIVE	Mutter kochte damals jeden Tag fünf Pfund Kartoffeln.
ACTIONAL PASSIVE	Bei uns wurden früher jeden Tag fünf Pfund Kartoffeln gekocht.
STATAL PASSIVE	Als ich nach Hause kam, waren die Kartoffeln schon gekocht.
	Wenn die Kartoffeln schon gekocht gewesen wären, hätten wir sofort essen können.

PERFECT

INTRANSITIVE	Die Kartoffeln haben noch gar nicht gekocht.
TRANSITIVE	Hast du auch genug Kartoffeln gekocht?
ACTIONAL PASSIVE	Bei uns sind noch nie soviel Kartoffeln gekocht worden wie in den letzten Tagen.

INFINITIVES

Ingelheim will *Die Frau mit dem Flamingo* an den Exotica-Verlag verkaufen.
Ingelheim soll *Die Frau mit dem Flamingo* an den Exotica-Verlag verkauft haben.

In Kanada darf *Die Frau mit dem Flamingo* nicht verkauft werden.
Im letzten Jahr sollen über 100.000 Exemplare verkauft worden sein.
Die ganze erste Auflage soll schon verkauft sein.
Haben Sie gehört, die ganze erste Auflage soll schon nach vier Wochen verkauft
gewesen sein.

[2] Distinction between Actional and Statal Passive Forms

SEE
ANALYSIS
198–199
(pp. 447-449)

Bei uns werden alle Briefe mit der Maschine geschrieben.
Diese Briefe sind mit der Maschine geschrieben.

Wann ist das Pulver denn erfunden worden?
Das weiß ich nicht. Als ich geboren wurde, war es schon erfunden.

Dieses Zimmer ist aber kalt. Ist das Zimmer nicht geheizt, oder kann es nicht
geheizt werden?

Ich höre, das Haus neben der Kirche soll verkauft werden.
Es ist schon verkauft.

VARIATIONS

Change the following statal passive sentences to the actional passive.

Das Haus ist schon verkauft.
Ist die Stadt wiederaufgebaut?
Das müßte verboten sein.
Ist meine Schreibmaschine schon repariert?

[3] "Transformations" from Active Voice to Actional Passive

SEE
ANALYSIS
200
(pp. 449-450)

Wer hat denn den Bunsenbrenner erfunden?
Der Bunsenbrenner ist von Bunsen erfunden worden.
Bunsen soll den Bunsenbrenner erfunden haben.
Der Bunsenbrenner soll von Bunsen erfunden worden sein.

*Die Trans-Pacific-Eisenbahn
wurde nicht an einem Tag gebaut*

**Auch die
Frankfurter Stadtbahn
braucht ihre Bauzeit**

Wer hat Amerika entdeckt?
Amerika ist von Kolumbus entdeckt worden.
Schon die Wikinger sollen Amerika entdeckt haben.
Amerika soll schon von den Wikingern entdeckt worden sein.

Die Polizei sucht ihn.
Die Polizei soll ihn suchen.
Er wird von der Polizei gesucht.
Er soll von der Polizei gesucht werden.
Die Polizei suchte ihn überall.
Er wurde von der Polizei gesucht.
Hat ihn die Polizei nie gefunden?
Ist er nie gefunden worden?
Doch! Die Polizei soll ihn gestern gefunden haben.
Doch! Er soll gestern gefunden worden sein.

Eine einzige Bombe hat das Haus zerstört.
Das Haus ist durch eine einzige Bombe zerstört worden.
Das Haus soll durch eine einzige Bombe zerstört worden sein.
Eine einzige Bombe soll das ganze Haus zerstört haben.

VARIATIONS

Transform the following sentences to the statal and the
actional passive. Leave out the agent.

Man hat die ganze Stadt zerstört.
Er hat das Haus verkauft.
Er soll das Haus schon verkauft haben.
Wir haben ihn gerettet.

[4] Dative Objects

SEE
ANALYSIS
201

(p. 450)

Wir konnten ihm nicht helfen.
Dem Manne kann geholfen werden. (Schiller, *Die Räuber*)
Ihm ist nicht zu helfen.
Man half ihm sofort.
Ihm wurde sofort geholfen.
Jemand hat mir gesagt, ich sollte um drei Uhr hier sein.
Mir wurde gesagt, ich sollte um drei Uhr hier sein.
Es wurde mir gesagt, ich sollte um drei Uhr hier sein.

[5] Passive Forms to Express Activity as Such

SEE
ANALYSIS
202

(p. 451)

Wir waschen nur mit Persil.
Bei uns wird nur mit Persil gewaschen, denn Persil bleibt Persil.
Hier wird gearbeitet.
Jeden Samstag abend wird dort getanzt.
In meinem Elternhaus ist viel musiziert worden.
In Kalifornien wird fast nur mit Gas geheizt.
Bei euch im Büro wird viel zu viel geredet.
Wann wird denn hier morgens gefrühstückt?
In diesem Hotel wird nur vom 15. September bis zum 1. Mai geheizt.
Ingelheim ist mir zu sentimental; in seinen Romanen wird auf jeder dritten
    Seite geweint.
Es wird gebeten, nicht zu rauchen.

VARIATIONS

Change to actional passive, expressing "activity as such."

Wir arbeiten hier schwer.
Man hat hier noch nie getanzt.
Und um eins essen wir hier zu Mittag.
In unserer Familie lachen wir viel.

[6] Syntactical Variations

zeigen

SEE
ANALYSIS
197–204

(pp. 447-452)

Der neue schwedische Film wird jetzt auch in Deutschland gezeigt.
Könnte man ihn nicht auch in den Vereinigten Staaten zeigen?
Während der internationalen Filmfestspiele in Berlin wurde auch der neue schwedische
    Film gezeigt.
Der Film soll sehr gut sein, aber in Amerika ist er noch nicht gezeigt worden.
Es wäre besser, wenn dieser Film auch in Berlin nicht gezeigt worden wäre.
Es tut mir leid, daß der Film gezeigt wird. Ich wollte, er würde nicht gezeigt.

Express in German.

When is it supposed to be shown here? _____

It can never be shown here. _____

einladen

So, ihr seid schon wieder bei Schultes eingeladen?
So, Schultes haben euch schon wieder eingeladen?

Ich werde leider nie eingeladen.
Mich haben sie noch nie eingeladen.

Warum warst du denn gestern abend nicht bei Schultes?
Ich war nicht eingeladen.

Ich wollte, ich würde auch einmal eingeladen.
Ich wollte, ich wäre damals auch eingeladen gewesen.

Den Eugen Wilke treffe ich wahrscheinlich heute bei Schultes. Er soll auch eingeladen
sein.
Karola Kirchhoff soll eingeladen worden sein, in Stuttgart die Desdemona zu spielen.
Natürlich freue ich mich darüber, daß ich eingeladen bin, hier in Stuttgart die Desdemona zu spielen. Aber ich bin nicht überrascht. Ich wäre sehr enttäuscht gewesen,
wenn ich nicht eingeladen worden wäre.

Express in German.

I wish they would invite us.	Ich wollte, _____.
I wish we were invited.	Ich wollte, _____.
I wish Ingrid had invited us.	Ich wollte, _____.
I wish we had been invited by Ingrid.	Ich wollte, _____.
I wish we had been invited.	Ich wollte, _____.

reden

Meine Herren, Sie wissen, ich bin hier neu; aber eines habe ich schon festgestellt. Hier
wird zu viel geredet, zu viel geraucht, zu viel Kaffee getrunken und zu wenig gearbeitet.

Auf dem Weg nach Hause redeten wir kaum ein Wort miteinander.
Auf dem Weg nach Hause wurde kaum geredet.
Auf dem Weg nach Hause wurde kaum ein Wort geredet.

Express in the actional passive.

Wir haben genug geredet; jetzt müssen wir etwas tun.

lösen

Es wurde zwar schon im Altertum angenommen, daß sich die Materie aus gewissen
„Elementen" zusammensetzt, aber das Problem, aus welchen Elementen die Materie
tatsächlich zusammengesetzt ist, konnte viele Jahrhunderte lang nicht gelöst werden.

Man konnte das Problem lange nicht lösen.

Das Problem war einfach nicht zu lösen.

Man glaubte, das Problem wäre nicht zu lösen.

Das Problem ließ sich lange nicht lösen.

Das Problem ist erst vor wenigen Jahren gelöst worden.

Das Problem konnte erst vor wenigen Jahren gelöst werden.

Ohne die Entdeckung des Radiums hätte das Problem nie gelöst werden können.

Im Mittelalter war das Problem noch nicht gelöst.

Erst die moderne Wissenschaft hat das Problem gelöst.

Heute ist das Problem gelöst.

ändern   *to change something, to enforce change*
sich ändern   *to become different, to change in nature or character*
sich verändern   *to change in physical appearance or behavior*

Ich habe meine Meinung geändert.

Der Mantel ist mir viel zu groß; den muß ich ändern lassen.

Haben Sie meinen Mantel schon geändert?

Ja, der Mantel ist schon geändert.

Bei uns gibt es nichts Neues; bei uns ändert sich nie etwas.

Der Marktplatz ist noch immer der alte, und nichts scheint sich hier geändert zu haben.

Morgen soll sich das Wetter endlich ändern.

Du hast dich aber verändert, Otto.

Gnädige Frau, Sie haben sich gar nicht verändert.

Die Maria hat sich aber verändert; die muß ja mindestens fünfundzwanzig Pfund abgenommen haben.—Ja, verändert hat sie sich, aber geändert hat sie sich nicht; es ist immer noch dieselbe alte Maria.

Express in German.

Of course I've changed; I'm ten years older.   Natürlich _____.

Karl has really changed; he doesn't drink   Karl hat _____
anymore.   _____.

[7] The Impersonal es

Be prepared to produce these and similar sentences orally.

SEE
ANALYSIS
205

(pp. 452-455)

Niemand war zu Hause.

Es war niemand zu Hause.

Jemand hat heute nachmittag nach Ihnen gefragt.

Es hat heute nachmittag jemand nach Ihnen gefragt.

Leider meldete sich niemand.

Es meldete sich leider niemand.

Jetzt werden wieder Häuser gebaut.
Es werden jetzt wieder Häuser gebaut.

Viele Leute waren nicht *da*.
Es waren nicht viele *Leute* da.

Ach Emma, du bist's!
Wer ist denn da?—Ich bin's, Emma.
Meyer kann es nicht gewesen sein.

Es regnet schon seit Tagen.
Hier regnet es schon seit Tagen.

Es hat schon wieder gehagelt.
Hier hat es heute schon wieder gehagelt.

Es hat die ganze Nacht geschneit.
Heute morgen hat es ein bißchen geschneit.

Es hat stundenlang gedonnert und geblitzt, aber geregnet hat es nicht.

Wie geht es denn deinem Vater?—Danke, es geht ihm gut.
Dem Anton geht's immer gut.
Mir geht es heute gar nicht gut; mir geht's schlecht.
Guten Tag, Herr Müller. Ich habe Sie lange nicht gesehen; wie geht's Ihnen denn?

Vor hundert Jahren gab es noch keine Flugzeuge.
Da oben ist ein Flugzeug.

Was gibt's denn zum Mittagessen?
Es gibt jeden Tag Schweinebraten.
Das ist doch kein Schweinebraten, das ist Kalbsbraten.

Wieviele Hotels gibt es denn hier?
Heute gibt es nicht mehr viele Familien mit neun Kindern.

[8] The Impersonal **es** Anticipating a Subject Clause

Es ist nicht gestattet, während der Fahrt mit dem Wagenführer zu sprechen.
Natürlich ist es nicht gestattet, während der Fahrt mit dem Wagenführer zu sprechen.

SEE ANALYSIS 205 (pp. 452-455)

Es ist leider nicht erlaubt, vor dem Rathaus zu parken.
Leider ist es nicht erlaubt, vor dem Rathaus zu parken.

Es ist verboten, die Türen während der Fahrt zu öffnen.
Ist es verboten, die Türen während der Fahrt zu öffnen?

Es wurde berichtet, daß Ingelheim spurlos verschwunden wäre.
Heute wird aus Kairo berichtet, daß die erste Meldung auf einem Irrtum beruhte.

Es muß leider angenommen werden, daß er nicht mehr am Leben ist.
Leider muß angenommen werden, daß er nicht mehr am Leben ist.

Es wurde vorgeschlagen, eine neue Brücke über den Rhein zu bauen.
Von allen Seiten wurde vorgeschlagen, eine neue Brücke über den Rhein zu bauen.

Es wird oft behauptet, daß Männer besser Auto fahren können als Frauen.
Früher wurde oft behauptet, daß Männer besser Auto fahren könnten als Frauen.

Es wurde beschlossen, endlich eine neue Klinik zu bauen.
Gestern abend wurde beschlossen, endlich eine neue Klinik zu bauen.

Leider konnte nicht festgestellt werden, wer der Dieb ist.
Es konnte nicht festgestellt werden, wer der Dieb ist.
Wer der Dieb ist, konnte bis jetzt nicht festgestellt werden.

Invent anticipating clauses with **es** for the following subject clauses.

_____, das Kind in eine Privatschule zu schicken.
_____, Ingelheim hätte sich scheiden lassen.
_____, daß er nicht gerettet worden ist.
_____, hier ein Bürohaus zu bauen.

[9] Pre-Noun Inserts

Note that the parentheses are added here only to indicate the
pre-noun inserts; they are not normally written.

SEE
ANALYSIS
207
(pp. 456-458)

Mein Chef, der gottseidank nicht sehr intelligent ist, weiß gar nicht, daß es in Berlin auch
billigere Hotels gibt.
Mein (gottseidank nicht sehr intelligenter) Chef weiß gar nicht, daß es in Berlin auch
billigere Hotels gibt.

Der Winter, der selbst für Norwegen ungewöhnlich kalt war, wollte gar kein Ende
nehmen.
Der (selbst für Norwegen ungewöhnlich kalte) Winter wollte gar kein Ende nehmen.

Die Fluggäste, die soeben mit Lufthansa Flug Nummer 401 aus Frankfurt angekommen
sind, werden gebeten, den Warteraum nicht zu verlassen.
Die (soeben mit Lufthansa Flug Nummer 401 aus Frankfurt angekommenen) Fluggäste
werden gebeten, den Warteraum nicht zu verlassen.

Karthago, das von den Römern zerstört wurde, ist nicht wiederaufgebaut worden.
Das (von den Römern zerstörte) Karthago ist nicht wiederaufgebaut worden.

Aloys Hinterkofer, der seit Wochen von der Polizei gesucht wird, soll gestern in der
Regina-Bar gesehen worden sein.
Der (seit Wochen von der Polizei gesuchte) Aloys Hinterkofer soll gestern in der Regina-
Bar gesehen worden sein.

Die Züge, die im Sommer von München nach Italien fahren, sind meistens überfüllt.
Die (im Sommer von München nach Italien fahrenden) Züge sind meistens überfüllt.

Alle Studenten, die an dem Projekt interessiert waren, das Professor Behrens vorgeschlagen hatte, wurden gebeten, sich am nächsten Tag auf dem Sekretariat zu melden.
Alle (an dem von Professor Behrens vorgeschlagenen Projekt interessierten) Studenten
wurden gebeten, sich am nächsten Tag auf dem Sekretariat zu melden.

If you can figure out the next sentence, you have really mastered the
last few units:

Meine Damen und Herren, es handelt sich hier um ein (von der Wissenschaft bis heute
noch kaum beachtetes und, soweit ich das aufgrund meiner Untersuchungen beurteilen
kann, immer wichtiger werdendes) mathematisches Problem.

Reading

Wie oft läßt sich ein Körper teilen?

Die Frage, wie oft sich ein Körper teilen läßt, ist schon im Altertum
gestellt worden. Was geschieht zum Beispiel, so fragte man, wenn
man ein kleines Körnchen Salz mit immer feineren Messern in immer
kleinere Teile teilt? Auch das kleinste Teilchen wäre ja kein mathe-
matischer Punkt. Auch von dem kleinsten Teilchen müßte immer 5
noch ein gewisser, wenn auch sehr kleiner, Raum ausgefüllt werden;
und rein theoretisch müßte sich dieser Raum, und damit der Körper,
von dem dieser Raum ausgefüllt ist, weiter teilen lassen.

Nach Demokrit kann ein Körper nicht unendlich oft geteilt werden.
Bei einem letzten Schnitt entstehen zwei Teile, die sich nicht weiter 10
teilen lassen. Diese kleinsten Teilchen nannte er Atome; und er
scheint gelehrt zu haben (seine Lehre ist uns nur durch die
Schriften seiner Gegner überliefert), daß es außer diesen Atomen
nur blinde Kräfte, wie z.B. die Gravitation, gibt, aber keinen Geist,
der „über" der Materie steht. 15

Aristoteles ging von dem Gegensatz zwischen „Form" und „Stoff"
aus. Nach dieser Lehre, von der auch das Denken des Mittelalters
beherrscht war, ist der Unterschied zwischen dem Element Wasser
und dem Element Luft auf den Unterschied zwischen der „Form"
(oder Struktur) des Wassers und der „Form" (oder Struktur) der 20
Luft zurückzuführen. Wird z.B. ein Tropfen Wasser immer weiter
geteilt, so muß schließlich ein Augenblick kommen, wo die für das
Wasser charakteristische Struktur zerstört wird. Das letzte Teilchen

das Körnchen, – little grain

rein   pure(ly)

die Lehre, –n   teaching
der Gegner, –   opponent
überliefern   transmit
die Kraft, ⁻e   force
der Geist, –er   spirit
die Materie   matter
der Stoff, –e   substance, matter
beherrschen   to rule
der Tropfen, –   drop

Wasser kann also zwar noch geteilt werden, aber das Resultat wären
nicht zwei noch kleinere Tröpfchen Wasser, sondern vielleicht zwei
Teilchen Luft oder Feuer, von denen jedes die für die Luft oder für
das Feuer charakteristische „Form" (oder Struktur) hätte. Nach
dieser Lehre kann die formlose oder strukturlose Materie, die 5
materia prima, nicht als solche existieren. Alle Körper enthalten
zwar *materia prima,* aber sie sind das, was sie sind (Luft, Feuer,
Erde, Wasser, Gold), nicht durch die in ihnen steckende Materie,
sondern durch die für sie charakteristische Form.

enthalten to contain

steckend existing, contained

Bei den Versuchen der Alchimisten, Blei in Gold zu verwandeln, 10
war die Lehre von dem Gegensatz zwischen *materia prima* und
forma stets vorausgesetzt. Wir wissen heute, daß die Alchimisten
im letzten Grunde recht hatten. Die von ihnen vorausgesetzte Ein- 15
heit alles Stofflichen ist heute sichergestellt, ja, sogar die Verwandlung eines Metalls in ein anderes, z.B. von Natrium in Magnesium,
ist bereits Tatsache geworden.

das Blei lead
verwandeln transform
**die vorausgesetzte
Einheit** the presup-
posed unity
sicherstellen to secure
das Natrium sodium
das Magnesium
magnesium
die Tatsache, –n fact

Aber den Alchimisten fehlte die wissenschaftliche Methode, d.h.
eine Methode, die Natur durch gut ausgedachte Experimente dazu
zu zwingen, eine ihr gestellte Frage so zu beantworten, daß diese
Antwort durch weitere Experimente geprüft und bestätigt werden 20
kann.

prüfen to test
bestätigen to confirm

Vor allem aber fehlte den Alchimisten die Geduld. Sie wollten das
Gebäude der Wissenschaft sozusagen mit dem Dach anfangen. Es
ist das große Verdienst Robert Boyles (1627–1691), seine Kollegen
dazu gebracht zu haben, daß sie sich zunächst einmal mit dem Bau 25
des Fundamentes beschäftigten, d.h. mit der Frage, wieviele Elemente es denn eigentlich gibt. Wir können uns heute kaum noch
vorstellen, wieviel Boyle von seiner Zeit verlangte, als er das Spekulieren über die *materia prima* beiseite schob und lehrte: In dem roten
Mineral Zinnober stecken tatsächlich die beiden Stoffe Schwefel und 30
Quecksilber. Der Zinnober besteht aus ihnen, so wie etwa ein Haus
aus Steinen und aus Holz besteht. Diese Behauptung schien paradox
zu sein, denn von den Eigenschaften beider „Elemente" ist ja nichts
mehr wahrzunehmen, sobald sie sich „verbunden" haben.

das Verdienst, –e
merit
der Bau, –ten build-
ing, construction
das Fundament, –e
foundation
das Spekulieren
speculation
beiseite aside
der Zinnober cinna-
bar
der Schwefel sulfur
das Quecksilber
mercury, quicksilver
die Eigenschaft, –en
characteristic
wahrnehmen to ob-
serve, perceive, notice

Aber erst als man sich entschloß, dieses Paradox zunächst einmal— 35
obwohl noch ungelöst—zu vergessen, wurde es möglich, durch lang-
same Arbeit die 92 Elemente zu entdecken, aus denen die materielle
Welt besteht. Als mit dieser Entdeckung das wissenschaftliche
Fundament gelegt war, konnte die Frage gestellt werden, ob diese
92 Elemente vom Wasserstoff bis zum Uran sich vielleicht doch 40
noch weiter „teilen" lassen.

der Wasserstoff hy-
drogen
das Uran' uranium

Die Suche nach dem Glück

Wir wollen hier nun endlich die Frage stellen, ob das Suchen nach
dem Glück wirklich ein sinnvolles Suchen ist. Das Glück hängt ja
nicht nur von materiellen Dingen ab, es hängt vor allem ab von
der Empfänglichkeit des Menschen, davon, ob er fähig ist, glücklich
zu sein. Diese Glücksfähigkeit aber leidet unter dem Suchen nach 5
Glück: Sie ist am größten, wenn ein geschenktes Gut nicht gesucht
war; sie ist am geringsten, wenn dieses Gut leidenschaftlich gewünscht wurde. Das Wünschen selbst, so scheint es, zerstört den
Glückswert des Gewünschten, und das Erreichen wird illusorisch,
weil das Erreichte für den Wünschenden nicht mehr dasselbe Glück 10
ist, das er suchte und das er erwartete. Das wirkliche Glück kommt
immer von einer anderen Seite als man es meint; es liegt immer da,
wo man es nicht sucht. Es kommt immer als Geschenk und läßt sich
dem Leben nicht abzwingen. Denn das Glück liegt in den Werten
des Lebens, die zwar immer da sind, die aber nur der findet, der 15
diese Werte selbst sucht und nicht das Glück, das sie versprechen.
Das Glück begleitet diese Werte, aber wer nur dem Glück nachläuft
und nicht die Werte selbst sucht, dem bleibt das Glück für immer
ein Phantom.

(nach Nicolai Hartmann, Ethik) 20

die Empfänglichkeit, –en receptivity

am geringsten least
leidenschaftlich passionate(ly)
der Wert, –e value

Im Jahr 2000 nur ein Stehplatz im Grünen?

Für Trabantenstädte, Vorortsiedlungen, Industrieanlagen,
Straßen, Autobahnkreuzungen und Landepisten wird die
Bundesrepublik Deutschland bis 1980 jährlich rund
45 000 Hektar freie Landschaft verlieren.

Wohnungsbau, Industrie und Verkehr sind nicht allein 5
angeklagt. Es kommen hinzu der erhöhte Rohstoff- und
Energieverbrauch, die Zunahme der Abfälle, Abgase und
Abwässer, die fortschreitende Veränderung in der Bodenbewirtschaftung und der steigende Flächenbedarf für
Freizeit und Erholung. Das Vermögen der Landschaft, 10
diese Eingriffe und Belastungen ökologisch auszugleichen,
wird immer geringer. In vielen Teilen der Bundesrepublik
Deutschland ist die Natur den Ansprüchen, die der
Mensch an sie stellt, nicht mehr gewachsen, die Grenzen
ihrer Belastbarkeit sind weit überschritten. 15

der Stehplatz, ̈e standing room
im Grünen in the countryside
der Trabant, –en satellite
die Siedlung, –en development
die Anlage, –n plant
die Kreuzung, –en intersection
die Landepiste, –n runway
jährlich annually
der Wohnungsbau residential construction   **anklagen** to accuse
erhöht increased   **verbrauchen** to
consume   **die Zunahme** increase
der Abfall, ̈e waste
das Abgas, –e waste gas
das Abwasser, ̈ waste water
fortschreitend progressive
die Bodenbewirtschaftung use of
land   **der Flächenbedarf** space re-
quirement   **die Freizeit** leisure
die Erholung recreation
das Vermögen capacity
der Eingriff, –e inroads
die Belastung, –en burden
ausgleichen to balance **gering** small

„Wenn wir nicht rechtzeitig vorbeugen, wird unseren Enkeln Landschaft nur gegen Eintrittsgebühr geliefert. Sie werden einen Stehplatz im Grünen vorfinden." Wird sich diese Prognose erfüllen? Dazu ein nüchternes Zitat aus einer amtlichen Broschüre des Bundesministeriums [5] für Ernährung, Landwirtschaft und Forsten: „Ohne lenkende Maßnahmen kann der gesamte Naturhaushalt den wachsenden Bedürfnissen der Industriegesellschaft nicht mehr genügen. Die Bundesregierung ist der Überzeugung, daß dem Schutz der Natur mehr Aufmerk- [10] samkeit gewidmet werden muß." Der letzte Satz ist ein Auszug aus der Regierungserklärung von Bundeskanzler Willy Brandt am 28. Oktober 1969, damals in seiner gesamten Tragweite kaum beachtet, doch seitdem oft zitiert, da er zur Initialzündung des umfassenden Bonner [15] Umweltprogramms wurde, das in den Jahren 1970/71 zunehmend an Aktualität gewann. Heute ist man in der Bundesrepublik Deutschland nicht mehr gewillt, den hohen Tribut zu zahlen, den das Eindringen der Industrie in Reservate der Natur, die planlose Zersiedlung der [20] Landschaft, die Erschließung bisher unberührter Gegenden für touristische Invasionen, die Landflucht und die Verstädterung fordern. Naturschutz wird nicht mehr als Luxus angesehen, auf den man gegebenenfalls verzichten kann. Naturschutz ist auch keine rückwärtsge- [25] richtete Tätigkeit mehr, die lebende Museen kultiviert. Es geht vielmehr darum, die Voraussetzungen für das Leben, manche sagen sogar für das bloße Überleben, zu bewahren. Naturschutz heißt auch nicht nur Schutz der Natur, sondern vor allem auch Schutz der Natur für den [30] Menschen. Hier darf nichts dem Zufall oder irgendeinem Marktmechanismus überlassen bleiben. Es bedarf der übergreifenden Planung, die auch vor ungewöhnlichen Schritten nicht zurückschreckt.

---

vorbeugen to take precautions
die Gebühr, –en fee
liefern to furnish   **erfüllen** to fulfill

nüchtern sober   **das Zitat, –e** quotation   **amtlich** official

lenkende Maßnahmen directive measures   **gesamt** entire
der Naturhaushalt ecology
das Bedürfnis, –se need
die Gesellschaft society   **genügen** to suffice   **der Schutz** protection
die Aufmerksamkeit attention
widmen to devote   **der Auszug, –̈e** excerpt   **die Erklärung, –en** statement   **die Tragweite** significance
beachten to notice   **zitieren** to quote   **die Zündung** trigger
umfassend comprehensive
die Umwelt environment
die Aktualität importance
das Eindringen intrusion
die Zersiedlung destruction by subdivision   **die Erschließung** opening-up   **unberührt** unspoiled
die Landflucht flight from the country   **die Verstädterung** urbanization   **gegebenenfalls** if need be
verzichten to dispense with
rückwärtsgerichtet backward-looking   **darum gehen** to be a question of   **vielmehr** rather
die Voraussetzung, –en prerequisite
bloß mere   **das Überleben** survival
bewahren to preserve

überlassen to leave to
bedürfen to take
übergreifend all-encompassing
der Schritt, –e step
zurückschrecken to be afraid

Analysis

197 Active Voice and Passive Voice

Compare these two groups of sentences:

We feed him once a day.	He is fed once a day.
We fed him once a day.	He was fed once a day.
We have always fed him once a day.	He has always been fed once a day.
We ought to feed him once a day.	He ought to be fed once a day.
We ought to have fed him once a day.	He ought to have been fed once a day.

The comparison shows that the forms of the transitive verb *to feed* (*a dog*)—that is, of a verb that can take a direct object—fall into two groups, called the *active voice* and the *passive voice*.

	ACTIVE VOICE	PASSIVE VOICE
PRESENT	he feeds	he is fed
PAST	he fed	he was fed
PRESENT PERFECT	he has fed	he has been fed
PRESENT INFINITIVE	to feed	to be fed
PAST INFINITIVE	to have fed	to have been fed

It is easy to see why the terms "active" and "passive" were chosen to identify these forms. In sentences like *We feed our dog*, the grammatical subject acting upon the object is an "active agent," whereas in *Our dog is fed once a day*, the grammatical subject plays the role of a "passive patient" who "suffers" the agent's activity.

198 Action and State

The phrase *was fed* in the two sentences

> The dog was fed well

and

> The dog was well fed

refers to two fundamentally different situations; for *was fed well* expresses the repeated action of feeding the dog, whereas *was well fed* refers to the state resulting from this action. However, though the difference between state and action is expressed in this particular case by word order, English has not developed a system which forces the speaker to differentiate at all

times between an action and the state resulting from this action. Thus the sentence

The house was built on a hill

can refer both to the action of building the house "from scratch" and to the accomplished fact that the house had been built and was sitting on a hill. In contrast to English, German forces the speaker to select his passive-voice forms in such a way that they refer either to an action or to the state resulting from this action. An ambiguous form comparable to English *was built* simply does not exist. Actions are expressed by the *actional passive*—a form of **werden** plus a participle—and the resulting state is expressed by the *statal passive*—a form of **sein** plus a participle used as a predicate adjective.

ACTION	STATE
Das Haus wird morgen verkauft.	
Das Haus ist gestern verkauft worden.	**Das Haus ist schon verkauft.**

The forms of the actional passive and those of the statal passive are never interchangeable. In the case of some verbs, the actional passive and the statal passive occur with equal frequency. Thus it makes linguistic sense to say either

Die Stadt war zerstört	The city was (already) destroyed (as the result of previous bombings)

or

Die Stadt wurde zerstört.	The city was destroyed. (during the war by bombing)
Die Stadt ist zerstört worden.	

However, in cases like **Das Haus war nicht versichert** (*The house was not insured*), the speaker is usually more interested in the state; and therefore the actional passive

Das Haus wurde versichert	The house was (going through the act of being) insured

hardly ever occurs.

199 The Forms of the Statal and Actional Passive

	STATAL PASSIVE	ACTIONAL PASSIVE
PRESENT	ist enttäuscht	wird enttäuscht
PAST	war enttäuscht	wurde enttäuscht
PERFECT	ist enttäuscht gewesen	ist enttäuscht worden
FUTURE	wird enttäuscht sein	wird enttäuscht werden
INFINITIVE	enttäuscht sein	enttäuscht werden
	enttäuscht gewesen sein	enttäuscht worden sein

NOTE: The participle of **werden**, when used as an auxiliary, is **worden,** not **geworden.**

200 Choice between Active and Passive Voice

In order to describe the difference between *His father punished him* and *He was punished by his father,* it is sometimes stated that the direct object (*him*) of an active verb becomes the grammatical subject (*he*) of the passive verb. This is true. However, it is necessary to point out two things.

First, the German passive is used only if there is a situation in which an "active agent" somehow focuses his action or attention on an object. German is much more rigid in this respect than English. It is perfectly acceptable English to say

Ingelheim was killed in an accident

although this statement does not mean that some "active agent" killed him. German, on the other hand, because there is no "active agent" involved, cannot use a passive and will use the intransitive verb **verunglücken** (*to die in an accident*) instead.

Ingelheim ist gestern verunglückt.

Second, if the sentence *My sister has adopted a child,* which does contain both an agent and a patient being acted upon, is transformed into the state-

ment *A child was adopted by my sister,* this indicates a change in the speaker's focus of attention.

When I say *My sister adopted a child, my sister* is not only the grammatical subject, but also the focus of my attention. I am making a statement about my sister, not a statement about a child. Conversely, the attention of a nurse in a home for orphans is focused on the children under her care. She might, therefore, say, *Last week we got six babies; three have already been adopted. One was adopted by my sister.*

Nobody ever mentally forms an active sentence and then transforms it into a passive sentence. Such transformations are only classroom exercises. Nevertheless, the term "transformation" is not useless, as long as one realizes that one does not transform an active sentence into a passive sentence, but rather shifts the focus of attention from the "agent" to the "patient."

201 Dative Objects

The event reported by the English sentence *They gave him a pill* can also be reported by saying *He was given a pill.* The indirect object *him* of the active clause has been "transformed" into the grammatical subject *he* of the passive clause.

In German, no dative object (of verbs like **helfen** *and* **folgen***) can be transformed into a nominative subject. Not ever!* **Nie!**

> *Beware!*
> *Americanism!*   **[Ich wurde sofort geholfen.]**   DO NOT USE!
> CORRECT   **Der Arzt half mir sofort.**

However, to shift the focus from the doctor to myself, the active sentence **Der Arzt half mir sofort** can be changed into **Mir wurde sofort geholfen.** The result is a sentence without a subject; **wurde geholfen** is an impersonal form not depending on **mir**.

If the speaker wants to place this **mir** in the inner field, he cannot leave the front field empty; for that would change the statement into the question

> **Wurde mir sofort geholfen?**

The declarative force of **mir wurde sofort geholfen** can be maintained in such a case by putting the meaningless filler **es** into the front field.

> **Es wurde mir sofort geholfen.**

This **es** has only one function: it preserves verb-second position. It disappears as soon as the front field is occupied.

> **Natürlich wurde mir sofort geholfen.**

202 Use of the Actional Passive to Express Activity as Such

German verbs like **arbeiten, tanzen, schießen, warten** do not normally govern an accusative object and therefore cannot be used to describe situations in which an agent acts upon a patient. One would not expect them, therefore, to appear in passive sentences. But they do!

The question *What is going on here?* is frequently answered in German by a form of the actional passive.

QUESTION **Was ist denn hier los?**   ANSWER **Hier wird gearbeitet.**
                                                     Hier wird getanzt.

Note that such short sentences do not contain a grammatical subject. The form **wird gearbeitet,** structurally not possible in English, denotes the activity of **arbeiten** as such. **Hier wird gearbeitet** means "The activity of working is going on here."

Further examples:

In meinem Elternhaus wurde viel musiziert.
Bei uns wird auch sonntags gearbeitet.
Seit heute morgen wird zurückgeschossen. (Hitler, on September 1, 1939)

203 The Use of **von, durch,** and **mit** in Passive Sentences

A large percentage of German passive sentences contain only the "passive patient" (the grammatical subject) and no active agent.

If a personal agent is mentioned, **von** is used.

Jerusalem wurde von den Römern zerstört.
Jerusalem was destroyed by the Romans.

Mit is used for things "handled" by a personal agent.

Abel wurde von Kain mit einem Stein erschlagen.
Abel was slain by Cain with a rock.

Das ganze Zimmer war mit Blumen geschmückt.
The whole room was decorated with flowers.

Abstract causes, impersonal causes, and impersonal means of destruction are introduced by **durch.**

Sie wurden durch ein neues Gesetz gezwungen, das Land zu verlassen.
They were forced by a new law to leave the country.

Lissabon wurde durch ein Erdbeben zerstört.
Lisbon was destroyed by an earthquake.

Dresden wurde durch Bomben zerstört.
Dresden was destroyed by bombs.

204 Examples Illustrating the Difference
between Action and State

The difference between action and state was introduced in connection with
the reflexives. It was pointed out that **Fritzchen ist schon gebadet** denotes
the state resulting from **Fritzchen hat sich gebadet.** We now have to point
out that **ist gebadet** may also be the state resulting from the actional passive
Er ist gerade gebadet worden. Of course, **Fritzchen ist schon gebadet** can
also denote the state resulting from an active statement such as **Ich habe
Fritzchen schon gebadet.**

	EVENT	STATE
ACTIVE VOICE	**Die Polizei hat ihn gerettet.** (Perfect)	
ACTIONAL PASSIVE	**Er ist gerettet worden.** (Perfect)	**Er ist gerettet.** (Present)
REFLEXIVE	**Er hat sich gerettet.** (Perfect)	
ACTIVE VOICE	**Sein Vater hatte ihn gut vorbereitet.** (Pluperfect)	
ACTIONAL PASSIVE	**Er war gut vorbereitet worden.** (Pluperfect)	**Er war gut vorbereitet.** (Past)
REFLEXIVE	**Er hatte sich gut vorbereitet.** (Pluperfect)	

205 The Impersonal **es** in the Front Field

Before discussing the impersonal **es** in the front field, it is necessary to recall
that an **es** in the front field cannot be a normal accusative object. For if the
es in the sentence

   Ich weiß es nicht

is shifted into the front field, it becomes **das.**

   Das weiß ich nicht.

Compare English *I don't know it* and *That I don't know.*

The impersonal **es** in the front field has one of three functions: It can (a) be
a meaningless filler to preserve verb-second position; it can (b) be the
grammatical subject of impersonal verbs; and it can (c) be used to anticipate a following dependent clause.

The Use of **es** as a Filler

In a short sentence like

Niemand war zu Hause

the inner field is empty. Both **war,** the first prong, and **zu Hause,** the second prong, are position-fixed. If the speaker, in order to put greater news value on **niemand,** decides to put **niemand** in the inner field, he must put something else in the front field; otherwise he would come up with the question

War niemand zu Hause?

Verb-second position, in these cases, can be preserved by filling the front field with a meaningless **es.**

Es war niemand zu Hause.
Es hat niemand angerufen.

This use of **es** as a filler is rather frequent in connection with the passive voice.

Es werden wieder Häuser gebaut.
Es wird wieder gearbeitet.

In all these cases, **es** disappears when the front field is occupied by another unit.

Gestern war niemand zu Hause.
Gestern hat niemand angerufen.
Hier werden wieder Häuser gebaut.
Hier wird wieder gearbeitet.

NOTE:

1. The **es** used in identification sentences was discussed in **78.** This **es** is not a meaningless filler that disappears when the front field is filled; it can appear either in the front field or immediately behind the first prong.

Es war nicht mein Bruder.
Mein Bruder war es nicht.

The **es** in such sentences means "the thing to be identified." **Ich bin's** corresponds to *it's me,* which cannot be expressed by [**Es bin ich**] or [**Es ist ich**]. Similarly: **Du bist's, er ist's,** and so on.

2. **Es** as a filler is also used in the standard introduction of German fairy tales and folk songs. **Es war einmal ein König** corresponds to *Once upon a time there was a king.* Since the entire news value is concentrated in **ein König,** the subject cannot stand in the front field.

Es war einmal eine alte Geiß.
Es war ein König in Thule.
Es waren zwei Königskinder.
Es steht ein Baum im Odenwald.

es as the Grammatical Subject of Impersonal Verbs

The verbs most frequently used with the impersonal subject **es** are:

> **Es regnet, es schneit, es donnert, es hagelt.**
> **Es geht mir (ihm, ihr, etc.) gut.**
> **Es geht mir (ihm) schlecht.**
> **Es ist mir zu warm (zu kalt, zu heiß).**
> **Es ist zehn Uhr (schon spät, noch früh).**
> **Es gelingt mir.**

In all these cases, the **es** must appear in the inner field if the front field is occupied by some other unit.

> **Es hat gestern geregnet.**   **Gestern hat es geregnet.**
> **Es schneit schon wieder.**   **Schneit es schon wieder?**
> **Es ist mir hier zu warm.**   **Hier ist es mir zu warm.**

Also, the idiom **es gibt** belongs to this group of impersonal verbs. **Es gibt,** translatable by either *there is* or *there are*, and roughly meaning "the situation provides," governs the accusative. In connection with a food term, it expresses what will be served. In other cases, it expresses that certain things exist as a permanent part of the environment or of nature.

> **Heute mittag gibt es Kartoffelsuppe.**
> **In Afrika gibt es noch immer wilde Elefanten.**
> **Gibt es hier ein Hotel?**

Unlike the English *there is,* **es gibt** can never be used to point at a specific thing or person.

> *Beware!*
> *Americanism!*   **[Da oben gibt es ein Flugzeug.]**   DO NOT USE!
> CORRECT   **Da oben ist ein Flugzeug.**

The Anticipating **es**

The use of **es** to anticipate a following dependent clause is comparable to the use of English *it* in

> I have *it* on good authority that Smith will be our next boss
> *It* simply is not true that she has gone to college

where the *it,* which cannot be left out, anticipates the following *that*-clause.

The German anticipatory **es** refers forward to a dependent (subject) clause, and **es** is the grammatical subject of the main clause.

> **Es ist möglich, daß Ingelheim noch lebt.**
> **Es ist nicht wahrscheinlich, daß Ingelheim noch lebt.**

Es ist nicht leicht, mit einer Frau wie Ilse verheiratet zu sein.
Es tut ihm leid, daß ich gestern nicht kommen konnte.
Es wird berichtet, daß Ingelheim spurlos verschwunden ist.
Es freut mich, daß Sie kommen konnten.

As long as this anticipatory **es** precedes the clause it anticipates, it does not disappear when the front field is occupied by some other unit.

Natürlich ist es auch möglich, daß Ingelheim noch lebt.
Wahrscheinlich ist es allerdings nicht, daß Ingelheim noch lebt.
Natürlich tut es mir leid, daß ich gestern nicht kommen konnte.

Only the actional passive in such phrases as **Es wird berichtet, daß . . .** becomes **Gestern wurde berichtet, daß . . .**

If the dependent clause precedes the main clause, the anticipatory **es** disappears, because there is nothing left to anticipate.

Daß Ingelheim noch lebt, ist ganz unwahrscheinlich.

206 jetzt and nun

Though both **jetzt** and **nun** are frequently equivalent to English *now*, they are not always interchangeable. **Jetzt** is an adverb of time without any implications.

Es ist jetzt zwölf Uhr fünfzehn.
Meyer wohnt jetzt in München.

Nun, on the other hand, always implies a reference to something which precedes; it therefore contains the idea that one state of affairs is superseded by another.

Und nun wohnt er in München.
(He used to live elsewhere.)

Und nun ist er schon drei Jahre tot.
(He used to be so full of life.)

Bist du nun zufrieden?
(I know you were dissatisfied before.)

Und nun hören Sie zum Abschluß unserer Sendung „Eine kleine Nachtmusik" von Wolfgang Amadeus Mozart.
And now we conclude our broadcast with Mozart's "Eine kleine Nachtmusik."

Because of the connotation "this is something new," **nun mal (nun einmal)** has the flavor "you might as well get used to it."

Das *ist* nun einmal so.
That's the way it is.

Ich *bin* nun mal nicht so intelligent wie du.
You might as well accept the fact that I'm not as intelligent as you are.

Na und? Ich *bin* nun mal kein Genie.
So what? I'm not a genius, and that's that.

207 Pre-Noun Inserts

Syntactical units like *a child* can be separated by adjectives, which are placed between the article and the noun. We shall call such inserted adjectives *pre-noun inserts*. For the sake of clarity and illustration, pre-noun inserts are placed within parentheses in this section.

In English, one can speak of *a (healthy) child* or even of *a (healthy but somewhat retarded) child.* However, one cannot speak of

> a (by a series of unfortunate childhood experiences somewhat retarded, but otherwise quite healthy) child

English speakers don't have that long a syntactical breath. In German, prenoun inserts of considerable length are a standard characteristic of expository prose and academic lectures.

Man sollte dieses** (durch eine Reihe von unglücklichen Kindheitserlebnissen leider etwas zurückgebliebene, aber sonst ganz gesunde) **Mädchen nicht der Gefahr aussetzen, von** (gleichaltrigen, nicht zurückgebliebenen) **Kindern unfreundlich behandelt zu werden.	*One should not expose this girl,* (who, though quite healthy, is unfortunately retarded by a number of unhappy childhood experiences,) *to the danger of being treated in an unfriendly way by children* (of the same age who are not retarded).

Both in English and in German, pre-noun adjective inserts can be viewed as shorthand versions of dependent clauses, usually relative clauses. Thus

This . . . . child, who is   really very beautiful

becomes

This   really very beautiful   child

and

Dieses . . . . Kind, das   wirklich sehr schön   ist

becomes

Dieses   wirklich sehr schöne   Kind

The example shows that

1. When a German dependent clause is transformed into a pre-noun insert, it drops its subject and the inflected verb belonging to it.

2. Since this transformation changes a predicate adjective or a participle into an attributive adjective, the adjective acquires an ending.

As far as German is concerned, pre-noun inserts, with the exception of (5) below, consist of an inner field plus a second prong. The usual word order is preserved. Pre-noun inserts can originate in the following ways:

1. The second prong is a predicate adjective.

> Dieses . . . . Mädchen, das sehr intelligent ist

becomes

> Dieses sehr intelligente Mädchen

2. The second prong is the participle of an intransitive verb like **ankommen, fallen, sterben,** or **zurückbleiben,** which forms its compound tenses with **sein.**

> Dieses . . . . Kind, das leider etwas zurückgeblieben ist

becomes

> Dieses leider etwas zurückgebliebene Kind

3. The second prong is the participle used to form the actional or statal passive.

> Diese Stadt, die während des letzten Krieges zerstört wurde (Actional Passive)

becomes

> Diese während des letzten Krieges zerstörte Stadt

> Diese Stadt, die noch nicht wiederaufgebaut ist (Statal Passive)

becomes

> Diese noch nicht wiederaufgebaute Stadt

> Diese (während des letzten Krieges zerstörte) und (noch nicht wiederaufgebaute) Stadt war einmal ein wichtiges Kulturzentrum.

4. The second prong is the participle belonging to a reflexive verb.

Der Gast, der sich   betrunken   **hat** (event)

The guest who got drunk

and

Der Gast, der   betrunken   **ist** (state)

The guest who is drunk

become

Der   betrunkene   **Gast**

5. As long as it makes sense, any present and past form of the *active* voice may be changed into a **-d** adjective. This **-d** adjective, preceded by its inner field, can then be used as a pre-noun insert.

Das Kind, das   laut schrie

becomes

Das   laut schreiende   **Kind**

Die allgemeine Frage, die (hinter diesem speziellen Problem steckt)
The general question which stands behind this special problem
　　Die (hinter diesem Problem steckende) **allgemeine Frage**

Die Bevölkerung Chinas, die (immer schneller wächst)
The population of China, which is growing faster and faster
　　Die (immer schneller wachsende) **Bevölkerung Chinas**

Der Weg, der (vom Dorf aus in den Wald) **führt**
The path which leads from the village to the forest
　　Der (vom Dorf aus in den Wald führende) **Weg**

Exercises

A. Change the following short sentences from the active voice to the actional passive. Do not change the tense. Omit the subject of the active sentence.

| **Man brachte ihn zurück.** | **Er wurde zurückgebracht.** |

1. Man führte uns durch den Garten.
2. Man trennte die Kinder von ihren Eltern.
3. Um acht Uhr schloß man das Tor.
4. Mich nimmt man nie mit.
5. Man suchte ihn, aber man fand ihn nicht.
6. Man schickte ihn nach Hause.
7. Man hielt ihn für einen Spion und erschoß ihn.
8. Man brachte uns im Löwen unter.
9. Man hat uns wieder im Löwen untergebracht.
10. Man hat ihn schon wieder gebeten, eine Rede zu halten.

SEE
ANALYSIS
200

(pp. 449-450)

B. In the following sentences, change the present actional passive forms into (a) present statal passive forms and (b) perfect actional passive forms.

| **Die Stadt wird zerstört.** | **(a) Die Stadt ist zerstört.**
(b) Die Stadt ist zerstört worden. |

1. Die Brücke wird schon gebaut.
2. Die Schweine werden gefüttert.
3. Der Brief wird schon geschrieben.
4. Es wird beschlossen.
5. Es wird gefunden.
6. Die Tür wird geschlossen.

SEE
ANALYSIS
198–199

(pp. 447-449)

C. Change the following active sentences into actional passive sentences. Omit the subject of the active sentence.

| **Wir zeigen den Film jetzt auch in Deutschland.**
Der Film wird jetzt auch in Deutschland gezeigt. |

1. In den Vereinigten Staaten trinkt man mehr Bier als in Deutschland.
2. Mich lädt nie jemand ein.
3. In unserem Elternhaus haben wir viel musiziert.
4. Kolumbus hat Amerika 1492 entdeckt.
5. Sie konnten nur wenige retten.
6. Wann hat Ihr Vater denn dieses Haus gebaut?

SEE
ANALYSIS
200

(pp. 449-450)

D. In the following sentences, supply **von, mit,** or **durch.**

1. Die Stadt wurde _____ ein Erdbeben völlig zerstört.
2. Die Stadt wurde _____ einen Bombenangriff völlig zerstört.

SEE
ANALYSIS
203

(p. 451)

3. Die Stadt wurde _____ den Russen zerstört.
4. Er ist _____ einem Stein erschlagen worden.
5. Er ist _____ seinem Bruder erschlagen worden.
6. Der Brief ist mir _____ meinem Vater nachgeschickt worden.
7. Er hat den Brief zwar unterschrieben, aber der Brief ist nicht _____ ihm selbst geschrieben worden.
8. Er hat alle seine Briefe _____ der Schreibmaschine geschrieben.
9. Ich wurde _____ meinem Chef nach Afrika geschickt.
10. Amerika ist _____ Kolumbus _____ Zufall entdeckt worden.

E. In the following sentences, supply either a form of **werden** or a form of **sein**.

SEE
ANALYSIS
198–199

(pp. 447-449)

1. Daß die Erde sich um die Sonne bewegt, _____ schon lange bewiesen.
2. Die Stadt _____ im Jahre 1944 zerstört.
3. Im Jahre 1950 _____ die Stadt noch nicht wieder aufgebaut.
4. Der weiße Mercedes _____ schon verkauft.
5. Das Haus neben der Kirche soll nächste Woche verkauft _____.
6. Der Film hat mir gar nicht gefallen. Ich _____ wirklich enttäuscht.

F. Change the following relative clauses into pre-noun inserts.

SEE
ANALYSIS
207

(pp. 456-458)

1. Der Zug, der soeben aus München angekommen ist, fährt in zehn Minuten weiter.
2. Für einen jungen Menschen, der in einem Dorf in den bayerischen Alpen großgeworden ist, ist es nicht leicht, sich an die Großstadt zu gewöhnen.
3. Hans ist jetzt Arzt, aber sein Bruder, der viel intelligenter ist, hat nie seinen Doktor gemacht.
4. Ingrids Vater war ein Architekt, der auch in Amerika bekannt war.
5. Die Städte, die während des Krieges zerstört wurden, sind heute fast alle wieder aufgebaut.
6. Die Douglas-Maschinen, die in Amerika gebaut werden, sieht man heute auf allen deutschen Flughäfen.
7. Der Juwelendieb, der seit Wochen von der Polizei gesucht wird, soll gestern in München gesehen worden sein.
8. Der Preis, der für diesen Rembrandt bezahlt worden ist, ist nach meiner Meinung viel zu hoch.
9. Seine Mutter, die noch immer in Berlin wohnte, hatte er seit Jahren nicht gesehen.
10. Er sah sie mit einem Blick an, der viel sagte.

Basic Vocabulary

abhängen von	to depend upon
begleiten	to accompany
bereits	already
berichten	to report
sich beschäftigen mit	to occupy oneself with
beschäftigt sein	to be occupied; employed
die Beschäftigung, –en	occupation
beschließen	to decide, to determine
bestehen aus	to consist of
beurteilen	to judge, to make a judgment
blitzen	to lighten; flash
der Blitz, –e	lightning
brennen	to burn
das Ding, –e	thing
donnern	to thunder
der Donner (*no pl.*)	thunder
einzig	only, sole, single
entdecken	to discover
entstehen	to originate; to come into being
enttäuschen	to disappoint
erfinden	to invent
fähig	capable
feststellen	to determine; to find out
das Feuer, –	fire
fragen nach	to inquire about
eine Frage stellen	to ask a question
eine Frage beantworten	to answer a question
füllen	to fill
überfüllt	overcrowded, packed (trains)
das Gebäude, –	building
geboren werden	to be born
der Gegensatz, ¨e	contrast
gelingen (*impersonal*)	to succeed
es gelingt mir (*plus infinitive*)	I succeed (to do)
gestatten (*formal term*)	to permit
gewöhnlich	usual
der Grund, ¨e	reason; ground
aufgrund (*prep. with gen.*)	on the basis of
das Holz, ¨er	wood
der Irrtum, ¨er	error
das Jahrhundert, –e	century
jedenfalls	at any rate
der Körper, –	body
langsam	slow
leid tun	to feel sorry
sie tat ihm leid	he felt sorry for her
es tut mir leid	I feel sorry about that
leiden	to suffer
los	loose
Was ist los?	What's the matter? What's going on?
der Markt, ¨e	the market (place)
sich melden	to report
da meldet sich niemand	nobody answers (telephone)
das Mittelalter	Middle Ages
der Raum, ¨e	room; space
der Warteraum	waiting room
schieben	to shove
soeben	just, just now
der Stoff, –e	matter; material
stofflich (*adj.*)	material
die Suche	search
unendlich	infinite
die Vereinigten Staaten	the United States
die Verwandlung, –en	change, metamorphosis
vorbeigehen	to pass, to pass by
wiederaufbauen	to reconstruct
die Wissenschaft, –en	science
wissenschaftlich	scientific

Additional Vocabulary

abnehmen	to decrease; to take off (weight)	beruhen auf (*with dat.*)	to be based on
abzwingen	to gain by force	die Bombe, –n	bomb
das Altertum	antiquity	braten	to roast, to fry
die Auflage, –n	printing, edition	der Braten, –	roast
aussetzen	to expose	der Schweinebraten, –	pork roast
beachten	to note, to notice	der Kalbsbraten, –	veal roast

Strong and Irregular Verbs

abhängen, hing ab, hat abgehangen, es hängt ab	to depend
beschließen, beschloß, hat beschlossen, er beschließt	to decide, to determine
bestehen, bestand, hat bestanden, er besteht	to consist
braten, briet, hat gebraten, er brät	to roast, to fry
brennen, brannte, hat gebrannt, er brennt	to burn
entstehen, entstand, ist entstanden, er entsteht	to originate; to come into being
erfinden, erfand, hat erfunden, er erfindet	to invent
erschlagen, erschlug, hat erschlagen, er erschlägt	to slay
gelingen, gelang, ist gelungen, es gelingt	to succeed
leiden, litt, hat gelitten, er leidet	to suffer
schieben, schob, hat geschoben, er schiebt	to shove
vorbeigehen, ging vorbei, ist vorbeigegangen, er geht vorbei	to pass, to pass by

Principal Parts of Strong and Irregular Verbs

NOTE: Many compound verbs, such as **aufmachen** and **ausgehen,** are not included in this table. The principal parts of such verbs will be identical in basic form with those of the corresponding simple verbs (**machen, gehen**).

abhängen von to depend upon
  hing ab von, hat abgehangen von, es hängt ab von
anfangen to begin, start
  fing an, hat angefangen, er fängt an
ankommen to arrive
  kam an, ist angekommen, er kommt an
annehmen to accept; to assume
  nahm an, hat angenommen, er nimmt an
anrufen to call up (on the telephone)
  rief an, hat angerufen, er ruft an
aufstehen to get up, to rise
  stand auf, ist aufgestanden, er steht auf

backen to bake
  backte (also **buk**), **hat gebacken, er bäckt**
befehlen to order, command
  befahl, hat befohlen, er befiehlt
beginnen to begin, start
  begann, hat begonnen, er beginnt
begreifen to comprehend
  begriff, hat begriffen, er begreift
behalten to keep, retain; to remember

behielt, hat behalten, er behält
bekommen to get, receive
  bekam, hat bekommen, er bekommt
beschließen to decide, determine
  beschloß, hat beschlossen, er beschließt
beweisen to prove
  bewies, hat bewiesen, er beweist
bitten to ask for, request
  bat, hat gebeten, er bittet
bleiben to stay, remain
  blieb, ist geblieben, er bleibt
braten to roast; to fry
  briet, hat gebraten, er brät
brechen to break
  brach, hat gebrochen, er bricht
brennen to burn
  brannte, hat gebrannt, er brennt
bringen to bring
  brachte, hat gebracht, er bringt

denken to think
  dachte, hat gedacht, er denkt
dürfen to be permitted to
  durfte, hat gedurft, er darf
einladen to invite
  lud ein, hat eingeladen, er lädt ein

empfangen to receive
  empfing, hat empfangen, er empfängt
empfehlen to recommend
  empfahl, hat empfohlen, er empfiehlt
sich entschließen to decide, make up one's mind
  entschloß sich, hat sich entschlossen, entschließt sich
entsprechen to correspond to
  entsprach, hat entsprochen, es entspricht
entstehen to originate, come into being
  entstand, ist entstanden, er entsteht
erfahren to find out, learn
  erfuhr, hat erfahren, er erfährt
erfinden to invent
  erfand, hat erfunden, er erfindet
erhalten to receive; to sustain
  erhielt, hat erhalten, er erhält
erkennen to recognize
  erkannte, hat erkannt, er erkennt
erscheinen to appear
  erschien, ist erschienen, er erscheint
erschrecken to be frightened
  erschrak, ist erschrocken, er erschrickt
ertrinken to drown

ertrank, ist ertrunken, er
ertrinkt
sich erweisen to turn out;
show
erwies sich, hat sich er-
wiesen, es erweist sich
essen to eat
aß, hat gegessen, er ißt

fahren to drive; go (by train,
boat, plane, car)
fuhr, ist gefahren, er fährt
fallen to fall
fiel, ist gefallen, er fällt
finden to find
fand, hat gefunden, er
findet
fliegen to fly
flog, ist geflogen, er fliegt
fliehen to flee, escape
floh, ist geflohen, er flieht
fließen to flow
floß, ist geflossen, er fließt
fressen to eat (said of animals)
fraß, hat gefressen, er frißt
frieren to freeze; to be cold
fror, hat gefroren, er friert

geben to give
gab, hat gegeben, er gibt
gefallen to please
gefiel, hat gefallen, er gefällt
gefangennehmen to capture,
take prisoner
nahm gefangen, hat ge-
fangengenommen, er
nimmt gefangen
gehen to go; walk
ging, ist gegangen, er geht
gelingen to succeed
gelang, ist gelungen, es
gelingt
geschehen to happen, occur
geschah, ist geschehen, es
geschieht
gewinnen to win
gewann, hat gewonnen, er
gewinnt
greifen to grasp
griff, hat gegriffen, er greift

haben to have
hatte, hat gehabt, er hat
halten to hold; to stop
hielt, hat gehalten, er hält
heißen to be called; to mean
hieß, hat geheißen, er heißt
helfen to help
half, hat geholfen, er hilft

kennen to know, be ac-
quainted with
kannte, hat gekannt, er
kennt
klingen to sound
klang, hat geklungen, es
klingt
kommen to come
kam, ist gekommen, er
kommt
können to be able to
konnte, hat gekonnt, er
kann

lassen to let; to leave
ließ, hat gelassen, er läßt
laufen to run
lief, ist gelaufen, er läuft
leiden to suffer
litt, hat gelitten, er leidet
lesen to read
las, hat gelesen, er liest
liegen to lie (flat); to be situated
lag, hat gelegen, er liegt
lügen to tell a lie
log, hat gelogen, er lügt

mögen to like
mochte, hat gemocht, er
mag
müssen to have to
mußte, hat gemußt, er muß

nachdenken to reflect, meditate
dachte nach, hat nachge-
dacht, er denkt nach
nehmen to take
nahm, hat genommen, er
nimmt

raten to advise, to guess
riet, hat geraten, er rät
reißen to tear
riß, hat gerissen, er reißt
rennen to run

rannte, ist gerannt, er rennt
rufen to call
rief, hat gerufen, er ruft

scheinen to seem; to shine
schien, hat geschienen, er
scheint
schieben to push, shove
schob, hat geschoben, er
schiebt
schießen to shoot
schoß, hat geschossen, er
schießt
schilaufen to ski
lief Schi, ist schigelaufen,
er läuft Schi
schlafen to sleep
schlief, hat geschlafen, er
schläft
schlagen to beat; hit
schlug, hat geschlagen, er
schlägt
schließen to close
schloß, hat geschlossen, er
schließt
schneiden to cut
schnitt, hat geschnitten, er
schneidet
schreiben to write
schrieb, hat geschrieben,
er schreibt
schreien to scream, cry
schrie, hat geschrie(e)n,
er schreit
schweigen to be silent, say
nothing
schwieg, hat geschwiegen,
er schweigt
schwimmen to swim
schwamm, ist geschwom-
men, er schwimmt
sehen to see
sah, hat gesehen, er sieht
sein to be
war, ist gewesen, er ist
senden to send
sandte, hat gesandt, er
sendet
singen to sing
sang, hat gesungen, er singt
sinken to sink
sank, ist gesunken, er sinkt
sitzen to sit
saß, hat gesessen, er sitzt
sollen to be supposed to

sollte, hat gesollt, er soll

spazierengehen to go for a walk
    ging spazieren, ist spazierengegangen, er geht spazieren

sprechen to speak, talk
    sprach, hat gesprochen, er spricht

springen to jump
    sprang, ist gesprungen, er springt

stehen to stand
    stand, hat gestanden, er steht

stehenbleiben to stop (walking or moving)
    blieb stehen, ist stehengeblieben, er bleibt stehen

stehlen to steal
    stahl, hat gestohlen, er stiehlt

steigen to climb
    stieg, ist gestiegen, er steigt

sterben to die
    starb, ist gestorben, er stirbt

streichen to spread; to stroke; to paint
    strich, hat gestrichen, er streicht

tragen to carry
    trug, hat getragen, er trägt

treffen to meet; to hit
    traf, hat getroffen, er trifft

treten to step
    trat, ist getreten, er tritt

trinken to drink
    trank, hat getrunken, er trinkt

tun to do
    tat, hat getan, er tut

sich unterhalten to converse, have a conversation
    unterhielt sich, hat sich unterhalten, er unterhält sich

verbieten to forbid
    verbot, hat verboten, er verbietet

verbinden to unite; to compound
    verband, hat verbunden, er verbindet

verbringen to spend (time)
    verbrachte, hat verbracht, er verbringt

vergessen to forget
    vergaß, hat vergessen, er vergißt

verlassen to leave
    verließ, hat verlassen, er verläßt

verlieren to lose
    verlor, hat verloren, er verliert

verschwinden to disappear
    verschwand, ist verschwunden, er verschwindet

versprechen to promise
    versprach, hat versprochen, er verspricht

verstehen to understand

verstand, hat verstanden, er versteht

verzeihen to pardon, excuse
    verzieh, hat verziehen, er verzeiht

vorschlagen to suggest; to propose
    schlug vor, hat vorgeschlagen, er schlägt vor

wachsen to grow
    wuchs, ist gewachsen, er wächst

waschen to wash
    wusch, hat gewaschen, er wäscht

werden to become
    wurde, ist geworden, er wird

werfen to throw
    warf, hat geworfen, er wirft

wissen to know
    wußte, hat gewußt, er weiß

wollen to want to
    wollte, hat gewollt, er will

wiegen to weigh
    wog, hat gewogen, er wiegt

ziehen to move (from one place to another)
    zog, ist gezogen, er zieht

ziehen to pull
    zog, hat gezogen, er zieht

zwingen to force
    zwang, hat gezwungen, er zwingt

Vocabulary: German-English

This vocabulary is intended primarily for quick reference; it is not meant to be a substitute for a dictionary of the German language. The English equivalents given here do not include all the meanings of the corresponding German words that are found in a German dictionary. Most of the translations are limited to the meanings in which the German words are used in this book.

NOUNS

All nouns are preceded by the definite article to show their gender and are followed by an indication of the plural form. Thus the entries

der Mann, ⁔er	man
die Blume, –n	flower
das Fenster, –	window

mean that **Mann** is masculine and its plural is **Männer, Blume** is feminine and its plural is **Blumen,** and **Fenster** is neuter and is unchanged in the plural. Nouns for which no plural form is shown are not used in the plural. If two case endings are listed, the first indicates the genitive singular and the second the nominative plural.

ACCENTUATION

An accent mark shows the pronunciation of words with an unusual accentuation in German (e.g., **Schokola'de**). If the stress shifts to another syllable in the plural, the complete plural form is shown with an accent mark indicating the stress (e.g., **der Doktor, die Dokto'ren**). Stress is not indicated for words in which the first syllable is an unaccented prefix such as **be-** or **er-** or for compound verbs.

VERBS

The vowel changes of strong verbs are indicated (e.g., **schreiben, ie, ie**), the vowels given being respectively the stem vowels of the past indicative and the past participle. With verbs that have a change of stem vowel in the present, the third person singular present is also given (e.g., **schlafen, ie, a, er schläft**). Strong verbs which change their stems have their principal parts given in full (e.g., **stehen, stand, gestanden**). For further reference a summary list of strong and irregular verbs used in this text precedes this vocabulary.

466

Verbs that require the auxiliary **sein** to form the perfect tenses are indicated by (**ist**) [e.g., **bleiben, ie, ie, (ist)** stay].

In compound verbs written as one word a dot between the complement and the verb (e.g., **aus·gehen, nach·denken**) indicates that the two parts are separated in the present and past tenses (**er geht aus, er denkt nach**).

With irregular or strong verbs that have separable prefixes the prefix is not repeated but the principal parts are given thus: **auf·stehen, stand –, –gestanden.**

ABBREVIATIONS

The following abbreviations are used in the entries:

acc.	= accusative	*gen.*	= genitive
adv.	= adverb	*pers.*	= person, personal
colloq.	= colloquial	*prep.*	= preposition
conj.	= conjunction	*sent. adv.*	= sentence adverb
dat.	= dative	*trans.*	= transitive
demonstr.	= demonstrative		

ab off
ab und zu now and then; off and on
der Abend, –e evening
  abends evenings
  gestern abend yesterday evening, last night
  heute abend this evening, tonight
  morgen abend tomorrow evening
  Guten Abend! Good evening!
das Abendessen, – supper
aber but; however
ab·fahren, u, a, (ist), er fährt ab to depart, leave
ab·hängen, i, a, von to depend upon
ab·holen to pick up
das Abitur' final examination in secondary school
ab·nehmen, nahm –, –genommen, er nimmt ab to lose weight; to decrease
ab·zwingen, a, u, er zwingt ab to gain by force
ach oh
  ach so oh, I see
die Achse, –n axle; axis
acht eight

achtzehn eighteen
achtzig eighty
adressie'ren to address
  die Adres'se, –n address
Ägyp'ten Egypt
ähnlich similar
alle all, all of us
  alle all gone
allein alone
allerdings' however; admittedly
allgemein' common; general
  im allgemeinen in general
alles everything
die Alpen the Alps
als than; when; as
also therefore; well; in other words
alt old
das Altertum antiquity
alt'modisch old-fashioned
der Amerika'ner, – American
an on; at
ander– other
  eins nach dem anderen one after the other
  anders different
(sich) ändern to change
an·fangen, i, a, er fängt an to begin, start
  der Anfang, ̈e beginning, start

an·gehen, ging –, –gegangen, (ist) to begin; go on
der Anglist', –en, –en Anglicist
die Angst, ̈e fear, anxiety
  Angst haben vor to be afraid of
an·kommen, kam –, –gekommen, (ist) to arrive
  die Ankunft arrival
an·nehmen, nahm –, –genommen, er nimmt an to accept; to assume, take on
an·reden mit to address by
an·rufen, ie, u to call up (on the telephone)
sich etwas an·schauen to look at something
an·schnallen to fasten seat belts
  die Schnalle, –n buckle
an·sehen, a, e, er sieht an to look at
  sich etwas an·sehen to look at something
die Ansicht, –en view; opinion
antworten (*with dat. of pers.*) to answer
  die Antwort, –en answer, reply
an·zeigen to announce

sich an·ziehen, zog –, –gezo-gen to get dressed
angezogen sein to be dressed
der Anzug, ⸚e suit
der Apfel, ⸚ apple
der April′ April
ara′bisch Arabic
arbeiten to work
die Arbeit, –en work
sich ärgern über to be angry about, mad at
arm poor
der Arm, –e arm
die Armee′, die Arme′en army
der Arzt, ⸚ physician, doctor
der Ast, ⸚e branch
atmen to breathe
auch also, too
auf on, on top of; up; open
auf·sein to be up; open
auf (die Tür) zu toward (the door)
die Aufführung, –en performance
auf·geben, a, e, er gibt auf to give up; mail, post (a letter)
auf·gehen, ging –, –gegangen, (ist) to rise (sun, moon); to open
aufgrund′ (prep. with gen.) on the basis of
auf·hören to stop
die Auflage, –n printing
auf·legen to put down the receiver
auf·machen to open
die Aufnahme, –n picture, photo
sich auf·regen über to get excited about
aufgeregt sein über to be excited about
auf·schließen, o, o to unlock
zu·schließen to lock
auf·schreiben, ie, ie to write down, note
auf·springen, a, u, (ist) to jump up
auf·stehen, stand –, –gestanden, (ist) to get up; stand up

der Aufzug, ⸚e elevator
das Auge, –n eye
der Augenblick, –e moment, instant
augenblicklich momentarily; instantly
der August′ August
aus out, out of
aus·geben, a, e, er gibt aus to spend
aus·gehen, ging –, –gegangen, (ist) to go out
aus·kommen, kam –, –gekommen, (ist) to get along
die Auskunft, ⸚e information
aus·lachen to laugh at, make fun of
das Ausland foreign countries
er lebt im Ausland he lives abroad
sich aus·ruhen to rest; to get a rest
ausgeruht sein to be rested
(sich) aus·schlafen, ie, a, er schläft (sich) aus to get enough sleep
aus·sehen, a, e, er sieht aus to look, appear
außer besides, except for
außerdem moreover
aus·setzen to expose
aus·sprechen, a, o, er spricht aus to pronounce, utter
aus·steigen, ie, ie, (ist) to get out (of a vehicle)
aus·wandern to emigrate
sich aus·ziehen, zog –, –gezogen to undress
ausgezogen sein to be undressed
das Auto, –s car

backen, backte or buk, gebacken to bake
der Bäcker, – baker
baden to bathe
das Bad, ⸚er bath
die Badewanne, –n bathtub
der Bahnhof, ⸚e railway station
zum Bahnhof to the station
im Bahnhof within the station
auf dem Bahnhof on the platform

bald soon
die Bank, ⸚e bench
die Bank, –en bank
der Bart, ⸚e beard
der Bauch, ⸚e stomach, belly
bauen to build
der Bauer, –n peasant, farmer
Bayern Bavaria
der Baum, ⸚e tree
beachten to note, notice
der Beamte, –n, –n civil servant, (government) official
die Beamtin, –nen official (female)
beantworten (trans.) to answer (a letter)
bedeuten to mean, signify
bedienen to serve
die Bedienung service
beenden to conclude, finish
befehlen, a, o, er befiehlt (with dat. of pers.) to command, order
beginnen, a, o to begin, start
begleiten to accompany
begreifen, begriff, begriffen to comprehend
behalten, ie, a, er behält to keep, retain
behaupten to maintain, claim
bei at, at the home of; near; with
bei Schmidts at the Schmidts'
beim Essen while eating
beide both
das Bein, –e leg
das Beispiel, –e example
zum Beispiel (z.B.) for example
bekannt well-known
der Bekannte, –n, –n acquaintance
bekommen, bekam, bekommen to get, receive
bellen to bark
bemerken to notice, mention, note, say
sich bemühen um, bemüht sein um to be concerned about, with
benutzen to use
beobachten to observe, watch

bereit ready
  bereits already
der Berg, –e mountain
berichten to report
der Beruf, –e profession
  Was sind Sie von Beruf?
    What is your profession?
beruhen auf to be based on
(sich) beruhigen to calm
    down
  beruhigt sein to be calmed
    down
sich beschäftigen mit to oc-
    cupy oneself with
  beschäftigt sein to be oc-
    cupied; employed
  die Beschäftigung, –en oc-
    cupation
beschließen, beschloß, be-
    schlossen to decide, de-
    termine
beschreiben, ie, ie to de-
    scribe
besetzen to occupy
  besetzt busy (telephone)
besonder– special
  besonders especially
besser better
bestehen aus, bestand, be-
    standen to consist of
bestellen to order
bestimmt definite(ly)
besuchen to visit
  der Besuch, –e visit
betrachten to look at, observe
das Bett, –en bed
beurteilen to judge, make a
    judgment
bevor (conj.) before
sich bewegen to move
  die Bewegung, –en move-
    ment
beweisen, ie, ie to prove
bezahlen to pay
die Bibliothek', –en library
das Bier, –e beer
das Bild, –er picture
billig inexpensive; cheap
bis until, up until; up to, as
    far as
  bis gestern until yesterday
  bis Köln as far as Cologne
  bis zum Winter (up) until
    winter

bis zum Bahnhof as far as
    the station
  zwei bis drei two to three
ein bißchen a bit, a little
bisher' until now
die Bitte, –n request
bitte please
bitten um, bat, gebeten to
    request, ask for
blau blue
bleiben, ie, ie, (ist) to stay,
    remain
blicken to look, glance
  der Blick, –e look, glance;
    view
blitzen to lighten
  der Blitz, –e lightning
blöd(e) stupid
blühen to bloom, blossom,
    flower
die Blume, –n flower
das Blut blood
  der Blutdruck blood pres-
    sure
der Boden, ⸚ ground; floor
die Bombe, –n bomb
böse mad, angry at; evil
  (jemandem) böse sein to
    be angry (mad) at
    somebody
braten, ie, a to roast, fry
  der Braten, – roast
  der Kalbsbraten, – veal
    roast
  der Schweinebraten, –
    pork roast
brauchen to need
braun brown
die Braut, ⸚e bride
  der Bräutigam, –e bride-
    groom
brechen, a, o, er bricht to
    break
breit broad, wide
brennen, brannte, gebrannt
    to burn
der Brief, –e letter
  die Brieftaube, –n carrier
    pigeon
  der Briefträger, – mailman
bringen, brachte, gebracht
    to bring
  ich bringe dich nach Hause
    I'll take you home

das Brot, –e bread
  das Brötchen, – hard roll
die Brücke, –n bridge
der Bruder, ⸚ brother
der Brunnen, – well, fountain
das Buch, ⸚er book
buchen to reserve a seat
der Buchstabe, –n, –n letter
    (of the alphabet)
die Bühne, –n stage
die Bundesregierung Federal
    Government (Germany)
das Büro', –s office
der Bus, –se bus
die Butter butter

das Café, –s café
der Chef, –s boss

da there; then; under these
    circumstances; (conj.)
    since
  dabei at the scene; in the
    process
  da drüben over there
  daher therefore; from
    there, from that place
  dahin there; toward that
    place
das Dach, ⸚er roof
damals at that time
die Dame, –n lady, woman
damit (conj.) so that
dankbar grateful, thankful
danken (with pers. dat.) to
    thank
  danke thank you, thanks
  danke schön thank you
    very much
  vielen Dank thank you
    very much
dann then
darum for that reason
das that (demonstr.)
daß that (conj.)
dauern to last; take (time)
die Decke, –n ceiling; blanket
denken, dachte, gedacht to
    think
  sich etwas denken to
    imagine
denn for (conj.)
dersel'be the same (see 161)
deshalb therefore

Deutsch German (language)
   Deutschland Germany
   Deutsch können to know German
der Dezember December
dicht thick, dense
dick thick, fat
der Dieb, –e thief
dienen to serve
   der Dienst service; official working time
Dienstag Tuesday
dieser, diese, dieses this
   diesmal this time
das Ding, –e thing
doch (*see* 39)
der Dok'tor, die Dokto'ren doctor
der Dollar, –s dollar
der Dom, –e cathedral
donnern to thunder
   der Donner (*no pl.*) thunder
der Donnerstag, –e Thursday
das Dorf, ̈er village
dort there
   dorthin to that place; there
draußen (*adv.*) outside
sich drehen um to turn (around something), to revolve; to concern, to be a matter of
   sich um·drehen to turn around
drei three
dreißig thirty
dreizehn thirteen
der Dritte the third (of a series)
das Drittel, – third (fraction)
dumm stupid, dumb
   der Dummkopf, ̈e dumbbell, fool
dünn thin
dunkel dark
durch through
drüben over there
drucken to print
durch·machen to go through, suffer
durstig thirsty
   der Durst (*no pl.*) thirst
dürfen, durfte, gedurft (*see* 52 ff.)

eben just
die Ecke, –n corner
egoi'stisch egotistic, selfish
das Ei, –er egg
eigen (*adj.*) own
eigentlich actually, really
sich eilen, sich beeilen to hurry
einander each other
sich etwas ein·bilden to imagine something
   eingebildet sein to be conceited
eineinhalb one and a half
einfach easy, simple
ein·fallen, fiel –, –gefallen, (ist), es fällt ein to remember; occur (to one's mind)
   es fällt mir ein I've just remembered
ein·holen to catch up with
einige some, several, a few
ein·laden, u, a, er lädt ein to invite
einmal (*colloq.* mal) once; at some time
   zweimal twice
   dreimal three times
   viermal four times etc.
   (noch) nicht' einmal not even
   nicht ein'mal not once
   noch einmal once more
sich ein·ordnen (traffic) to get into the correct lane; to merge
eins one (cardinal number)
ein·schlafen, ie, a, (ist), er schläft ein to fall asleep
ein·steigen, ie, ie, (ist) to enter, board (a plane or train)
ein·wandern to immigrate
der Einwohner, – inhabitant
die Einzelheit, –en detail
einzig only, sole
die Eisenbahn, –en railroad
das Element', –e element
elf eleven
die Eltern (*no sing.*) parents
empfangen, i, a, er empfängt to receive

der Empfang, ̈e reception
empfehlen, a, o, er empfiehlt to recommend
das Ende, –n end
   zu Ende to an end, to a conclusion
endlich at last, finally
eng narrow
entdecken to discover
entfernt distant
sich entschließen zu, entschloß, entschlossen to decide, make up one's mind
   entschlossen sein zu to be determined
(sich) entschuldigen to excuse (oneself)
   entschuldigt sein to be excused
entsprechen (*with dat.*)**, a, o** to correspond to
entstehen, entstand, entstanden, (ist) to originate, come into being
enttäuschen to disappoint
entweder . . . oder either . . . or
erben to inherit
das Erdbeben, – earthquake
die Erde, –n earth
erfahren, u, a, er erfährt to find out, learn; experience
erfinden, a, u to invent
   die Erfindung, –en invention
der Erfolg, –e success; result
erfreut sein to be pleased, glad
erhalten, ie, a, er erhält to receive
sich erholen to get a rest
   erholt sein to be well rested
erinnern an to remind of
   sich erinnern an to remember
   die Erinnerung, –en memory
sich erkälten to catch a cold
   erkältet sein to have a cold
erkennen (an), erkannte, erkannt to recognize (by)

erklären to explain
sich erkundigen to inquire
erlauben to allow, permit
erleben to experience
   das Erlebnis, –se experience
erreichen to reach, attain, achieve
erscheinen, ie, ie, (ist) to appear
erschlagen, u, a, er erschlägt to slay
erschrecken, erschrak, erschrocken, (ist), er erschrickt to be frightened
erst first; not until, only
   erst dann not until then, only then
   erst gestern not until yesterday, only yesterday
   zuerst at first, first
erstaunt astonished, amazed
erstens first(ly)
   zweitens second(ly)
   drittens third(ly)
   viertens fourth(ly)
   etc.
ertrinken, a, u, (ist) to drown
erwachsen (adj.) grown-up, adult
erwarten to expect
sich erweisen, ie, ie to turn out, show
erzählen to tell, relate
essen, aß, gegessen, er ißt to eat
   das Essen, – food; meal
etwa about; by any chance
etwas something; somewhat
Euro'pa Europe
   europä'isch European
das Exemplar', –e copy (of a book, etc.)

die Fabrik', –en factory
fähig capable
fahren, u, a, (ist), er fährt to drive, go (by train, boat, plane, car)
   fahren lernen to learn to drive
   die Fahrkarte, –n (train) ticket

das Fahrrad, –̈er bicycle
fallen, fiel, gefallen, (ist), er fällt to fall, drop
   der Fall, –̈e case; fall
   auf jeden Fall in any case, at any rate
   auf keinen Fall in no case, under no circumstances
falsch false, wrong
falten to fold
die Fami'lie, –n family
die Farbe, –n color
   die Lieblingsfarbe, –n favorite color
   färben to color; dye
   farbig in color, colored
fast almost
der Februar February
fehlen to be missing
der Fehler, – mistake
fein fine
der Feind, –e enemy
das Feld, –er field
das Fenster, – window
die Ferien (pl.) vacation
fern far away, distant
   die Ferne distance
fern'·sehen, a, e, er sieht fern to watch TV
   das Fernsehen television
   der Fernseher, – TV set
fertig ready, complete, finished
das Fest, –e festival, celebration
fest firm(ly)
fest·stellen to determine; find out; conclude
das Feuer, – fire
das Fieber fever
der Film, –e movie, film
das Filmfestspiel, –e film festival
finden, a, u to find
der Finger, – finger
fischen to fish
   der Fisch, –e fish
die Flasche, –n bottle
   eine Flasche Wein a bottle of wine
das Fleisch (no pl.) meat
fliegen, o, o, (ist) to fly
   der Flieger, – flyer
   der Tiefflieger, – strafing

plane
fliehen, o, o, (ist) to escape, flee
fließen, o, geflossen, (ist) to flow
der Flug, –̈e flight
   der Abflug, –̈e departure
   der Fluggast, –̈e passenger
   der Flughafen, –̈ airport
   der Flugschein, –e plane ticket
   das Flugzeug, –e airplane
flüstern to whisper
die Flut, –en flood
folgen (with dat.) to follow
fort away
fragen to ask
   fragen nach to inquire about
   die Frage, –n question
   eine Frage stellen to ask a question
   eine Frage beantworten to answer a question
Frankreich France
die Frau, –en woman, wife; Mrs.
   das Fräulein, – young lady; Miss
frei free; unoccupied
der Freitag, –e Friday
freiwillig voluntary
fremd strange, alien
fressen, a, e, er frißt to eat (said of animals)
die Freude, –n joy, pleasure
   sich freuen auf to look forward to
   sich freuen über to be happy (glad) about
der Freund, –e friend (male)
   die Freundin, –nen friend (female)
frieren, o, o to freeze
   ich friere I am cold
frisch fresh
froh glad, joyful, happy
   fröhlich joyous, merry
früh early
   früher earlier; formerly
   frühestens at the earliest
der Frühling, –e spring
frühstücken to breakfast, have breakfast

das **Frühstück,** –e breakfast

fühlen to feel

das **Gefühl,** –e feeling

führen to lead, guide

der **Führer,** – leader; guide

füllen to fill

überfüllt overcrowded (train)

fünf five

fünfzehn fifteen

fünfzig fifty

für for

furchtbar terrible, frightful

fürchten to fear

ich **fürchte, morgen regnet es** I am afraid it will rain tomorrow

der **Fuß,** ⸚e foot

der **Fußabdruck,** ⸚e footprint

füttern to feed

ganz whole, entire

ganz gut pretty good, not bad

den **ganzen Tag** all day

die **ganze Nacht** all night

gar nicht (kein, nichts) not (no . . . , nothing) at all

der **Garten,** ⸚ garden

das **Gas,** –e gas

der **Gast,** ⸚e guest

der **Gasthof,** ⸚e inn, restaurant

das **Gasthaus,** ⸚er inn, restaurant

das **Gebäude,** – building

das **Hauptgebäude,** – main building

geben, a, e, er gibt to give

es **gibt** there is (are) available

aus·geben, a, e, er gibt aus to spend (money)

geboren born

ich bin **geboren** I was born

geboren werden to be born

die **Geburt,** –en birth

der **Geburtstag,** –e birthday

der **Gedanke,** –ns, –n thought, idea

auf den Gedanken kommen to hit upon the idea

die **Geduld** (*no pl.*) patience

geduldig patient

die **Gefahr,** –en danger

gefährlich dangerous

gefallen, gefiel, gefallen, er gefällt to please

das **gefällt mir** I like it (that pleases me)

der **Gefallen,** – favor

gefangen·nehmen, nahm –, –genommen, er nimmt gefangen to capture, take prisoner

gegen against

gegen sechs Uhr around six o'clock

die **Gegend,** –en area

der **Gegensatz,** ⸚e contrast

gegenseitig each other; mutual

gegenü'ber (*with dat.*) opposite

die **Gegenwart** (*no pl.*) present; presence

gegenwärtig present

geheim secret

das **Geheimnis,** –se secret

gehen, ging, gegangen, (ist) to go; walk

gehorchen to obey

gehören (*with pers. dat.*) to belong to (property)

gehören zu to belong to (membership)

die **Geiß,** –en goat

der **Geist** intellect, mind, spirit; ghost

das **Geld** money

gelingen, a, u, (ist) to succeed

es **gelingt mir** I succeed

das **Gemüse,** – vegetable

genau exact

der **General',** ⸚e general

genug enough

das **Gepäck** (*no pl.*) baggage

gerade just; straight

gern(e) gladly

ich esse **gern(e)** I like to eat

ich möchte **gern(e) etwas essen** I'd like to eat something

der **Gesandte,** –n ambassador, envoy

das **Geschäft,** –e business; store

geschehen, a, e, (ist), es geschieht to happen, occur

das **Geschenk,** –e present, gift

die **Geschichte,** –n story; history

das **Gesetz,** –e law

das **Gesicht,** –er face

das **Gespräch,** –e conversation

gestatten to permit, allow

gestern yesterday

gestern abend last night, yesterday evening

gesund well, healthy

die **Gewähr** guarantee

gewinnen, a, o to win

gewiß certain

sich **gewöhnen an** to get used to

gewöhnt sein an to be used to

gewöhnlich usual

das **Glas,** ⸚er glass

der **Glaube,** –ns (*no pl.*) belief; faith

glauben to think, believe

glauben an (*with acc.*) to believe in

gleich equal, same, like; (*time adv.*) immediately, presently

das **Glück** (*no pl.*) happiness; luck, good luck; fortune

Glück haben to be lucky

glücklich happy

glücklicherwei'se fortunately; happily

gnädige Frau formal way of addressing a married woman

das **Gold** gold

der **Gott,** ⸚er god

Gott God

gottseidank' thank heavens, thank goodness

gratulie'ren to congratulate

grau gray

greifen, griff, gegriffen to

grasp; reach out (for something)

die Grenze, –n border

groß big, great, tall

die Großstadt, ⁀e large city, metropolis

der Großvater, ⁀ grandfather

grün green

der Grund, ⁀e reason; ground

aufgrund' (*with gen.*) on the basis of

grüßen to greet

der Gruß, ⁀e greeting

die Gruppe, –n group

gut good

das Gymna'sium, die Gymna'sien German secondary school, grades 5–13

das Haar, –e hair

haben to have

hageln to hail

halb half

die Hälfte, –n half

die Halle, –en hall, lobby

halten, ie, a, er hält to hold; stop

halten für to consider

halten von to think of

die Hand, ⁀e hand

handeln to act

sich handeln um to be a matter of

handeln mit to deal with (objects)

handeln von to deal with (subject matter)

der Händler, – dealer

die Handschrift handwriting

der Handschuh, –e glove

die Handtasche, –n handbag

hart hard

hassen to hate

Haupt– main

der Hauptbahnhof main station

das Haus, ⁀er house

ich gehe nach Hause I go home

ich bin zu Hause I am at home

heilen to heal

geheilt healed, well

heiraten to get married, marry

verheiratet married

ich bin verheiratet I am married

heiß hot

heißen, ie, ei to be called; to mean

heizen to heat

die Heizung heating system; radiator

die Zentral'heizung central heating

helfen (*with pers. dat.*), a, o, er hilft to help

hell light, bright

das Hemd, –en shirt

her toward the speaker (in the sense of *hither*)

heraus' out

herbei' here

herein' in

her·kommen to come here

sich heraus·stellen to turn out, become apparent

der Herd, –e stove

der Herr, –en (*gen., dat., and acc. sing.:* **Herrn**) gentleman

herum' around

das Herz, –ens, –en (*dat.:* **dem Herzen**) heart

der Herzog, ⁀e duke

heute today

heute abend this evening, tonight

heute morgen this morning

hier here

die Hilfe help

der Himmel heaven, sky

himmlisch heavenly

hin away from the speaker

sich hinaus·lehnen to lean out

hinein' in

hin·fahren, u, a, (ist), er fährt hin to go there

sich hin·setzen to sit down

hinten (*adv.*) in the back

hinter (*prep.*) behind, beyond, on the other side of

der Hintergrund, ⁀e background

hinun'ter down

den (Rhein) hinunter down the (Rhine)

die Hitze (*no pl.*) heat

hoch high

höchstens at the most

der Hof, ⁀e court, yard

der Hofgarten the Royal Gardens

hoffen to hope

hoffentlich I hope (*sent. adv.*)

die Höhe, –n height

in die Höhe upward

holen to get, fetch

das Holz, ⁀er wood

hören to hear

der Hörer, – telephone receiver; listener

die Hose, –n trousers, pants

das Hotel', –s hotel

hübsch pretty

der Hund, –e dog

hundert hundred

der Hunger hunger

ich habe Hunger I am hungry

hungrig hungry

der Hut, ⁀e hat

die Hypothek', –en mortgage

die Idee', die Ide'en idea

immer always

immer noch, noch immer still

immer wieder again and again

in in

In'dien India

der In'der, – (East) Indian

der India'ner, – (American) Indian

der Ingenieur', –e engineer

intelligent' intelligent

die Intelligenz' intelligence, intellect

interessant' interesting

sich interessie'ren für, interessiert sein an to be interested in; to like to acquire

inzwi'schen meanwhile, in the meantime

irgendetwas something, anything

irgendwo somewhere

irgendwohin somewhere

der Irrtum, ⸚er error

Ita′lien Italy

italie′nisch Italian

ja yes; indeed

das Jahr, –e year

jahrelang for years

das Jahrhun′dert, –e century

der Januar January

je, jemals ever

jedenfalls at any rate

jeder, jede, jedes each, every

jemand somebody, someone

jetzt now

die Jugend (*no pl.*) youth (*collective noun*); time of youth

der Ju′li July

jung young

der Junge, –n, –n boy

der Ju′ni June

der Kaffee coffee

das Kalb, ⸚er calf

kalt cold

die Kälte (*no pl.*) cold

kämmen to comb

kämpfen to fight

der Kampf, ⸚e fight, battle

das Kapi′tel, – chapter

die Karte, –n map; ticket

die Landkarte, –n map

die Fahrkarte, –n (train) ticket

die Rückfahrkarte, –n round-trip ticket

die Kartof′fel, –n potato

die Kasse, –n cash register, cash box

der Kasten, ⸚ chest, box

die Katze, –n cat

kaufen to buy

kaum hardly

kein no (not any)

der Keller, – cellar

der Kellner, – waiter

der Oberkellner, – headwaiter

Herr Ober normal way of addressing a waiter

kennen, kannte, gekannt to know, be acquainted with

kennen·lernen to meet, become acquainted with

das Kind, –er child

das Kino, –s movie house

die Kirche, –n church

ich gehe in die Kirche I go to church

klar clear

die Klasse, –n class

der Klatsch gossip

das Klavier, –e piano

das Kleid, –er dress

klein little

klettern to climb

das Klima climate

klingeln to ring (bell)

klingen, a, u to sound

klopfen to knock

an·klopfen to knock (at the door)

das Knie, – (*pl. pronounced with two syllables,* **Kni-e,** *the* **-e** *serving as ending*) knee

kochen to cook; boil

der Koffer, – suitcase

komisch funny; odd; comical

das Komma, –s comma

kommen, kam, gekommen, (ist) to come

der König, –e king

können, konnte, gekonnt, er kann (*see* **52** ff.)

das Konzert′, –e concert

der Kopf, ⸚e head

die Kopfschmerzen (*pl.*) headache

der Körper, – body

kosten to cost

krank sick

die Kreide chalk

der Krieg, –e war

kriegen (*colloq.*) = **bekommen** to get

die Küche, –n kitchen

die Kugel, –n ball, globe; bullet

der Kugelschreiber, – ballpoint pen

die Kuh, ⸚e cow

sich kümmern um to take care of; to be concerned with

der Künstler, – artist

kurz short

die Kusi′ne, –n (female) cousin

küssen to kiss

die Kutsche, –n coach; jalopy

lächeln to smile

das Lächeln smile

lachen to laugh

das Lachen laughter

das Land, ⸚er country; land

auf dem Land in the country

die Landschaft, –en landscape

der Landstrich, –e region

landen to land

die Landkarte, –n map

lang long

lange for a long time

jahrelang for years

fünf Jahre lang for five years

langsam slow

längst, schon längst for a long time, a long time ago

lang′·weilen to bore

sich langweilen, gelangweilt sein to be bored

langweilig boring

der Lärm (*no pl.*) noise; din

lassen, ie, a, er läßt to let, leave

die Kinder zu Hause lassen to leave the children at home

die Later′ne, –n street light

laufen, ie, au, (ist), er läuft to run

laut loud

leben to live, be alive

das Leben, – life

am Leben sein to be alive

ums Leben kommen to lose one's life

das Leder leather

leer empty

legen to lay, place
 sich legen to lie down
lehren to teach
 der Lehrer, – teacher
leicht easy; light (in weight)
leiden, litt, gelitten to suffer
leider unfortunately (*sent. adv.*)
leid tun to be sorry
 es tut mir leid I am sorry
 er tut mir leid I am sorry for him
leise soft, without noise
sich leisten to afford
leiten to lead
 der Leiter leader, person in charge
 die Leitung, –en people in charge; (power or gas) line
lernen to learn
lesen, a, e, er liest to read
letzt– last
 letzten Mai last May
 letzte Woche last week
 letztes Jahr last year
leuchten to shine
die Leute (*pl.*) people
der Leutnant, –e lieutenant
das Licht, –er light
lieb dear
 lieber rather (*adv.*)
 am liebsten (to like) most of all
 lieb·haben to love
lieben to love
 die Liebe love
lieblich lovely
der Liebling, –e darling, favorite
das Lied, –er song
liegen, a, e to lie (flat); to be situated
link– left
 links to the left
die Lippe, –n lip
 der Lippenstift, –e lipstick
lochen to punch (a ticket)
 das Loch, ¨er hole
der Löffel, – spoon
der Lohn, ¨e wage(s), pay
die Lokomoti've, –n locomotive
los loose

was ist los what's the matter
lösen to solve; dissolve
die Luft, ¨e air
 die Luftpost airmail
lügen, o, o to tell a lie
die Lust pleasure
 Lust haben zu to want to
lustig cheerful

machen to make; to do
 es macht nichts it doesn't matter
 an·machen to turn on
 aus·machen to turn off
das Mädchen, – girl
die Mahlzeit, –en meal
der Mai May
das Mal time
 dieses Mal this time
 diesmal this time
 einmal once
 zweimal twice
 noch einmal once more
 manchmal sometimes
 jedesmal every time
 zwei mal zwei two times two
malen to paint
man (*dat.:* einem; *acc.:* einen) one (*pron.*)
mancher many a (*see* 155)
 manchmal sometimes
der Mann, ¨er man, husband
der Mantel, ¨ coat, overcoat
die Mark mark
 zwei Mark two marks
der Markt, ¨e market; market place
die Maschi'ne, –n machine; typewriter
die Mate'rie (*no pl.*) matter
die Mathematik' mathematics
die Medizin' medicine; science of medicine
das Mehl flour
mehr more
 mehr als more than
 nicht mehr no longer
mehrere several
die Meile, –n mile
meinen to mean; be of the

opinion; say; have an opinion
 die Meinung, –en opinion
meist– most
meistens usually; mostly
sich melden to report (to somebody); to answer (the phone)
die Menge, –n quantity; mass, crowd
 jede Menge any amount
der Mensch, –en, –en man, human being
merken to notice
das Messer, – knife
das Meter, – meter
die Milch (*no pl.*) milk
mild mild
die Milliar'de, –n billion
die Million', –en million
mindestens at least
die Minu'te, –n minute
mit with, along
mit·machen to go along, cooperate
der Mittag, –e noon
 der Nachmittag, –e afternoon
das Mittagessen, – dinner (noon meal, the main meal in Germany)
mit·teilen to inform, let know, report (something)
das Mittelalter Middle Ages
Mitternacht midnight
der Mittwoch, –e Wednesday
die Möbel (*pl.*) furniture
modern' modern
mögen, mochte, gemocht, er mag (*see* 146 ff.)
möglich possible
 unmöglich impossible; (*sent. adv.*) not possibly
 möglicherweise possibly
 die Möglichkeit, –en possibility
der Mo'nat, –e month
der Mond, –e moon
der Montag, –e Monday
der Morgen, – morning
 heute morgen this morning

morgen tomorrow

morgen abend tomorrow evening

das Motorrad, ⸚er motorcycle

müde tired

der Müller, – miller

der Mund, ⸚er mouth

mündlich oral

das Muse'um, die Muse'en museum

musizie'ren to make music

müssen, mußte, gemußt, er muß (*see* **52** ff.)

die Mutter, ⸚ mother

Mutti Mom, Mommy

na so was! (expression of astonishment) you don't mean it, what do you think of that

na und? so what?

nach to, toward; after

der Nachbar (*gen.:* des Nachbars or des Nachbarn; *pl.:* die Nachbarn) neighbor

nachdem' (*conj.*) after

nach·denken über, dachte –, –gedacht to reflect, meditate about

nachher afterward

der Nachmittag, –e afternoon

nach·schicken to forward (mail)

nächst– next

nächstes Jahr next year

nächstens in the near future

die Nacht, ⸚e night

heute nacht this coming night; last night

but: **gestern abend** last night (before going to bed), yesterday evening

nah near, close by

die Nähe proximity, closeness, nearness

nähen to sew

der Name, –ns, –n (*dat.:* dem Namen; *acc.:* den Namen) name

der Vorname, –ns, –n first name

der Nachname, –ns, –n last name

nämlich namely; that is to say; you know

die Nase, –n nose

die Natur' nature

natür'lich naturally, of course

neben next to, beside

der Nebel fog

neblig foggy

nebenan' next door

nee (*colloq.*) = **nein** no

nehmen, nahm, genommen, er nimmt to take

nein no

nervös' nervous

nett nice

neu new

das ist mir neu that's news to me

die Neuigkeit, –en news

neugierig curious

neulich recently

neun nine

neunzehn nineteen

nicht not

nicht mehr no longer

noch nicht not yet

nichts nothing

nicken to nod

nie never

niemand nobody, no one

nirgends nowhere

noch still

noch nicht not yet

noch einmal once more

der Norden the north

nördlich northern

die Nordsee the North Sea

normalerweise normally

Norwegen Norway

der November November

null zero

die Nummer, –n number

nun now

nur only

nutzlos useless

ob whether; if

oben up (above); upstairs; on top

obligato'risch obligatory

das Obst (*no pl.*) fruit

obwohl although

oder or

der Ofen, ⸚e oven; stove

öffentlich public

der Offizier', –e officer

(sich) öffnen to open

geöffnet sein to be open

offen (*adj.*) open

oft often

ohne (*with acc.*) without

der Onkel, – uncle

die Oper, –n opera; opera house

operieren to operate

die Ordnung order

in Ordnung in order, all right, O.K.

der Ort, –e town

der Vorort, –e suburb

der Osten the east

östlich eastern

das Paar, –e pair, couple

ein paar a few

das Paket', –e package, parcel

das Papier', –e paper

parken to park

die Partei', –en party

der Paß, die Pässe passport; pass

passieren to happen

die Pause, –n pause, intermission, break

das Persil' a German detergent

die Person', –en person

persön'lich personal

der Perso'nenzug, ⸚e local train

der Pfarrer, – pastor

der Pfennig, –e pfennig, penny

das Pfund, –e pound

die Physik' (*no pl.*) physics

der Plan, ⸚e plan

die Platte, –n (phonograph) record; plate; flagstone

der Platz, ⸚e place; plaza, square; seat

der Sitzplatz, ⸚e seat

Platz nehmen to sit down, have a seat

plötzlich suddenly

plus plus, and
Polen Poland
   polnisch Polish
die Polizei′ (*no pl.*) police
   der Polizist′, –en policeman
die Post mail; post office
der Preis, –e price; prize
prima (*colloq.*) wonderful
das Problem′, –e problem
der Profes′sor, die Professo′-
   ren professor
Prozent′ per cent
die Psychologie′ psychology
das Pulver, – powder; gun-
   powder
der Punkt, –e point; period
putzen to clean

das Rad, ⁼er wheel
sich rasie′ren to shave
   rasiert sein to be shaved
raten, ie, a, er rät to advise;
   give counsel; guess
   der Rat advice, counsel;
   council; councilor
   das Rathaus, ⁼er town
   (city) hall
rauchen to smoke
der Raum, ⁼e room; space
reagie′ren auf to react to
rechnen to figure, to calculate
recht right; correct
   rechts to the right
   das ist mir recht that's all
   right with me
   recht haben to be right
   mit Recht rightfully
rechtzeitig on time
reden to talk, speak
die Regie′rung, –en government
   die Bun′desregierung
   Federal Government
   (of Germany)
regnen to rain
   der Regen rain
reich rich
die Reihe, –n row; series
   ich bin an der Reihe it's
   my turn
   ich komme an die Reihe
   I am next

reisen to travel
   die Reise, –n trip
   eine Reise machen to take
   a trip
die Reklame advertising
reißen, riß, gerissen to tear
rennen, rannte, gerannt, (ist)
   to run
reparie′ren to repair
reservie′ren to reserve
retten to save
der Rhein the Rhine
richtig correct; accurate
die Richtung, –en direction
der Ring, –e ring
der Rock, ⁼e jacket, coat;
   skirt
rollen to roll
der Roman, –e novel
die Rose, –n rose
rot red
die Rückfahrkarte, –n
   round-trip ticket
rufen, ie, u to call
ruhig quiet, restful; (*sent.
   adv.*) it won't bother
   me, I'll stay calm about
   it
   unruhig restless
   die Ruhe rest; quietness
   in aller Ruhe at leisure
rund round
russisch Russian
Rußland Russia

die Sache, –n thing, matter
der Saft, ⁼e juice
sagen to say
das Salz, –e salt
der Samstag, –e Saturday
   samstags on Saturdays
sanft soft
der Sänger, – singer
schade too bad
der Schalter, – (ticket) window
schalten to switch
   um·schalten to switch
   over
der Schauspieler, – actor
schauen to look, gaze
sich scheiden lassen von to
   get a divorce from

geschieden sein to be divorced
scheinen, ie, ie to seem; to
   shine
   er scheint zu schlafen he
   seems to be asleep
schenken to give (as a present); present
   das Geschenk, –e present,
   gift
schicken to send
schieben, o, o to push, shove
das Schiff, –e ship, boat
schi·laufen to ski
der Schinken, – ham
schlachten to butcher,
   slaughter
schlafen, ie, a, er schläft to
   sleep
schlagen, u, a, er schlägt to
   beat, hit
   der Schlag, ⁼e beat, stroke
schlank slender, slim
schlecht bad
(sich) schließen, schloß, ge-
   schlossen to close
   geschlossen sein to be
   closed
schließlich finally, after all
schlimm bad, disagreeable
schlucken to swallow
   der Schluck sip
der Schluß, die Schlüsse
   end; conclusion
der Schlüssel, – key
schmücken to decorate
die Schnalle, –n buckle
schnarchen to snore
der Schnee (*no pl.*) snow
schneiden, schnitt, ge-
   schnitten to cut
   der Schnitt, –e cut
schneien to snow
schnell fast, rapid
die Schokola′de chocolate
schon already
schön beautiful, pretty;
   good, O.K.
der Schrank, ⁼e cupboard,
   wardrobe
schrecklich terrible
schreiben, ie, ie to write
   die Schreibmaschine, –n
   typewriter

schreien, ie, ie to scream, cry
   der Schrei, –e scream
der Schriftsteller, – writer
der Schuh, –e shoe
die Schule, –n school
   auf der Schule in school
der Schüler, – pupil, (Gymnasium) student
die Schulter, –n shoulder
der Schuß, die Schüsse shot
schwach weak
der Schwager, ̈ brother-in-law
schwarz black
der Schwarzwald Black Forest
schweigen, ie, ie to be silent, say nothing
das Schwein, –e pig; swine
   das Schweinefleisch (no pl.) pork
die Schweiz Switzerland
schwer hard; heavy; difficult
die Schwester, –n sister
schwimmen, a, o, (ist) to swim
   das Schwimmbecken, – swimming pool
sechs six
sechzehn sixteen
sechzig sixty
der See, –n lake
die See (no pl.) sea, ocean
sehen, a, e, er sieht to see
sehr very
die Seife soap
sein, war, gewesen, (ist), er ist to be
seit since
   seitdem (conj.) since; (adv.) since then, since that time
   seit langem for a long time
   seit Anfang Mai since the beginning of May
die Seite, –n page; side
der Sekretär', –e secretary
selbst, selber –self (see 178); even (see 180)
selten rare, seldom
seltsam strange, peculiar
das Seme'ster, – semester
senden, sandte, gesandt to send; broadcast
   der Sender, – sender; broadcasting station

sentimental' sentimental
der September September
setzen to set
   sich setzen to sit down
sicher certain, sure; probably
sieben seven
siebzehn seventeen
siebzig seventy
der Sieg, –e victory
singen, a, u to sing
sinken, a, u, (ist) to sink
der Sinn, –e sense
   sinnvoll meaningful; sensible
die Situation', –en situation
sitzen, saß, gesessen to sit
   der Sitzplatz, ̈e seat
so so
   so etwas something like this
sobald' (conj.) as soon as
soe'ben just, just now
das Sofa, –s sofa
sofort' at once, immediately
sogar' even
der Sohn, ̈e son
solan'ge (conj.) as long as
solcher such (see 156)
der Soldat', –en, –en soldier
sollen (see 52 ff.)
der Sommer, – summer
sondern but
die Sonne, –n sun
der Sonntag, –e Sunday
   jeden Sonntag every Sunday
   sonntags on Sundays, every Sunday
sonst otherwise
soviel so much, as much; (conj.) as far as
sowieso anyhow, anyway
spät late
spätestens at the latest
spazie'ren·fahren, u, a, (ist), er fährt spazieren to go for a ride
spazie'ren·gehen, ging –, –gegangen, (ist) to go for a walk
speisen to eat (formal term)
   die Speisekarte, –n menu
der Spiegel, – mirror

spielen to play
der Sport (no pl.) sport, sports, athletics
sprechen, a, o, er spricht to speak, talk
   die Sprache, –n language
springen, a, u, (ist) to jump
   auf'springen to jump up
die Spur, –en trace
   spurlos without a trace
der Staat, –en state
die Stadt, ̈e town, city
stark strong; heavy
starren to stare
statt (with gen.) instead of
   statt . . . zu (kaufen) instead of (buying)
stecken to stick; put
stehen, stand, gestanden to stand
   auf·stehen, (ist) to arise; stand up, get up, rise
stehen·bleiben, ie, ie, (ist) to stop
stehlen, a, o, er stiehlt to steal
steigen, ie, ie, (ist) to climb
   ein·steigen to enter, board (a train or plane)
der Stein, –e stone
stellen to place, put (upright)
   die Stelle, –n place
   die Stellung, –en position; job
sterben, a, o, (ist), er stirbt to die
still quiet, still
die Stimme, –n voice
stimmen to be correct
   das stimmt nicht that's wrong
der Stock, ̈e stick; floor (of a building)
   im ersten (zweiten, etc.) Stock on the second (!) (third, etc.) floor
der Stolz (no pl.) pride
   stolz proud
stören to disturb
die Straße, –n street
die Straßenbahn, –en streetcar
streichen, i, i to spread; to stroke; to paint

das **Stück**, –e piece; play
  das **Goldstück**, –e gold coin
der **Student**, –en, –en student (masculine)
  die **Studentin**, –nen student (feminine)
studie′ren to study
  das **Stu′dium**, die **Stu′dien** studies, course of study
der **Stuhl**, –̈e chair
die **Stunde**, –n hour
suchen to look for, seek, search
  die **Suche** search
der **Süden** the south
  südlich southern
die **Sünde**, –n sin
die **Suppe**, –n soup

der **Tabak**, –e tobacco
der **Tag**, –e day
das **Tal**, –̈er valley
die **Tante**, –n aunt
tanzen to dance
  der **Tanz**, –̈e dance
die **Tasche**, –n pocket; bag, handbag; briefcase
die **Tasse**, –n cup
tatsächlich actual(ly), indeed, as a matter of fact
tausend thousand
das **Taxi**, –s; or: die **Taxe**, –n taxi
der **Tee** tea
teilen to divide
  geteilt durch divided by
  der **Teil**, –e part
das **Telefon**, –e telephone
  telefonie′ren (mit) to talk on the phone (with), to make a phone call (to)
das **Telegramm′**, –e telegram
die **Terras′se**, –n terrace
das **Testament′**, –e last will
teuer expensive
das **Thea′ter**, – theater
das **Thema**, die **Themen** topic; subject; theme
das **Tier**, –e animal
tippen to type
der **Tisch**, –e table
die **Tochter**, –̈ daughter
der **Tod**, –e death
  todschick elegant; "great"

das **Tor**, –e gate
tot dead
tragen, u, a, er **trägt** to carry; to wear
träumen to dream
  der **Traum**, –̈e dream
treffen, traf, getroffen, er **trifft** to meet; to hit
trennen to separate
die **Treppe**, –n staircase
treten, a, e, (ist), er **tritt** to step
trinken, a, u to drink
trocken dry
trotz (*prep.*) in spite of
trotzdem (*adv.*) in spite of, despite, nevertheless
tun, tat, getan to do
die **Tür**, –en door

üben to practice
über over
überall everywhere
überfüllt′ overflowing
überhaupt anyway; at all
sich **überle′gen** to think about, meditate, consider
übernach′ten to spend the night
überra′schen to surprise
überre′den to persuade
überset′zen to translate
  die **Überset′zung**, –en translation
(sich) **überzeu′gen** to convince (oneself)
  überzeugt sein von to be convinced
übrigens by the way, incidentally
die **Uhr**, –en clock, watch
  sechs Uhr six o'clock
  wieviel Uhr what time
um around; about; at
um . . . zu in order to
um·kommen, kam –, –gekommen, (ist) to perish
um·werfen, warf –, –geworfen, wirft – to knock over
um·ziehen, zog –, –gezogen, (ist) to move
  sich **um·ziehen** to change (clothes)

umgezogen sein to be changed
unbedingt absolute(ly), by all means
und and
der **Unfall**, –̈e accident
unendlich infinite
ungefähr approximate(ly), about
die **Universität**, –en university
unmöglich impossible
unruhig restless
der **Unsinn** nonsense
unten (*adv.*) down, down below, downstairs
(sich) **unterbre′chen**, a, o, er **unterbricht** to interrupt
unter·bringen, brachte –, –gebracht to put up, lodge
unter·gehen, ging′ –, –gegangen, (ist) to sink, perish; to set (sun, moon)
sich **unterhal′ten**, ie, a, er **unterhält sich** to converse, have a conversation
unter·kommen, kam –, –gekommen, (ist) to find a place to stay
unterrich′ten to teach, instruct
der **Unterschied**, –e difference
untersu′chen to investigate
der **Urlaub** (*no pl.*) furlough; vacation
die **Ursache**, –n cause

die **Vase**, –n vase
der **Vater**, –̈ father
sich **verändern** to change
  verändert sein to be changed, different
verbieten, o, o to forbid, prohibit
(sich) **verbinden**, a, u to unite; to compound; to connect
verbringen, verbrachte, verbracht to spend (time)
verdienen to earn; deserve

die **Vereinigten Staaten** the United States

sich **verfahren,** u, a, er ver**fährt sich** to lose one's way (driving)

vergessen, vergaß, vergessen, er vergißt to forget

vergeuden to squander

vergiften to poison

sich **verheiraten** to get married

verkaufen to sell

der **Verkehr** traffic

der **Verlag, –e** publishing house, publisher

verlangen to demand

verlassen, verließ, verlassen, er verläßt to leave (somebody or something)

sich **verlassen auf** to depend, rely upon

sich **verlaufen,** ie, au, er ver**läuft sich** to lose one's way (walking)

der **Verleger,** – publisher

jemanden **verletzen** to hurt somebody

sich **verlieben in** to fall in love with

verliebt sein in to be in love with

verlieren, o, o to lose

sich **verloben mit** to get engaged to

verlobt sein mit to be engaged to

verlobt engaged

der **Verlobte, –n** fiancé

das **Vermögen,** – wealth, fortune, estate

die **Vernunft** reason (intellect)

vernünftig reasonable

verreisen to go on a trip

verrückt crazy

verschwinden, a, u, (ist) to disappear

verschwunden (*adj.*) lost

versichern to insure; to assure

die **Verspätung, –en** delay

Verspätung haben to be late, not on schedule

versprechen, a, o, er ver-

spricht to promise

der **Verstand** (*no pl.*) mind; reason

verstehen, verstand, verstanden to understand

versuchen to try, attempt

der **Versuch, –e** try, attempt; experiment

verunglücken to die in an accident

die **Verwandlung, –en** change, metamorphosis

verwandt related

der **Verwandte, –n, –n** relative

verwöhnen to spoil somebody (by being too good to him)

verwunden, ie, ie to injure, wound

verzeihen, ie, ie to pardon, excuse

die **Verzeihung** pardon

der **Vetter, –n** cousin (male)

viel much

viele many

soviel so much, as much

zuviel too much

vielleicht' perhaps

vier four

vierzehn fourteen

vierzig forty

das **Visum, die Visen** visa

das **Volk, ∸er** people

voll full

völlig completely

von from

von mir aus as far as I am concerned

von (Paris) aus from (Paris)

vor before; in front of; ago

vor einem Jahr a year ago

vor allem above all

vorbei' (*adv.*) gone, past

vorbei'•gehen, ging –, –gegangen, (ist) to pass

sich **vor•bereiten auf** to prepare for

vorbereitet sein auf to be prepared for

vorgestern day before yesterday

vorher (*adv.*) before, earlier

vorhin' a little while ago

der **Vorname, –ns, –n** first name

vorne in front

vor•schlagen, u, a, er schlägt **vor** to propose, suggest

der **Vorschlag, ∸e** suggestion, proposal

die **Vorsicht** (*no pl.*) caution

vorsichtig careful

sich **vor•stellen** (*dat. reflexive*) to imagine

(sich) **vor•stellen** (*acc. reflexive*) to introduce (oneself)

wachsen, u, a, (ist), er **wächst** to grow

erwachsen (*adj.*) grown-up, adult

wagen to dare

der **Wagen,** – car; wagon

wählen to choose; to dial

wahr true

während during (*prep.*); while (*conj.*)

wahrschein'lich probably

der **Wald, ∸er** woods, forest

die **Wand, ∸e** wall

wandern to wander; migrate; hike

aus•wandern to emigrate

ein•wandern to immigrate

wann when

warm warm

warten auf (*with acc.*) to wait for

warum why

was what

was für what kind of (*see* 162)

waschen, u, a, er **wäscht** to wash

das **Wasser** water

der **Wechsel,** – change

wecken to awaken

der **Wecker,** – alarm clock

weder ... noch neither ... nor

weg away

weg•fahren, u, a, (ist), er **fährt weg** to drive away, leave

der **Weg, –e** way, path

wegen because of
sich weigern to refuse
Weihnachten Christmas
weil (*conj.*) because
der Wein, –e wine
weinen to cry, weep
weiß white
weit far
welcher which
die Welle, –n wave
   die Dauerwelle, –n permanent
die Welt, –en world
wenig little
weniger minus; less
wenigstens at least
wenn when; whenever; if
wer who
werden, wurde, geworden, (ist), er wird to become
werfen, a, o, er wirft to throw
   um·werfen to knock over
der Wert, –e worth; value
weshalb for what reason, why
der Westen the west
   die Westfront western front
   westlich western
das Wetter weather
wichtig important
wie as; like; how
   wie gesagt as I said
wieder again (i.e., second or third time); back (to the place of origin)
wiederauf'bauen, ich baue wieder auf to reconstruct
wiederho'len to repeat
wieder·sehen, a, e, er sieht wieder to see again
   auf Wiedersehen good-by
   auf Wiederhören good-by (telephone)
wiegen, o, o to weigh
Wien Vienna
die Wiese, –n meadow
wieviel how much
   wieviel Uhr what time
wild wild
der Winter, – winter
   im Winter in the winter

wirklich really
   die Wirklichkeit, –en reality
der Wirt, –e innkeeper; landlord
wissen, wußte, gewußt, er weiß to know (as a fact)
   wissen Sie you know (*sent. adv.*)
das Wissen knowledge
die Wissenschaft, –en science
wissenschaftlich scientific
die Witwe, –n widow
wo where
die Woche, –n week
woher from where
wohin where, where to (direction)
wohl well; probably
wohnen to reside, live
   die Wohnung, –en apartment
der Wolf, –e wolf
wollen, er will (*see* 52 ff.)
das Wort, –er (*also* –e) word
die Wunde, –n wound
das Wunder, – miracle; wonder
   wunderbar wonderful, marvelous
sich wundern über to be amazed at
der Wunsch, –e wish
wünschen to wish
die Wurst, –e sausage; cold cuts
   das Würstchen, – sausage
wütend mad, angry

zahlen to pay (in a restaurant)
zählen to count
   die Zahl, –en number
der Zahn, –e tooth
der Zaun, –e fence
zehn ten
das Zeichen, – sign
zeigen to show
sich zeigen (*impersonal*) to turn out; show
die Zeile, –n line (of print, poetry, verse)

die Zeit, –en time
   eine Zeitlang for a while (*not:* for a long time)
die Zeitung, –en newspaper
zerstören to destroy
ziehen, zog, gezogen to pull; (**ist**) to move (from one place to another)
   er hat gezogen he has pulled
   er ist nach (Köln) gezogen he has moved to (Cologne)
ziemlich rather, quite
   ziemlich weit quite far
die Zigaret'te, –n cigarette
die Zigar're, –n cigar
das Zimmer, – room
zittern to tremble, shake
zögern to hesitate
der Zoll, –e customs; duty
der Zoo, –s zoo
der Zorn anger
zu to; too; at
   zuviel too much
zuerst first, at first
der Zufall, –e accident, coincidence
   durch Zufall by accident
   zufällig by coincidence, by chance, accidentally
zufrie'den (*adj.*) satisfied, content
der Zug, –e train
die Zugspitze highest mountain in Germany
zu·hören to listen to
die Zukunft (*no pl.*) future
zunächst' first, first of all
zurück' back
   wieder zurück back, back again
zusam'men together
sich zusam'men·setzen aus to be composed of
zwanzig twenty
zwar to be sure
zwei two
der Zwerg, –e dwarf
zwingen, a, u to force
zwischen between
zwölf twelve

Vocabulary: English-German

able: to be able to können
to accept annehmen
accidentally zufällig
to act (as if) tun (als ob)
afraid: to be afraid (of)
    Angst haben (vor)
after all doch
again wieder
airport der Flughafen
alone allein
along mit
already schon
also auch
although obwohl
always immer
to answer antworten
apartment die Wohnung
approximately ungefähr
arm der Arm
to arrive ankommen
to ask fragen
aunt die Tante
away weg

back zurück
bank die Bank, –en
to bathe, take a bath (sich)
    baden
beautiful schön
because weil
to become werden
bed das Bett
to begin anfangen
   beginning der Anfang
to believe glauben; denken
   to believe in glauben an
to belong to gehören
bench die Bank, ¨-e
birthday der Geburtstag
book das Buch
bored: to be bored sich
   langweilen

to break brechen
breakfast das Frühstück
brother der Bruder
to build bauen
but aber; sondern
to buy kaufen

to call (up) anrufen
called: to be called heißen
to calm down sich beruhigen
car der Wagen
to catch a cold sich erkälten
chair der Stuhl
to change (sich) ändern;
   (sich) verändern
to change (clothes) sich
   umziehen
child das Kind
church die Kirche
city die Stadt
coat der Mantel
coffee der Kaffee
cold kalt
to come kommen
correct: to be correct
   stimmen
to count zählen
of course natürlich
cup die Tasse

darling Liebling
daughter die Tochter
day der Tag
dead tot
to deal with sich handeln um
   (*impersonal*)
dear lieb
to decide sich entschließen
to die sterben
different(ly) ander–; anders

dinner das Essen; das
   Mittagessen; das
   Abendessen
to disappear verschwinden
divorce: to get a divorce sich
   scheiden lassen
to do tun
doctor der Arzt; der Doktor
dog der Hund
door die Tür
downtown in die Stadt
to drink trinken
to drive fahren
dumbbell der Dummkopf

each jeder, jede, jedes
early früh
to eat essen
end das Ende
engaged: to get engaged
   sich verloben
every jeder, jede, jedes
everything alles
excited: to get excited (about)
   sich aufregen (über)
to expect erwarten
expensive teuer
to experience erfahren
eye das Auge

far weit
father der Vater
to feel fühlen
few wenige
   a few ein paar; einige
to fight kämpfen
finally endlich; schließlich
flower die Blume
to fly fliegen
footprint der Fußabdruck
for (*conj.*) denn
to forget vergessen

482

free frei
friend der Freund, die Freundin

garden der Garten
girl das Mädchen
to give geben
to go gehen
gold piece das Goldstück
good gut
haircut: to get a haircut sich die Haare schneiden lassen
to happen geschehen; passieren
happy glücklich
hat der Hut
to have haben
   to have to müssen
healthy gesund
to hear hören
to help helfen
here hier
hole das Loch
home (adv.) nach Hause
   at home zu Hause
to hope hoffen
hot heiß
hour die Stunde
house das Haus
how wie
human being der Mensch
hungry hungrig
to hurry up sich eilen; sich beeilen
husband der Mann

if wenn
to imagine sich vorstellen; sich (etwas) einbilden
immediately sofort
important wichtig
instead of statt . . . zu
intelligent intelligent
to intend to wollen
interested: to be interested in sich interessieren für
interesting interessant
to introduce (oneself) (sich) vorstellen
to invite einladen

just gerade

key der Schlüssel
to knock klopfen
to know (a person) kennen
   to know (facts) wissen

large groß
last letzt–; zuletzt
at last endlich
late spät
law das Gesetz
to learn lernen
least: at least mindestens, wenigstens
to leave lassen; abfahren
to let lassen
letter der Brief
to lie liegen
life das Leben
light das Licht
little klein; wenig
to live wohnen; leben
living room das Wohnzimmer
long lang; (adv.) lange
to look aussehen
to look forward to sich freuen auf
to lose one's way sich verlaufen; sich verfahren
to love lieben
to fall in love with sich verlieben in

mad: to be mad at sich ärgern über
to make machen
many viele
married: to be married verheiratet sein
to marry, to get married heiraten
to meet kennenlernen
mistake der Fehler
moment der Augenblick
money das Geld
more mehr
mother die Mutter
movie (house) das Kino
much viel

to need brauchen
never nie
new neu
newspaper die Zeitung
nice nett

nobody niemand
not nicht
   not until erst
   not yet noch nicht
nothing nichts
novel der Roman
now jetzt

o'clock: at (three) o'clock um (drei) Uhr
often oft
old alt
once einmal; früher
only nur; erst
order: in order in Ordnung
in order to um . . . zu
other ander–
overcoat der Mantel

to pay bezahlen
people die Leute
perhaps vielleicht
permitted: to be permitted to dürfen
to pick up, meet abholen
picture das Bild
please bitte
to prepare (oneself) for (sich) vorbereiten auf
to promise versprechen
to put setzen; stellen; legen

quite ganz

to rain regnen
rather lieber
to reach erreichen
to read lesen
really wirklich
to remember sich erinnern an
to rest sich ausruhen
restless unruhig
to ring (a telephone) klingeln
reason die Vernunft
   reasonable vernünftig
to recognize erkennen
relative der Verwandte
room das Zimmer

shoe der Schuh
school die Schule
to scream schreien
to see sehen
to seem scheinen

to send schicken
several mehrere
to shave sich rasieren
to show zeigen
sick krank
silent: to be silent schweigen
simple einfach
sister die Schwester
to sit sitzen
to sleep schlafen
   to get enough sleep (sich)
     ausschlafen
small klein
to smoke rauchen
soldier der Soldat
some einige; ein paar;
   manche; etwas
somebody jemand
something etwas
somewhere irgendwo;
   irgendwohin
son der Sohn
to speak sprechen
to stand stehen
station der Bahnhof
to stay bleiben
still noch
stone der Stein
stop halten; stehenbleiben
story die Geschichte
student der Student, die
   Studentin
to study studieren

such solch
suddenly plötzlich
to suggest vorschlagen
Sunday der Sonntag
supposed: to be supposed to
   sollen
swimming pool das
   Schwimmbecken
to switch off ausmachen

table der Tisch
to take nehmen
to talk reden; sprechen
teacher der Lehrer
to tell sagen; erzählen
to thank danken
thief der Dieb
to think (of) denken (an)
time die Zeit
   at the time damals
tired müde
today heute
tomorrow morgen
tonight heute abend
too auch
trace die Spur
   without a trace spurlos
train der Zug
to try versuchen
to turn off (light) ausmachen
to turn out sich herausstellen
   (impersonal)

to understand verstehen
to undress sich ausziehen
unfortunately leider
until bis
to get used to sich gewöhnen
   an

very sehr
to visit besuchen

to wait for warten auf
wall die Wand
to want to wollen
war der Krieg
watch die Uhr
week die Woche
weekend das Wochenende
well gesund; gut
when wann
where wo; wohin
whether ob
why warum
wife die Frau
wine der Wein
winter der Winter
without ohne
woman die Frau
to work arbeiten
writer der Schriftsteller

year das Jahr
yesterday gestern
young jung

Index